THEY LEFT THEIR MARK

Surveyors and Their Role in the Settlement of Ontario

For Peter Pavlin

THEY LEFT THEIR MARK
Surveyors and Their Role in the Settlement of Ontario

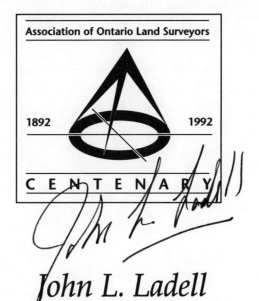

Association of Ontario Land Surveyors

1892   1992

C E N T E N A R Y

John L. Ladell

DUNDURN PRESS
TORONTO & OXFORD
1993

Editing: Margaret Hoogeveen
Design and Production: Andy Tong
Printing and Binding: Gagné Printing Ltd., Louiseville, Quebec, Canada

The writing of this manuscript and the publication of this book were made possible by support from several sources. The publisher wishes to acknowledge the generous assistance and ongoing support of The Canada Council, The Book Publishing Industry Development Program of the Department of Communications, The Ontario Arts Council, and The Ontario Publishing Centre of the Ministry of Culture and Communications.

Care has been taken to trace the ownership of copyright material used in the text (including the illustrations). Credit for each quotation is given at the end of the text. The author and publisher welcome any information enabling them to rectify any reference or credit in subsequent editions.

J. Kirk Howard, Publisher

Canadian Cataloguing in Publication Data

Ladell, John L., 1924–
   They left their mark: surveyors and their role
in the settlement of Ontario

Includes bibliographical references and index

ISBN 1-55002-160-5

1. Surveyors - Ontario - History.   2. Surveying - Ontario - History.
3. Ontario - Surveys - History.   I. Title

TA523.05L3 1993   526.9'2'09713   C92-095299-2

Dundurn Press Limited
2181 Queen Street East
Suite 301
Toronto, Canada
M4E 1E5

Dundurn Distribution
73 Lime Walk
Headington, Oxford
England
OX3 7AD

To the memory of

WILLIS CHIPMAN

B.A.Sc. (McGill), D.L.S., O.L.S.

1855-1929

CONTENTS

"Γεωμετρης Αγωνιστης"

The frontispiece is from the published proceedings of the first meeting of the Association of Provincial Land Surveyors held in Toronto in February 1886.

Freely translated, the Greek tag reads "A Surveyor in His Struggle," possibly a gloss on John Milton's *Samson Agonistes*. That it was assumed that a late-nineteenth-century surveyor could read Greek is of interest.

FOREWORD

In 1992 the Association of Ontario Land Surveyors celebrated its one hundredth birthday as a legally incorporated professional body. In 1991 the province of Ontario was two hundred years old, for it was on 19 June 1791 that King George III gave his royal assent to the Constitutional Act that divided the old province of Quebec into two, thus bringing Upper Canada – the Ontario of the future – into being. The coincidence in the timing of the centenary of the Association of Ontario Land Surveyors and the bicentenary of the province is singularly appropriate; it was surveyors who created the physical framework of the province in which we now live. To use a theatrical analogy, we act out our lives on a set that was designed and constructed by the province's early surveyors.

The first two centuries of Ontario's recorded history belong to the French. It was Samuel de Champlain and then the priests of various religious orders, principally the Jesuits, who started to elucidate the geography of the province. They established the general size and shape of the Great Lakes and how the lakes were connected. They became familiar with the St. Lawrence and Ottawa rivers, and how to reach Georgian Bay via the latter and the French River. They learned that the Grand River led to Lake Erie, that the Detroit River existed, and that Lake St. Clair was connected to Lake Huron. And they made maps of everything they found, which increased in accuracy as time passed.

However, inland from the Great Lakes lay what was virtually *terra incognita* to both the French and the British when they first came. Later, because the British were responsible for the defence of the province, Admiralty hydrographers would chart the Great Lakes, and army officers would explore the hinterland between the Ottawa River and Georgian Bay in hopes of establishing a more direct line of communication between them. But it was land surveyors acting for the Crown who laid out the first townships in the province, and it was crown surveyors who eventually carpeted virtually all of Ontario south of the French River, and much of northern Ontario, with a mosaic of roughly rectangular townships.

Out of the township system, with its gridlike pattern of roads, come the many parallel roads and crossroads – and, until recent times, its many hair-raising right-angled corners – that characterize rural Ontario. These roads, moreover, run straight, sometimes in total defiance of topography, such as those on the Niagara Peninsula that run southward from the Lake Ontario shore and then straight up and over the escarpment. Not so long ago, it was estimated that over 80 percent of all the roads in southern Ontario follow the road allowances laid down in the original township surveys. And it has been pointed out that, in downtown Toronto, the orientation of the east-west streets parallels very precisely the standard direction – in terms of the compass bearing – of the north shore of Lake Ontario commonly used by early surveyors from Belleville westward. This bearing, in turn, governed the direction of all the north-south roads built at right angles to the shoreline.

Land surveyors were the shock troops of settlement. Dispatched into what was often wilderness unseen by any European, the surveyor was the first to examine the land in detail, noting its quality and its suitability or otherwise for settlement. Where the land seemed good, they laid out – on the instructions of their political masters – the first townships and then subdivided these into the lots that the early settlers took up. In many cases the surveyor selected the location for a future town. Some of the chosen town sites came to nothing, but on many others villages were established, some to grow into the towns and cities we live in today. Surveyors also explored and decided on the routes that canals should take. In the more recent past, surveyors played a key role in the design and construction of the St. Lawrence Seaway.

It was surveyors who chose the best route for the railways, which played such a decisive role in shaping the economy of southern Ontario in the mid-1800s and which later spearheaded the opening of the North. Like the roads, the railways, too, led to the growth of villages and towns along the right-of-way. Other centres came into being, quite literally, at the end of the line; Collingwood, for example, grew around such a terminus in the bush on the shores of Georgian Bay. And later on, surveyors had a great deal to say about the routes of the first hydro lines, which now loom so large on our landscape. Surveyors also selected the routes for the first major highways, which we now take for granted and which are so much a part of our lives.

Although, as suggested above, the surveyors set the stage on which we now live, it is equally true that, like the set designer whose name on the theatre program is rarely noted, let alone remembered, the names of individual surveyors and what they accomplished remain largely unknown to the general public. To help rectify this is one of the aims of this book.

The surveyors were surprisingly few in number. To lay out the land for the reception of the Loyalist refugees after the American Revolutionary War, the authorities had less than a dozen surveyors they could call on, of whom about half were in the military. And even by 1800, when the population of Upper Canada had grown to 50 000 or so, the total number of land surveyors that had worked in the province at one time or another came to less then forty. The bulk of the work fell on the perhaps half-a-dozen commissioned deputy land surveyors, as they were then known, who were working at any one time.

Some of the earliest surveyors, such as the Loyalist officers who helped survey the first settlements, had no formal training at all. Others were self-taught. Some of the early surveys, carried out hurriedly in order to lay out lots for the reception of the relentless tide of settlers, were not as well done as they might have been, to the despair of both later landowners and the surveyors

trying to set things to rights. But in the main, the men who first took on the job of laying out the first townships did astonishingly well, considering how primitive their instruments were and their working conditions.

Even by 1860, less than four hundred surveyors had worked in the province since its founding. Yet by that date they had laid out close to five hundred townships to meet the needs of a population that had grown to about 1.4 million. In 1886, when the Association of Ontario Land Surveyors was formed, there were about two hundred. It is only a guess, but even by 1930 less than a thousand surveyors had been active in the province since the beginning. By that time they had laid out, in 147 years, over 2500 townships, of which nearly 1100 were fully subdivided into concessions and lots; they had also laid out the province's towns and cities, its roads and highways, its railways and canals, and its hydro lines and airfields, not to mention having satisfied the many private surveying needs of a rapidly growing urban population. Ontario surveyors had also, over the years, laid out interprovincial boundaries, district or county boundaries, boundaries of native reserves, and participated in the location and running of the international boundary between Canada and the United States. By any standards, a remarkable accomplishment by a small band of skilful, tough, and resourceful men.

Reading early surveyors' letters, diaries, and reports, one wonders why these men kept on surveying. For a start, they worked under appalling conditions. To meet deadlines – spelled out by budgets that were often ludicrously small – and to make enough money to live on, they worked in all types of weather. Beset by flies and mosquitos – no insect spray at the corner store in those days – they had to work, often as not, in extremely inhospitable country. When you and I go for a tramp in one of the more sparsely settled parts of the province – in Algonquin Park, perhaps, or even in a wilder part of a conservation area – and we are suddenly confronted with what seems an impene-

trable portion of a forest, an extensive tangle of underbrush, or a very wet-looking marsh, we quite sensibly look for an alternative route. This is just what a surveyor on the job could not do. If his compass told him that his survey line would take him through a forest or a tangle of underbrush, then through it he had to go. Likewise, he would have to go through a swamp, even if a sight had to be taken in the middle of it as he stood there waist deep in icy water.

The running of a "base line" was particularly rigorous. This was a line upon which future surveys would be based, and no deviation from the preselected compass course was tolerated. Thus, in 1856 a provincial land surveyor by the name of Albert Salter was instructed to start from what is now Sturgeon Falls and run a base line due west until he reached the northeastern shore of Lake Superior, some 160 miles (257 km) away. He and his men were also required to run "meridians" at stated intervals and of stated lengths. These were north-south lines upon which future townships would be "erected," to use the terminology then in vogue. It took Salter and his survey parties two seasons to finish the work. Today, Salter's Line is still used by land surveyors as a reference line in that part of northern Ontario.

Nineteenth-century surveyors were often men of prodigious energy and endurance. In 1860 Thomas Herrick, while carrying out the first exploratory survey north of Lake Superior, covered over 400 miles (644 km) in a single season, and this through some of the most rugged terrain in North America. In 1872 Hugh Wilson, instructed to lay out one of the first townships south of Thunder Bay, began his survey report with the laconic statement: "I started from Toronto on the 10th of February last, for Thunder Bay, Lake Superior and Duluth (Minnesota), and walked from Duluth to Prince Arthur's Landing, distant by the coast about 250 miles."

The diaries and reports of surveyors exploring or laying out townships in northern and northwestern

Ontario tell of working in the depths of winter when the working parts of their instruments were so stiff with cold as to be all but immovable. One surveyor apologized in his report for some possible inaccuracies; he was working for much of the time, he explained, in 4 feet (1.2 m) of snow. Surveyors' reports tell of working through sleet and snow, and of crossing ice of varying degrees of treachery; they tell of working in summer through apparently unending rain – and always accompanied by flies, which are described as "bad," "very bad," "terrible," and "fearful." The reports tell, too, of building rafts to cross lakes; of toting supplies; of walking 20 miles (32 km) or more to get back to camp; of encountering cliffs impossible to climb and round which a way must be found somehow; and of working in terrain that is "broken," "very rough," "mountainous," or merely "difficult of access in the extreme."

Sometimes the surveyors' reports describe a struggle to get a sick or injured man out of the bush. Scurvy was a constant risk where men were living for months on salted meat, flour, and dried beans, or "pease." Some reports tell of survey parties so short of food that they were literally starving. Robert Bell and his party, running a base line across the southern fringes of what is now Algonquin Park in 1847, were only saved from starvation by a rescue team that brought them meat on the hoof by driving oxen up the line that the surveyors had cut. And occasionally a report will tell of a drowning, or perhaps more than one.

In pioneer days, a deputy provincial surveyor, who was proud to add the letters "D.P.S." after his name, was a direct agent of the Crown. Trained and knowledgeable surveyors were the *sine qua non* of land settlement. The future of the province depended on the rapid and orderly settlement of many thousands of immigrants. These had come to Upper Canada in search of land – land that would be legally theirs. To give them legal title to a property – without which there would be chaos – required that the land be sur-

veyed and described in a manner that the law recognized. Only certified surveyors were allowed to carry out such surveys and prepare such descriptions. Early surveyors had, then, a certain status in society. For all that, they were only moderately paid – and in the eighteenth century their pay was often in arrears into the bargain. Empowered by their formal "instructions," surveyors would hire many assistants, such as chainmen and ten or more axemen to clear lines of sight. However, the surveyor was likely to be left at the end of the survey without the cash to pay his employees. And like it or not, he might remain out of pocket for months until his accounts were examined and approved by the parsimonious authorities.

A disrupted home life, little chance of making a quick fortune, poor working conditions – why did surveyors keep on surveying? There was, of course, the obvious attractions of the work: an open-air life, independence, and a measure of responsibility. But there was more to the job than that. For a start, in the late eighteenth and early nineteenth century, surveyors with their knowledge and technical expertise were members of an intellectual elite that included the infant province's doctors, lawyers, and clergymen.

With their knowledge – and being essentially practical men – surveyors often found themselves undertaking work that today would be considered a task for civil engineers. As towns and cities grew, so did the need for roads, bridges, and, in time, water works and sewage systems. Willis Chipman, the man who played a leading role in the formation of what is now the Association of Ontario Land Surveyors, became a world authority on the construction of water works and sewage systems. In fact, he was to design and install the first of these systems in just about every town in Ontario. From the earliest days, land surveyors did private work. And as the towns and cities grew, the demand for private work grew, encouraging many surveyors to establish private practices and form partnerships and surveying firms. Many surveyors went on to

play a wider role in the history of Ontario. Two became distinguished senators, another an eminent divine. Others went on to become prominent businessmen and bankers. Some became judges, while not a few became county registrars or other local government officials.

Their status in a pioneer society apart, there must have been something else to keep the early surveyors doing their difficult job. That "something else" applies to surveyors today, as well. When asked why they took up surveying, surveyors often speak of a love of mathematics. Reduced to its simplest form, this amounts, perhaps, to a compulsive desire to set things in order. A certain satisfaction can be gained by wrenching the apparent chaos of the natural landscape and its manmade accretions – or a jumble of city streets – into an understandable form such as a plan or map. Surveyors also possess a lively sense of history or at least a sense of historical continuity. They must have this. For, of necessity, today's surveyor may well be basing his work on what his predecessor did, perhaps last week, perhaps last year, perhaps a century ago. Thus surveys made as long ago as the 1790s may still be considered "working" documents and may be referred to as a matter of course. That there may be something innate in a surveyor's make-up is borne out by the fact that surveying tends to run in families. Ontario's surveying history is full of father and son teams. At one point, all five brothers in the Code family were practising land surveyors. And surveyor's tended to marry into surveying families, while today there is at least one instance of surveyors marrying.

From the earliest days, not only was the land-settlement process governed by appropriate legislation, but so were the professional qualifications required of surveyors and the manner in which the surveys of townships, concessions, and lots were to be carried out. By the same token, any transaction today that involves the purchase or transfer of land, or of the size and exact location of buildings, say for mortgage purposes, requires a survey made by a qualified surveyor. Which brings us to one of the subjects of this book, the Association of Ontario Land Surveyors. With its authority first granted by the Ontario legislature in 1892, this body was set up to maintain, as a self-regulating body, the standards of the profession and to examine student surveyors, pronounce upon their professional competence, and, in effect, grant them their licence to practise. All of this is symbolized by the letters "O.L.S." that only a duly qualified Ontario Land Surveyor is allowed to use after his or her name, and without whose signature surveys have no validity in law.

In recent years the professional land surveyor in Ontario has had to meet a new challenge. The need to face the rigours of the climate in rugged and inhospitable country has given way to the need to adapt to recent advances in science such as those in photogrammetry, computer technology, and remote-sensing from satellites. There are new ways of measuring distances – and this to an accuracy that would have astonished a surveyor of a hundred years ago. All these advances have had a profound impact on the profession. At the time of writing, the Association of Ontario Land Surveyors is re-evaluating its function and its form in the light of such changes. However, with an active membership of 798 as of April 1992, the association is vigilant, as ever, to its responsibility under provincial legislation to maintain the standards of the profession, in order – as the Surveyors Act prosaically puts it – "that the public interest may be served and protected."

ACKNOWLEDGMENTS

Firstly, I wish to thank the Association of Ontario Land Surveyors for the opportunity of writing this book and, in particular, Lorraine Petzold, O.L.S., then executive-director of the association, for her help and suggestions.

Many Ontario Land Surveyors patiently answered my many queries, among them Charles Gibson, Steven Gossling, Robert G. Holder, Martin H. Kaldeway, Lenox T. Lane, Robert L. Lemon, Hunter Mackenzie, Grenville Rogers, Wilfred J. Ryan, M. Neil Simpson, Leonard P. Stidwill, and the late John F. Weston. Regretfully, many interesting reminiscences recounted by the above and much local surveying history had to be excluded for reasons of space.

Of the members of the association's Archives Committee, David M. Churchmuch, Danny P. Quinlan, and William C. Yates were of particular help. W. John Quinsey drew my attention to surveyors' diaries of particular interest and loaned me material of his own. Sandy Chapman, Daphne Kuehn, and Janie Heffernan in the association office were unfailingly helpful.

I am indebted to Sydney G. Hancock, O.L.S., for an interview and for material on the history of Steep Rock Iron Mines, Ltd. William J. Daniels, O.L.S., gave valuable advice on early surveying instruments and supplied illustrative material.

In collaboration with William D. Ratz, Bruce Wright, and T. Spence Foreman (all now retired Ontario Land Surveyors), Harold S. Howden, O.L.S., produced an extremely useful summary of the survey history of the Department of Highways (now the Ministry of Transportation). Further thanks are due to Harold Howden for the photograph of a painting in the Ministry of Transportation library at Downsview and for obtaining the ministry's permission to include it in the book.

The staff of Ontario's Ministry of Natural Resources were generous in supplying information, assistance, and advice, among them the surveyor general, Pier (Peter) L. Finos, O.L.S., C.L.S., James A. MacIntosh, O.L.S., Barry W. Costello, O.L.S., J. Morgan Goadsby, O.L.S., Michael B. Smart, Dennis E. Jeanes, and Allan Day. John Schragge and Greg Barber of the Ontario Ministry of Transportation supplied information and material.

J.E. Hietala, O.L.S., senior project manager of Marshall Macklin Monaghan, sent me unpublished material on the survey history of northern Ontario.

Jean Trapido-Rosenthal, librarian, the St. Augustine Historical Society, St. Augustine, Florida, furnished information on early Spanish surveying and on Frederick Haldimand's military career in Florida. Bruce S. Elliott of Ottawa drew my attention to a deficiency in John Stegman's survey in what is now Nepean Township and loaned me his article on the subject.

My thanks to Ron Orasi, archivist, Inco Limited in Sudbury, for material on the early history of the mining industry in Sudbury and on John D. Evans, O.L.S. My thanks also to M.A. McAllister of the Anderson Farm Museum in Lively for additional material on the founding of Sudbury.

I am indebted to Dr. Gordon Gracie, director, Centre for Surveying Science, Erindale Campus, University of Toronto, for information about the Centre and to the late Professor D.C. Kapoor, O.L.S., for statistics on enrolment. Professor David W. Lambden, O.L.S., C.L.S., also of the Centre, enlightened me on the background history of the association's Survey Review Department, the workings of which were kindly explained to me by Andrea E. Tieman, O.L.S.

Robert G. Code, O.L.S., a former surveyor general of Ontario, supplied information and material on the Ontario Co-ordinate system and the adoption by the province of the Universal Transverse Mercator Grid. Robert O. Semper, secretary-treasurer of the Canadian Council of Land Surveyors, supplied information on the founding of the council.

The staff of the Archives of Ontario gave assistance and advice on innumerable occasions. Leon S. Warmski, Karen Bergsteinsson, and Christine Niarchos-Bourolias were of particular help. Michael Moir, archivist, the Toronto Harbour Commission, supplied information and material on early surveys of Toronto harbour.

Dr. Alec C. McEwen, then commissioner of the Canadian Section of the International Boundary Commission, Ottawa, read part of an early draft of the book and made helpful comments and suggestions.

Several maps were drawn by Sherry C. Niemetz, C.S.T., of the City of Scarborough's Engineering and Surveys Division, thanks to the good offices of David Churchmuch, O.L.S., C.L.S., the division's assistant director.

Above all, I am indebted to Lou M. Sebert, C.L.S., who not only read and commented exhaustively upon succeeding drafts of the book, but lent me much of his own material. For this and for his continuing interest, encouragement, and enthusiasm for the project, my very sincere thanks.

Lastly, I owe more than I can say to my wife, Monica, for her patience, advice, and encouragement during the many months it took to research and write this book, and for her help in locating and obtaining illustrations and maps.

INTRODUCTION

Writing in about A.D. 540, Magnus Cassidorus, a Calabrian historian who was secretary to the king of the Ostrogoths, one of the tribes then overrunning the Roman Empire, wrote a remarkable tribute to the surveyors who had helped build that empire. He commented on the high esteem in which Romans held surveyors, and then went on, in a passage that rings down the centuries both as a tribute to the land surveyor and as a summary of his work that could scarcely be bettered:

> The land surveyor is like a judge; the deserted fields become his forum ... You would fancy him a madman when you see him walking along the most devious paths. But in truth he is seeking for the traces of lost facts in rough woods and thickets. He walks not as other men walk. His path is the book from which he reads; he shows what he is saying; he proves what he has learned; by his steps he divides the rights of hostile claimants; and like a mighty river he takes away the fields of one side to deposit them on the other.[1]

Boundaries were considered by the Romans to be so important that one of their deities presided over them. His name was Terminus, and his symbol, appropriately enough, was a stone.

By Roman times, land surveying in the western world was already thousands of years old. Virtually from the dawn of civilization, rulers of cities, principalities, and states have raised money by taxing landowners, and because that land had to be measured or surveyed, it follows that the profession of surveying is a very ancient one indeed. Still surviving from 1000 B.C. and even earlier are Sumerian boundary stones and clay tablets showing the layout of cities and adjacent agricultural areas.

Not much is known about the methods used by the earliest surveyors. A Theban tomb inscription, dating to about 1400 B.C., seems to show surveyors using a slit in a palm leaf as a sighting device – the forerunner of the slit and hair sights that would be developed in medieval Europe. Egyptian land surveyors were kept particularly busy because the annual flooding of the land tended to obliterate boundary marks. Egyptian surveyors used a slit palm leaf in combination with a plumb line as a way of establishing a required line. For measuring right angles, the Egyptians used a set square and may also have used a cross made from the ribs of palm leaves with plumb bobs hanging from each of the four ends. The device was apparently meant to be suspended from the hand from a loop of cord tied to the intersection of the cross. Cords were used for measuring distances. In fact, Egyptian land surveyors were known as *harpedonaptae,* or "rope-stretchers," while in Babylonia "stretching a field" meant measuring it. Indeed, before they were superseded by metal chains in the early 1600s, cords would be used in Europe and in early colonial America to measure distances. They were stretched beforehand and then waxed to reduce shrinkage from the damp.

In their primitive way, the Babylonian and Egyptian surveyors were engaged in what is now known as "cadastral" surveying. Though "cadastral" sounds like it has something to do with the stars, the word has its roots in the French word "cadastre," meaning a register of property. Thus cadastral surveyors are primarily concerned with the location and size of parcels of land and buildings in connection with transfer of ownership or their evaluation for tax or mortgage purposes. Today, many of Ontario's land surveyors spend much of their time in cadastral surveying, now often termed "legal surveying."

The instruments used by Roman land surveyors or *agrimensores,* literally "land measurers," seem to have been crude – at least from what we know of them, which isn't a great deal. To measure right angles, it seems that the Romans commonly used what was called the *groma,* an adaptation of a device known as a

"Grecian star," which in turn was a more solidly built version of the surveyor's cross used by the Egyptians. For levelling, the Romans used a plumb bob suspended from a triangle for small jobs, water troughs, or *chorobates,* for larger. The latter remained in essence the standard method for centuries.

Crude though their instruments may have been, the Romans accomplished wonders. It was in Roman times that the close connection – one might well call it the symbiotic relationship – between surveying and what we now call civil engineering was first established. Aqueducts were one product of this connection, such as the Gier aqueduct serving Lyon, 47 miles (75 km) long and incorporating four inverted siphons, one of them about 400 feet deep no less. Things didn't always go right, though, even for the Romans.

The knowledge of mathematics that is the basis of all but the crudest forms of land surveying came from the Arabs and the Greeks, much of it developed in connection with the growing science of astronomy. With advances in astronomy came a growing interest in the shape and size of the earth and ways of defining the position of features on the earth's surface – which brings us to the Greeks and the great Greek school of learning at Alexandria founded in 331 B.C. by Alexander the Great. The western world's first text on land surveying was written by Heron of Alexandria, probably in about A.D. 100. Euclid, who wrote his famous works on geometry in about 300 B.C., taught mathematics at the school at Alexandria. Among the other teachers was Eratosthenes, the Greek astronomer, mathematician, and geographer born about 276 B.C. and who had been brought to Alexandria to superintend its great library.

In about 500 B.C. Pythagoras had concluded that, as the sun and moon was round, the earth was probably also round and not flat as was generally believed. A century later Aristotle became convinced that Pythagoras was right. Eratosthenes went further and, in so doing, founded the science of geodesy, that is to say, the branch of mathematics that deals with the shape or figure of the earth. Eratosthenes devised an ingenious method for measuring the circumference of the earth. Using nothing but the sun's shadow, a wooden pole, a protractor, and his powers of reasoning, he arrived at a figure for the circumference of the earth that may well have been correct within a few hundred miles.

Eratosthenes was also the first to come up with the concept of the "meridian," a term we shall hear much of in the pages that follow and which refers to an imaginary circle around the earth that passes directly over an observer's head and through both celestial poles, or, to put it more simply, a circle passing through places with the same longitude, or to put even more simply, an imaginary line on the ground pointing to the true, as opposed to the magnetic, north. Of necessity, such lines converge, unlike parallels of latitude, which never do. A degree of longitude equals 69.17 miles (111.32 km) at the equator and zero at the poles, resulting in a convergence that is measurable even over a matter of miles and which, depending on the east-west extent of the land being surveyed, the latter-day land surveyor must take into account.

Roman Surveyors Had Their Troubles Too

An inscription from northern Africa dating about A.D. 153 tells the somewhat hair-raising story of Nonius Datus. This retired surveyor from the III Legion *Augusta* had been brought in to salvage a tunnelling project that had gone badly wrong. The plan had called for a 1400 foot (427 m) tunnel that was to carry water through a hill in the coastal city of Saldae (now Bejaia). Tunnelling had gone forward from both sides of the mountain, but the two tunnels hadn't met. So Nonius Datus was hauled out of retirement and sent to put things right.

On their way to Saldae, Datus and his party were set upon by bandits who stripped them of their clothes and left Datus wounded. Undaunted, they reached Saldae where, according to Datus, he was taken to the hill "where those doubtful of the undertaking were lamenting." And with good reason. The tunnel borings were longer than the hill was wide. Not only had the two halves of the tunnel not met, but "the true direction had wandered over the hill from east to west." In the end, the work was begun again. Datus carried out the levelling and set troops to work to re-dig the tunnel, following which he handed over the project to be completed by a civilian contractor. (The relevant inscription has been variously translated. See, for example, Kiely, *Surveying Instruments*, 42–43.)

Alexander the Great: Town Planner

Alexander, a Macedonian and former pupil of Aristotle, had made himself master of Greece, Syria, Palestine, and Egypt in a matter of three years. He had a habit of naming cities after himself. On the western side of the Nile Delta he saw an excellent site for a city; such was his enthusiasm that he sat down immediately to plan it himself. The story goes that he was in so much of a hurry to get his new city built that he laid out the outer walls of the city himself using cornmeal from his soldiers' packs. Leaving Egypt, Alexander went on to occupy Persia and much of modern Pakistan, all this before he died at the age of thirty-three. The university, or school, established at Alexandria became the principle seat of learning in the ancient world. It survived well into the Christian era.

A century or so after Eratosthenes, Hipparchus, the first great astronomer, initiated the science of trigonometry and was the first to set astronomy on a sound geometrical basis. He had followed up Eratosthenes's idea of meridians and suggested defining the geographical position of places using imaginary lines of latitude and longitude. Of all the teachers at Alexandria, however, none would have a greater impact on European thought and the course of overseas discovery than Claudius Ptolemy, an astronomer and geographer who worked at the school between about A.D. 140 and 160. Following Hipparchus's method of locating places on the earth's surface, he listed some eight thousand places in the known world together with their latitudes and longitudes. Finally, though it is not known whether he actually drew the maps himself, he produced an atlas known as the *Geographia*, which included nearly thirty maps of different regions, one of them a map of the world, and nearly seventy other maps of smaller areas. The maps were drawn to scale, making Ptolemy the first to stress the importance of this procedure.

However, Ptolemy's world map had serious flaws. Disregarding Eratosthenes's estimate of the earth's circumference, Ptolemy chose to use the figure arrived at by Posidonius, a Greek astronomer and philosopher whose estimate of the world's circumference of the earth fell short by nearly 7000 miles (over 1100 km). Furthermore, Ptolemy overestimated the size of Euro-Asia, which, according to him, stretched about halfway around the world. Missing altogether was the American continent, not to mention the Pacific Ocean and Australasia. Dusted off and re-examined in fourteenth-century Europe, Ptolemy's *Geographia* would mislead monarchs, statesmen, and early navigators alike for over a hundred years.

Some of the instruments developed by early astronomers were adapted for navigational use when European mariners first ventured onto the open ocean. Among these was the earliest of all scientific instruments, the astrolabe, which appeared in about the third century B.C. The astrolabe in its simplest form, namely a disk with 360 degrees* marked on its perimeter and with a sight or alidade pivoted at its centre, was used by mariners and explorers, such as Samuel de Champlain, to determine latitude by measuring the altitude (that is, the angular distance) of the sun or other heavenly bodies. Land surveyors found little use for this instrument. However, a derivative of the astrolabe, known as the quadrant, came to be widely used by surveyors.

As its name implies, the quadrant was basically a quarter-circle with 90 degrees marked on its rim and which was first described in a Moslem work about A.D. 800, by which time it was already apparently in general use. By the seventeenth century, the quadrant was in common use by navigators and land surveyors for the measurement of vertical angles. And, later, quadrants would be built into more complex surveying instruments when these came to be developed.

Of all the navigational devices that came to be used by land surveyors, none was of such fundamental importance as the magnetic compass. The compass was probably being used in Europe in the late 1100s and possibly earlier – historians still argue the point. Compass variation, or departure from the true north, was first noted in the fifteenth century. This variation arises from the fact that the magnetic north pole does not correspond with the north pole itself. Not only that, but the position of the magnetic pole is constantly changing. In a sense, Canada owns the magnetic pole. Since the early 1830s when its position was first accurately determined, the magnetic pole has wandered northward at about 5 miles (8 km) a year and is now on Bathurst Island, one of the Queen Elizabeth Islands in the Northwest Territories. The magnetic compass is subject to other causes of variation. Mineral deposits may alter the local magnetic field, as may the material used to house the compass. So early surveyors using magnetic compasses to lay out their courses were urged to check the variation of their compasses frequently, by comparing the north as indicated by the compass with a meridian indicating the true north.

The first instrument designed specifically for surveying appeared early in the sixteenth century. Apparently capable of measuring angles on both the horizontal and vertical planes, it was called a

How Eratosthenes Measured the Earth

Eratosthenes knew that at Syene (now Aswan) the sun was directly overhead at the summer solstice when it shone down a well without casting a shadow. He determined that on the same day in Alexandria the sun at its zenith lay at an angle of 87 degrees, or 7 degrees from the vertical, as estimated from the shadow of a vertical pole. He reasoned that this 7 degrees bore the same relation to the 360 degrees covered by the earth in one complete revolution as the distance from Alexandria to Syene did to the earth's circumference. He reckoned that Alexandria was 5000 stadia from Syene, a distance based, it is thought, on the time taken for a camel caravan to travel between them. This gave him a figure for the earth's circumference of 225 000 stadia, the modern polar value of which is now placed at 24 860.53 miles (40 008.05 km). However, as the length of his stadia is now the subject of scholarly argument, all we can say today is that he was either right within 0.5 percent or over today's accepted value by about 15 percent. Either way it was an astonishing feat considering the crudity of his equipment.

*Why 360 degrees in a circle? No one knows for sure. Chaldean or Babylonian astronomers, a thousand years or more before Christ, worked with circles divided into 360 degrees, this being an approximation, it is assumed, of the number of days it takes the earth to make its annual circuit around the sun. The Chinese, until they learned something of European science from Jesuit missionaries in the 1600s, divided their circles more accurately into 365.25 degrees.

"polimetrum," and was thought to have been used by a cartographer and surveyor named Martin Waldseemüller to produce maps of Lorraine and the Upper Rhine, which he published in 1511. And in 1529, Gemma Frisius, a student at the University of Louvain (now Leuven not far east of Brussels in modern Belgium), then a noted centre of learning, devised an instrument that he called an "epipedometron," consisting of a modified astrolabe mounted on a compass.

Gemma Frisius's epipedometron was built in connection with a new approach to land surveying, or, to be more precise, large-scale mapping, which he described and which came to be known as triangulation. Over distances of about 12 miles (19 km), the principles of plane geometry as used in cadastral surveying cannot be applied without serious error because of the curvature of the earth. The branch of surveying that takes the shape of the earth into account is known as geodetic surveying and until the years following the Second World War when new methods of determining positions on the earth's surface using satellites were developed, triangulation was the principal method used by geodetic surveyors.

As a method, triangulation is extremely simple. First, a base line is laid down, the length and geographical position of which is accurately determined. Then, from each end of the base line, bearings are taken on a selected visible point or survey station. The position of that point, which may be a considerable distance from the base line, is given by the intersection of the two bearings. The distances between each end of the base line and the point observed may be calculated from the length of the base line and the observed angles or bearings. This results in a triangle, of which the position of the apices are known as well as the length of its sides. These sides become in effect two new base lines, from the ends of which observations may be made on further points or survey stations. In this way a triangulation net may be built up across the area or region being triangulated.

As far back as the late 1700s, France and Britain had embarked on a systematic triangulation of their respective countries with a view to producing detailed topographic small-scale maps, and by the close of the nineteenth century a number of industrialized nations were doing the same – including a newly emerging Japan and several countries in what was then the British empire. For example, Sir George Everest, one-time surveyor general of India and the man after whom Mount Everest is named, completed the first monumental triangulation of India (the Himalayas excepted) in the mid-1800s.

But, astonishingly enough, Ontario – indeed Canada as a whole – got by without any systematic geodetic or topographic mapping until the twentieth century.[2] Such early provincial maps as were produced in Ontario were pieced together from the cadastral surveys of individual townships turned in by crown surveyors, later augmented by information provided by private surveyors who produced various county "atlases." No elevations were taken in such surveys. And apart from precise determinations of latitude and longitude made by British Admiralty hydrographers when surveying the Great Lakes and a few similar determinations made elsewhere by happenstance, the precise location and elevation of the province's towns, cities, rivers, and lakes, or any other feature for that matter, man-made or otherwise, remained unknown until well into the 1900s. The lack of a national geodetic survey would become a scandal until the federal government was finally shamed into it by various scientific and professional bodies, notably the Association of Ontario Land Surveyors.

In Waldseemüller's polimetrum and Frisius's epipedometron we see the forerunners of the theodolite that would be developed in England. Up until a few years ago when it was replaced by electronic distance-measuring instruments, the theodolite was the basic instrument used by land surveyors throughout most of the nineteenth and twentieth century. Basically, the theodolite consisted in its final form of a telescope fitted with cross-hairs mounted over a compass in such a way that both horizontal and vertical angles could be accurately measured. In North America, the theodolite came to be known as a "transit," this following an American modification in the early 1800s.

A Triangulation of Elizabethan England?

While Gemma Frisius is usually considered to be the first to enunciate the principles of triangulation, it has been pointed out that much the same idea had been propounded in an English manuscript dating from the 1300s. And it may well have been in England that triangulation was first used in a major mapping project. In the early 1570s, a young English surveyor, Christopher Saxton, was commissioned by Elizabeth I's secretary of state, William Cecil, Lord Burghley, to produce a detailed map of England and Wales. After only five seasons of mapping, Saxton had completed the field work, from which he produced thirty-four maps showing not only county boundaries but cities, towns, villages, rivers, and parks as well. How did he complete the field work so quickly?

Surviving are royal instructions to local authorities to allow Saxton access to towers, castles, hills, and other "highe place[s]" – those places, in fact, that formed the national network of warning beacons that would be lit to signal the arrival of the Spanish Armada. It is thought that Saxton may have used these "highe places" to map by triangulation, using a plane-table and an early form of theodolite. Saxton's completed work was published in atlas form in 1579. Saxton's reward from the queen: a ten-year monopoly on the publication and sale of his atlas, together with his very own coat-of-arms.

The early history of land surveying in England was connected not with scientific progress or with advances in cartography, but rather with changes in the pattern of agricultural landholding. And because it was in England that the feudal system first started to break down, with a consequent change in the pattern of landholding, it was there that modern land surveying started to emerge as a profession. The close connection between land surveying and the law developed in England at a very early date – the earliest English survey map still extant was made in about 1300 in connection with a dispute between three barons over land ownership.

With the Normans the process known as the "enclosures" began, whereby the open fields of the Anglo-Saxons were divided by ditches, fields, and roads. The enclosures led to so many disputes over land titles that manorial courts came to include courts of survey, where such matters could be thrashed out by a surveyor, who would arrive at a decision after viewing the land and hearing evidence under oath. Still in common use today is the English medieval term used to denote a type of legal description of an irregularly shaped parcel of land, known as a "description by metes and bounds."

In those very early days, the task of measuring land in England was not made any easier by the multiplicity of the terms and units used. "Rods," "poles," or "perches" were used interchangeably. A rod, pole, or perch was the equivalent of 12 feet (3.7 km) in southern England, in the north it was 22 feet. And rods might differ in length according to the type of land being measured – whether it was arable, pasture, or woodland. An acre, originally the amount of land that a yoke of oxen could plough in a day, was defined as being 160 square rods, whatever the length of the rod being used. This happy state of Anglo-Saxon confusion ended in 1277 when Edward I standardized weights and measures – though the modern mind might wonder whether Edward I went far enough. The rod was set at 16.5 feet, which was a German measure of length

called the "ruthen," which the Angles or Saxons had brought with them. A statute acre, as before, was set at 160 square rods.

It was in England that the methodology used by the land surveyors in what is now Ontario – and throughout the English-speaking world for that matter – was developed. The very first English text on land surveying, written in 1523 by Anthony Fitzherbert (though some say it may have been his brother John), had no real title. It started off "Here Begynneth a right Fruteful Mater and hath to name the boke Surveynge Improvementes ..." and stressed the importance of what came to be called a surveyor's diary, instructing the surveyor to keep a small book, wherein to record his findings. While the book had little or nothing to say about practical surveying, it did touch on a range of important matters, such as the law concerning land ownership, that are still pertinent to the education of a land surveyor over four hundred years later.

Increases in land values in sixteenth-century England, which resulted from the on-going process of

---

Descriptions by Metes and Bounds

"Metes" is a Middle English word meaning a boundary or boundary stone, and "bounds" means a territorial limit, such as a river or other natural feature. Starting at what the land surveyor calls the "point of commencement," the boundaries of the parcel are traced by means of measured distances and stated "courses," or compass bearings, from one corner to the next. Having traced (or "traversed") the perimeter, the surveyor eventually gets back to where he started from, thus "closing" his survey. Given straight sides, the boundaries of the parcel may well describe the geometric figure known as a polygon, the internal angles of which should add up to 180(n-2) degrees, thus supplying the surveyor with a check on his work. If they don't so add up, the error is distributed among the various angles. A traverse around the perimeter of a parcel is known as a "closed" traverse. Closed traverses might also be carried out around a lake, while the course of a river might be plotted by an open-ended traverse.

In earlier days, a surveyor's "point of commencement" in a legal description was often a tree, which, disappearing in the course of time, would result in many a headache for a later surveyor trying to make sense of the earlier surveyor's description. Likewise, earlier township or lot corners might well be wooden posts which rotted and disappeared. In northern Ontario, wooden survey posts were apt to be burned in forest fires, which sometimes made it extremely difficult to locate an earlier survey line.

Theodolite: What's in a Name?

The word "theodolite" is certainly a shortened form of "theodolitus," but where did "theodolitus" come from? From the Greek words for "I view" or "I behold" together with that for "visible" or "clear"? The Oxford English Dictionary suggests it might. Another theory has it that "theodolitus" is a tribute to Theodulus, a minor Greek mathematician. Or did the word come from a poem in Old French entitled "Theodolet," which in turn is a translation from a Latin poem entitled "Theodulus"? In fact was the word made up at all? Perhaps it came from "althelida," a word already being used by early Oxford scientists to denote an index or sight, a corruption, in turn, of the Arab word "alhidada" for the same device – which is certainly where our word "alidade" comes from. So as far as the origin of the term "theodolite" goes, your guess is as good as anyone's.

enclosures, led to a growing need for more accurate descriptions of land, which in turn led to a greater demand for both more surveyors and for more precise ways of measuring land. At the same time, the general level of education among all but the upper classes remained abysmally low. To help remedy this situation, several men brought out books in the mid-1500s. The most notable was Leonard Digges. A mathematician who dabbled in optics (with a claim to the invention of the telescope), Digges was also an educator who wrote widely on applied mathematics and related military subjects. Drawing on the latest in European science and technology, he published *A Book Named Tectonicon* in 1556.

In 1571 Leonard Digges's second book came out, which may be said to be famous for no other reason than it was the first English text to use the name "theodolitus" from which the word theodolite would be derived. Entitled *Pantometria,* the book was published by Leonard's son, John, one of the leading English mathematicians of his day. In his book, Digges describes how to build what he called an "instrument topographicall," using which there was "no manner, altitude, latitude, longitude, or profunditie can offer it selfe, howsoever it be situate, which you may not both readily and exactly measure."[3] Incorporated in his instrument was a "theodolitus." It bore little resemblance to what we call a theodolite. No compass is shown as part of the instrument, though Digges mentions that one should be used to align the instrument to the north-south meridian. Digges advised that the instrument should be mounted on a flat surface attached to the top of a pole with a sharp point to allow it to be stuck in the ground – the tripod had yet to be invented.

Meanwhile other English surveying texts published in the late sixteenth century touched on methodology. Thus Valentine Leigh, a professional surveyor, stressed in a book published in 1577 the importance of writing all measurements in a "paperbooke" wherein the surveyor should also note the number of houses on a parcel of land along with information on standing timber, mills, the presence of minerals, and anything else of particular interest or importance. We have here the forerunner of the standard "Instructions" that, in the course of time, were to be issued to all crown surveyors in Ontario.

In his text on practical surveying written in 1590, Cyprian Lucar, a surveyor, mathematician, and self-styled "gentleman," included an illustrated list of a surveyor's equipment at the time. There is a plane table,* which he calls a "geometricall table," mounted on a short pole with three short spikes on the end to help hold it firmly in the ground, a frame for holding the paper "which covereth the geometricall table," a carpenter's square to ensure right angles, a draughtsman's compass for measuring distances on the table, a "keeler" or pencil and a "sharp pointed cole" (coal) to draw with, a stool to sit on, and, surprisingly, a military side-drum. This was possibly used in a crude form of triangulation, wherein drums were placed on the top of three or more hills and lines of sight drawn directly on the faces of the drums. Finally there is a surveyor's "chain" to measure lengths – this to be made out of a four perch or 66-foot (20-m) length of wire, divided into links, each 1 foot long, which should be painted different colours to expedite and reduce errors in measuring.

By the close of the sixteenth century, the circumferentor had made its appearance. This hand-held instrument for measuring horizontal angles would become the standard workhorse of the land surveyors who laid out the first settlements in what became Ontario – and all of colonial America for that matter. Consisting simply of a magnetic compass with a centrally mounted sight or alidade, its great advantage was

its portability, hence its name, derived from the Latin, meaning "to carry about." The name was coined by John Godwyn, who taught mathematics in London, and who, according to some contemporary surveyors, invented the instrument, even though something close to it was undoubtedly already being used in mainland Europe. Simple and cheap to make and repair, the circumferentor remained in everyday use until well into the nineteenth century.

While it was Ralph Agas who first mentioned using the circumferentor, the first English surveyor to describe it was John Norden, a crown surveyor who surveyed Windsor, among other places. In a book published in 1611, Norden pointed out how the circumferentor differed from more complex instruments, such as Digges's "instrument topographicall." Whereas bearings with the latter were obtained with a movable sight after the instrument had been positioned with respect to the meridian, the reverse was true with the circumferentor. In the circumferentor the sights were fixed to the instrument, so that after sighting by moving the whole instrument around, the required bearing was read off the compass or "wandering needle."

Norden called his book *Surveyors Dialogue* because, like several other English surveying texts at that period, it was written in the form of a dialogue. In a five-way dialogue between the lord of the manor, a farmer, a tenant, a bailiff, and the surveyor himself, Norden explains to the public just what a surveyor does and why he does it, just as the Association of Ontario Land Surveyors is still doing some four hundred years later.

Thus by the time Europeans were starting to make the first charts and maps of North America, land surveying was emerging as a profession in northern Europe, surveying methodology was well advanced, and more sophisticated surveying instruments were starting to appear.

---

*First described by Abel Foullon in a book published in Paris in 1551, the plane table is essentially a drawing board on which a map or plan can be drawn directly to scale in the field, using one or more alidades or sights. Requiring a minimum of mathematical knowledge, it soon became very popular with English surveyors.

Come the Renaissance in the fourteenth century Ptolemy's *Geographia* was dusted off and re-examined, misleading world map and all. About 1375, what is known as the *Catalan Atlas* appeared, which consisted of a number of maps showing the world as it was then thought to be. The atlas was apparently based on the *Geographia*, with modifications based on information on Asia brought back by Marco Polo and others. By the early 1400s then, charts for the use of mariners were appearing, together with maps of the world – with America still missing. So with this flawed view of world geography and a belief that the earth was much smaller than it was, it came as no great surprise to Christopher Columbus when in 1492 he found himself off the coast of what he thought was Japan after only thirty-three days' sailing.

Columbus had hardly returned from his voyage than the Spanish claim to all the lands beyond the western ocean was disputed by the Portuguese who maintained that their seamen had sighted Brazil in the process of rounding the Cape of Good Hope to reach the Far East. In 1494, with what seems to us now as breathtaking presumption, the two countries signed the Treaty of Tordesillas, which in effect divided the world in two. With the exception of lands already under the sway of Christian princes, Spain and Portugal claimed all the land east and west, respectively, of a meridian passing through a point 370 leagues west of Cape Verde, a line roughly approximating longitude 45°W. For the most part, Spain and Portugal were to abide by their treaty. England and France took no notice of it at all.

It seems that, in 1480, some Bristol merchants financed an abortive attempt to find new markets in North America. But England's involvement in the New World is commonly assumed to have begun with the voyages of John Cabot in 1497 and 1498. Cabot, born Giovanni Caboto in Genoa, had been living in Bristol since 1490, then one of England's largest and most prosperous cities. English fishermen had been sailing to Iceland since the mid-1400s to buy fish. It is reasonable to suppose, then, that English fishermen had learned something of the northeastern coast of Canada from the Icelanders and may have even found themselves fishing off that coast themselves. At any rate, Cabot seemed to know what he was about when he persuaded Henry VII to underwrite a voyage, which, like that of Columbus, had as its object the discovery of a shortcut to the Far East.

Cabot sailed from Bristol in May 1497 in the *Matthew*, a tiny ship with a crew of only eighteen, and he got back in August. No one knows for sure what land he reached. It may have been Labrador, Newfoundland, or Cape Breton Island. But wherever it was, he landed, planted a large cross, and claimed the land for England. His was the first recorded landing on mainland North America since the Norsemen came centuries before. The next year he set off again, this time with five ships. He landed in Greenland, and then sailed south, possibly reaching Chesapeake Bay before turning for home. However, on the way back, three or more of Cabot's ships were lost with all hands; among them was Cabot himself. Henry VII and the merchants of Bristol were discouraged, and for the time being England lost interest in North America.

However, Cabot's first voyage had attracted the attention of King Manuel of Portugal. He reasoned that if Cabot had indeed reached the eastern shore of Asia, then he, Manuel, would not be breaking his treaty with Spain if he found out more about this region. According to Cabot, it was rich in much-needed fish. Manuel commissioned Gaspar Corte-Real and members of his family to have a look at the coasts that Cabot had sailed along. They made two voyages in the early 1500s. But beyond the fact that they reached Newfoundland, little is known about their voyages, though the information they brought back confirmed the basic geography of the region. Other Portuguese ships explored the northeastern coasts of Canada in the early 1500s. The story goes that on one such ship there was a *lavrador*, or farmer, and that it was he who first sighted an unknown coast. By way of a jest, the land was called *Terra del Lavrador*, from which comes the modern name of Labrador.

In 1515 Francis I became king of France at the age of twenty-one. It was under this young and energetic king that France first ventured into the New World. However, when he came to the throne, France was in the middle of a costly on-again-off-again war involving the Italian republics, Spain, and the Holy Roman Empire. Short of money, Francis I persuaded the silk merchants of Lyon to finance a voyage of discovery, who hired Giovanni Verazzano, a Genoese like Cabot, to make the voyage upon which French claims to North America were ultimately to be based.

Sailing in 1524, Verazzano reached the West Indies and then sailed north up the eastern seaboard of North America, explored Long Island Sound, had a look at the Hudson River, and then sailed north again towards Newfoundland. Standing well out from land, he missed the all-important strait that would have led him to the St. Lawrence. However, he did help establish that the east coast of North America was unbroken. Estaban Gomez, a Spaniard, explored the eastern seaboard the year after Verazzano and came to the same conclusion.

Meanwhile something of the true dimensions of the world had been revealed by Ferdinand Magellan, a Portuguese seaman who, convinced that he could find a less arduous route to the Far East, set sail with five ships in 1520 and found his way into the Pacific via the strait at the southern tip of South America that now bears his name. Magellan himself was killed in a fracas with natives in the Philippines, but one of his five ships sailed around the Cape of Good Hope to reach Europe three long years after it had left it.

China appeared to be at least twice as far from Europe as monarchs and merchants hoped it was. But surely a shorter and more practicable route than Magellan's was there for the finding? It was to search for that route that Francis I of France dispatched Jacques Cartier in 1534. He was instructed by Francis I to sail to the "New Lands" on the other side of the North Atlantic "to discover ... islands and territories where, it is said, are great quantities of gold and other riches." In dispatching expeditions to the New World, European monarchs, perennially short of bullion as they were, gave a very high priority to finding sources of gold and silver.

Cartier made three voyages. In the first – like Cabot he seemed to know where he was going – he headed for the northeast coast of Newfoundland, followed the coastline north until he reached and entered the northern end of the Strait of Belle Isle, and then sailed southward, hugging the Labrador coast, which in its barrenness he compared to the land that God gave Cain, reached Prince Edward Island, and continued south to land on the Gaspé Peninsula, where, at or near the Baie de Chaleur, he planted a cross and claimed the land for France.

Returning to the area the next spring, Cartier spent several months exploring, assisted by the two natives who had accompanied him to France and back (the French were very keen on what we now call cultural exchanges). Cartier took a look at Anticosti Island, and it was here on 10 August 1535 that he named a bay Saint Lawrence, after the saint whose feast day it was. This name came to be applied to the river that Cartier soon found himself sailing up, eventually encountering impassable rapids in the vicinity of an imposing hill which he called Mont Royal, the site of the future Montreal. Climbing the hill, Cartier glimpsed the upper St. Lawrence flowing from the southwest, while from his native guides he learned of the existence of the Ottawa River and of indescribably large bodies of water to the northwest.

On his third voyage in 1541, Cartier sailed as second-in-command to Jean-François de la Rocque, Sieur de Roberval, who had been charged with the establishment of a French colony on the St. Lawrence. The two

men sailed independently and Cartier went sadly astray. He was sidetracked by deposits of iron pyrites, or "fool's gold," which he found upstream from present-day Quebec city. He hurried back to France with his cargo of iron pyrites and lumps of pure quartz, which he mistook for diamonds. Meanwhile, left in the lurch, Roberval made a brave attempt to carry out his instructions, sailing up the "Rivière du Canada" and wintering upriver. But things went badly, and in the summer of 1543 the colony, such as it was, was abandoned and Roberval sailed for home.

Back in France, Cartier's treasures had been exposed for what they were, giving rise to the derisive expression "As false as a Canadian diamond."* While Cartier's exploring days may have ended in a cloud of tragicomedy, he had established a French "sphere of influence" in North America and had made an enormous contribution to Canadian geography. More pertinent to the immediate subject, his explorations pointed the way into the heart of the continent. In the years ahead, Cartier's countrymen, missionaries and laymen alike, would follow his path and in so doing would start to open up the country that is now Ontario.

Cartier's discoveries enabled several French mapmakers to depict the northeast coast of America with a little more accuracy, notably, Pierre Desceliers, an artist and map-maker living near Dieppe, who produced a map in the late 1540s on which the gulf of the St. Lawrence and the name "Canada" appears, both approximately in the right place. Francis I, however, did not follow up Cartier's voyages. Like Henry VII of England he was disillusioned with voyages of discovery. He was getting deeper into debt with his foreign wars. Further, there was a mounting tide of religious dissent to worry about. In 1515, two years after Francis I came to the throne, Martin Luther had nailed his protest against the excesses of the Roman Catholic

Church to the door of a church in Wittenberg, an act that is usually taken as the start of the Reformation. Eight years later the first French Protestants were being burnt at the stake. This was the start of a period of religious strife that was to rend France for the next 150 years.

Much as the Pilgrim Fathers later succeeded in doing, French Protestants, or Huguenots, attempted to found a colony in America where they could practise their religion unmolested. Early attempts to found settlements in Brazil were scotched by the Portuguese. Then, in 1562, a trading post was built on the South Carolina coast. The settlement didn't last long. The colonists fought among themselves, gave up, built a ship, and sailed for home. Undaunted, the Huguenots tried again in 1564, building a fortified trading post called Fort Caroline near the mouth of the St. John River in Florida.* Fort Caroline was far too near Spanish trade routes for comfort, so Philip II of Spain ordered its elimination. This was speedily done, with all Huguenot prisoners executed – the Spaniards boasted that they had killed not just 150 Frenchmen but 150 heretics as well. It was following this intrusion into their territory that the Spanish founded St. Augustine in 1565, the oldest European settlement in the United States.

More or less coinciding with the destruction of Fort Caroline and the founding of St. Augustine, the Spanish government enacted two laws governing the method of settlement to be followed in the Americas, the first in 1563 and the second ten years later. These resulted in the appearance of the first townships or municipalities in North America. These townships were to be not less than 144 square miles (373 km²) laid out in lots of sufficient size to sustain a peasant or

---

*In spite of all this, Cartier continued to be held in some esteem by the king and retired to his native town of St. Malo, where he was to die of the plague in 1557. He was buried there in the cathedral.

*Curiously enough, it was at Fort Caroline that Sir Richard Hawkins first saw men smoking: he took pipes and tobacco back with him to England and so started what some might now call the first drug craze in England – the craze which half a century later enabled England's first North American colony, Virginia, to survive and prosper.

foot soldier. Central to each municipality was a town plot, laid out grid-fashion, surrounded by 50-by-100 foot (15-by-30 m) market-garden plots. The so-called Dorchester township – a township plan that Lord Dorchester would attempt to introduce in what is now Ontario in the late 1780s – was remarkably similar to the Spanish "municipality."

The idea of finding a shortcut to China had remained very much alive in sixteenth-century England. One of Henry VIII's advisors told him that it could be reached by simply sailing over the pole, and in 1527 John Rut tried it, only to hit pack ice somewhere off Labrador. With attempts failing to reach the Far East along Russia's north coast, interest in finding a way around North America was renewed. And so began the search for The Northwest Passage, a search that Britain would make peculiarly her own and which would lead to the progressive elucidation of the geography of the eastern Canadian Arctic.

The search for the Northwest Passage began with Martin (later Sir Martin) Frobisher, a Yorkshireman. He had spent many years as a merchant seaman. He had been thinking about finding a shortcut to the Far East for some time, in his words, "the only thing in the world left undone whereby a notable mind might be made famous and remarkable."[4] Financed by a private company, he sailed on his first voyage in June 1576. One of his three ships foundered and another was abandoned, but Frobisher sailed on in the 25-ton *Gabriel* to sight the Labrador coast at the end of July. He then sailed north to find himself in the bay named after him at the southeastern end of Baffin Island. There he found some "fool's gold," and, much as Cartier had been, he was led down the garden path by it, organizing abortive mining expeditions in 1577 and 1578. However, in 1578 he did sail part way up the strait that Henry Hudson was to explore three decades later and which would be named Hudson Strait.

Frobisher pointed the way for John Davis, his successor in the search for the Northwest Passage. By this time the search for the passage was deemed a matter of national importance, so Davis received the royal sanction to search for a way to China. He sailed with two ships, charmingly named *Sunneshine* and *Mooneshine,* early in 1585. On the way, he did some hydrographic work in the Scilly Isles, using a small boat to chart some of the islands, together with their "rockes and harboroughs" – taking care on his chart to add "lynes and scales thereunto convenient." Arriving off the west coast of Greenland in July, he sailed north, to reach latitude 66°40', just inside the Arctic Circle, before crossing the strait named after him and thence to Baffin Island. He followed much the same route on his second trip a year later, with *Mermaiyde* and *North Starre* added to his little fleet.

In his third and final voyage to Davis Strait he got as far north along the coast of Greenland as latitude 72°12'N before crossing over to Baffin Island as before and then returning to England. Though he failed to find the Northwest Passage, his explorations did much towards elucidating the geographic puzzle that the Canadian Arctic then presented to England's cartographers. On his return, Davis wrote a couple of books, one of them on navigation, while later years found him in the Far East where, at Bintang near Singapore, he was killed by Japanese pirates in 1605.

The first English attempt to found a colony in North America may be said to have begun with Sir Humphrey Gilbert, who was granted a charter from Queen Elizabeth I to found a colony in lands not already possessed by "any Christian prince or people." In 1578 he set off with his half brother, Walter

---

The First English Surveyors in North America

Having sent a fleet to reconnoiter the North Carolina coast, Sir Walter Raleigh decided to found his colony inside the Outer Banks on Roanoke Island. With Queen Elizabeth I's permission, he called it Virginia. Landing in 1585, the hundred or so colonists survived one winter and then were taken home at their request by Sir Francis Drake the following summer.

While the attempt failed, it did take the first English surveyors to North America. Raleigh had selected two men to chronicle the expedition. His choice was inspired. One was Thomas Hariot, variously described as a surveyor, astronomer, mathematician, and master navigator. The other, also sometimes described as a surveyor, was the water colour artist, John White, who, interestingly enough, had painted the Inuit when a member of Frobisher's 1577 expedition. On his return Hariot published *A Brief and True Report of the New Found Land of Virginia*. With illustrations by White, Hariot described the native animals, classified food ources and building materials, and gave an account of the local Algonquins and their way of life, which, it is said, no other Englishman was to equal for accuracy for a century.

Raleigh's second attempt led to perhaps the greatest mystery in the annals of North American settlement. In 1587 he sent more colonists to Roanoke Island, eighty-four men, nine women, and nine children. Because of war with Spain and the Spanish Armada, the progress of the colony wasn't checked until 1590. All that was found were some rusting armour, pillaged chests, and rotting maps. The only clue to the colonists' fate were the letters "CRO" inscribed on a tree and the word "Croatoan" carved on a post, the name of an island to the south of Roanoke. Were they all killed, or were those that survived a native attack carried off and assimilated by a local tribe? Historians have been debating the question ever since. The site of the colony is now a U.S. national historic site not far from Manteo, North Carolina.

Raleigh, on an expedition that ended disastrously, with Gilbert losing all his – and his wife's – money. But in 1583 he tried again, with the idea of founding a trading post and colony on the coast of Maine. On the way there and almost as afterthought he looked in at St. John's, Newfoundland, and claimed that island for Queen Elizabeth, telling the assembled fishermen of various nationalities, no doubt much to their surprise, that they were now the Queen's subjects, thus establishing England's earliest claim to that island.

Sailing south, Gilbert sent one of his four ships home and lost another on Sable Island. With his remaining ships battered by gales, he became discouraged and turned for home. He was in the pinnace *Squirrel,* a vessel of only 10 tons, which went down one night in heavy seas taking Gilbert and all on board with her. Sir Walter Raleigh, as he now was, inherited his half brother Gilbert's charter and made two attempts in the 1580s to found an English colony on mainland America. Both failed, though the first was instrumental in bringing the first English surveyors to North America. It would be another twenty years before the English tried again and, this time, succeeded.

So What Was So Special about the Beaver?

In the sixteenth century both men and women made much use of fur in their dress. Men used it, among other things, to trim their cloaks and collars or as a turn-back on sleeves. Favourite furs were lynx, wolf, and sable. Then in the late 1500s, a way was discovered to felt the short hairs of beaver skins. Its water-repellent qualities made this felt the perfect material for hats; these soon became immensely popular. The traditional source of furs was Russia. Transported overland, for the most part, Russian fur was expensive. And then for political reasons this source dried up. So the finding of an alternative source – and a much cheaper one at that – came at an opportune moment.

Since 1562, France had been laid virtually prostrate by the series of civil wars known as the Wars of Religion. (An early victim was Roberval, Cartier's erstwhile commander. A Huguenot, he was killed in a street brawl in 1560.) The wars went on in a welter of political intrigue and assassinations for forty years. They ended in 1598 when Henry of Navarre came to the throne as Henry IV. By his Edict of Nantes, Henry gave a measure of religious freedom to the Huguenots – though it was not to last. Henry also ended an ongoing war with Spain, and so gave France a peace she had not known for the better part of a century. And so, with Spanish power on the wane and both England and Holland now bustling with maritime enterprise, the eyes of Henry and the French court turned once more to North America.

Canadian furs had been trickling into France since the early 1580s when three St. Malo ships sailed up the St. Lawrence as far as the Lachine Rapids to bring back a profitable cargo. About the same time, Rouen merchants sent a ship to trade off the east coast from Cape Breton southward. Thereafter trade in Canadian furs intensified. But it became increasingly clear that a local base of operations was required if the trade was to be put on a firm footing. In 1599, Henry IV gave Pierre de Chauvin a trading monopoly on condition that he built a "stronghold," or fort and actually lived in the country, in other words, that he should found a French settlement in North America.

Pierre de Chauvin built his stronghold at Tadoussac where the Saguenay flows into the St. Lawrence. He survived a single winter in Canada, though most of his small party did not, and he had a couple of years of successful trading. Then he died and was succeeded in his venture by a colleague, a Huguenot sea captain experienced in the fur trade, variously known as François Pontgravé or François Gravé Du Pont. With Pontgravé, as he headed for Tadoussac for the 1603 fur-trading season, was one Samuel de Champlain. And it is at this point that Champlain steps onto the stage of Canadian history. It was Champlain who, using an explorer-surveyor's eye, first made astronomical observations in what is now Ontario, and so it is with Champlain that the story of land surveying in Ontario begins.

Part 1

Early Days of Exploration and Settlement

CHAPTER ONE

Samuel de Champlain

There are some curious gaps in our knowledge of Samuel de Champlain. For one thing, no one knows what he looked like, "authentic" likenesses and heroic statues notwithstanding. Even the date of his birth is uncertain. Most historians give the year as 1670. However it *is* known that he was born in Brouage, a seaport some 19 miles (30 km) south of the port of La Rochelle, France. At the time, La Rochelle was literally a bastion of Protestantism in France, fortified by royal permission. So was Champlain a Huguenot by birth? Again, no one knows. His Christian name, some argue, shows that he was. Later he married a Huguenot, doing so at a time when mixed marriages were not exactly encouraged. There is no firm evidence one way or the other. But whether Protestant or Catholic, he was beyond doubt a zealous Christian by the standards of his time.

In his late twenties, Champlain made a voyage that took him first to Spain and then to the West Indies. A couple of years later he got a chance to sail with Pontgravé to the St. Lawrence, apparently as a passenger. Sailing in March 1603, they reached Tadoussac towards the end of May. A verbal exchange then took place between the French and the Montagnais that was to have far reaching consequences in the years ahead.

At a native meeting marking the return of two Montagnais who had been visiting France, a message from the king was relayed to the natives. The king of France, they were told, wished the Montagnais well and desired to people their country. Moreover, he wished to make peace with their enemies and, failing that, would send forces to defeat them. Fateful words. In reply, the Montagnais leader said that they were happy to have the French settling in their country and, further, that they were content to have their king making war on their enemies. As indeed they might.

The Montagnais, the Algonquin, and the Huron, whose homelands lay between what is now Lake Simcoe and Nottawasaga Bay (in what we now call Huronia) were in loose alliance against the Iroquois confederacy, whose territory bordered the south shore of Lake Ontario. In Champlain's time there were five nations in the confederacy. To the west were the Seneca and Cayuga, who gave their names to two of the Finger Lakes in what is now upper New York state. Farther east were the Onondaga and the Oneida, the latter around the present lake of that name, while to the east of them again came the Mohawk who lived in the Mohawk Valley, through which the Mohawk River flows east into the Hudson. About 1720 the Tuscarora trekked north from Carolina to join the Five Nations, thereby making the Six Nation Confederacy, whose remnants now live chiefly around Brantford. Though the French did not realize it at the time, by casually allying themselves with the Montagnais, Algonquin, and Huron, they were to incur the lasting enmity of the Iroquois. This was to cost them dearly in the next 150 years.

As Cartier had done some seventy years earlier, Champlain travelled up the St. Lawrence. Upriver from Quebec, Champlain noted enthusiastically – much as Cartier had done before him – that the country got "finer and finer." As Cartier had found earlier, the rapids below the island of Montreal proved impassable, so the travellers went on by skiff "constructed on purpose for passing the said rapid," but unlike the natives in their canoes, they soon ran into trouble. Eventually they made it to the Lachine rapids. On seeing them, Champlain pronounced upon the absolute necessity of using easily portaged canoes, rather than European boats, to explore the country. Using the "canoe of the savages one may travel freely and quickly throughout the country," Champlain commented, adding optimistically, "so that by directing one's course with the help of the savages ... a man may see all that is to be seen, good and bad, within the space of a year or two."[1]

Again much as Cartier had done, Champlain learned something of the geography of the hinterland from the natives with the help of crude maps, "which I made them draw by hand," perhaps in the sand. What follows is the first description of the Great Lakes by a European, based on what Champlain gleaned from the natives.

They told us, that beyond the first rapid we had seen, they go up the river ... to a river [the Ottawa] which extends to the dwelling-place of the Algonquins ... and then they pass five rapids ... Then they come to a lake [Lake St. Francis], which may be fifteen or sixteen leagues long [about 43 miles, but actually about 28 miles]. Beyond it they enter a river [the St. Lawrence], which may be a league broad, and travel some two leagues up it; and then enter another lake ... at the end of which they pass five other rapids [beginning with the Long Sault above Cornwall], the distance from first to last being some twenty-five or thirty leagues ... [say, 75 miles, but actually only about 37 miles before the construction of the St. Lawrence Seaway.]

Then they come to a lake [Lake Ontario] which may be some eighty leagues in length [about 236 miles: a good approximation. It's actually about 196 miles long], and in which there are many islands, and at the extremity of which the water is brackish [a puzzle to translators and others] and the winter mild. At the end of the said lake they pass a fall [Niagara Falls] which is somewhat high, and where little water flows over ... From here they enter another lake [Lake Erie], which may be some sixty leagues long [180 miles: a gross underestimate. Lake Erie is about 250 miles long] and the water is very brackish. [This could make some sense, especially if the

level in the lakes were low – which might also account for the lack of water passing over the falls]. Having reached the end of it [Lake Erie] they come to a strait [the Detroit River] which leads into the interior.

They told us that they themselves had passed no further, and had not seen the extremity of a lake [beyond the strait] because it was so vast that they will not venture to put out into the same, for fear that some storm or gale should surprise them. They say that in summer the sun sets to the north of this lake, and in winter it sets as it were in the middle of it; and that the water there is very salt, like that of the sea.[2]

Presumably the reference to salt water was that of Hudson Bay of which the natives had heard. But Champlain, on mulling over what he had been told, concluded through a somewhat muddled train of reasoning, that the huge lake of which the natives had spoken, might well be the Pacific Ocean.

Pontgravé and Champlain sailed for France in the middle of August, arriving home to find that another French venture to North America was being planned. The brainchild of a Huguenot nobleman, Sieur de Monts, it was to be a trading monopoly again, but one granted by the king to a joint-stock company after the English fashion, the king to get 10 percent of the profits. In return for their monopoly, the company agreed to establish a settlement, look for minerals, and convert the heathen. De Monts asked Champlain to take part in his venture. And so Champlain set off on his third trans-Atlantic voyage, this time as an accredited geographer and cartographer.

Believing that the winter on the Atlantic coast would be milder than along the St. Lawrence, the two-ship expedition headed for what is now the coast of Nova Scotia. Leaving in April 1604, they made a landing a month later at a place they named La Have, now

with a river and island of the same name, about 62 miles (100 km) south of present-day Halifax. And it was there that Champlain made his first chart in mainland Canada. Not only that, it was the first modern chart made in North America (see figure 1.1).

Looking for a suitable site for a settlement, the two ships cruised southward and then northward into the Bay of Fundy, where Port Royal was briefly noted and named. They then continued southward along the Atlantic coast, coming to a large river on the Feast of St. John and naming it after him. Heading south again, they found themselves in what is now Passamaquoddy Bay and then into and up another large river where they finally fetched up on an island they called L'Isle Sancte Croix. Here the adventurers decided to pass the winter, building a storehouse and some houses, the remains of which were to play their

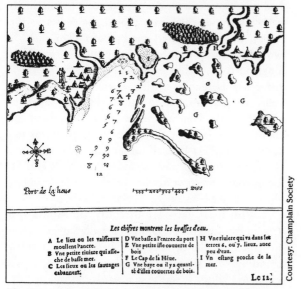

Figure 1.1 Champlain's chart of Port de la Have. Drawn in 1604, it was the first modern chart made in Canada. Note soundings and the use of symbols to indicate wooded areas and native villages. (From Biggar, *The Works of Samuel de Champlain*.)

part in determining the Canadian–United States border nearly two hundred years later.

After passing an appalling winter on L'Isle Sancte Croix, de Monts decided to look for a better site for the settlement. Leaving their island, they cruised south once more, inspecting the coasts of present-day Maine. After exploring the Kennebec River, and with Champlain busily charting as they went, they eventually arrived at Cape Anne just north of what is now Gloucester and Boston. They got a cool reception from the natives, though Champlain did manage to extract enough information from them to include Boston harbour in a small-scale map of the region that he produced a year later. Still moving south, they found a fine harbour towards the end of July, which they called Port St. Louis and which Champlain duly mapped.

Some ten years earlier, Captain John Smith, who had much to do with the survival of Virginia in its early days and who had explored the coasts to the north, had named the same harbour Plymouth. It would be Smith's enthusiastic account of the New England coast, published in 1616, that would catch the eye of a group of English religious dissenters later called the Puritans, and so lead the Pilgrim Fathers to set off for the New World in 1620. Bound for the mouth of the Hudson, they were driven by storms and forced to make a landfall, or landing, at Cape Cod. There they finally settled around Champlain's Port St. Louis some fifteen years after he charted it, founding the first of the New England colonies in the process.

With local natives unfriendly, de Monts and Champlain left Port St. Louis to inspect the inside arm of Cape Cod. Shortly afterward, there was a misunderstanding with the natives, violence erupted, and a sailor was killed. It was now towards the end of July. So, with time running out and many possibly hostile Indians in the area, de Monts ordered a retreat to L'Isle Sancte Croix. Arriving there he made a snap decision to relocate the settlement back to Port Royal where he hoped the winter would be more benign. This they

The de Monts Settlement on St. Croix and the International Boundary

Nearly two hundred years after de Monts abandoned the short-lived settlement on L'Isle Sancte Croix, it played a crucial role in setting the international boundary between Canada and the United States after the Revolutionary War. In both the Proclamation of 1763 and the Quebec Act of 1774 the St. Croix River was named as being the boundary between the American colony of Maine and Britain's new colony of Quebec. So in the Treaty of Versailles of 1783, which recognized American independence, the international boundary was placed along the same river. The only trouble was that in 1783 there was no river of that name. Excavations were carried out on Dochet Island in the Schoodie River, as a result of which, artifacts were brought to light that confirmed the British claim that the island was indeed the site of the old French settlement – and that the St. Croix River and the Schoodie were one and the same.

did. With the building of that settlement, the long and troubled history of Acadia began.

De Monts soon returned to France. Some forty or so men remained at Port Royal under Pontgravé who had turned up with supplies. Among them was Champlain, who wanted to try to realize a long cherished dream of reviving the old French trading post in Florida. The dream finally faded in October 1606, when an expedition on its way south had a bloody confrontation in which both natives and Frenchmen were killed. Once more a discouraged expedition returned to Port Royal. Worse was to come the following year. Back home in France, de Monts's monopoly was revoked, the result of lobbying by independent traders. On hearing the news, the settlement at Port Royal was abandoned and the would-be settlers set sail for France.

Even as the French were dismantling their settlement at Port Royal in 1607, English settlers to the south of them were founding the colony of Virginia. After various setbacks, the colony was to survive, though it wasn't until 1613, when the colonists found they had a valuable export in the form of tobacco, that Virginia started to thrive. In Virginia, the first professional English land surveyors in North America went to work – Virginia even had a surveyor general as early

as 1621. In early Virginia, prices and salaries were expressed in terms of tobacco. Thus, land surveyors in 1624 were paid 10 pounds (4.5 kg) of tobacco per 100 acres surveyed. Later this became 20 pounds, to be doubled again in 1666.

Back in France, Champlain persuaded de Monts that yet another attempt should be made to establish a French settlement in North America. This time, Champlain insisted, it should be on the St. Lawrence with the important proviso that it should be upstream from the post at Tadoussac, thus short-circuiting the post's supply of furs from the upper St. Lawrence. In spite of opposition from the independent traders, the king gave de Monts his monopoly but only for one year. Champlain was appointed commander of the proposed expedition and thus was on his own for the first time.

On this expedition, which left in the spring of 1608, Champlain founded a settlement at Quebec – the first permanent French settlement in North America and thus of the Canada that was to come. And it was also on this expedition, that the fateful decision was made to honour Henry IV's promise to the Montagnais and their allies to help them in their war against the Iroquois. Champlain and two Frenchmen joined a raiding party, that made its way up the

Richelieu River, reaching the lake to which Champlain gave his name. Here they bumped into some Iroquois, and, in the resulting fracas, Champlain and his men killed several of them. The Iroquois never forgot; for several decades to come the upper St. Lawrence and what is now upstate New York would be a "no-go" area for the French. Later the animosity felt by the Iroquois for the French was to be put to good use by the British.

Just about the time when Champlain was heading up the Richelieu for his ill-fated encounter with the Iroquois, Henry Hudson, sailing on behalf the Dutch, was cruising south along the Maine coast much as Champlain had done three years earlier. Hudson remains something of a mystery man. He emerged from obscurity in 1607 when, in service with the Dutch, he made the first of two unsuccessful voyages in search of a "north-east passage" to China. Then, in 1608 and still in Dutch service, he was dispatched to look for the Northwest Passage. In search of this he sailed first northwest and then west to find himself off Newfoundland. Turning south, he eventually reached Cape Cod in the spring of 1609, where he landed just as Champlain had done, and then continued southward around the coast to fetch up in what is now the harbour of New York. And even as Champlain was sailing home in 1609, Hudson was making his slow way up the river that bears his name, getting as far as present-day Albany – which the Dutch would call Fort Orange – before returning downstream. Back in the Netherlands, Hudson reported that the area would yield a good profit in furs, and before long Dutch traders were busy along the Hudson River.

Back in France, Henry IV declined to renew de Mont's monopoly. However, the latter persuaded some Rouen merchants to help keep the post at Quebec going, and in April 1610 Champlain set off once more for New France. One of the more impressive things about Champlain was the extraordinary energy of the man; like a trans-Atlantic yo-yo he regularly commuted from his homeland to spend his summers – the exploring season as it were – in New France.

Champlain's 1610 expedition was virtually a carbon-copy of his previous one except that a lot more Iroquois were killed, this in a French-assisted assault by the Algonquin and their allies on an Iroquoian fort at the mouth of the Richelieu River. And that was about all that came of that expedition, except that in a "cultural exchange" a Huron was swapped for a young Frenchman, thought to be Étienne Brûlé, who went to live among the Indians.

Back in France, Henry IV had been assassinated and was succeeded by his son Louis XIII. Louis was only nine years of age, so until 1614 France was ruled by a regent in the person of his mother, Marie de Médici, who declined to give de Monts or Champlain the royal ear. However, de Monts was still prepared to back Champlain personally, who set off for New France once more, in the spring of 1611, leaving behind his newly married twelve-year-old wife. Soon after his arrival, Champlain attempted to reach the northern, "inland" sea via the St. Maurice River that flows into the St. Lawrence at what is now Trois-Rivières. But the Algonquin, who wanted no white men in their territory, declined to co-operate. In any case, the river peters out in the hills after about 62 miles (100 km).

So Champlain, his hopes now pinned on getting up the Ottawa River, moved up the St. Lawrence to Lachine. While waiting at a prearranged rendezvous for the Algonquins, Champlain did a bit of exploring at the confluence of the Ottawa and St. Lawrence rivers, for the first time seeing country not reached by Cartier. The Algonquins finally arrived, and Champlain traded back his Huron visitor for Brûlé (if Brûlé it was), who had spent the winter in Huronia. But Champlain's hopes of ascending the Ottawa were frustrated yet again. The Algonquins were unco-operative, though Champlain did acquire further information on the geography of the interior. Presumably Champlain must have also learned much from the putative Brûlé. By the fall of 1611 the indefatigable Champlain was back in France.

For the first time in years, Champlain spent a summer in his native country. De Monts had no money left and had had no luck in regaining his monopoly from Louis XIII. It was in France that Champlain heard the unwelcome news that Henry Hudson, now backed by English merchants, had explored the great northern bay that is named after him (see figure 1.2). Retained to search for the Northwest Passage, Hudson had sailed his *Discovery* up the strait that Frobisher and Davis had seen a few decades earlier and had finally entered the bay to sail down its eastern side. The onset of winter in 1610 found Hudson in what came to be called James Bay. It is thought that he stopped near the mouth of the Rupert River, which flows west from Quebec into Rupert Bay. Here he beached his ship and passed the winter. After Hudson announced his intention do go on looking for the Northwest Passage, a mutiny erupted, ending tragically, with Hudson, his son, and seven others set adrift in an open boat to meet their fate. Two of the three ringleaders of the mutiny were killed by natives, the third starved to death.

Robert Bylot sailed *Discovery* back to England, taking with him the charts Hudson had made. It was on these charts that, for the first time, any part of what is now Ontario appeared on a European map. On *Discovery*'s arrival in England, four of the nine survivors were tried for murder but reprieved – with their knowledge, these men were too valuable to hang. Among them was Bylot, who would later return to the Arctic with William Baffin.

Late in 1612, Champlain's fortunes took a dramatic turn for the better when he received a royal licence to return to New France. It was on this trip that he travelled up the Ottawa River and first set foot – and made the first observations for latitude – in what is now Ontario. He sailed early in 1613, taking with

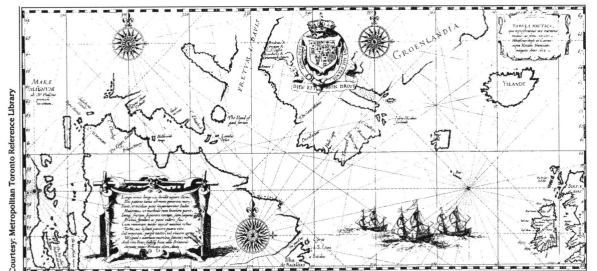

Figure 1.2 Published in 1612, the map, based on Henry Hudson's voyage, showed part of Ontario's northern shore line for the first time. The entrance to James Bay is clearly shown (bottom left), as is the entrance to Hudson Bay from Hudson Strait. The unseen western shore of Hudson Bay was conjectural. Note the strait already named for John Davis. Note also the cross marking the east on the compass roses. Denoting the Holy Land, such crosses commonly appeared on English compass roses until the eighteenth century.

him one Nicholas de Vignau, who had wintered with the natives in previous years and who Champlain had employed in his earlier explorations. De Vignau had turned up in France in 1612 with an exciting story: he had reached Hudson Bay via the Ottawa River and had seen the wreckage of an English ship on the shore, presumably Hudson's.

This, Champlain decided, he must see for himself. Heading for an Algonquin camp near present-day Pembroke, Champlain, four Frenchman including de Vignau, and a native left a small island opposite Mont Royal on 27 May 1613. They passed the rapids at La Chine "partly by portage, partly by tracking, and were forced to carry our canoes, clothes, provisions, and arms on our shoulders, which is no small labour for those who are not used to it."[3] Not long after they entered the Ottawa, they met some

Algonquins coming downriver and from them obtained a guide.

They were soon at the mouth of the north-flowing Petite Nation River. "The river is very attractive," Champlain observed, "on account of the beautiful islands in it, and of the lands along its banks covered with fine open woods. This land is suitable for tillage." Which is exactly what Loyalists were to think some 170 years later when they applied to have the area surveyed for settlement.

By 4 June they reached the mouths of the Gatineau and Rideau rivers, and, commenting on the falls at the mouth of the latter, Champlain called it "wonderful" and added, "It falls with such impetuosity that it forms an archway nearly four hundred yards in width."[4] They then arrived at the Chaudière Falls, which Champlain placed at 45°38'N (actually

45°25'33"N). Up to this point they had kept to the eastern bank of the Ottawa. But on 6 June they crossed over to the western, or Ontario, side of the river on the advice of the natives (de Vignau was already turning out to be something of a broken reed as a guide) who were to take them to the Algonquin camp in the Pembroke area via a chain of lakes that included the 8-mile (13-km) Muskrat Lake. Here, at what is now Gould's Landing north of Renfrew, Champlain made another observation for latitude, the first ever made in Ontario. He made it 46°40' (actually 46°34').

The going was not good.

We had much trouble in taking this route overland, being laden for my part alone with three arquebuses, an equal number of paddles, my cloak and some small articles. I encouraged our men, who were somewhat more heavily laden, but who suffered more from mosquitoes than from their loads ... Their pertinacity is so great that it is impossible to give any description of it.

The next day we passed along this pond [since identified as a small lake just southeast of Cobden in Renfrew county] ... and then made our way through more difficult country than we had yet seen, on account of the wind having blown down pine-trees on top of the other, which is no small inconvenience; for one must go now over, and now under, these trees.[5]

It may well have been while they were struggling through these windfalls that Champlain lost his astrolabe. It would be found again over 250 years later near Green Lake, northwest of Renfrew.

Finally arriving at the Algonquin settlement, matters took an ugly turn. The Algonquins suspected Champlain of wanting to contact the Nipissings

The Finding of Champlain's Astrolabe

In August 1867, a man and his teenage son were clearing land on the rear half of Lot 12, Second Concession, of Ross Township, this near Cobden, which lies on Highway 17 about halfway between Renfrew and Pembroke. The father had sawn up a windfall, an old red pine. The son was using oxen to drag the timber away. The last log was embedded in moss, and, in dislodging the log the son saw "a round yellow thing, nine or ten inches across."

He showed his find to his father who put it on a stump. Later that day his employer, one Captain Overman, turned up to see how the work was going, and the astrolabe was passed on to him. Overman gave it to Richard Cassels, president of the Ottawa railroad and forwarding company for which he worked. Cassel kept it until his death, when the astrolabe passed on to his son, Walter. In 1897 Walter Cassels offered it to the city of Quebec for $1,000. The city turned the offer down, as did the federal government. In 1901 Cassels sold the astrolabe for $500 to Samuel Hoffman, an American antiquarian, who bequeathed it in 1942 to the New York Historical Society, in whose keeping the astrolabe remained for many years. It is now in the Canadian Museum of Civilization, Hull, Quebec. While some have questioned its authenticity, there is little doubt that it really is Champlain's astrolabe.

The astrolabe found near Cobden, Ontario, in 1867. It is now in the Canadian Museum of Civilization, Hull, Quebec.

upriver in order to bypass the Algonquins as middlemen in the Ottawa River fur trade. This was probably true. They recognized de Vignau, accusing him of treachery and the French of breaking their promise to help them in a foray against the Iroquois the year before. Then, to further confuse the situation, de Vignau broke down and admitted he had never been to Hudson Bay and had been hoodwinking Champlain all along. The Algonquins threatened violence. Escorted downriver to the St. Lawrence, a discouraged Champlain lost no time in returning to France.

In 1610 the little settlement at Port Royal had been reoccupied, and in 1613 a mission had been set up on Mount Desert, an island off the coast of Maine. However, these had scarcely been established before an English expedition sailed north from Virginia and put an end to them – the long conflict between England and France in North America had begun. The English were now also laying claim to Hudson Bay. Clearly, if something was to come of New France, a new approach was necessary.

In putting together a promotional package for his next venture to Canada, Champlain offered not only its settlement but the promise of the cultural and religious conversion of the "heathen." Not a nomadic people, the Hurons were selected as promising converts. In his newly found zeal for the religious conversion of the aboriginals, Champlain had the support of the Recollet missionaries, four of whom joined him in Canada when he returned there in 1615. One of them, Father Joseph Le Caron, was so anxious to begin his ministry that, new to the country though he was, he decided not to wait for Champlain; he set off for Huronia virtually alone except for one guide. And so it was Le Caron, and not Champlain, as some histories imply, who pioneered the historic route to the upper lakes by way of the Ottawa River, Lake Nipissing, and the French River.

Two weeks later Champlain was paddling up the Ottawa in Le Caron's wake. He was not impressed by the country around Pembroke, describing it as an "ill-favoured region full of pines, birches, and a few oaks, very rocky, and in many places rather hilly. Moreover it is quite a wilderness, being barren and uninhabited, except for a few Algonquin savages."[6] However, this "frightful and abandoned region" was redeemed in his eyes by wild fruit, among them the blueberry, and he gave them the name "bluet," by which they are still known to Francophones. The country around Mattawa, which he placed on latitude 46°N (actually 46°18'), he thought was "very pleasant to look at, although unproductive."

Passing through Lake Nipissing and the French River, about which he had little to say, Champlain reached Lake Huron, which "in view of its size" he named the "Freshwater Sea." Reaching the vicinity of present-day Midland he noted a "great change in the country ... very fine, mostly cleared, with many hills and streams, which make it an agreeable district. I went to look at their Indian corn which at that time was far advanced in season."[7]

Once in Huronia Champlain was sidetracked yet again into a foray against the Iroquois. A village near present-day Syracuse was to be attacked by a joint force, with Champlain and his natives reinforced by Susquehannoks from Virginia brought north by Brûlé. (Probably the first European to see Niagara Falls, Brûlé is thought to have got as far as Chesapeake Bay on his trip to Virginia.) Things went badly wrong. Brûlé and his Susquehannocks didn't turn up, and, forewarned, the Iroquois made a spirited defence. After heavy losses and with Champlain himself wounded in both knee and foot, the attackers retreated. Unable to walk, Champlain pleaded in vain to be taken back to his own people on the St. Lawrence. Instead, he was carried back to Huronia where he overwintered, returning to the St. Lawrence in the summer of 1616 and thence back to France. With his many wounds and now nearly fifty, his exploring days were done.

In 1624 the fortunes of New France took an upward turn with the emergence of Duc de Richelieu as Louis XIII's chief minister. A giant of a man, he was to guide France's destiny for the best part of two decades. While the flow of furs from New France seemed satisfactory enough in 1624, the trading posts themselves were in a ramshackle condition; compared to the now flourishing English colony of Virginia, New France was only progressing slowly as a settlement. In 1627, Richelieu got around to doing something about it. He formed the Compagnie des Cent-Associés, or Company of One Hundred Associates, to

Figure 1.3 Samuel de Champlain's map of New France published in 1632.

set New France on its feet, the associates being of the bourgeois class. Under the terms of Richelieu's agreement, the company was given not only a monopoly over the fur trade but feudal rights to all of New France, which was defined as stretching from Florida to the Arctic Circle and westward as far the Great Lakes. In return, the company was required to transport settlers to New France.

All this was welcome news for Champlain, who had been appointed lieutenant-governor of New France in 1625. His vision of a thriving French colony in Canada was, it seemed, about to be realized. But, as fate would have it, the first convoy transporting emigrants to New France was intercepted by English ships

– this in an operation set in train by Charles I and financed by businessmen who had their own plans for the St. Lawrence valley. Under the command of David Kirke, the force took Tadoussac and then sailed just off the Quebec coastline, demanding Quebec's surrender. After Champlain finally capitulated, Quebec passed into English, or, to be precise, Scots hands for a couple of years, with Champlain spending a short time in England as a prisoner before he was returned to France.

When the dust had settled, Quebec was restored to France. A newly nominated governor of New France turned the job down, so Champlain was brought out of retirement and sent in his place. In

March 1633 he set sail once again for his beloved Quebec, only to die three years later on Christmas Day, 1635. He was sixty-five. Where he was buried, no one knows.

Perhaps Champlain's greatest legacy to those who would, quite literally, follow in his footsteps is his map of New France, compiled in 1632 when he was still an exile in France (see figure 1.3). Drawing on his own knowledge and reconciling this with information supplied by Brûlé and the northern native people, Champlain made a map that portrays, with some accuracy, the lower reaches of the Ottawa River and its relationship with Lac St. Louis, his name for Lake Ontario, though he greatly underestimated its size.

Georgian Bay on the other hand is shown as a large lake in its own right. He called it Mer Douce, with "douce" not used in its sense of gentle or mild, but as in "eau douce," the French term for fresh water. West of Mer Douce is Grand Lac, apparently a composite of Lakes Huron and Superior. Lakes Erie and St. Clair are indicated by small bodies of water, though interestingly enough they are shown as being connected with both the western end of Lac St. Louis (or Lake Ontario) and the upper Great lakes. Hudson Bay (unnamed) is more or less in its true position. And south of the upper St. Lawrence, and somewhat bigger than it should be, is the lake that commemorates his name, Lac de Champlain.

Hard-hit by the temporary occupation of the Quebec trading post by the English, the Company of One Hundred Associates, lacking the means to organize the settlement of New France themselves, passed on this responsibility to men on the spot. And so, starting in 1634, the seigneurial system came into existence.* Under this system, the company granted a large parcel of land to an individual – who immediately

---

*The seigneuriel system was very similar to that set up some five years earlier by the Dutch West India Company in the New Netherlands, later New York. There, the "seigneurs" were known as "patroons."

Seigneuries and the Ontario-Quebec Boundary in Southern Ontario

Excluding seigneuries in Labrador and the Gaspé, some small urban seigneuries, and those along Lake Champlain that passed into American hands after the Revolutionary War, there were nearly two hundred seigneuries in existence by 1791 when Upper Canada was formed. Four of them lay in the angle between the Ottawa and St. Lawrence Rivers, which is why the boundary between Upper and Lower Canada, when it was formed, strikes north between the two rivers (see figure 5.1).

---

acquired the enviable title of seigneur, or lord, in the process – on the principal condition that it be placed under agricultural production. These parcels or seigneuries varied in size but in the main were oblong, about 9 miles (15 km) in depth and 3 miles wide. Besides the seigneuries themselves, there were *augmentations* corresponding to the English term "additional" that came to be attached to some townships in Upper Canada. The attraction of owning a seigneurie, besides the title that went with it, was, of course, the income it would produce. If he wished, the seigneur could farm his land himself, but it was common practice to subdivide it and grant or concede land to others who held it under a rental system.

With some exceptions the seigneuries were subdivided into *rangs*, or ranges, of long narrow lots running back from rivers, reflecting a pattern of land use commonly found in Normandy, from which many of the early settlers came. Often about ten times as long as they were broad, an average farm lot was roughly 75 acres with a river frontage of about 575 feet (175 m). As a system of settlement the seigneuries offered several advantages. They were easy and cheap to survey and subdivide. Every farmer had direct access to the water, which offered an easy method of transport for produce both in summer and winter. The narrowness of the lots made for closeness of neighbours, while each farmer got a fair share of different types of terrain, these tending to change with distance from the river. The subdivided land became known to early French lawyers as

"concessions," a term that was to be carried over into what is now Ontario and is still, of course, in common use today. The way that the seigneuries were laid out would have a profound influence on the method used to subdivide the first townships in Ontario. Furthermore, seigneuries had been granted in the angle formed by the confluence of the Ottawa and St. Lawrence rivers, thereby determining where the Ontario-Quebec boundary in southern Ontario is today.

Meanwhile, as efforts were being made to put New France on its feet, English navigators had continued their unsuccessful search for the Northwest Passage and, in the process, had further elucidated the geography of the eastern Canadian Arctic. Hudson had been followed by others such as William Baffin and Robert Bylot. Baffin acted as navigator for an expedition that explored the west coast of Greenland in 1612, and which reached latitude 67°N before turning back. In 1615, acting this time as Robert Bylot's navigator, Baffin examined Hudson Strait and the east coast of Southampton Island. Returning to the region the following year, he explored the coast of Baffin Island and established the nature and extent of Baffin Bay – the great body of water between Canada's eastern Arctic and Greenland. (Baffin is reputed to be the first navigator to use celestial observations to determine longitude at sea. With only crude lunar tables and a pendulum clock to go by, however, his results were far from accurate.)

After a lull of some years, the search for the Northwest Passage was resumed in 1631 by Luke Foxe and Thomas James. They were friendly rivals, with Foxe sailing two days after James, Foxe from London, and James from Bristol, the merchants of which city were underwriting his voyage. Leaving in early June, James reached Hudson Bay a couple of months later and, after exploring part of its western coast, sailed south along it to Cape Henrietta Maria, at the mouth of the bay that now bears his name – the cape itself is named after James's ship. Here, quite by chance, he bumped into Foxe, and the two dined together on James's ship on 30 August. Leaving Foxe, James continued south into James Bay, having named the country round about "New South Wales," presumably in honour of his patrons. And it was on Charlton Island, which lies towards the head of the bay and athwart the seaward extension of the Ontario-Quebec boundary, that James used astronomic observations to determine the longitude, the first time this had been done on Canadian soil. (Charlton Island is now in the Northwest Territories.)

James observed and timed an eclipse of the moon, due in October of that year. This was done in collaboration with Henry Gellibrand, the Savilian professor of astronomy at Oxford who had shown James how to go about it. James also observed and timed the difference between the culmination of the moon (that is, the point at which the highest point is reached on the meridian) and that of various stars. Using James's observations of the moon culminations, Gellibrand placed Charlton Island at longitude 78°30'W, which is about 42.5 miles (68 km) east of where it actually is. However, Gellibrand accepted the longitude as derived from his and James's observations of the eclipse as being correct, this being considered the more reliable method of the two. This method placed Charlton Island at longitude 79°30' – which is where it is on modern maps.

In mid-winter, the pendulum clock that James was using to give local time froze with the cold so he had to give up his astronomic observations. But he and his men survived – the first Europeans to voluntarily winter in the Arctic. After digging their ship out of the ice in May and repairing it, they eventually got back to Bristol in October 1632. Some have suggested that Coleridge based his *Rime of the Ancient Mariner* on James's account of his voyage.

In the meantime, in 1631 Luke Foxe had sailed east through the channel between Baffin and Southampton islands, later called the Foxe Channel, and on into what came to be called the Foxe Basin. Unable to get farther west, he returned to England. With the failure of both James and Foxe, Britain's search for the Northwest Passage was to languish until the nineteenth century.

CHAPTER TWO

The Jesuits and Other Explorers

The geography of what is now Ontario, which Champlain had begun to elucidate, became rapidly clearer following the arrival in Quebec in 1632 of members of the Society of Jesus, or Jesuits for short. The Jesuits were more than just teachers and missionaries. They were a superbly trained elite with a thorough grounding, not just in the humanities but in all branches of learning. Indefatigable travellers and observers, their knowledge of the country grew steadily. To this knowledge they added what they learned from others to produce an on-going synthesis, which, through their published *Relations* soon passed into the public domain. The first Jesuits arrived in New France in 1625, and a year later they were in Huronia – all before Richelieu had even formed his Company of One Hundred Associates. With the formation of that company the Recollets had been eased out of the missionary picture.

With the English occupation of New France at an end, the Jesuits returned in 1632 with ambitious plans for the Hurons. No sooner had they arrived in Quebec than the first Jesuit left for the *pays d'en haut,* as the French called the western wilderness, a term corresponding to the English "up-country," and in 1639, under the direction of Father Jérôme Lalemant, a mission was built that became known as Ste. Marie Among the Hurons, this near Midland on the bank of the Wye River. Though it didn't last long, it was the first inland European settlement in North America.

The Jesuits in Huronia were the first to make estimations for longitude in southern Ontario. In the absence of a speedy and reliable method of determining longitude, reliance was still being placed on the land equivalent of "dead-reckoning" to calculate east-west

Saint-Marie Among the Hurons Today

An exploratory excavation of the site was carried out in 1855 by Father Felix Martin, S.J., but serious work did not start until the early 1940s, on behalf of the Royal Ontario Museum and the Jesuit order. Money ran out, but in the late 1940s the University of Western Ontario resumed the work for the Ontario government with actual reconstruction beginning in 1964. It is now a tourist and interpretive centre. Though heavily criticized in academic circles, Sainte Marie Among the Hurons remains an evocative and deeply impressive place to visit. From the summit of a nearby hill, where a Martyrs' Shrine now stands, there is a magnificent view of the shore of Georgian Bay, down which it is easy to imagine the Jesuits paddling south in their canoes some 350 years ago.

The Jesuit "Relations"

Sooner or later anyone with an interest in early Canadian history will come across a reference to the Jesuit *Relations.* What exactly were they? Between 1611 and 1768 each Jesuit missionary in North America was required to send to his Canadian Superior in Quebec an account of his year's activities. There they were combined into a single "relation," the French word for a narrative or narration. The complete *Relations* was forwarded to the provincial of the order in Paris, with those between 1632 to 1673 being printed and published. Then as now, they were an invaluable source of information on New France. In one of the greatest projects of modern scholarship, an American historian, Reuben Gold Thwaites, translated the *Relations* into English at the turn of the twentieth century. Published between 1896 and 1901, there are seventy-three volumes.

distances. The basic unit on land was a league, equivalent to the distance a fit man could walk in one hour, that is, just over 3 miles (5 km). Thus, with allowance for latitude, Champlain had assigned an east-west distance of 17.5 leagues to each degree of longitude in New France, that is, about 52.5 miles.

Using the same basic approach, Lalemant estimated that Huronia lay 12°, or 200 leagues (roughly 620 miles [1000 km]), west of Quebec, an overestimate of roughly 125 miles. He also estimated that Huronia lay just over 74° west of France. It is, in fact, about 80°, so he was not too far off. Later, other Jesuits were to make estimations of Huronia's longitude based on celestial observations, the closest being Father Francesco Bressani (see figure 2.1) who placed Huronia six hours, or 90° west of Rome, an underestimation of only 2°30' – it being remembered that until 1884, when an international conference agreed that the prime meridian should be that passing through Britain's Royal Observatory at Greenwich, all that could be said was that one place was so many degrees east or west of another.

By 1640 the Jesuits at Ste. Marie Among the Hurons already knew quite a lot about what is now southwest Ontario. Where had the information come from? It is conjectured that it came, perhaps, from a Recollet who, fifteen years earlier, had visited the Neutrals, a nation whose homeland is thought to have been around the western end of Lake Ontario; perhaps from Brûlé or Jean Nicolet who, like Brûlé, had lived among the natives and whose explorations had taken him as far as Green Bay at the northern end of Lake Michigan; or perhaps from itinerant French fur traders. At any rate, Fathers Jean de Brébeuf and Pierre Chaumonot set off in the fall of 1640 to spend that winter with the Neutrals. And while they were there they visited Niagara Falls as well as another nation not positively identified but which seems to have lived near present-day Windsor. Chaumonot did make a map of the region, but it disappeared. It seems likely

that the two priests got as far west as the Detroit River in that winter of 1640–41.

Their findings were duly described by Father Lalemant in his *Relation* of 1640–41 from Ste. Marie Among the Hurons, in which he not only clarifies the geography of the southern lakes, but spells out the strategic significance of Lake Ontario and the upper St. Lawrence if the Iroquois menace were to be nullified:

This stream or River [the Saint Clair] is that through which our great lake of the Hurons ... empties; it flows first into the lake of Erie, or of the Nation of the Cat, and at the end of that lake ... it enters into the territory of the Neutral Nation ... until it empties into the Ontario or lake of St. Louis, whence finally emerges the river that passes before Quebec, called the St. Lawrence. So that, if once we

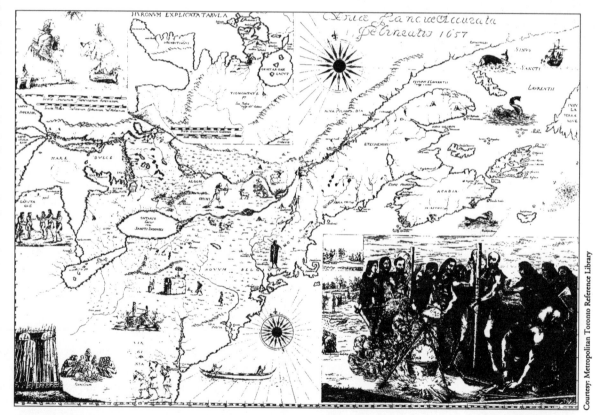

Figure 2.1 Map of Huronia and New France published in 1657 and attributed to the Jesuit Francesco Bressani, who worked among the Hurons from 1645 to 1649. The inset map of Huronia (top) shows the Bruce Peninsula and Lakes Simcoe and Couchiching. Lakes Erie and Huron are shown as connected. Stressing the religious theme, the martyrdom of Fathers Brébeuf and Lalemant is shown bottom right.

were masters of the coast of the sea nearest the dwelling of the Iroquois, we could ascend by the river St. Lawrence without danger, as far as the Neutral Nation, and far beyond, with considerable saving of time and trouble.[1]

In the late 1640s, Iroquois raids on Huronia intensified. In March 1649, the Iroquois attacked and burned an outlying mission where Fathers Brébeuf and Gabriel Lalemant met atrocious deaths. With further Iroquois attacks, the Jesuits abandoned and burned the mission at St. Marie. An attempt was made to re-establish the mission on Christian Island in Georgian Bay, but with a total of five Jesuit fathers murdered, the mission was finally withdrawn to Quebec in 1650.

The Iroquois then turned on the Hurons. With their numbers more than halved by European diseases and with the Iroquois now being armed by Dutch and English traders, the Hurons were easy prey. Those that weren't killed or made prisoner took refuge with the Ottawa and other nations. Three hundred finally gathered together at Lorette near Quebec where their descendants live to this day. Having dispersed the Hurons, the Iroquois went on to destroy the Petuns and the Neutrals. Emptied of its native people by the early 1650s, southern Ontario remained a virtual desert for half a century until the Mississaugas and other Ojibwas drifted south and appropriated it. Thus, when the Loyalists came, it would be these relative newcomers who possessed southern Ontario.

The dispersal of the Hurons by the Iroquois had an immediate and disastrous effect on the fur trade. Only a few years before, in 1651, the One Hundred Associates had passed on its monopoly to a locally based co-operative that called itself the Community of the Habitants of New France. The community now faced ruin. When the western Iroquois headed by the Onondaga turned up in Montreal in 1653 and suggested that a peace be negotiated, the French were all too happy to agree. The French also agreed to establish a trading post and mission among the Onondagas. This the Jesuits did on a site at the southern end of Lake Onondaga where Syracuse, New York, now stands. But the mission lasted only two years. The peace had been a shaky one at best and, warned that trouble was brewing once more, the fifty or so French at the new mission returned to Quebec. Full-scale war with the Mohawk broke out again.

However short their stay had been south of Lake Ontario, the Jesuits had made good use of their time from the geographic standpoint. They had explored the Finger Lakes in upstate New York for the first time. And for the first time, they had been able to travel up the St. Lawrence above Montreal. Father Simon le Moine made the first recorded passage of the upper St. Lawrence in 1654, nearly a century and a quarter after Cartier had first gazed on it from the summit of Mont Royal.

Cartographers in the mother country made good use of the geographical information flowing out of New France. From the 1620s onward, thanks to Richelieu, France had a ministry of marine to oversee its expanding colonial affairs, a revitalized merchant fleet, and a growing navy. The climate was right for the growth of French cartography, with the Sanson family leading the way. What was to amount to a cartographic dynasty was founded by Nicholas Sanson, born in 1600 and who, at the age of thirty, was appointed *Géographe ordinaire du Roi*, the king's geographer. With his two sons, Adrien and Guillaume, Nicholas produced a profusion of excellent maps in the middle years of the seventeenth century, among which were maps of North America that were published in 1650 and 1656, these based on the explorations of the Jesuits and other sources touched on above. For the first time, the Great Lakes are fully recognizable. Champlain's Lake St. Louis is shown with its alternative name, Lake Ontario. Lake Erie is there, as are the northeastern approaches to Lake Michigan and Manitoulin Island. Also shown is the narrow link between Lakes Erie and Huron via Lake St. Clair, giving credence to the supposition that Fathers Brébeuf and Chaumonot explored the region in the winter of 1640–41 in the days of Sainte-Marie Among the Hurons. However, only the eastern end of Lake Superior is depicted, named as such by the French not because of its grandeur or size, but simply because it was the "topmost" lake. In fact its extent was still unknown – but not for long.

In the same year that Father le Moine travelled up the St. Lawrence from Montreal, a large party of Ottawas and displaced Hurons had taken advantage of the temporary peace to bring a load of beaver down the Ottawa. Their arrival set in train a chain of events that led to the formation of the Hudson's Bay Company, which had far-reaching consequences, not only for Ontario but for the whole of Canada. The Ottawas and Hurons had come down from the upper lakes, a hitherto untapped source of furs and clearly one to be investigated. So when they returned up-country in 1654, one Médard Chouart des Groseilliers went with them, the governor of New France having granted his permission. Groseilliers returned two years later, having got as far west as Green Bay and the southwestern shore of Lake Superior. He brought back fifty canoe loads of furs and glowing accounts of the possibilities that the northwest offered in terms of both trade and missionary work.

A further bonanza in furs came in from the west in 1657. But with the Iroquois active once more, this new source of furs started to dry up with only six canoe loads appearing in 1659. These furs were brought in by Mississaugas, who made it clear that further furs depended upon French protection. Groseilliers wanted to go back with them. The governor refused permission, but Groseilliers went anyway, this time accompanied by the other half of perhaps the most famous exploration team in early Canadian history, Pierre-Esprit Radisson, by now Groseilliers's brother-in-law.

The pair were away a year, having got as far west as the Pigeon River, which today divides Canada from the United States just west of Lake Superior. They returned with sixty canoe loads of furs but also with a lot to tell about the western Great Lakes and the upper Mississippi valley. From the Crees they had learned of the rich trapping grounds north of Superior and the great northern south-reaching bay that gave access to it. It required no great leap of the imagination to envisage northern furs being transported directly to France via Hudson Bay, and thus beyond the reach of the Iroquois. This leap officials in New France were unable to make. And in spite of the much-needed economic boost that their furs and the native traders had brought the shaky colony, Radisson and Groseilliers were arrested for illegal trading, with the latter doing a spell in jail. To cap it all, their furs were confiscated.

Understandably put out, Groseilliers and Radisson took their ideas to the English in Boston and eventually to England itself. Their scheme of trading directly into Hudson Bay eventually caught the attention of Charles II's cousin, Prince Rupert, and in 1668 two English ships set out on a trial run. These were the *Nonsuch* and the *Eaglet*, with Groseilliers in the former and Radisson, needless to say, in the latter. *Eaglet* had to turn back, but a year later *Nonsuch* got back to England loaded with furs. A few months later, in May 1670, Charles II granted a charter to the "The Governor and Company of Adventurers of England trading into Hudson's Bay," thus making what is now commonly called "The Bay" the oldest joint-stock company in the English-speaking world. The company was given wide powers over what was called Rupert's Land, a vast territory that included all the land drained by rivers flowing into Hudson Bay. Just how vast, time was to show.

Groseilliers and Radisson had hardly got back to New France from their trip up-country when Father René Ménard was dispatched to open a mission near the western end of Lake Superior, some traders going

So What Became of Groseilliers and Radisson?

Both spent several years with the Hudson's Bay Company, helping to set up posts on Hudson and James bay. In the mid-1670s they were lured back into French service with generous cash offers, and they became involved in the Compagnie du Nord, which had been set up to challenge the Hudson's Bay Company. They now took to destroying the very Hudson's Bay posts they had helped build. Getting into trouble for this and for evading French taxes on furs, they went to France in a vain attempt to win their case. Here their ways parted. Groseilliers retired to die in New France, it is thought in about 1696 when he would have been seventy-eight. Radisson served with the French Navy and then in another bewildering *volte-face* not only rejoined the Hudson's Bay Company but persuaded his nephew, then in charge of the French trading post on the Nelson River – which he himself had established – to hand the posts over to the Hudson's Bay Company. Whereupon he ran the post himself. By now thoroughly and quite understandably *persona non grata* with the French authorities, he retired with his family to London where after writing his memoirs he died in 1710.

with him. The mission, known as St. Esprit, was at the foot of Chequamegon Bay in northern Wisconsin. It lasted ten years before it was abandoned because of Sioux hostility. Ménard himself was drowned early in his mission, but it was continued in 1665 by Father Claude Allouez, one of the most indefatigable of the Jesuit explorers. The following is from Allouez's first journey to the west, which took him past what was called the Ste. Marie Sault and later, Sault Ste. Marie:

> On the eighth of August, in the year 1665, I embarked at three Rivers with six Frenchmen, in company of more than four hundred savages of various nations, who, after transacting the little trading for which they had come, were returning to their own country ... Towards the beginning of September, after coasting along the shores of the Lake of Hurons, we reached the Sault; for such is the name given to a half-league of rapids that are encountered in a beautiful river which unites two great Lakes – that of the Hurons and Lake Superior. This river is pleasing, not only on account of the Islands intercepting its course and the great bays bordering it, but

because of the fishing and hunting, which are excellent there.

A few days later, Allouez entered Lake Superior, its form, in his words,

> nearly that of a bow, the southern shore being much curved and the northern nearly straight. Fish are abundant there, and of excellent quality; while the water is so clear and pure that objects at the bottom can be seen to the depth of six brasses. One often finds at the bottom of the water pieces of pure copper.[2]

Between 1665 and 1667 Father Allouez travelled around almost the entire periphery of Lake Superior, with side trips to Lake Nipigon and into northern Wisconsin. By 1668 three more missions were established on the upper Great Lakes, with one of them, St. Ignace near Michilimackinac, founded by Father Jacques Marquette, becoming a major base from which further missions were to be undertaken around southwestern Lake Michigan, which Allouez had also explored. Father Allouez spent a quarter of a century on the upper Great Lakes and rose to become vicar-general of the western missions. And it was the findings of Father Allouez and others that enabled Father Claude Dablon, by then Superior of the Canadian missions, to draft the first map showing Lake Superior in its entirety (see figure 2.2).

Meanwhile, back in France Richelieu and Louis XIII had died within a year of each other, with the latter succeeded in 1643 by Louis XIV, whose reign lasted seventy-two years. Raising an army that would reach the hitherto undreamed of size of 400 000 men, this egregious monarch embarked on a series of wars of aggrandizement that, before his reign was over, would embroil practically every state and country in Europe. To further overseas expansion, Jean Colbert, his first minister, added over one hundred ships to the French navy in little over fifteen years and established schools of marine engineering, cartography, and hydrography.

As the minister for marine, Colbert also rationalized the administration of France's colonies. In the process, New France became a royal province in 1663 with Jean Talon installed as its intendant two years later. Regular troops were sent to New France to "take out" the Iroquois, to use the modern phrase. By 1667, their mission was accomplished: all five nations were brought to terms and for a decade all of the Iroquois lands south of Lake Ontario were open to the French.

Paradoxically, after all these years the least known of the Great Lakes were Ontario and Erie. Quite a lot was already known about the country bordering the upper Great Lakes, as we have seen, but what we now call southwestern Ontario was still *terra incognita*. With Lake Ontario open to peaceful travel, at least temporarily, these gaps in geographical knowledge were quickly filled in, largely through the efforts of René-Robert Cavalier de la Salle. Possibly the most controversial figure in the history of New France, La Salle was an heroic explorer to some – to others he was something of an adventurous scoundrel and an incompetent scoundrel at that. Whatever his character and short-comings, La Salle organized the first major voyage of exploration led by a layman, and it was through him that what is now southwestern Ontario was first opened up.

Arriving in New France in 1667, La Salle set off from Montreal two years later with twenty others to find a way to China via a river that would lead to the "Southern Sea" – in the minds of many, a preposterous idea. Accompanying him was a Sulpician priest, François Dollier de Casson and a Sulpician deacon, René Bréhant de Galinée, who had "some smattering of mathematics, and enough to put a map together after a fashion."[3] It was Galinée who was to chronicle the expedition. It took them a month to get up the St. Lawrence to Lake Ontario. Hugging the south shore of Lake Ontario, they fetched up at a Seneca village where they hoped to find a guide to the Ohio country.

After a month of stalling by the Seneca, another of the Iroquois offered to lead them to his village, a

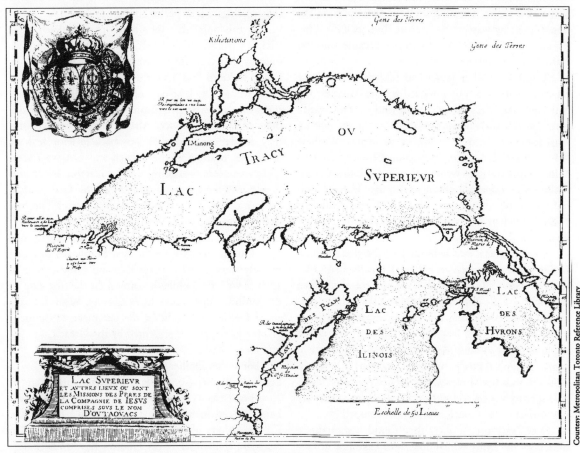

Figure 2.2 Lake Superior as shown on a map included in the *Relation* of 1670–71, submitted by Father Dablon, who may also have drafted the map. Remarkably accurate, it summarizes the findings of Father Allouez and other Jesuits up to that time.

hunting camp a few miles north of present-day Hamilton. There, they were assured, they would learn of a much easier route to the Ohio than the cross-country one used by the Seneca. At this camp – and quite by chance – they bumped into one Jolliet, now thought to be Adrien, brother to Louis, who was returning from an official prospecting trip to find the source of the copper of which the Jesuits had heard so much. Jolliet told them that in return for saving an Iroquois from the Ottawas, the Iroquois had shown him a new way of reaching the St. Lawrence from the upper lakes: by way of the Detroit River to Lake Erie. By taking this route, Adrien Jolliet became the first European to travel that river.

Inspired by what Jolliet had told them of a large northern nation as yet unvisited by missionaries, the two Sulpicians decided to go and find it. This wasn't what La Salle had in mind at all, so the party split up with some of the men returning to Montreal where they were derided as the "men from China" – later La Salle's property near Montreal became known as La Chine and it remains Lachine to this day. La Salle himself apparently did not get back to Quebec until late 1670. Just where he went remains a matter of scholarly argument.

At any rate, it was without La Salle that Galinée, Dollier, and five others set off on 1 October 1669 for what we now call the Grand River and travelled down it, reaching Lake Erie ten days later. They then "proceeded three days along this lake ... during which we made only 21 or 22 leagues, we found a spot which appeared to us so beautiful, with such an abundance of game, that we thought we could not find a better in which to pass our winter ... We looked for some favorable spot to make a winter camp, and discovered a very pretty river at the mouth of which we camped."[4]

The "very pretty" river they found is thought to have been the Lynn, which flows into Lake Erie at Port Dover. It was too windy to camp by the lake, so they went inland a short way and "chose a beautiful spot on the bank of a rivulet," and there they passed the winter. On Passion Sunday, 23 March 1670, they planted a cross on the lakeshore "in memory of so long a sojourn of Frenchmen as ours had been" and took possession of the land in the name of Louis XIV. With the ice clearing from the lake they continued westward along the shore and "proceeded as far as a long point [and] landed there on a beautiful sand beach on the east side of the point."[5] This was Pointe Pélee, so named by the French because of the absence of trees on the eastern side which gave it a "peeled" or bare look.

At this point disaster struck. They had left their packs at the water's edge for the night and slept so soundly that they did not hear the wind get up. They finally woke to find a northeast gale blowing and the water rising. The best part of their baggage was gone, including all their provisions and, what was worse, their entire altar service. After debating what to do, they decided to make their way back to Montreal via Sault Ste. Marie and the French and Ottawa rivers. They were soon paddling up the Detroit River and thence into the yet-to-be-named Lake St. Clair which, Galinée observed, "was called by M. Sanson The Salt Water Lake, but we saw no sign of salt in it."[6] From there Dollier and Galinée made their way north into Lake Huron and so were the first Europeans to travel the waterway between Lakes Erie and Huron, at least as far as we know, while the latter drew the first map of the peninsula that is now Essex County. With the travels of Dollier and Galinée, the last piece of the geographic jigsaw puzzle presented by the Great Lakes fell into place.

Soon after Dollier and Galinée got back, in 1672, Louis de Buade, Comte de Frontenac, turned up in New France as its governor. By now, New France was being boxed in by what had recently become the English colony of New York. The English were also establishing themselves on Hudson Bay, and English traders were soon ranging beyond the Appalachians. Not only did they pay more for furs, but their trade goods were cheaper, thus presenting a tempting market not only to native traders but French *coureurs de bois* as well. The Iroquois, too, were doing their best to divert furs into their own hands for resale to the English in upper New York. Thus it was to short-circuit the English and the Iroquois that Frontenac established a trading post and fort on the Cataraqui River in 1673 – and so the city of Kingston had its beginnings.

After Fort Cataraqui had been established, La Salle, whose path had crossed Frontenac's soon after the latter's arrival, went to France and, backed by Frontenac, had obtained a grant that made him the seigneur of Cataraqui and ennobled him into the bargain. He renamed the trading post Fort Frontenac in his patron's honour. Though La Salle's seigneurie was never subdivided, it became active in the fur trade with, it's said, Frontenac as La Salle's silent partner.

Meanwhile, in 1669 Frontenac had given official blessing to an expedition that was to explore the regions south and west of Lake Michigan. Led by Louis Jolliet and accompanied by Father Marquette, the party was on the Mississippi River a month after leaving Michilimackinac. They travelled down the Mississippi to within about 280 miles (450 km) of what is now New Orleans before turning back. Worn out by his exertions, Father Marquette died not long after.

In 1679 La Salle was once more in the news. He had been back to France and obtained the king's permission to explore all the western lands between New France, Florida, and Mexico. He then returned to New France with a small army of craftsmen, and, on Cayuga Creek above Niagara Falls, they built the 45-ton *Griffin*, the name honouring Frontenac, on whose coat of arms that mythical bird appears. All this happened before the unbelieving eyes of his many detractors who thought La Salle insane.

On 7 August 1679 *Griffin* was launched and the first sailing vessel on the Great Lakes set sail on her maiden voyage with La Salle and thirty-one others on board. With Lake Michigan as their destination they sailed up the Detroit River to reach Sanson's Salt Water Lake on 12 August, which they named Lake Claire, after St. Clair of Assisi whose feast day it was (it would later be anglicized to Lake St. Clair, and was called Lake Sinclair at one point). Eventually *Griffin* passed through the Straits of Mackinac to take on a load of furs on the western shore of Lake Michigan. She sailed for Niagara in mid-September and was never seen again. She was wrecked, some say, off Tobermory.

La Salle, however, had left the ship in Michigan to go exploring and would go on to build trading posts on the Illinois River. Later, in 1681, he followed in the steps of Jolliet and Marquette to make his historic voyage down the Mississippi. On the coast of the Gulf of Mexico below New Orleans he claimed the entire Mississippi basin for France, naming it Louisiana. Later still, in 1684, he was to return to the area directly from France, this time as a commander of a four-ship expedition, complete with soldiers and even some settlers. Just about everything that could go wrong did go wrong, and eventually La Salle was murdered by his own men. As one modern historian has put it, it was a wonder that they had not done so long before.

Frontenac, long at loggerheads with the governing council, the governor of Montreal, and several of the leading families in the colony, was finally recalled to France in 1682. He would return in 1689, somewhat but not entirely chastened, in time to save Quebec from the English.

In the closing decades of the seventeenth century, the pattern of French geographical discovery was increasingly dictated by military necessity and the needs of the fur trade. In a matter of only twenty years, a handful of colonial French – with New France as their springboard – had made themselves masters of the Mississippi valley from its upper tributaries to the Gulf of Mexico, thus fencing in the English colonies with a population ten times that of New France. It was an astonishing achievement. However, the day of the great Jesuit explorers in the future Ontario was over. Soldiers, surveyors, and traders would take over the task of filling in the picture, for which men such as Allouez, Brébeuf, Chaumonot, Jogues, Ménard, le Moine, and Marquette, with their skills, endurance, and immense courage, had provided the frame.

CHAPTER THREE

The First Land Survey in the Province and the Anglo-French Wars

In 1608, science took a giant step forward with the invention of the telescope, usually ascribed to Hans Lippershey, a Dutch spectacle maker. Galileo Galilei built his first telescope a year later. For a long time telescopes were too long and unwieldy to be incorporated into surveying instruments, and even then there was the difficult matter of fitting them with internal sights. However, the first steps towards this had been taken by Johannes Kepler, the great German astronomer.

Kepler added a "positive" lens to the telescope, thus making it possible for the later incorporation of a reticle with cross-hairs and for the introduction of a tachymeter or micrometer into the telescope. The tachymeter was invented in 1638 by William Gascoigne, an English mathematician and astronomer, and consisted of two movable parallel vertical wires mounted in the focal plane of a telescope. Winding them in or out by means of a worm gear allowed one to measure the angular distance between two distant objects. Gascoigne was killed a few years later in the civil wars then convulsing England, and in 1664 the tachymeter was reinvented by two French astronomers, Adrian Auzout and Jean Picard.

Picard was the first, it is thought, to think of using the telescope in a surveying instrument as opposed to an astronomical instrument, though it remains doubtful that instruments so fitted were widely used. As for fitting sights in a telescope, it is said that this was first done in 1689 by one John Flamborough, who placed spider webs in the focal plane of a telescope to form cross-hairs. But again, it was to be some years before the idea of cross-hairs caught on. Meanwhile, the early 1600s had also seen the appearance of the vernier, which takes its name from Pierre Vernier who, in 1631, first described the device and its application to astronomical quadrants.

Instrumentation and surveying methods both continued to be refined and improved in seventeenth-century England. Arthur Hopton, a surveyor and an applied mathematician and instrument designer, tried to improve on Leonard Digges's topographical instrument, which he described in his *Speculum Topographicum: The Topographicall Glasses*, published in 1611. It incorporated a compass, among other

Aaron Rathborne's theodolite. While he referred to the whole instrument as a theodolite, the term came to be applied to the angle-measuring device surmounting it. Detail from the cover of his *The Surveyor in Foure Bookes*, published in 1616. (From Kiely, *Surveying Instruments: Their History*.)

things. Hopton's instrument was mounted on a tripod – an idea borrowed from a French instrument maker, Philip Danfrie, who had described it in 1579. Five years later, in 1616, in *The Surveyor in Foure Bookes,* Aaron Rathborne also described a surveying instrument. He called it a "theodolite"; thereafter the name stuck. It was much like Digges's "topographicall instrument." For use on level ground, a ruler with sights was attached to the circular planisphere. On uneven ground a quadrant was substituted, again with a sight attached. Rathborne was the first English surveyor to show how a fieldbook should be laid out in columns.

As we have seen, Cyprian Lucar described a type of surveyor's chain in 1590. Rathborne had also come up with a type of chain. Borrowing from a French work on mathematics, he invented, used, and described a decimal chain, whereby the statute pole, or perch, of 16.5 feet (5 m) was divided into 100 links. However, the type of chain that came to be adopted throughout the English-speaking world was devised by Edmund Gunter, who first described it in 1620. Curiously enough, Gunter was not a surveyor but a professor of astronomy, though he had a strong interest in the prevailing movement to bring mathematics to the masses.

The appeal of Gunter's chain lay in the ease with which areas could be derived from linear measurements. Gunter's chain was 66 feet (20 m) long and was divided into a hundred links. Eighty chains made one mile; ten square chains made one acre; and fractions of an acre could also be easily calculated, there being 100 000 square links to an acre. Gunter's chain would become the standard measure of length throughout the English-speaking world for the better part of the next 300 years, not being entirely superseded until the steel tape gained acceptance early in the twentieth century. Gunter's chain measure crops up in the most curious places; a cricket pitch, for example, is 22 yards or 1 chain long. To this day, the size of many farm lots and the width of the rights-of-way along many of Ontario's roads and city streets are based on Gunter's 66-foot chain.

From the mid-1600s on, there would be increasing stress in England on the mathematics involved in land surveying. Thus, in *The Compleat Surveyor: Containing the Whole Art of Surveying of Land,* published in 1653, William Leybourn discussed the use of logarithms and trigonometry in calculating area. He recommended the theodolite and circumferentor for large areas; the plane table for small. And he also discussed levelling.

Levelling had long been carried out using plumb bobs and water trays that differed little from those used by the ancients. Then, in about 1500, a type of level was introduced that consisted of a U-shaped glass tube containing liquid. Levels could be ascertained by the difference in the level of the liquid in the upturned

Aaron Rathborne's plane table. First described by Abel Foullon in a book published in Paris in 1551, the plane table required little knowledge of mathematics and came to be widely used by English surveyors. (From Kiely, *Surveying Instruments: Their History.*)

Courtesy: Carben Surveying Reprints

ends of the tube. In the early 1660s, however, Leybourn was still recommending a covered 5- or 6-foot water trough (about 1.7-m), or a copper tube of similar length with cups fitted to the ends "into which the water must issue to set the level truly," a device similar to that used by the Romans. Not long after, in 1666, Melchisédech Thevénot published a description in France of a sealed bubble level, though it was to be some time before the difficulty of manufacturing them allowed bubble levels to be used generally.

In 1688 the first English text to deal with surveying in North America came out. This was John Love's *Geodasia: Or the Art of Surveying and Measuring Land Made Easie.* Love wrote his book after working as a surveyor in North Carolina, as well as in Jamaica. It became a very popular text, with more than eleven editions coming out in England, and two later editions appearing in the 1790s in what was by then the United States – it was probably the first surveying book to be published there. Significantly, Love was one of the first to consider his plots as maps, rather than as mere representations of discrete tracts of land. In America, where the tracts were large, especially in thickly forested areas, he advocated the use of the circumferentor and Gunter's chain.

In the same year that John Love's book came out, William of Orange became king of England. Meanwhile, Louis XIV had outraged Protestant Europe by his virtual expulsion of French Protestants from their native land, and then went on to invade the Rhine Palatinate, laying waste to it. Many thousands of Palatines, as they came to be called, fled to England, some three thousand of whom were resettled by the British government in New York, where many of their descendants would remain loyal to the British during the American revolution. This is why such a high proportion of the Loyalists who pioneered the settlement of Upper Canada were of German ancestry.

With Louis XIV now threatening William's native Holland, William declared war on France in 1689.

The Huguenots

In 1685, Louis XIV revoked the Edict of Nantes, by which, some ninety years earlier, French Protestants or Huguenots had been granted a measure of religious freedom. Outlawed in their own country, over a quarter of a million French Protestants left France for good. Some forty to fifty thousand emigrated to England where, known as *refugiés*, they added the word "refugee" to the English language. Many were artisans and instrument makers and, as such, contributed materially to the development of surveying and other scientific instruments in England. Some were soldiers – one Huguenot would become commander-in-chief of the British army in the mid-1700s. And many were seaman, some of whom would found British naval dynasties. From one such family came Alexander Vidal, one of the first land surveyors to work in northern Ontario and who later became a senator. Also of Huguenot descent was Edward DeCou who practised on the Niagara Peninsula.

Ending in 1697, what was called the War of the League of Augsburg was followed closely by the War of the Spanish Succession, which broke out in 1701 and went on until 1713. In North America, the two wars became known as King William's and Queen Anne's War, respectively, and were fought, on this continent, on a different timetable and for more immediate reasons. King William's War may be said to have begun in North America in 1686 when Jacques-René de Brissay de Dennonville, then governor of New France, sent an overland expedition to capture the Hudson's Bay trading posts at Moose Factory, Fort Rupert, and Fort Albany. The latter was recaptured by the English in 1693, but the others stayed in French hands until the Treaty of Utrecht of 1713.

Again, even before war broke out in Europe, Louis XIV had been preparing to invade New York.* The command of the expedition was given to Frontenac, who was also appointed governor of New France in place of Dennonville, who had asked to be replaced, pleading exhaustion. By the time Frontenac reached New France in 1689, however, it was too late in the season to mount the planned assaults on Manhattan

---

*Louis's plans for New York included the expulsion of all non-Catholics as possible subversives, this to New England and Pennsylvania. The British were to expel the Acadians for much the same reasons.

and Albany, so instead he sent Franco-native forces to raid outlying English settlements. In doing so, Frontenac set the pattern of savage raids and counter-raids that were to characterize the King William's and Queen Anne's wars in North America.

The New Englanders, predictably enraged at the French raids, vowed to put an end to New France. In 1690 the New Englanders took Port Royal, following this up with what was supposed to be a two-pronged attack on the heart of New France, with Montreal to be taken by land and Quebec by sea. The former plan was abandoned when a New England force came down with smallpox upon reaching Lake Champlain. The latter plan came to nothing when Frontenac declined to surrender Quebec to the New Englanders. A second attempt to take Quebec during the Queen Anne's War would also fail.

There had also been prewar skirmishes between the French and English centring on what the French called *Le Détroit* – the word "détroit" meaning a strait and which was originally applied to the whole waterway between Lakes Erie and Huron, Lake St. Clair included. Following its discovery by Dollier and Gallinée in 1669, it wasn't long before English traders started using this waterway to reach the upper lakes. In 1686 the French decided to build a fort on the waterway to try to keep the English out, selecting a site on the west, or American, side of the Detroit River where it flows out of Lake Huron. Called Fort St. Joseph, it was situated where Port Huron, Michigan, now stands opposite Sarnia.

This was followed by the building in 1701 of a fort on the north (now the American side) of the Detroit River. First named Fort Pontchartrain du Détroit – the Comte de Pontchartrain then being Louis XIV's chief minister – it became commonly known as Détroit, which was used to describe both the fort and the settlement that grew around it. Meanwhile, throughout the two wars the French had vigorously pursued a program of expansion into the Illinois country where posts were established at Cahokia in 1699 and Kaskasia in 1703, in the vicinity of present-day St. Louis, with the latter growing into a thriving settlement.

Another aspect of the Anglo-French conflict in North America involved the Iroquois. After devastating raids on their homelands south of Lake Ontario, the French finally succeeded in bringing the Iroquois to terms. A treaty signed in 1701 finally ended the Franco-Iroquois conflict so carelessly begun by Champlain some ninety years earlier. Under the terms of the treaty the French hoped, at least, to keep the Iroquois neutral. The English colonists, however, wanted the Iroquois as an allied buffer state between them and the hated Canadians. This led to a spectacular public relations coup brought off in 1710 by the governor of New York, who took several Mohawk sachems to London. Here, in their native costumes and trappings, the natives became an overnight sensation. The governor of New York's ploy worked, with the Iroquois becoming Britain's formal allies.

In Europe, Louis XIV was finally brought to a halt in 1704 at a place called Blenheim, roughly halfway between Munich and Stuttgart. There, in a battle considered to be one of the most decisive in history, the French army met its first major military defeat in over two generations, at the hands of John Churchill, Duke of Marlborough, and Prince Eugene of Austria. Louis's strength was spent. Following further military defeats he was back much where he had started fifty years earlier. Peace returned to Europe with the signing of the Treaty of Utrecht in 1713. France's claim to the St. Lawrence Valley and to the land in the Mississippi Basin was recognized. But Newfoundland, captured earlier by the French, and the Hudson's Bay Company posts went back to Britain. And France finally lost Acadia. Recaptured by the French, it had been captured again by the English in 1710 when Port Royal was renamed Annapolis Royal, after Queen Anne. Two years after the treaty was signed, Louis XIV died, leaving his country so exhausted and impoverished that it would take decades to recover.

Wars have always spurred the emergence of new technology. In the case of the Anglo-French wars, it was the development of the marine chronometer to facilitate the estimation of longitude. In late seventeenth-century England it was thought that the most promising method of determining longitude was by the angular displacement, or distance, of the moon from other celestial bodies. The method required accurate timetables of such displacements at a place on a known meridian. To make the observations necessary for constructing the lunar tables, the Royal Observatory at Greenwich was founded by Charles II in 1675. The lunar method was laborious at best.

As Britain's navy grew in the eighteenth century, an easier way of "discovering the longitude" became a matter of increasing urgency. Warships, whether French, Dutch, or British, relied heavily on local pilots in coastal waters. Marine charts were still notoriously unreliable. For the best part of that century British ships (as those of other nations) were never quite sure where they were once they were out of sight of land, a fact spectacularly demonstrated in 1707 by a British admiral with the delightful name of Sir Cloudesley Shovel. Returning from Gibraltar in overcast and foggy weather, he put his entire fleet aground on the Scilly Isles, with the loss of four ships and nearly 1000 men, Sir Cloudesley among them.

It was largely because of this disaster that the British Admiralty established a Board of Longitude in 1714, which offered a reward of ten thousand pounds for the development of any practical device capable of determining longitude within one degree after a six-week voyage to Jamaica (where a degree of longitude is roughly equivalent to 60 miles [97 km]) and double that sum for a device that would give the longitude within 30 minutes or half a degree. The importance attached by the Admiralty to the speedy and accurate determination of longitude may be gauged by the size of the reward – £20,000 would amount to something like $2 million in today's money. The man who eventually claimed the reward in the 1760s was a Yorkshire carpenter and clockmaker named John Harrison who literally devoted his life to perfecting his chronometer.

Meanwhile, the task of the navigator had been eased considerably by the development of the marine sextant.[1] For centuries, one of the chief difficulties facing the navigator trying to make accurate observations was, quite simply, that both horizon and object being observed were heaving up and down with the motion of the ship. With the sextant, the navigator could concentrate on the horizon and "bring down" the sun or other heavenly object to it. It seems that what was then called a "reflecting octant" was invented by both Thomas Godfrey and John Hadley in the early 1730s. However, it was Hadley's instrument that came into use, its development assisted by British naval commanders, many of whom were by then becoming navigational enthusiasts. Later, the sextant would be widely used by land surveyors, particularly in exploratory work.

The mid-1700s saw the beginnings of England's so-called ordnance survey, and also witnessed the country's agricultural revolution, which, among other things, resulted in the consolidation of many small holdings into larger parcels that could be farmed more

Harrison "Discovers the Longitude"

As far back as 1530, Gemma Frisius had suggested that the simplest way of determining longitude would be to carry a clock from place to place, comparing its time with local time as determined by observations of the sun. All that was needed was a really reliable and accurate clock. And this John Harrison set out to build, keeping in mind the reward offered by the Admiralty. Harrison started in 1714 when he was twenty-one. It took him twenty-two years to build a prototype. Known as H.1, it was tested on a barge in the Thames. It was impractically large, but it kept a degree of accuracy hitherto undreamed of.

It was a nervous Admiralty that allowed this "secret weapon" to be tested at sea. After five years the prototype had been reduced in size to a 5-inch (130-cm) diameter watch called H.4. In 1759 it was tested on an eighty-one-day voyage to Jamaica when it erred by only five seconds, corresponding to a longitudinal error of about 1.5 miles (2.5 km). In a second trial in 1764 it gave an error in time of only fifteen seconds after five months spent mostly at sea. In the late 1760s and early 1770s, Captain James Cook used Harrison's "sea clock" to make his epoch-making voyages to the South Seas. Cook called it "our never failing guide." Harrison applied for the full reward of £20,000. After making a lot of fuss, including a personal appeal to George III, he finally got his money, some fifty years after he first set hand to the project.

efficiently, a process hastened by parliamentary legislation. This, together with a change in the general pattern of land ownership, led to an increase in the demand for land surveyors and for more accurate surveys. This, in turn, hastened the development of more accurate instruments. Jonathan Sisson, a London instrument maker, started making what might be called the first modern theodolites in the 1720s. With their shorter telescopes, Sisson's late-model theodolites were extremely rugged and compact; a bubble level was built in, and there was an attachment for a vernier. Although the scales were hand-divided, Sisson's later theodolites were accurate, it was said, to within 6 minutes of arc.

By the mid-1700s hand-cut scales of great precision were being produced by English instrument makers. Pre-eminent in this field and in his day was a contemporary of Sisson's, George Graham, who as early as 1725 had produced an 8-foot (2.5-m) iron quadrant for the Royal Observatory, which, with a vernier, allowed measurements to within 15 minutes of arc. Later there was John Bird, who died in 1776 and with whom hand-dividing is said to have reached its zenith.

Bird built some of the instruments used by Charles Mason and Jeremiah Dixon in surveying their famous line. Bird's method of hand-dividing, somewhat modified, was also used in the late 1770s by John Troughton, the co-founder of the firm Troughton and Simms, which survived under that name until well on into the twentieth century.

The 1770s also saw the appearance in England of a new way of measuring distances, this through the "stadia," as it came to be called. In 1778 William Green, a London optician, showed in his *Description and Use of an Improved Refracting Telescope with Scale for Surveying*, that if equidistant threads were mounted in the focal plane of the telescope, they could, following calibration, be used to measure the distance to a rod showing clearly marked divisions, also pre-calibrated – a principle, in essence that of a range-finder, first enunciated by Geminiano Montanari, an Italian astronomer, in the 1600s and apparently rediscovered by Green. Offering a direct way of measuring distances quickly, the stadia came to be popular with some surveyors working in rugged or hilly country, both in Britain and, later, Canada.

The Great Triangulation

Following Bonnie Prince Charlie's defeat at Culloden in 1745, the task of subduing the Highlands was made more difficult by the lack of good maps. And so the British army set to work to produce them, using compass traverses to locate main roads and field sketches to fill in topographic features. The officer who took over the direction of the survey in Scotland was William Roy, who was also put in charge of all military surveys in Britain, which were administered by the Board of Ordnance.

The work of mapping Britain was in abeyance during the American Revolutionary War. After it, Roy made a start on Britain's first geodetic survey, with triangulation stations at the Greenwich Observatory, Arthur's Seat, and Cotton Hill. In 1783 the French astronomer, César Cassini de Thury, suggested linking the royal observatory in Paris with its counterpart at Greenwich by means of a precisely triangulated survey. Work began in Britain under Roy on what became known as "The Great Triangulation" in 1784 – the same year that saw the first mass settlement of the Loyalists around Cataraqui and along the St. Lawrence – with a 15.5-mile (25 km) base line laid down on Hounslow Heath. Following measurements on forty-five triangles in southern England, the survey was tied into the French base line at Dunkirk. In 1791, triangulation work in Britain became the Trigonometrical Survey, again administered by the Board of Ordnance, both then housed in the Tower of London. The first 1-inch-to-1-mile maps of Britain appeared in 1801. From that time on, the Trigonometrical Survey of Britain became known as the "Ordnance Survey" and to this day Britain's popular official topographical maps are known as "Ordnance maps."

The problem of eliminating the human error in dividing scales was finally solved by Jesse Ramsden who produced his first "dividing engine" in 1768 and a second, improved version in 1775. Meanwhile, Ramsden, who had apprenticed himself to an instrument maker in 1758, had become renowned the world over for his instruments. With machine-divided scales and with the compound achromatic lens, which allowed the construction of short refracting telescopes with incorporated cross-hairs, the modern theodolite might be said to have arrived.

Six years after the Treaty of Utrecht had been signed in 1713, the French began construction on the massive fortress of Louisburg on Ile Royale, now Cape Breton Island. A fort was also built at Niagara to replace earlier ones. This substantial three-storey affair is arguably one of the most historic forts in North America; it still stands, with its later British accretions, on the American side of the Niagara River opposite Niagara-on-the-Lake. At the same time, a small trading post called Fort Rouillé was built at Toronto, though it only lasted a few years. Later, in 1750, a more permanent structure was built, its site now covered by the grounds of the CNE. The British response to Forts Niagara and Rouillé was to build a fort at Oswego on Lake Ontario's southeastern shore.

Meanwhile, in the 1730s and 1740s, members of the remarkable family of La Vérendrye were opening up the country from Lake Superior westward. The head of the family, Pierre Gaultier de La Vérendrye had a fixation on a "western sea," thought by some to be a great gulf reaching inland from the Pacific, which, if found, would prove to be the long-sought shortcut to the Far East. He passed his fixation on to his four sons and between them they made a number of expeditions in which exploration was combined with fur trading and establishing a chain of forts. The first, Fort St. Piérre, was built in 1731 on the site of present-day Winnipeg. A year later Fort St. Charles was built on the northwest arm of the Lake of the Woods near Rat Portage, which was subsequently renamed Kenora. Forts on Lake Winnipeg followed (see figure 3.1).

The search for the inland sea went on: the elder La Vérendrye headed southwest from the southern end of Lake Manitoba in 1738 to reach the Missouri; Louis-Joseph, his eldest son, and his brother, François, followed this up with an exploratory sweep through what is now Wyoming and South Dakota. About this time another brother and a cousin were killed by natives on Massacre Island on the Lake of the Woods. The senior La Vérendrye was planning to explore the Saskatchewan River when he died in the late 1740s. His son, Louis-Joseph, fought in the Seven Years' War and eventually died in a shipwreck off Cape Breton.

In 1740 the second of the two pairs of Anglo-French wars broke out. In what is known in Europe as the War of the Austrian Succession and as King George's War in North America, New England militiamen, backed by a few British ships, laid siege to Louisburg. Following a naval defeat off Cape Finisterre, no help was forthcoming from France so Louisburg finally surrendered, only to be given back to France under the Treaty of Aix-la-Chapelle, which ended the war in 1748 – much to the anger of the New Englanders. To counter Louisburg, the British started to build the naval base at Halifax a year after the war ended. With the arrival of settlers from Britain, the colony of Nova Scotia came into being.

Before King George's War had even ended, the seeds of another Anglo-French conflict in North America were being sown. There is a connection between the cause of that war and the first land survey carried out in what is now Ontario. Following the Treaty of Utrecht of 1713, Britain's American colonies had grown rapidly; the population had quadrupled from 350 000 in 1713 to some 1 500 000 in the 1750s. With good land on the coastal plains increasingly hard to come by, the tide of settlement swept inland, and in 1747 a group of land companies were formed by prominent Virginians to acquire land in the Ohio Valley, which they claimed lay within the boundaries of the colony's original charter. Seasoned traders were sent to the Ohio to sound out the natives with a view to acquiring their land. This alarmed the French, who saw their lines of communication with the Mississippi and Louisiana threatened. They decided to build posts along the Ohio.

Up to this point the south, or Canadian, shore of the Detroit River, opposite what was by now a substantial French settlement around Fort Detroit, was

---

Admiral Anson Gets Lost

During the Anglo-Spanish war that immediately preceded King George's War, the British had planned a pincer movement on the Isthmus of Panama, with Admiral Vernon taking Porto Bello on its eastern coast, and Admiral Anson rounding the Horn to attack the Isthmus from the west. In heavy weather and out of sight of the Horn, Anson thought he had rounded it, only to find when he sailed north that he was still to the east of it. He eventually managed it, but then his flagship was suddenly stricken with scurvy. With his men dying before his eyes, Anson decided to make for the Juan Fernandez islands off the Chilean coast, there to land his sick. But he couldn't find the islands, not knowing his longitude. He then adopted the old seaman's trick of sailing along the appropriate latitude. Having reached the latitude of the islands, he sailed west. Not finding them, he backtracked and sailed east. Fetching up on the Chilean coast, he realized he had been right the first time. So he backtracked once more, at last finding the islands. This delay cost not only the lives of eighty seamen but the success of the whole operation. Admiral Vernon had captured Porto Bello, but without Anson's support could not hold it and was forced to abandon the enterprise.

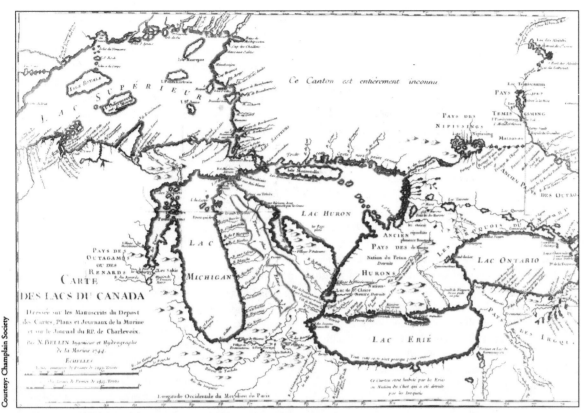

Figure 3.1 Map of the Great Lakes made by the noted French cartographer Jacques-Nicolas Bellin in 1744. It was partly based on maps made by Father P.F.X. Charlevoix. Later, Mrs. Simcoe would comment on the accuracy of Charlevoix's map of southwestern Upper Canada.

from La Rivière aux Dindes, now Turkey Creek, north to Le Ruisseau de la Vielle Reine, a stream now buried under the southern outskirts of Windsor (see figure 3.2). The lots were just over 100 acres and were typically long and narrow. From a later, undated report it seems that de Léry was assisted in his survey by de Sabrevois, the commandant, and further, that it wasn't done all that well. "These lands ...," reads the report, "have been laid out ... in no great regularity. I believe they will be found fully three arpents too large." The report hastened to add that this was not the fault of

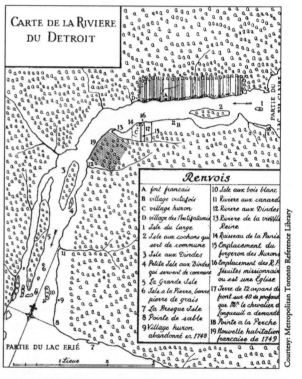

Figure 3.2 Carried out in 1749 by Gaspard Chaussegros de Léry, a military engineer and surveyor, the first cadastral survey in Ontario was of the French settlement on the Canadian side of the Detroit River, numbered 19 on the key. (From Lajeunesse, *Windsor Border Region*.)

unoccupied save for some native encampments and a mission. It was now decided to place settlers there, both in order to help raise food for the forts farther south and to reinforce the French presence in this vital area. The settlement scheme got under way in the spring of 1749 when families were induced to leave the safety of the St. Lawrence Valley for the uncertainties of frontier life at Detroit with promises of free land, seeds, and tools. At the same time Gaspard Chaussegros de Léry, a military engineer and surveyor,

was sent by the governor of New France to examine and report on the area and make the necessary surveys. At the end of July 1749, he reached Detroit where, according to his report, he "began surveying and obtaining the necessary information for rendering an exact account of the position, the quality of the lands and the things to be done in order to farm them."[2]

In this, the first land survey in the province, de Léry laid out some twenty lots along a 2.5-mile (4-km) frontage along the Canadian side of the Detroit River,

the surveyors. "In case an examination of these limits shall be made in the future, the defects of this survey can only be attributed to the negligence, ignorance or bad faith of the peasants who carried the poles which have been used for measuring these cessions."[3]

With further lots laid out in the next decade the settlement grew southward until, by the time the British came in the 1760s, it extended some 6 miles (10 km) along the Detroit River. Known by then as the Petite Côte, the settlement consisted of over sixty farms with over 500 acres under cultivation. Pre-dating the Loyalist settlements by a quarter of a century, the French settlement along the Petite Côte is the oldest continuous settlement of non-natives in what is now Ontario.

While the first French farmers were settling in on the land opposite Fort Detroit, a French expedition was sent into the Ohio Valley to take possession of it, and by 1753 a chain of forts had been built along the Allegheny River and the upper Ohio. This led to an Anglo-French confrontation that was to result in the Seven Years' War, called the French and Indian War in North America. George Washington, then twenty-one and a major in the Virginia militia, had been sent by the governor of Virginia to protest the presence of the French in what was considered British territory. The outcome was a series of incidents, in one of which several French soldiers were killed and which ended with Washington and his men surrendering to the French. The French, meanwhile, had destroyed a half-built British fort at the confluence of the Allegheny and the Monongahela rivers, where Pittsburgh now stands, and built one of their own, which they called Fort Dusquesne.

All this was being followed closely in Britain. Hoping to confine hostilities to North America and to oust the French from the Ohio Valley, Britain sent a mixed force of British regulars and Virginians under the command of Major General Edward Braddock into the Ohio Valley, where, within a few miles of Fort Duquesne, Braddock's force was surprised and routed by a mixed force of French and natives, with Braddock himself being killed. Waking Britain to the French threat to her American colonies, Braddock's defeat has been called the Pearl Harbor of the Seven Years' War, which broke out a year later and which finally led to the loss of New France to Britain.

War was finally declared in 1756. On one side were Britain, Prussia, and Hanover; on the other, France, Austria, Sweden, Saxony, and Russia. At first all went well for the French. By August 1757 they were in possession of Fort Oswego on the southeast shore of Lake Ontario, along with nearby Forts George and Ontario, as well as Fort Bull at the mouth of the Mohawk River and Fort William Henry at the southern end of Lake George in the Hudson Valley. Elsewhere, in what is sometimes called the first world war, French forces were in the ascendant.

Then, in 1758, William Pitt the Elder, later the Earl of Chatham, became, as secretary of state, the virtual prime minister of Britain and revived the spirits of a country depressed by a sense of failure. He saw the elimination of France's colonies as the key to victory, placing his faith in sea power. Paying the Prussians and Hanoverians to get on with the land war in Europe, Pitt planned a naval war that would combine a blockade of French ports with military expeditions against France's overseas possessions in Africa and the West Indies, but with the principal thrust directed at New France. By 1758 the tide was beginning to turn against the French.

Meanwhile, a new regiment had been formed in the British army and this, curiously enough, in a roundabout way was to have profound effect on the settlement and surveying history of Ontario. Following the Braddock fiasco, it was felt that the British forces in North America should be augmented by a body of light infantry, especially trained to fight under frontier conditions. About the same time it was suggested that a new regiment be recruited among the Swiss and German settlers in Pennsylvania, and that it should be officered by such German-speaking soldiers in other European armies as might be persuaded to serve the British crown. The result was the formation in 1755 of the Sixty-second (later the Sixtieth) Regiment of Foot, or Royal Americans – a regiment, it may be added, that at the time of writing still lives on as the Second Green Jackets, the King's Royal Rifle Corps.

Among the ninety or so who joined this regiment were Frederick Haldimand and Samuel Holland. Haldimand would become the governor of Quebec and Holland his surveyor general; between them they would oversee the first mass settlement of Loyalists in the future Ontario and, in the process, initiate the township system that now blankets all of southern Ontario and much of the north.

Frederick Haldimand was born in Yverdon, Switzerland, in 1718. Before he was twenty, he joined a Prussian infantry regiment and had seen much action in the War of the Austrian Succession. Later he transferred to the Swiss Guards and, rising to the rank of lieutenant-colonel, received the same rank in the Royal Americans, which he joined in 1756, he then being in his late thirties.

Ten years younger than Haldimand, Samuel Johannes Holland was born in Nijmegen in the Netherlands, and had served in the Dutch army before emigrating to England in 1754 and joining the Royal Americans as lieutenant. Both men were to suffer in the early stages of their careers in the British army from prejudice against foreigners. Both succeeded in spite of it: Haldimand by sheer ability, first as a soldier, which led him to become perhaps the best general that Britain had in North America, and then as a skilled and compassionate administrator; Holland by his outstanding skills as a surveyor and military engineer.

The two men were of contrasting character. Haldimand was an austere man. A life-long bachelor, it may be said that he married the army, swallowing the many disappointments that came his way but doing his duty, always. Holland, on the other hand, was far from austere. A personable man, he quickly found his way around London society, and his abilities as a draughtsman and map-maker soon attracted the attention of his senior officers. For a man with a bent for surveying, England must have been an exciting place to be. As we have seen, instruments such as the theodolite were being steadily improved. There was a growing number of highly skilled instrument-makers in the country. And with Britain's growing navy, there was an intense interest in improving navigation, with the sextant coming into general use and with Harrison's improved chronometer about to undergo its first sea trials.

In June 1756 some forty officers of the fledgling Royal American Regiment arrived in New York, Haldimand and Holland among them. Also with the Royal Americans was Henry Bouquet, Haldimand's best friend and confidant, an outstanding soldier who would save Fort Pitt in the Pontiac uprising and who was instrumental in building the first British ships on Lake Erie. Among other things, these ships would make the first, if rudimentary, hydrographic surveys on that lake.

The first objective in the campaign against New France was the reduction of Louisburg, by now a heavily fortified town, naval base, and fishing port, garrisoned by three thousand or so regulars and a thousand militia. Active preparations for the operation began in the spring of 1758 with the arrival in Halifax of British troops under Major-General Jeffrey Amherst. Meanwhile, the Royal Americans who had arrived in North America a year or so earlier had been busy training their men, recruited for the most part from German and Swiss settlers. Haldimand's battalion was scheduled to take part in the Louisburg operation, and he was in Philadelphia supervising its embarkation for Louisburg when he was persuaded by Major-General James Abercromby, then commander-in-chief in North America, to transfer to another bat-

---

Early Hydrographic Surveys on Lake Erie

In the summer of 1760 Henry Bouquet, then in command of the Sixtieth Royal Americans, probed northward from Fort Pitt to emerge on the shore of Lake Erie. It struck him that ships would be required on the lake, and he wrote headquarters in New York to that effect. His idea was taken up; in an operation that must have involved some mind-boggling portages, canvas, ropes and cordage, tools, and all the necessary marine hardware – including anchors – arrived at Niagara in June 1761 via the Hudson, Lake Oneida, and Lake Ontario, along with workmen and seamen. Construction of the *Huron* and *Michigan* began at once with the first ship launched towards the end of August – the first vessel to sail on the Upper Lakes since La Salle's *Griffin*. Soon after the launch of the *Huron* in the early summer of 1761, Lieutenant Robertson was taking soundings on the Niagara River near the eastern end of Lake Erie. Sent in a bateau by the commandant at Detroit to explore and sound the St. Clair River, with hopes of establishing communications with the Mackinac, he and his party were ambushed by natives and all but two were killed or taken prisoner.

---

talion, which was to take part in an assault against Fort Carillon, a major French post near the attenuated southern end of Lake Champlain.

The assault on Carillon was a disastrous failure. British regulars supported by colonial militia were bloodily repulsed; among the many wounded was Haldimand, who had been selected to lead units of the prestigious British grenadiers, no less. A couple of months later, however, Fort Frontenac (or Cataraqui) was taken and burned, while in the Ohio Valley, the French abandoned Fort Duquesne and retreated upriver in the face of an advancing British force. The French fort was rebuilt as Fort Pitt, around which the future city of Pittsburgh was to grow.

Holland had also become involved in the proposed assault on Fort Carillon to the extent that he carried out some of the preliminary reconnaissance work. However, by this time his abilities as a engineer, surveyor, and draughtsman had already attracted the attention of his superiors. He was appointed assistant engineer in the Louisburg venture and, as a member of Brigadier-General James Wolfe's staff, prepared plans and charts in preparation for the assault and offered engineering advice to his chief. After several weeks' siege directed by the cautious and methodical Amherst,

Louisburg, cut off to landward by a besieging force of 13 000 and with over a hundred British ships to seaward, finally fell at the end of July 1757.

Following months of preparation, the reduction of Quebec began in the spring of 1759 when a 150-ship expeditionary force assembled in the Gulf of St. Lawrence and started upstream. At the end of June the siege of Quebec began with the landing of British troops on the Île d'Orléans. Holland, by now a captain-lieutenant, spent his time surveying and preparing plans for the use of Wolfe, whose protégé he had now become. Promoted during the siege to full captain, Wolfe presented him with a pair of duelling pistols. It was to be one of the great griefs of Holland's later life that one of his sons was killed when using them for the unhappy purpose for which they were intended.

Meanwhile, the Carillon fiasco had a fortunate outcome, at least as far as the British were concerned, in that Abercromby had been immediately recalled, to be replaced as commander-in-chief by Amherst, who, notwithstanding Wolfe's derring-do at Quebec, was the principal architect of the downfall of New France. Amherst had planned a pincer movement on Quebec, with an advance up the Hudson Valley from New York led by himself intended to coincide with Wolfe's arrival

---

The Mitchell Map

What is often described as the most important map in the history of North America was published in 1755 by John Mitchell, a Virginia-born botanist-cum-doctor. Packed off to school in the mother country, Mitchell studied medicine at Edinburgh and then returned to practise at Urbanna, some 30 miles (50 km) north of Williamsburg, Virginia. Plagued by ill health, he returned to England in 1746 where he pursued his interest in botany. Then, for no clear reason, he took to cartography in 1750 and made a map of North America that impressed the Lords Commissioners of Trade and Plantations.

With the commissioners' backing, Mitchell produced a second and better map in 1755 (see figure 3.3). It was based on maps of the various British colonies and provinces that the commissioners had ordered their governors to make. Mitchell also used French maps, as well as latitudes and longitudes as logged by ships of the Royal Navy. The result was a 1:2 000 000 scale map on eight sheets with the partial title "Map of the British and French Dominions in North America, with Roads, Distances, Limits, and Extent of Settlements ..." The British army relied heavily on Mitchell's map during the Seven Years' War. Later it was used to define the new British province of Quebec. And after the American Revolutionary War it was used – with all its errors – to draw the boundary between British North America and the United States. Later still, Mitchell's map was to figure in the bitter dispute over Ontario's western boundary in the mid-1800s.

Known in his own day as "the man who made the map," Mitchell died in England in 1768, aged fifty-seven. One of the founders of Kew Gardens, Mitchell has a plant named after him – the partridge berry, *Mitchella rubens*.

Samuel Holland and James Cook

After the fall of Louisburg, H.M.S. *Pembroke,* one of the offshore squadron, came in from sea. *Pembroke* was commanded by Captain John Simcoe, father of John Graves Simcoe, destined to become the first lieutenant-governor of Upper Canada, then a small boy in England. *Pembroke*'s sailing master was the thirty-year-old James Cook who, a decade later, would make the first of his famous exploratory voyages to the Pacific.

Many years later Samuel Holland told John Graves Simcoe how he met Simcoe's father, which came about through a chance meeting with Cook. Holland was surveying along the shore using a plane table. Cook approached him and asked Holland to explain what he was doing, thus the latter becoming, at least to some degree, Cook's mentor. Hearing of this meeting, Captain Simcoe asked Holland to bring his plane table on board so he, too, could examine it and be instructed in its use. Captain Simcoe died not long after and was buried at sea off Anticosti Island. Later, his son, John Graves Simcoe, would rename what is now Lake Simcoe in his memory.

at Quebec. Moving north, Amherst captured the French forts in the valley though he didn't reach Quebec as planned, which, in any case, fell to Wolfe on 13 September 1759, when the battle on the Plains of Abraham was fought. In the meantime, New France's outer defences continued to crumble. Fort Niagara had fallen in July; Fort Rouillé at Toronto was abandoned, as were forts in the Ohio Valley. However, in the spring of 1760 the British in Quebec, now themselves besieged, made a massive sortie from the city, only to be defeated at the Battle of Ste. Foy. Following the battle, the British retired once more into the city to await the arrival of British ships when the ice went out – which they duly did.

Only Montreal remained. Surrounded by seventeen thousand British, it surrendered on 8 September 1760. And with that surrender, New France passed into British hands. The man who took formal possession of the town was the French-speaking Haldimand. Some two months after the surrender of Montreal, a small British force commanded by a Loyalist officer, Major Robert Rogers, set off for Detroit bearing a letter for the commandant from the last French governor of Montreal with instructions to surrender, which he did. It was from Rogers, who learned about it on his way to Detroit, that the British first learned of the shortcut to the upper Great Lakes via the Humber River, later called the Toronto Passage, and which would be duly explored some twenty years later.

The Seven Years' War, sometimes called the first world war, went on for three years after the fall of New France. In the end, France had little choice but to sue for peace. This France did, with the war coming to an end with the Treaty of Paris signed in 1763. Under the terms of the treaty, France lost all her possessions in North America except the islands of St. Pierre and Miquelon.

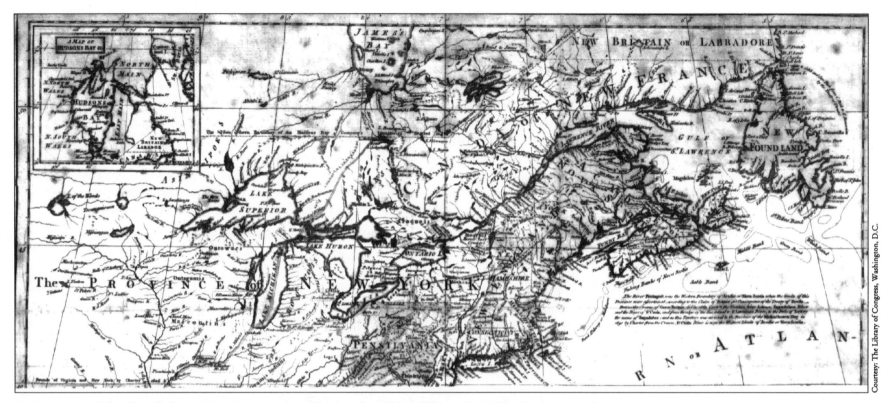

Figure 3.3 Part of John Mitchell's map of 1755. His map was used by the military during the Seven Years' War and after it to define the boundary of Quebec. Later, inaccuracies in his map would lead to problems in defining the international boundary with the U.S. Later still, it would figure in the Ontario-Manitoba boundary dispute.

CHAPTER FOUR

Holland, Collins, and Haldimand

In anticipation of a peace settlement at the end of the Seven Years' War that would leave New France in British hands, Brigadier General James Murray, then military governor of Quebec, ordered Captain Holland and other military engineers and surveyors to undertake an extensive survey of the settled areas of New France. The surveys went forward during 1760 and 1762, with the *Murray Atlas* as the result, a compendium of forty-four topographical maps of the St. Lawrence and adjacent lands. The *Murray Atlas* has been described as being "probably the most elaborate topographical survey and mapping project to be found anywhere within the British Empire up to that time."[1]

Taking some of his maps with him and armed with a recommendation from Murray, Holland went to London in 1762 to suggest to the Lords Commissioners of Trade and Plantations, who then presided over colonial affairs, that there should be a survey of all British possessions in North America in order to facilitate their further settlement. (The word "plantations" here refers to the overseas settlement of people, not plantations in the botanical sense.)

With the Seven Years' War finally over, the Lords Commissioners of Trade and Plantations followed up Holland's recommendation and, in February 1764, submitted a proposal to George III, which was almost certainly written by Holland. By this time Holland had learned that he was to be appointed surveyor general of the new British province of Quebec at a salary of £300 a year. The commissioners wrote: "... we find ourselves under the greatest difficulties arising from want of exact surveys of these countries, many parts of which have never been surveyed at all, and others so imperfectly that the charts and maps thereof are not to be depended upon."[2]

So much for colonial surveyors. The commissioners went on to suggest that "no time should be lost in obtaining accurate surveys of all your Majesty's North American dominions, but more especially of such parts as, from their natural advantages, require our immediate attention." Said dominions should, they suggested, be divided into two districts, a northern and a southern,

---

Surveys in Early Colonial America

By the 1660s, the survey fabric in Virginia was in a sad state of confusion. As the House of Assembly put it, "many contentious suits are dayly incited and stirred up about bounds of land for which noe remedy hath yet bin provided." Compounding the confusion were poorly marked or unmarked boundaries, not to mention bad surveying. Resurveying was not the answer, it seems, for as the assembly complained, "the least variation of a compasse alters the scituation of a whole neighbourhood" (quoted in "The College of William and Mary and Surveying in Early Virginia," *ACSM Journal of Surveying and Mapping*, June 1958). Matters improved with the foundation of the College of William and Mary in 1693. As instructed in its royal charter, the college assumed the functions of the surveyor general including the examination and licensing of land surveyors. Among their more illustrious graduate surveyors was George Washington. The college was offering courses in surveying as recently as the 1940s.

Maryland had similar troubles. Decades of laxness in the distribution and survey of land grants eventually led to such confusion that in 1699 Maryland's House of Assembly passed an act aimed at sorting things out. The preamble started with a dig at early surveyors, referring to them as being "but very meanly skillful" with boundaries "generally expressed in such uncertain terms [that] many chargeable and tedious suits in law happen about such bounds" (quoted in Clement, "Public Land Surveys," *ACSM Journal of Mapping and Surveying*, June 1958). All this led to a five-man commission, which sat in 1715 to hear and settle individual disputes. A similar, if short-lived, commission would be set up in Upper Canada in the 1830s.

Samuel Holland, known as the "father of Canadian surveying," was Dutch by birth. After serving with the British army, he was appointed Quebec's first surveyor general. The first surveys of the Loyalist settlements were made under his direction. (Miniature on ivory by C. Lewis.)
Courtesy: McCord Museum of Canadian History, Montreal, M4083

with the Potomac as the dividing line, and with a surveyor general in each.

The commissioners then laid before His Majesty "annexed proposals offered to us by Captain Samuel Holland, who has great knowledge of the northern parts of America, and who has distinguished himself as a brave and active officer, and able engineer ... but also as a skilful surveyor, in the accurate map he has made of the settled parts of your Majesty's Colony of Quebec."[3] They went on to tell the king that Holland had offered to direct the proposed survey of the north-

ern district himself, and this, moreover, without any extra pay – a proposal that must have set the commissioners, and probably the king as well, blinking in surprise.

The annexed proposal consisted of a budget, drawn up by Holland, for a proposed survey of the northern district. It is not clear whether the total cost is for the whole proposed survey or for the year 1764 only. The considerable costs totalled £1,117 12s. – possibly a quarter of a million dollars in today's terms. They included a £100 allowance for a deputy surveyor general to take over when Holland was working outside Quebec, 7s. a day for each of two assistant surveyors, pay for a sergeant, corporal, and ten private men "to assist in such survey as camp, colour and chainmen, and to make signals along shore and on the tops of mountains," and 5s. a day for a draughtsman. Finally, £416 15s. or nearly half the total requested, was set aside for two sets of instruments. Good instruments did not come cheap in those days. The commissioners made a point of backing up Holland's request for *two* sets of instruments "lest the work should be interrupted by any accident happening to these."[4]

The commissioners recommended that Holland's proposals be acted on. Within four days the king had approved them and directed the Admiralty to provide Holland with a ship, whereupon the Board of Survey, under whose orders Holland now came, furnished him with a 200-ton survey vessel, H.M.S. *Canceaux*. Appointed surveyor general of Quebec as of 6 March 1764, Holland recrossed the Atlantic, arriving at Quebec in the summer. He carried with him, for delivery to Murray, a set of directives regarding the civil administration of the province. These included the establishment of a legislative council, to which Murray appointed Holland in his capacity as surveyor general. Holland attended its inaugural meeting in August 1764. And so the most experienced and skilful surveyor in North America embarked on his civilian career,

which, in the course of time, would see him playing a leading role in the early surveys of Ontario-to-be.

Even more closely connected with the early surveys was his deputy, "Mr. John Collins, a gentleman qualified for the business. He has been imployed for many years as a Deputy Surveyor in the southern colonys and was recommended to me by Governor Murray and several other gentlemen."[5] That's about all we know of Collins's early life, though it is thought that he was in business in Quebec in the interim. Appointed by Holland on 8 September 1764, Collins had many duties, including the "admeasuring, surveying, setting out of roads and lands in the Province of Quebec," and for which he was to be paid not just his salary but "a moiety, or half part, of all salaries, fees, perquisites, profits and advantages thereunto belonging or appartaining to [his] office."[6] Collins was also made deputy surveyor of roads. On 2 May 1775, after the passing of the Quebec Act, his appointment as deputy surveyor general was confirmed by Guy Carleton (later Lord Dorchester), then governor of the province.

The Treaty of Paris, which ended the Seven Years' War, was followed by a royal proclamation that established distinct and separate governments in the four new territories that Britain had acquired in North America: Canada, East and West Florida, and Grenada. What became known as the Proclamation of 1763 gave these governments the authority to grant land in their respective territories on terms that would be advantageous to both government and grantees. There were two general provisions that would bear directly on the settlement of what is now Ontario. The first of these authorized, indeed directed, that the "conduct and bravery of the officers and men of our armies" be rewarded with grants of land. A scale was laid down. Field officers were to receive 5000 acres, captains 3000, subalterns 2000, non-commissioned officers 200, and private men 50 acres.

The second general provision pertinent to the settlement of Ontario established a principle that was to affect the whole course of Canadian history. The purchase of native land by private persons was forbidden. Native land could only be bought by the Crown and only at a "public meeting or assembly" of the native nation involved. However much one may decry the pitifully small amounts that were to be paid for native land, and the cynicism that sometimes accompanied these purchases, at least an attempt was made to deal fairly with the aboriginals. Five years after the proclamation, a treaty signed at Fort Stanwix in 1768 confirmed that the native people owned all the land north and west of the line that followed the Ohio and Alleghany rivers, and thence to the headwaters of the Mohawk River.

Late in 1763, particular instructions[7] reached Murray in Quebec, with Murray himself appointed first civil governor of the province. According to the definition of native land in the proclamation, the western boundary of Quebec was placed on a line joining Lake Nipissing and the intersection of the forty-fifth parallel and the St. Lawrence, essentially the Ottawa River. Apart from the settlement at Detroit, now placed in a curious legal limbo because of its location beyond the proclamation line, the future Ontario was to be a native reserve, remaining much as it was in the days of the French. This former *pays d'en haut* was a wilderness peopled only by natives, soldiers, and licensed traders – though from now on the latter would be working for British, or, to be more precise, Scots masters, who came to dominate the Montreal-based fur-trading empire.

Murray was also issued with instructions regarding land settlement. While at that time there was no question of settling what is now Ontario, the instructions must nevertheless have loomed large in Frederick Haldimand's mind when he came to make the first hurried decisions regarding the settlement of the Loyalists. Murray's instructions, like those sent to the governors of East and West Florida and Nova Scotia, were virtually identical to those that had been issued to the governors of Georgia and both North and South Carolina in the mid-1750s. Crown lands were to be available to bona fide settlers, black or white, "on reasonable terms."

After a settler had established his or her good faith, a warrant would be issued to the surveyor general "or other proper officers, impowering him or them to make a faithful and exact survey of the lands ... petitioned for," said warrant to be returned within six months, "with a plot or description of the lands so surveyed thereunto annexed." Following this, the grant would be made out. Settlers had to register a grant within six months at the Register's Office, as well as lodge a "docquet" with the Auditor's Office. That the British civil service of the 1760s was a stern task master is emphasized by a further proviso: copies of *all* entries arising out of the transaction were to be forwarded regularly to the Board of Trade in London.

Included in Murray's instructions (as they had been in those sent to the governor of Georgia in 1753) were the terms under which land was to be granted. The basic unit of land grant was to be 100 acres, with that amount to be granted to each petitioner, plus 50 acres for each additional member of the household, black or white. Up to 1000 acres of additional land could be bought, cash down, for 5s. an acre provided the purchaser could show an ability to cultivate it. After two years, all land was subject to an annual quit rent of 2s. per 100 acres. The settler also had to build a house at least 20 feet (6 m) long and 16 feet wide within three years. Also within three years, he or she was required to place three "neat cattle" on every 50 acres of land. In the foregoing we see the origins of the terms governing land grants in Upper Canada.

Of primary importance were Murray's instructions regarding surveys and the size of townships. He was "to take especial care, that in all surveys hereafter to be made, every surveyor be required ... to take particular notice, according to the best of his judgement and understanding, how much land is plantable, and how much of it is barren and unfit for cultivation; and accordingly to insert in the survey and plott [sic] by him to be returned into the Register's Office, the true quantity of each kind of land."

As for the laying out of townships, these were to be "about 20 thousand acres" and were to be laid out "having, as far as may be, natural boundaries extending up into the country and comprehending a necessary part of the St. Lawrence." In so far as these instructions had a bearing on the size of townships that came to be laid out in what became Ontario, it is of interest that 20 000 acres is equivalent to 31.25 square miles, roughly the same size as a 5.6-mile-square township, thus approximating the 6-mile-square townships laid out in New England.

Metrication

An historical work on land surveying inevitably contains many measurements taken in years past. In the interest of simplicity and accuracy, usually the original imperial measurement will be cited alone. Metric conversions are provided where they might be of use to the reader, as in measurements of distances.

Today's land surveyors often find themselves working on surveys originally made when distances were measured in "chains." A chain (66 feet or 20.1 m) made for extreme simplicity in the calculation of areas from lineal measurements – a virtue still appreciated by many surveyors. Throughout much of Ontario's settlement history the standard lot was either 200 or 100 acres. Suffice it to say that 200 acres is equivalent to 81 hectares, 100 acres to 40.5 hectares.

Murray was instructed that in each township a place should be marked out for a town "sufficient to contain such a number of families as you shall judge proper ... taking care that the said town be laid out upon or as near as conveniently may be to some navigable river or the sea coast." Land was also to be reserved in each township for military purposes, a church, and a school, along with specified acreages for the support of a minister and schoolmaster respectively – the origins here, perhaps, of the province's notorious "clergy reserves."

Of particular interest in light of the design of the first townships laid out in what is now Ontario were instructions relating to the siting of individual lots and their proportions. Virtually identical instructions, it may be added, had been given the governor of New York as early as 1708:

In all Grants of Land to be made by you ... regard be had to the profitable and unprofitable acres, so that each Grantee may have a proportionable number of one sort and the other; as likewise that the breadth of each tract of land ... be one third the length of such tract; and that the length of such tract do not extend along the banks of any river, but into the main land, that thereby the said Grantees may have a convenient share of what accommodation the said river may afford for navigation or otherwise.[8]

Finally, Murray was instructed

to give strict orders to the surveyors whom you shall employ to mark out the said townships to make returns to you of their surveys as soon as possible with a particular description of each township and the nature of the soil within the same. And you are to oblige all such persons as shall be appointed to be sur-

veyors of the said lands in each township to take an oath for the due performance of their offices and for obliging them to make exact surveys of all lands required to be set out.[9]

The French were less than enthusiastic about the new type of land grant, even though the quit rents worked out to be cheaper than those laid down in most seigneurial contracts. And so, in 1771, the seigneurial system was reinstated; its retention was confirmed by the Quebec Act of 1774, the act that reaffirmed the right of French-speaking Canadians to their Roman Catholic religion and provided for a dual legal system, with British common law co-existing with French civil law. By the same act the boundaries of the province were enlarged, with Quebec now becoming a huge L-shaped area, stretching from Labrador to Lake Superior with one arm reaching southward to include all or part of what are now the states of Michigan, Ohio, Illinois, Minnesota, and Wisconsin. Thus the settlement at Detroit and the other western posts were drawn into the province once more, *de jure* as well as *de facto*.

As for Governor Murray's now superseded land-granting procedures laid down in the Proclamation of 1763, they remained, if not a blueprint, at least a signpost showing the way that would be followed in the years ahead in what would become Ontario. In later years the role and duties of the land surveyor and the manner in which land was to be registered became increasingly refined – and also more complex – yet the basic system was put into place in British North America long before the first British land surveyor had even set foot in the future province of Ontario.

After he had appointed John Collins to act in his place in September 1764, Holland left Quebec for St. John's Island where he spent the next three years or so super-

vising the surveys of the future Prince Edward Island, the Magdalen Islands, and Cape Breton.

In Holland's absence, Collins had been busy running the first section of the boundary between the provinces of Quebec and New York, which some twenty years later was to become international. This line ran along the forty-fifth parallel eastward from the intersection of that parallel with Lake St. Francis. According to his accounts for the year 1765, which totalled £578 4s. 3d., it took him and his assistant seventy-nine days, from 2 March to 19 May 1765, to run the line between Lake St. Francis and Lake Champlain. Among other items in his account was "taking charge of the King's Highways and Streets in the Province giving all necessary orders for having them kept in good repair."[10] for which he was paid £100.

Whether or not the instruments that Holland and Collins used in their early surveys were their own or supplied by government is not clear. Some thirty years later in early 1791 – the year that Upper Canada was founded – when asked by Lord Dorchester to furnish a list of the instruments held by the Surveyor General's Office, Collins replied flatly that "There are no instruments ... which belong to the Government." Collins went on to list his own instruments: one Rowley theodolite, one achromatic telescope, one Hadley's quadrant, one mason's level, one English chain, and one French chain. "The Deputy Surveyor and the Assistant Surveyors furnish their own instruments for the ordinary business of surveying lands."[11]

Holland replied in much the same vein:

As no allowance of instruments has ever been made to the Land Surveyor-General of the Province of Quebec, of course, there are no instruments appertaining to his office, those made use of in his department being the private property either of himself or his deputies, and of the number in their possession I can only mention such as were commissioned out from London by me about six years ago, and sent me by Messrs. Watson and Keshleigh, being ... the best improved horizontal theodolites [with] circular protractors of the same divisions and dimensions of the instruments, with bar needles, agate cap'd ... and I have now ordered three more.[12]

A "horizontal" – as opposed to an "azimuthal" – theodolite was not equipped to measure vertical angles. It would be several decades before "modern" theodolites would come into general use.

Speaking for all land surveyors, then as now, Holland went on to explain why he liked to own his instruments. He "should be loth," he wrote, "to trust in any unskillful hands my capital set of instruments," and went on to enlarge on what might happen if his instruments were to fall into "unskillful hands," such as those of Mrs. Holland, by whom they "were much deranged" when she removed them from their boxes "to prevent their being carried off by the Americans, while she and her family were their prisoners in the year 1776." However, all turned out well as Holland took the principal ones to England where "they underwent a thorough repair."[13]

In 1767 Holland returned briefly to Quebec. He then surveyed the Atlantic coastline between the St. John River and New York and was working in New England when the American Revolutionary War broke out. Resisting pleas from the Americans to stay in the colonies, Holland fled to Britain.

Meanwhile, what of Frederick Haldimand? Following the fall of New France, he had served first as acting military governor and later as governor, of Trois-Rivières. He went on to serve as the general in command of the Southern Department where he remained until 1772 when he was transferred to New York under General Thomas Gage. When Gage spent a year on leave in England, Haldimand acted as commander-in-chief in his place, thus adding to his already considerable experience in administration, both civil and military. After Gage's return and subsequent departure for Boston following the "Boston Tea Party," Haldimand remained in New York, but when the situation worsened in Boston he was ordered to join Gage there, along with troops from New York. With Gage busy with his duties as governor, Haldimand became, in effect, the military commander in Boston.

After the start of the American Revolutionary War in April 1775, Haldimand was superseded; his foreign birth, he was told, made him unsuitable for a senior command in what had become a civil war. He left Boston the day before the Battle of Bunker Hill and returned to London where, as an expert on North America, he was well received. Meanwhile, Murray had

been succeeded as governor of Quebec by Guy Carleton, the future Lord Dorchester. On Carleton's sudden resignation, Haldimand, with his long experience in North America, both as soldier and administrator, was appointed governor in his place, arriving in Quebec in June 1778.

In the meantime, Holland returned to New York with the rank of major and in the somewhat surprising

Born in Switzerland, Frederick Haldimand, later knighted, rose to senior rank in the British army during the Seven Years' War and later became governor of Quebec. He defended the province during the American Revolutionary War and was in charge of settling the Loyalists in what became Upper Canada. (Painting by Sir Joshuah Reynolds, 1723–92, in the Raydon Gallery, New York, N.Y.)

Photo by Laszlo Studio, New York, N.Y.,
courtesy, Alexander R. Raydon, Raydon Gallery, New York, N.Y.

Holland's Home Life

Mrs. Holland must have been one of the first surveyors' wives to follow her husband into the field. Born Marie-Josephe Rolette, she had followed Holland while still in her early twenties to St. John's Island, where she and Holland lived in a makeshift house at what is now Holland Cove near Charlottetown. It was there that their first son, John Frederick, was born, the first British subject to be born in what became Prince Edward Island. At this point, however, Marie-Josephe was not Samuel's legal wife – in fact, he had a legal wife and daughter in Europe whom he was still supporting. A ruling obtained in New Hampshire in 1772 finally allowed Samuel and Marie-Josephe to get married, by which time they had some half-a-dozen children. They went on to have ten.

role of British *aide-de-camp* to the commander of the Hessian troops that formed part of the British forces in America. Four months after he arrived in Quebec, Haldimand summoned Holland to resume his duties as surveyor general. Holland's arrival in the spring of 1779 completed the three-man team of Haldimand, Holland, and Collins, who together were to deal so efficiently with the first mass settlement of Loyalist refugees.

The first land surveys under the British flag in what was to become Ontario were made in the Detroit area, apparently in the early 1770s. The early settlement history of what is now Essex County is confusing, largely as a result of breaches, sometimes well intentioned, sometimes criminally inspired, of the rules laid down in the Proclamation of 1763 regarding the private acquisition of native land. The resulting tangle of claims and counter-claims would take the rest of the century to sort out.

These troubles started early. It seems that in 1770 or thereabouts the British military authorities then governing Detroit took it upon themselves to grant land, presumably to local French farmers. Surveys may have been made in connection with these grants, though who made them is unknown. The commandant at Detroit told General Gage, then commander-in-chief in New York, what had been done. He got his knuckles rapped for exceeding his authority, and the grants were declared null and void.

The earliest firm evidence of land-surveying activities in the Detroit area under the British is a note written on a later survey by Thomas Smith, a notary and part-time surveyor who lived in Detroit. It refers to lots opposite Peach Island at the eastern end of the Detroit River where it enters Lake St. Clair, now a northeastern suburb of Windsor. According to this note, the settlement began on the site in about 1774, by permission of one Major Bassett of the Tenth Regiment of Foot, who was then commandant. In 1780, Major Arent

de Peyster of the Eighth Regiment and also commandant authorized a surveyor by the name of J. Porlier Benac to survey the settlement. This he did, giving a certificate of survey to each proprietor. A copy of one of them appears on Smith's survey already referred to. This, the first known surveyor's description to be written in Ontario, runs (in translation) as follows:

> Three arpents in front by eight arpents in depth. I, the undersigned, being duly authorized, certify that I measured the front of the land that the Ottawas gave to Mr. Louis Peltier (No. 134) of three arpents' frontage, which land adjoins on the west the land of Jacques Peltier (No. 133) and on the west the land of J.B. Paré (No. 135). I also planted some pickets on the side of the road designated as the King's Road. The side line of the said land runs south 10 degrees east. In witness thereof I have given the present to serve as needed. Detroit, June 20, 1780.
>
> J. Porlier Benac[14]

An *arpent* equals about 191.8 feet, so the lot would have been about 575 feet by 1534 feet or, roughly, 9 chains wide and 23 chains deep

Following the outbreak of the American Revolutionary War, Haldimand was pondering, like the French before him, on the logistics of supplying Detroit and other western posts. Out of this was to come the first land survey of consequence in Ontario. Since 1777, Fort Niagara, now near Lewiston in the state of New York, had been the operational base of Butler's Rangers, a Loyalist corps raised after the outbreak of the American Revolutionary War by Captain John Butler.

The official strength of Butler's Rangers was 500. Add men of the Indian Department, detachments of British regulars and of other Loyalist formations, fur traders and others concerned with the 9-mile (14-km)

portage around Niagara Falls, and a growing number of civilian refugees fleeing the now embattled American colonies and the number of mouths that needed feeding at Niagara was considerable. Vegetables were already being grown in the military garden, but the great bulk of Niagara's needs had to be supplied, at enormous expense and with great difficulty, from Quebec.

During his time as regimental officer in the Revolutionary War, Haldimand had become acquainted with the excellence of the vegetables grown in the Niagara area. After becoming governor, he wrote to Lieutenant-Colonel Mason Bolton, the commandant at Niagara, suggesting that the refugees might be usefully employed growing vegetables around the fort. Bolton replied in the spring of 1779, by which time Butler had built a range of barracks for his rangers on the western, or Canadian, side of the Niagara River. Bolton was not enthusiastic about Haldimand's idea. He said it would take seven years to bring enough land under cultivation to supply the garrison. He felt that, in any case, it was inadvisable to "encroach on the lands of the Six Nations, as we have informed them that the Great King never deprived them of an acre."[15] However, he *had* learned that the soil was more fertile on the west (or Canadian) side where, moreover, the land was owned by the Mississaugas. Haldimand urged him to get on with it.

As it turned out, the summer of 1779 saw Bolton – and Haldimand – preoccupied with other matters. A massive punitive expedition was mounted by the Americans, which had as its object the destruction of the homelands of the Senecas and Cayugas around the Finger Lakes, who had remained staunchly pro-British. The British and Iroquois were unable to stem the American advance, and, by the fall of 1779, some 5000 Six Nation Indians driven from their lands were encamped around Fort Niagara clamouring for food and supplies, placing further strain on British supply lines. Thus, in September 1779 we find Haldimand writing to the colonial secretary in London urging that more consideration be given also to "raising grain and all kinds of stock at Detroit." He continued, "The same plan is very practicable at Niagara, and there is nothing wanting but a beginning."[16]

A beginning was made the following summer. In July 1780, the colonial secretary approving, Haldimand directed Bolton at Niagara to "reclaim the land granted by the Mississaugas to Sir William Johnson for the Crown, situated on the southwest side of the river opposite the fort [where Niagara-on-the-Lake now stands] ... which land will be divided into several lots."[17] The lots were to be held on a temporary basis. Haldimand was referring to a 14-by-4-mile tract centred on the Niagara River originally ceded by the Senecas after the Seven Years' War to bring the all-important portage around Niagara Falls under British control. However, there had been no mention in the treaty of anyone settling there. Haldimand directed that a 4-mile tract on the west side, stretching from Lake Ontario to Lake Erie, be bought from the Mississaugas for a temporary settlement.

Haldimand had already asked Butler, who had a sound knowledge of farming, to help him get men cultivating the land at Niagara, knowing that he had "some good farmers in his corps who, either advancing in years or having a large family, he [Butler] could dis-

pense with." By December 1780, according to Butler, there were "four or five families settled and they have built themselves houses." And so the first Loyalist settlement in Ontario was founded, a settlement that antedated those at Cataraqui and along the St. Lawrence by some four years.

It was not until the following spring, on 9 May 1781, that a meeting was held with the Mississauga and Chippewa (with the Seneca as observers, just in case) at which land was bought for settlers on the Canadian side of the Niagara River. This was the first purchase of native land for white settlement made in Ontario. The tract was described by Lieutenant Terrot of the Royal Artillery, who planted posts on Lakes Ontario and Erie, as "beginning at a large white oak tree forked 6 feet from the ground," which grew on the shore of Lake Ontario 4 miles in a straight line west of Fort Niagara. This 4-mile strip hugging the west side of the Niagara River was bought from the natives for the value of three hundred suits of clothes.

On 25 August 1782, a survey of the settlement at Niagara showed sixteen families on the land, totalling sixty-eight men, women, and children. They had cleared 236 acres and owned 49 horses, 42 cows, 30 sheep, and 103 hogs. Either that summer or the following spring a survey was made of the settlement, the first of its kind in Ontario. On Butler's orders the set-

tlement – apparently containing seventy lots – was surveyed by Allan McDonell, one of the settlers.[18] Not much is known of McDonell, though he seems to have known what he was about. His account – probably the first account to be submitted by a British surveyor in Ontario – ran as follows:

Allan McDonell

April 4 [no year given]

	£	s	d
2 chain bearers & 1 marker at 4/- for 24 days —	14	8	0
24 days for surveying — 10/–	12	0	0
3 days draft draw'd — 20/–	3	0	0
for expenses	2	14	0
	£32	2	0

In early May 1783, Butler forwarded McDonell's plan of the settlement to Haldimand. Butler also enclosed McDonell's account for payment because both the superintendent of Indian Affairs and the commandant of the fort at Niagara declined – in forcible terms – to have anything to do with it. McDonell would not be the last surveyor in the province to have difficulty in getting paid for his work. On a return of the settlers at Niagara, dated 1 December 1783, Allan McDonell's name appears as McDaniel. As far as is known, his work on the Niagara settlement was the last survey he undertook – and also may have been his first.

In the midst of dealing with all his other worries, Haldimand found time to dispatch the first British exploratory party to have a look at the Toronto Passage, as it became known, the shortcut between Georgian Bay and Lake Ontario via Lake Simcoe and the Holland River. As mentioned earlier, Major Rogers

Haldimand's Canal

In order to eliminate time-consuming and tedious portages around the worst rapids on the upper St. Lawrence and so speed the transport of supplies to the western posts, Haldimand ordered the construction of the first successful canal on the St. Lawrence. This was at Côteau-du-Lac, now a small town about 19 miles (30 km) east of the Ontario-Quebec boundary. Construction began in 1779 under the direction of a Lieutenant William Twiss of the Corps of Engineers, later the Royal Engineers. On its completion in 1781, the canal was 900 feet (274.3 m) long with three locks, each about 40 feet long, 6 feet wide, and 2.5 feet deep. With its warehouses and its fortifications, Côteau-du-Lac not only catered to the needs of the military but played an important civilian role in facilitating the shipment downstream of furs, wheat, and other produce. Now being restored, the canal at Côteau-du-Lac, with its related buildings, is now a national historic site.

had learned of the Toronto Passage when on his way to Detroit in 1760. Presumably Haldimand was concerned, as other senior British military men would be later, at the vulnerability of the long line of communication with Detroit, not to mention the obstacle represented by Niagara Falls. No doubt he was pressured by fur-trading interests anxious to find a cheaper route to the upper Great Lakes.

The officer dispatched on this mission is now thought to have been Captain Peter Hare of Butler's Rangers, who completed his exploratory survey in the summer of 1780. His journal is incomplete, and, while his route takes some reconstructing, it is believed he took his party from Toronto to Lake Simcoe and some distance down the Severn River before striking north to emerge eventually on Georgian Bay at Honey Harbour. The party then came south to the Severn again and so back to Lake Simcoe and Toronto. Nothing much came of this venture at the time. Not until the War of 1812 were serious efforts made by the military to find a shortcut to the upper Great Lakes.

CHAPTER FIVE

Haldimand and the First Townships

By the time the first Loyalist farmers were settling in across the river from Fort Niagara, the American Revolutionary War was coming to an end, though the final treaty, usually called the Treaty of Versailles, would not be signed until September 1783. By then Governor Haldimand had fresh worries on his mind. Since the early days of the war, refugees had been turning up at Niagara and Detroit and making their way to Montreal and its environs, where by 1778 the number of destitute Loyalist refugees was becoming a serious problem. To help resolve the immediate difficulty, Haldimand started housing them at Sorel and other temporary camps.

Early in 1783 Haldimand received details of the preliminary peace treaty from London and was instructed to make arrangements to resettle the Loyalists, who now had no hope of returning to their former homes. By this time Haldimand had upwards of 6000 men, women, and children – some say as many as 10 000 – on his hands. His first thought was to form a single, large Loyalist settlement across the river from Detroit. However, the British government advised him to settle them in what were later called the Eastern Townships, where some Loyalists had already asked to go. Haldimand disagreed. In his view, that part of Quebec should be left for the expansion of the French population. Haldimand could not forbid Loyalists from settling there – and many did – but he later refused them the provisions and supplies that were doled out to the bulk of the Loyalists.

At this juncture Haldimand was starting to worry that the British base on Carleton Island near present-day Kingston would end up in U.S. territory when the international boundary came to be drawn (see figure 5.3). To replace that base, he began to think in terms of rebuilding the French fort at Cataraqui and of placing a military settlement around it.

Haldimand also found he had another class of displaced persons to provide for – the Six Nation Indians whose homelands to the south of Lake Ontario had now come under American jurisdiction and who had taken refuge in British territory. Unable to impress upon the home government, which was at that point indifferent to the fate of the Six Nations, the seriousness of the situation, Haldimand was on his own. Indeed, he received no instructions of any kind regarding the native people. During the winter of 1782–83 he learned that their leader, Joseph Brant,[1] would not be averse to his people settling north of Lake Ontario. In May 1783 an impatient and angry Brant travelled to Quebec to find out how the Six Nations stood. In response Haldimand suggested that they might settle north of the lake, perhaps around Cataraqui, and that the surveyor general would take a look at this area with the Six Nations in mind.

Haldimand then wrote to London, seeking endorsement for his action, which in due course he received. After talking to Brant, Haldimand ordered Holland to make the necessary exploratory surveys. On 26 May 1783, with both the rebuilding of the old French fort at Cataraqui and the resettlement of the Six Nations in mind, Haldimand issued his instructions to Holland – instructions that, as it turned out, were to set in motion the whole process of survey and settlement in what is now Ontario:

> As it is necessary that I should be informed of the nature of the country from the last concessions [i.e., in Quebec (see figures 5.1 and 5.2)] to Cataraqui and thence to Niagara on the north side of Lake Ontario, you are hereby directed to set off immediately for Montreal and to proceed to Cataraqui where you will minutely examine into the situation and state of the fort formerly occupied by the French, and the land and country adjacent.[2]

Holland set off for Montreal immediately, taking Captain Brant and another Six Nation Indian with him. A month later Holland was back in Quebec and writing, although no one knew it at the time, the province's first survey report – the first of many thousands. He stated on 26 June 1783 that he had examined the country carefully with a view to settlement and that

> from the supposed bounds of the Seigneurie of Soulange, the property of Monsieur de Longueille on Lake St. Francis, the lands are low towards the water side, and fit for meadows, but at the same distance the soil is exceeding good tillage. From the upper part of Lake St. Francis to the Long Sault [above Cornwall] no land can be more promising ...
>
> From the head of the Long Sault to the top of the uppermost rapid, where the navigation begins, the country has a most favorable appearance. From hence to Cataraqui ... though the shore appears rough and uninviting the soil is rich at some distance – fit for all purposes of agriculture, as I have been informed [presumably by natives].[3]

Holland went on to say that, having reached Carleton Island on 10 June, he went on to Cataraqui two days later, where he started the first surveys at

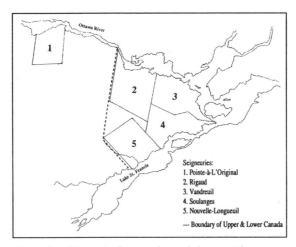

Figure 5.1 Seigneuries lying in the angle between the Ottawa and St. Lawrence rivers. They affected the location of the Loyalist townships on the St. Lawrence and later the position of the boundary between Upper and Lower Canada. Pointe-à-L'Orignal (1 above) became Longueuil Township in Prescott County. (Based on a map by William Vondenvelden and Louis Charland, London, 1803, reprinted in *Historical Atlas of Canada*, Volume 1, University of Toronto Press, n.d.)

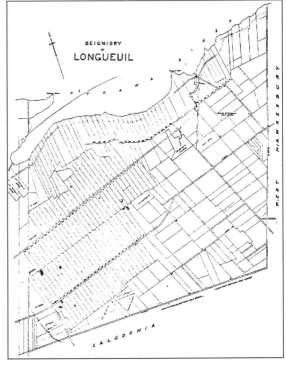

Figure 5.2 The only seigneury in Ontario, now Longueuil Township in Prescott county, as it was in the early 1900s. Originally granted to François Provost, the mayor of Quebec, in 1674, it was bought in 1791 by J.D. Le Moyne de Longueuil, after whom the township is named. De Longueuil sold the seigneury to one N.H. Treadwell for 1,000 guineas, whose grandson, Charles Platt Treadwell, disposed of it parcel by parcel. (From Wilkie, *The Seigniory of Longueuil.*)

Tinling, Peachey, and La Force

William Tinling was a British regular with the Twenty-ninth Foot. James Peachey was a skilled artist, besides being a surveyor and draughtsman. Described by Holland as being "on the footing of a gentleman, of which he made himself deserving of, as well by his conduct & improvements and drawing and painting," Peachey first worked for the Crown in Boston in about 1774, returning to North America in 1780 when he was presumably taken on by Holland. A few years after he accompanied Holland on his historic exploratory survey, he obtained a commission in the Sixtieth Foot, the Royal Americans, to die in the late 1790s in Martinique, probably during an epidemic. Captain René-Hypolite Pepin, otherwise known as La Force, was a Quebec-born Frenchman who had sworn allegiance to the British Crown after the conquest and had helped defend Quebec against the Americans. Since 1777 he had been in command of British ships on Lake Ontario.

what is now Kingston. He found the area to be quite favourable, as did Brant and several of the Six Nations who "seemed to be well satisfied with the country." Holland also made arrangements to have men and materials sent from Carleton Island to Cataraqui to start work on the new fort there; such work was to go forward under Lieutenant Tinling, with Lieutenant Holland (Samuel Holland's son, John Frederick) as his assistant. In addition, "Captain La Force, Mr. Cotte, and Mr. Peachy proceeded to survey the north shore of Lake Ontario, all the way to Niagara having received my instructions for that purpose." On his return to Montreal, Holland sent Haldimand a plan of the fort, which he was planning, apparently, to call Fort Haldimand, thus perpetuating Haldimand's name "to all posterity."[4]

Even as Holland was busy at Cataraqui, Haldimand heard from Sir Guy Carleton in New York that he was shipping several hundred Loyalists to Quebec. These came in two parties under Michael Grass and Peter Van Alstine, later referred to by an exasperated official as "so-called captains." It was the intention of the Associated Loyalists, as they called themselves, to settle at Cataraqui, which Grass had got to know as a prisoner of the French during the Seven Years' War. These Loyalists proved to be nothing but trouble for the over-burdened Haldimand from the moment of their arrival. It was found that they had brought smallpox and measles with them, necessitating their quarantine at Sorel with armed guards posted to try and contain the diseases.

On 23 July 1783 Holland supplied Haldimand, at the latter's request, with a sketch of a town to be laid out at Cataraqui. A few days later this was forwarded by Haldimand's secretary, Captain Robert Mathews, to Major John Ross, then in command at Oswego and the senior military man in the area, with instructions to speed the dismantling of the fort and buildings on Carleton Island and to transfer as much as possible to Cataraqui. He was also to "have the sur-

vey mentioned in Major Holland's letter immediately undertaken." Mathews added a revealing postscript. "His Excellency not having yet received the least information or instructions concerning the settlement of Loyalists in this Province, and having it only in view to place them in such situations as appears to him most eligible, desires you will not mention anything of the present scheme to any person whatever."[5]

At the end of July, Major Ross arrived from Oswego to take charge at Cataraqui, where he found Tinling had already received instructions directly from Holland regarding the proposed survey of the new fort. By early September, Ross and Tinling had finished the

survey of the site for the proposed fort, though, as Ross explained at some length to Haldimand it was not to be where Holland had suggested. Meanwhile, Haldimand had come increasingly to rely on and confide in Sir John Johnson, superintendent of Indian Affairs, who was fast becoming the unofficial spokesman for the Loyalists. Thus it was he who wrote Haldimand in August that the Mississauga had no objection to the white men settling among them but, interestingly enough, that they were distinctly uneasy at the thought of the formidable Six Nations doing so.

On 1 September 1783 Haldimand tells Johnson that he is preparing "to send off a surveyor and proper

"A view of the ruins of Fort at Cataraqui," painted by James Peachey. Peachey was one of the surveyors who accompanied Holland on his first exploratory survey of the upper St. Lawrence and the Bay of Quinte. Fort Cataraqui had been destroyed during the Seven Years' War.

"Encampment of Loyalists at Johnstown," painted by James Peachey. Named after Sir John Johnson, Johnstown became New Johnstown and, later, Cornwall.

proportion of lands I propose to grant to each family Viz 120 acres of which six are to be in front which will make 19 chains in front and 63 chains 25 links in depth – so that every township will have 25 lots in front and four chains 75 links will remain for roads, with 7 Concessions in depth – 58 links will remain for a road by which distribution each Township will contain 175 lots of 120 acres.

It being recalled that one chain equals 66 feet (20 m) and that there are 100 links to a chain, the "four chains 75 links" left over for roads, when divided by seven (the number of concessions), gives road allowances between the concessions of just under 45 feet. Within the 6-mile (10-km) breadth of the township, twenty-five lots of 19 chains left room for five side roads, each one chain wide.

persons to explore and mark lands for the intended settlement at Cataraqui" and that land must be bought from the Mississauga for the Six Nations. He also told Johnson of his determination that lots should be distributed by means of a lottery. "I know," he wrote, "there are many who are speculating for large grants, in order to turn land-jobbers, a system I shall entirely discourage."[6] Ten days later, on 11 September, Haldimand issued instructions to Collins that included directions for laying out what were to be the first of many townships in Ontario, presumably after consulting Holland and probably Collins himself. Addressed to John Collins, Esq., they began as follows:

> Sir: It being my intention to establish settlements for the provision of part of the distressed Loyalists resorting to this Province at and in the neighbourhood of Cataraqui upon Lake Ontario – you are hereby directed to proceed to that place without loss of time for the purpose of surveying and laying out the

several lands in townships and lots agreeable to the following instructions.[7]

That Haldimand began his instructions the way he did makes it clear that the momentous decision to settle the Loyalists around Cataraqui was his and his alone. Considering the pressure of events and the continuing absence of precise instructions from Britain, he could scarcely have done otherwise. The first two paragraphs of the instructions emphasize the military aspects of the proposed settlement and deal with the layout of the fortifications and harbour. The third paragraph of Haldimand's letter instructed Collins to make provision for a 400-acre common, which was to be reserved for the use of the townspeople.

The fourth paragraph contained what might be termed the surveying meat of Collins's instructions:

> The method of laying out townships of six miles square I consider as the best to be followed as the people to be settled there are most used to it, and it will best answer the

Sir John Johnson

Sir John Johnson was the son of Sir William Johnson, who had settled near Albany, New York, where he had became superintendent of the Indian Department. It was largely through Sir William's efforts that the Mohawk remained loyal to Britain during the Seven Years' War. He married the daughter of a German missionary, by whom he had three children, one of whom was John Johnson. Sir William died soon after the start of the Revolutionary War, during the early stages of which his son, Sir John, fled to Montreal where he raised the King's Royal Regiment of New York, also known as the Royal Yorkers or just plain Yorkers. In March 1782 he was appointed superintendent of Indian Affairs. After the war, Sir John emerged as leader of the Loyalists and subsequently led the campaign that resulted in the formation of Upper Canada. He was Lord Dorchester's nominee for lieutenant-governor of the new province, but he lost out to John Graves

Haldimand went on to tell Collins that he would be assisted by Captain Justus Sherwood, Lieutenant Lewis Cotté,[8] and Captain Michael Grass, and that "these gentlemen will be attended with ax men etc proper for the occasion." Collins is to begin his survey by laying out a "township on each side of the bay and transmit it [i.e., the survey] to me together with your remarks." He is instructed to report his progress "from time to time."

Even today a surveyor may find himself measuring a choice parcel of land and earmarking it, as it were, for himself. In earlier days this happened frequently. Haldimand knew this. As he delicately put it, "As it is not impossible in exploring these lands, some of the persons employed may make choice of particular situations and make preparations accordingly – to prevent which you are to signify to them that my intentions are to distribute the lots impartially by drawing for them." With the phrase "Wishing you success, etc.," Haldimand ends his letter.

We do not know how Haldimand (presumably after consulting Holland and perhaps Collins) arrived at the basic design and layout of his township. There were certain precedents. There were the instructions regarding the surveying, layout, and granting of lands that had been sent by the Board of Trade to Governor Murray in 1763, which called for the laying out of townships of "about" 20 000 acres in extent. Haldimand's townships were to be 6 miles square (this had emerged in New England as the most satisfactory size), equal to a shade over 23 000 acres. But why did Haldimand decide that the size of the lots in the township be an awkward 120 acres, when the Proclamation of 1763 that followed the Seven Years' War and even earlier British "planting" schemes had 100 acres as the base unit? It is an interesting point and one of Ontario's minor surveying mysteries. The 1763 instructions state, however, that the breadth of lots should be one-third the length, which is more or less the size of Haldimand's lots. He stipulates a width of

19 chains, which, being multiplied by three, gives 57 chains – this at least approaches the length of 63 chains, 25 links that Haldimand laid down.

The 1763 instructions also required that lots on a river be laid out in such a manner that their length extend into "the main land." This harks back to the instructions sent to the governor of New York as far back as 1708, which in turn reflects the general layout of the *seigneuries*, though there is no evidence of a direct connection. In fact, common sense would dictate such an arrangement. One can only assume that the final design was an amalgam of the New England experience; of earlier British colonial survey layouts, which Haldimand may well have observed during his years in Florida; and the French seigneuries. All Haldimand's concerns were tempered by the need for surveys that could be easily and cheaply carried out. This last must have weighed heavily with Haldimand, who was forever urging the importance of economy.

With Cataraqui the centre of activity, the north shore of the St. Lawrence above Lake St. Francis had so far received only passing attention. About the same time as Haldimand was sending Collins his instructions, Captain Sherwood was sent with a party to explore and report on the settlement possibilities along the St. Lawrence and round the Bay of Quinte. Sherwood left on 19 September. In his own words he "left Mountreal with Lt. Johns & two men of the King's Rangers, Ensn Bottum and 7 men of the Loyal Rangers proceeded up the St. Lawrence in a boat." Sherwood's report on the quality of the land was generally favourable, with the exception of a stretch of "broken land" east of Cataraqui. He concluded, "The climate here is very mild & good, and I think the Loyalists may be the happiest people in America by settling this country."[9]

During all this, Haldimand had not forgotten the possibility of placing settlers along the Ottawa River, then called the Grand, and in the hinterland between that river and the St. Lawrence. He decided to send an

Gunter's chain as used by early surveyors. Chains stretched with use and from the mid-1800s onwards had to be tested against a standard length. Chains were not superseded by steel tapes until the twentieth century. Many road allowances in the province are still one chain (66 feet) wide.

exploratory expedition up the Ottawa, which would then work its way south to the St. Lawrence. The expedition was led by Lieutenant Gershom French of the Loyal Rangers. He left Montreal on 29 September, paddling up the Ottawa with seven Loyalist soldiers, two Canadians, and a native guide, all in two canoes, reaching the Rideau two days later, having briefly explored both shores of the Ottawa along the way. They then went up the Rideau to reach the Rideau Lakes. From here they worked their way to the Gananoque River, and so down to the St. Lawrence, which they reached on 14 October – two weeks or so after they left.

While French was away, the ever-careful Haldimand wrote to Major Ross instructing him to send a party to meet French. Haldimand added, "Our plans of this country are very imperfect, according to them I should conjecture that due north from your post the Grand River lies some 150 miles distant." In fact it is less than a hundred miles (160 km) – an illustration of the ignorance then prevailing of the inland geography of the province.

Collins arrived at Cataraqui early in October, having had "excessive bad weather" almost every day since leaving Quebec. He reported to Major Ross who advised him to mark time until the land required for the townships was bought from the Mississaugas. Under the direction of Sir John Johnson, the negotiations had been in the hands of Captain William Crawford, an American-born Loyalist with Sir John Johnson's King's Royal Regiment of New York (KRRNY). These discussions led to a meeting with the Mississaugas on Carleton Island where, on 9 October 1783, Crawford bought all the land from what is now the Quebec-Ontario border westward to the River Trent – virtually all the land in the present-day counties of Glengarry, Stormont, Dundas, Leeds and Grenville, Frontenac, Lennox and Addington, and Hastings.

As soon as the purchase had been made, Ross dispatched several officers of the garrison at Cataraqui to explore inland. Ross reported that they found "the lands in general of a very excellent quality, easily cleared and intersected with rivers on which there are several falls where mills can be conveniently erected." Meanwhile French's party had come in, having, it seems, missed the relief party that Ross had sent out. French was less enthusiastic about the land on the upper Gananoque than he was about those along the Rideau, describing it as very barren.

With the land purchases made, Collins and his men got down to work. Initially there were to be four townships. These were No. 1, or Kingston Township;

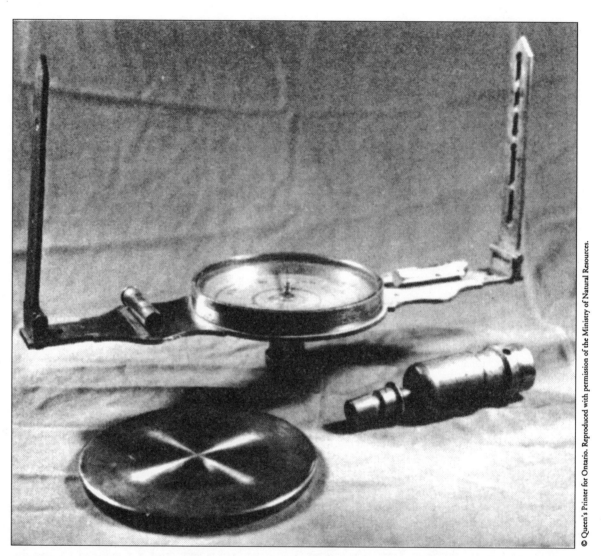

Circumferentor or sighting compass used by early surveyors. Also shown is its cover and a staff head onto which the instrument fitted.

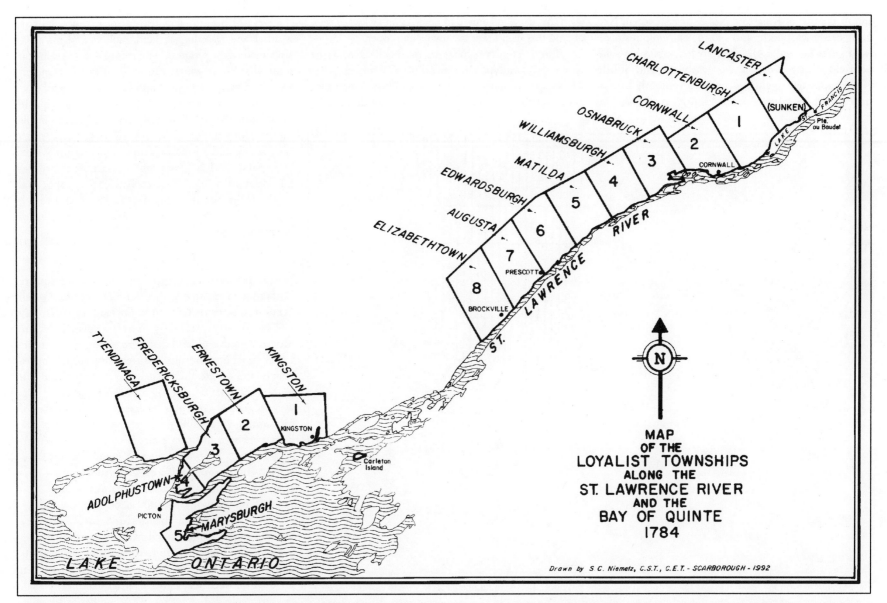

Figure 5.3 The first Loyalist townships along the St. Lawrence and around the Bay of Quinte. At first numbered, they were named later. The township of Tyendinaga was reserved for the Six Nations and is now occupied by the Mohawks of the Bay of Quinte.

and to the east of Kingston, No. 2, or Ernestown; No. 3, or Fredericksburgh; and No. 4, or Adolphustown (see figures 5.3 and 5.4). Later, Fredericksburgh would be divided into North Fredericksburgh and South Fredericksburgh townships, while a southerly extension would be called Fredericksburgh Additional, a term that came to be used to describe an awkward tract of land that didn't rate as a township proper.

The first survey post in township No. 1, or Kingston Township, was planted on 27 October 1783. The lots were numbered from west to east, which suggests that the first post planted was some distance to the west of present-day Kingston. Plagued by bad weather and waterlogged land, Collins and his assistants made slow progress. The record is unclear, but it seems that before winter had set in, they had completed at least part of Kingston and Ernestown townships.

While Collins was at work around Cataraqui in the fall of 1783, the first steps were being taken in the surveys along the St. Lawrence. In September, apparently acting under Johnson's orders, Lieutenant Walter Sutherland, KRRNY, was sent to examine the shoreline westward from Pointe au Baudet – the spot that marked the western border of the last French seigneurie and which now lies on the Ontario-Quebec border (see figure 5.3).

Work had hardly begun on the 6-mile-square Cataraqui townships with their 120-acre lots when Haldimand's instructions from England, dated 16 July 1783, finally arrived. These specified the various amounts of land that were to be granted to the Loyalists. The amounts – surely not surprising to Haldimand – were almost identical to those laid down in the Proclamation of 1763. Civilian heads of families were to get 100 acres plus 50 acres for each member of his family, with single men getting 50 acres. Ex-soldiers were on a different scale. Private soldiers were to get 50 acres plus 50 acres for each member of his family, non-commissioned officers 200 acres, warrant officers and lieutenants 500 acres, captains 700 acres, and those of more senior rank 1000 acres.

The land was to be divided into "distinct seigneuries or fiefs, to extend from two to four leagues in front, and from three to five leagues in depth, if situated upon a navigable river, otherwise to be run square, or in such shape and in such quantities, as shall be convenient & practicable."[10] At 3 miles to a league, these instructions therefore called for seigneuries or townships on navigable water that were to be from 6 to 12 miles (10 to 19 km) along the front and from

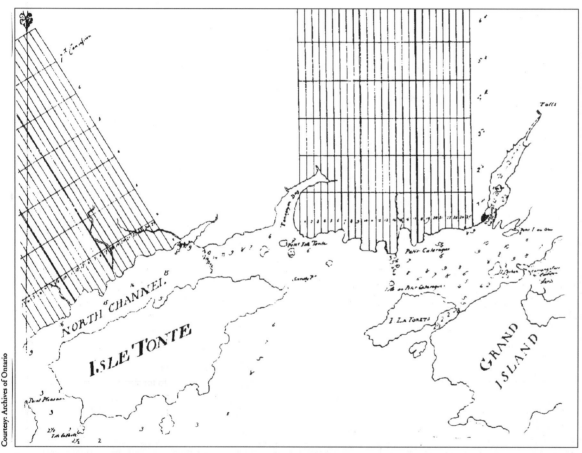

Figure 5.4 Kingston township, the first township laid out in the province. Lots were numbered from west to east suggesting that the surveyors started work some distance to the west of present-day Kingston. Isle Tonte is now Amherst Island, Grand Island became Wolfe Island. (Detail from a "Survey of the north side of Lake Ontario from Cataraque [sic] to Niagara by Tinling, Kotte and Peachey, under the direction of Samuel Holland." Copied by Lieut. Prevost, 1784. AO, Cartographic Records Collection, R-L.)

9 to 15 miles deep. The fresh instructions received by Haldimand also confirmed that land granted to the Loyalists were to be held under the seigneurial system, even those around Niagara. In other words the Loyalists would be tenants of the Crown and subject after ten years to quit rent of a half-penny per acre, such rent being in lieu of service under the seigneurial system. That they would not own their land outright was not welcome news to the Loyalists.

Faced with the new size of land grants based on 100-acre units, Haldimand – again after consultations, presumably, with Holland and Collins – decided to change the standard lot from 120 to 200 acres sometime during the winter of 1783–84. This change led to less upset than might have resulted had the township surveys been further advanced than they were. In such townships as had been begun with lots in the first concession marked only by corner posts 19 chains apart, all that was done was to increase the depth of the lots to 105.25 chains, which, multiplied by 19 chains, gave the 200 acres required. However, the increase in lot size also meant that fewer people could be accommodated in a township. So in order to locate the same number of settlers in a township, the size of the standard township was increased to 9 miles (15 km) in width and 12 miles in depth. This corresponded exactly with the average dimensions of a seigneurie as required in Haldimand's new instructions.* And so the basic 9-by-12-mile townships with 200-acre lots that now typify much of southern Ontario came into being.

With lots in the first concession laid out along the shoreline, and with one dwelling per lot in each of the concessions inland, the end result was akin to a modern street with houses along only one side of it, with the empty land opposite it belonging to the house on the next parallel street. This method of laying out a township later became known as the "Single-Front System," of which Haldimand's township was the prototype. The system did not make for cohesive communities. Nor did farmers have neighbours across the road to help them keep the concession roads open in winter. With all its faults, however, the single-front system remained the standard until 1818 (see figure 5.5).

*It is ironic that the Americans would adopt the 6-mile-square township as their standard at just about the time when it was being abandoned in Canada. It would be reintroduced into Ontario in the mid-1800s.

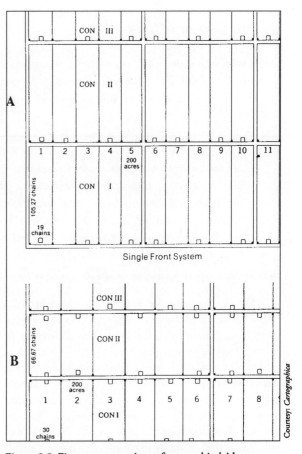

Figure 5.5 First two concessions of a township laid out according to the single-front system (A). Small solid squares along the front of each concession indicate the position of the survey posts planted. No lot sidelines were run in the initial survey. To make sure they were on their own land, settlers usually placed their house (larger open squares) near the road. The single-front system did not make for cohesive communities and made road upkeep difficult. These disadvantages were partly overcome by the introduction in 1818 of the double-front system (B). (From Sebert, *Land Surveys of Ontario*.)

Up to this point the Loyalists requiring resettlement consisted of civilians and their families, along with a miscellany of ex-soldiers from a number of units. Yet to be settled were the men, many with families, of the various Loyalist regiments based in and about Montreal, in Niagara, and on Carleton Island, which was due to fall on the U.S. side of the international boundary as Haldimand had foreseen. (Carleton Island is now in private hands. To the locals, the site of the British fort is known as Fort Haldimand.) With the signing of the definitive peace treaty in September 1783, Haldimand received orders to disband all these Loyalists by Christmas Day.

Haldimand, as was his wont, chose to modify his instructions in the light of immediate realities. It was too late in the season to disband the troops up-country; there was, in any case, not enough surveyed land for them to settle on. As it turned out, Haldimand postponed the release of the Loyalist troops until the following June. The only exception was the First Battalion of the KRRNY, then in barracks in Montreal, which Haldimand ordered to be replaced immediately by regular troops.

Towards the end of January 1784, Sir John Johnson was already becoming concerned that land for the disbanded soldiers had not yet been surveyed. He informed Haldimand that the men of the First Battalion alone would need four townships. He offered the services of two men to help lay out townships along the St. Lawrence. One of them was Lieutenant Walter Sutherland mentioned above; the other was William Coffin (also a lieutenant in the KRRNY) who hailed from Boston, where his father was a merchant. It was arranged that these two would join forces with two surveyors furnished by Holland: Lieutenant Lewis Cotté and Patrick McNiff. Up to this point all surveying had been carried out by Holland, Collins, and various British regular officers, with Loyalist officers working alongside them. McNiff, therefore, was the first strictly civilian surveyor employed by the Crown in Ontario.

Initial surveys along the St. Lawrence under the direction of Johnson apparently started in mid-February 1784, by which time Sutherland was engaging

men and working with a survey party. On 1 March, McNiff set off up the St. Lawrence in bateaux taking twenty-six men with him, meeting Johnson by arrangement to select two possible sites for a town. This they did. Ten days later Johnson instructed Cotté, who had been sent downriver from Cataraqui on Haldimand's instructions, to make the final choice. He settled on the site, and before long Johnson was calling it New Johnstown; it was later renamed Cornwall.

Shortly afterward, McNiff started laying out townships along the St. Lawrence from Pointe au Baudet westward. The first township east of Pointe au Baudet was considered too waterlogged for settlement and was quickly passed over, though later in 1784 McNiff and James McDonell would return to the township and start laying it out. At first it had various names, denoting various degrees of dampness, one of which was the "Sunken Township" – it later became Lancaster Township.

From the western boundary of the Sunken Township, the front concessions of eight more townships were run. On Haldimand's instructions these were to be called "Royal Seigneuries" and were to be numbered from one to eight. Later they would be renamed, from east to west: Charlottenburgh, Cornwall, Osnabruck, Williamsburgh, Matilda, Edwardsburgh, Augusta, and Elizabethtown – where the town of that name grew up, renamed Brockville in 1813. The 40-mile-or-so (65-km) stretch between Elizabethtown and Cataraqui, which we now know is characterized by outcrops of Precambrian granite extending southward from the Canadian Shield, was found to be too "broken" for settlement, as indeed Sherwood and others had pointed out earlier.

To get the settlers onto their land quickly, the initial surveys were minimal. As Haldimand himself put it "running a few lines will sufficiently define them [the lots] for every man to know his own." This is one of the reasons why early settlers built their houses and farm buildings so close to the road that marked the concession line – they wanted to make quite sure that they built on their own land.

As if he did not have enough on his plate in early 1784, Collins received instructions from Haldimand in the middle of May to organize a Loyalist settlement near Sorel. After he had finished there, Haldimand ordered him to "join Major Holland at Montreal and proceed with him in settling the Loyalists upwards to Cataraqui." After this, Collins was to get on with the surveys at Cataraqui where the Second Battalion of the Royal Yorkers had also decided to settle. Though survey work in the townships along the St. Lawrence was going ahead briskly enough in the early months of 1784, nothing much was being done on the townships west of Cataraqui. Not until mid-June could an

increasingly anxious Ross report to Haldimand that Collins had arrived. And Holland was not to turn up until even later in the season.

Meanwhile, in May 1784, the complex operation of moving the Loyalists onto their land began. Holland had been ordered by Haldimand to send Lieutenant Tinling from Cataraqui to Niagara "to lay out the ground lately purchased at that place," this for the reception of the men of Butler's Rangers. It had become clear that the 4-mile strip bought earlier was not going to be adequate for all the Rangers and other Loyalists at Niagara who were in need of a place to settle. There was another reason why this tract would be insufficient, Tinling was instructed that part of the tract at Niagara would be reserved for military use. The Americans had been demanding that the British posts at Oswego, Niagara, Detroit, and Michilimackinac – all of which were now in U.S. territory – be handed over. However, pending instructions from Britain, Haldimand took it on himself to order that none of the posts were to change hands "until Indian affairs are in a more settled state, and ... our traders in the interior can withdraw their property." Haldimand's decision was to be upheld by the British government, to the growing resentment of the Americans. Because of the inevitable transfer, Haldimand was giving thought to the re-establishment of the posts on the British side of the border, and hence the need for more space at Niagara. In the event, the American posts remained in British hands for another twelve years.

Haldimand now learned that Brant was averse to settling his Six Nations on the Bay of Quinte. Instead, he wanted to take them to the Grand River to settle on land that the government would purchase from the Mississaugas. About a hundred Mohawk elected to settle on the Bay of Quinte as originally planned, which they did in the township of Tyendinaga under their leader, John Deserontyon, after whom Deseronto is named. Their reservation is known today as that of the "Mohawks of the Bay of Quinte." However, Brant

took most of the Six Nations to the Grand River. By 1785 some 1840 natives had settled there, of which more than 400 were Mohawk. It was then decided to purchase a large enough tract of land to accommodate both the Six Nations and the Loyalists. At first Haldimand considered purchasing all of what is now southwest Ontario at one go. But this, it was thought, would frighten the Mississaugas, so land requirements were scaled down. Even so, the tract bought on 22 May 1784 at a well-attended meeting at Niagara was impressively large. It consisted of all the land lying inside the following borders: the Lake Ontario shore from what is now Niagara-on-the-Lake to Burlington Bay; a line drawn northwest from Burlington to the Grand River; the Grand itself to Lake Erie; and the Lake Erie shore eastward to the land bordering the Niagara River that was purchased earlier.

Out of this, a 12-mile (19-km) tract centring on the lower reaches of the Grand River was handed over to the Six Nations. The Six Nations thus obtained what was found later to be about 570 000 acres or nearly 900 square miles (2330 km²). Following the purchase, the first range of lots along the front at Niagara was laid out for the Loyalists by Tinling, with their distribution supervised by Lieutenant-Colonel Arent de Peyster, then commandant at Fort Niagara. Tinling was also told to lay out Brant's settlement on the Grand.

Back in the east, Sherwood was busy laying out New Johnstown – and "lotting the people's land" as he called it. As he wrote to Mathews on 2 July,

I have been continually employed here since the 5th of last month in laying out a town half a mile square into lots of 8 rods [132 feet or 40 m] square – and in laying out the second concessions. Giving the people the necessary oaths and their Certificates etc which has and will for some time require my constant attention ... upwards of 50 of the lots are already settled and nearly cleared. The settlement of our three townships 6, 7 and 8 [i.e., from present-day Cardinal to Brockville] goes on very rapidly.[11]

About a week later (10 July 1784), Johnson reported that 1568 men and 626 women were now on their land, along with 90 servants and 1492 children – such was the fecundity of the times. He told Haldimand that he had left Cataraqui where he had been supervising the settlement of the four townships there. Surveys of three of them were as yet incomplete, while the survey of Adolphustown had just begun. Peachey and Lieutenants Samuel Tuffe and Henry Holland (Samuel Holland's son*) were apparently assisting Cotté at that point, but Cotté had fallen sick. Johnson reports that "Major Holland was preparing to set off on that business [to complete the surveys] the day after I left ... Mr. Collins had begun a township on the peninsula on the opposite side of the Bay ... for the Germans and men of the established [i.e., regular] regiments." The Germans he was referring to were men of the German formations who had chosen to take their discharge in Canada as had some of the British regulars. The township that Collins had just started would become Marysburgh, now in Prince Edward County, later to be divided into North and South Marysburgh townships.

July 1784 also saw the beginnings of civil government in the new settlements with the appointment of John Ross and Neil Maclean as Justices of the Peace, an interim measure to stay in place until "a regular Police can be established," as Mathews put it. As the summer went on, Collins and Holland continued their

survey of the Cataraqui townships, at the same time trying to deal with dissatisfied settlers who wanted to change locations. At the beginning of August, Mathews told Holland that "His Excellency" was pleased that he had stayed at Cataraqui and asked him to remain there until the settlement was making good progress. He was to expedite this by employing "every surveyor or persons that can be found useful."

Collins laboured on at Cataraqui until early October. "Mr. Collins leaves this place for Quebec," wrote Ross to Haldimand on the tenth, "his personal exertions ... to promote the service on which he was employed has given universal satisfaction. I wish," added Ross pointedly, "he had been better supported, as some of the people are not yet on their lands."[12]

And so some eighteen months of hectic surveying and exploration came to an end and with it the establishment of the first settlements along the St. Lawrence and around the Bay of Quinte. That those settlements were as successful as they were was due in no small way to the surveyors concerned. These men were called on, not just to run their lines, but to act as the personal and humane agents of government as they supervised the actual process of settlement, a process that was to require, with its multitude of problems, all their wisdom and tact to help bring about a successful conclusion.

By the fall of 1784, concern was being expressed about the Loyalists bound for the St. Lawrence settlements who were not yet on their land. Should they be housed in barracks over the winter? Also to be dealt with – and an augury of problems to come – were the refugees still arriving at the camps and posts, not just in and around Montreal but at Niagara and Detroit as well.

But Haldimand would not be there to help them. On 16 November 1784 he sailed for England on indefinite leave, something he had intended to do for some time. He never came back. Haldimand's great

and continuing concern for the welfare of the Loyalists and the Six Nations was particularly remarkable considering that in the summer of 1782 he learned from Lord Shelburne, then Britain's prime minister, that he was to be replaced by Carleton, this because of a possible invasion of Quebec by France. Haldimand's pride was deeply wounded. As he pointed out, Carleton had been junior to him in rank for forty-three years. There was also the question of his health; he was still recovering, he said, from a fall the year before which needed treatment not available in Canada. Nonetheless, he agreed to stay until the spring of 1783. In the event, the threatened French invasion did not materialize, Carleton did not want to come to Canada – at least not at that point – and Shelburne was replaced. Haldimand reiterated his determination to take indefinite leave. However, he stayed on, as we have seen, until the Loyalists, both native and non-native, were beginning to settle in their new homes.

Before he left, he reported that 6152 Loyalists had been settled, of whom 5576 were drawing full rations. Remaining the official governor of Quebec, Haldimand took up residence in London, to be knighted in 1785 in recognition of his services to the Crown. It was in London that he spent his remaining years, this as an accepted and relatively well-to-do member of London society, a bachelor to the last. Occasionally he would visit his birth place in Switzerland, and during one of these visits he died on 5 June 1791 at the age of seventy-three, only two months or so before the new province of Upper Canada was to be formed, the province that he had done so much to help bring into being.

---

*Two of Holland's sons took part in these first surveys. John Frederick, Holland's eldest son, who had been taught surveying by his father, was a lieutenant with the KRRNY and became acting engineer at Cataraqui during the winter of 1783–84. Henry, his second-eldest son, was a lieutenant in a British regiment, apparently the Seventieth Foot, and had been seconded for surveying work on a half-pay basis.

CHAPTER SIX

Settling In

The process of land procurement, survey, and settlement had gone forward in a fairly orderly fashion at the eastern end of the province and at Niagara. At Detroit, however, the process had been far from orderly.

It will be remembered that in the mid-1770s the commandant at Detroit had got into trouble for obtaining native land illegally. Subsequently, Henry Hamilton, who had been appointed lieutenant-governor at Detroit, got his knuckles rapped by Haldimand for placing refugees on native-owned land – although, to be fair, Hamilton had made it clear to the refugees that this was a temporary arrangement. In 1778 Hamilton led an ill-advised expedition against the Americans, in which he was captured. (He eventually reached Quebec again via England.) This left Major Arent de Peyster, the commandant at Detroit, on his own; he took it upon himself to allow the private acquisition of native land – himself obtaining 5000 acres. Such irregular goings-on came to Haldimand's ears in 1784, at which time he ordered the notarial register, in which land sales were recorded, to be sent to Quebec for examination.

In the meantime, Captain Matthew Elliott of the Indian Department and Captain William Caldwell of Butler's Rangers had taken swift advantage of the newly promulgated instructions regarding the allotment of land to ex-officers by acquiring large tracts on the Canadian side near the mouth of the Detroit River. Other officers planned on settling on the shore to the south, on the understanding that the natives had no objection and that the land would be purchased by the Crown in due course.

However, it came to light that Jacob Schieffelin, secretary of the Indian Department, had already bought some 7 square miles (18 km²) of this land by a secret treaty with some Objibwas – apparently in order to resell it at a profit. It was rumoured that Schieffelin had plied the natives with drink before concluding the deal. When this information reached Haldimand, he

exploded. Schiefflin's deal was declared null and void, and he lost his job.

In June 1784 the Hurons and "neighbouring Chiefs" deeded the same tract to a mixed group of ex–Indian Department men, Loyalists, and ex-regulars, following which Caldwell journeyed to Quebec to see Haldimand and obtain his approval for the proposed settlement along the lower Detroit. Haldimand gave it in August with the reservation that the land purchase must be regularized by a legal treaty approved by the natives in full council, which was done two years later.

In 1785 Philip Frey was sent to Detroit to survey the land acquired by Caldwell near the mouth of the Detroit River. Frey, or Fry, was one of two deputy surveyors commissioned in that year, the other being Alexander Aitken. Aitken was the first British-trained land surveyor to be taken on as a deputy surveyor, hailing, it is thought, from Berwick-upon-Tweed where he was probably trained by his father. Frey was from Canajoharie, New York. There, in his early twenties, he had served with a regular regiment, the Eighth, and then transferred to Butler's Rangers in which he served as an ensign. He was living in Detroit when Holland, whose protégé was apparently Frey, wrote a personal letter to him in January 1785 telling him that he had been appointed a resident surveyor for Niagara and Detroit. Holland went on to tell Frey the latest news: Sir Guy Carleton would be arriving from England as "our Viceroy." He mentions hearing from "William Smith, Esq., late Chief Justice of New York, who comments that "settlers will flash [into] the Province from all quarters of America, and will make work enough for surveyors."[1]

Frey's commission is one of the oldest on record, being dated 30 March 1783.

To Philip R. Frey, Gentleman:
By virtue of the power and authority to me given by His Majesty I do hereby constitute and appoint you to be one of the deputy

surveyors of Lands, for making surveys in the Upper District of the Province of Quebec; authorizing and requiring you to execute and perform the duties of a deputy surveyor, agreeable to the orders and instructions hereunto annexed, or to be annexed, by his Excellency the Governor or Commander-in-Chief, or from the Courts of Judiciary, or from me, or from the deputy surveyor-general of this Province, hold, exercise and enjoy the same during pleasure, together with the fees and advantages thereunto belonging or appertaining; and you are to make your surveys agreeable to the justice and the rules of the science of surveying.

The oath follows. "I, Philip Frey, do solemnly swear on the holy Evangelists of the Almighty God that I will act impartially and do justice between man and man, as far as my knowledge doth extend in the science of surveying."[2]

Frey completed his survey by mid-March 1785 (before he was sworn in), the first in what is now the township of Malden. There were only about a dozen lots in all, fronting on the river south of present-day Amherstburg and extending to marshy land at the river's mouth (see figure 6.1). But the lots were large — and they were all spoken for, mostly by officers and interpreters of the Indian Department. So where were the bulk of the Loyalist refugees and ex-soldiers to go? Once again it was Caldwell who took the initiative. Caldwell had invited the men of Butler's Rangers to join him along the Detroit River after their discharge. Now, disappointingly, it seemed there was no land for them, and for want of anything better, many had become tenant farmers.

With these people in mind, Caldwell obtained more land from the natives. He chose a tract on the Lake Erie shore that extended from a creek 4 miles (6.5 km) east of the Detroit eastward some 18 miles to the site of present-day Kingsville, just south of Jack Miner's well-known bird sanctuary (see figure 6.1). In the summer of 1787 the land was accepted on behalf of the Crown by Major Mathews, Haldimand's ex-secretary, who had gone on to command at Detroit. Later that summer a range of ninety-seven lots was laid out

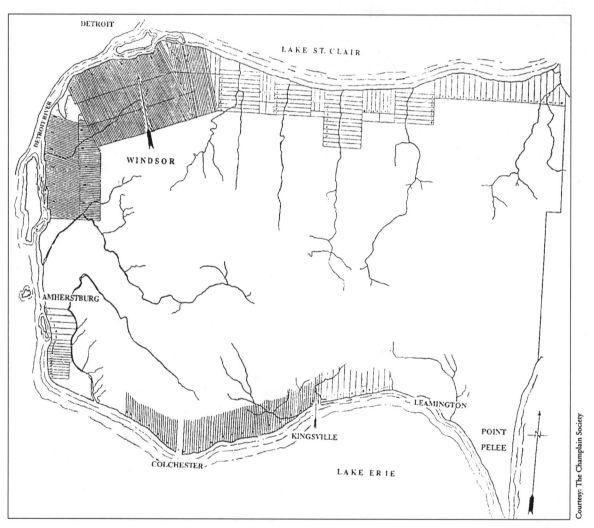

Figure 6.1 Waterfront surveys in Essex County during the late 1780s and 1790s. Modern place names added. Lots on the Detroit River south of present-day Amherstburg were acquired by officers of the Indian Department. Captain Caldwell obtained a tract south and east of these. He later obtained land for the settlement of ex-Butler's Rangers on the Lake Erie shore. (After Lajeunesse, *Windsor Border Region*.)

fronting the lake by Thomas Smith working under the direction of Mathews himself, who had, he said, "some 60 fine fellows" to place on the land. Smith, a notary, as mentioned above, apparently functioned as a deputy surveyor, though there is no record of his appointment. Later he acted as secretary for the Land Board.

The range of lots was later extended, and a second concession was laid out, though it was to be a number of years before the rear lots were taken up. Three lots were reserved for the Crown for later use as a town plot, the first such plot in Essex County. The town that grew up there was Colchester, while the settlement became known as the New Settlement to distinguish it from the old French settlement opposite Detroit. Later the settlement became known as the Two Connected Townships, as part of it lay in Colchester Township, and part in Gosfield Township.

With the founding of the New Settlement, the last of the four nuclei came into being from which the Loyalist settlements would grow. To the east were the Royal Townships along the St. Lawrence, with a 45-mile gap between them and those at Cataraqui and around the Bay of Quinte. Then, after a long stretch of Lake Ontario shoreline, came the settlement at Niagara, separated in turn by the full length of Lake Erie from the New Settlement and the settlements along the Detroit River. The next few years would see the tide of settlement spread west from the River Trent to coalesce with the settlement on the Niagara Peninsula. The settlement of the Lake Erie shore from the Grand River westward would not come until much later.

At the eastern end of what was now being called the "Upper District," the years immediately following Haldimand's departure were primarily those of consolidation. On 18 June 1785, Collins wrote a report for Haldimand on the state of the townships along the St. Lawrence and around the Bay of Quinte. Though in England, Haldimand was still officially governor of the province (his functions in Canada having been assumed by Henry Hamilton, by now back in Canada). Having met "all the principal persons" in the townships, Collins wrote that he found them "extremely well satisfied." He went on to say that only the second township was "regularly surveyed." This was New Johnstown or Cornwall, where we saw Sherwood busy doing his "lotting." The rest of the townships "have nothing more than a front line run with a single picket set up on each side [of] the lot."

Collins appended a list of immediate survey requirements. In three townships, the front of the second, third, and fourth concessions still needed to be run. In three others, including the Sunken Township, only the front of the second and third concessions needed running. He had "given orders," he said, "to Messrs McNiff and Jessup to complete the same without loss of time."[3] On the same day, Collins ordered McNiff to get on with these, "leaving roads of forty feet wide between each concession, and taking care to sett up two posts to serve as a government [or guide] to the inhabitants to divide their lands."[4] He was also to lay out a road along the St. Lawrence shore from Côteau-du-Lac to the western boundary of Matilda Township, nearly as far as present-day Cardinal – though it is not clear whether he did this.

Collins's report also dwelt on the possibility of reaching the upper lakes via the Trent River system – something the Montreal fur traders had found to be of increasing interest since the end of the Revolutionary War. The American occupation of Fort Niagara might threaten the vital portage around the falls, and, furthermore, with Detroit in American hands, the source of supplies and provisions upon which the fur traders in the west had long relied might disappear.

The upshot was an exploratory survey carried out of the Trent–Georgian Bay route by Collins late in the summer of 1785, a survey in which, at Hamilton's request, he took particular note of water depths and the place and length of the portages involved. Collins also took a look at the Toronto Passage, which Captain Hare, if Captain Hare it was, had explored five years earlier. Whatever use Collins's surveys may have been to the fur traders, which probably wasn't a great deal, it at least helped clarify the geography of these regions.

The year 1785 also saw the appearance of the first legislation bearing specifically on surveying and surveyors, with the passing of An Ordnance Concerning Land Surveyors and the Admeasurement of Lands (25 Geo. 3, c. 3) by the legislative council of the province, of which Holland had now been an influential member for some twenty years. This ordnance would be the basis of all subsequent surveying legislation in what is now Ontario. Some of its provisions merely codified part of the instructions issued by the Board of Trade in 1763 and which were already being followed after a fashion: surveyors should keep field books and make plans of their surveys, for example. However, surveyors were now required to ensure that these field books be lodged with the surveyor general after their death. The size and shape of boundary monuments were specified. Surveyors were to take an oath of allegiance and be examined before their appointment. A list of qualified surveyors was to be kept, this to be published from time to time in the official gazette. Instruments had to be tested before use, and three test meridians were to be established by which compasses could be calibrated. These were to be at Quebec, Trois Rivières, and Montreal, the latter being the usual jumping-off place for westbound surveyors. Clearly instigated by Holland, the establishment of test meridians was a measure far ahead of its time.

In England it had been confirmed that Haldimand's successor was to be Guy Carleton, who would come to Canada as Lord Dorchester. Meanwhile Brigadier General Hope had taken over from Hamilton on the latter's departure for England – Hamilton would later become the governor of Bermuda where he gave his name to its capital. With Lord Dorchester's arrival imminent, Holland was asked by Hope in the winter of 1785–86 to report on the state of his department and to come up with estimates of future survey costs. As he mentioned in the preamble to his Instructions to Deputy Surveyors, dated 18 January 1786, he had laid before Hope "plans and proposals for the better regulating of that Department so as to prevent for the future any expenses to be added to the enormous sum already accumulated on that amount."[5]

Holland's proposals foreshadowed the creation of four districts by Lord Dorchester two years later, and thus it was Holland who took the first step in streamlining the administration of the Upper District. In his instructions, mentioned above, Holland translated his proposals into action by issuing a series of virtually identical orders that allotted specific districts to various surveyors.[6] Essentially, McNiff was to be responsible for the townships along the St. Lawrence; Cotté was to take care of the surveying needs of the townships around Kingston, the Bay of Quinte, and in what became Prince Edward County; while Philip Frey was to handle surveys at Niagara and Detroit, as we have already seen. Curiously enough, there is no mention of Alexander Aitken.

These deputy surveyors were to be paid 7s. 6d. a day when surveying in the field; 4s. a day when not. Accounts for the previous six months' work had to be in by 10 April 1786. Government would no longer pay for chainmen or axemen. Much as McNiff had suggested, "... those wanting their lands surveyed" must apply to Stephen De Lancey (now inspector of Loyalists) who will "require of them ... at least 6 men or more" to assist the surveyor. These would, however, receive "one Royalist ration pr. day."[7] And there was to be no exchanging of lots without permission.

In the summer of 1785 Collins surveyed the front of Little, or East, Lake in Ameliasburgh on the Lake Ontario side of the county[8] – this before Ameliasburgh was subdivided into several townships, while on the Bay of Quinte side, front lots in Sophiasburgh and Ameliasburgh were being drawn for by "proprietors" from Fredericksburgh in the same year. The front of Ameliasburgh was run by Cotté who, it seems, was inclined to be difficult. As Neil Maclean, deputy inspector of Loyalists, put it in a letter to Holland in 1786, he had found himself frustrated in his efforts to locate settlers by "want of maps" of Marysburgh, Sophiasburgh, and Ameliasburgh. And Cotté, who had run the first concession of the latter township, wasn't being of much help. Wrote Maclean crossly, "I find he is not inclined to give any information ... than he can withhold."

According to a plan submitted later to Lieutenant-Governor Simcoe, the townships of Marysburgh and Sophiasburgh were surveyed by Collins and William Chewett in 1784 and 1785 – a plan that, according to a note appended to it, "may not be depended on for accuracy" as the "original minutes of this survey having been damaged and in part destroyed by a storm on the way down," presumably to Quebec. Whether or not Chewett was in fact active in the Loyalist settlements as early as 1784 is open to question – not that he was not a qualified land surveyor. He received his commission in 1774, thus giving him a seniority that was second only to Collins himself. So where was Chewett when the need for surveyors became critical in 1783?

Born in London in 1753, where he trained as a hydrographer for the East India Company, Chewett had fetched up in Quebec in 1774, he then being twenty-one, after missing his ship because of smallpox. Taken on by Holland in the Surveyor General's Office, Chewett was in Quebec when it was besieged by the Americans in the winter of 1775–76 and served throughout that siege in the militia. After this he acted as paymaster for various military and naval departments until 1783 at which time he was transferred back to the Surveyor General's Office. It is probable that his first appearance in the Loyalist settlements was in 1785, when he and McNiff started surveying what

was termed the "residue" of Charlottenburg, Cornwall, Osnasbruck, Williamsburg, and Matilda townships. Chewett then went on to work on Edwardsburgh, Augusta, and Elizabethtown townships, along with Jeremiah McCarthy and Edward Jessup, who had raised a Loyalist unit later known as Jessup's Corps.

In 1786 Chewett was laying out a range of lots in what are now known as the Eastern Townships, when he was asked to locate the Quebec–New York boundary that Collins had run some twenty years before, a boundary that, with the peace, had attained a new importance as an international one. He couldn't find it. Reporting from New Johnstown on 19 August 1786 he wrote: "The Indians could not show, nor could I find out the stone, or any remains of the boundary of the Province, the brush having grown up, and the Indians having cut down all the blazed trees and all the others for a mile around."

Chewett went on to say that De Lancey, the inspector of Loyalists, had ordered him to "detain [his] party to lay out the road from Riviere aux Raisin [not far east of Cornwall] to Coteau du Lac."[9] This is what McNiff was supposed to have done but presumably hadn't. Assuming Chewett carried out his orders, he laid out the far eastern portion of Ontario's first major road, which in years to come would become part of Highway 2.

Towards the end of 1786, McNiff produced what is probably the most widely consulted map in the Archives of Ontario. Popularly known as the "McNiff Map," it shows the extent of settlement in the six townships along the St. Lawrence between the present Quebec border and the town of Cardinal. Lots are shown as far back as the Second Concession in Lancaster, the Second Concession north of the Raisin River in Charlottenburgh, the Eighth Concession in Cornwall, the Third Concession in Osnabruck, and the Second Concession in Williamsburg and Matilda. McNiff carefully inscribed the names of the owners of each lot, and it is these names that are scrutinized by the many people who consult the map in search of the names of their ancestors.

In October 1786 Sir Guy Carleton, now Lord Dorchester, arrived in Quebec as its new governor. He found the province rife with discontent. From the beginning, the Loyalists had objected to both the seigneurial system of land tenure and the French form of civil law, with which they were not familiar. They wanted freehold land, British laws, and an assembly of their own, in short all the British institutions for which they had fought and for which many of them had died. A formal petition to that effect had been signed by Sir John Johnson and a group of Loyalist officers as early as April 1785. It was to be followed by many similar petitions in the next few years.

Dorchester was also faced with the problem of the so-called late Loyalists. If the coming of peace had not seen Americans exactly "flash" into the province, as Holland had put it, there had certainly been a steady stream of would-be settlers coming north. This group's loyalty to the Crown was questionable, thus placing the security of the province at risk. These fears were to persist, thereby affecting land settlement policies for the next twenty-five years or so. They were not to be laid to rest until a flood of emigrants came from the United Kingdom following the ending of the Napoleonic Wars in 1815.

The question of loyalty was taken seriously. But how, as one historian has put it, to distinguish the children of light from the children of darkness? It was on a fact-finding mission to help resolve these problems that Collins and William Dummer Powell, a native of Boston who would eventually become acting chief justice of Upper Canada, were sent into the settlements in the spring of 1787. Collins was authorized to grant a bonus of 200 acres to all those who had improved their lands. On the face of it, this was to discourage speculation and squatting. But the bonus was also to be with-held from those who had "doubtful principles and reputations" – a means of discouraging would-be settlers of doubtful loyalty. What became known as "Dorchester's Bounty" was supposed to be discontinued after July 1790 but in fact remained operative for seven years after that.

While Collins and Powell reported that there were in fact few undesirables in the new settlement, there did exist a "very dangerous jealousy and want of confidence" between the settlers and their late officers. This stemmed in part from the sometimes inequitable distribution of land between them. In spite of Haldimand's directive, officers tended to get better lots (i.e., on the waterfront). Also, arrangements for dispensing justice in the new settlements were inadequate. And, because it was required that their suitability, that is, their loyalty, must be ruled upon by the Land Committee in Quebec, new settlers faced interminable delays in the processing of their applications for land.

Dorchester could not give the Loyalists their own province, but in July 1788 he went some way towards meeting their demands by dividing the new settlements into four districts. Each district was to have a court of common pleas complete with three judges. Following the lead given by Holland, and with boundaries that ran between them due north and south, the four districts were, from east to west: Luneburg, extending from the eastern boundary of Lancaster Township to the Gananoque River; Mecklenburgh, from the Gananoque to the Trent; Nassau, from the Trent to Long Point on Lake Erie; and Hesse, from Long Point to Detroit – all names connected with the royal house of Hanover (see figure 6.2).

While the internal threat to the security of the province by possibly disloyal former Americans was one of Dorchester's concerns, another was the province's military preparedness. Accordingly, in May 1788, Dorchester ordered Captain Gother Mann to inspect and report on the state of the province's defences in the west. Mann, who was English-born, his name notwithstanding, had been in command of the Royal Engineers in Canada since 1785. In the course of a busy summer, which took him as far west as Sault Ste. Marie and Detroit, Mann carried out the first British hydrographic surveys of importance on the Great Lakes, charting among other things stretches of the Georgian Bay shoreline. He recommended a site for a fort on the Canadian side of the Detroit River, should one be required. He also noted that the site of present-day Toronto would make an admirable military base, and prepared a pleasingly imaginative town plan to go with it. Dorchester, however, had already sent Aitken there in 1788 to lay out a town and settlement (see figure 6.3). As it turned out, with no townships laid out on the Lake Ontario shore west of the Trent, both Mann's and Aitken's plans were shelved, at least for the time being.

Having created the four districts, Dorchester followed this up by issuing "Rules and Regulation for the Conduct of the Land Department" on 17 February 1789, which established land boards in each district in order to expedite settlement procedures. One of the duties of the boards was to receive petitions for land and, if satisfied of a petitioner's loyalty, to give a certificate to a deputy surveyor, which authorized him to assign to the petitioner a single lot of about 200 acres, the boundaries of which would be duly described. The deputy surveyor, in turn, would locate the settler and issue a signed certificate describing the land he or she had been granted. The land boards were also authorized to grant an additional 50 acres for each family member. Larger acreages had to be referred to the governor-in-council for a decision. The formation of the new districts had little effect on survey arrangements, which, as has been pointed out, predated the formation of the districts, except that it became necessary to appoint a resident surveyor to the district of Hesse, which centred on Detroit. The finger fell on McNiff, who by the spring of 1790 was already engaged in the first of his many battles with the Land Board in Detroit

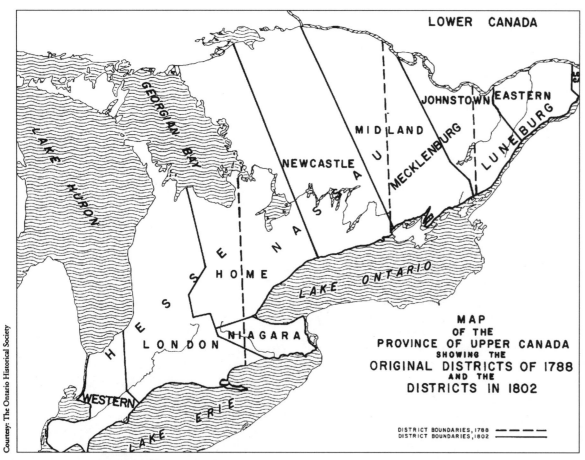

Inside the map:

LOWER CANADA

GEORGIAN BAY

LAKE HURON

JOHNSTOWN EASTERN

MIDLAND

MECKLENBURG

LUNENBURG

NEWCASTLE

NASSAU

HESSE

HOME

LAKE ONTARIO

NIAGARA

LONDON

WESTERN

LAKE ERIE

MAP
OF THE
PROVINCE OF UPPER CANADA
SHOWING THE
ORIGINAL DISTRICTS OF 1788
AND THE
DISTRICTS IN 1802

DISTRICT BOUNDARIES, 1788 — — —
DISTRICT BOUNDARIES, 1802 —————

Figure 6.2 Districts established by Lord Dorchester in 1788 and as reorganized and renamed in 1802. (After Spragge, *The Districts of Upper Canada.*)

In October 1789 Dorchester ordered the land boards in October to make up lists of Loyalist families, this in order to make it easier to distinguish between desirable settlers and possibly disloyal newcomers. Families that had demonstrated their loyalty to the Crown before the war ended in 1783 would have the letters U.E. placed after their name to show that they "had adhered to the Unity of the Empire." In fact it seems no such lists were made at that time, though "U.E." did appear after the appropriate names on militia rolls.[10] Dorchester further directed that 200 acres be given to the sons of such Loyalist families when they came of age and to daughters when they married, such lands to be free of survey and patent fees. It seems clear that Dorchester had in mind only sons and daughters that were already in the province. But the land boards took Dorchester's directive as applying to all Loyalist families whenever they arrived, or might arrive, in the province. The result was a controversy that would go on for decades and an enormous loss in land revenue. Some 3,300,000 acres or over 5,000 square miles (13,000 km²) of Crown land was eventually given away with losses in land revenue that have been calculated at £75,000. All of this came to a head in the 1820s, at which point Crown revenue and land-settlement problems were partly solved by the formation of the Canada Company.

The immediate result of the U.E. grants was to increase the demand for surveyed land, a demand that had already risen sharply following Dorchester's "bounty," and which had risen again in 1788 when he directed that all ex-Loyalist officers should receive land according to the scale laid down for those of the Eighty-fourth Regiment. Raised in the early days of the Revolutionary War and first known as the Royal Highland Emigrants, its officers had joined on the understanding that they would be rewarded with land on their discharge on a scale that ran 2,000, 3,000, and 5,000 acres for lieutenants, captains, and field officers respectively, and this they were given – acreages that were from three to five times more land than anyone else's. Not unnaturally, the difference between the size of their land grants and those of officers from other regiments had been bitterly resented by the latter, until, as we have seen, Dorchester ordered that land grants to all officers be bumped up to the higher level. Thus, at this point in time, it was no inrush of new emigrants that set surveyors scrambling to put in new townships and to complete the surveys of townships already started, but a demand on the part of Loyalists who had been granted successive bonanzas of land, in many cases much more than they could possibly improve.

By the late 1780s, several of the Loyalists who had helped out on the first surveys had retired into private life, so Holland and Collins were seeking new blood. This search, one imagines, was conducted with a certain desperation in view of the amount of work to be done. Jesse Pennoyer was taken on as a deputy surveyor in 1788, as were William Fortune, Hugh McDonell, and Daniel Hazen. A year later came Theodore De Pencier and James Rankin. Pierre Marcoullier, commissioned in 1788, and Marie d.d.G. Devens and Louis Perrault, commissioned in 1789, all Francophones, were put to work in the Eastern Townships.

William Fortune had been a deputy surveyor in South Carolina in 1773. He received his commission in Quebec on 4 July 1788, when he was already probably over fifty. He was given the nod by Dorchester who signed his commission himself. It ran in part as follows:

> Whereas William Fortune, late of South Carolina, now of the Province of Quebec, Gentleman, hath petitioned to obtain a Commission of Surveyor of Lands in the Province of Quebec, and John Collins, deputy surveyor General for the said Province hath certified to me this day, that he hath carefully examined the said William Fortune, respecting his fitness and capacity as a Surveyor of Lands, and the sufficiency of his surveying instruments, and the said instruments have been duly regulated and rectified by the meridian near the Town of Quebec, and that the variation has been found equal to twelve degrees and thirty minutes west, and that [he] is a person of proper character and well qualified for the said office of Surveyor of Lands.[11]

Hugh McDonell, who had served with the KKRNY, was soon to combine his surveying with politics: he became one of the first representatives for Glengarry county in Upper Canada's first legislature. Later he left Canada for England, there to pursue a career in the British army. Jesse Pennoyer was of Loyalist stock, whose family had emigrated from

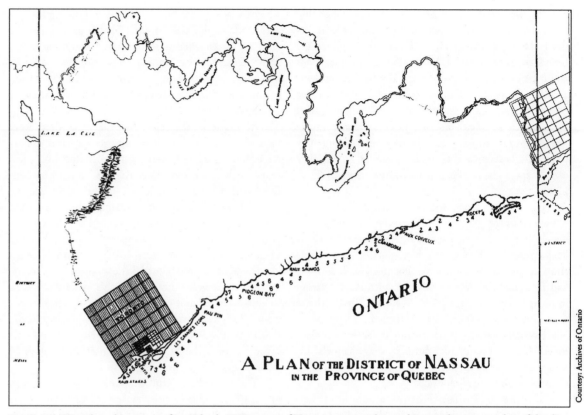

Figure 6.3 Though nothing came of it, Aitken's 1788 survey of Toronto town and township was shown on a plan of the district of Nassau made in 1790. Note soundings along the shore between the Trent River and Toronto. (Part of a plan of the district of Nassau in the Province of Quebec, signed by Samuel Holland and John Collins, AO, Cartographic Records Collection A-16. As reproduced in Fraser, Third Report of the Bureau of Archives, 1905.)

southern England to Massachusetts in the seventeenth century. During the Revolutionary War, he had come north with his wife from Dutchess County, New York, and settled in Quebec, where the Pennoyers were to bring up thirteen children – which must have taken some doing on a surveyor's salary. Pennoyer was to die in Quebec, at Compton, in 1825 and was buried at Hatley.

By now the cost of getting the Loyalists settled was being carefully monitored. Surveyors' provisions were provided either directly by the government or by a requisition to be presented to a named private supplier. And it had become usual for surveyors to be advanced money to pay their men. However, all too often unexpected expenses gobbled up the surveyors' advances, and they found themselves with empty pockets. How did they survive? One clue is afforded in the letters that passed between Jesse Pennoyer and Collins late in 1791. With no money to pay off his men in Montreal, Pennoyer rushed his accounts to Collins in Quebec pleading for speedy payment. There was no suggestion in Pennoyer's letter of a personal advance or loan, yet this is the way Collins took it. "I have so far assisted my friends that I have not left five pounds in my house, nor will it be in my power to advance any further until the accounts are paid ..." Collins replied.[12] So it seems that when his surveyors were really strapped, Collins loaned them money to tide them over. Just how much money were surveyors making at that stage? Assuming they were actively employed at the daily rate of 7s. 6d., they could expect about £80 a year, compared to Collins's £200 or so.

Even the military found it difficult to extract money from the government for survey work done on behalf of the surveyor general's department. In 1791, Major John Smith of the Fifth Regiment, then in garrison at Detroit, wrote to say that the year before, he had furnished the deputy surveyor with survey parties in order to lay out land for the Loyalists. "But as this is a work of such fatigue," he continued, "I applied to His Excellency that the troops might receive payment for it." He went on to ask "through what channels" his men were to be paid.[13] One can only hope that such a channel was eventually found.

Writing to William Fortune a couple of days before he was commissioned, Holland urged economy, "... as your accounts will undergo a strict scrutiny ... You will guide yourself accordingly and I make no doubt acquit yourself satisfactorily. Indeed a strict attention to the above cannot fail of redounding to your credit and of furnishing you a surety of future constant employment."[14] In other words, whatever else, keep your accounts straight and government will love you.

It was sound advice. For Theodore De Pencier, his apparent inability to keep track of his expenses eventually proved to be his undoing. Of Swedish extraction, De Pencier first came to Canada in 1776 as a captain in a German mercenary regiment. He was later discharged in England and returned to Canada in 1784

where he was granted land near Sorel. Finding himself with none of the skills needed for life as a settler, he drew on his knowledge of mathematics to bone up on surveying and so was granted his commission. That he was bilingual helped no doubt. However, he was soon running into serious trouble with his accounts, of which more below.

As was to be the case down the years, there were men who were given their commissions as land surveyors only to disappear from the records after just a few years. Such a one was James Rankin,* not to be confused with Charles Rankin who in the 1800s became one of Upper Canada's most distinguished surveyors. In 1789 James Rankin was dispatched up the Ottawa and then, roughly following the route taken by Lieutenant French five years earlier, he worked south via the Rideau river and lake system to the St. Lawrence. However, unlike French's exploratory trip, Rankin traversed and measured his way up the Ottawa from L'Orignal above what is now Hawkesbury to the mouth of the Rideau River and thence inland and south to reach the St. Lawrence after many days of atrociously difficult surveying.

The immediate result of Rankin's survey was to open up the Rideau river system to settlement. In February 1790 De Pencier was instructed to lay out a township, this to "satisfy a number of Loyalists now waiting for their locations."[15] This was Malborough, Ontario's first truly inland township. Now in the Regional Municipality of Ottawa-Carleton, Marlborough Township fronts the Rideau River. Kemptville in Oxford Township on the other side of the river lies opposite Malborough's southeastern corner. De Pencier's instructions contained the directive that, in modified forms, was to become very familiar to Ontario's land surveyors in the years that lay ahead:

---

*That the land surveyors of the day tended to move in the same circles, is attested to by the fact that Rankin married John Collins's daughter, Mary, with Jesse Pennoyer acting as a witness.

You are to commence and proceed in the execution of this work with all diligence, accuracy and fidelity in conformity with the General Rules & Regulations ...

You are to keep journals & field books, inserting therein whatever is observable for its singularity and value towards the public utility as water falls, minerals, quarries, the quality of the lands, timber, etc and likewise accounting for the time spent upon such service with such minuteness and certainty as will shew the work of each day, and enable you to answer questions upon oath in respect thereto if the same shall be required, reporting all such journals and field books under your signature to this office after the completion of the work, together with protractions thereof both to [this office] and to the Land Board of the District in which you shall have been employed.

You are to pay a very strict attention to economy ...[16]

Marlborough was to be 10 miles square conforming to "an inland township as approved by His Excellency the Governor." This was a reference to what has been called the "Dorchester Township." Included in Dorchester's "Rules and Regulation for the Conduct of the Land Department" issued a year earlier, were plans to be followed in laying out waterfront and inland townships respectively. In designing these townships, Dorchester, if Dorchester it was, had apparently harked back to instructions as given in the Proclamation of 1763, in which a town plot was called for in each 20 000-acre township, along with reserves of one kind or another. Thus, an inland township, which was to be 10 miles square with 200-acre lots in ten concessions, was now to have a town plot in its centre. And in a waterfront township which was 9 miles (15 km) along the front and 12 miles deep

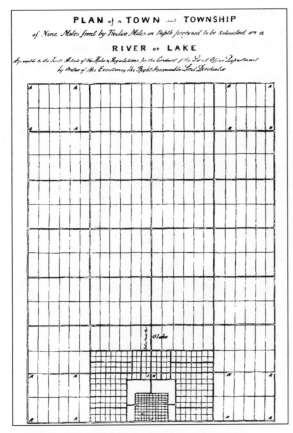

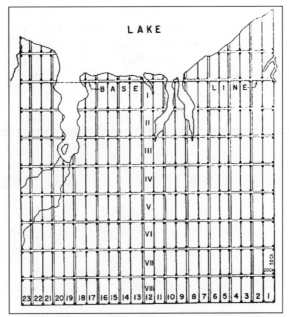

Figure 6.4 Specimen plan of a waterfront "Dorchester" township as issued to surveyors in 1789. A block (marked by 'A's) was reserved for the Crown in each corner. These reserves plus the town plot meant only two standard lots were available to settlers on the waterfront, the choicest location. The inland "Dorchester" township had similar crown reserves with the town plot in the centre. Only a few "Dorchester" townships were laid out and in no case did a town appear in the designated location (see figure 6.7). (From Patterson, *Land Settlement in Upper Canada*.)

Figure 6.5 In the front-and-rear township survey system all four corners of lots were picketed by the surveyor (small black squares). Abandoned because it was too expensive, only thirteen townships, all on the Niagara peninsula, were laid out using this system. (From Sebert, *Land Surveys of Ontario*.) Courtesy: *Cartographica*

with 200-acre lots ranged in fourteen concessions, the town plot was to be on the front itself. In both types of townships, there was also to be Crown reserves in each corner, while around the town there were to be 1-acre lots for the use of townspeople who wanted to try their hand at market gardening (see figure 6.4).

The design of the Dorchester townships caused some misgivings, particularly for a waterfront township which was left with only two 200-acre lots available for general settlement along the front – the best location. In the event, in no case did towns emerge based solely on Dorchester's township plans. A start had been made

on Cornwall as far back as 1784. And while a start had also been made on Johnstown, where Sir John Johnson came to live, now on the outskirts of Prescott, a proposal in 1790 that the survey of the town plot and its boundaries be completed was turned down by the Land Committee. They were "not apprized," they said, "of the immediate want of any more surveys in this township [Edwardsburgh]." In May 1789 Dorchester ordered the Land Board of Hesse in Detroit to lay out a township to be called George Town opposite the island of Bois Blanc. On being informed that the site of the proposed town was already occupied by Captain Caldwell, Dorchester did not press the matter but told the board to issue deeds to Caldwell and other bona fide settlers in the immediate area.

In Marlborough Township, in his instructions mentioned above, De Pencier had been ordered to "mark every third line of concession, reserving the site of the town, the glebe and Crown lands, etc." But no town ever grew up there. Quite apart from the faulty assumption that a town can be brought into being by simply putting it on a plan without a *raison d'etre* and without reference to any physiographic features that might render the location desirable, a town has to have someone to live in it. It was to be a number of years before any but the first few concessions were taken up. And in fact Marlborough township remains almost totally rural to this day.

In the meantime, a new system of laying out townships was being used on the Niagara peninsula, though who initiated it remains unknown. It may have been Philip Frey who became the "resident" surveyor at Niagara in 1785, or perhaps it was the newly arrived Augustus Jones, later to become one of province's most noted surveyors. Jones acted as one of Frey's chainmen when Frey was ordered by the commandant, Major Archibald Campbell, in 1787 to lay out a second township upriver, which was given the name of Stamford. Whereas in the single-front system only the front corners of individual lots were marked, in this new system both the front and rear corners of each lot were marked. Hence the name by which it became enshrined in survey legislation was the "Front-and-Rear System." (See figure 6.5.)

With all four corners of his lot marked, the settler knew exactly where he was. Gone was the need for the settler to run the side lines of his lot and with it the risk of argument with his neighbors if he placed them wrongly. Because in this new system, the side lines of lots there were run and not the concessions. As he went along, the surveyor picketed front and rear corners of lots (lots were 20 by 50 chains to give 200 acres), leaving room for a concession road between the rear of one lot and the front of the one behind it. As in the single-front system, there was a road between each concession.

In theory the surveyor ran up and down the side lines of the township like a "shuttle in a loom," as it has been put, until the township was complete. Apparently it wasn't quite like that, at least in the first front-and-rear townships. In about 1790 Holland and Collins made a plan of the Niagara settlements which shows several townships in various stages of completion (see figure 6.6). Niagara and Stamford fronting the Niagara River are complete. Louth Township behind Niagara and fronting Lake Ontario, now partly covered by St. Catharines, is completely outlined and the concession lines *have* been run. As per textbook, the surveyor has completed a number of lots on the Niagara side of the township, surveying the township

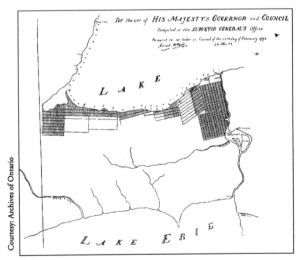

Figure 6.6 Townships on the Niagara Peninsula in 1790. (Part of a plan of the district of Nassau in the Province of Quebec, signed by Samuel Holland and John Collins, AO, Cartographic Records Collection A-16. As reproduced in Fraser, *Third Report of the Bureau of Archives*, 1905.)

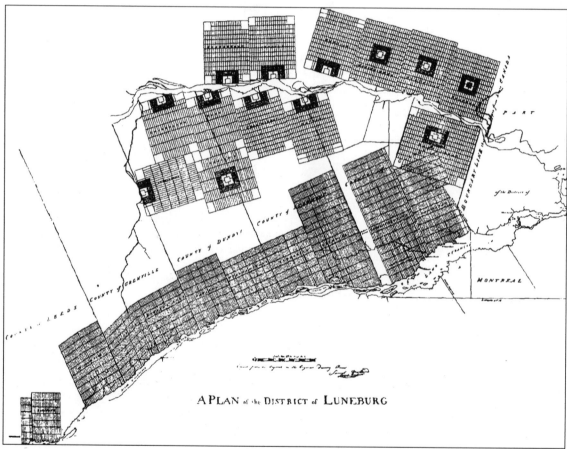

Figure 6.7 The district of Luneburg in 1790. Note that several "Dorchester" townships have already been laid out, though nothing would come of the town sites surveyed. Note also that the district had apparently already been divided into counties, though these would not be officially promulgated until 1792. (Part of a plan of the district of Luneburg copied from an original in the Surveyor General's Office, 1790, AO, Cartographic Records Collection A-9, Repro. no. AO 1313. As reproduced in Fraser, *Third Report of the Bureau of Archives*, 1905.)

from its side inward. The same is happening in other partly completed townships to the west. Because of the time and expense involved, the front-and-rear system was used in only thirteen townships, all on the Niagara Peninsula, and was finally abandoned in 1813.

Among the items approved for the 1790 survey season was the tracing of a "highway" (the first appearance of this term) between Cornwall and Kingston, the distance being given as 80 miles (129 km). Jesse Pennoyer was to handle the job with a ten-man party. It was estimated that it would take sixty days and was costed accordingly to give a total budget of £103 15s. Rankin, now the resident deputy surveyor for Luneburg, was to run the western boundaries of the old French seigneuries on the Ottawa and St. Lawrence, which, in the event, would shortly become part of the boundary between Upper and Lower Canada. Rankin was also to survey the boundary between the districts of Luneburg and Mecklenburg, which, interestingly enough, were referred to as "counties." Aitken was to put in more townships north of Kingston. Frey was to be given the job of surveying and laying out all "the land lately purchased by Sir John Johnson from the Missesaga Nation in the District of Nassau from the Bay of Quinte to Toronto." It was assumed optimistically that this daunting task would take Frey and ten men only sixty days at a cost of £432 9s. 2d. The proposal was modified. Frey was to lay out only the front line of townships between Trent and Cornwall with the side lines carried back one mile "well marked."[17] Frey didn't finish the job and in 1791 it was reassigned to Augustus Jones.

A far-sighted proposal by Collins, which was rejected in 1790, could have considerably eased the task of producing an accurate map of the province. Collins's proposal ran thus:

In order to correct the several surveys which compose the general plan of this Province it will be necessary to ascertain with exactitude, both the latitude and longitude of the lakes, rivers, fords, settlements, etc in all such parts as may be worthy of observation between the entrance of Lake Superior and the town of Montreal.[18]

The verdict of the Land Committee was that "this work does not appear to be immediately expedient." Collins himself sat on the Land Committee. Presumably and most unfortunately, he must have been voted down.

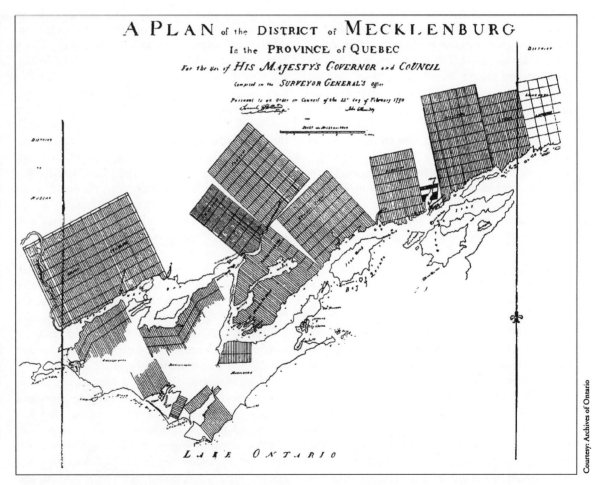

Figure 6.8 The district of Mecklenburg in 1790. Much of present day Prince Edward county had yet to be laid out. (Part of a plan of the district of Mecklenburg in the Province of Quebec, signed by Samuel Holland and John Collins, AO, Cartographic Records Collection B-27. As reproduced in Fraser, *Third Report of the Bureau of Archives*, 1905.)

By 1790, Frey was apparently turning out to be something of a broken reed. On 31 July 1788 – after Frey had already been on the job a couple of years – Collins wrote to Frey at Niagara, recapitulating some of the survey procedures that he should be using. In the interests of economy, he is to do no more work than was strictly necessary. Thus, for example, he is to survey only as "much of the exterior lines of the township ... as will guide these grantees in extending the side lines of their own lots to the rear in that concession ..." He also advises Frey to make sure of "the two capital stations for the breadth of the town" and that healthy trees should be blazed for that purpose ... using such an instrument as is used by coopers in making casks ..."[19] Surely this was all pretty elementary stuff for a deputy surveyor who had been on the job for several years?

When Frey was first appointed to Niagara, Detroit fell within his bailiwick. But it came to light he had not been to Detroit for nearly two years and his work had been done for him by Thomas Smith. Frey had also kept Collins waiting for a map of his district for no less than three years. From 1790 onwards his name starts to disappear from the survey records, and he left the province not long after. Collins could not have been sorry to see Frey go.

Frey's replacement as the deputy surveyor for the district of Nassau was Augustus Jones, of whom was written in 1923 "Every Land Surveyor who has practised in Toronto, Hamilton and the Niagara Peninsula during the last hundred years has had occasion to refer to [Jones's] field notes and plans ..."[20] Born in 1757 or 1758, Jones was of Welsh descent. His forebears settled on the Hudson River, probably in Dutchess County, New York, before the American revolution. They then went to live near Newburgh, at which point Jones got some training as a land surveyor. After the restoration of peace in 1783, the Jones family came north to settle on the Niagara Peninsula, where Jones and his father, together with several of his brothers and sisters, were granted land in Saltfleet township, the survey of which Jones himself was later to complete. He was sworn in as a crown surveyor on 11 June 1787 when he would have been a man of thirty or thirty-one. However, it was not until the following winter that he was officially taken on as one of Frey's assistants at a salary of 2s. 6d. per day.

The summer of 1791 saw other inland townships surveyed in the east. The covetous eyes of various ex-officers had fallen on the land bordering the South Nation River to the southeast of Ottawa. To accommodate them Rankin was instructed to lay out Cambridge Township, now in Prescott and Russell County, complete with a town plot, glebe, and crown reserves.[21] There is now a village named Casselman in the township, though it is not at its centre. Rankin was then to lay out the adjacent township of Roxburgh (now Roxborough in Glengarry Township). Rankin was provisioned for five months in the bush, being given a government order on a private supplier for his food. This was the usual practice in the absence of government stores. Failing both these, deputy surveyors got 1s. 3d. a day subsistence allowance. Rankin's food for five months consisted of five barrels of pork, ten bushels of peas, and 2250 pounds of flour, all of which must have taken some carrying.[22] Pennoyer, De Pencier, and Chewett were similarly provisioned, though for four months only. Collins told Pennoyer that "the pork ... arrived a few days past from London [England] and must assuredly be good ..."[23]

That same summer, Jones at Niagara was told to lay out, on the west side of the Niagara River and according to the instructions of the Land Board, a "county town of the District to be called Lenox [later Newark, later still Niagara-on-the-Lake]." He was also instructed to do what Frey should have done the previous year and lay out townships between Trenton and Toronto (the district of Nassau, to which he was attached, stretching as it did from Trenton to Long Point on Lake Erie). Jones was ordered to lay out Murray (immediately to the east of Trenton) "and the rest as they follow in proceeding westerly ..." These were Cramahe, Haldimand, Hamilton, Hope, Clark, Bristol, Norwich, Edinburgh, Glasgow, and Dublin. The last five townships, covering the stretch between Newcastle and Toronto, would acquire new names in the course of time, with the last three becoming Pickering, Scarborough, and York.

In 1791, we catch our first glimpse of a surveyor by the name of John Stegman, to use the name he is generally known by – he himself always spelled his name "Stegmann." Stegman was one of the few ex-German army officers who elected to take their discharge in Canada after the Revolutionary War and had been granted a standard 200-acre lot on the third concession of Osnabruck Township in Stormont County. After teaching himself surveying to bring in some much-needed cash, Stegman was engaged in some private work when De Pencier stumbled across him, though exactly where is not clear. Stegman had his own way of doing things, and what he was doing when his and De Pencier's paths crossed, provoked the latter into writing a long, rambling, and extremely agitated letter to Collins on 13 August 1791 (the original is in French):

It is my duty, sir, to acquaint your Honor of the very particular manner Mr Stegman goes on working in several seigneuries. He pays no regard to the running of the seigneurial lines being the limits of each seigneury, and with which the lines of division between the lands [lots] of the inhabitants must naturally be parallel. No, sir, he forcibly traces [side] lines [of a lot] from the boundary of a concession to that of another [lot in the next concession] bearing the same number ... Instead of dividing the lines so that [the lots] may form [rectangles] they will form trapeziums that will differ in form and magnitude.

De Pencier went on to say that "several proprietors will lose land belonging to them, others will have more than belong to them; finally it is introducing confusion and discord in the settlement ..." Concluding his letter De Pencier refers to resurveys at private expense of earlier crown surveys, which apparently was not uncommon even at that early date. "And besides, the injustice – How many persons are there who have paid surveyors to trace their lines anew. I have traced several of them myself, faithfully parallel to the seigneurial lines, Mr. Stegman [adding insult to injury] inspects them, I do not know by what authority ..."[24] In replying, Collins said that as Stegman was not employed by the surveyor general's department he was unable to interfere. The matter "sits entirely with the Land Board of the District who ought to put a stop immediately to such illegal proceedings which if suffered to go on will throw the whole settlement into confusion ..."[25]

In fact, what Stegman was trying to do, in his dogged way, was to wrench lots in successive townships into their theoretical position one behind the other or, to put it another way, where they should have been had the side lines of the lots been run continuously from front to rear of the township. This is exactly what the procedure was in the front-and-rear system, initiated three years before on the Niagara Peninsula, and which Stegman perhaps had heard of – or even personally observed.

In February 1791 it was finally announced that Quebec was to be divided into the two provinces of Upper and Lower Canada, with the necessary bill, the Constitutional Act, often called the Canada Act, receiving royal assent on 19 June 1791. By this time the first lieutenant-governor of Upper Canada had already been selected in the person of John Graves Simcoe, though he was not to arrive in Canada until November of that year.

Meanwhile, with the creation of the new province imminent, authorities in Quebec decided it was time to take stock and to start winding down the extremely costly operation of settling the Loyalists. The days of taking on supernumerary surveyors was over. An order-in-council was issued early in 1791: "... as soon as the business of settling the Loyalists and reduced troops ... should be brought to a conclusion, there could be no further occasion for the employment of extraordinary surveyors ... at stated daily allowances."[26] These allowances would cease at the end of the next season with a final deadline of December 1792. Thereafter all survey services would be provided by the surveyor general's department following the approval of annual estimates.

At the same time and in line with the new dispensation, Collins was asked to prepare a list of surveys yet to be completed in the upper districts and their total cost. His proposals were considered not by the Land Committee – which in any case was shortly to be abolished – but a committee of the whole governing council, which included both Holland and Collins. Surveys proposed for 1791 would cost £1350 10s. Collins's list, which shows the status of survey work on the eve of the creation of Upper Canada, included proposed new townships (all as yet unnamed) immediately to the north of Charlettenburgh, Cornwall, and Elizabethtown, one on the Little Nation River where some ex-officers liked the look of the land, two more on the Rideau, and four more north of Kingston. In the latter, side lines were to be carried back "one mile well-marked." At Niagara "it will only be required to run the third concession line in the 5th, the 7th and 9th [townships] and the back boundary line ... which will be a saving to Government of one half of the work."[27] Also outstanding, apparently, were the front lines of townships between Burlington Bay and Toronto. In these, too, the sidelines were to be carried

---

A Surveyor in Love

Ingenuous soul that he must have been, Chewett had written to Collins from Cornwall on 22 April 1791 as follows. He was thirty-eight at the time.

Dear Sir,
Having found a girl whom I mean to make a partner for life, and without which it is impossible to exist in this settlement, having no settled place to retire to after the fatigues of a survey, or take care of the little property I have (this, I hope you will not think unreasonable at the time of life I am come to, as it does not proceed from motives of folly, but of a mature and deliberate consideration), I therefore must pray you as my friend, to obtain a licence for me and Isabella McDonnel (she is of the family of major Archibald McDonnel, of the Long Sault), to be sent by the first opportunity; and in so doing you will oblige an old servant who is, with the greatest respect, Dear Sir,
Your most obedient, humble servant, [signed]
    W. Chewett

   The date of the marriage is not known. However, their first child, a son, arrived on 20 May 1792. (Letter from AC, "Biographical Sketch of the Late Colonel Chewett," in *APLS*, 1890.)

back only a mile. Surprisingly, the interior of Prince Edward County was as yet still unsurveyed – the second and third concessions of Marysburgh, Sophiasburgh, and Ameliasburgh still needed running, as did the back concessions of Lancaster, the "Sunken Township."

The cutback in the number of full-time surveyors, as adumbrated by Dorchester's order-in-council, started to take effect at the end of the 1791 season. An early victim was Chewett, who had been working in the Luneburg District, and who had married earlier that year. Upon learning that he had been laid off, Chewett wrote an anguished letter to Collins from his home in Matilda Township. "I now find," he wrote, "I have been serving my whole life for nothing ... There has been no surveyor, in the same line as myself, that has the same right to expect a continuation ... However, I trust, you will be able to find me some employment, either in our Department, or some other ..."[28]

McNiff in Detroit also worked himself into a great state on hearing of the same order-in-council. If the "dismission of surveyors on daily state subsistence from Government" included him, he told Collins in a long and somewhat distraught letter, he would have been "much better off for the time past with my family in the middle or lower parts of the Province ..." And now that he was at Detroit where everything cost three times as much and "with a numerous and helpless family [in] the heart of a wilderness near one thousand miles from the seat of Government." If the order-in-council *did* apply to him, there was nothing for it, he concluded, but "to convey my infants from here to some place where they may not perish for want of the necessities of life."[29] Presumably McNiff was told that his job was safe. At any rate he stayed on at Detroit. At least for a time.

With the economy the new watchword, accounts were being very carefully scrutinized and awkward questions were being asked of the Surveyor General's Office. This is when De Pencier's financial troubles started to deepen. "How comes Mr. De Pencier's provisions to be charged so high, say pork at 5 pounds a barrel, when Mr. Peachey charges his 5d pr. lb and all other Deputy's 4 pounds a barrel?" Answer: "We are unable to say why the provisions supplied to Mr. De Pencier are charged higher than the others ... Whether the provisions furnished by [this supplier were] of a superior quality we are unable to say. Mr. De Pencier should have undoubtedly taken care his provisions should be charged at a reasonable rate particularly as the person who supplied them was recommended by himself."

There were other questions, such as: "What is the usual allowance of time you make to the deputy surveyors to come to Sorel from Quebec?" Answer: No particular time because the "same distance will sometimes require a greater and sometimes a lesser number of days according to the weather, the state of the road [if going by land] and according to the wind if going by water – we should however think that a person in health might easily walk from Sorel to Quebec in a week ..."[30] It's about 100 miles from Quebec to Sorel – and that's as the crow flies.

Presumably it was also with the coming of the new lieutenant-governor in mind that Dorchester told the Land Board in January 1791 to make sure that the maps and plans in the Surveyor General's Office were in a fit state for inspection. It transpired that they were far from being in that state and Collins was hauled over the coals for being laggardly in setting matters to rights. Collins was also supposed to prepare a list of ex-officers who had applied for grants of land. That hadn't been done either.

That all was not as it should be in Collins's office was not surprising. We have no idea how old he was, the date of his birth being unknown, but by 1790 he must have been advancing in years; his handwriting had grown more spidery, his letters full of corrections. Four years later he would be dead. While Holland may have been the master land surveyor, the real hero of the Loyalist settlements was surely Collins himself. Not only did he labour mightily in the field, and this when he was no longer young, but he also did his best to encourage his surveyors when things looked bleak, lent them money when they were broke, and comforted them when things went wrong.

Part 2

Upper Canada

CHAPTER SEVEN

John Graves Simcoe

Upper Canada's first lieutenant-governor, John Graves Simcoe, was a career soldier who had seen much hard service during the Revolutionary War, being wounded three times and at one point taken prisoner to face execution as a hostage before his exchange was providentially arranged. After serving with two regular regiments, he was given command of a Loyalist regiment, the Queen's Rangers, a regiment to which he gave his heart. Simcoe and his Rangers were with Cornwallis when he surrendered at Yorktown, but Simcoe himself was allowed to return to New York because of ill health. Returning to England, he married Elizabeth Gwillim, then the sixteen-year-old ward of Simcoe's godfather, Admiral Graves, from whom Simcoe got his middle name. Elizabeth's mother had died at the time of her birth – hence her rather curious middle name of Posthuma. Mrs. Simcoe was an accomplished artist; her sketches and watercolours were to complement a remarkable diary that she kept while she was in Canada. She was also interested in maps and map-making; one wonders if this interest, unusual for a woman of her time, had helped the romance along.

After getting married, the couple went to live in Devon. Simcoe kept himself abreast of events in North America and was soon pestering his contacts in Whitehall with suggestions as to how the remnants of Britain's North American empire could be made secure and prosperous. It seems that it was these suggestions that brought his name to the fore when candidates were being considered for the post of lieutenant-governor of the new province of Upper Canada. Lord Dorchester had his own candidate in Sir John Johnson, but by the time his recommendation reached London in 1790, Simcoe had already been appointed.

Simcoe, his wife, and their two youngest children – they left the four eldest behind – arrived in Quebec City on 11 November 1791. It was too late in the season to travel farther, and, in any case, Simcoe could not be sworn in as lieutenant-governor of Upper Canada until a quorum of his newly appointed executive council could be assembled, and the chief justice, William Osgoode, and the receiver general, Peter Russell, were not due until the following spring. So the Simcoes spent the winter in Quebec. Not long after his arrival, Simcoe went to Montreal to confer with Sir John Johnson, returning with a Lieutenant Thomas Talbot, whom he had taken on as his aide-de-camp. Dancing attendance on Mrs. Simcoe, Talbot became virtually part of the Simcoe family while it was in Upper Canada. Later, after an absence from Canada of a few years, Talbot was to return and found the Talbot Settlement, which was instrumental in opening up southwestern Ontario.

On 26 December 1791, the Constitutional Act was proclaimed in Quebec City by Sir Alured Clarke, the lieutenant-governor of Lower Canada, Dorchester being absent in England. The act defined the boundaries of the new province of Upper Canada. Its southern boundary followed the international boundary as defined in the Treaty of Paris. The border with Quebec struck north from the St. Lawrence, skirting the seigneuries in the angle of the St. Lawrence and Ottawa rivers, and then followed the Ottawa to Lake Timiskaming and thence due north to James Bay. There was no clear western boundary. From its eastern boundary, Upper Canada comprehended "all the territory to the westward and northward" of the Quebec and U.S. borders respectively "to the utmost extent of the country commonly called or known by the name of Canada." There was, however, a tacit recognition that the western boundary impinged somewhere in the northwest on the territory claimed and administered by the Hudson's Bay Company, that is, all the land draining into Hudson Bay.

Right from the start, Simcoe had been determined that Upper Canada should have its own surveyor general to preside over what he saw as a rapidly expanding department. (See appendix B for all provincial surveyors general.) It transpired later that this was not the view of the Colonial Office. Henry Dundas, the colonial secretary, saw no necessity for such an appointment or for setting up separate surveying arrangements for Upper Canada. "It is proposed," he was to write to Simcoe on 15 August 1792, "that the surveyor-general of Lower Canada shall likewise fill the same situation in Upper Canada, but without any additional salary. The attention of the surveyor-general may certainly be bestowed at proper seasons on both provinces."[1] But these instructions had not arrived in early 1792. Had Lord Dorchester, who was to veto many of Simcoe's ideas, been there, he might well have ordered Simcoe to wait until instructions on the subject had been received from England. But he wasn't. And so Simcoe went ahead, with Upper Canada the beneficiary.

Soon after his arrival in Quebec, Simcoe started discussing possible appointees to the post of surveyor general with Holland, who approved of the idea. It seems that Simcoe had approached a Lieutenant-Colonel Provost to take on the job, but he wouldn't come to Canada. Having put forward the name of his eldest son, John Frederick, as a candidate for the post – whom Simcoe turned down – Holland then recommended Chewett, who had applied for the post. Holland had supplied Simcoe with a list of deputy surveyors then working in what was now Upper Canada, which included Chewett, Aitken, Jones, McNiff, Stegman, Fortune, De Pencier, Pennoyer, and Joseph Bouchette, the last then in his late teens and newly attached to the Surveyor General's Office. Simcoe was not impressed by any on Holland's list. On 21 June 1792, just before he left Quebec for Upper Canada, he wrote to Dundas on the subject of a surveyor general for Upper Canada, an office that

> requires great professional abilities and equal integrity. It was on the conviction of the important qualities necessary for this office that I did not venture to recommend to you

any of the numerous persons who applied to me ... and I greatly fear through the incompetence of persons who Major Holland, that able servant of the Crown, has been formerly obliged to employ in Upper Canada, I shall have considerable difficulty, if I may judge from the documents before me, in the prevention of mischievous litigations.[2]

Surely a sweeping and unfair generalization if there ever was one. And Simcoe wasn't too happy with Holland or Collins either. Of Holland, he was to write "that good and faithful servant of the Crown is worn out in body, though in full possession of his intellect." Collins, he added, "possesses neither strength nor intellect."[3]

Chewett got the nod. In March 1792 he was summoned to Quebec, where Simcoe, in Chewett's own words, "promised him employment." A couple of weeks later, Simcoe's plans for a separate surveyor general's office hit a civil service roadblock. There was no provision for such an office in the proposed civil service establishment of the new province. Instructed by Simcoe to transfer Chewett to Niagara where Simcoe planned to set up his temporary capital, Holland did not know how this could be done – so he referred the matter to the acting governor, Clarke. Clarke was equally baffled. Simcoe decided to mark time "until," in Chewett's words, "he took possession of his Government when he would have everything at his command."[4] In the event, Chewett was appointed acting surveyor general as of 10 April 1792.

Until Simcoe left Quebec for Upper Canada in June, he had Chewett scurrying around, supplying him with the many maps and plans that he wished to see. Simcoe also ordered Chewett to appear before a special meeting, along with other surveyors then in Quebec, to cross-examine them on the time, and thus money required, to run the outlines of a 10-mile-square (26-km^2) township fronting on a river. They came up with

the following table, which, with the pay rates given as well as the required "implements," throws light on the survey procedures then being followed.

	Days
Running the front on a river	15
" one side line	10
" one rear line	10
Returning to the first station in order to finish the closing line	1
For the closing line	10
Allowance for bad weather and other casualties	14
Total days	57

Such a survey would require one surveyor at 10s. a day (possibly wishful thinking; pay was to remain at 7s. 6d. a day for a while yet), two chain-bearers at 2s. a day each, and 8 axemen at 1s. 6d. a day. "Provisions for the party to be allowed the same as the Deputy Surveyor-General was allowed, 1/3d per day for each man. Implements [required]: 6 New England axes, 4 tommy-hawks, 1 oil cloth, 1 batteaux or canoe, and all contingencies to be sworn to."[5]

Simcoe also put Chewett to work copying all the instructions relating to "settling the Upper Country – buy a book for the same," noted Chewett, "and charge it to the surveyor-general." The day of 20 June 1792 saw Chewett happily packing what he always called his "little baggage" for Kingston, where Simcoe and his family were also bound.

Simcoe arrived in Canada at a time when the safety of the new province was under increasing threat from the Americans. American anger was mounting at the continuing reluctance of the British to vacate the forts and posts on the American side of the border. They were also angered by British support of the native nations resisting American encroachment on their lands south of Lake Erie, though such support was to stop short of military assistance.

Before he even left England, Simcoe had roughed out what proved to be intertwining strategies for the defence and future settlement of Upper Canada. He envisaged a thriving Upper Canada that would have its political and commercial centre of gravity in the southwest. Such an Upper Canada would come to dominate the mid-west and might even, as some suggested, wean away newly emerging American states west of the Appalachians. In Simcoe's view the ideal site for a capital would be on the river that the French called La Tranche, which he decided to rename the Thames, where a town called Georgina would be founded. For the moment, however, he decided that the settlement at Niagara, to be called Newark, would be the province's temporary capital. On second thought he decided it to call his proposed capital on the Thames New London, which, with Chatham as a naval dockyard established downstream, would form a pleasing parallel with the London and Chatham on England's River Thames.

There remained the need to establish a major military base on Lake Ontario. While Kingston was already fortified, it was, in Simcoe's view, too dangerously close to the United States to be an effective base. Examining Mann's reports and maps among others, Simcoe decided that Toronto, with its harbour protected by a curving spit, would be an excellent site for a naval base and military arsenal.

Along with the necessity of increasing Upper Canada's military preparedness, there was an urgent need for immigrants to populate the new province. Simcoe foresaw these would come from the United States. While he detested republicanism and "popular" democracy, he had been greatly impressed by what he had seen during the Revolutionary War of the industry and skills of American farmers. So even before his administration was inaugurated and with Americans principally in mind, he issued a proclamation in February 1793 that outlined the land-granting system that would be applied in Upper Canada. The proclamation was published in English and West Indian newspapers, whence, it was hoped, the message would reach American ears. And to make quite sure, Simcoe wrote to the British consul at Philadelphia in the hope of luring Quakers to Upper Canada, a people that had especially impressed him, and to whom he promised exemption from bearing arms should they come.

According to the terms of Simcoe's proclamation, the settlement of Upper Canada was to proceed, as before, on the basis of townships. If abutting navigable waters, these were to be 9 miles (14 km) along the front and 12 miles deep, inland they would be 10 miles square – dimensions presumably arrived at by Simcoe following consultations with Holland and Collins. Basic lot size would be 200 acres, as before, though an additional 1000 acres could be granted at the discretion of the government. Land would be granted freehold and free of all expenses, save for fees paid to officials involved with passing and recording the patents. To obtain a grant, petitioners had to swear loyalty to the Crown and give assurances that they would cultivate and improve their land.

Early in June 1792, the officials arrived for whom Simcoe had been waiting; he and his family set off for Upper Canada travelling in a bateau up the St. Lawrence, reaching Montreal on 13 June,* and what was now being called Kingston on 1 July. With his officials duly assembled in Kingston, Simcoe took the oath of office on 8 July 1791. In effect this marked the beginning of Upper Canada's first administration.

On 16 July Simcoe issued a proclamation that, for purposes of political representation, the province was to be divided into nineteen counties (see figure 7.1). Roughly speaking, the boundaries of the counties along the St. Lawrence and Lake Ontario shore ran at right-angles to the shoreline. In southwestern Ontario, however, the arrangement was somewhat different. Essex included all of the extreme southwest of the province with its eastern boundary at Pointe au Pins, now in Rondeau Provincial Park. However, a 4-mile (6.5-km) strip along the Detroit River and the south shore of Lake St. Clair fell into Kent County, which, apart from this strip, had the Thames as its southern boundary. Its northern boundary was undetermined; to all intents and purposes it included all the northernmost parts of the province. East of Essex came Suffolk, then virtually unsettled, which extended from Pointe au Pins to the Niagara Peninsula (see figure 7.6). Later, these counties would be subdivided as the spread of settlement warranted. Just how big the province was in geographical terms was still imperfectly known.

With the business done at Kingston, Simcoe and his family took ship for Niagara, arriving at Navy Hall on 25 July. He renamed the settlement there Newark (now Niagara-on-the-Lake), and it was there that Simcoe opened the first session of the first provincial parliament on 17 September 1792. One of the statutes enacted at the first session renamed the old districts of Luneburg, Mecklenburg, Nassau, and Hesse. They were now to be known as the Eastern, Midland, Home, and Western districts respectively and were retained primarily to serve a legal function. The old land boards were abolished, being replaced by seven new boards. These would deal with applications for land in thirteen out of the nineteen new counties. Applications for land in the other six – Ontario, Northumberland, Durham, York, Norfolk, and Suffolk, covering the Niagara Peninsula and western Lake Ontario, all considered to be "sensitive" from the military standpoint – were to be considered by Simcoe himself and his executive council.

---

*Mrs. Simcoe was much taken by the spaciousness of Government House, but her pleasure was checked by the heat, which she found "more insufferable than I had ever felt. The thermometer continued at 96 for two days, and the heat was not ill-described by a centinal who exclaimed 'There is but a sheet of brown paper between this place and hell.' "

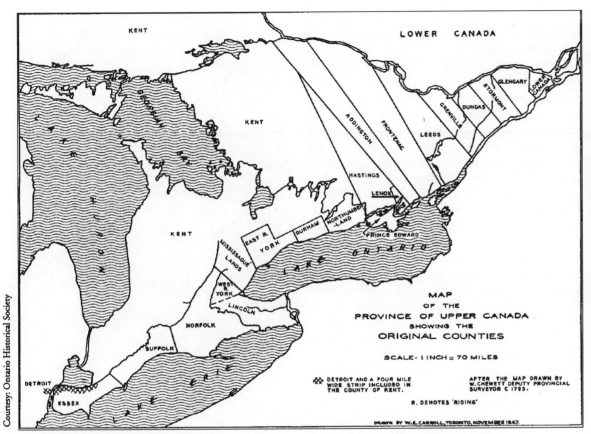

Courtesy: Ontario Historical Society

MAP
OF THE
PROVINCE OF UPPER CANADA
SHOWING THE
ORIGINAL COUNTIES

SCALE · 1 INCH = 70 MILES

✕✕ DETROIT AND A FOUR MILE
WIDE STRIP INCLUDED IN
THE COUNTY OF KENT.

AFTER THE MAP DRAWN BY
W. CHEWETT DEPUTY PROVINCIAL
SURVEYOR C 1793.

R. DENOTES 'RIDING'

DRAWN BY W.E. CARROLL, TORONTO, NOVEMBER 1947.

Figure 7.1 First nineteen counties established by Lieutenant-Governor Simcoe. Note extent of Kent County. (From Spragge, *The Districts of Upper Canada*.)

Another Chance Missed

In the absence of methodical determinations of latitude and longitude, the precise dimensions of the province would remain unknown for more than a century. On 4 October 1792, Samuel Holland's son, John Frederick,* wrote to Simcoe offering to take part personally in a general survey of the new province, which would include determinations of latitude and longitude of "the most principal places" in the province. He pointed out that it would be useful to know the exact position and length of Lake Superior, and, were these known, it would be possible to arrive at an estimate of the continent itself, now that Captain Cook had established the position of the West Coast. Holland's proposal, like a very similar one put forward by Collins some years earlier, was unfortunately not followed up. The Great Triangulation was well under way in Britain, but a similar survey of Ontario would not be made until the early 1900s. (John F. Holland to John Graves Simcoe, 4 October 1792, photostat, *Instructions to Surveyors, 1764–1791*, vol. 1 [Survey Records, MNR], 130.)

*That this handsome offer was made by John Frederick and not by his father, Samuel Holland, as is sometimes stated, was brought to my attention by Lou Sebert, C.L.S.

Chewett, along with Jones and Aitken, had spent a few days at Kingston while Simcoe was there, going over more maps and plans with him. For Chewett, who was now signing himself as acting surveyor general, there was also the matter of handing over his post as deputy surveyor of Luneburg to his successor, Hugh Macdonell. This done, Chewett turned up at Niagara on 4 September 1792, ten days after Simcoe arrived. During those ten days, unbeknownst to Chewett, Simcoe had found a potential surveyor general who

was much more to his liking in the person of Lieutenant David Smith.

Smith was the only son of Major, later Colonel, John Smith, of the Fifth Regiment, Northumberland Fusiliers, then in garrison at Niagara. This was the same Major Smith who had written to Collins from Detroit a year or so earlier about getting his men paid for survey work, his regiment having been subsequently transferred to Niagara from Detroit. Born in England in 1764 and privately educated by military

tutors, David William Smith – later to become Sir David – had joined his father's regiment and, in 1792, had been in Canada only about two years. D.W. Smith, as he came to be known, must have made a good first impression on Simcoe; they were soon meeting socially. Simcoe and his wife dined with Major Smith and his family at Fort Niagara four days after their arrival. Recording the occasion in her diary, Mrs. Simcoe commented: "Lt. Smith ... is married to a beautiful Irish woman" (born Anna O'Reilly from County Longford). She went on to say that Mrs. Smith, with whom she quickly struck up a close friendship, had two tame raccoons.

Though only twenty-eight, Smith was clearly an up-and-coming man, ambitious, energetic, and, if his letters at that stage are anything to go by, unusually literate. At the time of the Simcoe's arrival in Newark, Smith was busy contesting the seat for Essex and Suffolk in the province's first general election. He won his seat, becoming one of the sixteen members to sit in the first session of Ontario's legislature – and he would go on to serve as Speaker for all four sessions of the second assembly and for two sessions of the third. While his regiment had been stationed in Detroit, he had served in various administrative posts – and he may even have taken part in the surveys mentioned above. The competence with which the regiment was run had already impressed Simcoe, another plus for Smith in Simcoe's eyes. And, in addition, Smith had served on the land board of Hesse, becoming its clerk. According to Simcoe, when he recommended him to the Colonial Office for the post of surveyor general, D.W. Smith was the "efficient person of that board."

Smith had first-hand experience in the work of a land board, some experience in the political arena, as well as possibly some practical surveying experience (Mrs. Simcoe mentions that "Lt. Smith has drawn a fine map of the La Tranche River"), not to mention obvious social acceptability. It is perhaps not surprising that Simcoe submitted his name to the Colonial Office as his choice for surveyor general. There was another important consideration; as there were no provision for this post within the civil service establishment at this time, there could be no possibility of a salary for the new surveyor general or of his receiving any of the fees accruing to the office. But Smith had army pay. On 28 September 1792, following the first meeting of the provincial legislature, Simcoe appointed Smith as acting surveyor general "till His Majesty's pleasure is known."* As it turned out, the appointment would not

*In further references, the word "acting" is omitted for the sake of brevity.

be confirmed until 1 January 1798, at which time Smith got all back pay owed him as surveyor general, back-dated to 1 July 1792.

Chewett was to be unhappily surprised of Smith's appointment. Since his arrival in Newark, Chewett had found Simcoe strangely elusive and was given little or nothing to do. Then on 30 September when he "attended" the governor at a *levée*, Simcoe told him – and it must have been a shock, poor man – that the coveted post was not going to be his after all. He would serve as assistant surveyor general instead.

The post of surveyor general was to elude William Chewett all his life. It was to be again almost within his grasp some ten years later. The man who would beat him to it then was already in government employ at Newark when Chewett arrived there to join Simcoe in 1792. This was Thomas Ridout, then a thirty-eight-year-old clerk with the army Commissariat Department. Ridout had left his native Dorsetshire in 1774 to join his elder brother in what was then still the British colony of Maryland. He arrived to find the colonies in an uproar over the tea that the British government had wished on them, with the Boston consignment dumped overboard in the climactic Boston Tea Party. However, in spite of this and the outbreak of the Revolutionary War that followed – from which he somehow remained aloof – Ridout set himself up in the importing business.

In December 1787 Ridout joined a party bound for Kentucky, then being opened up to settlement. They never got there, being ambushed on the Ohio River by Shawnees with nearly all, Ridout among them, taken prisoner or killed. After three months of captivity, Ridout was allowed to make his way northward to Detroit, then still in British hands and garrisoned by the Fifty-third Regiment. The regiment was about to be relieved, and when they were, Ridout went with them to Montreal, stopping on the way at Niagara where he met, and apparently made an impression on, the commandant, Colonel Peter

Personally selected by Simcoe, D.W. Smith, later knighted, was Upper Canada's first surveyor general.

© Queen's Printer for Ontario. Reproduced with permission of the Ministry of Natural Resources.

Hunter. In the course of time, Hunter would be appointed lieutenant-governor of Upper Canada and would back Ridout's efforts to obtain the post of surveyor general, Ridout by then being a clerk in the Surveyor General's Office. Thus it was in this somewhat extraordinary and convoluted fashion that Thomas Ridout came to be surveyor general in the crucial years that followed the ending of the Napoleonic Wars and the War of 1812 when settlers would come pouring in from Britain.

It had been laid down in the Constitutional Act that land must be set aside for the support of the Protestant church in "due proportion" to all the crown land already granted. And, further, that one-seventh of all land granted in the future must be reserved for the same purpose. Later, the British government decreed that a similar proportion of land must be set aside in order to provide governors with an additional source of revenue.

While it was stated in Simcoe's proclamation that land would be granted in new townships only after they had been surveyed and one-seventh had been reserved for clergy and Crown respectively, the precise location of these reserves was yet to be decided. When he was in Quebec, Simcoe had been advised that it would be best to place the reserves in a single block in each township. However, the Constitutional Act had stipulated that the reserves should be land of "like quality" to the rest of the township. After discussing the matter, Simcoe and Smith decided that the reserves must be scattered in 200-acre lots throughout the township, with block reserves made only in townships surveyed before the act came into force in 1791, such to be placed between adjoining townships.

Smith went to work, producing a basic township design that was to be followed from then on by deputy land surveyors, as they were now starting to be called. This showed a township 9 miles (14 km) wide along the front and 12 miles deep – the dimensions stated in Simcoe's proclamation. There were no planned town plots as featured in Dorchester's townships. Simcoe's standard township was to be divided into fourteen concessions with concession roads between each – thus perpetuating the single-front system of laying out townships, which Haldimand had pioneered. Each concession was to be subdivided into twenty-four 200-acre lots to give a township total of 336 lots. Of this, two-sevenths, or 96 lots, had to be reserved. Distributed equitably, these would come to 6.86 lots per concession. To make things simpler, it was decided to reserve seven lots in each concession, creating two more

reserved lots per township than was strictly required. These were to be additional crown reserves. There were various exceptions to the standard layout of the reserves, an important one being that there must be an unbroken front along major roads. All this was worked out and approved by the executive council within a month of Smith taking office. Surveyors were to follow this "Chequered Plan" for the next forty years or so (see figure 7.2).

The reserves, which came to be detested by settlers, compounded the faults already inherent in the single-

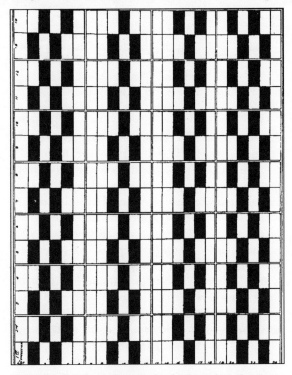

Figure 7.2 Specimen plan issued to land surveyors showing the distribution of crown and clergy reserves throughout a township. The reserves (shown in black) contributed to the lack of cohesion in communities and so compounded the faults of the single-front township survey system. (From Patterson, *Land Settlement in Upper Canada*.)

front system of laying out townships, militating further against the formation of cohesive communities and making the upkeep of roads even more difficult. And to cap it all, no matter how desirable and fertile was the land in the reserves, it was forever beyond a settler's reach. By the mid-1790s, the idea of selling crown and clergy reserves to bring in much-needed revenue was proved to be impractical in view of the amount of land on the market. Measures were eventually introduced to allow crown reserves to be leased, at first on a twenty-one-year lease, later for longer. On the face of it, this removed one of the objectionable features of Simcoe's checkered township. Now at least a farmer could make use of the land – if he could afford the rent.

Another measure brought in towards the end of Simcoe's time in Upper Canada would militate further against the cohesion of the settlements as a whole. This was the practice of granting land to leading officials and deserving citizens as a reward for services rendered. No lover of popular democracy, Simcoe hoped in this way to build up a land-owning aristocracy in the province; this idea was central to his vision of a thoroughly British Upper Canada. The grants were at times as large as 5000 acres. Some officials amassed huge tracts in this way. Smith himself accumulated 20 000 acres in twenty-one townships, and he was accused of using his position to select the best land for himself. It was said that the initials "D.W.S." on a lot was a reliable indicator that it was a choice one.

There was as yet no legal basis for the conduct of land surveys in the new province – such would not come until 1798 – and in the interim such surveys went forward by default under the general provisions of An Ordnance Concerning Land Surveyors and the Admeasurement of Lands, which, it will be recalled, had been passed in Quebec in 1785. Land surveyors were required to take an oath of allegiance and an oath of performance. As they had been used to doing, they kept all their field books and in due course lodged them as required with the Surveyor General's Office.

Borrowing the boat used by the surveyor Lewis Grant, the Simcoes rowed up the Lake Ontario shore and saw the Scarborough Bluffs for the first time, an event commemorated by a 2000-square-foot mural at 2384 Kingston Road, Scarborough, painted by Risto Turunen in 1992. Courtesy: Risto Turunen

That some land surveyors of the period were not above tinkering with their field books before sending them in, is hinted at in a letter written in April 1800 by William Vondenvelden of the Surveyor General's Office in Lower Canada to William Osgoode, chairman of the permanent committee of the executive council. It concerned shortcomings in the surveys of ten townships in Lower Canada. The committee suspected that both diaries and plans had been fudged, or "cogged," to use the expression then current.

That the letter found its way to the office of the surveyor general in Upper Canada suggests that even as late as 1800 the two surveyors general at least kept in touch. Certainly the break between them was not complete. Thus a circular issued from Quebec in June 1792 also found its way to Smith's office, then still in Newark. Addressed to deputy surveyors, part of it touched on the number of trees felled during a survey, something that was evidently causing some concern. "You will therefore avoid," deputy surveyors were enjoined, "every unnecessary expence and delay that may be occasioned by cutting down the trees where the deviation of your needle shall not absolutely require it."[6]

The act of 1785 required, in very general terms, that prospective surveyors be examined by the surveyor general. Such examinations were, of necessity, cursory in early days, indeed if they were carried out at all. But Simcoe, who could not abide incompetence, took what may be thought of as the first steps towards formalizing such examinations. On his way up to Newark in 1792, Simcoe ordered Chewett to examine Lewis Grant. Grant must have been the first land surveyor whose commission applied specifically to Upper Canada. The examination lasted three days, from 25 to 27 August 1792, and was conducted on the "Grand River, in the County of Stormont." Chewett's report on Lewis, addressed to Simcoe, gives us a good idea of what was required of a land surveyor at that time and the instruments he was likely to use:

I have examined [wrote Chewett] Mr. Lewis Grant ... viz.:

In the necessary parts of arithmetic.

In the necessary parts of geometry and trigonometry.

In the necessary parts of surveying, such as:

Viz. – Surveying a regular or irregular field by the circumferentor or chain, and finding the contents of the same.

Surveying a small river on the ice, and protracting the same, by the theodolite and traverse table.

Surveying a large river, intersecting its opposite side, and protracting the same by the theodolite and traverse table.

Surveying and laying out a township, regular or irregular, and protracting the same, by the theodolite, traverse table and sector.

In fixing a meridian, and finding the variation of the compass.

In finding the latitude by the sun's meridian altitude.

In levelling, for the purpose of making aqueducts, etc., etc.

W. Chewett
Act. Surv. Gen.[7]

Shortly after Grant was given his commission, John Stegman reappeared on the surveying scene. On 27 October 1792 he wrote to Smith asking for work. Stegman's bold and elegant hand make his letters a delight to read – quite apart from his insecure grasp of English spelling and syntax. His letter to Smith ran as follows:

Sir,

Since I have not had the honor to be personally acquainted with you I beg that you will pardon the liberty I take to trouble you with my writing, and to make myself knowing to you.

My name is John Stegmann, late Lieutenant in the Hessian Regiment of Lossberg, commanded by Major Gen'l DeLoos, and served during the whole war in America till the reduction took place in the month of August, 1783, and by the favour and indulgence of His Excellency Lord Dorchester I obtained land in this new settlement and township of Osnabruck, and an appointment as surveyor in the Province, which I take the liberty to make appear by my revived commission [He dusted it off and enclosed it with his letter?]. But having no resource or any means of supporting myself except my own industry, having a wife and small family to provide for, and the struggles natural in a new country augmented to me by being a stranger, and engaged in a calling to which I hithertoo [was] intirely ingnorant of. But am in hopes that you soon will employ an number of surveyors in this Province. Therefore take the liberty to offer you my

humbly service and beg that you will have the goodness to employ me. I have the honour to be with due respect, Sir, Your most obedient and most humble servent,

John Stegmann[8]

Given to understand that if he wanted work he had best move nearer to the seat of government, he moved with his wife and three children to Newark.

Simcoe's proclamation on settlement inviting settlers to Upper Canada soon started to pay dividends. As early as November 1792 Simcoe had reported that many settlers had come daily from the United States, "some even from the Carolinas, about 2,000 miles." Shortly after that, Simcoe walked from Newark to Burlington Bay and back, just to take a first-hand look at the settlements along the Lake Ontario shore, along which Mennonites and others of the Plain People were already settling.

Soon after his arrival at Newark, Simcoe initiated another type of settlement scheme. Under this scheme, roughly modelled on the way that new townships were opened up in New England, a whole township would be granted to leaders of "associations," to be called "nominees," who would receive up to 1200 acres in return for bringing their settlers in. There was a similar scheme in Lower Canada. For a while, applications for townships poured in, with some would-be proprietors asking for tracts of as much as thirty townships at a time. By July 1793 over thirty townships had been granted to assorted nominees. But the scheme soon ran into trouble. Deprived of the fees that otherwise might come to them, land board officials didn't think much of Simcoe's idea. And while the nominee was supposed to guarantee that his prospective settlers were of demonstrable loyalty, the scheme was much resented by the Loyalists, who saw themselves placed on the level of any Johnny-come-lately.

To meet the demand for land on the part of both bona fide settlers and nominees, six new townships

were opened up in 1792, eight in 1793 (including what became York, North York, and East York townships), thirteen in 1794, and nineteen in 1795.[9] Many of the townships that were started by crown surveyors on behalf of Simcoe's nominees from 1793 onward were outlined only. It was up to the nominees to have the townships subdivided.

Meanwhile, as land surveying went steadily forward in the central and eastern parts of the province,

John Stegman in 1790. Self-taught, Stegman first worked in the eastern part of the province. He later made many surveys in and about York, on the Niagara Peninsula, and in the southwest. He was drowned in 1804 when on his way to serve as an expert witness in a murder trial.
Courtesy: AOLS Archives

progress was far from steady in the far southwest. McNiff had been at odds with the Land Board at Detroit ever since his arrival. The Land Board complained of his obstructionist attitude and his tardiness. McNiff, for his part, said he had great difficulty in extracting men, canoes, paper – and even pencils – out of the Land Board. The Land Board had its own troubles. Faced with a growing number of petitions for land, the board found it had virtually no land at its immediate disposal. The earlier Loyalist settlements along the Detroit River had been on native land and, as noted in a previous chapter, had gone forward on the understanding that the land would be purchased from them in due course. As of 1790 this had not yet been done. So in order to regularize the existing situation and to make more land available for settlement, steps were taken to buy the land from the natives.

As required by government decree, a full council of native people was summoned, attended by the Chippewas, Pottowatamys, and Hurons on the native side and various officials and military officers on the British. At Detroit on 19 May 1790, virtually all of what is now southwest Ontario west of Rondeau Provincial Park was purchased for £1,200 worth of trade goods. Two reserves were left in native hands. One was a triangular parcel on which stood the Huron Church; the other and larger one fronted the river north of Amherstburg.

Surveying the newly purchased lands was one of the first jobs given to McNiff by the Land Board. Ordered to undertake the survey on 22 May 1790, three days after the purchase was completed, McNiff was slow off the mark, complaining – with some justification, one would have thought – that, apart from anything else, his instructions contained no point of commencement. Once this was provided, McNiff went to work and laid the survey before the board on 30 July. However, even after the native land had been bought, the Land Board was not much better off. In the absence of any roads to speak of, lots that fronted

water were a virtual necessity. The only vacant ones were in the New Settlement on Lake Erie, where, as McNiff was to report to the board in 1790, there were many abandoned farms and, to add to the general confusion, numerous unauthorized transfers of land. In response to a call from the Land Board for holders of the original location tickets to exchange them for certificates, only about a third came forward to claim their lots. Apart from such waterfront lots that had become available in the New Settlement, there were few others worth settling. The land at the southern end of the Detroit River had long been settled by officers of the Indian Department and other Loyalists. Then, moving north and then clockwise, came the native reserve, the old French settlement, and the Huron Church Reserve, while the land fronting the south shore of Lake St. Clair to the mouth of the Thames was also taken up and there were squatters on the Thames itself (see figure 6.1).

It was not until 1793 that the first steps were taken to locate settlers on the back concessions, by which time Upper Canada had been formed and the jurisdiction of the Land Board confined to the new counties of Essex and Kent. On 5 February 1793 the Land Board instructed McNiff to lay out the land inland south of the Huron Church reserve. His report, of which part appears below, speaks volumes about the nature of the terrain he had to squelch through:

I did on the 13th of February last commence between the Church Land and the Indian Reserve and run back S28d, 30E. the distance of six concessions, at which distance the land proved so wet and swampy could not continue that line to its end. I therefore proceeded to the head line of the third concession and run it to a distance of nine miles marking and numbering the lots as I went, chiefly low wet land, few lots fit for culture. That line ended, I commenced at the head line of the 4th concession, and run it to the end of the 14th lot

which terminated in a swamp full of water ... I then commenced at the head line of the 5th concession and continued it to the end of the 8th lot ending in a swamp.[10]

McNiff then had a look at the land farther back from the Lake St. Clair shore, land intersected by several north-flowing rivers. He suggested a departure from the standard dimensions for 200-acre lots – as had by now been laid down in Simcoe-Smith's checkered township plan – which involved a narrower frontage on the respective rivers and their tributaries, with the 200 acres arrived at by increasing the depths of lots, though even so, he pointed out, most lots would include a sizeable acreage of swamp. Following up his suggestion, the board ordered him on 29 March 1793 to make the survey, with a reminder not to forget the clergy and crown reserves. His survey marked the beginnings of what would become the townships of Maidstone, Rochester, and Tilbury North. His report of 11 April 1793 again says much about the land. McNiff says that the tributaries "with their very serpentine courses, render it impossible to front lots on any of them, without crossing them [the lots] in several places."[11] Not exactly the easiest land to survey and lay out.

In his report on another survey he made shortly after, in response to a petition from the inhabitants of the old French settlements to have a second concession run behind them, McNiff again speaks of being "obstructed by the marshes ... which marshes," he continues, "I could not pass either with, or without a canoe – there being not sufficient water for a canoe, and the mudd too soft to pass on foot."[12] As it turned out, McNiff's "mudd" had enormous agricultural potential, though it would be many years before draining would allow that potential to be realized. And there in his "mudd," we must leave an increasingly exasperated McNiff, at least for the time being.

While Simcoe's scheme of granting townships was destined to run into trouble, so was the basic land-granting procedure as outlined in his proclamation. It will be recalled that bona fide settlers received their land free of expenses, except for the fees connected with the processing of their deeds or patents. These fees went to augment the somewhat meagre salaries of the various officials involved. On the processing of a single claim, no less than nine officials got a cut. Thus for a patent on the standard grant of 200 acres, the patentee had to pay £4. This was distributed on a descending scale from £1 10s., which went to the keeper of the Great Seal, down to the governor's secretary who got a shilling per patent issued. The fees went up with the size of the grant.

While from the officials' point of view these fees added up nicely, for the possibly impoverished settler the fee for patenting his land, small though it was, was an expense he preferred to avoid. So after having obtained his location ticket, he often left it at that. Very soon, a trade in location tickets developed, with speculators acquiring them in order to build up their holdings, among them various undesirables frowned on by the authorities. With the idea of screening these out more efficiently, the land boards, originally established in 1788 to rule on the eligibility of would-be emigrants, were abolished as of 6 November 1794. The responsibility for making such rulings was transferred, at least as far as the run-of-the-mill 200-acre grants were concerned, to local magistrates, who, as officers of the Crown under their respective county lieutenants, might be expected to act more zealously. In order to assign his lot to a settler, all that the deputy surveyor required was the recommendation of a magistrate. In unusual cases, petitions were to be dealt with by the lieutenant-governor or his executive council. However, this system didn't work either, as magistrates proved to be even less efficient at screening applicants than the land boards. It was effective for only a year. Finally, in the hope of bringing the land-granting process under control, Simcoe issued a proclamation on 21 August 1795 calling in all outstanding location tickets or certificates of occupation for their replacement by legal patents.

From henceforth all petitions were to be addressed directly to the lieutenant-governor-in-council. While this may have led to more careful screening of those petitioning for land, the result was a bottleneck in the land-granting procedures. This, together with growing confusion over land titles and the still undecided future of the townships granted under Simcoe's nominee scheme, amounted to a major problem that landed in the lap of Simcoe's successor.

Early in February 1793, with both the Americans and his new capital in mind, Simcoe set off with Smith, five other officers, and twenty men to inspect the location of his proposed capital and the defences at Detroit. Detroit was duly reached and on the way, Simcoe, as his wife put it, "was confirmed in his opinion that the forks of the Thames is the most proper scite for the capital of the country, to be called New London on a fine dry plain without underwood but abounding in good oak trees."[13] Simcoe was away for five weeks, having walked most of the way to Detroit and back, a total distance of some 600 miles (nearly 1000 km). Having dispatched a surveyor to the first

Joseph Bouchette. He made the first survey of Toronto harbour in 1792. Appointed surveyor general of Lower Canada in 1804, he died in 1841. *Courtesy: AOLS Archives*

Joseph Bouchette

Born in Quebec in 1774, Joseph was the son of Commodore Jean Bouchette, who swore allegiance to the British crown after the fall of New France and commanded British naval forces on Lake Ontario from 1783 until his death in 1804. Joseph followed in his father's footsteps and joined the navy. In about 1790 he started working as a draughtsman in the office of the surveyor general, Holland being his uncle. Until 1796 he carried out hydrographic surveys of the most important harbours on Lake Ontario, that of Toronto included, combining the career of a surveyor with that of a naval officer. When the provincial navy was partially reduced, he switched to the army. Holland died in 1801, and Bouchette succeeded him as surveyor general of Lower Canada in 1804. At the end of the War of 1812, he was nominated by the British to preside over the commission set up to resolve differences over the Canada–United States boundary. Later he produced and published several maps and in 1831 published *The British Dominions in North America*. He died in Montreal in April 1841.

fork of the Thames, Simcoe then took his first look at Toronto. He had already ordered a survey of its harbour, which had been completed by Joseph Bouchette late in November 1792. There, too, he was well pleased with what he found. On his arrival back in Newark in mid-May, he wrote:

> I lately ... examined this harbour ... and upon minute examination I found it to be without comparison the most proper situation for an arsenal in every extent of that word that can be met with in this province ... At the bottom of the harbour [i.e., at the eastern end] there is a situation admirably adapted for a naval arsenal and dock yard and there [is a] river [the Don] the banks of which are covered with excellent timber. Upon this river I purpose to build a sawmill ... I have fixed upon the scite for a town on the main shore – and another [for] barracks for the King's troops."[14]

The following month, on 26 June, he ordered Aitken and Jones to lay out the southern part of the township of York and lay out a town on the north side of Toronto harbour. It will be recalled that, in 1790, Frey had been ordered to lay the eleven townships west of the Trent, which he failed to do. Jones, stepping in to do the job the next year, followed the general lie of

the Lake Ontario shore, and fronted his townships on a general bearing of S74°W. This was fine until he reached the last two townships of the series, then called Glasgow (renamed Scarborough by Simcoe) and Dublin (renamed York). With the shoreline suddenly veering to the south, Jones found that his line through Scarborough Township was taking him farther and farther from the lake. By the time he reached the township's western boundary he found he was some 3.5 miles (5.5 km) from the lake. So Jones then turned left 90 degrees, ran the Glasgow-Dublin boundary (now Victoria Park Avenue) to the lake, and continued westward on his old bearing – along what is now Queen Street – across Dublin Township, the western boundary of which he placed on a line that ran north and south through today's High Park.

When Aitken laid out his town as instructed by Simcoe in June 1793 (Jones, it is thought, was busy running the concessions at the time), he naturally established the east-west axis of his town on the magnetic bearing that Jones had used when he ran the front of Dublin (York) Township. Correspondingly, the north-south axis followed the bearing of the township boundaries – bearings, it may be added, that are perpetuated in the orientation of the principal streets of present-day downtown Toronto. Aitken's plan for York called for ten blocks, with lots one chain wide and two chains deep, bounded on the north and south by what are now Adelaide and Front streets, with Ontario Street on the

west and George Street on the east.

In late July 1793, men of the Queen's Rangers arrived on the site from Niagara and started clearing the land (Simcoe had managed to get his old regiment resuscitated before he left England), and with that the modern history of Toronto may be said to have begun. Apart from the men of the Rangers, the first residents of Toronto were the Simcoes themselves, who had their famous canvas house erected there, in which they lived for the rest of the summer of 1793, throughout the next winter, and into the spring of 1794. An arrangement, it might be added, that hardly speeded the task of government, whose officials were loathe to leave the comfort of their homes in Newark.

Late in July 1793 Mrs. Simcoe arrived from Newark to join her husband in Toronto. The following Sunday, the couple went exploring. Walking on the "Peninsula" they came across "Mr. Grant's [the surveyor's] boat. It was not much larger than a canoe but we ventured into it & after rowing a mile we came within sight of what is named in the map the high lands of Toronto. The shore is extremely bold & has the appearance of chalk cliffs but I believe they are only white sand. They appeared so well that we talked of building a summer residence there and calling it Scarborough."[15] And so the Scarborough Bluffs and Scarborough itself were named.

By this time, news had reached Upper Canada that Britain was once more at war with France. The French Revolution had broken out in 1789, and while it was welcomed in republican America, it was decried in Britain, which reacted in horror to the Reign of Terror and the death of Louis XVI under the guillotine. Having invaded Holland, France declared war on Britain on 1 February 1793. This was the start of what became the Napoleonic Wars, which, except for one short break, were to go on for twenty-two years and which, with the aftermath, were to have a profound effect on the settlement and development of the province of Upper Canada.

Late in August 1793 the news reached Upper Canada that the Duke of York, George III's second son and then commander-in-chief of the British army, had emerged victorious in a series of rather minor engagements with the French. Simcoe renamed Toronto "York" in his honour on 26 August 1793. (York reverted to its old name of Toronto when the town was incorporated in 1834.) The outbreak of war with France added a new sense of urgency to the task of making the province defensible. The Americans, already in sympathy with revolutionary France, were soon vociferously denouncing Britain for interfering with American commerce in the West Indies, where, on the outbreak of war, the Royal Navy had quickly instituted a blockade of the French West Indies. With the increasing possibility that the Americans would invade the province, so increased the need for better communications with the southwest.

And so on 23 September 1793 a party of a hundred Rangers started to clear a road that eventually was to reach the Thames. It took them only a week to cut the first 20 miles (32 km) – to where Port Credit is today – of what Simcoe had already named Dundas Street after Henry Dundas, the British secretary of state for war and the colonies. The survey of Dundas Street, commonly known as "The Governor's Road" and which much later became Highway 5, became associated primarily with the name of Augustus Jones, who worked on it for two years. Observed Mrs. Simcoe: "From what has been surveyed, it is proved that [Pierre] Charlevoix, the French explorer's map, describes the country with great truth. If the line from the road to the river La Tranche was laid down according to its true bearings on any map but Charlevoix's, it would strike Lake Erie instead of La Tranche."[16] Which tells us something, not only about the superior quality of French maps but about Mrs. Simcoe's breadth of expertise as well.

Two days after the Rangers left to start work on the new road, the indefatigable Simcoe left with a party of soldiers and some natives to explore the Toronto Passage. Overtaking the advance party on the Humber, Simcoe and his men portaged to what was then called the Missisaga Creek and which Simcoe renamed Holland River after Samuel Holland. From here they travelled to Lac au Claies, which Simcoe renamed Lake Simcoe in memory of his father, Captain John Simcoe. Simcoe and his party reached Georgian Bay via Lake Couchiching and the Matchedash River (the Severn), eventually returning to Toronto by the same route, with Simcoe returning on foot from "the Pine Fort" on the east branch of the Holland River, following the route that Yonge Street would take when it was begun a year later.

In all his comings and goings, Simcoe was to attend the annual sessions of the provincial legislature, besides presiding over numerous meetings of his executive council. He would not only set up the basic apparatus of government and the legal system, but a multiplicity of other matters had to be attended to if the province was to become a going concern – everything from the regularization of marriages performed in earlier days without benefit of clergy, to millers' tolls, to placing a bounty on wolves. Arrangements also had to be made to regulate the medical and legal professions. The first statutes were passed regarding the building and maintenance of highways and roads. These became the responsibility of local authorities, a system which kept, in the words of one historian, "the roads of this Province a disgrace to civilization for a century."

Late in 1793, Lord Dorchester returned to Canada only to pour cold water on several of Simcoe's schemes, including his new capital and the fortification of his "arsenal" at York. In any case, Simcoe had more immediate problems on his mind. War with the United States seemed likely. Dorchester ordered Simcoe to rebuild Fort Miamis on the Maumee River (where Toledo now stands), an old fort dating from the Revolutionary War. Simcoe went down to Detroit to see to this, returning by ship to Fort Erie. It was a nerve-racking spring and summer, as all available men and guns were sent to Detroit, gunboats were built on the Thames, and ships on the Great Lakes were placed on a wartime footing. Mrs. Simcoe and the children were packed off to Quebec for safety, and there was even talk of shifting the provincial capital to Cornwall should the Americans invade.

The climax came in late August. An American general, Anthony Wayne, and his 3000-man army defeated a mixed force of natives and renegade Loyalists at the Battle of Fallen Timbers, not far from Fort Miamis. The Americans then surrounded the fort in the hopes of intimidating its small garrison and forcing its surrender. But the British under Major William Campbell stood firm, and after a show of strength Wayne went away. From then on tensions were to ease, especially after Jay's Treaty was signed in November. Under the terms of the treaty, Britain agreed to evacuate the western posts by 1 June 1796, while the Americans were to set up a commission to look into the debts, outstanding since the Revolutionary War, owed to Britain and the Loyalists. The Mississippi was to remain open to both nations, and traders would have free access to western land on both sides of the border. Joint commissions would be established to try and settle outstanding differences over the international boundary, with that between Maine and New Brunswick the first to be given attention. In the United States, the war hawks, eager for war with Britain, greeted the news of the treaty with howls of rage, with even Washington himself booed in the streets. They would make their voice heard again less than two decades later in 1812.

By 1796 it had become abundantly clear that many of the nominees who had applied for and obtained townships under Simcoe's township granting scheme had done so for solely speculative purposes; the scheme was a failure. So in May of that year Simcoe proclaimed that those nominees who had failed to produce settlers would forfeit their townships, giving them until 1 June 1797 to produce evidence to the contrary. Otherwise their townships would be thrown open to general settlement.

However, Simcoe's scheme, in a roundabout fashion, brought William Berczy and his German settlers to Upper Canada, where they came to be associated with the beginning of Yonge Street and the founding of what is now Markham. German-born and a man of many talents – as a painter he exhibited at the Royal Academy in London – he became involved with the Genesee Association, set up by some British speculators to bring settlers to the Genesee country in New York state. Arriving there with some 200 German emigrants Berczy found the local agent to be unco-operative, so he went to New York where he helped form the German Company, together with some men who had already bought three townships in Upper Canada. Berczy then went to Newark where, in April 1794, he petitioned for a grant of a million acres on the north shore of Lake Erie. He was awarded 64 000 acres west of the Grand River, with a promise of more land to come. However, Simcoe diverted Berczy and his settlers eastward to speed the growth of York, offering him a township to the north of it.

Meanwhile, early in 1794, anxious as he was to see a "road of communication" built from York to Lake Simcoe, Simcoe had ordered Augustus Jones to survey and map the route. This done, a start was made on laying out the townships of Markham and Vaughan. These were opposite each other and fronted the line of the proposed road. And it was to Markham that Berczy and his settlers came, where, by November 1794, they were finally located by Abraham Iredell, then newly commissioned, who had surveyed the township as far back as the seventh concession. In the meantime, a start had been made on cutting out the road by the Queen's Rangers, but as the war crisis deepened during the summer of 1794, they were withdrawn for sterner duties at Niagara and Detroit. So, in September,

Simcoe contracted the work of opening the road to Berczy, who was given a year to put it through to the Pine Fort. What with sickness among his settlers, who were hard pressed anyway to set their settlement on its feet, Berczy failed to complete the work on time. His settlement was to go through some very hard times, and when in May 1796 Simcoe decided to foreclose on all those who had acquired townships and whose obligations remained unfulfilled, Berczy lost his land – a perceived injustice that he was to fight until he died in New York in 1813.

With Berczy's failure to open up the road by September 1794, the task reverted to government, with Jones again put on the job. By now, Simcoe had decided to name the road "Yonge Street" after his friend Sir George Yonge, a rather shadowy figure who was then secretary of state for war and who had been the M.P. for Honiton in Devon where the Simcoes lived in England. Thus on 18 February 1796 Mrs. Simcoe wrote: "The party who were to cut the road ... called the Yonge Street, are returned after an absence of seven weeks. The distance is 33 miles and 56 chains."[17] Two days later, Jones himself recorded that he "had waited on His Excellency the Governor, and informed him that Yonge Street is opened from York to Pine Fort Landing, Lake Simcoe."[18] The "Pine Fort" became Gwillimbury, Gwillim being Mrs. Simcoe's maiden name, and that name also lives on in the township names of East and West Gwillimbury.

On 1 December 1795 Simcoe applied for a leave of absence on grounds of ill health. But there was more to it than that. His relations with Dorchester had become increasingly sour as the former vetoed many of his schemes. And after the danger of war with the United States eased in November 1794, Dorchester had withdrawn all troops from Upper Canada, save for the Rangers and the men of the Royal Artillery. With all his Rangers required for garrison duties, Simcoe's many

plans became even more difficult to carry out. Furthermore, his idea of building a new capital had hardly endeared him to the influential merchants of Kingston, who saw their own town in that role. Even Simcoe's proposal to free the slaves in the province (as had already been accomplished in Britain) met widespread opposition from the many Loyalists who "owned" them. In the end he had to be content with a compromise that forbade any further importation of slaves.

With his leave of absence granted, Simcoe left York for Quebec and England on 21 July 1796, having the day before appointed the sixty-three-year-old Peter Russell, by this time the senior executive councillor, to take over in his absence. Simcoe officially remained lieutenant-governor of Upper Canada until April 1799, but he never returned. After military service in the West Indies and in England, he was on his way in 1808 to join a British force in Portugal when he became ill and was taken back to England; here he died shortly after his arrival. Elizabeth Simcoe survived him by forty-four years.

While Simcoe remains a controversial figure, the fact remains that in only four and a half years he set Upper Canada on its feet. For much of what we now take for granted we have Simcoe to thank. His Dundas and Yonge streets, radiating from the hub that was York, marked the beginnings of a road system that would open up the central and southwestern regions of the province, with York itself emerging as its capital. He left Upper Canada with a workable system of government, and, thanks to his insistence, the province acquired its own surveyor general. This key decision led to the founding of the Office of the Surveyor General, the government department that would play the principal role in the orderly settlement of the province for the next half century. And in his choice of David Smith as Upper Canada's first surveyor general, Simcoe left that office in the capable hands of an energetic, honest, and public-spirited man.

CHAPTER EIGHT

Before and During the War of 1812

Peter Russell, who became administrator of Upper Canada when Simcoe left, had been a soldier. He had met Simcoe during the American Revolutionary War, and it was on Simcoe's recommendation that he was appointed receiver and auditor general of the new province, to emerge, as already mentioned, as the senior executive councillor at the time of Simcoe's departure, Russell then being fifty-nine.

The British evacuation of the American forts, stipulated in Jay's Treaty to take place by 1 June 1796, more or less coincided with Simcoe's departure and went off without incident. When Detroit became American, a number of its citizens chose to remain British subjects, crossing the river to live on the Canadian side. Patrick McNiff was not among them. When the land boards were abolished in November 1794, McNiff was informed that his services would no longer be required. A year later he became involved in a huge land speculation scheme in northern Ohio, which failed. He died in Detroit as an American citizen a few years later – a curious end for a surveyor who had done so much in earlier days to further the first Loyalist settlements along the St. Lawrence.

One of the residents of Detroit whose name appeared on a list of 118 who elected for British citizenship in 1796 was Abraham Iredell, who had first been appointed a deputy surveyor in 1794. He was asked to lay out the town of Sandwich, which Peter Russell had instructed should be built to accommodate the citizens who had crossed the river. The proposed site was the Huron Church Reserve, which Russell directed should be bought from the Hurons. This was eventually done in 1800 when over a thousand acres was bought from the Hurons for 300 pounds, leaving them with only 60 or so acres near their church. Meanwhile Iredell laid out Sandwich in 1797, now part of Windsor.

In spite of opposition from officials, Russell insisted on carrying out Simcoe's plan to move the seat of government from Newark to York and to enlarge the town of York. So in 1796 Chewett was instructed to extend the town westward. In making his survey he had great difficulty in locating any of the marks and monuments from Aitken's earlier survey, so much so that D.W. Smith posted a notice, dated 8 November 1796, that read in part: "Whoever shall attempt to move or throw down any Boundary will be prosecuted with as much vigor as the law permits – and if any person throws down a boundary by accident in clearing his lot, he is to make immediate application to the surveyor's office there to have it fixed in its proper place."[1]

Smith himself had built a house at the corner of King and Ontario streets, which he named Maryville Lodge. And here, in the northwest corner of the lodge, he set up his office, where he was assisted by William Chewett, his deputy, and a minuscule staff headed by Thomas Ridout as chief clerk. Chewett acquired two of the town plots in York: one at the southeast corner of present-day King and York and the other just east of York on what is now Wellington. On this last site he built his family home for himself, his wife Isabella, and their three children, one of whom, James Grant Chewett, would follow in his father's footsteps, as did so many land surveyors' children. James was to receive his commission in 1819. Ridout's son, Samuel, also qualified as a land surveyor, in 1806, though it seems he did little work in the field. Taken on by his father to work in the office, he was to serve as his chief clerk until his father died in 1829. From these small – one might say "family" – beginnings the Surveyor General's Office was to grow in the next fifty years into what would become the province's most powerful arm of government. It was the only arm of the provincial government that dealt solely in land matters, and these were the very stuff of the settlement process by which the province was to grow.

The duties of the office were manifold. It reported on petitions for land received by the lieutenant-governor-in-council. On these being verified, the surveyor general would order the requisite surveys, preparing the

View of Maryville Lodge, Toronto, Smith's home and office

D.W. Smith, Upper Canada's first surveyor general, worked out of his home, Maryville Lodge, at the corner of King and Ontario streets. © Queen's Printer for Ontario. Reproduced with permission of the Ministry of Natural Resources.

formal instructions by which the surveys were initiated and issuing them to a deputy surveyor. On completion of the survey, the results had to be entered and checked for accuracy, and, if necessary, a check survey was ordered. All being well, a plan was drawn, and a formal description of the parcel was drawn up for the patent or deed, copies of which were made, entered in the books, and duly forwarded to the persons concerned. The surveyor general and his staff had other duties as well. There were annual returns to be made of patents issued, while the treasurers of each district also required annual returns in connection with tax assessment. And there were to be other returns of one sort or another, as required by the legislature, besides regular returns of vacant or grantable lands required by the lieutenant-governor himself. All these activities, without which the orderly settlement of the province could not go forward, rested ultimately on the land surveyors. As we have seen them so far – warts and all – they were men as other men, plying their skills as best they knew how.

Though Russell and Smith did not get along that well, between them they did what they could to improve the arrangements for land settlement. In June 1797 an Heirs and Devises Commission was set up to enquire into the state of Simcoe's township grants. Smith had discovered that only six of over thirty such townships had significant numbers of settlers on them. Berczy's and other township grants had already been cancelled by Simcoe. The commission now rescinded all of them, opening them to general settlement, with compensation only where there had been actual settlement. This took the form of a 1200-acre grant to those proprietors who could show that they had brought in a significant number of settlers, provided that they, the proprietors, became residents of the province.

One of these proprietors had been Asa Danforth, who had been granted four townships in what became Northumberland County. He now claimed he had placed over two hundred settlers in his townships – and was duly granted 1200 acres. However, he then joined a group led by William Berczy who were taking legal action against the executive council for granting land in townships they regarded as theirs, whereupon an angry council rescinded Danforth's grant. A year or so later Danforth apologized for his action and got his 1200 acres back. Meanwhile, two of his settlers had complained that he had substituted his name for theirs on lots they had settled and improved. An investigation into Danforth's townships followed, as the result of which Danforth and his associates were accused of fraud.

In the middle of this imbroglio, Russell awarded a contract to Danforth to build a road from York to what is now Trenton. The first step in making such a road (first mooted by Simcoe as an easterly extension of his Dundas Road) was taken in the summer of 1798 by the legislative assembly, which, after exhaustive discussion, sent Russell a report that outlined ways and means of building the road. In March 1799, Asa Danforth offered to build it. Surprisingly – considering he was already at odds with the provincial government – he got the contract, which called for its completion by 1 July 1800. John Stegman began surveying the western section of the road in April 1799. It began at the end of King Street near the mouth of the Don River, eventually turned up present-day Kingston Road, turned north on Victoria Park Avenue – now the western boundary of the city of Scarborough – and then veered westward, following the route taken by the eastern portion of the Danforth Road today. The western portion of today's Danforth Road was not part of the original road.

Danforth started work in June 1799. By January 1800 he had completed about half of the 120-mile (193-km) road. Short of capital and with payment for his work slow in coming, Danforth returned to the United States in March of that year, where he was jailed for debt. Getting back to Upper Canada, he got an extension on his contract and finally completed what became known as the Danforth Road in

December 1800. The executive council found it wanting and withheld payment. After another brief sojourn in the States, Danforth came back to Upper Canada in 1801 in hopes of salvaging something from both his townships and his road. In this he was disappointed. Now an embittered man, he left Upper Canada for good in 1802, and when last seen in 1821, Asa Danforth was in New York, hiding from the sheriff.

Badly built as it was, his road – by which Danforth is so perversely remembered – soon deteriorated to the point at which stretches of it passed into disuse. In order to keep the road open, Danforth had suggested placing settlers along it, who could be made responsible for keeping it in a good state of repair. This was the principle of "colonization roads" that was so successful in opening up much of both southern and northern Ontario, and it is much to Danforth's credit that he conceived it. As it happened, there were only three settlers along the first 30 miles (48 km) of road, so Danforth's scheme came to nothing.

In 1798 Upper Canada's first survey act was brought in, an act upon which all subsequent survey acts in the province were based. Entitled An Act to Ascertain and Establish the Boundary Lines of the Different Townships of this Province, the act (38 Geo. 3, c. 1) provided for the planting of monuments of stone or other durable materials at the corners of townships and at governing points. These monuments would henceforth govern courses and distances, regardless of what these might have been in earlier grants and patents. The boundary markers were not to be planted as a matter of course but were to follow an inspection by the surveyor general, who would then apply to the lieutenant-governor for his sanction to erect the same. It was perhaps because of Smith's annoyance at having the "boundaries" in York disappear that the act came down so heavily on people tampering with the monuments: "If any person or persons," the act read, "shall, knowingly and wilfully, pull down, deface, alter or

remove any such monuments so erected, he, she, or they shall be adjudged guilty of a felony, and shall suffer death without benefit of clergy."

It was also in 1798 that Russell and Smith together brought in measures to tighten up the conditions imposed on a settler before a patent was granted. As of July 1794 the only requirement was that the land be occupied and a house built on it within a year. Largely on Smith's initiative, further conditions were imposed in 1798. These required that at least 5 acres be cleared and the land fenced. In line with this tough new policy, Smith ordered Jones in 1798 to report on the settlements along Yonge Street. Jones found much that needed doing, and in 1801 Stegman was ordered to make another inspection. The result was a voluminous report. Of the stretch flanking Markham Township, Stegman's comments ranged from a flat "Non-Compliance" (to the settlement regulations) to "Clearing completed with nothing done to the street." The road in front of many lots was apparently still littered with logs. Stegman expressed the opinion that "the most ancient inhabitants on Yonge Street have been the most neglectful [and] that some trifles [sic] with ... the Government in respect of clearing the Street."[2]

Earlier in the 1790s Stegman had worked in the eastern end of the province, where, among other things, he laid out part of Wolford and Montague townships, which lie astride the Rideau River above Smiths Falls. In the central part of the province he often worked in association with Jones. Thus in 1798 they both worked on Glanford, Burford, Oxford, and Blenheim townships, as well as on a stretch along the Niagara River. The year 1799 saw Stegman working on King Township, on Dundas Street, and on the Lakeshore Road, east of York. In the next couple of years, he was variously employed in laying out more concessions on the east side of Yonge Street and in reporting on the number of unclaimed lots in York Township and the condition of town plots in York itself. In 1801 Stegman also worked on a plan of part

of York and completed the township of Markham, which so far had been surveyed only as far back as the Sixth Concession. He also laid out the village of Coote's Paradise, later renamed Dundas. Without questioning the orders given to him by the Surveyor General's Office, he duly laid out the village in defiance of topography, with half the village on top of the Niagara Escarpment, the other half on the flats below. The year after that, he completed the survey of Whitchurch Township just north of Markham and, going back east, put in Finch and Elmsley townships just to the west of present-day Smiths Falls.

Still working in the east in 1803, Stegman made the surveys of what became Nepean, Osgoode, Gloucester, and North Gower. It was in Nepean that he found himself surveying in a "tedious swamp" as he put it in his report – nice phrase. In the course of this work he managed to produce a "phantom lot" through a survey error. This was an unnumbered lot in Concession B, Rideau Front, Nepean Township, the existence of which was first brought to light by John McNaughton when resurveying in Nepean Township in 1824–25. This lot led to a series of legal disputes that began in the mid-1840s and were not finally resolved until 1860.

By this time new names were appearing on the roster of deputy surveyors. One was William Fortune's son Joseph, commissioned in 1796. The father had laid out some half-a-dozen townships in the Rideau River District and he was an old man with dimming eyesight when Joseph joined him. Together they went on to subdivide parts of Alfred, Plantagenet, and East and West Hawkesbury in what is now the county of Prescott and Russell, the fronts of which McNiff had laid out in 1788. By 1805, William Fortune's name disappears from the official records, and it is thought that he died soon after, with his body eventually buried, some say, in Hawkesbury.

Thomas Walsh, sometimes spelled Welch, commissioned in 1793, was active on the Niagara

Peninsula and then in several townships in the vicinity of Long Point, where he settled in 1796 and where he was made registrar of deeds for Norfolk County. Later he would become a judge of the district and surrogate court. Born in 1775, Reuben Sherwood came to Upper Canada in 1784 with his Loyalist father, Thomas, who had taken up Lot 1 in the First Concession in Elizabethtown and thus claimed to be the first settler in that township. Reuben Sherwood was commissioned sometime in the late 1790s, exactly when it is not known. Retiring in 1820, he spent most of his working life in the townships at the eastern end of the province and was to number among his students several land surveyors who went on to make a name for themselves, among them Richard Birdsall, who was to become well known in the Peterborough area.

John Ryder, who had the unhappy distinction of having only one arm, was also the son of a Loyalist who had been granted land near Kingston. Commissioned in 1800, Ryder worked in and around Kingston and in Prince Edward County. He made the first survey of Bath, opposite Amherst Island, and, among other townships, he put in Marmora and Madoc in the interior of Hastings County in 1819 and 1820 respectively. By then, townships were being surveyed by contract; that for Madoc had actually been won by one Daniel McIntyre of York, who was given 1200 acres of land in payment, but he subcontracted Ryder to do the actual work. Ryder would continue to work until 1832, when he died at the age of fifty-seven from pneumonia – the result, it is said, of walking on ice in moccasins when on survey on Wolfe Island opposite Kingston.

Shown erroneously on the crown lands list of land surveyors issued in 1857 as being commissioned in 1813, Joseph Kilborn qualified in 1792. However, though he was licensed in Upper Canada, he did most of his work in the Eastern Townships, where Nathaniel Coffin was also employed when he was not surveying out of Kingston. Kilborn came from a long line of surveyors. His ancestors had come from England to settle in Connecticut in the early 1600s, where one of them acted as a land surveyor for most of his life, as did Kilborn's grandfather. Joseph's sister Polly married the land surveyor Reuben Sherwood, while his brother William became the father of yet another land surveyor, William Henry Kilborn, who was to be commissioned a land surveyor in 1821.

Meanwhile, what of Theodore De Pencier? Between 1792 and 1795 he had worked for the Royal Engineers near Sault Ste. Marie where he surveyed the strait formed by the St. Mary's River and St. Joseph Island. Unable as always to control his expenses, he ended these surveys out of pocket. He then went on to get even deeper into the red over other surveys in Lower Canada. From 1799 onward he got no further work from government, though he did work for local authorities in and about Sorel, while continuing to fight for the money he claimed the government owed him. By 1814, and by now probably insane, he became a recluse at his home in Sorel. There he died, it is thought in 1817, almost certainly the only Ontario surveyor to be driven out of his mind by the exacting demands of British civil service accountants.

Alexander Aitken was kept busy throughout the 1790s. He remains a somewhat shadowy figure. A dedicated surveyor and lifelong bachelor, he acquired a town plot in Kingston where he helped support his local church. After Simcoe's arrival he worked on the new town plan of York, and later years saw him working on Yonge and Dundas streets and the harbour at Penetanguishene. By the late 1790s his health started to give way. He seems to have had malaria, and his

---

Getting Squibby

Surveyors had at least the mental challenge of their exacting work to help them forget the sometimes appalling conditions in which they worked, but their axemen and chainmen had no such distraction from the hardships and monotony of their poorly paid jobs. Many took refuge in alcohol. To be fair, it should be remembered that diseases such as cholera were practically endemic, and it was thought that adding whiskey to water would reduce the risk of infection. In any case there was little that a surveyor could do about drinking if he wanted to keep his men happy. When Reuben Sherwood was engaged in 1819 in surveying the township of Nelson, in which Burlington now lies, and Nassagaweya, the township inland from it, he wrote in his diary (in part) as follows:

Monday, 25th February: A snowy morning, the party all employed in arranging for bread, axes, pease, etc. ... Gave the men one quart of whiskey in the morn, and gave them one quart of spirits on the way up.
Saturday, 14th March: Snowing again in the morning. I go out with the party and finish the 2nd concession line to 15 and road. Return again at 7 p.m.
Sunday, 15th March: A cold day. The boys go out and bring three packs of biscuits in, and all get drunk.
Tuesday, 23rd March: Go out and find all my men *squibby,* having drunk up my whiskey and their own, and they had not moved the camp.
Friday, 9th April: A fine day. We move down to the east angle of the township again to commence the town line.

Completing the survey of the two townships some nine weeks after he started, Sherwood set off for York to report to the surveyor general on 3 May. He returned eleven days later to settle his accounts. He found "all hands *squibby.*" (AC, "Biographical Sketch of Reuben Sherwood," in *APLS, 1886.*)

---

death was hastened by a fall from a carriole and then by tuberculosis. He died in Kingston in 1800, where he was buried in St. George's (now St. Paul's) cemetery. Poignantly, his land holdings, totalling some 1500 acres, were left to his father in the border country of Scotland, which he had left some fifteen years earlier.

The outstanding surveyor of the 1790s, indeed of the early history of Upper Canada, was Augustus Jones. Sometimes working alone, sometimes with others such as Stegman, he laid out over a quarter of the 101 townships (not counting Amherst Island) listed as wholly or partially surveyed by the end of 1799. These included a number of townships on the Niagara Peninsula and in the central part of the province, including York, Scarborough, and Pickering, and from the head of Lake Ontario to what became St. Thomas. He also explored the sources of the Thames, worked on both Yonge and Dundas streets as well as the Lake Shore Road, and in the Six Nation Reserve on the Grand River. But then, possibly because of his close association with the Six Nations (of which more below), no more government work came his way except for a resurvey of part of Dundas Street, which he was asked to do in 1825. Jones must have been singularly blessed with capable assistants. Even so, his was an astonishing performance – one only possible for a man of the extraordinary energy and iron constitution that Jones so obviously had. Even a broken collarbone, sustained when his horse threw him, did not deter Jones for long.

Closely associated with the Mohawk since he first worked in Upper Canada, Jones became a close friend of Joseph Brant, whose home in Wellington Square (now Burlington) was near Jones's home near Stoney Creek in Saltfleet Township, which he had laid out himself. In 1798 Jones married Sarah, the daughter of Tekarihogen, a Mohawk chief to whom Brant himself was related by marriage. Jones had eight children by Sarah and at least two others by another Sarah, daughter of a Mississauga chief – which lead much later to Jones being publicly denounced by Sir Francis Bond Head as an adulterer.

Nonetheless, Jones became Brant's and Tekarihogen's trusted ally and adviser in their fight against the authorities (and others of the Six Nations) for the right to sell or lease Six Nation land. Brant took the view that the Six Nation land was theirs to do what they liked with. In fact, deeds had been issued to various settlers since 1787. Others of the Six Nations took the traditional view that land was not just another commodity to be bought and sold. As government saw it, the Six Nations could only sell their land with the approval of the Crown, and after Simcoe arrived in 1791 matters became deadlocked when he refused Brant permission to sell. He feared the Six Nations would become prey to speculators, though he did go so far as to prepare a patent that gave the Crown first refusal on any sale. However, Brant refused it on principle, and there matters stood when Simcoe left.

Russell agreed with Simcoe, but eventually his hand was forced when Brant hinted that if the war with France spread to North America, Russell could not rely on the loyalty of the Six Nations. Brant had already been negotiating with various buyers; all that was required of Russell was for him to issue the necessary deeds. This he did, and on 5 February 1798 the Six Nations parted with six parcels of land on the upper reaches of the Grand amounting to over 380 000 acres, well over half the magnificent tract that they had acquired less than fifteen years earlier. It turned out that Simcoe had been right. The Six Nations got next to nothing for their land. They agreed to 30 cents an acre (in today's money), but they were not to receive even that.

Mennonites from Pennsylvania, on hearing of the sale of the Six Nation lands, formed what they called the German Company and hurried north to buy a 60 000-acre tract that had been sold to a Colonel Beasley for the price of £10 000. Beasley, however, had neglected to tell them that the land was mortgaged; it

Courtesy: AOLS Archives

Augustus Jones, the outstanding surveyor of the 1790s. Either working alone or with other surveyors, he laid out over a quarter of the townships surveyed by 1799. He also explored the sources of the Thames River and worked on Yonge and Dundas streets.

was not until 1805 that, with government intervention, the German Company finally obtained clear title to the land. The company went on to acquire another of the Six Nation parcels, this to the north of the first. As with every one of the original six parcels, there were difficulties over legal ownership. When these were ironed out, the Mennonites added another 45 000

Courtesy: Scarborough Archives

Thought to have been built between 1793 and 1795, Augustus Jones's cabin still stands on its original site in Scarborough, now in the grounds of the Guild Inn. (From the Richard Schofield Historical Collection, Scarborough Archives.)

Street. The three others were Brighton and Murray, both fronting Lake Ontario just west of present-day Trenton, and Harwich Township fronting Lake Erie where Rondeau Provincial Park is now situated. In 1801 only one township survey was ordered, this being the completion of Markham Township, while in the next three years only three new townships were opened up: Whitchurch, North Gwillimbury, and Dover fronting the western shore of Lake St. Clair, these in 1802, 1803, and 1804 respectively. And only two new townships followed in 1805, South Gosfield on Lake Erie and Uxbridge to the east of Whitchurch.

Hunter also identified a major bottleneck in the land-granting system in the person of William Jarvis, the provincial secretary. The underpaid Jarvis was unwilling to spend the time required to process land patents because he lost money doing so, the scale of fees being what they were. While reprimanding Jarvis, Hunter introduced a new scale of fees, which almost doubled them. They now came to nearly 5 pounds sterling on the standard 200-acre lot. Hunter also introduced a measure that required the prompt payment of fees. Thus a settler had only three days to pay the fee after his grant was confirmed, and three weeks to take out – and pay for – a patent once it had been drawn up. However, while these measures pleased the officials involved, the higher fees were not exactly welcomed by would-be settlers. A faster settlement process was achieved only by abandoning the more stringent settlement conditions that Smith had laboured to bring in.

Hunter also tried to reduce the amount of land that was being doled out as free grants to those on the U.E. list. He ordered a drastic revision of the list, which resulted in nearly a thousand names being struck off. At the same time he placed a time limit on claims. Those not appearing before a commission set up to examine claims would forfeit their land. These last measures provoked howls of rage throughout the province, and, after Hunter's death, no time was lost in

acres to their holdings in an area that included the future cities of Kitchener and Waterloo. They subdivided the land themselves, resulting in anomalies in the survey fabric. As a result, Waterloo is still shown as a blank on crown township maps.

◦◦◦

In 1799 Peter Hunter was appointed to succeed Simcoe as lieutenant-governor of Upper Canada. As an army man through and through, he was to run Upper Canada – as historians are wont to put it – as just another regiment. With Britain at war, Hunter's prime responsibility was the safety of Canada, and he spent

much of his time in Quebec. Despite his long absences from the province, Hunter accomplished much – though his forthright approach to problem-solving did little to endear him to his subordinates. He gave high priority to dealing with the shortcomings in the land settlement process.

For a start, he decreed that no new townships should be opened up until those already surveyed were fully occupied. As a result, the number of new townships fell from eleven in 1799 to six in 1800, three of them in the vicinity of a rapidly growing York to which settlers were now flocking: Scarborough, King, and East Gwillimbury at the northern end of Yonge

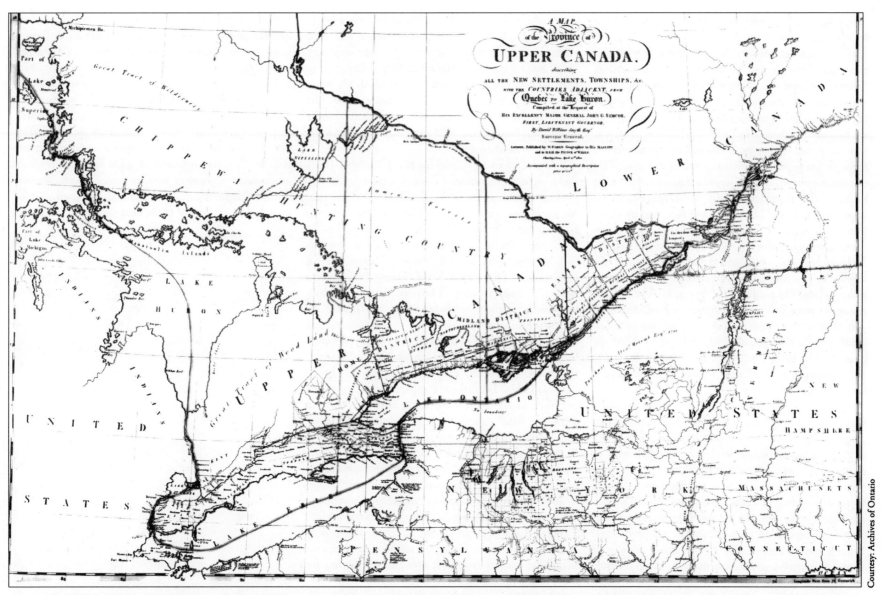

Upper Canada in 1800, originally compiled by D.W. Smith at Simcoe's request. Much of the western part of southern Ontario is still a blank described as a "Great Tract of Wood Land."
Northern Ontario (a "Great Tract of Wilderness") is noted as being "Chippewa Hunting Country." (AO, Cartographic Records Collection A-9, Repro. no. 492.)

removing the time limit, and some years later the U.E. list was again opened up.

As a soldier responsible for the safety of the province, Hunter was much alive to the need, as Simcoe had been, for improving communications both within and into the province; he pushed, for example, for the completion of the Danforth Road, though, as we have seen, it wasn't to be of much use even after it was completed. However, in 1801 a new road was cut through Scarborough Township nearer the lake. This was the beginning of the Kingston Road. Incorporating parts of the Danforth Road, a straightened and improved road would link York and Kingston by 1817. Hunter also ordered Colonel Mann to make an immediate inspection of the system of canals and locks on the St. Lawrence, which Haldimand had built a quarter of a century earlier. Mann found these to be in serious need of upgrading. On receiving his report, Hunter ordered repairs to some locks on the system, the rebuilding of part of the canal system, and the construction of a new canal near Île des Cascades, which began in 1804. In charge of the project was John By, a twenty-five-year-old lieutenant in the Royal Engineers, whom Upper Canada was to see again.

Hunter, who had been suffering from gout and stomach ailments for some time, died suddenly in August 1805. Peter Russell had hopes that he would again be appointed administrator, but the post went to Alexander Grant, an elderly naval officer, who was soon superseded by a new lieutenant-governor, Francis Gore, who arrived in 1806. In any case, Russell's influence was on the wane. In his seventies, without a pension, and unable to cash in on his land holdings, Russell couldn't even afford the passage money to England, so he lingered on as attorney general, eventually dying in York in 1808.

Smith's influence, too, had waned, and his attempts to tighten up on the settlement regulations had made him unpopular with the larger landowners. His Irish wife, whose looks Elizabeth Simcoe had so

much admired, had died in 1798 at the age of only twenty-eight. Though Smith's competence had even been praised by Hunter, who was a hard man to please, Smith saw no future for himself in Upper Canada and went back to England on sick leave in 1802. He never came back. In England he remarried, became the chief administrator of the Duke of Northumberland's estates, was knighted in 1821, and died near Alnwick, Northumberland, in 1837.

According to an official list dated 25 April 1805, there were then fourteen deputy surveyors in the province (see appendix A). Interestingly enough, Augustus Jones's name is on the list, *persona non grata* as he apparently was. The others, in no particular order, were William Fortune (nearing the end of his life), his son Joseph, Abraham Iredell, Thomas Welch, Lewis Grant, Richard Cockerell, Henry Smith, John Ryder, Aaron Greeley, Thomas Fraser, Reuben Sherwood, Solomon Stevens, and Samuel Wilmot.

Wilmot was to become one of the busiest and most widely known of early land surveyors. His family had left England to settle in Connecticut in the seventeenth century. When the Revolutionary War broke out, his father, Lemuel, was apparently living in the province of New York, where Samuel was born in 1774. His father joined a Loyalist regiment commanded by Beverly Robinson, whose sons, John Beverly and Peter, would both achieve prominence in Upper Canada in the years to come. Perhaps this connection with the Robinson family was what brought Samuel Wilmot to Upper Canada in 1796, where he settled in Richmond Hill. Two years later he married Mary Stegman, John Stegman's eldest daughter. Presumably about the same time, he started studying land surveying under his father-in-law, eventually receiving his commission in 1804.

In 1808, after working in several townships north of York, Wilmot made the first exploratory surveys around Penetanguishene where a naval base would be established. Three years later, in 1811, he surveyed the

first line for a new road that would connect Penetanguishene with the head of Kempenfeldt Bay on Lake Simcoe, a road, it might be added, that was urged on the government by the North West Company, irate at American customs officers at Niagara who took to interfering with the company's cargoes. The company had already contributed £12,000 in 1799 towards improving Yonge Street. The road link between Penetanguishene and Lake Simcoe would be a further step in the improvement of what was essentially a modernized version of the Toronto Passage. Wilmot finished his survey in 1812 and laid out town plots at each end of it. One of them became Barrie, the other,

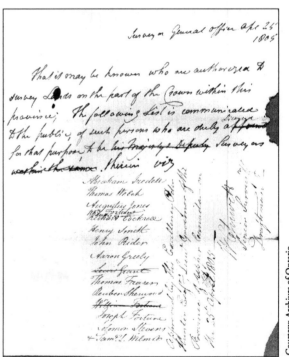

List of authorized surveyors, dated 25 April 1805. Possibly a draft, it is signed by William Chewett, who describes himself as "Senior Surveyor and Draftsman." Few such lists still survive. (AO, RG1, CB-1, Box 43, Miscellaneous Records.)

Penetanguishene. In 1814 Wilmot's road was built by the military, while a start was made that same year on building a naval base at Penetanguishene.

Sadly, John Stegman's name is also missing from the 1805 list of surveyors. He had been drowned the previous fall in the line of duty. In 1804 Stegman had become an "expert witness" in connection with a murder that had taken place at a trading post on an island on Lake Skugog, north of Oshawa. The manager of the post had been murdered by a Mississauga, apparently in retaliation for the earlier killing by a white man of his brother, about which the authorities had done little or nothing. A Mississauga chief discovered the identity of the murderer and handed him over to the authorities. The accused's lawyer argued that the trial could not be held in York because the crime had been committed in the district of Newcastle.

And this is where Stegman comes into the picture. In August 1804 he was ordered to establish the precise position of the murder site in relation to the boundary line of York with Newcastle. On 6 August 1804 he drew and signed for what were probably his last office supplies: "Two sheets of drawing paper, two blank memorandum books – 1 quire paper & 2 black lead pencils."[3] Pencils were valuable in those days. He carried out the survey and on 28 August 1804 he wrote what was probably his last survey report.

> Gentleman,
> In obedience to your Instruction bearing date the 15th inst. have the honore [sic] to report that the same is complied with. That the exact and positive situation of the house of Moody Farwell [the murder site] is seven miles eastward of the division line between the townships of Whitby and Darlington and that all the oeconomy [sic] of time and expenses have been made use of. The protraction of the work will shew the real situation.
> I am with respect, gentleman,
> Your most obedient and humble servent [sic]
> John Stegmann
> Dy. Surveyor[4]

As a result of Stegman's survey, the court was ordered reconvened at Smithfield, not far west of Trenton. Accordingly, all concerned – including the prisoner, the solicitor general, the high constable, the judge, and various witnesses, including Stegman – embarked on the *Speedy*, a government schooner, to make the trip to Brighton, the nearest port to Smithfield. Sailing on 7 October 1804 and last seen the following evening off Presqu'ile, the *Speedy* foundered in a storm that same night and took all on board with her, an event now commemorated by a provincial plaque at the eastern tip of Presqu'ile Provincial Park.* And so, in these somewhat bizarre circumstances, died one of the province's equally bizarre, if endearing, land surveyors.

On 13 April 1795 John Collins died suddenly at his house in St. Louis Street in Quebec and was buried in St. Louis Gate Cemetery, which is no longer in existence. His name is commemorated in Collins Street in Quebec and in Collins Bay near Kingston. But perhaps his most fitting memorial is the plaque in Kingston that marks the beginning of the first crown survey (under civil authority) in what is now Ontario.

Samuel Holland died on 28 December 1801 at Holland House, which stood on his farm on the road to Sainte Foy outside Quebec. He was seventy-three. His health, as Simcoe had noted in 1792, had been giving way for some time, and early in 1801 he handed over his duties as surveyor general of Lower Canada to William Vondenvelden, who, because of Holland's failing health, had already been performing them on an informal basis. Given a military funeral, Holland was buried on his farm next to his son, Samuel Lester, who had been killed in a duel using the pistols that Wolfe had given his father in the action-packed days that preceded the capture of Quebec. With his insistence on meticulous accuracy and his uncompromising professional integrity he had, in his day, set new standards for both surveying and cartography in both Canada and northeastern North America. And his influence was

Samuel Wilmot studied surveying under John Stegman and married Stegman's daughter, Mary. Wilmot was one of the busiest surveyors of his day.

*At the time of writing, it is thought that scuba divers have located the wreck of the *Speedy*. Ontario Land Surveyors have greeted the news with much interest.

long lasting. To Willis Chipman, who was to be instrumental in the founding of the Association of Land Surveyors eighty-five years after Holland's death, he was the land surveyor *par excellence*.

With Smith's return to England in 1802, Holland's passing in 1801, the death of Collins in 1795, McNiff's defection to the United States the year after, the fall from grace of Jones in 1799, and the deaths of Aitken in 1800 and that of Stegman in 1804, the era of pioneer surveying in Upper Canada may be said to have ended. Of the old-time "greats" only Chewett, with his commission dating from the early

Courtesy: AOLS Archives

Thomas Ridout. Appointed surveyor general in 1810, he held the post until he died in 1829.

1770s, remained in harness. And as of 1800, he still had a half-century of life, less one year, to go.

With Smith gone, a new home for the Surveyor General's Office had to be found. This was to be in the new Parliament Building that, thanks to Peter Hunter, had now been built at the foot of Parliament Street. Pending the arrival of a new surveyor general, Thomas Ridout and Chewett had carried on in tandem in an acting capacity, with the latter holding some hope of obtaining the post. But once again Chewett was to be disappointed. The home authorities appointed one C.B. Wyatt, who arrived from England in 1805. Apparently a headstrong young man, he soon became embroiled in an on-going dispute between the legislative assembly and the executive council. He also quarrelled with Ridout's son, Samuel, then serving his father as his chief clerk, and dismissed him, only to be overruled by Gore. Wyatt was also accused of substituting his own name for someone else's on a survey. Gore had enough. He suspended Wyatt early in 1807, who returned to England where he was to sue Gore for libel – and win his case.

By now Thomas Ridout was a rising figure. He had been made registrar of York County in 1796 and two years later was appointed sergeant-at-arms to the assembly. And in 1800 he had been made clerk of the peace for the Home District. On Wyatt's disappearance from the scene, Ridout made his move and went to England, where, with Gore's support, he was successful in his bid for the post of surveyor general, though it would not be until 1810 before his appointment was confirmed.

As mentioned above, the rate at which new townships were being opened up had fallen markedly during General Hunter's time. Thereafter, this low rate was to be maintained until the outbreak of the War of 1812, though for different reasons. As the war against Napoleon intensified, fewer emigrants reached Upper Canada from Britain, while the rate of immigration from the States fell off as tensions between the United

States and Britain mounted. And following the policy laid down by Hunter, land for these immigrants was found by completing the subdivision of townships already started. Of the twenty-five township surveys ordered from 1806 to 1812 inclusive, nine, or something like a third, were for the completion of existing townships. The year 1811, however, saw a sudden upsurge in surveying activity with nine new townships started. Of these, five were on the Niagara Peninsula, much of which, interestingly enough, had remained unsubdivided all these years. In 1812, township surveys were confined to Hallowell Township in Prince Edward County and Thorold Township on the Niagara Peninsula in Welland County.

By now more names were appearing on the roster of deputy land surveyors. Thomas Ridout's son, Samuel, was commissioned in 1806, though, as already mentioned, he was to do little or no work in the field. Duncan McDonell started surveying in 1808 after training with his uncle, Hugh McDonell. His forty-four years of land surveying saw him working in townships from Georgina on the south shore of Lake Simcoe to the township of Kenyon in Glengarry County, besides carrying out such diverse surveys as one on the Madawaska River in 1847 and a survey of some islands in the St. Lawrence, which he carried out four years before his death at his home near Alexandria, Glengarry County, in 1865.

Duncan McDonell and Jonathan Rogers also received their licences in 1808; William Graves and Colonel Talbot's *protégé*, Mahlon Burwell, in 1809; Simon Zalotes Watson in 1810; Daniel Everitt, Robert McLean, and Wilson Conger in 1811; and Shubal Park in 1812. Joseph Kilborn was licensed in 1813, and after that no more deputy land surveyors would be appointed until 1816.

The war against Napoleonic France resulted in a phenomenal growth of the Royal Navy. To help man that

navy, Britain exerted what she saw as her right to impress any British seamen found on foreign ships, American ships included. For this and other reasons, tension between Britain and the United States mounted as the war against Napoleon went on. All this had been watched in Upper Canada with increasing unease – an unease heightened by the old worry that settlers from the United States might prove to be of doubtful loyalty. It was a legitimate concern. Modern estimates place the population of Upper Canada at that time at about 100 000, of which four-fifths were American born. To make it worse, the make-up of the population was becoming increasingly polarized. The eastern end of the province was predominantly Loyalist. But it was the more productive land around York and to the west that had attracted most of the American newcomers. And so, when two men approached the British government with plans for settlements in the southwest that would stress the British element, the authorities were very willing to listen.

One was Lord Selkirk. In 1804 he placed 111 Highlanders on the land in a settlement he named Baldoon, near present-day Wallaceburg. It did not prosper. By 1805, nearly half the settlers had died from malaria or dysentery. Eventually, a combination of mismanagement and sickness led to the collapse of the venture, and, though Selkirk tried to set things right, he had by this time become absorbed in a new project in the northwest that resulted in the establishment of his Red River colony in 1812.

The other man who found a sympathetic ear in the British government was Simcoe's erstwhile private secretary and Mrs. Simcoe's companion, Thomas Talbot, who had thrown up his army career and returned to Upper Canada in 1801. During a visit to England, he approached the government with a settlement scheme of his own devising. It was approved. He would be given a field officer's grant of 5000 acres in Dunwich and Aldborough townships (which William Hambly had started to lay out in 1803), on which he would place carefully screened settlers. For every 50 acres of his own land so settled, he would be rewarded with 200 acres for himself, such to come from land reserved for the purpose elsewhere in the two townships. Assuming he filled up his original 5000 acres with settlers, he stood to gain 20 000 acres for himself.

In May 1803 Talbot and five assistants made their way by boat down the Lake Erie shore to land 40 miles (64 km) from the nearest settlement, at a mouth of a creek some miles west of present-day Port Stanley. Here he and his men started to clear land, building sawmills and grist mills a year later. He called the place Port Talbot, and it was here that he would live virtually for the rest of his life. His settlement got off to a very slow start – only twenty families would be placed by 1808.

He soon started to depart from the terms of the original agreement by using his 200-acre reward to build up his holdings around his home. As he explained to the lieutenant-governor, Francis Gore, he liked to keep his settlers at a comfortable distance. His aversion to dealing directly with his settlers got to the point where he would only do business with them through a small wicket that he had built into a window of his house. By about 1809 he also got permission to place his settlers and transfer land without reference to the Surveyor General's Office. Extraordinary as it may

The Self-Taught Robert McLean

Not long after he was commissioned in 1811, Robert McLean of Elizabethtown was called in to rerun a line that was the subject of dispute between no less than five parties. The line in question was down the centre of Lot 29 in the Third Concession of Elizabethtown. It had been run previously by William Graves and Reuben Sherwood, who had chained in a predetermined distance from the side of the township at both front and rear of the concession to establish the centre of the lot and then joined the two points. But McLean came up with widely differing results. Commenting on all this in a letter to Thomas Ridout, the surveyor general, McLean wrote: "I have not found a town line straight through a concession yet ... [and] the want of parallellism among concession lines, besides their being very crooked in numberless instances, render it next to impossible to ascertain equal distances from the town line on the front and rear of concessions even allowing that it were possible to measure accurately."

Working from the town line, the exact position of which he established by lining up pickets ("sharply pointed with a pen-knife") after clearing all obstructions, McLean established its angular relation to a meridian based on celestial observations – using a "sextant" with a 30-inch (76-cm) radius he had made himself. Repeating the process in reverse, as it were, he then established a parallel line that passed through the centre of the lot as measured along its front. At the rear of the concession, his line passed 5 chains to the west of Graves's line and 10 chains to the west of Sherwood's. It seems McLean's line was eventually accepted.

An inavoidable source of error in those days was imprecise instrumentation. For instance, McLean pointed out that, with sights set from 7 to 10 inches apart, the "horsehair" in the aperture of a theodolite was thick enough to hide a four-foot (1.2-m) diameter tree at 10 chains, so that at that distance "a picket set anywhere within the four feet will be hid by the hair." McLean's solution was to build his own, larger theodolite.

Ending his long and erudite letter, McLean apologizes for his "verbosity" and "ignorance." He concludes: "As I never had the advantage of being an hour at school in my life, and when 17 years of age could not write my name, I hope you will not criticize severely" (Robert McLean to Thomas Ridout, 25 February 1812, RG1 A-1-1, vol. 7; also quoted in"Early Surveying in Upeer Canada," *The Canadian Surveyor*, June 1977, supplement).

Commissioned in 1809, Mahlon Burwell surveyed the Talbot Road (now Highway 3) and carried out many other surveys in southwestern Ontario. He also worked in the Huron Tract. Port Burwell is named after him.

sound, Talbot managed to keep his settlement maps away from the prying eyes of the surveyor general until sometime in the 1830s.

Having got himself appointed a district road commissioner in 1804, Talbot then approached Gore and got him to approve a plan that involved building a new road into his settlement. Along both sides of this road, settlers would be granted 200-acre lots, provided that within two years they had built a house, cleared and fenced 10 acres, cleared all trees within 100 feet (30 m) of the road, and, most importantly, cleared and stumped half the width of the road facing their property.

Talbot's plan was approved by Gore in February 1809, and on Talbot's own recommendation the job of surveying and laying out the new road was offered to Mahlon Burwell, who was thereupon appointed a provincial land surveyor. The son of a Loyalist, who had come north to settle in Bertie Township in 1797, Burwell had no formal training and his knowledge of mathematics was poor. When he had first applied for a post as deputy surveyor in 1805 he had not been successful. However, it was clear in 1809 that he had learned much in a few years.

Burwell's instructions of 24 March 1809 required him to survey and lay out a road, which became known as Talbot Road East, through the townships of Southwold, Yarmouth (which Jones had started on in 1799), and Houghton "in breadth one Gunter's chain" and to lay out lots "thereon of twenty chains in breadth on each side of the same, leaving a road on the side lines [of townships] and a road between every five lots ... of one Gunter's chain."[5] He was given "rough plans" of the townships, which were not yet laid out, and he was to locate his road with reference to the side lines of these townships and to Lake Erie. He was advised to consult Chewett if he encountered difficulties in understanding his instructions.

Instructed to commence his survey at Port Talbot and work eastward, Burwell and his party travelled down the Lake Erie shore to Port Talbot by rowboat. What with storms that threatened the safety of the open boat and putting ashore each night to look for men to hire, it took them over three weeks to reach Port Talbot from Fort Erie. Working all that summer and part of the next, Burwell took the road as far as what is now Delhi, roughly 60 miles (100 km) from where he began. Later, the road would be continued eastward to reach the settlements on the Niagara Peninsula. He was also instructed to survey the land between Yarmouth and Houghton and divide it into the two townships of Malahide and Bayham. In the latter he selected some land for himself at the mouth of Big Otter Creek, where Port Burwell was to grow.

In 1811 Gore bypassed his executive council and authorized two extensions of the Talbot Road – one north to the Thames, the other west to Amherstburg – and at the same time gave Talbot permission to locate settlers as far east as Yarmouth Township. Moving quickly, Talbot had Burwell start on the westerly extension of the Talbot Road. Talbot also started locating settlers along it, this on land that had already been allocated by the surveyor general. The result was a furor that was only partly stilled by Gore's departure for England, his replacement by Major General Isaac Brock, and the outbreak of the War of 1812.

To anticipate, Burwell resumed work on the road in 1816, taking it on to Sandwich, though it was 1824 before he sent in his final report. By the end of the 1820s the nearly 300-mile (483-km) Talbot Road (now Highway 3) was the finest highway in the province, thanks to Burwell, to the settlers who built it, and to Talbot, who, in his own curmudgeonly, way kept his settlers up to the mark.

Meanwhile Talbot himself continued to be a thorn in the side of the provincial government. In 1815, urged to do so by Gore, Talbot finally let the surveyor general have a look at his records. He had settled 350 families up to that point. By 1817, the total was over 800, most of whom Ridout, the surveyor general, had never even heard about. Moreover, Talbot had failed to pass on some £4,000 worth of settlement fees to the government. When the government took steps to expedite the recovery of these fees from his settlers, Talbot went to England and, after gaining the ear of Lord Bathhurst, the colonial secretary, had all his actions endorsed. Not only that, Talbot was then awarded over 65 000 acres in his original townships of Dunwich and Aldborough as a reward for his services in the cause of Upper Canadian settlement.

However, in 1828 the provincial government refused to allow Talbot to add any more land to his personal holdings, by which time – by virtue of his settlers along the Talbot Road – his settlement extended some 130 miles (209 km) along Lake Erie and covered all or part of twenty-nine townships. By 1831 even the British government was suggesting that Talbot's affairs be looked into, and in 1836 the provincial assembly did just that, discovering that, apart from Talbot's own holdings in Dunwich Township, he had located settlers on over 3000 lots, with a total settled area of nearly 520 000 acres. Of the total, 63 percent had not been reported to the surveyor general and only a quarter of the land had been actually patented.

It all ended in 1838 when Talbot was ordered to wind up his settlement and turn it over to the province. Talbot remained relatively poor, and he was granted a pension that was part of the Canada Company deal, as noted below. Talbot died in 1853 in London in what had become Canada West. He was eighty-three. When the new county of Elgin was carved out of Middlesex in 1851, he was disappointed it was not called Talbot. However, St. Thomas was named after him, with the prefix "Saint" added, it has been said, for the sake of euphony. The Talbot Settlement itself, though, remained an abiding memorial. It was by far the most successful settlement in the history of Upper Canada.

As might be expected, the War of 1812 brought the process of laying out new townships to a virtual halt, with only one township surveyed in 1813 – that of Stamford in Welland County – none in 1814, and only one in 1815 – Wolford in Grenville County. Contributing to the slowdown was the American occupation of York in the spring of 1813, which saw the new Parliament Building set ablaze and government cash boxes carried off. Chewett, in his capacity of colonel commanding the Third Regiment of West York Militia, was one of those who had been left in the town to deal with the Americans when the British

troops withdrew. It seems his militia did not distinguish themselves militarily. Samuel Wilmot also saw action at York.

Several other land surveyors saw active service with their respective militia regiments during the war. Thomas Welch, for example, took part in the bitterest battle of the war, fought on a sultry July night in 1814 within earshot of Niagara Falls and remembered thereafter as the Battle of Lundy's Lane. Mahlon Burwell served in the First Middlesex Militia Regiment (which Talbot commanded on a routine basis), and he may have seen action on the Niagara frontier. At any rate he was taken prisoner by the Americans on one of their sweeps through southwestern Upper Canada in 1814, to be released later that year on parole. He went back to surveying and pursuing his political career, which had seen him first elected to the provincial assembly in 1812, and to looking after his business interests in the port that was named after him.

Besides McNiff, two other Upper Canadian land surveyors ended up on the wrong side in the war. One was Aaron Greeley, who was a school teacher in New Hampshire until he came north in about 1795 to settle near Carrying Place. On being commissioned a deputy surveyor, he apparently became involved with Asa Danforth's land settlement schemes. When those schemes finally came to nothing he returned to the States in 1806 to start surveying out of Detroit.

Margaret Greely, his wife, decided to join him and had a boat built at Presqu'ile. In it she, her child, her brother-in-law, and one other managed to get as far as Queenston. She then took ship from Chippewa to Detroit. On the outbreak of war, Greeley joined the U.S. army and was captured. Released on parole through Margaret's efforts, he and Margaret went to live first in Buffalo and then in New Hampshire. At the war's end, Margaret returned to Upper Canada with what were now four children and settled in Grafton. However, Aaron went back to Detroit, where he presumably took up surveying again, dying

on the job, or so 'tis thought, a few miles south of Detroit.

And then there was another American-born land surveyor, Simon Zilotes Watson, who, after surveying in Lower Canada, came east. As noted above, he had been taken on in Upper Canada as a deputy land surveyor in 1810. Having made a few surveys, he ran afoul of Talbot in connection with a settlement scheme of his own that he was trying to promote. Frustrated in this and vowing vengeance on Talbot, he joined the Americans when they invaded the southwest in 1812. He was last seen, as it were, by General Brock himself, who reported that the American cavalry "was being led by one Watson, a surveyor from Montreal, a desperate character."[6]

CHAPTER NINE

Postwar Expansion

Not the least of the difficulties faced by British naval vessels on the Great Lakes during the War of 1812 was a lack of adequate charts. Thus, when Sir Edward Owen was appointed commodore in command of British naval forces on the Great Lakes in 1815, the year the war ended, he lost no time in remedying this deficiency, appointing as chief hydrographer his younger brother, Captain William Fitzwilliam Owen. Starting in March 1815, Captain Owen charted from the upper St. Lawrence to Sault Ste. Marie, with more than fifty charts forwarded to the Admiralty at the end of the season. In the course of his work Captain Owen charted the sound that bears his name, and he all but gave us a sixth Great Lake in the body of water he called Lake Manitoulin, later to be renamed Georgian Bay in honour of George IV, who succeeded George III in 1820.

The following season, that of 1816, Captain Owen was assisted by Lieutenant Henry Bayfield, who Owen found to be an apt pupil. Working out of Kingston, they surveyed the upper St. Lawrence and the Lake Ontario shore, with plans to return to the upper lakes the following year. Owen, however, had to return to England in 1817, so he persuaded Bayfield to carry on the Great Lakes survey, which he did for the next nine years. With the Admiralty retrenching after the war, Bayfield was left with a single midshipman, Philip Collins, as his assistant, along with two small boats. They completed Lake Erie in 1817 and then spent four years charting Lake Huron and Georgian Bay. In the course of this work they charted some 20 000 islands.

Moving on to Lake Superior in 1823, Bayfield and Collins spent three summers there, using Fort William as their winter quarters. Bayfield then spent another two years in England perfecting his charts of Lakes Erie, Huron, and Superior, together with his plans for various harbours and the Lake St. Clair–St. Clair River–Detroit River system. Promoted to commander in 1826, Bayfield returned to Canada where

he and Collins started on their surveys of the lower St. Lawrence. Bayfield gave his name to Bayfield Sound and to the village of Bayfield, south of Goderich. Captain J.G. Boulton, who came after Bayfield, spoke of Bayfield and his work in glowing terms. "The Admiralty Survey Service has produced good men from Captain Cook onwards but I doubt whether the British Navy has ever possessed a more gifted and zealous surveyor than Bayfield."[1] Apart from their worth to navigators, the charts produced by Bayfield, with their near perfect accuracy and meticulously plotted shorelines, were to establish the exact geographical bounds of Upper Canada, something that the provincial government had never got around to doing.

The 1812 war also spurred on the British military to look for shortcuts to Lake Huron. They were especially intrigued by the possibilities of the Severn River, first explored in 1780, it will be recalled, by the party dispatched at Haldimand's command to examine the Toronto Passage. If the Severn with its seven falls could be made navigable, this river would figure largely both in an Ottawa River–Lake Huron route and in one linking Lake Simcoe with the Trent River system, a goal that had never been lost sight of since the 1780s when John Collins made his exploratory survey on behalf of both government and fur-trading interests.

Captain Owen had been instructed in 1815 to pay particular attention to the Severn. In 1819 Lieutenant Joseph Portlock of the Royal Engineers was sent to have another look at it. And in that same year, another Royal Engineer lieutenant, James Catty, while pursuing orders to find a water route between Lake Simcoe and the Ottawa, took his party up the Talbot River, which flows into Lake Simcoe on its eastern side, and eventually reached and travelled down the Madawaska River to the Ottawa at Arnprior (see figure 9.1).

Catty's original map is now lost, so just how Catty reached the Madawaska remains unclear. Be that as it may, he and his party were the first white men to travel through what we now call Haliburton. The information

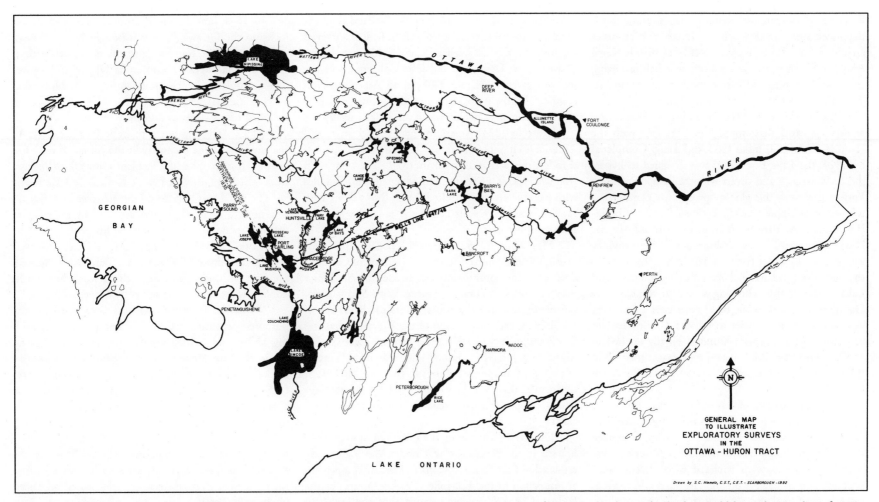

Figure 9.1 River systems explored in early efforts to find routes from Georgian Bay to the Ottawa River and the Bay of Quinte. Also shown: the Carthew-Baddeley exploration line of 1835 and Bell's Line of 1847–48. Modern place names added.

that Catty brought back established that the likelihood of finding a practicable water route to the Ottawa was remote, though this did not prevent the British government from trying again in the mid-1820s.

In the meantime, the military had been following up the possibility of building a canal to link the St. Lawrence and Ottawa rivers, the War of 1812 having amply demonstrated the vulnerability of the upper St. Lawrence as Upper Canada's only lifeline. The first steps in building what became known as the Rideau Canal were taken in 1814, when Lieutenant-Colonel George Macdonell, following in the footsteps of Lieutenant French and James Rankin, examined and roughly surveyed a route connecting the Rideau and Cataraqui rivers. This was followed in 1816 by a more detailed survey of the route that was made by Lieutenant Joshua Jebb, R.E. After this, civilian contractors began construction of a lock at the Ottawa

River end of the proposed system. Then nothing much happened until 1818 when the Duke of Richmond arrived in Canada as governor-in-chief of British North America. Work began, but it came to a halt following the duke's death in 1819 from the bite of a rabid fox. The project then hung fire for several years.

In 1817 the state of New York began construction work on a canal that would link Lake Erie with the Hudson River, 350 miles (563 km) away. Completed by 1824, the Lake Erie Canal was designed to bypass the St. Lawrence and divert Montreal's trade to New York. Faced with this gloomy prospect, a commission was set up in Upper Canada to consider ways of building Canadian canals to upgrade the whole St. Lawrence system. It wasn't long before the province was gripped by canal fever. In 1823 a passage was cut through the sand bar between Burlington Bay and Lake Ontario, thus allowing access to what is now Hamilton Harbour, while three years later a company was incorporated in order to build a 4-mile canal to link Burlington Bay with Dundas. Finally opened in 1837, it proved redundant and its remains now lie in the Coote's Paradise section of the Royal Botanical Gardens in Hamilton.

In 1824 the idea of linking the west end of the Bay of Quinte with Lake Ontario by a canal at Carrying Place was also resurrected – it had first been mooted in the early 1790s when the route was surveyed by Jones – with Richard Birdsall and Seth Watkins sent to make a preliminary survey. Known as the Murray Canal and destined to become something of a political football, the canal was eventually completed in 1882.

Of greater consequence was the construction of the Welland Canal. This had its genesis in 1818 when William Hamilton Merritt, who owned mills and a distillery on Twelve Mile Creek east of present-day St. Catharines, wondered whether he could get more water to run his mills by tapping the Chippewa, or Welland, River. From this grew the idea of linking Lake Erie with Lake Ontario via the Welland River. It would be pleasant to record that a Canadian surveyed the route for the first Welland Canal, which would run between Port Dalhousie and Port Colborne, but the job was given to Hiram Tibbets, an American civil engineer. Furthermore, following the incorporation of a private company, which was given its charter by the legislature in 1824, American money paid for it and American engineers built it. The first ships passed through the Welland Canal in 1829. But what with wooden locks in constant need of repair, and troubles with water levels that required the addition of a feeder canal, it was many years before the canal was successfully completed.

Meanwhile, in 1825 the British had set up a commission to examine and report on the state of Canada's defences. The commission was headed by Sir James Smyth, a senior military engineer. With Smyth's recommendation and the full support of the Duke of Wellington, the construction of the Rideau Canal was finally authorized in 1826. And here we meet Gother Mann and John By again. Mann was now General Mann and inspector-general for the Board of Ordnance and it was he who selected By, now a lieutenant-colonel, to superintend the construction of the canal.

On leaving Canada in 1810, By had distinguished himself in the Peninsular War under Wellington. He returned to Canada in September 1826. After a personal inspection of the 120-mile (193-km) route for the Rideau Canal, he recommended that the locks, of which there were to be forty-seven, should be enlarged in order to accommodate the steam vessels that were then coming into use. He recommended that the length of the locks be increased from 100 to 150 feet (30 to 46 m), and their width from 22 to 50 feet. The greater cost that this would involve caused consternation in London. However, a compromise was finally reached, with an agreement that the locks should be 134 feet long and 33 feet wide.

In 1826 land in the vicinity of the head of the locks on the Ottawa River was bought by the Crown to house construction workers; there two settlements grew up that became known as Upper and Lower Town. Construction began in late 1827. By November 1831 the canal was virtually complete. The system included fifty-two dams and forty-seven locks, with all of the locks and most of the dams built of masonry. All the work was done manually in the course of only five seasons, this in spite of a virulent outbreak of malaria from which hundreds of workers died, and By nearly so. The canal was an astonishing achievement. But on returning to England, By was censured by the treasury for over-spending, and, in spite of his protests that he had acted on the instructions of the Duke of Wellington himself, he was never publicly vindicated. He was still under an official cloud when he died in 1836, it is thought at the age of fifty-seven.

While the Rideau Canal was never used for the purpose it was intended, its building led to the founding of Bytown, which would later become Ottawa, while the canal brought prosperity to the region through which it passed. Land values increased twentyfold, and there was a boom in what we now call the construction industry with many availing themselves of the skills of the many masons that had been attracted to the area. What with the Perth and Lanark settlements (of which more below), the building of the Rideau Canal, and a rapidly growing lumber industry, the settlement of far eastern Ontario was far advanced by the early 1830s.

The ending of the War of 1812 refocused attention on various international boundary problems, some of which had remained outstanding since the ending of the Revolutionary War. The exact location of the boundary west of Lake Superior gave rise to several difficulties and their resolution would result in a curious jog in the international boundary at the Ontario-Manitoba border where Minnesota juts north into the Lake of the Woods in tonguelike fashion. Known as the Northwest Angle, its story is an integral part of that of the international boundary itself, while later in the century the Northwest Angle would loom large in the on-going and increasingly bitter dispute among the Dominion, Manitoba, and Ontario over the latter's western boundary.

In the provisional treaty signed by Britain and the United States in 1782, it was agreed that the western-most part of the international boundary – based on John Mitchell's map of 1755, then the most accurate map available – should run though Lake Superior "northward of the Isles of Royal and Philippeaux, to the Long Lake, and the water communication [the Pigeon River] between it and the Lake of the Woods; thence through the said lake to the northwestern point thereof, and thence due west to the river Mississippi."[2] The definitive treaty of 1783 was to say much the same thing. All very well, but which and where was the "Long Lake"? And which the "northwestern point" of the Lake of the Woods? As for a line drawn due west from any part of the Lake of the Woods reaching the Mississippi, this was an impossibility. Indeed, that this might be the case was recognized in the Treaty of London signed in 1794, wherein it was stated that if such a due west line did not strike the Mississippi, then "the two parties will thereupon proceed by amicable negotiation to regulate the boundary in that quarter."[3] Following the War of 1812, the need to resolve the position of the boundary west of Superior had become urgent. Apart from anything else, Lord Selkirk had established his colony on the Red River the same year that war had broken out. Britain and the United States finally agreed, in the Convention of 1818, that the boundary west of Lake of the Woods should be along the forty-ninth parallel, even though this might involve a jog in the boundary at the longitude corresponding to the northwestern point of the Lake of the Woods mentioned in earlier treaties.

An international joint boundary commission was established in 1822. The job of exploring and survey-ing the boundary between Lake Superior and Lake of the Woods was given to David Thompson, by now a veteran western explorer and surveyor of renown, who in 1812 had retired with his wife and family to live in Upper Canada.

And so, at the age of fifty-two, David Thompson was appointed to lead the Canadian survey party that, under the general instructions of the joint British-American commission, set out to find the "Long Lake" mentioned in the treaties of 1782 and 1783, thereby establishing a tentative international boundary between Lake Superior and Lake of the Woods. It took him until 1825, with the position of the contentious Northwest Angle on the Lake of the Woods being ten-tatively identified and established by Dr. J.C. Tiarks, a British astronomer. Deciding on the northern shore of a bay now known as Northwest Angle Inlet, he placed a monument there, the position of which was carefully determined. It lies some 25 miles (40 km) north of the forty-ninth parallel, causing the international boundary to run south to reach that parallel – and hence that curious jog in the international boundary.

Thompson submitted his findings to the joint commission at the end of 1826, which failed to agree on the boundary. They were also used, however, in the Webster-Ashburton agreement of 1842, which finally defined the international boundary between Lake Superior and Lake of the Woods. As for the monu-ment placed at the Northwest Angle, it was to become lost and then eventually found – and argued about all over again – some fifty years later, when in 1872 British and American surveyors started to run the international boundary along the forty-ninth parallel west of the Lake of the Woods.

As we have seen, before the War of 1812 had even ended, the British government had become interested in building what became the Rideau Canal. The need to guard this, together with the postwar concern over the number of American settlers in Upper Canada, led Lord Bathurst, secretary of state for war and the colonies, to devise a scheme in 1815 for a military set-tlement in the Rideau District where both immigrants from Britain and discharged servicemen would be granted land. Using ships that were being sent to Canada to bring back regular troops, emigrants would be given free passage to Upper Canada, where they were to be joined on the settlement by discharged sol-diers from both British and Canadian regular regi-ments, such as the Canadian Fencibles and the Glengarry Light Infantry. The first immigrants were 250 Scots who arrived in Brockville in the fall of 1815. An advance party went inland where they established a base camp on the Pike River, which they renamed the Tay. The settlement that grew up there was called Perth. As a predominantly military affair, the Perth set-tlement was stage-managed by the commander-in-chief in Lower Canada, something that did not endear the plan to Francis Gore, now back as lieutenant-governor of Upper Canada. Be that as it may, a start was hastily made on putting in the necessary townships, with part of Bathurst Township surveyed early in 1816 and oth-ers the following year.

By way of reinforcing the Perth settlers, Lord Bathurst followed it up with another government-sponsored settlement scheme to its north. The first body of settlers consisted of nearly 1200 Scots who arrived in 1820 and moved into Lanark Township, which had been started earlier in connection with the Perth settlement. They were joined a year later by 1800 others. Meanwhile another government-assisted scheme was in the making, this one designed to allevi-ate distress in some of the poorest districts in Ireland. The establishment of the settlement was placed in the hands of Peter Robinson, brother of Upper Canada's attorney general. In 1823 the first contingent of 570 Irish immigrants was placed immediately south of Arnprior in Pakenham Township, which had been sur-veyed in 1822. This was followed in 1825 by some 2000 more Irish immigrants who established a settle-ment north of Rice Lake. This became centred on a village that grew up on the Otonabee River that was named Peterborough in honour of the man who had brought the settlement into being. The Peterborough settlement was the last to be sponsored by the British government. They were just too expensive.

In 1815 Lord Bathurst had directed that routine land grants in Upper Canada should be reduced from 200 to 100 acres, this being considered all that immigrants fresh out of Britain could reasonably cope with, at least at the start. In the years to come, 100 acres became the standard land grant throughout the southern part of the province.

As originally specified, the dimensions of 200-acre lots were 105.27 chains deep and 19 chains broad. The only way of obtaining the 100-acre lots commonly in demand, while still retaining access to a concession road, was to divide the lots down the middle. This resulted in lots that were ten times longer than they were broad, an extremely impractical shape for efficient farming. So in 1793, the dimensions of the 200-acre lots were changed to a more sensible 20 by 100 chains. After a series of modifications, the standard lot became 30 chains wide and 66 2/3 chains long – with the concession roads that divided each range of lots coming closer to each other in consequence.

As noted earlier, the single-front system compounded by the clergy and crown reserves made for far from cohesive settlements. This had been abundantly clear for a long time. At last, in October 1818, something was done about it when Thomas Ridout introduced a modification of the single-front system that eradicated that system's shortcomings, while at the time recognizing the trend to the 100-acre lot as the basic unit of land grants. Concession roads would be the same distance apart as they were in the single-front system, that is, 66 2/3 chains, and the lots would still be 30 chains wide, but settlers would now be placed on both sides of the road, hence the name "Double-Front System" by which Ridout's modification became known (see figure 5.5). The new system also recog-

nized what Talbot had so effectively demonstrated: placing settlers on both sides of a road was an efficient way of maintaining them.

However, as before, only the township outline and the concession lines were run by the surveyor. The bearing of the side line of the township was used to guide the side lines of lots. But with lot side lines running in from the concession roads, likely as not they didn't meet in the middle of the concessions. Thus when side roads came to be opened, they often resulted in a jog halfway across a concession. Such jogs, perpetuated in some parts of southern Ontario to this day, may come as an unpleasant surprise to the motorist, though they are less common than they once were.

In 1818 – the same year that the double-front system was introduced – a new survey act was passed. Its ponderous title confirms that the act passed in 1785 in Quebec was believed to apply to the "Upper District," though this was not apparent from the wording of that act. The title of the 1818 act: An Act to Repeal an Ordinance of the Province of Quebec, Passed in the Twenty-fifth Year of His Majesty's Reign [i.e., 1785], Entitled an Ordinance Concerning Land Surveyors and the Admeasurement of Lands, and Also to Extend the Provisions of an Act, Passed in the Thirty-eighth Year of His Majesty's Reign [i.e., 1798] to Ascertain and Establish on a Permanent Footing the Boundary Lines of the Different Townships of this Province, and Further to Regulate the Manner in Which Lands are Hereafter to be Surveyed.

For the first time, it became a legal requirement that prospective land surveyors be examined by the surveyor general or his deputy, who would rule on a candidate's suitability and examine him on his knowledge of the theory and practice of surveying. If successful, he would be given an appointment to act, following which he would be granted a licence on posting two sureties for £500 and would be required to subscribe to an oath. And, for the first time, provision was made for swearing in chainmen. Among the survey procedures

laid down, the front of each concession was declared to be the boundary nearest the township boundary from which the concessions are numbered. All lines run and monuments planted in the first survey were unalterable. The boundary lines of each concession, when these had been run on the same bearing, would govern all division and side lines.

With the new act came a major change in the ground rules by which deputy land surveyors worked. From 1819 onward, township surveys were let out on contract, with payment either in the form of land or a combination of money and land. By now the basic rate of pay for land surveyors had been increased to 10s. a day, though for a long time their pay had been augmented by grants of land. Under the new arrangement such payments in kind, as it were, were now formalized. Burwell, for instance, usually worked for a straight 4.5 percent of the area he surveyed – and it is said that he amassed over 40 000 acres in this way, mostly in Essex County.

This new way of recompensing surveyors had a disastrous effect on the accuracy of the surveys, as both contractors and surveyors scrambled to get as much land surveyed as they could in any given season. In 1829, land surveyors were once again placed on a daily rate. But the damage had been done. By the 1830s there were so many disputes resulting from deficiencies in the survey fabric that, much as had been done in colonial Maryland in 1715, boards of boundary line commissioners had to be set up. Under the Boundary Line Commissioners Act of 1838 (1 Vict., c. 19), a board was to be established in every district (see figure 9.2), with three commissioners to a board.

The new boundary act had hardly been passed before it was rescinded in 1842. But the idea of setting up legal machinery to deal specifically with boundary disputes was to persist. Not long after the formation of the Association of Ontario Land Surveyors, and on subsequent occasions thereafter, members agitated for the reintroduction of legislation specifically aimed at settling boundary disputes. But such would not be brought in until 1959.

❧

Upper Canada being naturally loath to grant land to Americans in the years following the War of 1812, there was some concern as to how to people the province if it was to hold its own against the burgeoning republic to the south. As it turned out, the problem resolved itself. The ending of the Napoleonic Wars was followed in Great Britain by a massive industrial slump that started a wave of emigration. Britons left by the shipload for Canada, Australia, and South Africa. By 1830 the population of Upper Canada doubled to over 200 000. By 1842 it would double again to reach 487 000, with most of the emigrants coming from the United Kingdom, which included Ireland after 1806.

Up to the end of 1815, a total of 141 townships had been laid out in the province either wholly or in part. Following the war, the number of new townships surveyed steadily increased to accommodate the rising tide of immigrants. In the twenty-six years between the end of the 1812 war and the union of the two Canadas in 1841, a further 189 townships were laid either partially or wholly. All this in addition to resurveys and the completion of townships started earlier. This represented a formidable effort on the part of the Surveyor General's Office and was made possible only by the appointment of a steadily increasing number of land surveyors. By 1838 there would be 106 on the government roster (see appendix A).

In the years immediately following the war, two land surveyors were licensed in 1816, John Booth and Thomas Caldwell; four more in 1817 and 1818, Gabriel Lount, James Nickalls, Richard Bristol, and Mahlon Burwell's son, Lewis; and then, with pressure rising on the surveyor general to produce more surveyed land, twelve in the year 1819 alone, including Richard Birdsall, John Bostwick, and William Chewett's son, James.

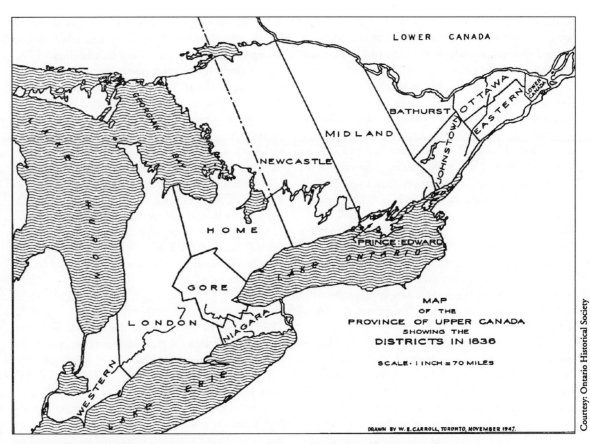

Figure 9.2 Districts in Upper Canada as of 1836. (From Spragge, *The Districts of Upper Canada*.)

Courtesy: Ontario Historical Society

Gabriel Lount, originally from England, had settled in Pennsylvania, whence he had come north to Upper Canada in 1811 with his three sons, Samuel, George, and James, to settle on Yonge Street just north of Aurora. George qualified as a land surveyor a couple of years after his father, and it was together that the two of them took on their first job with the government, which was the subdivision of West Gwillimbury and part of Tecumseth Township immediately to the west. It seems that it was George who did the work. At any rate, it was he who was paid for it – in land. He got 1900 acres in West Gwillimbury and over 2300 acres in Tecumseth.

In 1820, under a contract that was apparently awarded to one George Pearson (Gabriel Lount's son-in-law), Gabriel, and his son George worked on the survey of Innisfil Township, which lies on the west side of the southwestern arm of Lake Simcoe – for which George again got paid in land, this time to the tune of over 3800 acres. According to one account, Gabriel was assisted on this survey not only by George but by one or perhaps both of his other sons, Samuel and

James – which, if true, would make Samuel Lount the only land surveyor (albeit unofficial) in Ontario to be hanged for treason – which he would be for his part in the Mackenzie Rebellion of 1837.

Also assisting the Lounts on that survey of Innisfil Township in 1820 was Richard Birdsall, then twenty-one and newly arrived in Upper Canada. Trained in his native Yorkshire, he was apparently too conscientious for the Lounts' liking, who saw their profits going down the drain. There was a quarrel, following which George Lount took over the compass from Birdsall, with the latter ending up tallying for the chainmen and making up the field notes. A year later, Birdsall bought over 900 acres of land north of Rice Lake from the Honourable Zacheus Burnham, whose daughter he married, and it was in that area that he settled, taking up Lot 1 on the First Concession in a township that he named himself, calling it Asphodel because the trilliums reminded him of that "immortal flower of Elysium."

In 1825 Birdsall and his father-in-law contracted to lay out the town of Peterborough, then merely a village known as Scott's Mills, with Burnham as the sleeping partner. Birdsall went on to become the accredited surveyor of what was then known as the Newcastle District, in which Peterborough then lay, with a long list of surveys to his credit both in the district and elsewhere. Described as "upright as a wand," Birdsall was a prodigious walker. It was during one bit-terly cold morning in 1852, when he set out to walk to Cavan, a village over 19 miles (30 km) away, that he contracted the pneumonia from which he died.

In the early 1820s a private settlement scheme somewhat similar to Talbot's had been set in train by William Dickson, a Scottish lawyer. After the war, Dickson had bought a 94 000-acre tract in what became Dumfries Township – now divided into North and South Dumfries. One of the six parcels originally sold by the Six Nations, it was purchased by Dickson with American settlers in mind. Balked of these after the War of 1812, Dickson advertised his settlement in Scotland with great success. His assistant was a young Pennsylvanian named Absalom Shade, and it was around the village of Shade's Mills that the settlement grew, to be subsequently renamed Galt after John Galt, of whom more below.

The War of 1812 had given the citizens of Upper Canada a new sense of pride in themselves in that the Americans had been repulsed, though admittedly this was very largely due to British military might. And apart from those on the Niagara Peninsula and in the southwest who had had property destroyed by the Americans, the province had done well during the war. In the British army, farmers had found a customer who paid well and on time, and military movements had given a fillip to road building. But now those halcyon days were over, and following the war a depression had set in. What with this and Upper Canada receiving less than a fair share of customs dues collected in Quebec – a long-standing grievance – the provincial coffers were bare. And there was little hope of help coming from the British government, which was still paying for a very long and costly war.

At the same time, the feud between the assembly and the so-called Family Compact was deepening, with the former increasingly unwilling to grant the government money to carry on the business of governing. This was the situation that confronted Sir Peregrine Maitland when he arrived as the province's new lieutenant-governor in 1818. It soon became clear to him that the root of the province's problems lay in the profligate land settlement policies of the past.

It was to be found in 1824 that no less than eight million acres had been given away to private individuals – about one-quarter of all the land in southern Ontario. It had gone not just to Loyalist settlers and senior military men but to civil servants, judges, and land surveyors. Of this eight million acres, only three million were occupied, the balance being held by speculators. And of this three million, only about one-sixth, or half-a-million acres, were actually being farmed. All this not counting some three million acres of crown and clergy reserves. The whole sorry mess was perhaps best summed up by William Chewett's son, James, who was asked in 1839 to testify before a parliamentary committee set up in connection with Lord Durham's findings. "I cannot help remarking," he said, "that the system upon which lands have been granted, was the greatest prostitution of the Sovereign's Bounty ever practiced in any country."[4]

Maitland tightened up on land-granting procedures and raised both settlement fees and the tax on wild land in an effort to discourage speculators and to increase government revenues. But it soon became clear that something more drastic was needed if the province was to become economically self-sufficient. Clearly, it was

Birdsall Returns from the Bush

Wrote Frances Stewart in 1823: "One very wet day I saw two men walk past my window; one had a blanket about his shoulders, a pair of snowshoes in his hands, and a small fur cap. The other was dressed in ragged sailor's clothes. I took the foremost for an Indian ... but to our surprise we found this was Mr. Birdsall, a very smart young Englishman who is surveyor of the township in this district, and his assistant; they had with them five other men as chain-bearers, etc. I found that they had all been living in the woods for the months of March and April, which accounted for the ragged and weatherbeaten appearance of the whole party" (quoted in Guillet, ed., *Valley of the Trent*, 26).

time to cash in on the crown and clergy reserves if a way could be found to do it. Somewhat improbably, the answer was to come from a Scottish novelist, John Galt, who had become involved in Upper Canadian affairs when he agreed to lobby the British government on behalf of those claiming compensation for damage incurred during the 1812 war. Hard up for cash at the time, he agreed to do this for a 3 percent commission on whatever he could wheedle out of the government. He got the British government to meet part of the amount claimed, but only if Upper Canada would match their contribution pound for pound. This it could not do, and matters reached an impasse. It was then that Galt came up with the idea of forming a company that would buy the crown and clergy reserves, which in turn would settle them. For its part, the provincial government would get some much needed cash.

The upshot of all this was the formation in London of the Canada Company in 1824, to which the Crown would convey all its reserves, with some exceptions, and half the clergy reserves. In the event, the clergy reserves were left out of the final deal. Instead, the company got a 1.1-million-acre tract that had been previously purchased from the Chippewas. Roughly triangular in shape, with its base on the Lake Huron shore and with its truncated tip nudging the German Company land around Waterloo, what became known as the Huron Tract comprised most of what are now Huron and Perth counties. For this and 1 384 013 acres of crown reserves, the company paid at a flat rate of 3s. 6d. an acre (roughly 90 cents an acre at the rate of exchange then prevailing). The final price they paid was £344,375 7s. 2d. although part of this was withheld against capital improvements in the Huron Tract. Of the money paid to the government, some went to crown officials to compensate them for lost fees, some went to the Roman Catholic and Presbyterian churches and a college, and some went to providing a pension to a now near-indigent Colonel Talbot.

Reaching Upper Canada in late 1826 as the superintendent of the company, Galt founded Guelph the following spring with the assistance of his irrepressible sidekick, "Tiger" Dunlop, and a somewhat rowdy party of axemen from the Dickson settlement, who cheered Galt on as he ceremoniously felled the first tree. Guelph itself was planned by John McDonald, a graduate civil engineer from Scotland hired by Galt, and it was under McDonald that surveying arrangements went forward in the Huron Tract, at least in their earlier stages. Early in May 1827 McDonald and Dunlop were joined by Mahlon Burwell and his assistants, who were to make an exploratory survey designed to push through a road from Guelph to Lake Huron and establish a proof line through the tract – which, as it happened, was later abandoned.

Accompanied on and off by McDonald, Dunlop, and some natives, Burwell struck out for Lake Huron on a line parallel to, but a few miles south of, the northern boundary of the tract, which runs roughly northwest and southeast. What with bad weather, swamps, and the denseness of the underbrush, it took them eleven days to reach the Lake Huron shore, arriving on it a little north of the mouth of the Menesetung, now the Maitland, River.

A couple of days later, on 29 May 1827, Burwell surveyed a half-acre square on the left bank of the river and had his men clear the underbrush, cut some logs, and start building the foundations of the first house in what would become Goderich. On 1 June he started to lay out what he called the Bridle Road back to Wilmot Township. Having worked through constant rain, he became ill and returned to the town site after a few days only to find that Galt and some others had turned up by ship in his absence. They, along with Dunlop, had had a little party to celebrate the founding of the town that Galt had called Goderich after Viscount Goderich, who happened to be chancellor of the exchequer and who the Canada Company was anxious to please. Burwell finally got back to Wilmot

Township on 13 July after laying out the Bridle Road. He got his maps, reports, and notes into the Surveyor General's Office by 1 August.

Burwell had hardly caught his breath when he was sent back to run the northern boundary of the tract. He started on 4 October at the northwest corner of Garafraxa Township, where Arthur now stands. What with rain, hail, and snow, densely wooded swamps, and the headwaters of the Menesetung, which they had to cross and recross nearly twenty times, it took them twenty-four days to cover the 60 miles (97 km) to Lake Huron. On the return journey in November, which took them six days through the river now in flood because of storms, they found their caches of food had been destroyed by bears.

Burwell was no longer a young man, and by the 1830s rheumatism had brought his surveying days to an end. His road surveys had included, besides the Talbot roads, both East and West, the northerly extension of the same towards London, the so-called Middle road (a road first suggested by Smith when he was surveyor general) that followed the high ground and wound its way through the swamps east from Sandwich, and the Brock Road, which connected Guelph and Burlington. He had laid out all or part of

Tiger Dunlop

Dr. William Dunlop was a massive, hard-drinking, red-headed Scot who had served with the army during the War of 1812 and then gone to India where his alleged prowess at getting rid of unwanted tigers earned him his nickname. Becoming a journalist, he had met Galt in London, who made him his "Warden of Woods and Forests." Later made superintendent of the Lachine Canal, he died in Montreal in 1848. He was buried on a bluff overlooking the Maitland River and the Goderich he had helped to found.

Courtesy: AOLS Archives

*I have the honor to be
Dear Sir
Your most Obed.
humble Serv.
W. Chewett*

William Chewett. In government service for fifty-eight years, he died in 1849. A deputy land surveyor since 1774, the coveted post of surveyor general eluded him all his life.

some twenty-eight townships in southwestern Ontario. He had resurveyed Chatham, and in 1826 he laid out the town of London. He had also surveyed several native reserves in Middleton and Lambton counties. He died in 1846. Variously described as ambitious, egotistical, and vindictive, he is reputed to have made more enemies than friends – a bird of a feather with Talbot perhaps. And maybe that's why they got on together, by and large. But whatever else, Burwell was a man of integrity – which was just one of the qualities that made him such an outstanding land surveyor.

Burwell's Bridle Road was followed up the following year by a survey party under McDonald and Dunlop. Working in the most appalling weather, they laid out and cut the Huron Road, now part of

Highway 8, and on which Stratford was to grow. On reaching Goderich, McDonald left Dunlop to clear and widen the road, while he laid out a second road designed to connect the Huron Tract with the Talbot settlement to the south. Starting at what is now Clinton, and becoming known as the Clinton Road, McDonald's road eventually became Highway 4. As he had done on the Huron Road, McDonald marked the corners of future townships. The next year, that of 1829, he laid the front posts of the 100-acre lots that would front the Huron and Clinton roads.

The township survey system that McDonald was using marked a complete break from those used in the past. The directors of the Canada Company in London wanted the Huron Tract laid out into 1-mile-square blocks as used in the American 6-mile-square township system. However, what was at first used in the Huron Tract was a modification of the American system that was called the "2400-Acre Section System" and was presumably devised by Thomas Ridout and William Chewett with the Canada Company breathing over their shoulders. However, after twenty-two years as surveyor general Thomas Ridout died in 1829 at the age of seventy-five, and so it was Chewett, who had stepped into the breach yet again as acting surveyor general, who was responsible in the spring of 1829 for the order-in-council that authorized the 2400-acre section township.

In Chewett's system, the dimensions of the standard lot was 30 by 66 2/3 chains, as in the previous systems used in Upper Canada, but these would now be incorporated into 2400-acre sections, each forming a 181 by 133 1/3 chain rectangle, thus giving 12 lots per section (see figure 9.3). To the layman, this may seem an unnecessarily complicated way of going about things. In fact, under this new system the surveyor went about his survey much as he had in the double-front system, but he now surveyed a township section by section, including the side roads, and he closed each section as he went, thereby vastly improving the accu-

racy of his survey. The average size of the township was to be much the same as before, that is, about 110 square miles, but the system was readily adaptable to irregular areas, with, for example, more sections fitted into the front of the township than in its rear. However, Chewett's system had a major shortcoming in that it did not recognize the need for smaller lots, as first adumbrated by the Perth settlement of 1816, and which the Canada Company had stressed. They wanted 100-acre lots with a simple standard size of 20 by 50 chains that were suitable for the type of untried settler of limited means they were hoping to lure to the Huron Tract.

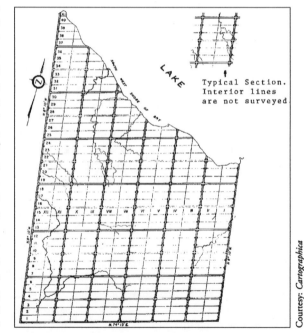

Typical Section. Interior lines are not surveyed.

Courtesy: Cartographica

Figure 9.3 The 2400-acre sectional township survey system introduced in 1829 in partial emulation of the American 6-mile-square township system. The perimeter of each section was "closed" by the surveyor as he went along, thus increasing the accuracy of the survey. (From Sebert, *Land Surveys of Ontario*.)

And so, only six years later in 1835, yet another system was brought in. This was a modification, in which the "section" was reduced to 1000 acres, comprised of ten lots, each 20 by 50 chains (see figure 9.4). From the Huron Tract, this "1000-Acre Sectional System," went on to be used in Bruce County, Muskoka, Haliburton, Nipissing, and Parry Sound. Only thirty-five townships were laid out using the 2400-acre section system though it co-existed with the 1000-acre sectional system until 1854. The 1000-acre sectional system was not to be discontinued until 1906 (see figure 9.5).

In three years alone, between 1830 and 1833, the population of Upper Canada increased by nearly 50 percent. This phenomenal increase was partly due to the efforts of Sir John Colborne, who had succeeded Maitland as lieutenant-governor in 1828. Seeing in the newcomers a useful counterweight to the American settlers once again flocking into the province, Colborne took it upon himself to assist British immigrants, even to the extent of granting 50 acres to those who were indigent, with no payments to be made for three years. In the summer of 1832 over 50 000 would-be settlers

arrived in Quebec from Britain. They brought cholera with them – thereby adding to the problems posed by the enormous influx. That the province coped with the difficulties as efficiently as it did, providing food, shelter, and medical care, constitutes one of the most stirring stories in the history of Upper Canada, one in which the surveyor Roswell Mount played a prominent role.

By 1828 Upper Canada's political troubles were coming to a head. William Lyon Mackenzie, now the undisputed leader of the Reform party, had been elected to the assembly as the member for York County.

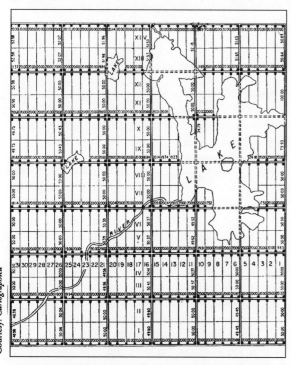

Courtesy: *Cartographica*

Figure 9.4 The 2400-acre sectional township survey system which resulted in 200 acre lots was soon superseded by the 1000-acre sectional system shown above because the Canada Company wanted 100 acre lots more suitable to immigrant farmers. Solid black squares denote survey posts planted. (From Sebert, *Land Surveys of Ontario*.)

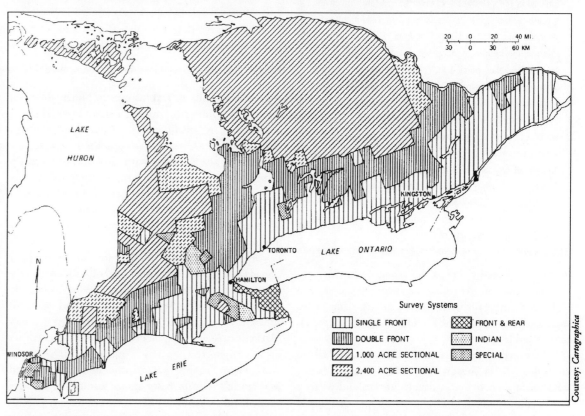

Courtesy: *Cartographica*

Figure 9.5 Distribution of the various township survey systems in southern Ontario. Note that the 2400-acre system was confined to the Huron Tract and other areas in the west. The 1000-acre system that replaced it was later used in the Ottawa-Huron Tract. (From Sebert, *Land Surveys of Ontario*.)

Colborne Lodge in Toronto's High Park

As Torontonians flock in their thousands to enjoy walking or picnicking in High Park, few realize what they owe to a provincial land surveyor named John Howard, Toronto's first city surveyor. He owned all the land that High Park now occupies, built a house there, which he named "Colborne Lodge," and then deeded the land to the city in 1873. Born in London, England in 1803, Howard went to sea when he was fifteen but, because of chronic seasickness, later apprenticed himself to an architect. Emigrating to Upper Canada in 1832 with his wife, Jemima, the couple found cholera raging in Quebec and Montreal, so they hurried to York where Howard became drawing master at Upper Canada College and went on to become a deputy land surveyor in 1836. Appointed Toronto's chief surveyor by William Lyon Mackenzie, Howard occupied the post for over twenty years. He surveyed the harbour and what are now the Toronto Islands in 1834 and 1846, the grounds of Osgoode Hall in 1843, the city south of Bloor Street in 1847, while in 1853 he surveyed The Esplanade in connection with the new Northern Railway. He also made the surveys and plans for Toronto's first waterworks system, construction of which began in 1842.

Roswell Mount

Trained by Mahlon Burwell, and licensed in 1820, Roswell Mount – like Theodore De Pencier before him – found it difficult to keep track of money. Elected to the legislature in 1830, Mount became a friend of Peter Robinson, who in 1832 got him appointed the crown lands agent in the Western District with an office in Port Stanley.

Almost at once, Mount was inundated by immigrants, many with cholera. Mount was responsible for feeding, sheltering, and seeing to the medical needs of these destitute people before settling them in the then empty townships of Warwick and Adelaide. In July 1832 he processed 400; in August over 800 arrived. And they kept coming. Despite Robinson's warning that he might be overspending, Mount continued to do as much as he could. Sir John Colborne had budgeted the relief effort in 1832 at £5,000. When he came to examine the accounts, he found £13,000 had been spent – over half of it by Mount.

Mount was replaced and an enquiry followed. In January of 1834, with his 1832 accounts still unsettled, Roswell Mount suddenly died. He was only thirty-seven. A pauper at his death, which took place in York, his funeral expenses were paid by Mahlon Burwell – who subsequently asked to be reimbursed by Robinson.

Thrown repeatedly out of the assembly for his venomous attacks on the ruling oligarchy, he was thrown right back in again by his constituents. One of his most active assistants was David Gibson, a prosperous farmer and land surveyor.

Destined to found a remarkable dynasty of land surveyors, David Gibson came from a Scottish family who made their living as tenant farmers and weavers in the country north of Dundee. In hopes that David might better himself, they articled him when he was fifteen to a land surveyor and civil engineer by the name of Blackadder. On completing his five-year apprenticeship, he turned his eyes to North America, eventually joining his uncle, Alexander Milne, in Markham. After qualifying as a deputy land surveyor that same year, Gibson was appointed as a deputy surveyor of roads. What with this, some township survey work, and a growing private practice he was soon doing well. Marrying his cousin, Eliza Milne, in 1828, he bought a farm on Yonge Street at Willowdale the next year and then became interested in politics.

Apparently disappointed at finding that Upper Canada was not the egalitarian land of milk and honey that he had been led to expect, and having the sternly moral Calvinist background that he had, Gibson apparently found a man after his own heart in the fiery Mackenzie. At any rate, he became one of Mackenzie's firmest supporters. So it was not surprising that in 1834 when Toronto was incorporated as a city and Mackenzie's Reform party gained control of the city council with Mackenzie himself elected mayor, Gibson should find himself appointed city surveyor.

Elected to the assembly on a Reform ticket in 1836, Gibson became even more deeply involved with the radical Mackenzie. However, when push came to shove in 1837 and Mackenzie, with a motley and somewhat pathetic little army, raised the flag of armed rebellion at Montgomery's Tavern on the evening of 7 December, it came as a shock to Gibson. He had heard of the planned uprising only two days before. By the time it was over, his house and farm buildings had all been burned, following which Gibson hid in Oshawa for a month and then fled across the lake to find safety in Rochester, New York. So ended part one of his surveying career in the province. Others were not so lucky: in spite of petitions in their support and appeals for clemency, two of Mackenzie's supporters, Samuel Lount and Peter Mathews, were executed on 12 April 1838.

Gibson subsequently settled in Lockport, New York, where his family joined him and where he lived for over ten years, having got a job as an engineer on the Erie Canal. Though pardoned in 1843 for his part in the rebellion, he remained in Lockport, where he had prospered and bought a farm, and in 1846 he applied for U.S. citizenship. However, in 1848 he lost his job on the canal and decided to return to his farm in Willowdale, which had been looked after by relatives in his absence, and took up land surveying in Canada again. Thus began part two of Gibson's surveying career in what, in his absence, had become Canada West, of which more below.

While David Gibson was busy getting himself into trouble in Toronto, Charles Rankin was starting to make a name for himself as a competent surveyor. Of Irish extraction, Rankin came from a very different background than did Gibson. His was a relatively well-to-do professional family. Two of his brothers became doctors, while a third, Arthur Rankin, would qualify as a land surveyor in 1836. Licensed in 1820 at the age of twenty-three, Charles Rankin first worked out of Malden. However, in contrast to those surveyors who were content to work in and about the counties in which they lived, Charles Rankin courted variety and must have soon become known to the Surveyor General's Office as a reliable land surveyor of the "go anywhere–do anything" variety. In 1830 he was working on Eldon and Fenelon townships on the edge of the Canadian Shield north of Lindsay. The following year he surveyed Presqu'ile Point, now a provincial park. In the years that followed he worked variously in Loughborough Township north of Kingston, and on the Niagara Peninsula. The mid-1830s saw him carrying out the first surveys in the Nottawasaga Bay area that would make his name synonymous with the opening up and settlement of Grey and Bruce counties.

In 1833 Rankin set out by boat from what had become a naval base at Penetanguishene, where he had hired his men, and made his way around Nottawasaga Bay to establish himself in a log cabin he built near the mouth of the Beaver River where Thornbury now stands. Working out of his cabin, Rankin surveyed Collingwood and St. Vincent townships, both of which front on Nottawasaga Bay. The bay was still fringed with the dense pineries that would bring loggers flocking to the area in the 1850s when, after half-a-century of merciless exploitation, the forests on the Canadian Shield had been all but stripped of its

John G. Howard surveying Toronto harbour in 1835, painted by G. D'Almain. Note his theodolite, used for measuring both horizontal and vertical angles, and by then in general use.

merchantable trees. Then, starting in 1837, he laid out the Garafraxa Road to open up the so-called Queen's Bush that lay to the north of the Huron Tract. Striking north from Arthur through what are now Mount Forest and Durham along what is now part of Highway 6, the Garafraxa Road led to Owen Sound. Here, in 1840, Rankin laid out a town at the mouth of the Sydenham River, which flows into the sound. First called Sydenham, the town was later renamed Owen Sound.

Efforts by the British military to find a practicable water route between Lake Simcoe and the Ottawa had been reactivated by the Smyth commission in the mid-1820s. Surveys were ordered as a follow-up to Lieutenant Catty's explorations of 1819, such to go forward under the direction of Colonel Elias Durnford, who commanded the Royal Engineers in Canada. Accordingly, in February 1826, Lieutenant Henry Briscoe, R.E., and Ensign Durnford of the Sixty-eighth Light Infantry were sent to explore both the Talbot River, which Catty had followed in 1819, and the Black River, which flows into Lake Couchiching from the northeast.

Advised by a native guide, Briscoe and Durnford set off in early September in an entirely different direction. From the Severn, they worked their way north to Lake Muskoka and thence by a branch of the Muskoka River eastward to the Lake of Bays, thus becoming, as far as is known, the first white men to cross the *terra incognita* that we now call Muskoka. Travelling via tributaries of the Madawaska and a series of lakes, they eventually found themselves in the heart of what is now Algonquin Park. They had now been travelling almost three weeks. With only ten days worth of rations remaining, they took the advice of a native and crossed over to the Petawawa River, travelling down it to the Ottawa. They then went downriver to arrive, no doubt thankfully, at Fort Coulonge, thus concluding

their minor exploratory epic, which had seen them cover over 170 miles (270 km) as the crow flies in just over a month.

In the meantime, Lieutenant William Marlow, R.E., and a lieutenant of the Royal Artillery were sent to explore the Black River, which reaches Lake Couchiching from the northeast and which, it was thought, might prove to be the key to a practicable Lake Simcoe–Ottawa River water route. In the course of proving that it wasn't, they struggled through to the Gull River system some 19 miles to the east before turning back.

Reporting on Marlow and Briscoe's exertions, Smyth concluded that it would be better to concentrate on building locks and canals to make the Severn navigable, while he surmised that the Talbot River could no doubt form part of a water route linking Lake Simcoe to the Bay of Quinte. He also made a point of saying that even though Briscoe had not followed his instructions, both he and Marlow had done rather well. The Duke of Wellington disagreed. Violently. Commenting on the survey reports, he wrote in a minute dated 10 January 1827 that he had "read them with pain. They afford," he went on, "a fresh proof of the inaccuracy with which all the military business of this country [i.e., Canada] is done. The reason is that nobody does his own." He then lit into poor Briscoe and Marlow.

Here are certain officers in time of peace ordered to make specific reconnoissances. They do not arrange matters as to procure to a certainty the provisions necessary to enable them to perform their duty; nor do they, where guides are requisite, take measures for providing such guides as are capable of conducting each officer on the road he is to go.

The consequences is that they go wandering over the country they don't know where, and report upon any thing excepting

what they were sent to examine and report upon.

Let these surveys be made again next season.[5]

So in the summer of 1827, Lieutenant Briscoe was sent back to do it all over again, this time in company with Lieutenant William Greenwood of the Royal Artillery. With specific instructions to stick to the Madawaska this time, he returned to report that, with its numerous falls and rapids, the difficulty and expense of rendering it navigable would be enormous – a conclusion, Briscoe stressed, that Catty had already arrived at in 1819. As for the country through which Briscoe passed, it was "uniformly of a sterile nature, the bed of the river, and the banks thereof, which are generally steep, being one continued line of granite, to within a few miles of the Ottawa."[6]

Also undertaken that same season as a direct result of Wellington's order, was a further exploratory survey of the Talbot River route to the Madawaska. This by Lieutenant John Walpole. It is somewhat surprising that all these military surveys had gone ahead with apparently little or no co-operation from the Surveyor General's Office. Civilian land surveyors had, after all, much local experience and knowledge to contribute had they been asked. So it comes as something of a surprise to learn that Walpole's companion on this survey was James Chewett. However, he went as a volunteer. Both Briscoe and Walpole had been ordered to look out for a river that Catty had mentioned as flowing south towards Kingston. Needless to say, neither found such a river. Walpole's observations on the country he passed through agreed with Briscoe's. It bore, he wrote, "a most barren and cheerless aspect."

Following these surveys the British military lost interest in the possibility in finding a shortcut from the Ottawa to Lake Huron. However, they had scarcely done so before their interest was re-aroused by Charles

Sherriff (also spelled Shirreff, Shirrif, and Sheriff) and his sons. Charles Sherriff was a Scottish merchant who had settled at Fitzroy Harbour on the Ottawa in 1818, where he and his four sons became prominent in the development of the area. Charles was a canal enthusiast, as well as something of a visionary. This was made evident in a proposal he submitted to Colonel By in 1829, who passed it on to Durnford, the senior royal engineer at Kingston. Sherriff claimed he had it on good authority from some natives that there was indeed a shortcut from the Ottawa to Lake Huron via what seems to have been the Lake of Bays. Sherriff went further. He claimed that the route could be made navigable for steamboats at a cost of less than a thousand pounds. Not only that, he claimed that what he called the Huron Canal would pass through "an extensive tract of good land" that would attract settlers, while the canal itself would bring commerce to the region. He went on to describe the Great Lakes as "a new Mediterranean," which could be looked on as a "new and vast field for enterprise affording an additional opening for the commerce of Great Britain protected from all foreign intrusion by carriers composed of her own colonies."[7]

As a result of this panegyric, official sanction was given to Sherriff's son, Alexander, to make an exploratory journey through the Ottawa-Huron Tract. Travelling from east to west to reach Georgian Bay by way of Lake Muskoka and the Severn and then back again, Alexander concluded that there was no better way of reaching Lake Huron from the Ottawa than by Lake Nipissing and the French River – which, of course, the native people and the French had known from time out of mind. And he snuffed out his father's dream of building the Huron Canal.

However, he did come back with some electrifying news. North of the "barren rocky range" traversed by earlier exploring parties it appeared "almost certain ... that immediately to the north of these explored tracts, the country becomes less elevated and more fertile."

Basing his opinion, quite erroneously, on the prevalence of white pine, he came up with the astonishing statement that "on the whole, every thing that I have seen or heard, enables me to state that in this, hitherto, unnoticed part of Canada, a fine habitable country will be found, to the extent of millions of acres."[8]

This statement resulted in an excited provincial legislature deciding in 1834 that it was time that the region between the Severn River and Lake Nipissing be properly explored, with a view to assessing both its suitability for agricultural settlement and its mineral potential. The upshot was the dispatch of a joint military and civilian survey party, which was given the ambitious goal of laying down a base line (with lateral excursions) from the township of Rama on the east side of Lake Couchiching, partly surveyed in 1835, northwest through Muskoka and what is now the district of Parry Sound, all the way to the French River, over a hundred miles (160 km) away. The resulting line would roughly parallel the eastern shore of Georgian Bay, though some distance inland (see figure 9.1).

Lieutenant John Carthew, R.N., was in charge of the party, which consisted, besides the requisite chainmen, axemen, and *voyageurs*, of Lieutenant Frederick Baddeley, R.E., who was to act as geologist, and two provincial land surveyors, who were actually to run the line, one the veteran Samuel Richardson, licensed in 1821, the other, William Hawkins, licensed in 1832. Leaving York for Lake Simcoe on 16 July 1835, the party reached Lake Couchiching in early August. Thereafter the party split up. While the two officers ranged into the hinterland, doing much towards elucidating the geography of Muskoka, the two land surveyors laboured at their work of laying out the line, supervised off and on by Carthew.

In November, with winter coming on, food in short supply, and supply problems worsening, the line was abandoned. It had been run some 77 miles (124 km) and was short of the French River by a matter of only 30 miles. The remarkable achievements of

Carthew, Baddeley, Richardson, and Hawkins should be better remembered.

Alexander Sherriff may have scotched his father's idea of a commercial canal linking the Ottawa with Georgian Bay, but as far as the province was concerned, hopes of finding a route for such a canal died hard. In March 1837 the provincial legislature passed an act empowering the lieutenant-governor to set up a commission to oversee further exploratory surveys of the waterways in the Ottawa-Huron Tract. Heading the resulting commission was the Honourable John Macaulay, who at that point was surveyor general in the dying days of the office. Also appointed were John S. Cartwright and Captain Frederick Baddeley, R.E. In the summer of 1837, they dispatched three exploratory survey parties. The first party, headed by a Lieutenant David Taylor, was sent to recheck the old route to the Ottawa via the French River, Lake Nipissing, and the Mattawa. William Hawkins was instructed to take a party up the Magnetawan River, which flows into Georgian Bay some distance north of Parry Sound, and then eastward to Allumette Island on the Ottawa, from where he was to return to Georgian Bay by Lake Nipissing and the French River.

The third assignment, which was to explore the route to the Ottawa by way of Lake Muskoka and the Madawaska River, was given to David Thompson, not long back from the west. Curiously enough, Baddeley had doubts about "Mr. T.," as he called him, questioning his veracity, of all things. And he balked when Thompson wanted to be paid for time spent after his return on the preparation of reports and maps. "This seems to me to be a *feeler*," wrote Baddeley. "In my opinion he is bound to furnish report [and] calculations and both free of expense ... He seems throughout to be trying to make the best bargain for himself."[9] Hardly surprising, considering he was nearly seventy and desperately short of money. In any case, one might ask, why shouldn't he be paid for his time?

By July 1837 Thompson was at Holland Landing supervising the building of his own cedar canoes, this to the disgust of Baddeley, who wanted him to use the new-fangled tin ones. By mid-August Thompson was on Lake Muskoka and spent ten days producing the first accurate surveys and maps of that lake, along with Lakes Rosseau and Joseph. Then he moved northeast to the Lake of Bays and thence to Canoe Lake (in the southwest corner of what is now Algonquin Park) where he paused for a couple of weeks to build himself two new canoes. He then worked his way through to the Madawaska and so down to the Ottawa, which he reached at the end of September.

Astonishingly, Thompson's report and maps, once read, were shelved and forgotten. Over twenty years later, John Stoughton Dennis was to make what he thought was the first survey of the Muskoka Lakes, apparently unaware of Thompson's earlier survey. In 1862 the "recent discovery" of Lake Joseph was hailed as bringing to light a lake so far unknown to white men. That Thompson's reports and maps could be thus forgotten perhaps tells us something of the morass of inefficiency in which the Crown Lands Department, of which by that time the Survey Branch was a part, was to become increasingly enmired in the years ahead. The Duke of Wellington, had he been around, would no doubt have had something suitably acid to say about it all.

While the results of all three exploratory surveys had dashed provincial hopes of a commercial canal to the Ottawa, the idea had been revived of building one from Georgian Bay to Lake Ontario by means of the Severn and the Trent River system – the possibility that the British government had never lost sight of. It was with commercial applications in mind that in 1833 the provincial government retained a consulting civil engineer, one N.H. Baird, to take a closer look at the problems involved. He came up in the mid-1830s with two schemes, one using canals alone – probable cost about half a million pounds – the second, a com-bined road and canal route, costing less than half that. The legislature voted some money to get the scheme going, but nothing much was done. It was not until the twentieth century that the Trent Canal system finally came into being – long after the railways had made such a system economically redundant.

In 1825 Lord Bathurst made a sweeping proposal that would change the basis of land settlement in Upper Canada. Influenced by the ideas of Gibbon Wakefield, an English social reformer, a new type of settlement scheme had been initiated with some success in New South Wales. Land was sold to those who could afford it, with the proceeds going to assist the settlement of the less fortunate. Bathurst now suggested that the same scheme be instituted in Upper Canada and that the old system of gratuitous land grants be abandoned once and for all. The new system was not to be legally implemented until 1837 when the Public Lands Act was passed, but, in the interim, a step was taken to change the system with the appointment in 1827 of Peter Robinson as commissioner of crown lands, who would oversee the change. At the same time he was appointed surveyor general of woods and forests and a second land office was created to deal with the issuing of timber licences and revenues derived from the grow-ing lumber industry.

Following the death of Thomas Ridout in 1829, the changes in land settlement policies, and the cre-ation of the Crown Lands Office, which started to usurp many of the functions of the Surveyor General's Office, the latter office started to fall apart. In 1832, after only three years as acting surveyor general, Chewett retired when the new surveyor general was appointed in the person of Samuel Hurd. By this time, lax supervision on the part of a desperately overbur-dened Peter Robinson, poor bookkeeping by an over-worked staff, and declining morale brought both the new Crown Lands Office and Department of Woods and Lands into a state of near chaos. In 1836 Robinson's health finally gave way, and he was suc-ceeded by Robert Sullivan, one-time mayor of Toronto.

Under Hurd, the Surveyor General's Office, already disintegrating, started to suffer from a corrupt chief clerk, one John Radenhurst. He bid for crown lands on behalf of his friends, taking a commission for it, and let the business of his office go hang. Survey notes were lost, faulty descriptions were issued, and, to cap it all, illegal fees were levied to remedy the resulting disputes and errors. All this occurred at a time when land settlement procedures were being completely revamped and the office was reeling under the impact of a rising tide of immi-grants. Whereas in earlier years surveyors had laboured to lay out townships to accommodate set-tlers in their hundreds, immigrants were now arriving in their tens of thousands.

The sad state of the Surveyor General's Office was hardly improved by the post of surveyor general passing through four hands in thirteen years. Hurd retired for health reasons after less then three years in office, to be succeeded in 1836 by John Macaulay, who was also in office for only two years. Then in 1837 a new Public Lands Act was passed, giving legal teeth to the sweeping changes in the land settlement process that had followed Lord Bathurst's proposal made some years earlier. Henceforth, crown lands were to be sold at public auctions with an upset price set by the government. Such sales were to be handled by the commissioner of crown lands who would act through local land agents in each district. The agents would also collect installments on former sales of crown lands and rents on leased land. They would carry out inspections of land and see to the delivery of patents, besides giving out information on coming sales and grants of land.

With the commissioner of crown lands taking over so many of the functions of the Surveyor

General's Office, it seemed to the assembly that it was hardly worthwhile having a surveyor general at all. So, for reasons of economy, it was decided that money would be saved if Sullivan, the commissioner of crown lands, should take on the job of surveyor general as well. Whereupon the state of the Surveyor General's Office deteriorated even further. Sullivan was succeeded in 1841 by Thomas Parke, and in that same year the Surveyor General's Office moved to Kingston, chosen as the new seat of government following the union of the two Canadas.

On 17 March 1845 the Office of the Surveyor General was abolished by provincial statute (8 Vic., c. 11, s.1), its functions taken over by the commissioner of crown lands. And so the office was abolished that, since Samuel Holland was first appointed to it over eighty years earlier, had played such a vital and prominent role in the settlement of the province. After lying dormant for almost a century, the post of surveyor general would be revived in Ontario in 1928 within what was then the Department of Lands and Forests.

The ending of what had been a great surveying era was marked by the death in 1836 of perhaps the most outstanding of the old-time land surveyors, Augustus Jones. On leaving the government service in 1799, Jones farmed his land in Saltfleet Township until after the War of 1812 and then took his native wife to live among the Mohawks at Brantford. He then moved to a 1200-acre tract he had acquired at Cold Springs, near Paris. At the time of his death, though he was over ninety, he was planning a mill with town plots to be laid out around it. Buried at Cold Springs, his body was moved later to a cemetery in Brantford where he lies in an unmarked grave.

William Chewett, the date of whose appointment as a deputy land surveyor was antedated only by that of John Collins himself, finally retired in 1832 after fifty-eight years in government service. He lived out the rest of his life pleasantly enough in his home in Toronto.

He died there in 1849 at the age of seventy-nine. Meticulous to the last, he always wound his watch at noon. And the last entry in his diary, made a few hours before his tranquil death on the afternoon of 24 September, consisted of the two words "Wound up."

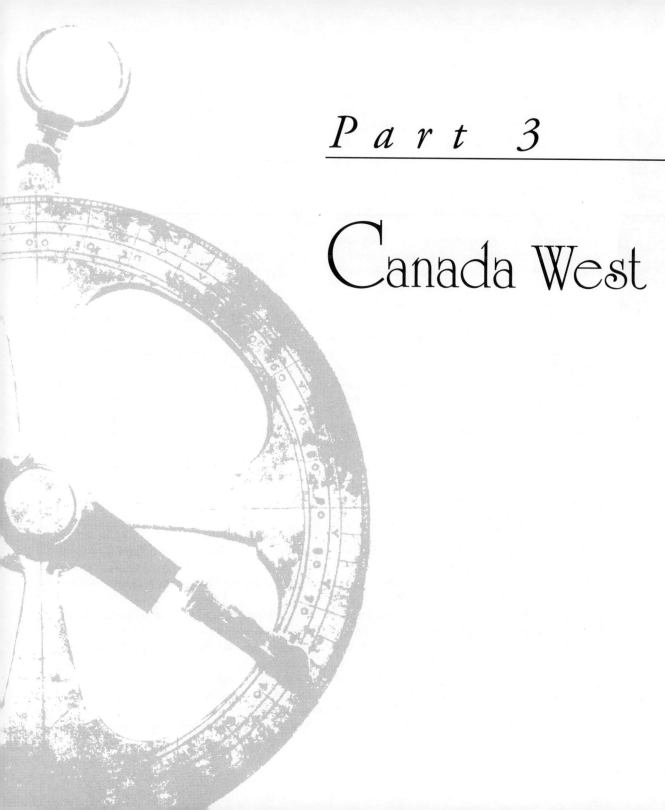

Part 3

Canada West

CHAPTER TEN

The Shield, the Railways, and a New Professionalism

A few years after the union of the two Canadas in 1841, the population of Toronto was nearing 20 000. Besides the many blacksmiths, wheelwrights, saddlers, and other artisans residing in the city, there were – according to a gazette published in 1846 – sixty-five lawyers, twenty doctors and surgeons, two dentists, nine chemists and druggists, two veterinary surgeons, four architects, six land agents – and two land surveyors.

One of the land surveyors was presumably Charles Rankin, who in 1840 had moved to Toronto where his wife Elizabeth ran a school for "young ladies" at the corner of present-day King and York streets. In 1846 the newly formed Provincial Agricultural Society held an agricultural exhibition and plowing match. Its venue was Toronto, with the exhibition held at Old Government House, where Roy Thomson Hall now stands. The animals were shown in a field behind Upper Canada College – then located in the same area. Perhaps impressed by the success of the agricultural society, Rankin in that same year became one of the prime movers in an attempt to form a professional association that would be open to all land surveyors, engineers, and architects in the province. If matters had gone as intended, the association would have been preceded only by the Law Society of Upper Canada, formed in 1797. In the event what came out of it was the Royal Canadian Institute.

Rankin's associates were Sandford Fleming, a recent arrival in Canada, and John Stoughton Dennis. Born in Kirkaldy, Fifeshire, in 1827, Fleming had studied surveying before coming to Upper Canada in 1845. He qualified as a provincial land surveyor in 1849 and then worked with the Northern Railway, becoming its chief engineer in 1857. Stoughton Dennis, as he was usually known, had been Rankin's pupil before qualifying in 1842, only two years before. Educated at Victoria College, then in Cobourg, Dennis was to have a distinguished career and became Canada's first surveyor general not long after Confederation.

After an abortive first attempt, Fleming and two other surveyors, Frederick Passmore and John O. Browne, eventually wrestled the association to its feet. Passmore became secretary of the association, Browne its vice-president, while Fleming served on the standing committee along with – among others – two architects, William Thomas and the notable Kivas Tully, and Thomas Richert, an engineer. The president was W.E. (later Sir William) Logan, a geologist and the most prestigious scientist in Canada. He had been

The Geological Survey

Efforts to set up a systematic survey of the geology of Canada culminated in 1841 when the first assembly of the united provinces voted some money towards starting such a survey. William Logan, a Montreal native of Scottish descent, came to the attention of Lord Stanley, then secretary of state for the colonies, with a recommendation that he be appointed to head the survey. And this he was, arriving in Kingston in 1842.

The survey was formally initiated by an act passed in 1845. One of the survey's earliest achievements was to focus attention on the economic possibilities of the petroleum springs and oily gumbo in southwestern Ontario, long known to the native people and commented on by Simcoe. One thing led to another, and, eventually, in 1858, North America's first producing oil well was sunk at Oil Springs in Lambton County.

A further act in 1856 authorized the survey to make and publish maps and to establish permanent benchmarks at accurately ascertained latitudes and longitudes, together with their altitudes. It was a source of chagrin to professional land surveyors in the province that the Geological Survey were allowed to do these things and that they were not.

knowledge ... connected with the Professions of Surveying, Engineering and Architecture."[1] However, it soon became less of an association for professionals than one aimed at educating the general public in matters scientific, much as the agricultural associations had been doing for farmers, though the arts were not forgotten.

The institute, which is still very much a going concern, has had various homes. In the late 1870s it was located at 58 Richmond Street East, a few blocks from Yonge Street. It was there, in 1879, that Sandford Fleming gave the two papers that led to the adoption four years later of standard time, an event commemorated by a small historic plaque on the northeast corner of the intersection of present-day Richmond and Berti streets. And, appropriately enough in view of the major role played by surveyors in bringing the institute into being, it was in the lecture room of that same building that both the Association of Ontario Land Surveyors and its forerunner, the Association of Provincial Land Surveyors, held their annual meetings for many years.

With immigrants still pouring in from the United Kingdom, a flood augmented, from the late 1840s onward, by the Irish fleeing their famine-stricken country, it became clear that the province was running short of the land needed to sustain the province's leading industry – agriculture. In the central part of the province all of present-day Simcoe County had been opened up, with a start made on the last township, that of Nottawasaga, in 1833. In the west, all but four of the fifteen townships in what is now Huron County had been laid out by 1845, and all but three out of eleven in Perth County. Of the twelve townships in Wellington County, only three were as yet unsurveyed, all in the north.

By the mid-1840s the only sizeable tract of land with good agricultural potential left in the province lay in the as yet uninhabited land in Grey and Bruce

Sandford Fleming in 1849. In 1846 he helped Charles Rankin and J. Stoughton Dennis found the first association of surveyors, architects, and engineers in the province. The association became the Royal Canadian Institute. Courtesy: AOLS Archives

J. Stoughton Dennis. After distinguishing himself as a provincial land surveyor, he went on to work for the Dominion government and became Canada's first surveyor general. Courtesy: AOLS Archives

appointed geologist to the Province of Canada in 1842, thus initiating the Geological Survey of Canada.

At that point, both Passmore and Browne had qualified not long before. Passmore was a Scot who had studied for the Royal Navy before coming to Canada in 1845 at the age of twenty-one. Qualifying in 1846, he would survey extensively in the southwestern part of the province and also resurvey Scarborough in 1864. Browne was from England, where he had

studied engineering under Robert Stephenson and the great Isambard Kingdom Brunell. Settling in Toronto, he qualified as a provincial land surveyor in 1848, to remain almost exclusively in private practice.

The association was incorporated by royal charter in 1851 as the Royal Canadian Institute, its object the "encouragement and general advancement of the Physical Sciences, the Arts and Manufactures ... and more particularly promoting the acquisition ... of

Charles Rankin worked extensively in Bruce and Grey counties and made the exploratory surveys that opened the Muskoka region to settlers.
Courtesy: AOLS Archives

Frederick Passmore. One of the most respected surveyors of his day, he worked extensively in the Southwest and resurveyed Scarborough Township in 1864.
Courtesy: AOLS Archives

counties south of the Saugeen (now the Bruce) Peninsula. Of the sixteen townships that would eventually comprise Grey County, only five had been surveyed – thanks largely to Charles Rankin's work on Nottawasaga Bay and in the Beaver Valley. A start would be made on the first of Bruce County's sixteen townships in 1849.

The settlement of these townships had been hastened, first, by the construction of "colonization roads" and, second, by the changes in the basic approach to land settlement, whereby crown land would be sold. By an order-in-council dated 17 August 1842 the price for all public land offered for sale was fixed at 8s. (provincial currency) per acre. A settler could now buy land on installments. Defaulters or those that failed in their settlement duties would lose their land, such to be resold. More important, all free grants would be reviewed by government. After 1 January 1843 no more claims for free grants would be entertained. However, a free grant of 50 acres could still be obtained along a government road or in a new settlement by a British subject who could show he was a genuine settler. Such settlers were also given the right to purchase an adjacent 150 acres if they wished.

The first colonization road was Toronto-Sydenham Road, which, from the military standpoint, provided a more or less direct line of communication to Owen Sound. Surveyed by Rankin, it was opened in 1848. From Toronto the road followed Dundas Street west and present-day Islington Avenue north, and then headed northwesterly. It then followed the road allowances along various townships to Mono Mills, following present-day Highway 9 and Airport Road. It then cut across Mono Township to Shelburne and then followed what is now Highway 10 to Owen Sound. The next colonization road was the Durham Road between Kincardine and the Garafraxa Road, which was begun sometime before 1853. And then came the Elora and Saugeen Road, which ran northwest from Elora and then north to Southampton, and which would be almost complete by 1855.

With most of the best agricultural land taken up, what was left? It had been clear for a long time that the settlements on the southern and eastern fringes of the Canadian Shield had reached their respective northern and western limits. Only the land on the shield was left, and, as early as 1826, thought was being given to putting in a further range of townships in upper Victoria and Peterborough counties. John Huston from Cavan, who had been licensed in 1821, and who later laid out the town plot of Lindsay, was instructed to report on the character of the country.

Receiving his instructions late in 1826, he dutifully set out without delay, winter though it was, though he didn't get much done.

By the severity of the weather on the 27th. of said Decemb [sic] was compelled to desist, during which time the woods was verry [sic] unfavorable by reason of the marshes, swamps and streams, not being frozen ... from the present depth of the snow it would be verry tedious and would encrease the expence to undertake to finish it now.[2]

He made his final report in June 1827. north of Verulam Township, he ranged far enough east and west up to the "line of waters surv [*sic*] by Lieut. Catty. Royal Engineer" to know the land to be "not fit for settlement" and "in general bad."

In spite of such negative reports, however, by the late 1840s the pressure to find land – any land – on which to place settlers had reached such intensity that it was decided to open up the marginal lands fringing the southern borders of the Canadian Shield and to do this by building colonization roads into them. Accordingly, on 8 July 1847, Publius Elmore, a long-time resident of Belleville, was sent appropriate instructions from D.P. Papineau, then commissioner of crown lands. Publius Virgilius Elmore, born in 1798 and licensed in 1821, had surveyed the boundaries of several townships in Prince Edward County. Elmore's instructions began as follows:

> Having been decided by order in Council of the 19th of April last to lay open the waste lands of the Crown in the rear of the Midland, Victoria and Colborne districts for settlement by the survey of certain lines of roads with double concessions fronting thereon ... I have chose you to perform the survey of the above mentioned line.[3]

So that matters would be made quite clear, Elmore was furnished with a sketch map, with point "A" marking his starting point, the northeast corner of Lake Township (roughly 19 miles south of present-day Bancroft), and "B," the spot he was to aim for on the Madawaska River. These were some 50 miles (80 km) apart, as the crow flies. In addition to his usual survey

Publius Virgilius Elmore in 1821. In 1847 he surveyed the first colonization road into the Ottawa-Huron Tract.
Courtesy: AOLS Archives

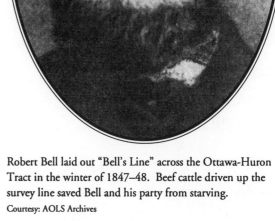

Robert Bell laid out "Bell's Line" across the Ottawa-Huron Tract in the winter of 1847–48. Beef cattle driven up the survey line saved Bell and his party from starving.
Courtesy: AOLS Archives

party, he was to take two "explorers" with him who had "a knowledge of the fitness of land for agricultural purposes and road making" and who knew how to read a compass and take notes. "You and your exploring assistants will avail yourselves of fit opportunities of viewing the country from tops of tall trees on top of elevated hill stations."

Elmore was also to "reopen and blaze the existing boundary line of the Township of Lake to the south-

easterly angle thereof, and thence ascertain the best line for a road to the settlement in Madoc or Marmora." He was to keep an eye open for the best places to bridge streams, estimate bridge lengths, and the probable cost of the "cheapest kind of a road practicable for wheeled carriages." He was also to collect geological specimens, "say from one to two cubic inches or larger ... attaching a number to each, and wrapping them in birch bark, or such suitable material to

After surveys in the Ottawa-Huron Tract, John Snow went out west where he figured prominently in the events that led to the first Riel uprising. Courtesy: AOLS Archives

Michael Deane was one of a number of skilled Irish surveyors who flocked to Upper Canada after Britain's railway-building boom ended. He became county surveyor in Victoria County. He also worked for the Dominion government out west, where he chanced to meet Louis Riel. On Riel being sentenced to death, Deane was among those who signed a petition for clemency. Courtesy: AOLS Archives

were to be marked by posts of "durable wood, six inches square, with a stone [monument] alongside."[4] His pay would be 16*s.* 6*d.* a day, his chainmen and explorers 5*s.* 3*d.*, other members of his party 4*s.* a day.

In the mid-1840s, further surveys were ordered with a view to opening up the rear of what were then Midland, Victoria, and Colborne districts to settlement (see figure 10.1), while, starting in 1845, a number of surveys were made of the watersheds of south-flowing tributaries of the Madawaska River, with the York branch of the river receiving particular attention. Among the surveyors involved were John Snow, Publius Elmore, and Thomas Devine, future head of the Surveys Branch of the Crown Lands Department.

In 1847, Robert Bell and John Haslett were instructed to lay out a base line through the southern fringes of the shield. Thought to have been born in Ireland, whence his parents had emigrated to New York, later to move north and take up land near Kemptville, Bell had qualified in 1843. He had worked in and about Bytown for three years and in the early part of 1847 surveyed the Snake and Chalk rivers. Later that year, when he had been qualified for only four years and was still in his early twenties, Bell began the survey that was to be one of the most remarkable in the history of land surveying in Ontario.

Bell and Haslett left Bytown with their parties on 9 August 1847 to reach Bark Lake on the Madawaska sixteen days later. After selecting a point on the north bank of the Madawaska in latitude 45°22'45"N, determined astronomically, the party divided. Haslett struck east while Bell set off westward for the northeastern boundary of the Home District over 80 miles (130 km) away, laying down his line on a predetermined true bearing of S70 1/2°W (see figure 9.1). As he went, he planted posts of cedar or other durable wood every 101 chains, and at every 808 chains (just over 10 miles) he planted stone monuments with a

be had on the spot," noting the exact location as well as "the dip and strike of the rock, if stratified." All this, however, was "not to materially retard the progress" of his survey.

It was intended, Elmore was told, that lots 10 chains wide would be laid out along the road, with a

one-chain road allowance between every tenth lot. However, all he was required to do at that stage was to plant posts along the road line at 101-chain intervals, while every 808 chains he was to plant posts marking future township boundaries, running the boundaries one mile back from the line. Township boundaries

foundation of broken glass and crockery to mark future township boundaries.

At first things went well. By 21 October Bell had run 35.5 miles (52 km) of the line. Then the weather broke with heavy rain that turned to snow. October 24 was a Sunday, which he made the most of by exploring south of the line to a distance of some 15 miles at which point he climbed "a steep rocky pinnacle ... The appearance of the country on all sides was beautiful," he recorded, "I never saw a finer quality of timber or apparently better soil."[5] The next day he fell sick and the unwelcome news reached him that some of the canoe men bringing up supplies had been badly hurt at some falls on their way up.

From then on, what with worsening weather, shortage of food, the increasing ruggedness of the terrain, and his own deteriorating health, Bell's progress slowed. He surveyed only a few chains on some days, a mile or so on others. October 29: "So unwell I did not go out, got some observations." October 30: "Fair until afternoon. Three of the axe men got back with their loads. The others had to be sent to Bytown, disabled – Ran 20 chs afternoon." Working through very bad weather and with the going sometimes "of the worst sort," he completed some 54 miles (87 km) of the line by Christmas Day.

By now, supply problems were becoming acute, with meat on the hoof – in the form of oxen – being driven in to them. On 30 December the unfortunate oxen were holding up the work. "Drove the cattle about three miles further, which took the whole forenoon, as the cattle were about fatigued out." Come January, with only a few more miles of the line run, winter set in. January 5: "Exceedingly stormy. The snow blew around & fell so thick it was quite impossible to see to carry on the line. Got some beef carried in & explored around the lakes. Clear night." A couple of days later, Bell fell sick again and was "unable to eat or rise" for some ten days. Meanwhile, the party was almost out of food and all of them, except one who

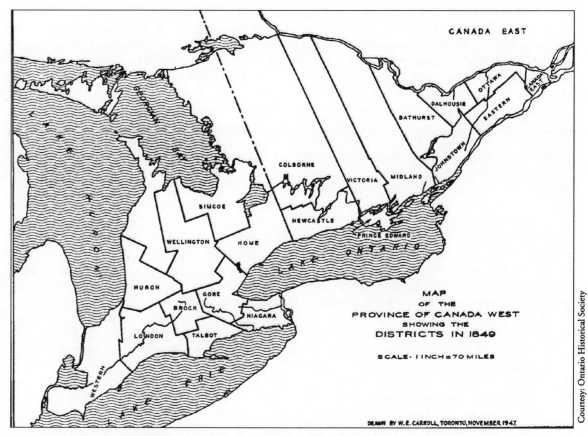

Figure 10.1 Districts in Canada West as of 1849. (From Spragge, *The Districts of Upper Canada.*)

remained with Bell, went back down the line to bring up flour.

On 25 January Bell abandoned theodolite for compass in order to speed his progress. Men were now leaving him "en masse." However, early in February, matters improved somewhat when more men came up the line to seek work. "The breaking up of the lumbering establishment on the Madawaska River," Bell noted, "had most fortunately thrown so many men out of employment that some had been found willing to engage in a service that was universally dreaded." On

4 February, with food supplies low again, Bell "required them to live almost entirely on beef." By 12 February and now working in extreme cold, Bell completed 79 miles (127 km) of line, to finally end the line on the north branch of the Muskoka River near present-day Bracebridge on 15 February 1848. Still referred to by local land surveyors as "Bell's Line," it remains a fitting memorial to both a monumental survey and the man who ran it.

However, on completing the line, Bell still had half his assignment to finish, which was to return more or less by the way he had come and lay out a tentative line for a road. This he did, planting posts every 101 chains and marking the intersections of the road and township lines with stone monuments. He also carried the township lines back one mile from the road. In his final report, submitted in September 1848, Bell analyzed the country he passed through in some detail and mentioned tracts of "good," even "excellent," land, an opinion apparently based, like Sherriff's, on the relative abundance of different types of trees. And while he stated that "the chief part of [the country] ... quite fit for settlement," he also admitted that "the greatest objection ... in respect of the whole territory is the great abundance of rocks."[6]

After such a promising start, Bell gave up his surveying career after only a few years. By 1849 he had bought a Bytown newspaper that was to become the *Ottawa Citizen* three years later. He also became an enthusiastic promoter of railways when these came along in the 1850s and was the prime mover in the construction of a line between Bytown and Prescott. Named secretary of the railway when it was chartered in 1851, he went on to become its president, a position he held for many years. He served on the Bytown town council and was elected to the provincial legislature in 1861. Later, he ran for what had become the House of Commons in Ottawa on Confederation but was defeated. With the bankruptcy of his railway, his failure in politics, and, finally, the death of his wife in 1868, he retired to Hull where he died in 1873. He was only fifty-two.

While most immigrants during the 1830s and 1840s settled on the land, the cities and towns were growing, thanks in part to the introduction of local government. This had been ushered in by the District Councils Act of 1841, which had established district councils. The act was the brainchild of Lord Sydenham, the first British governor of the united provinces, who had been instructed by the home government to prepare Canada for self-government. Thus, while the district councils were composed of elected officials, they were presided over by wardens elected by the governor himself.

In 1849 the Municipal Corporation Act was passed. With its broad definition of a "municipality" as "a locality the inhabitants of which are incorporated,"[7] elected councils of townships, villages, towns, cities, and counties were created under the act both to manage local affairs and to undertake improvements. The act was to have a profound effect on the livelihood of land surveyors, providing new sources of work ranging from municipal surveys of one sort or another to surveys needed for the location and construction of new roads and bridges – all the work, in short, that the new town or township engineers were going to do.

Meanwhile, two minor pieces of legislation dealing with surveying had been passed. In 1839 a short act (2 Vict., c. 17) dealt with the question of ejectment and compensation arising out of unskilful surveying. The second act was passed in 1841–42. This was An Act to Grant Authority to Licensed Surveyors in that Part of this Province Called Upper Canada, to Administer Oaths and to Protect Them While in Discharge of their Duties in Surveying Lands (4 & 5 Vict., c. 9). By this act, it became a misdemeanour, punishable by a fine or imprisonment, to hinder or molest any licensed surveyor carrying out his lawful duties – as it is to this day, with a reminder to that effect appearing on the back of the identification card now carried by all Ontario Land Surveyors. The act also gave land surveyors the right to administer oaths to anybody giving information about doubtful boundaries or lost monuments, and to obtain such information in the form of a signed statement that was to be filed in the county registry office to be subsequently used in court if required.

Then, in 1849, the same year that the Municipal Act was passed, a survey act was passed that marked the end of a fifty-year era in land surveying in the province, an era that had seen the land surveyor change from a direct servant of the Crown in his capacity as a deputy of the surveyor general to an independent professional responsible for his own actions. This was the Act to Repeal Certain Acts Therein Mentioned, and to Make Better Provision for the Admission of Land Surveyors and the Survey of Lands in this Province (12 Vict., c. 35). All previous legislation pertaining to land surveying was swept away and replaced by an act that recognized the united provinces. Of the act's fifty-two sections, twenty were applied to both Lower and Upper Canada (these names remained in both official and popular use until Confederation), ten applied specifically to Lower Canada and twenty-two to Upper Canada. For the first time, a board of examiners was to be set up. This would serve both Upper and Lower Canada and was to be headed by the commissioner of crown lands with six others appointed by the governor. Candidates had to be twenty-one and must have served for three years as a legally articled apprentice to a qualified land surveyor, on the completion of which they were examined in geometry, including six books of Euclid, mensuration, plotting, and map drawing. And they had to have sufficient knowledge of spherical trigonometry and astronomy to determine latitude and to lay down a meridian.

The Board of Examiners was to meet four times a year. It could appoint a secretary, who received remuneration in the form of fees based on the number of examinations and certificates granted. A bond had to be entered into by the surveyor, as before, and an oath of allegiance and duty taken. Chain bearers who could not be closely related to the interested parties were also sworn in. With the commissioner of crown lands taking the place of the surveyor general, monuments were now to be placed in the commissioner's name. The removal of stone monuments was declared a felony, the removal or defacement of any other mark, a misdemeanour.

The commissioner was also to keep two standard lengths in his office, one English, the other French, by which surveyors in Upper and Lower Canada respectively must measure their chains. Accordingly a standard English yard (a brass bar, now in the possession of the Association of Ontario Land Surveyors) was obtained from Troughton and Simms in London, wooden replicas of which, marked in both inches and links, were supplied to every licensed surveyor. With the passage of the act, new rates of pay came in: five dollars a day for surveyors and a dollar a day for chainmen. "Explorers" got three dollars a day. The ration allowance was fixed at a dollar a day per man. And henceforth, qualified land surveyors would be known as provincial land surveyors, entitled to add the letters "P.L.S." after their names.

By now, new and improved instruments were becoming available to land surveyors, thanks largely to the industrial revolution, now gaining momentum, with its emphasis on mechanization and the improvements in instrumentation that went with it. Thus in 1824 William Simms in England mechanized Ramsden's "dividing engine," thereby bringing a new and greatly improved precision to the scales incorporated in astronomical and surveying instruments. This was followed up in North America by William Young of Philadelphia, who also built a "graduating engine" and who in the early 1830s built the first "transit." In effect, this was a theodolite in which the telescope could be completely revolved, or transited, on its horizontal axis – hence its name – which eased the task of taking back sights. In North America, the term "transit" came to be synonymous with that of "theodolite" as used in Britain.

The artificial horizon for use with sextants had appeared early in the century. The prismatic compass was introduced in 1812. And in 1836 William Burt, a surveyor and instrument maker in Chicago, patented his solar compass, which eased the task of establishing a meridian. More popular in the United States than in Canada, these would be used by some Ontario Land Surveyors later in the century.

With the advent of the railway in England, levelling achieved a new importance, with the first manual on the subject appearing in 1836, namely *A Treatise on the Principles and Practise of Levelling* by Frederick Simms, with a second edition in 1842 and a third in 1846. Among other things, it discussed the use of the Y and "Dumpy" levels, the latter recently invented by William Gavatt. By the late 1840s, the determination of altitude was being carried out by aneroid barometers instead of the cruder mercury hypsometers.

The type of work carried out by most surveyors in what is now southern Ontario had been changing for some time. While government work was there to be had for those who wanted it, an increasing number of land surveyors were taking on private work – and finding enough of it to enable them to work close to home. Charles Kennedy, for example, joined his brother, George, in Equesing Township in 1818, qualified as a land surveyor the next year, and practised in Georgetown, named after his brother, until he died there in 1864. Also qualifying in 1819, George Benson lived out his professional life in Belleville. Among other things, he laid out the village of Napanee in 1831 and carried out surveys for government in Huntingdon, Thurlow, Bedford, Rawdon, and Hungerford townships, eventually dying in Belleville in 1876.

Commissioned in 1825, Dublin-born James West lived in Mountain Township, Dundas County, where he had a farm, as well as in Morrisburg and Winchester Springs. Before his death in Yarker in 1880, he became one of the best-known land surveyors in the east. Also working in the east was Angus Cattanach, licensed in 1820, who had been a surveyor in his native Scotland before coming to Upper Canada and settling in Lanark County, where he died at Dalhousie Mills in 1873.

Mahlon Burwell's son Lewis, a qualified land surveyor since 1818, as already mentioned, worked out of Brantford all his life. Following early surveys in Burford, Dumfries, Oxford, and North Southwold townships, he went on in the 1830s to work in Luther and Enniskillen townships and also laid out the town plot of Cayuga. In 1834 he worked on the northwest boundary of the Huron Tract, first laid out by his father seven years earlier. His later years were increasingly spent in Brant County. At the other end of the scale, as it were, was William Fairfield, commissioned in 1822. After a diligent search, Fairfield's would-be biographers discovered that he had done no surveying

Field Notes as a Stock in Trade

Land surveying is nothing if not a historical process, with each surveyor building on the work of his predecessor. As we have seen, townships in earlier days were rarely laid out all of a piece. Hence the importance of marks and monuments to a future surveyor, who would be lost if he could not find them. And hence, too, the importance of a surveyor's original field notes. These – if they were as clear and concise as they should be – were invaluable to a later surveyor in search of earlier marks in order to furnish him, for instance, with the all-important "point of commencement."

And so, as an increasing number of surveyors turned to private practice, the original field notes became a *sine qua non* for any surveyor practising in the area in question, and as such they became something to be bought and sold. To this day, you may well find on an Ontario Land Surveyor's letterhead something to the effect that so-and-so's field notes are in his possession. These may well have passed from one surveyor to another down many years. The firm of M.H. Kaldeway Ltd. in Brockville, for example, lists on their letterhead field notes from no less than fourteen land surveyors.

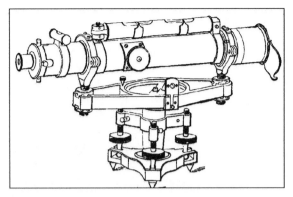

The development of precision instruments, known as "levels," to measure departures from the horizontal was hastened by the coming of the railways. Shown is a late nineteenth-century Y level, so-called because of the Y-shaped clamps. Note the bubble level mounted parallel to the telescope and another at right angles to it. (From Stanley, *Surveying and Levelling Instruments*.)

at all. (Though one of them thought he *might* have carried out a survey on Amherst Island.)

Since the earliest days, some surveyors combined their surveying pursuits with other activities. One good example is Thomas Walsh, sometimes spelled Welch, commissioned in 1793, who pursued his life as a land surveyor on the Niagara Peninsula and then in several townships in the vicinity of Long Point, where he settled in 1796 and where he was made registrar of deeds for Norfolk County. Later he went on to become a judge of the District and Surrogate Court. Thomas Ridout's son, Samuel, who came to acquire a farm on Yonge Street known as Summer Hill, combined his work in the Surveyor General's Office, first with that of sheriff of the Home District from 1815 to 1827, and then with that of registrar of the county of York, a post he held until his death in 1855, by which time he was living in downtown Toronto on "Park Lot No. 4." Qualifying in 1819, Josias Richey practised in Renfrew County until 1866, when at the age of seventy he was

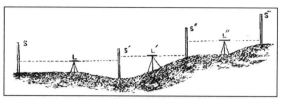

The use of a level is illustrated above. The difference in elevation between two or more points can be calculated from readings, as given by the level, on successive graduated vertical staffs (S above). (From Stanley, *Surveying and Levelling Instruments*.)

appointed lock master on the Rideau Canal at Smiths Falls. Still working at the age of seventy-nine, he lost his footing one day, and fell to his death in an empty lock.

Long before the days of town or township "engineers," more than a few early land surveyors ventured into the field of what we would now call civil engineering. Thus Edmund Decew, who had been one of Mahlon Burwell's apprentices and who qualified in 1836, became well known as both an engineer and a land surveyor on the Niagara Peninsula. The Decews or Decous were among the many Huguenot families that fled to England in the 1600s. From there, some of them emigrated to Vermont, from where Edmund's father, John, came north after the Revolutionary War to settle on land that included what became known as DeCew Falls on Beaverdam Creek. Here he built a substantial stone house (that still stands), which the British commander made his headquarters during the Battle of Beaverdam in June 1813. And it was to him, in John Decou's house, that Laura Secord delivered her famous message that, as tradition will have it, enabled the British – and their native allies – to win the battle. John held various municipal offices in the township of Thorold and he no doubt steered a variety of work in his son Edmund's way. Later in his working career, Edmund worked with his own son, also named John, who qualified in 1857. In their day the two of them

acquired a reputation as competent geologists. Edmund died in 1892 at the age of eighty.

Some surveyors went into business. At the time of the union of the two Canadas, James Chewett severed his connection with the Surveyor General's Office when it was moved to Kingston. His roots were firmly in Toronto, where he had become one of the city's first aldermen in 1835, the year after its incorporation. At about the same time, Chewett became involved in banking, first as vice-president of the Bank of Upper Canada, and then, from 1856 onward, as president of the Bank of Toronto, a position he held until his death in 1862.

Peter Carrol, whose nephew, Cyrus Carrol, would qualify as a land surveyor in 1860, also ended up as a banker. Qualifying in 1828, Peter Carrol worked from his farm near Ingersoll, spending many years as a land surveyor in the southwest before moving to Hamilton in about 1850 when he became a crown lands agent. He then went into road construction and became a gravel contractor, building a number of gravel roads in the vicinity of Hamilton. Expanding his business interests, he became a director of both the Gore Bank and the Bank of Brantford and in due course was also a director of the Great Western Railway and the Niagara Suspension Bridge Company. In 1876 he went on a visit to Europe in hopes of recovering his health. Ironically, he caught smallpox there, dying from it not long after his return.

Another land surveyor who became involved in banking was Alexander Vidal, whose career – perhaps the most varied and distinguished of any nineteenth-century land surveyor – was to take him to the Senate. Vidal came from a distinguished naval family, which, like the Decous, was of Huguenot stock. Born and educated in England, at eighteen he was to join the merchant marines when, in 1834, he was persuaded to accompany his father to Upper Canada. With his retirement from the navy imminent, his father had taken up land on the St. Clair River, land now occupied by the city of Sarnia.

In about 1840 Alexander Vidal apprenticed himself to John Wilkinson, then apparently living in Amherstburg. At that point, Wilkinson had not been qualified for very long himself. He, like the Vidals, had a service background, having come to Upper Canada as a half-pay officer after the Napoleonic Wars to settle in the Sandwich area. He represented the Western District in the provincial legislature for seventeen years, during which time he also worked as a civil engineer and then, after qualifying as a land surveyor in 1835, as a surveyor as well, working out of Sandwich and Amherstburg until he died in 1858. His son, Alexander John, also became a land surveyor, qualifying in 1843, eight years after his father.

After a year or so of apprenticeship under John Wilkinson, Alexander Vidal was ready to be examined. This meant travelling to the Surveyor General's Office in Kingston. All went well with the exam. In his own words: "Attended at Surveyor General's office and underwent an examination as to my ability for surveying, passed satisfactorily to Mr. Bouchette, and entered into a bond, conjointly with my father and Mr. Turguaned to discharge my duties faithfully; took the customary oaths and petitioned for a license."[8] He received it on 8 June 1842. He was among the last to receive his licence from the surveyor general before that office was abolished.

On getting home, Vidal worked for a short time in Sarnia and Moore townships and then in 1843 returned to Kingston to work in the Surveyor General's Office for six months. Then it was back again to Grey County where he surveyed the townships of Bentinck and Glenelg, which had been opened up to settlement by Charles Rankin's Garafraxa Road. Following this he became one of the first land surveyors to work in what is now northern Ontario.

The first land surveys in northern Ontario were made in the mid- to late 1840s in connection with mining claims. The location and survey of mining claims required specialized knowledge that not many

land surveyors possessed. When, in 1841, the Montreal Mining Company became interested in the mineral potential along the north shore of Lake Superior, they sent a large, well-equipped exploration party of their own, engaging Alexander Wilkinson to survey their claims, after which the company acquired extensive tracts of land in the area. In 1846 a claim was filed that eventually resulted in Canada's first commercially successful copper mine, located some 30 miles (50 km) east of Sault Ste. Marie at a place that became known as Bruce Mines. There were to be two mines, one called the Bruce, the other, the Wellington.

Up to that time, what little mining business there was had been handled directly by the provincial executive, with regulations drawn up by orders-in-council and exploratory licences issued directly by the secretary of the province. Then in 1846, the same year that the Bruce Mine claim was filed, mining affairs were transferred to the Crown Lands Department, the first of several accretions to a department steadily growing in importance.

After some dithering, the Crown Lands Department decided to undertake surveys of mining locations, as they were then known, in the northwest. Meanwhile, Vidal had already been instructed, late in 1845, to lay out mining locations (including that of the Bruce Mine) in the vicinity of Sault Ste. Marie. He was also to survey former North West Company posts in the area, which had become Hudson's Bay Company posts when the two companies merged in 1821. In addition, Vidal was instructed to lay out a town plot at Sault Ste. Marie, where, before long, American interests would start building a deep-water canal to bypass the rapids between Lakes Huron and Superior.

Vidal worked on these assignments for a couple of years, with supplementary instructions reaching him from time to time. For instance, in July 1846 he was told to reserve a one-acre site in the town for a customs house, while in 1847 he was told to survey mill sites

Alexander Vidal, one of the earliest surveyors to work in northern Ontario. He later became a distinguished senator.
Courtesy: AOLS Archives

along the St. Mary's River in addition to his mine-location work. By 1849 Vidal had apparently surveyed nearly thirty such locations along the north shore of Lake Huron and Lake George, as the Crown Lands Department was still calling Georgian Bay.

On finishing his assignment in 1848, Vidal had returned to his office in Sarnia. Writing from there in January 1849 he enclosed his accounts of his survey "of the Mining Tracts on Lake Huron," apologizing for the delay in forwarding his returns as his surveys were

Alexander Wilkinson. He acted as surveyor for the Montreal Mining Company in northern Ontario and made many surveys in Essex County. Courtesy: AOLS Archives

Albert Salter. He was a persistent advocate of the American 6-mile-square township survey system, and its eventual adoption was probably largely due to his efforts. He would later lay down the first base line in northern Ontario. Courtesy: AOLS Archives

"performed trigonometrically."[9] In May the commissioner acknowledged Vidal's plans, field book, diary, and report and added a rare accolade: "The assiduity and professional skill shown in your field work & the neatness and accuracy of your plans & field notes are highly creditable to you & satisfactory to this department."[10]

A couple of years later, in 1851, Vidal became the road surveyor for Lambton County. That same year saw him and his survey crew sailing north from Sarnia in a small schooner to spend four months laying out Saugeen Township, where Port Elgin and Southampton now stand. The following year, he gave up surveying for banking, becoming the manager of the Sarnia branch of the Bank of Upper Canada. When that bank failed in 1866, he switched over to managing the newly opened Sarnia branch of the Bank of Montreal. Meanwhile, he had become involved in politics. In 1861 he ran – unsuccessfully – as the Conservative candidate for the St. Clair division. Two years later he tried again and won. He held his seat until Confederation, at which point he retired from active politics. Appointed to the Senate in 1873, he served there with distinction as a leading advocate of the temperance movement until his death thirty-three years later, in 1906.

A few months after Vidal had been patted on the back for his surveys at the Soo, David Gibson was far from being congratulated for the work he had done on laying out the Durham Road. Gibson was not long back in Upper Canada after living in Lockport, New York, in self-imposed exile – at least since his pardon in 1843. He had returned to Willowdale in 1848 and had been reinstated as a provincial land surveyor. His assignment on the Durham Road was the first he had received on his return.

It seems Gibson's land-surveying skills had rusted. At any rate, we find the commissioner writing a frigid letter to him on 8 August 1849 pointing out a number of errors in his survey, which was followed by another on 20 October 1849 that questioned his accounts. Conceding that "the cost of the field work is greater than usual owing to the unfavorable weather," the commissioner went on to comment that "the charge for preparing your returns of survey is quite exorbitant – you have charged 64 days, 22 can be allowed ... The time charged for purchasing stationery cannot be allowed, but you will charge the cost of stationery and bindings."[11]

However, this poor start did not prevent Gibson from being appointed a member of the Board of Examiners only a couple of years later in 1851, a position he was to hold for the rest of his life. A year later, he tried to re-enter politics to run as a candidate for his old seat in the legislature. But he lost, and from then on he stuck to his surveying career, which until 1856 saw him at work laying out a number of townships in Simcoe, Huron, Grey and Bruce, and other counties. In this he was assisted by his sons, James and Peter Silas. It was to be the start of a notable family business.

By now, two other provincial surveyors had become involved in mining claim work in the north. One was John McNaughton, the other was Albert Pellew Salter. By 1847 McNaughton had surveyed over twenty mining locations at the western end of Superior, including one on the Pigeon River. McNaughton, the son of a soldier who had served in the Revolutionary War and been granted land in Charlottenburgh in Glengarry County, was by this time a veteran land surveyor in his mid-fifties. Qualifying in 1821, he had undertaken much of his work along and about the Ottawa River, where he laid out the townships of Pembroke, Ross, and Westmeath in Renfrew County. In his later years, McNaughton combined local surveying first with running a sawmill, which he built himself, and then with farming in Glengarry County. He would live on into his nineties, dying, apparently in Ottawa, in 1888.

Born in England, Albert Pellew Salter had come to Upper Canada in 1834. After living for some time in Lambton County, he moved to Sandwich were he taught in a grammar school. He then became interested in civil engineering and land surveying, perhaps because he had got to know the Wilkinsons. Salter also knew Vidal in Sarnia, who had studied under John Wilkinson. At any rate, Salter duly qualified as a provincial land surveyor in 1844, one year after Alexander Wilkinson did so.

It was perhaps Alexander Wilkinson (who had laid out mining claims for the Montreal Mining Company) who stimulated Salter's interest in the north. Salter was to play a leading role in opening up the lands north of Lake Huron. He may also have played a significant, if largely unnoticed, role in the adoption of the American 6-mile-square township as the basic survey system to be used in northern Ontario.

The Salter story may be said to have started in February 1846, when he wrote to the commissioner of crown lands, D.B. Papineau, on behalf of himself and Alexander Wilkinson. At that point, Salter had been qualified only a couple of years, Wilkinson, three.

Dear Sir:

Having been informed that it is the intention of Her Majesty's Government to survey the Crown lands, at present unexplored, situate on the northern shores of Lake Superior, we beg leave, respectfully, to tender you our services as Deputy Provincial Surveyors: and should you not have selected persons to perform that duty, we shall feel extremely obliged to your taking our application into consideration.

We also beg leave to submit, for your inspection, a small pamphlet, containing the instructions given by the several Surveyors General of the U. States to their Deputies, thinking that it contains some remarks which may be of service to the department.[12]

Salter then drew the attention of the commissioner to specific paragraphs in the pamphlet. What these referred to we don't know, but it's clear that Salter and Wilkinson had looked at the pamphlet with more than casual interest.

Salter's application was supported by a member of the legislature, who, writing to Papineau a few days after Salter had done so, stated that Salter was "a friend and supporter of his ... [and] that every confidence may be placed in him as a practical surveyor ... I will esteem it a personal favour," he concluded, "if Mr. Salter is promised such employment."[13]

Apparently nothing came of Salter's application, however, and in April Wilkinson wrote to the commissioner on his own behalf. Then, towards the end of that month, a James Henderson, who had acted as Salter's go-between in Montreal, wrote to Papineau in support of Salter's application, pointing out that "he is the gentleman who procured for the Commission of Enquiry into the Crown lands department the information respecting the disposal of public lands in the United States."[14] Henderson added that Salter refused payment for what he had done.

The following June, Salter finally got the nod. On 23 June 1847 he reported that he had arrived at Sault Ste. Marie and was ready to begin work on the survey of the mining locations assigned to him. He worked on these for two seasons, and then in 1849 he was instructed to lay out the township of Penryth fronting the St. Mary's River to the west of the Soo, his point of commencement to be the stone monument planted by Vidal "on the limit of the town plot of Ste. Marie." Penryth was the first township to be laid out in what is now northern Ontario, though it would disappear when the land was resurveyed a decade later.

In his survey report of 6 October 1849, Salter described the front of Penryth as being mostly swampy, though there were a few acres of good land. "The rear of the township," he added, "consists apparently of terraces of sand rising one above another for a considerable distance and terminating in a table land, but as far as the eye can reach the timber has been almost entirely destroyed by fire."[15] Forest fires would become the bane of surveyors working in the north, often destroying in a matter of minutes the blazed trees and wooden survey posts that represented months of careful and laborious work. Following this survey, Salter did not return to the north for some years.

In the meantime, in April 1848, at the suggestion of William Logan, the commissioner of crown lands had written to Captain Bayfield, then in Charlottetown, asking for copies of his "plottings" of the north shore of Lakes Huron and Superior and the St. Mary's River. The department had copies of his charts, but his actual "plottings" would help reduce the cost of the mining location surveys. No more land surveys were to be called for in the north until the mid-1850s.

The picture of a province relying on its roads and water-borne transport changed dramatically with the coming of the railways. The Liverpool and Manchester Railway, the world's first, had opened in England in 1830. It created an immense sensation, and Britain went railway mad. By 1840 the country had 500 miles (800 km) of track. Three years later there were 2400 miles. By 1848, there were some 5000 miles. This was not just a matter of putting down railway tracks. It has been written of those 5000 miles, that with "their cuttings, embankments, tunnels, bridges and viaducts, [they] included some of the most massive engineering works ever undertaken, and considered as a whole they were a feat of construction never previously equalled nor, perhaps, since surpassed."[16] Surveyors and surveyor-engineers played a vital role in bringing these mammoth projects to fruition. Some of them were to bring their expertise to Upper Canada – to Upper Canada's lasting benefit.

Almost from the start, Upper Canada got caught up in the British mania for railway building, with nine railway lines chartered by the legislature during the 1830s. In the event, only one was completed and even that was not a true railway. Running from Queenston to Chippewa 10 miles (16 km) away, and designed to bypass Niagara Falls, its grades were too steep for the power of any steam locomotive – the cars had to be drawn by horses. This unhappy outcome might have been avoided if the planners of the railway had had topographical maps to consult.[17]

Following this false start, interest in building railways waned until 1849 when the Guarantee Act was passed, which, as the name of the act implied, guaranteed government financial backing for railway companies. The result was a virtual explosion of railway construction, which, as far as the surveying profession in the province was concerned, was by far the single most important event of the mid-1800s. It was instrumental in bringing to the province a galaxy of notable land surveyors, among them Michael and William Deane, James Fitzgerald, Thomas Herrick, Thomas Molesworth, Clement Hanning, and George Kirkpatrick.

As William Deane put it in a letter urging his brother to come to Canada, the railway mania was on its last legs in England, whereas in Upper Canada it had just begun. He explains further that the railway lines' enormous lengths would require the services of many surveyors. Most of the land surveyors that came had a common background. They were Irish graduates of Trinity College, Dublin, where they received excellent training in both civil engineering and surveying. Most had cut their surveying teeth with the Irish Ordnance Survey, an extension into Ireland of Britain's prestigious Ordnance Survey. Following this, some had worked in England on railway and assorted municipal projects.

Such was the background of Michael Deane, who apparently took the advice of his younger brother, William, and came to Upper Canada to qualify as a surveyor in 1847, a year after his brother. William himself lived and worked out of Lindsay, and would later be one of the pioneer surveyors in the Ottawa-Huron Tract.

George B. Kirkpatrick, another of the Irish surveyors, was twenty-two when he came to Upper Canada in 1857 after leaving Trinity College. After two years on railway construction work, he served a three-year apprenticeship with A.B. Berry of Lennox and Addington County before qualifying in 1863. Later, in 1878, he would be appointed director of surveys for Ontario, and, in 1886, having lent his considerable professional support to the formation of what became the Association of Ontario Land Surveyors, he became the new organization's first president.

Stretching north from Toronto, the Northern Railway reached Aurora by 1852 and Barrie a year later. In 1855 it had reached Nottawasaga Bay at a point then known as Hen and Chickens Harbour. With the coming of the railway, a town sprang up there, which was named Collingwood. Like Collingwood, many of today's towns and villages in

---

William Deane Urges His Brother to Emigrate

In August 1847 William Deane wrote to his brother Michael, then still working in England, urging him to come to Canada. Of his own prospects, William said that "every day seems to bring with it fresh confidence. I have not the slightest doubt but in a few years we will be independent and have sufficient bona fide property to keep us the rest of our lives."

He discusses the price of instruments. "When I was in Montreal for my license last May I visited the only optician's shop in that city and found that a very good five inch instrument would cost 33 pounds ... Now taking these things into account, it would not be prudent to come without one. Any kind of a thing will do here. Because all you have to do is to measure one horizontal angle at a time ... a common circumferentor is very useful in this country, as it very often happens that you will be called to survey an irregular piece of ground, and triangulation ... is out of the question, there being so much woodland ... The surveyors in this country have all very poor instruments."

"In six months after you arrive ... you will be acknowledged a professional man, and then you can look back with pleasure at the toils and troubles you had to attain it" ("Michael Deane," in *AOLS, 1934*, 98–99). Within a few months of getting his brother's letter, Michael Deane was in Canada.

Ontario owe their existence to the fact that they were on the route selected by surveyors working for railway companies. For towns already established, the railways brought increasing prosperity. By the same token, places bypassed by the railway started to decline. The prosperous ports of Port Credit and Oakville, for example, declined with the building of the Great Western Railway.

Meanwhile, the Bytown and Prescott Railroad – to be renamed the Ottawa and Prescott when Bytown became Ottawa in 1855 – promoted by the erstwhile land surveyor Robert Bell, had been chartered. The first train arrived in Bytown on Christmas Day 1854. And by 1856 the Grand Trunk was linking Toronto and Montreal. The line was then extended to Sarnia via Kitchener and St. Marys. One of the many other surveyors who had been caught up in the railway boom was Stoughton Dennis, who surveyed a number of townsites along the routes to be taken by both the Great Western and Grand Trunk railways. By this time, Dennis was emerging as one of the foremost land surveyors in the province, having been appointed to the Board of Examiners in 1851.

From 1852 on, these major railway projects had been accompanied by a host of smaller ones following the passing of the Municipal Loan Fund Act, which offered financial assistance to municipalities who wanted to indulge themselves in railway building. Many invested in hopes of bringing instant wealth to their communities – until 1857 when financial panic set in and railway construction came to a sudden halt. Later, it was to be resumed once again at a more sober level. In the years ahead the province would be crisscrossed with a bewildering number of railways, some only a few miles apart, others destined to be short-lived. These would provide many land surveyors with employment, either on contract for planning and construction, or as permanent employees of railway companies.

The task of locating proposed railway lines in Upper Canada was made no easier by the continuing – and in retrospect, astonishing – lack of topographic maps. By this time several countries in Europe had carried out national geodetic surveys and had produced detailed contour maps of their territory. In France, Napoleon had followed up the *Carte Géométrique de la France,* begun as early as 1748, with an ambitious plan to map all of Europe on a 1:100 000 scale, which was well under way when his career was brought to an abrupt end at Waterloo in 1815. Switzerland began a national topographic survey in 1832, Austria even earlier. In Britain the first one-inch-to-the-mile sheet of the Ordnance Survey had been published in 1801. And when the series was completed later in the century, another was started at a scale of six inches to the mile.

The closest Upper Canada came to such maps were produced by private enterprise. These were based on township and county plans supplied by government, with further detail added by surveyors employed by the commercial map-maker concerned. These surveyors would inspect the area and add any creeks and ponds missed on the original township survey, as well as any newly constructed buildings. Though no actual survey work was carried out, they would often check the dimensions of farms. The result was maps that, in many cases, were more accurate than those produced by government. In the absence of data on altitude, however, no contours as such could be added.

For many years the only government agency producing topographic maps was the Geological Survey, which made these maps because its work would have been greatly hampered without them. In 1854, when asked by a government committee to enlarge on the difficulties faced by the survey, Logan observed that "independently of those [difficulties] incident to travelling in canoes in shallow rivers and on foot through forests, are those arising from the want of a good topographical map of the country."[18] That the government was so dilatory in carrying out topographic surveys was due not to inefficiency but to lack of money.

Immediate needs connected with the opening up and development of the country were paramount and would be for some decades to come.

CHAPTER ELEVEN

The Ottawa-Huron Tract, Muskoka, and Parry Sound

Up to 1850, logging on the Canadian Shield and around Georgian Bay, as well as prospecting for minerals on the upper Great Lakes, had all gone forward in the absence of any legal arrangement with any native people. But in that year – and about time, some might say – the Canadian government and the Ojibwas signed what became known as the Robinson Treaty. The latter surrendered all claims to virtually all of what we now call northern Ontario to the height of land* north of Georgian Bay and Lake Superior, together with so-far unceded land in Muskoka and Haliburton. All this in return for a cash settlement, hunting rights, and some reserves.

With native rights to the area now extinguished – at least to the satisfaction of the government of the day – Alexander Murray, Logan's assistant on the Geological Survey, was sent in 1853 on yet another exploratory survey through the shield country. Apparently unaware of David Thompson's earlier surveys, he travelled northward across the tract via Lake Muskoka, the Lake of Bays, and Canoe Lake – where he, like Thompson, also stopped to build a canoe, curiously enough – eventually descending the Petawawa to the Ottawa. He then recrossed the tract in a southwesterly direction.

Meanwhile, in 1849 the districts long used in Upper Canada for judicial and other purposes had been abolished. Their constituent counties under their respective county councils came into their own, and, following the Robinson Treaty, portions of the land now legally belonging to the Crown were annexed to them. As a result, Simcoe County suddenly found itself the possessor of all the land to its north as far as the French River. The county council quickly petitioned the governor general to have the area surveyed for settlement.

James Bridgland[1] (who would later become a superintendent of colonization roads) had, in fact, already been instructed to lay out the township of Carden to the east of Lake Simcoe. Having reported that the land was not worth subdividing, he was then told to run and open up two exploration lines through the heart of Muskoka. Bridgland ran his exploration lines in the summer of 1852, and on his return he wrote a devastating report on the suitability of the area for large-scale agricultural settlement.

*A "height of land" is an imaginary line between watersheds.

In 1852, James Bridgland ran exploration lines through the Muskoka country and reported that the Canadian Shield was unsuited for agricultural settlement. His report was unfortunately ignored. He later headed the Colonization Road Program. Courtesy: AOLS Archives

I must express my regret and disappointment ... The general quality of the land ... is extremely rocky and broken, so much so indeed, that, in a district explored of abt. five hundred square miles, not a portion, sufficient for a small township, could be obtained in any one locality, of a generally cultivatable nature.

The country northward of Black River, may be described as one vast field of granite rock.[2]

And so on. He concluded his detailed and largely negative report with this comment: "The only advantage, perhaps, which your department will realize from it, is, a knowledge, and a consequent safeguard, against incurring future expenses in the sub-division of a country into townships, and farm lots, which is entirely unfitted, as a whole for agricultural purposes." Wise words that were to be ignored in the decades ahead.

Calls for settlement of the newly acquired territories came at a time when the government was being pressured by the "lumber barons" in Ottawa, not only for settlements that would provide them with a closer and thus cheaper source of food, but for roads along which they could transport that food and extract their lumber. In response to these pressures, it was moved in the legislature in November 1852 by William Lyon Mackenzie, that an immediate survey be made of all the land south of the French River lying between the Ottawa and Georgian Bay – what soon came to be called the Ottawa-Huron Tract.

Interestingly enough, the motion specified exactly how the tract was to be laid out: using a township survey system resembling the American system. Could this have been due to Albert Salter's continuing advocacy of such, following his researches on behalf of the department only a few years earlier? It is reasonable to suppose so. Townships in the Ottawa-Huron Tract were supposed to be 7 miles (11 km) square with nine such townships forming one county. Each township would contain 49 sections, each of which were to be one mile square or 640 acres. Each section was to be subdivided into four quarter sections of 160 acres, with allowances for roads. However, as it turned out the system used in the tract was the 1000-acre sectional system, which had been introduced in the mid-1830s at the request of the Canada Company (see figure 9.4).

In 1853, the year after Mackenzie brought in his motion, a public-lands act was passed to further the settlement of the Ottawa-Huron Tract. It empowered the government to "appropriate as free grants any Public Lands in this province to actual settlers, upon which or in the vicinity of any Public Roads in any new settlements which shall or may be opened through the Lands of the Crown."[3] A colonization fund was set up under the act to pay for roads, land, and other costs associated with the scheme, such to be administered by agents of the Crown Lands Department. While the principle of colonization roads had already been applied with success in other parts of the province, it was only when such roads were built into the Ottawa-Huron Tract that colonization roads became an official program. As the government department responsible for immigration, the Bureau of Agriculture took over the Colonization Road Program in 1854, though it would be transferred back to Crown Lands in 1862, which had been virtually running the program all along.

In that same year of 1854, the British government had taken a step that was of particular significance to the future settlement of Canada: the clergy reserves were finally secularized. At the same time the British government gave up its right to disapprove of Canadian land bills. Canada was now mistress of her own settlement destiny and had taken an important step towards complete self-government.

Even before the passing of the lands act and setting up of the colonization fund in 1853, the

---

The Canada Land and Emigration Company

While it was primarily the government that attempted the settlement of the Ottawa-Huron Tract, private land settlement companies also tried. One such was the Canada Land and Emigration Company, incorporated in England in the early 1860s, with the Honourable Thomas Haliburton* as its first chairman. The company acquired nine townships in the county that Haliburton gave his name to, and one in Victoria County. It was finally agreed that some 260 000 acres in the ten townships were fit for settlement, and this the company paid for at 50 cents an acre.

The townships were outlined by crown surveyors, but their subdivision was the responsibility of the company. These went forward under Brooks W. Gossage, licensed in 1857, who at one point had a number of land surveyors working for him. From 1866, the company agent was Alexander Niven, a long-time resident of Haliburton, who had been licensed in 1859 and who would go on to become perhaps the province's most outstanding land surveyor.

The company had hardly got off the ground before the government started to implement its colonization roads scheme. With free land being offered in the same area, the company had understandable difficulty in selling its land. By 1870 it had sold or leased only a small fraction of its original acreage. Surprisingly, the company, after selling out and changing its name in the late 1880s, remained in existence for many years and was not finally wound up until the Second World War.

---

*A prominent judge and politician in Nova Scotia, Haliburton became Canada's first internationally known author, with his satirical series entitled *The Clockmaker; or the Sayings and Doings of Samuel Slick, of Slickville* eventually appearing in a book that ran into eighty editions.

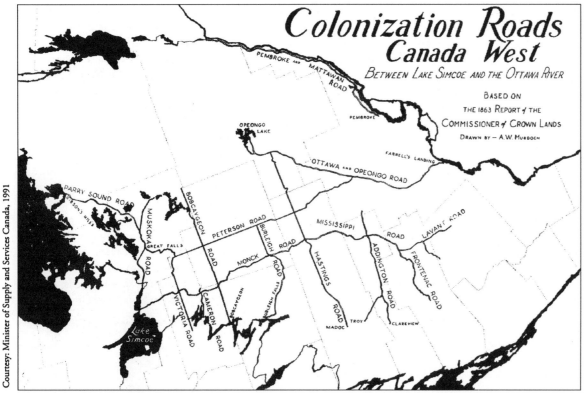

Courtesy: Minister of Supply and Services Canada, 1991

Figure 11.1 Designed to help lure settlers to the Ottawa-Huron Tract, this idealized version of the colonization road system in the tract was issued by the Department of Crown Lands in 1863. (From Thomson, *Men and Meridians*, vol. 1. Department of Mines and Technical Surveys no. 232-5238, Energy, Mines and Resources Canada.)

government had gone ahead with the survey and construction of roads into the Ottawa-Huron Tract. With lumbermen in mind, the government had completed a road from Arnprior to Pembroke in 1852, a road still known locally as the "Government Road." Similarly, work had also been done on the Opeongo Road – as it is still known today – which ran from the mouth of the Bonnechere River near Renfrew to Lake Opeongo in the heart of the tract. Originally intended to run clear across the tract to Georgian Bay, the Opeongo Road was more or less completed as far as Lake Opeongo by 1854 but was never extended as planned.

The government continued to dither over whether or not to actually open the Ottawa-Huron Tract to settlement until, in 1856, the Honourable Philip Vankoughnet, then acting commissioner of crown lands, pressured by lumbering interests, took it upon himself to set the ball rolling by committing his department to the policy of free land grants to settlers who would take up land along the roads. Following this, work went forward on the survey and construction of these roads, while at the same time efforts were made to open up the marginal land in the rear of the various counties fringing the southern borders of the tract.

In 1856 and 1857 Michael Deane ran exploration lines starting in Somerville Township, north of Fenelon Falls – one of them ran to Bell's Line. His comments on the fitness of the land for agriculture were guarded, though he did recommend building a road from Fenelon Falls to Bell's Line. While Deane was exploring the country in upper Victoria County in 1857, James Fitzgerald and John Lindsay were starting to outline a number of townships in the rear of Peterborough County, in the heart of what became known as the Haliburton District.

In that same year of 1857, a start was also made on opening up Muskoka, with Muskoka Township at the southern end of the lake partially laid out – this in spite of Bridgland's earlier comments on the unfitness of the land for settlement. In the ten years between 1856 and 1865, half of Hastings County's twenty-four townships were laid out, most of them at the northern end of the county. The same ten years saw eighteen of Renfrew's thirty-seven townships go in. Surveying activity was particularly intense in what is now the provisional county of Haliburton, with nineteen of the county's twenty-three townships surveyed in the five years between 1859 and 1863. An attempt would be made to promote a private land-settlement scheme in Haliburton County, but it came to nothing.

All this was accomplished in addition to surveys in connection with the location and laying out of the colonization roads themselves. In his report of 1863, the commissioner of crown lands was to include a map of the colonization road system (see figure 11.1). Designed to lure settlers, the map was inaccurate in that it included some roads that were only just begun and other roads that actually followed a somewhat more serpentine course. However, the map does give a good idea of the overall road system the commissioner envisaged.

South of the Opeongo Road, on which work was already going forward, as mentioned above, another east-west road was built. Originally, it was to follow the line laid out by Bell. As it turned out, another land surveyor, Joseph Peterson, suggested a better route one township to the south of Bell's survey line, and so what started off as the Bell Road became known as the Peterson Road. Local contractors began work from both ends. In the years ahead, contractors would find the building and repair of the colonization roads in the tract a lucrative source of income. As was to be the case with several of the roads, the Peterson Road was poorly constructed and maintained and, as early as 1865, was already being pronounced a failure. By the 1870s parts of it were so overgrown that they were closed to traffic.

The Bobcaygeon Road, started in 1856, ran north from present-day Fenelon Falls to Bell's Line following a line surveyed by Michael Deane, who also laid out a single tier of lots along it. In 1858 Stoughton Dennis did the same along the road north of Bell's Line. As originally planned, the Bobcaygeon Road was to be continued north to cross the projected western extension of the Opeongo Road, and in May 1859 John Roche was instructed to search out a line that would have taken the road through to Lake Nipissing. The son of a Royal Navy captain, Roche had emigrated to Upper Canada in about 1833, had been commissioned in 1841, and was on the first Board of Examiners set up under the act of 1849. He was a veteran land surveyor. Experienced in the bush as he was, he drowned on Balsam Lake when hurrying back in September 1859 to make a progress report on his survey.

Roche's survey was taken over by Crosbie Brady, who succeeded in running the line through to Lake Nipissing in the winter of 1859–60. Several of Brady's party contracted scurvy, and one of his assistants, John Roche's brother, David, died. Two deaths for a stretch of road that was never built is a steep price. The Bobcaygeon Road eventually got as far as the Oxtongue River, which flows into the Lake of Bays. The northern extension was abandoned. The southern part of the Bobcaygeon Road is now part of Highway

35, but north of Minden the modern highway follows a more easterly route.

Running roughly parallel to the Peterson Road but more to the south was the Monck Road. Though shown as apparently complete on the map of 1863, definitive surveys of the Monck Road did not begin until a year later when Peter Gibson surveyed it eastward as far as present-day Bancroft. At this point Thomas Weatherald took over, and then Robert Gilmour. They took the road as far as the north-south Hastings Road. Then in 1866 John Snow relocated the western end of the road, first surveyed by Peter Gibson, and supervised the beginnings of construction work where the road began in Mara Township on the northeastern shore of Lake Simcoe. At Bancroft, the Monck Road became the Mississippi Road, while feeding into the system from the south were the Frontenac, Addington, and Hastings roads, their names reflecting their respective counties.

Surveyed by Aylsworth Perry and William Rombough, construction of the Addington Road began in 1854, to be finally completed ten years later. The road followed a route close to present-day Highway 41, which runs north through Kaladar. Qualifying in 1842, Perry came of United Empire Loyalist stock and worked out of Kingston before moving to the village of Violet in Ernestown, where he was to live for the rest of his life. He outlined a number of townships in upper Hastings and Lennox and Addington counties for the Department of Crown Lands, as well as a survey of Presqu'ile. Later, when returning to survey in the Parry Sound District from Toronto, where he had gone to have a damaged instrument repaired, his canoe capsized in Georgian Bay. A nonswimmer, Perry clung to the canoe and eventually drifted safely ashore. It was said, however, that this incident broke his health. His constitution was further undermined by arduous surveying for the Kingston and Pembroke railways. Be that as it may, he was in his mid-seventies when he died in 1887.

John Roche, who was drowned when hurrying back from a road-location survey in the Ottawa-Huron Tract. He was one of many surveyors who worked in the tract.
Courtesy: AOLS Archives

The Hastings Road ran north from present-day Madoc to Bancroft, following a route somewhat to the east of present-day Highway 62. This road had its origins in the late 1840s when, it will be recalled, Publius Elmore explored a line for a road from Lake Township to the Madawaska River. Another north-south road was the Burleigh Road, a route first explored by James Fitzgerald in 1860. It ran north from Burleigh Falls to tie in, like the Bobcaygeon Road, with the Peterson Road.

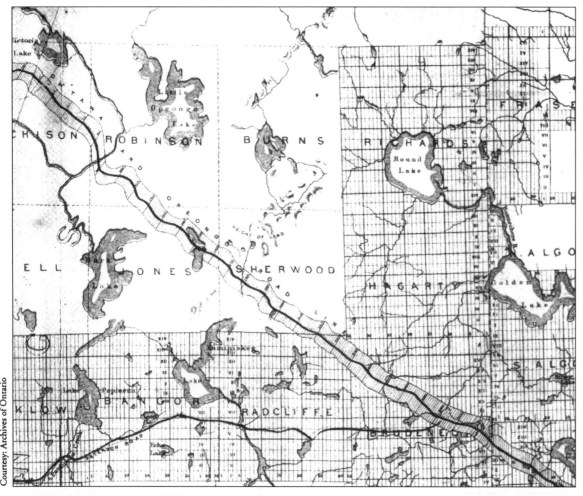

Figure 11.2 Lots laid out along the Opeongo Road, one of the colonization roads in the Ottawa-Huron Tract. Though widely advertised in Europe, the scheme to settle the tract was a failure. (Part of map of the Huron and Ottawa Territory, Upper Canada, Canada(s) Department of Crown Lands, 1861. AO: Crown Lands, 1861.)

By 1860, 481 miles (774 km) of colonization roads had been built, and efforts were made to persuade settlers to locate along them (see figure 11.2). But, with the promise of free grants, the best land was soon taken up and interest in settling among the rocks of the shield quickly waned. To keep the scheme alive, efforts were made to lure settlers from Europe with advertisements in German, French, and Norwegian, as well as in English. A few came, notably Kashub Poles who founded a settlement in the Barry's Bay area in 1864. Joined by other Polish settlers in the next thirty years, their descendants farm there to this day. But in general the scheme to settle the tract was a failure. With the American west opening up, it was a bad time to try and induce emigrants to come to Upper Canada. Even Upper Canadians were heading west in large numbers – so much so that for a while the exodus to the States was a matter of acute government concern. When Manitoba was opened to settlement later in the century, interest in the tract died once and for all.

Apart from the lack of emigrants, the colonization roads had in them the seeds of their own failure. Bogus settlers got their land, cut the trees off it, and then decamped to do the same elsewhere. On the one hand, legitimate settlers wanted roads they could use all year. The lumbermen, on the other hand, were interested only in winter hauling. And with too few settlers to keep them up, the roads quickly deteriorated. To cap it all, when the roads were finally complete, the lumbermen found that it was cheaper to bring in supplies in bulk, rather than buy them piecemeal from the settlers. With their market gone, many settlers abandoned their holdings and left.

C.F. Aylsworth, O.L.S., described the Hastings Road as he saw it in 1925: "In driving along the Hastings Road today, it is one, long trail of abandoned farms, adversity, blasted hopes, broken hearts, and exhausted ambition. And the mute evidence of it all is empty, dilapidated and abandoned houses and barns, orchards, wells ..." – all of it now being engulfed by the all-invading bush. The thin top soil soon disappeared to leave only "unproductive yellow silica sand."[4]

Today there are still traces of abandoned farmsteads and communities to be found along the erstwhile colonization roads in the Ottawa-Huron Tract, mute testimony not only to failed dreams but, let it be said, to the greed of the moneyed lumbermen who persuaded the government to undertake the colonization scheme in the first place. In retrospect it is clear that had the tract been properly surveyed and its agricultural potential thoroughly assessed, or had the advice of land surveyors such as James Bridgland been followed, then the scheme might never have been undertaken, with much money saved and, as far as the settlers were concerned, much suffering avoided.

Though little came of the efforts to populate the Ottawa-Huron Tract, the Colonization Road Program was to continue. Eventually it would figure largely in opening up northern Ontario in the 1900s. Transferred from the Bureau of Agriculture to the Department of Crown Lands in 1862 to become the responsibility of a newly formed Colonization Roads Branch, it remained there until 1900 when it was moved to the Department of Public Works. Not until 1947 did the government finally repeal the legislation governing colonization roads.

Of the many land surveyors involved in opening up the Ottawa-Huron Tract, Michael Deane would go on to become involved in railway work, taking part in the construction of the Toronto and Nipissing Railway and the branch line of the Grand Trunk from Kingston to Lindsay. The late 1870s and 1880s saw him working for the Dominion government and laying out townships in Manitoba. Retiring to Windsor in 1893, he died there four years later at the age of seventy-four. John Snow would go on to work in the West. His name became a household word throughout Ontario, when he became a central figure in the troubles that were to develop in the Red River colony.

As mentioned above, both Peter and James Gibson also became involved in the Colonization Road Program. Meanwhile, in 1853, the fortunes of their father, David Gibson, took a turn for the better. His friend, John Rolph, then commissioner for crown lands, appointed him inspector of various agencies in his department, including the Colonization Roads Branch. Gibson's work involved extensive travel, during which he found time to keep an eye on his farms in Willowdale and Lockport. By 1860 he was spending more time in the office in Quebec than in the field, and it was in a hotel in Quebec that he died in January 1864, it is thought of pneumonia.

Only in the case of the Muskoka Road did one of the original colonization roads lead, eventually – and both literally and figuratively – to other and better things. Trial lines for the road run by Charles Unwin in 1856 and 1857 were both too expensive. So David Gibson surveyed a third and more acceptable line northward from Washago at the tip of Lake Couchiching through present-day Gravenhurst to Muskoka Falls, then known as the Grand Falls, on the south branch of the Muskoka River. Construction of the road at its southern end began in 1858, with Charles Rankin laying off lots along it. The work was actually done by his partner, William Spry, who had qualified that same year and who would, twenty-eight years later, at the inaugural meeting of the Association of Ontario Land Surveyors in 1886, be the only person to speak against the formation of such an association.

While work went ahead on the road, Stoughton Dennis was instructed to carry out a series of exploratory surveys in Muskoka and Parry Sound. Assisting him on these surveys was John Oliver and two students. One was Milner Hart, who would receive his license in 1863 and who later, like many other land surveyors of this period, went to work out west. The other student was Vernon Wadsworth, who only three months earlier had sat for his preliminary examinations at the Parliament Buildings, then still at Front and Wellington streets.

Licensed in 1864, and destined to be made the association's first honorary president in 1931, Wadsworth would go on to become Brooks Gossage's partner in Toronto. On Gossage's retirement in 1868, Wadsworth then joined forces with Charles Unwin, who, apart from the then aging Frederick Passmore, was the only other licensed surveyor in Toronto at that time. The partnership of Wadsworth and Unwin lasted eight years and became noted for, among other things, compiling a map of the city of Toronto in 1872. Then in 1876 Wadsworth became an inspector for what was then The London & Canadian Loan and Agency Company, for which he worked for the rest of his life.

Dennis's first assignment was to extend the Muskoka Road from Muskoka Falls northeast and then east to connect with the Bobcaygeon Road. The beginning of July 1860 saw Dennis at Penetanguishene hiring axemen, a cook, and "packers" (i.e., load carriers). Later in July, the survey party assembled at Orillia, with what Wadsworth called the "staff" travelling north by the Northern Railway to Collingwood on 24 July.[5] They must have been among the first survey parties to start off by train – and they must have felt very much up to date.

From Orillia the party travelled north up the Muskoka Road to where it then ended at what is now Gravenhurst. They then took to canoes and eventually established a base camp near Muskoka Falls. Exploratory work on the Muskoka Road extension took them about a month. Searching for the best place to bridge the north branch of the Muskoka River, Dennis found none better than at what was then called the North Falls. The bridge (where Bracebridge was to grow) was soon being built. Dennis then, in the words of his report, "proceeded to connect this site with the Bridge which had lately been erected over the South Branch at the Grand Falls."[6] He then retraced his steps to the North Falls from where he took up the search for a line that would take the Muskoka Road northward.

After exploring the country north of Lake Vernon and Fairy Lake, he found the best place to bridge the north branch of the Muskoka (the Vernon) would be between the lakes. The construction of the bridge (where Huntsville was to grow) would not be completed until 1870. Having located this bridge site,

Dennis then worked northeast, but "although no pains were spared in exploring it was found impossible anywhere in the vicinity of the Survey to get a line however crooked upon which a road could be opened at any reasonable expense for construction ... "[7] He then continued his line out to that of the Bobcaygeon Road.

With the first part of his assignment completed, Dennis went on to his second, which was to run an exploration line for a road that would run west through present-day Port Carling to Georgian Bay where, at its terminus on the bay, he was to examine the possibility of establishing a harbour at the mouth of the Musquash River, which flows into the bay more or less opposite Penetanguishene. With that done, he was to have a look at Parry Sound as an alternative site for a harbour and then run an exploration line inland for some 50 miles (80 km) to meet the proposed extension of the Bobcaygeon Road.

Accordingly, Dennis took his party south again and, towards the end of September, explored the road line eastward to Georgian Bay, which he didn't think worth building, what with the many bridges and causeways required. Neither did he think much of the harbour at the terminus of the proposed road. The harbour was then used by ships bringing logs for the mills upriver, which they would exchange for sawn lumber. Dennis discovered such ships always had to make use of a pilot and, what's more, were often trapped in the harbour by contrary winds.

At the end of October, Dennis then took his party north once more, this to examine the harbour at Parry Sound. He was most impressed. "From my observations at this place together with information derived from the pilot ... and from mariners – all being corroborated by ... the gentleman in charge of the extensive mills erected by Mr Gibson, I am led to believe that this to be a commodious and safe harbour."[8] Dennis recommended in his report that a road be built to Parry Sound, following which, he received fresh instructions. He was to explore the country between Parry Sound and the line of the Muskoka Road with a view to putting in a road and, as was customary, examine the land with a view to possible settlement.

By July 1861 Dennis had established a base camp at the head of Lake Rosseau, and was surveying west to Parry Sound and east to the line of the Muskoka Road. The final road line was surveyed by Peter Gibson's brother, James, in the winter of 1862–63 with construction beginning about the same time. In modern terms, the Parry Sound Road left the Muskoka Road a few miles north of Bracebridge, ran north and then northwest through Rosseau, a route now roughly followed by Highway 141. Forty-five miles (72 km) long, the road was finally completed in 1867. By this time other roads were under construction. One was the Northern Road, which ran north and east from Parry Sound. The other, begun in 1864, ran from Rosseau by way of Magnetawan to Nipissing, a village on Lake Nipissing's south bay. Completed for winter traffic by 1873, it is still used by local traffic for much of its length.

As the Muskoka Road was being pushed northward, the first townships in Muskoka were being outlined and then either wholly or partially laid out. The first was Muskoka Township itself at the southern end of Lake Muskoka, begun in 1857 by Rankin. By 1869, two years after Confederation, all but five of the twenty-two townships in the original district of Muskoka had been laid out. With work going forward on the Parry Sound Road, a start was made on laying out the first townships in what is now the district of Parry Sound. McDougall and Foley, to the north and south respectively of Parry Sound itself, were surveyed in 1866, along with Humphrey Township, which included the north end of Lake Joseph and part of the tip of Lake Rosseau. Two years earlier, the township of Mattawan had been laid out on the Ontario-Quebec border east of North Bay. Though north of the Mattawa River and thus, strictly speaking, lying in northern Ontario, Mattawan came to lie in the modern district of Nipissing and was thus the first township of the no less than eighty-eight townships that were to be laid out in that district in the years ahead.

CHAPTER TWELVE

Upgrading the Profession and on to the Northwest

Plagued by inefficiency immediately prior to the union of the two Canadas in 1841, the state of the Crown Lands Department improved but little afterwards. This was hardly surprising. In the twenty-six years between the formation of the United Provinces and their separation again at Confederation in 1867, the post of commissioner of crown lands changed hands no less than eighteen times. Making matters worse, the Crown Lands Department was, it seems, forever on the move. From 1841 to Confederation, the seat of government changed seven times: from Toronto to Kingston; then to Montreal; then back to Toronto; then it was off to Quebec; back to Toronto once more; then back to Quebec; and finally, on Confederation, to Ottawa. As far as the Crown Lands Department was concerned, each change in the venue of the legislature involved the movement of four hundred or so employees, not to mention all their files and records. In the circumstances, one is amazed that any work was done at all.

At the same time the department started to grow. In 1846 it took on mining affairs, as already mentioned. In 1852 the Woods and Forests Branch was created to handle timber licences and dues. As the department got larger and more unwieldy, its inefficiency was compounded by interbranch jealousies, which poor supervision at the top did little to smooth. In consequence, the process of land settlement became bedeviled by land speculation. It was to transpire that not a few of the Crown Lands Department's own land agents were involved.

Another reason that the Crown Lands Department had got into such a mess was that its year-to-year operations had never been scrutinized by its political masters in the legislature, who had never been favoured with regular reports. Finally, in 1855 the legislature passed a resolution requesting the commissioner of crown lands to issue an annual report. The commissioner at that point was the Honourable Joseph Cauchon, who had been appointed on 27 January of that same year. Formerly a newspaper publisher and editor, Cauchon was not only ambitious, articulate, and aggressive, he was also a first-class administrator and something of a visionary.

On assuming office, Cauchon lost no time in taking measures that had three principle objectives: first, to reform the system by which crown lands were disposed of and to eliminate corruption; second, to restore public confidence in the Crown Lands

The Honourable Joseph Cauchon. As commissioner of crown lands, he advocated the settlement of northern Ontario and introduced much needed reforms in the Surveys Branch.
© Queen's Printer for Ontario. Reproduced with permission of the Ministry of Natural Resources.

Department, the Surveys Branch included, the efficiency of which was increasingly under fire; and third and most important, to promote the development of the northwest, thereby joining his influence and abilities to a cause that was quickly becoming a matter of public debate.

After two years in office and one year after a report on his department was called for, Cauchon produced a massive, book-sized document that not only

contained a detailed critique of the workings and efficiency of the department, including that of the Surveys Branch, but was also the vehicle for expounding Cauchon's own views on the need for western expansion, complete with suggestions as to how this might be brought about.

Cauchon's report for 1856 revealed, much to a modern reader's surprise, that the Surveyor General's Office had never been fully abolished. Listed on a

return of the officers and clerks of the department, under "Surveyor General's Office, late," appear the names of four clerks, headed by William Spragge, noted as having been appointed by Sir John Colborne in 1829. Unusually outspoken for a junior civil servant, Spragge had played a central role in uncovering the corruption that was plaguing the Surveyor General's Office in the late 1820s and thereby gained much respect. So here he was, still in harness, nearly thirty years later. What Spragge and his clerks did, beyond making out a few returns and reports, is not clear. Needless to say, the Surveyor General's Office was finally put to rest in the course of Cauchon's efforts to clean up and reorganize the Crown Lands Department.

Everybody's pay went up. In 1856 Andrew Russell, as the "Senior Surveyor and Draftsman," was getting £460 per annum. The next year he was appointed to the newly created post of assistant commissioner at a salary of £1,200. These and similar changes were the result of Cauchon's efforts to set up a permanent civil service, thus providing administrative continuity, the lack of which, as he made clear in his report, was largely to blame for the troubles then besetting the department. In 1857, not long after Cauchon resigned, a Civil Service Act was passed that introduced the concept of a deputy minister who, as a senior civil servant, would bridge the gap from one political administration to the next. Though it would be some years before the Civil Service Act would be fully implemented, Russell's appointment in effect made him deputy minister.

Thomas Devine, listed as "Assistant Surveyor and Draftsman" in 1856 with an annual salary of £300, took over Russell's position as senior surveyor in 1857 with his pay quadrupled to £1,200 a year. On becoming head of the branch, he replaced Russell as chairman of the Board of Examiners, a position he held until his resignation from the government in 1879. Devine, who had come to Canada from Ireland where he had worked on the Ordnance Survey under the Royal

Andrew Russell, senior surveyor in the Crown Lands Department. Cauchon appointed him assistant commissioner of crown lands in 1857, thus making him in effect the first deputy minister in the provincial government.
© Queen's Printer for Ontario. Reproduced with permission of the Ministry of Natural Resources.

Appointed senior surveyor in the Crown Lands Surveys Branch in 1857, Thomas Devine became a noted cartographer and compiled the first official map of Canada. He devised the split-line method of recording field notes.
© Queen's Printer for Ontario. Reproduced with permission of the Ministry of Natural Resources.

Engineers, had been a licensed land surveyor since 1846, though he had only worked once in the field – carrying out a survey of the York branch of the Madawaska River the year after he qualified.

From that time on, Devine had been attached to the Surveys Branch as a surveyor and a draughtsman. He was to become noted for his cartographic work. He supervised the drawing of a map of the northwest to accompany Cauchon's report of 1856, which is considered to be outstanding for its time. This was to be followed three years later by the first official map of Canada, covering the area from the Gulf of St. Lawrence to the Red River. Widely published and referred to, its excellence led to Devine's election to the Royal Geographic Society in 1860.

Judging by Cauchon's report and the annual reports that followed in the next few years, the public was becoming vociferous in its complaints over the inaccuracies of earlier surveys. Thus, in his report of 1856, Cauchon dealt at some length with the reasons for these inaccuracies and what was being done to set matters right:

> As no uniform mode was adhered to in laying out ... road allowances in the older surveys, much uncertainty exists as to their true position which has given rise to many lawsuits ... and has seriously retarded the improvement of the roads.
>
> Owing to the use of the magnetic needle and the inferiority of the surveying instruments used, and to the unskillfulness of some of the surveyors, who did not make allowances for the difference in the variation of the compass at different places, nor for the progressive change in the variation at the same place, and especially owing to the want of check lines, many gross errors were made in earlier surveys.
>
> In the year 1818, an attempt was made

to ensure greater accuracy ... but in consequence of the surveys at that period having been performed by contract and paid for by land, the attempt was not successful, for of all of the older surveys none have been found so defective as these.

Cauchon ended on an optimistic note: "As all the outlines of every section are now surveyed in the middle of the road allowances, the uncertainty as to the true position of roads and the errors in the areas of the lots so frequent in the older surveys, are avoided."[1]

This last was a reference to a new set of instructions that Cauchon had just issued to all provincial land surveyors in connection with surveys in the Ottawa-Huron Tract, and which were included in his report for the information of both the legislature and the public. These instructions covered a number of points besides the positioning of lines in the middle of road allowances. All bearings were to be checked by astronomical observations; detailed records of magnetic variation were to be kept; and back sights were to be taken at each station. The length of chains (the links of which tended to become worn and stretched with use) were to be checked frequently, and theodolites examined often "to prevent errors which would arise from the derangement of its adjustment."[2] The size, placement, and marking of posts for township corners, concessions, and lots were to be specified, with their positions in relation to the nearest tree, such a tree to be blazed and marked "B.T.," standing for "Bearing Tree." Original survey posts and marks were to be "diligently" searched for and original boundaries adhered to.

Eligible town sites were to be noted, all lakes traversed, and, where necessary, road allowances laid out around them. Finally, when the field work was completed, a 40-chains-to-the-inch plan of the survey was to submitted to the department, which had to show all natural features, including hills, swamps, meadows, lakes, and streams, as well as cleared land and build-

ings, sites for mills and town plots, harbours, and "other public improvements." The surveyor was also to furnish a map of the township with various types of timber shown in different colours, along with notes on their relative abundance. "Mount your drawing paper," the surveyor was instructed, "on thin linen or cotton, well stretched on your drawing table, previous to drawing your plan, and roll, not fold it, when you send it to this Department."

The surveyor was to keep a diary ("in the form transmitted herewith") in which he was to enter the number of chains surveyed each day, along with notes on the weather, and where and when men were hired, together with their names. A field book was also to be kept "in the accompanying form" for recording all astronomical courses of all lines run, the magnetic variations, and distances in chains and links, as well as all types of soil and timber, the topography of the country traversed, marshes, swamps, meadows, the width and depth of all rivers and "brooks" crossed, all "mines and minerals," all travelled roads, and, finally, "the tracts [tracks?] of hurricanes as shewn by the fallen timber."

The method used to measure the distance of an object from the survey line, or length of an offset, was also to be specified. The surveyor was told: "Your Report of Survey must contain a concise summary of your proceedings, with a few general observations on the physical geography of the country, its capabilities and the best mode of developing them." And there was a final exhortation. The report must be written on "paper of the same size as the printed forms of field notes and diaries, as it will be bound with them."[3]

The sample field book that was distributed to surveyors was laid out in a novel manner devised by Thomas Devine himself. As he was to make clear in the department's annual report for 1860 and 1861, he was disgusted at the haphazard methods used by earlier surveyors to make their field notes. In his "split-line method," as it came to be called, the taking of field notes was rationalized by placing the distance column

Frederick Passmore's camp when he was resurveying Scarborough Township in 1864. Note Union Jack flying above the camp. Passmore has a street in Scarborough named after him. (From the Richard Schofield Historical Collection, Scarborough Archives.)

sion. Section 2 of the act merely stated that no one could act as "a surveyor of lands" in the province unless he was legally authorized to do so, something that one would have thought had long been clear – yet it apparently needed to be spelled out once again. The act instituted a preliminary examination of would-be land surveyors before they could enter an apprenticeship. The examination was to be a rigorous one, intended to ensure that would-be students had a thorough knowledge of basic mathematics, including plane trigonometry. It was also designed to test the candi-

---

Surveys with Marriage Licences on the Cheap

A poster nailed to a barn in a village in southwestern Ontario and seen by Charles Unwin in 1865 is reproduced below. Unwin did not give the man's name.

Cheap Land Surveying

P.L. Surveyor, Conveyancer and Issuer of Marriage Licences

In returning thanks to his numerous friends begs leave to remind all in Kent and Essex that he is always on hand in the above line of business, all orders either verbal or written promptly attended to; for surveying or conveyancing he has a deputy to issue marriage licences at Rond Eau, please address Rond Eau, Chatham, Thamesville, Ridgetown, Romney, Morpeth, Florence, Kingsville, and Leamington Post Office – Can boast over all for cheapness and can adjust all difficult lines with the aid of the old field notes of Samuel Smith, Esq., and drawing meridian lines. Take notice – No extra charge for travelling, as he keeps a conveyance of his own. Charge, $4 a day.

Silver at par for issuing marriage licenses.

---

in the centre of the page, with natural features indicated by pictographs drawn to the left or right of the column as the case might be. Distances in chains and links were entered from the bottom up. Devine's split-line method came to be widely adopted and remains standard to this day.

That all was not well with the land surveying profession itself was also made obvious by the passage in 1855 of new legislation governing the profession. The surveyors act of 1849 had been modified in 1851–52 (14 & 15 Vict., c. 4), which very sensibly provided for

separate boards in Upper and Lower Canada, one meeting in Toronto, the other in Quebec, with the commissioner of crown lands presiding over both, but with separate secretaries and different members at large. In Upper Canada the number of members was now increased to eight. By the same token, standard lengths would now be lodged with both secretaries. The fee payable by a successful candidate for a certificate was doubled to £5.

The act of 1855 (18 Vict., c. 83), however, was clearly directed at upgrading standards in the profes-

date's reading and writing skills.

The act also responded to the many complaints coming in of the inaccuracy of early surveys. Should a municipality (on the application of half of those directly concerned) decide that a "concession or range" should be resurveyed, it could apply to have such a survey carried out under the authority of the commissioner of crown lands. Such monuments that were raised in the course of that survey should be "the true limits thereof, any law or usage to the contrary, notwithstanding." These provisions were enlarged on just a couple of years later when a further act was passed (20 Vict., c. 73) concerning the establishment of boundaries "in all cases in which concession Lines were not run in the original survey." Following the passage of these two acts, municipal resurveys under the auspices of the commissioner would be a steadily increasing – and profitable – source of work for many surveyors.

As far as professional standards went, the act of 1855 was followed by an amendment in 1857 (20 Vict., c. 37), which reduced the period of apprenticeship to one year for those who, after articling, attended a Canadian university and took two years of courses in "civil engineering, natural philosophy [i.e., science], geology, and the other branches of education required by law for admission as a land surveyor," and had obtained a "degree or diploma of qualification as a civil engineer or land surveyor." There was also provision for those who had been to university for less than two years.

That a knowledge of geology was now to be an important requirement was underscored by a circular, dated 24 December 1856, sent to all land surveyors by F.F. Passmore, then secretary of the Board of Examiners. This requirement was clearly made with northern mining potential in mind. However, the main burden of the circular were various irregularities that had been uncovered and what was to be done about them. This circular, too, was included in an appendix to Cauchon's report, by way of reassuring, one assumes, a public that had growing doubts as to the efficiency and integrity of provincial land surveyors. Having informed surveyors that their apprentices now had to know something about geology, Passmore went on to say that complaints had been received by the board that "many persons not duly authorized, are practising as land surveyors" and reminding whoever might read the circular that this was "a misdemeanour and punishable accordingly." He also asked all provincial land surveyors "to aid the board in its endeavours to put a stop to a practice so injurious both to the public and the profession."[4]

Passmore then dealt with another irregularity. The Board had "learned from the most reliable sources, that apprenticeships are in several instances only *nominal;* the surveyor in some cases has ceased to practise, and in others, the student does not reside with the Surveyor, nor even in the same locality, consequently is not *bona fide* serving with him." Further, some surveyors were allowing their apprentices to work, without supervision, as fully qualified land surveyors, this "to the injury of the duly admitted practitioner."[5] Passmore added that any provincial land surveyors found guilty of granting false certificates would be suspended or dismissed.

By way of a follow-up to all this, yet another circular concerning bogus land surveyors was issued by the Crown Lands Department. Dated 8 December 1857, and appearing over the name of Andrew Russell, assistant commissioner of crown lands, it ran as follows:

As complaints have been made ... an official list of the provincial land surveyors for Upper Canada, is enclosed herewith for your information and guidance. You will not employ any person to survey lands, not accept of plans, certificates, or returns of survey, from any one whose name is not in the accompanying list.[6]

Included on the list, which was arranged alphabetically, were the names of all the licensed land surveyors who had worked in the province since John Collins was commissioned in 1764. The one exception was Samuel Holland. There were 369 names on the list, of which some 225 were shown to be have been active at the time that the circular was issued. Over 140 surveyors on the list were shown as deceased as of 1857 (see appendix A).

That the list included dead surveyors at first seems odd. But presumably the list was not just for the benefit of anyone thinking of employing a land surveyor, but also for lawyers or anyone else dealing with past and possibly forged deeds and the like, which might have the name of a fictitious and conveniently dead land surveyor attached to it. Of the 369 land surveyors listed, 163, or well over 40 percent, had been licensed in the two preceding decades, in itself an indicator of the growth in the profession that had taken place since the union of the two Canadas.

Efforts to restore public confidence in the efficiency of provincial land surveyors and the results of their work were to continue. Thus in the department's annual report for 1860 Thomas Devine, in his capacity as head of surveys in what had just become the Department of Crown Lands,[7] enlarged at some length on how provincial land surveyors went about their work. He touched, for instance, on the type of surveying instruments used by land surveyors. "The instruments used in the various surveys belong to the surveyors, and are generally five-inch theodolites, or transit theodolites of that dimension, graduated to read single minutes, and Gunter's chains of 66 feet, or one hundred links."

Having mentioned the resurveys of older townships ordered that year (these had been going on since 1855), Devine enlarged on the reasons why this had been found necessary:

Between the years 1819 and 1827, about 50 townships of 64,000 acres each had been surveyed by contract into farm lots in Upper Canada. The surveys of these townships were performed in the most loose and careless manner ... It has been discovered by examination on the ground, that lines have been run in the most erroneous manner – some of the lots falling short of the quantity patented by as much as 20 acres.[8]

He claims, however, that all would be well from now on: "Since surveying by contract has been abandoned, and astronomical surveys adopted, few or no complaints have been made to the Department of erroneous surveys." For the first time, surveys would be audited, to use the official term, before the land was released for settlement, to make sure that the acreage of individual lots as returned by the surveyor was in fact there.

While land-surveying procedures and the profession itself benefited immeasurably when Cauchon shook up the department, the Surveys Branch included, the department as a whole continued to have troubles as it acquired new functions and grew steadily more unwieldy. In 1856, ordnance lands, that is, military reserves, were transferred by the imperial government to the province of Canada and were placed under the wing of the department. In 1857 a Fisheries Branch was formed to foster conservation and regulate catches at the various fishing stations along the St. Lawrence and on the Great Lakes. And in 1860 the department absorbed Indian Affairs, up to that point another imperial agency administered directly by the governor's office. The acquisition by the department of control over ordnance lands and Indian Affairs added to the workload of the Surveys Branch as both ordnance lands and native reserves had to be surveyed or resurveyed. Much of the work on the former, it may be added, was entrusted to one man: Stoughton Dennis.

By about 1850, with good land in Upper Canada increasingly hard to come by, both the British and Canadian governments were becoming seriously concerned at the number of emigrants ending up in the United States. At the same time, both governments started to give thought to developing the northwest. In fact, with the increasingly expansionist mood of the Americans, there were growing fears that unless something was done there might not be any British territory west of Superior to develop. Michigan had achieved statehood in 1837, Wisconsin in 1848, while farther west, American settlers from Minnesota, which would be admitted to the union in 1858, were drifting north into the Red River country. In 1856, with doubts rising as to the ability of the Hudson's Bay Company to resist American pressures, British troops were sent to the Red River settlement, this both to reinforce British sovereignty over the region and to help stabilize the situation in the settlement itself, then under the sway of the company.

Just how much more advanced was American settlement in the northwest at about this time can be seen in a report written in January 1861 by William Gibbard, a provincial land surveyor, who at that point was superintendent of fisheries on the upper Great Lakes. The season before, he had been instructed to tour, inspect, and report on mining locations on Lakes Huron and Superior. In his detailed report, he states that the white population along the Canadian shores of Lake Superior, excluding those at Hudson's Bay Company posts, consisted, in the spring of 1860, of precisely nine people, two of them women. Add in all those associated with the Hudson's Bay Company and the total still came to only 115. Gibbard contrasted this with the nearly seventeen thousand living on the south, or American, shore of Superior, a total established by census not long before.

There were only four Canadian ships on Lake Superior, compared with seventeen American steamships, not to mention over a hundred schooners, seven or so steam tugs, two steam dredgers and two fully armed revenue cutters. As for mining, there was intense activity on the American side, while no mines were operating on the Canadian – the Bruce and Wellington mines having temporarily shut down. Wrote Gibbard, "The difference in the prosperity and trade of the North and South shores of Lake Superior is quite disheartening."[9]

In 1855 two things happened that augmented the need to open up the Canadian northwest. First, the Northern Railway reached the small settlement on Nottawasaga Bay, which was renamed Collingwood, and, second, American interests com-

William Gibbard. He laid out the town plot of Collingwood and Meaford and was murdered in mysterious circumstances. Courtesy: AOLS Archives

pleted a shipping canal at Sault Ste. Marie. Within two years of its founding, Collingwood was to grow into a town of some two thousand people – it wasn't long before steamers were leaving it's new 800-foot (250-m) pier for Sault Ste. Marie and Fort William, and for Mackinac, Green Bay, and Chicago with onward connections to the American West. With Sault Ste. Marie starting to acquire a new importance, it was decided in the early 1850s to place settlers on St. Joseph Island to the southeast. Starting in 1852, the island was divided into three townships. Hilton and St. Joseph were completed by 1855. The third township, Jocelyn, was completed two years later. All three were laid out as 1000-acre sectional townships as in the south.

As a leading proponent of the development of the north and northwest, Cauchon, on becoming commissioner early in 1855, ordered an exploratory survey of the north shore of Lake Huron. The land surveyor selected was Albert Salter, who by now had moved to Chatham. Presumably Salter's enthusiasm for developing the north, together with his continued advocacy of the American way of laying out townships, was by now widely known.

Salter was not only to carry out the survey but to escort a certain Count de Rottermund, a French geologist who was to examine the mineral potential in the vicinity of the Soo. Instructions were issued to Salter on 18 June 1855 and were accompanied by an advance of £250, no small sum in those days and an indication of the importance attached to the survey.

Salter was on his way four days later, leaving Chatham on 22 June for Detroit, where he bought supplies and hoped to obtain some instruments. In this he was unsuccessful, so he sent an assistant to New York for them. On his assistant's return five days later with a sextant and some compasses, Salter and de Rottermund left for the Soo. After conducting a joint examination of the country around the Soo and the Bruce Mines, they separated, with Salter working his way east along the north shore and having a good look at the lower reaches of the Thessalon, Mississagi, Blind, Serpent, Spanish, and French rivers as he went.

The beginning of November found Salter and his party on Lake Nipissing. With the weather worsening, Salter discharged his party on 5 November and by 10 November he was back home in Chatham. He then got down to work preparing his returns, which he forwarded to the department by the end of January 1856.

In his report, Salter made much use of such phrases as the "country presents a very rugged and barren appearance," but he was sufficiently impressed with such well-timbered alluvial flats and valleys as he came across to suggest that they were sufficient for the establishment of "at least sixty fine townships of thirty-six square miles each, capable of producing to perfection, rye, oats, barley, maize, grass and all kinds of root crops." He then went on to speak of the region's vast timber resources, its rivers with "their magnificent water-power," and its mineral potential. Salter ended his report with a recommendation that the American system of survey be used to open up the region.[10]

In the summer of 1856 Salter was back in the North, laying down what was to be the first base line in northern Ontario, still familiarly known to local surveyors as Salter's Line (see figure 12.1). The line, which was to extend from Lake Nipissing to Sault Ste. Marie, was to be the first step towards putting in several tiers of townships along the North Shore. These were to be 6 miles (10 km) square, as in the American system.

Thus, some time during the winter of 1855–56 or in the spring of 1856, the decision had already been taken to change to that system. Salter's final report on his exploratory survey of 1855, with his reiterated recommendation that the American survey system be adopted, would have reached Cauchon in February

The Curious End of William Gibbard

William Gibbard had the dubious distinction of being murdered – that, at any rate, was the coroner's verdict. A graduate of Cambridge, he served with the Royal Engineers in India before emigrating to Canada in 1841 to qualify as a provincial land surveyor three years later.

As a justice of the peace in 1863, he took a posse of police to intervene in a dispute over fishing rights between a fisherman and native people on Manitoulin Island. Violence ensued, with the fisherman forced off the fishing grounds to take refuge in Little Current. Three men were arrested, and a riot followed. Gibbard and his policemen were forced to release their prisoners, but they went on to Bruce Mines where a native was arrested and charged. Returning by steamer to Collingwood with the prisoner, Gibbard disappeared in the night, with his body later found floating near Little Current. The coroner's verdict was "wilful murder by a person or persons unknown."

Scandal on St. Joseph Island

In the 1830s, St. Joseph Island had been the site of a short-lived settlement founded by a Major William Kingdom Rains, a retired British army officer. The island had long been a military reserve, and Rains bought land from the government at a shilling an acre. Rains's settlement failed, but Rains himself stayed on to become the object of scandal. After legally separating from his wife, he brought two attractive sisters with him to the settlement, eventually having children by both and building each a house.

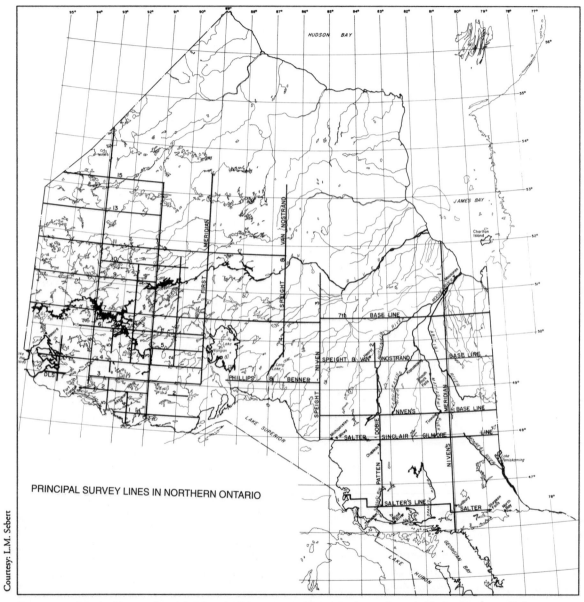

Courtesy: L.M. Sebert

Figure 12.1 Principal base and meridian lines laid down in northern Ontario. At first named after the surveyor who surveyed them, they were later numbered as shown. Meridian lines run north and south, base lines run east and west. Such lines are now known as "control lines." (After unpublished map by L.M. Sebert.)

1856. It is highly likely, then, that Salter's recommendation had a lot to do with the decision to adopt the new system, which, in the event, turned out to be a momentous one. Not only would the American system be used to lay out over 560 townships in northern Ontario but many on the prairies of the Canadian west as well. The system would be formally authorized in 1859.

For his base-line survey, which was to be both large and, thanks to Salter, well organized, Salter was assisted by two other provincial land surveyors, James

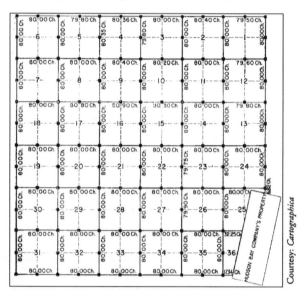

Courtesy: *Cartographica*

Figure 12.2 The 640-acre sectional township survey system introduced in 1859. A virtual carbon copy of the American system, townships were 6 miles square with 36 numbered sections of 640 acres. The township was surveyed section by section, thus increasing accuracy (black squares denote survey posts planted). On later modification, this system became known as the 640-acre sectional system, Pattern 2. Not shown is the Pattern 1 version of the system (with surveyed road allowances) as used by Dominion Land Surveyors to lay out some 20 townships flanking the Pigeon River. (From Sebert, *Land Surveys of Ontario*.)

Johnston and Arthur Jones, who was to act as "explorer." Leaving Penetanguishene on 10 June 1856, Salter reached the Sturgeon River, which flows south into Lake Nipissing in early July. Then, in his own words:

with the kind assistance of Mr. Murray, Assistant Provincial Geologist, I was enabled to get a set of lunar observations, from which I hope to deduce the longitude of the mouth of the Sturgeon River.

From the point of commencement in Latitude 46 degrees 22 minutes, 9 seconds N., by observation, immediately below the first fall which impedes the navigation of the Sturgeon River, I produced the line West, noting at intervals the variation of the magnet, and placing a post of cedar at the end of six miles [i.e., the width of one township], with the distance from the post at the point

of commencement marked thereon, and this system, I would here remark, was adopted throughout the survey, cairns of stones, where practicable, being piled around them, and the bearings and distances of trees taken.[11]

Having made a good start on the line, Salter left Johnston to get on with it, along with Jones, two chainmen, and eight axemen and packmen. He then returned to the extreme western end of Lake Nipissing and carried supplies inland to establish a cache on the latitude of the projected line. He did the same at two other places farther west – no meat on the hoof for him. He also laid down as his Principal Meridian a north-south line extending two townships north and south of the base line. To the south of his base line, his meridian passed through the eastern side of Round Lake, 12 miles (20 km) southeast of present-day Sudbury. To the north of the base line, the meridian

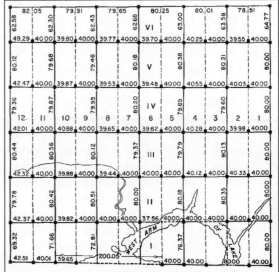

Figure 12.3 In 1874 the 640-acre sectional system was modified by reintroducing the concessions with which surveyors and settlers were familiar. Only concession and side lines of sections were surveyed with a post planted at the corners of the 320-acre half-sections. This survey system became known as the 640-acre sectional system, Pattern 3. (From Sebert, *Land Surveys of Ontario*.)

The 640-Acre Sectional System

The American system (see figures 12.2 and 12.3) was initially adopted virtually *in toto*, including the replacement of township names with numbers, though this was to change. Townships would be 6 miles by 6 miles (10 km by 10 km), divided into 36-square-mile or 640-acre sections, which the surveyor would close as he went along, thus ensuring accuracy. Each section was to be subdivided into four quarter-sections of 160 acres. There were no allowances for roads as in the older systems, but there was an area allowance of 5 percent for them, if and when they were required. There were no concessions. And the standard "lot," as the term was understood in the south, was now the quarter-section of 40 by 40 chains.

In 1874, after only fifteen years' use, the system was modified in deference to settlers and land surveyors long used to their familiar lots and concessions. Concessions were incorporated into the system, while each section was divided into two 320-acre lots instead of four 160-acre ones. Thus, in what is now northern Ontario, the "standard lot" would henceforth be one of 320 acres.

Meanwhile, in 1872, Dominion Land Surveyors working around the Red River settlement moved east into the Rainy River District, where they put in twenty-three townships using the same survey system they were already using, namely the "640-Acre Sectional System" introduced in 1859, but with the addition of surveyed road allowances around each section.

Thus there are three versions of the 640-acre sectional system. They are distinguished by their pattern number. To confuse matters, the original system of 1859 is now known as Pattern 2, the modification that reintroduced lots and concessions is known as Pattern 3, and the system used in by the Dominion Land Surveyors is known as Pattern 1.

passed through Whitefish Lake not far to the north of Round Lake.

And it was while running the meridian north of Whitefish Lake that a curious deflection of his compass drew Salter's attention to an outcrop of minerals so unusual that he made a point of mentioning them to Alexander Murray of the Geological Survey, then working in the area. Murray collected specimens, which on subsequent analysis were found to contain nickel, and copper. At that point no one was particularly interested in nickel, and Salter's find wasn't followed up. However, in 1900 the Creighton Mine went into production on the site of Salter's original discovery, a mine that for the next thirty years would be the world's leading nickel producer.[12]

On his Principal Meridian, Salter restarted the base line two townships to the north, to give a dog-leg with the base line continued westward at about the same latitude as Sudbury. By the end of September, with the weather worsening, Salter and his men concluded their work for the season. They had run about 90 miles (150 km) of the line, which took them as far as the Spanish River. Work was resumed the following season, that of 1857, with Salter directing the work of four other surveyors: Arthur Jones, Thomas Herrick, Thomas Molesworth,[13] and Philip Donnelly. The rest of the base line was run – a little over 100 miles of it. At its western end Salter made a couple of northward jogs that took the line north of Sault Ste. Marie and so ended it on the shore of Lake Superior.

While Salter and others were running the base line, Molesworth ran the Second and Fourth Meridian, with the former 18 miles (29 km) west of the Principal Meridian, and the latter 36 miles beyond it. Of the land he passed through on laying out the Second Meridian, Molesworth reported it as unfit for settlement. On running the Fourth Meridian, he thought that, in the vicinity of the Spanish River, south of the base line "A few townships might be ... suitable for a people coming from a mountainous country, who with economy and labour might make a good settlement."[14]

It was a stormy November before Molesworth finished his work. Procuring a sail boat to get himself and his party home after completing the Fourth Meridian, he got as far as Killarney where he was delayed for a week by storms. Eager to get home to Goderich, he set off into questionable weather, only to be driven ashore near the Saugeen River. He saved his field notes and instruments but lost his tent and all his provisions. The boat was a write-off, so he walked the 60 miles (97 km) or so back to Goderich.

The next year, Arthur Jones also had some difficulty getting home. After outlining four townships north of the eastern end of Salter's Line, he took his party back to Sault Ste. Marie, only to find that there was no money waiting for him to pay off his men. Eventually he managed to borrow enough to do this, but it was the following March before he could start back to his home in Chatham. Impatient to be gone, he and two assistants set off on foot with the mail carriers across the ice to Penetanguishene, nearly 300 miles (480 km) away. Although they were delayed by bad ice and storms, it still only took them seventeen days. However, Jones took sick on finally reaching home and was unable to work on his returns for several weeks. With apologies for the delay, he sent in his returns in late May. He also enclosed his final account. "I have included," he wrote, "four accounts paid for snow shoes, strings, and a train ... [as these] were indisputably necessary."[15]

In his final report, dated 20 January 1858, Salter stated that what he called the "range lines" (or future township boundaries) were all drawn parallel to his Principal Meridian with "due allowance being made for convergence," that is, on the North Pole. And that the "whole of the work was frequently checked by careful astronomical observations, and the variation of the magnet was consistently noted." In spite of the less than favourable reports brought in by his explorers, he still maintained that "there are extensive valleys of excellent land, well fitted for purposes of settlement."[16]

In 1857 Salter had been told that, on finishing his base line, he was to start laying out two townships at Sault Ste. Marie. The following year, that of 1858, a new district called Algoma was created. Eventually broken down into the separate districts of Timiskaming, Sudbury, Cochrane, Algoma, Thunder Bay, Kenora, and Rainy River, Algoma initially comprised virtually all of what is now northern Ontario, though its northern and western boundaries remained undefined. Sault Ste. Marie was made the judicial centre of the new district, and, with its importance thus enhanced, surveying activity there intensified.

By 1859 Johnston had laid out Awenge along the St. Mary's River, where Sault St. Marie now stands, and Korah to its north. Salter laid out another sliver of a township along the river, called St. Mary, Tarentorus to its north, and Aweres to the north of that. These and Pennefather to the north of Korah, completed by Joseph Burke in 1860, were the first of the 6-mile-square townships, being laid out according to the "640 Acre, Pattern 2" system as it came to be called. These and a survey of the Goulais River were apparently Burke's only surveys. By 1862 he was teaching mathematics at a girl's school in Toronto and in 1865 started to read for the ministry. He eventually became a canon.

Also completed in 1860 were Parke and Prince to the west of the Soo, these by Septimus Prince. Disappearing in the course of this work was the township of Penryth, first surveyed by Salter in the late 1840s. The third township, this one to the east, was Macdonald, laid out by Edward Miles. These would be followed in the next few years by a number of others, including the townships of Rose and Lefroy to the north and south of Salter's Line, surveyed by Clement Hanning in 1861, and one on the Spanish River, which was named Salter (one is glad to learn) and which was surveyed by Charles Unwin, who also laid out Esten and Spragge, also in 1861 (see figure 12.4).

By Confederation over twenty townships had been laid out in the vicinity of Sault Ste. Marie and along the North Shore. Meanwhile, Salter had been instructed to begin construction of what became known as the Great North Road (a road of "communication" rather than "colonization") that ran eastward from Sault Ste. Marie and which by 1860 had been located as far eastward as the Spanish River.

It is striking that, besides Vidal and Salter, most of the early surveyors in the north came from the south-

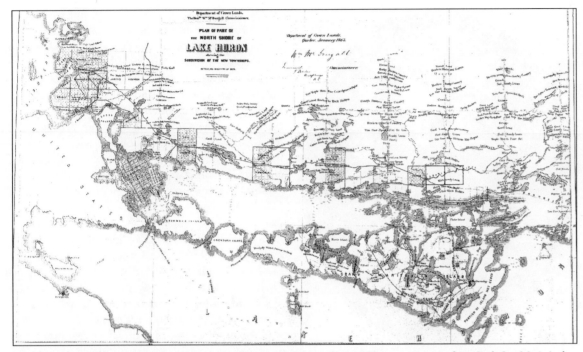

Figure 12.4 Plan of part of the North Shore of Lake Huron in 1863. The solid line running east from Sault Ste. Marie is the route of the proposed Great Northern Road route, then being located by Albert Salter. "Salter's Base Line" is faintly discernible on the plan. (AO, Cartographic Records Collection, B-47A, Repro. no. 1345.)

western region of the province, though perhaps this is not surprising considering the relative ease with which the north could be reached by water from Sandwich and Sarnia. It is also striking that, far from being veterans, several were carrying out their first surveys as newly qualified land surveyors. Presumably, for many of the older, more experienced hands, many of whom by now were established in their urban or local rural practices, the north was just too remote from civilization for comfort.

Sadly, several of the early surveyors in the North died young. Such a one was Septimus Prince. In 1860 his father, who was the first judge to be appointed in the newly created district of Algoma, moved to Sault Ste. Marie. Septimus had qualified as a provincial land surveyor the year before. As we have seen, Prince completed the surveys of two townships. Subsequently his health failed, and he had to return to his home in Sandwich. After two years of illness he died in 1867. He was only twenty-nine.

Also short-lived was Edward Miles, who spent much of his boyhood in Denmark. After a few years at sea, he came to Upper Canada in 1851, where he settled on a lot in Markham Township. Farming did not appeal, so Miles studied surveying under Stoughton Dennis, receiving his commission in 1857. In partnership with Charles Unwin, he laid out the township of Macdonald as mentioned above. He then became a surveyor with the Canadian Land and Emigration Company. By 1865, however, he had already given up surveying to become a partner in a woollen mill at Weston. A year later, at the age of thirty-one, he was injured in one of the machines, to die of what was diagnosed as tetanus not long after.

Molesworth went on to become heavily involved with railway location and construction, and in the mid-1860s he worked on surveys and plans in connection with the international bridge between Fort Erie and Buffalo. In the late 1860s he would be appointed chief engineer of public works for the province and as such became heavily involved in drainage schemes, especially in Kent and Essex. He died in 1879.

The survey of Rose and Lefroy townships east of Sault Ste. Marie was Clement Hanning's first job as a qualified land surveyor. He went on to lay out a road on St. Joseph Island. Later years saw him working on municipal surveys, including the preparation of plans for the town of Bowmanville and the villages of Orono and Newcastle in 1866 and 1867. From about 1870 onward he became almost exclusively involved with railway location and costing, right-of-way surveys, and roadbed construction for a number of railway companies. Coming to live in Toronto, he entered into partnership with Charles Murphy in the mid-1880s, later taking in Henry Esten, who would qualify in 1887 but who soon gave up surveying for law.

Charles Unwin was born in Nottinghamshire in 1829. His father died when he was six. A few years later an uncle sent for him and his sister to join him in Toronto. The two made the trip under the care of a family friend who was bound for the States, Unwin being thirteen at the time. His uncle lived with and worked for Samuel Ridout, who by that time (the early 1840s) was the registrar of Toronto and of the counties of York, Ontario, and Peel. Following his schooling at

Upper Canada College, Unwin was apprenticed to Stoughton Dennis and qualified in 1852. He worked on the Muskoka Road and later laid out the townships of Esten, Spragge, and Salter in the North, which were completed in 1861. By this time Unwin was already on the Board of Examiners. Among his many later surveys were of those of the Thousand Islands in the St. Lawrence, while the early 1880s would see him surveying in Manitoba. Later still, he would become one of Toronto's most prominent surveyors and a founding member of the surveying firm now known as Unwin, Murphy & Esten, Ltd. And in 1916, at the annual meeting of what became the Association of Ontario Land Surveyors, Unwin would preside over the association's first veterans' reunion.

Salter's report on his exploratory survey of 1856 provided just the sort of ammunition that Cauchon needed to further his campaign to settle and develop the north and northwest. In his report of that same year, Cauchon developed his arguments at some length, discussing the southern part of Upper Canada, region by region, stressing its lack of settlement potential. There was the as yet unopened land south of Lake Nipissing. This, he declared, was "unquestionably the best country for the growth of wheat still remaining unoccupied to the eastward of Lake Huron." As for northern Ontario, he cited Salter's findings and noted that there was a "large extent of country well adapted for settlement" north of Lake Huron. But after admitting that the north was not "equal in climate nor in general fitness for cultivation to the Western Peninsula of Upper Canada," Cauchon comments, with remarkable prescience, that this area "can only gradually become occupied through economic enterprise, or as the progressive demands of trade present a stimulus."

Cauchon then finally made the point he had been working up to all along, which was the need to settle

Charles Unwin was commissioned in 1852 and sixty-four years later would preside over the association's first Veterans' Lunch. He was a co-founder of the surveying firm Unwin, Murphy & Esten, Ltd., still in business. Courtesy: AOLS Archives

the west. "It is well known that not only very many European immigrants, but also a great and increasing number of the young men of the Province, and even the older settlers, prefer the easier livelihood that is to be earned by cultivating the prairies of the west, where the plough can be immediately used, and great crops be obtained with comparatively little labor."[17]

However the *sine qua non* of any settlements in the West was the elimination of the Hudson's Bay Company whose writ, by right of its ancient charter, ran to the height of land that hugged the northern shores of Lakes Huron and Superior. No one knew

exactly where that height of land lay. But wherever it was, the presence of the company, in Cauchon's eyes and in the eyes of those who shared his views, was an anachronism that had to be abolished.

In order to bring this about, Cauchon built up a massive case against the land claims of the company, arguing that various international treaties signed by Britain since the 1760s recognized that Britain's, and by extension, Canada's, authority extended beyond the height of land. It was up to Britain to re-examine the company's claims, and, if they were thought to be invalid, to terminate its charter in the interests of orderly settlement of the northwest, such to be overseen by the government of the province of Canada. And this Britain eventually did, with negotiations starting in the 1860s that led to the sale of Rupert's Land to Canada in 1870. About the same time as negotiations were opened with the company, the idea of Confederation was first mooted, but the Colonial Office at that juncture saw little point in it.

Meanwhile, the provincial government had dispatched a three-party expedition to explore the country west of Lake Superior, which arrived at Fort William in July of 1857. With his enthusiasm and experience in the north, Salter probably would have led one of the parties if he hadn't been busy completing his base line. Instead, the job was given to Simon Dawson, a Scottish civil engineer and surveyor who had worked for the government on a relatively minor project in Lower Canada. A second party was led by an engineer, W.H. Napier, and a third by Professor Henry Hind, a geologist and chemist from Toronto's Trinity College who had been primed by a memorandum from Sir William Logan, head of the Geological Survey. Acting as a chainman on the expedition was a future surveyor general of Canada, Lindsay Russell, not to be confused with Andrew Russell, by then assistant commissioner of the Crown Lands Department.

Initially instructed to explore the country west of Lake Superior and to determine the best route to the

Red River settlement, the expedition was told after its arrival at the Red River settlement in September to examine the country as far west as the Saskatchewan River. Dawson, as he had been asked to do, came up with recommendations on the best route through the 90 miles (145 km) of country between the Lakehead and the Red River settlement, while in their reports, which were accompanied by detailed large-scale maps, both Dawson and Hind dwelt on the suitability for settlement of the land west of the Red River settlement (the future Winnipeg).

Hind, in his report, paid tribute to the quality and accuracy of the maps of the international boundary made by David Thompson over thirty years earlier, remarking that "the labours of this remarkable man are only now beginning to be realised."[18] Thompson had died in Montreal only shortly before, in February 1857. Totally blind for the last ten years of his life, perhaps the greatest surveyor and map-maker that Canada had ever seen had died in poverty, his death unnoticed by press and public alike.

Following Dawson and company's expeditions to the Red River country and beyond in 1857 and 1858, the first exploratory survey was made of the country north of Lake Superior by Thomas Herrick. It was possibly the most arduous ever undertaken by a provincial land surveyor. It was certainly the longest single survey ever made in the province, in terms of both time and distance. It took Herrick and his assistants – they varied in the course of the survey – nearly two years to complete, during the whole of which time Herrick left the survey line only when it was necessary to organize supplies or hire more men.

From Sault Ste. Marie, the survey line followed a six-legged arc north of Lake Superior to end near Fort William. The length of the completed line was just on 400 miles (645 km) as the crow flies (see figure 12.5). In addition, over thirty lakes were mapped and a dozen or so rivers traversed.

Having hired men and two "explorers" in Quebec, Herrick reached Sault Ste. Marie in late August 1860. Here he was joined by Salter's erstwhile colleague, James Johnston, and another surveyor, one Davies, otherwise unidentified. Work on the survey line started on 7 September 1860, Herrick having tied in his point of commencement with a jog in "Salter's Exploring Line."[19] Three miles (5 km) from it and in latitude 46°42'53"N (determined from "Bayfield's chart"), Herrick commenced "Line No. 1" on a bearing of N 18°W (see figure 12.6).

In November Herrick returned to Sault Ste. Marie to arrange for supplies and to hire another axeman, leaving Davies working on the line and Johnston surveying lakes in the vicinity of present-day Agawa Bay. While Herrick was away disaster struck. The terse entry in his diary for 1 December reads: "This day Mr. Johnston was drowned in Trout Lake thro' the ice – Mr. Davies & J. Dyas nearly."

By this time winter was coming on. On 11 December, Herrick and his men woke to find "a foot of snow on our blankets." Coming up the survey line on 17 December Herrick saw Johnston's death "notified on tree." He got back to the head of the line to find that the men had become disorderly and "mutinous." He discharged four men and, a few days later, another

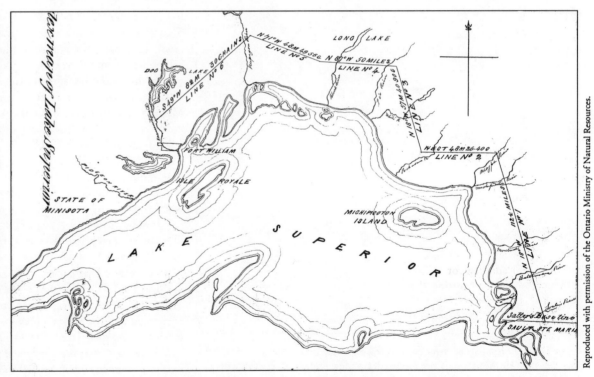

Figure 12.5 Principal survey line followed by Thomas Herrick in the first exploratory survey north of Lake Superior made in 1860–62. (From T. Herrick, *Report and Field Notes of the Survey of the Exploration Line from Sault St. Mary to Fort William, North Shore of Lake Superior*, 2 vols., nos. 1896 and 1908, Survey Records, Ministry of Natural Resources.)

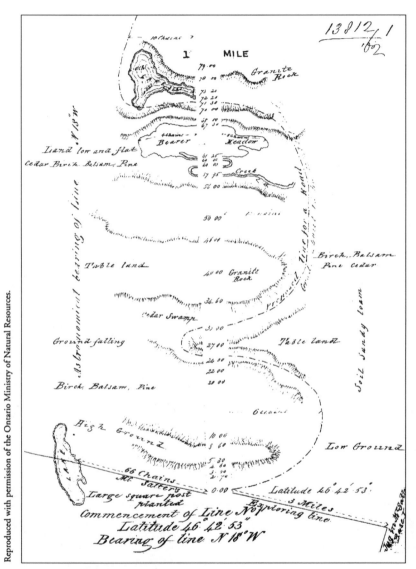

Figure 12.6 The first page of Herrick's field notes on his exploratory survey north of Lake Superior. He used Devine's new method of recording field notes. They are read from the bottom of the page upward. Note (bottom right) that Herrick tied in his point of commencement to Salter's Line. (From T. Herrick, *Report and Field Notes of the Survey of the Exploration Line from Sault St. Mary to Fort William, North Shore of Lake Superior*, 2 vols., nos. 1896 and 1908, Survey Records, Ministry of Natural Resources.)

four. On 6 January 1861, a search was made in Trout Lake for Johnston's body. They found it at "2 P.M. – hands & feet & face frozen – water 9 fathoms, 1/4 mile from shore – Mr. Wilson left with Johnston."

On 31 January they were able to supplement their diet with "cariboo" meat obtained from natives. It was a long and very hard winter – Herrick noting a temperature of -28°F on 18 March. And it seems it must have been a very late spring. "Hard frost at night," Herrick wrote on 13 July. Other troubles were in store. In late August there was an (unspecified) accident. "August 27. 2 men down river with wounded man." And then trouble of a different kind: "August 30. Woods on fire behind us for miles. Great fires ahead." Somehow, they got round the fires.

The party had been working on the line for a year and another winter was approaching. On 1 December there is the cryptic entry in Herrick's diary: "Getting own winter clothes made." Did he make his own? Or perhaps he got them from natives. "January 1 [1862], Suffering greatly from snow blindness – the cook very sick from scurvy, both his feet frozen also – cold night." The next night it was -30°F. Ley, the cook, got worse and by 5 January was very sick with "scurvy, rheumatism & frozen feet," while Herrick himself "lay in great pain" from his snow blindness. The party eventually went on, but Ley was left behind with someone to look after him.

In the meantime, Soublin, the replacement cook, also took ill. He got worse. On 16 January, he had a high fever, and Herrick bled the unfortunate man using a penknife. Meanwhile, the weather had got colder, with Herrick recording -39°F on 13 January. On the twentieth, Herrick went back down the line to check on Ley and "brought [him] up on a dog-train with great difficulty. Ley's body quite black & in agony from cold and pain." Eventually, one is glad to learn, Ley was taken down a river to a trading post. The last we hear of him, he had lost all his teeth and was "unable to move in his bed." Early in March, Davies had come down with scurvy as well, though he recovered. And by 15 April the whole survey party was too weak to work, "generally from scurvy."

Meanwhile, on 16 March, Herrick set out to walk to Fort William to arrange for supplies and reached it four days later. He returned to the line only to make another excursion in early April. "April 4th. Heavy snow at night – fine day – walked 35 miles to Hudson Bay Co. post on Dog Lake."

Early in July, and within a few miles of the end of the line, there was almost another disaster. A canoe with eight men in it upset, the men "nearly drowned." Lost was some equipment and the survey notes for the previous 11 miles, which Herrick had to reconstruct from his diary (see figure 12.7).

A few days later, the survey line reached the Kaministiquia River about 25 miles northwest of present-day Thunder Bay and, a month short of two years after he began it, Herrick completed his survey (see figure 12.8). The final chainage as recorded in Herrick's field notes was 59 386, or some 742 miles (1187 km). Add 570 miles of river traverses and the total distance covered by Herrick and his party amounted to a staggering 1312 miles – and this through some of the most difficult terrain in North America.

One might think that Herrick had earned himself a rest after his exertions. However, he was instructed to lay out two townships in the vicinity of Fort William forthwith. This he did, with the townships of

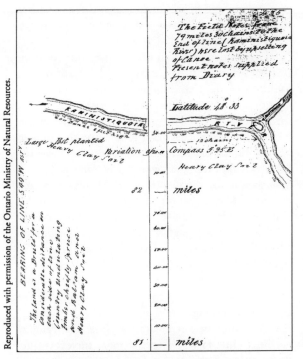

Figure 12.7 The last page of Herrick's field notes. He comments on the loss of field notes top right. The mileage refers to the last of the six courses run during the two-year survey. (From T. Herrick, *Report and Field Notes of the Survey of the Exploration Line from Sault St. Mary to Fort William, North Shore of Lake Superior*, 2 vols., nos. 1896 and 1908, Survey Records, Ministry of Natural Resources.)

Nee-bing and Pai-poonge (now spelled Neebing and Paipoonge) being the first on Thunder Bay.

Following Herrick's work, it would be another ten years before surveying would be resumed on or about Lake Superior. As for Herrick himself, he carried out further surveys north of the Michipicoten River in 1861, and thereafter his surveying career remains obscure. In 1872 he would die unmarried in Toronto at the age of forty-four.

On the eve of Confederation, the subdivision into townships of the forty-two counties of southern, or "old," Ontario was all but complete.[20] In the seventy-three years since John Collins had started on the first township of Kingston in 1783 a total of 453 townships had been laid out. Only seven townships were yet to be completed. Just to the north, of Haliburton's twenty-three townships, all but four were completed, of Muskoka's twenty-two townships, all but eight.

However, the opening up of the district of Parry Sound had barely begun. Eventually to be subdivided into forty-six townships, only the three townships near the sound itself had been completed before Confederation. There were no townships as yet in Nipissing District south of the French and Mattawa rivers, while to the north of those rivers, in what is now officially considered to be northern Ontario, there was but one isolated township, that of Mattawan.

Along Lake Huron's north shore, there was a scattering of six townships, although there were nine townships laid out in the vicinity of Sault Ste. Marie, together with a further five on Batchawana Bay not far to the northwest. There were three townships on St. Joseph Island, while in 1864 a start had been made on laying out Manitoulin, with eight townships completed by 1867. There were no townships on Lake Superior, save the two at Thunder Bay laid out by Herrick in the early 1860s. At Confederation, then,

only thirty-three townships had been laid out in northern Ontario, twenty-two if the townships on St. Joseph Island and Manitoulin are omitted. This was few indeed considering the immense distance from Mattawa to Thunder Bay – about 500 miles (800 km) as the crow flies.

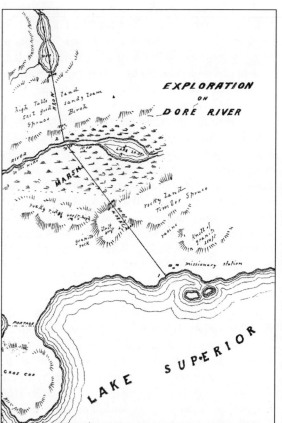

Figure 12.8 Part of one of the many maps made by Herrick and his party when making side traverses from the principal survey line. (From T. Herrick, *Report and Field Notes of the Survey of the Exploration Line from Sault St. Mary to Fort William, North Shore of Lake Superior*, 2 vols, nos. 1896 and 1908, Survey Records, Ministry of Natural Resources.)

While it rapidly became clear that the Ottawa-Huron Tract was largely devoid of the good farm land upon which the colonization roads program had, at least ostensibly, been predicated, it also became clear that such land was going to be equally hard to find in the north. It certainly wasn't to be found along the North Shore along which Salter had been pushing his road eastward from Sault Ste. Marie. It was in hopes of bringing those elusive tracts of good agricultural land to light that it was decided in 1866 to explore and map the hinterland well north of Salter's original line.

There were to be two parts to the survey. A traverse was to be run down the Montreal River, which runs southeast to peter out in Bay Lake 12 miles (20 km) or so west of Lake Temiskaming, not far from the present-day town of Cobalt. And at the same time an east-west exploration line was to be run along latitude 47°56'N from the Montreal River to Michipoceten on Lake Superior (near present-day Wawa) 200 miles away (see figure 12.1). Acting on instructions issued in September 1866, Alfred G. Forrest completed a 102-mile traverse of the Montreal River during the fall of 1866 and the ensuing winter, as well as running a further 27 miles of traverse line on various lakes, and exploring the country a few miles on each side of the river. He completed his survey without undue trouble.

The same cannot be said for the line that was run from the Montreal River to Michipoceten. It was an ambitious undertaking. The proposed line lay inland from the North Shore by more than 100 miles (160 km), which, to put it mildly, made it extremely difficult to bring in supplies. In the event, the project nearly brought disaster to all concerned. The plan called for Duncan Sinclair to start on the Montreal River and work west, and for Robert Gilmour to start at Michipoceten and work east. The two expected to meet near the headwaters of the Mississagi River, which flows generally southward to flow into Lake Huron near Blind River. In overall charge was Albert Salter, who was to help with supplies, running them north up the Mississagi and exploring the river at the same time.

Sinclair's troubles started before he even commenced his survey. On his way up the Ottawa River after leaving Ottawa on 20 September, one of his packers was drowned. Initially the rest refused to go on. However, he persuaded them to continue, and on 23 October, after determining the position of his point of commencement on the Montreal River, started west along the line. By 11 January 1867 he had run 104.5 miles (168 km) of line, which brought him to the Ivanhoe River, not all that far from present-day Chapleau. Here he turned back to explore and traverse a further 228 miles on the upper reaches of the Montreal River before the spring thaw brought survey work to an end. In all, in what was an unusually severe winter, he covered about 440 miles of extremely rugged ground, not counting exploratory side trips and the distance to and from Ottawa.

Gilmour, who was from the village of Paisley in Bruce County, travelled first to Chatham where he conferred with Salter. He eventually reached Michipoceten on 6 October, travelling via Toronto and Owen Sound. He started east on 17 October, accompanied by Salter. Held up by increasingly bad weather, with no more pork, beans, salt, or tea, with two members of the party seriously ill with scurvy and others suffering from rheumatism and dysentery, and with the spring break-up starting, they finally called a halt on 13 April 1867 after running 84 miles (135 km) of line. Although they didn't know it, they were within about 10 miles of the west end of Sinclair's line. They started back for Michipoceten, sending a few men on ahead to bring supplies back up the line. By the time they reached Michipoceten, two members of the party could no longer stand and had to be carried.

Meanwhile, Salter, who had remained with them until the middle of January, had turned back to cope with supply problems. He returned to Sault Ste. Marie and about the middle of February starting packing supplies up the Mississagi, exploring and surveying as he went. Unable to find further provisions at a Hudson's Bay Company post he was aiming for, he pushed north anyway until his frightened men refused to go farther, whereupon he turned his party south again. They ran out of meat and bread and for eleven days existed on gruel, tallow, and flour. On 24 March they got back to the mouth of the Mississagi suffering from both starvation and snow blindness.

Determined to get up to the survey line to ensure that both survey parties were safe, Salter went back to Sault Ste. Marie, picked up more supplies and, though the going was increasingly dangerous because of the spring thaw, set off up the Mississagi once more. Finally he met some natives who told him that the survey parties had finished and were returning. However, Salter wouldn't take their word for it. After picking up more supplies at the mouth of the Mississagi towards the end of May, he set off north for the third time. He abandoned his attempt to reach the line only after he failed to find a native guide. Officially, Salter only ran 130 miles (209 km) of survey line that spring. The actual distance he covered must have been several times that, and, in terms of personal achievement, Salter's epic performance during the survey was rarely, if ever, equalled in the long history of Ontario land surveying.

Following these exploratory surveys, this region of northern Ontario would see no more surveyors until the Canadian Pacific Railway was being built some ten years later. Following Confederation, the northwest became the focus of attention.

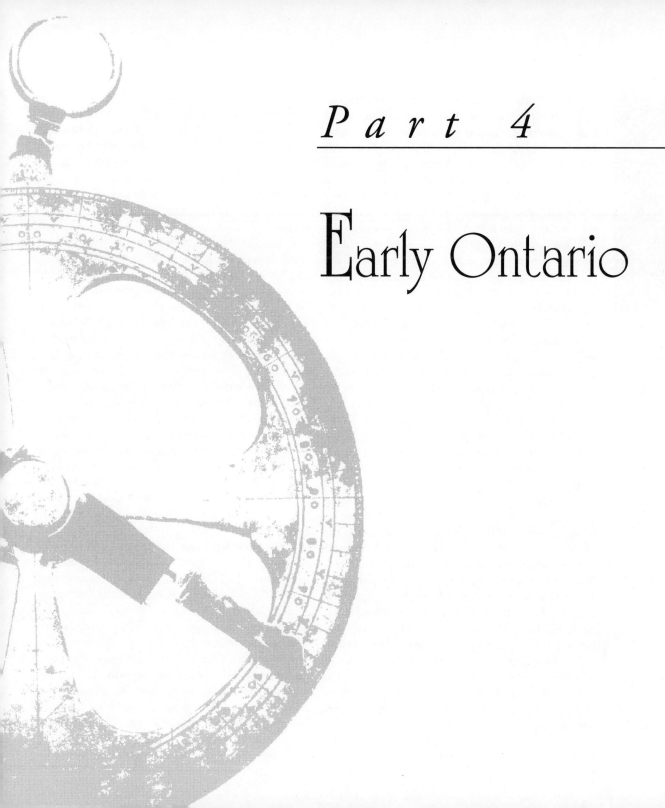

Part 4

Early Ontario

CHAPTER THIRTEEN

Ontario's Boundaries, Northern Surveys, and the CPR

The British North America Act, which brought Nova Scotia, New Brunswick, and the newly named province of Ontario into a confederation, received royal assent on 29 March 1867 and came into effect on 1 July of that year. Six months later, on 27 December, the new provincial legislature of Ontario sat for the first time with John Sandfield Macdonald as the premier.

The first speech from the throne dwelt on the need for local works and social improvement. More railways were required to sustain the growth of the lumber industry and to exploit the mineral resources of the new province, should these be brought to light. But the main thrust of the speech was the need to foster immigration and settlement, which were still seen as the *sine qua non* of the new province's economic wellbeing. The government called for more roads; this to help realize what was still being thought of as the great agricultural potential of Haliburton, Muskoka, Parry Sound, and Nipissing. To encourage immigration, new legislation was to be brought in.

This legislation took the form of the Free Grant and Homestead Act passed in 1868. In effect, the act reintroduced the principle of free land grants to desirable settlers that was first used to settle Loyalists after the American revolution. In certain designated townships, a 100-acre lot would be granted free to bona fide settlers, who could also buy a second lot for 50 cents an acre. As the scheme developed, heads of families would receive 200 acres, childless couples 100 acres. A patent would be issued after five years, provided at least 15 acres had been cultivated, the land continuously occupied, and a house of minimum size built. The first free-grant townships were in the rear of the counties along the southern borders of the shield, western Renfrew County, and in Muskoka, Parry Sound, and Haliburton districts. Later, there would be more such townships in Nipissing, around Sault Ste. Marie, and in the Rainy River District.

Confederation brought with it many other changes for the Department of Crown Lands. To start with, it was shorn of some of its powers. The Fisheries Branch became the federal Department of Marine and Fisheries. Ordnance lands and Indian Affairs became the responsibility of the secretary of state. What was left was divided between Ontario and Quebec. After the dust had settled, Ontario emerged with a much streamlined Department of Crown Lands. And gone were the days when each year seemed to bring a new commissioner. In 1873 Timothy Pardee was appointed commissioner of crown lands, a post he was to hold for sixteen years. Lawyer, successful politician, and popular man-about-town, Pardee's prime task was to improve the image of the department, which had long had the reputation of being in the pocket of the lumber barons – as witness the Ottawa-Huron Tract fiasco.

On Confederation, Andrew Russell stayed on as assistant commissioner and Thomas Devine continued as head of the Surveys Branch. One of Devine's two assistants at that juncture was George Kirkpatrick. In 1878 Kirkpatrick would become director of surveys for the department, a position he would occupy until his death in 1917. Later he would serve as the first president of the Association of Provincial Land Surveyors of Ontario, the forerunner of the Association of Ontario Land Surveyors.

From the legislative standpoint, surveying went forward in the new province under two acts that had been passed in 1859, minus the sections that dealt specifically with Lower Canada. Both acts had brought together all the scattered pieces of legislation that had been brought in during the preceding three decades. One of the 1859 acts dealt with the training, examination, and certification of land surveyors, along with such matters as the right of a surveyor to subpoena witnesses when ascertaining doubtful boundary lines, his right to enter or cross private land when surveying, and the penalty for obstructing him. This was An Act

Timothy B. Pardee. Appointed commissioner of crown lands in 1873, he held the post for sixteen years and did much to restore public confidence in his department.
© Queen's Printer for Ontario. Reproduced with permission of the Ministry of Natural Resources.

Respecting Land Surveyors and the Survey of Lands (22 Vict., c. 77).

The second act was An Act Respecting the Survey of Lands in Upper Canada (22 Vict., c. 93), which dealt with the minutiae of the cadastral land surveying process if the end result were boundaries that were, to use the key words in the act, "true and unalterable." It also dealt with the legal status and placing of survey monuments and boundary marks, including the penalty for their removal or defacement. Also defined by the act was the relationship between land surveyors acting for the Crown and those acting for municipalities. It spelled out the process by which the latter could apply to the Crown to have resurveys carried out and how they were to pay for them. Other sections of the act dealt with plans, their registration, and the duties of the registrar, while a two-line section stated that "No ... private survey shall be valid, unless performed by a duly authorized Surveyor."

Many sections of the act, with their mixture of surveying terms and legal jargon, are not easy for the layman to follow. Apparently they were not easily followed by the land surveyors themselves. In 1886, at the inaugural meeting of what became the Association of Ontario Land Surveyors, Villiers Sankey said of the act (which became Chapter 146 of the Revised Statutes of Ontario): "This is the act with which we are all familiar, and which I might almost say we could willingly see committed to the flames, with all reverence and respect however, for out of its venerable ashes it should be the aim and determination of every surveyor in the Province, to assist in the production of such an Act, as would at the same time be concise, simple and effective."[1]

John A. Macdonald, Canada's first prime minister, saw that the best way to counter the American threat in the West was to draw the Red River settlement and the western territories into Confederation. The threat to the Red River settlement in particular was a very real one. In Minnesota, for example, there were calls for the annexation of the Red River settlement just to the north. Accordingly, in December 1867, the Honourable William McDougall, the newly appointed minister of public works for Canada (under whose aegis federal land surveys would go forward for the next few years) passed a series of resolutions in the Commons calling for the immediate transfer of the Hudson's Bay Company territory, or Rupert's Land, to Canada. The British government co-operating, this would go forward with the date of transfer originally scheduled for 1 October 1869.

Meanwhile, work on the Red River Route, as it was then called, had begun in 1867. It had gone forward under the auspices of what was now the Ontario Department of Crown Lands, who suddenly found to its chagrin that, as of June of that year, well over half of the $92,460 set aside for the colonization roads program was to be diverted to the Red River project, "on the assumption that the amount so expended," to use the words in the annual report for that year, "would form a claim of the Province of Ontario upon the New Dominion of Canada." The work went ahead under the direction of James Bridgland, who had been in charge of the colonization roads program for many years.

A road was constructed from Prince Arthur's Landing to Dog Lake some 20 miles (32 km) to the northwest. The location and construction of the western end of the proposed road was to be carried out by John Snow, who was sent to the Red River settlement by McDougall. It was Snow's survey work on land claimed by the Métis that triggered the events that led to the first uprising under Louis Riel, an affair in which Stoughton Dennis was to play a leading if somewhat discreditable role.

On 10 July 1869 Dennis had been instructed by McDougall to proceed to Fort Garry (now Winnipeg), inspect the Red River area, recommend a suitable land-survey system, and proceed with the necessary surveys. Dennis proposed a modification of the American township survey system. Not waiting for an answer from Ottawa on this, Dennis started to lay out his Principal (later, the Winnipeg) Meridian. Working with him were two other provincial land surveyors from Ontario, Milner Hart and Adam Webb.

On 11 October 1869 in a first overt act of resistance, a band of Métis led by Riel came up to a party headed by Webb and brought surveying to a halt, this by the simple expedient of standing on their chain. Sensibly, Webb quietly withdrew. Dennis, however, insisted that an attempt be made to arrest and punish the Métis, an action that led the prime minister to write later: "The course taken by Stoughton Dennis in pressing for strong measures to be taken against parties interfering with his surveys was exceedingly injudicious. He is a very decent fellow and a good surveyor, and all that, but he has got no head and is exceedingly fussy."[2]

Late in November John A. Macdonald had informed the British government that Canada would not accept the transfer of Rupert's Land until this could be accomplished peacefully, thus voiding the 1 December takeover date. Unaware of this, McDougall was on his way west, having been appointed lieutenant-governor of the northwest late in September. He arrived in Pembina on 11 October – the same day that the Métis had stopped Webb's party. Dennis joined him there. Having unwisely taken Dennis's advice, McDougall had brought with him several hundred rifles and a quantity of ammunition, news of which quickly reached Riel, who a few days later ordered McDougall not to enter their territory without permission. This McDougall and Dennis tried to do on 2 November; they were turned back by a Métis patrol.

There matters stood until 29 November when Dennis went to the settlement with two proclamations that were to compound this tragic comedy of errors. One announced that McDougall would be taking over the settlement as of 1 December. The other concerned himself: Dennis had been transmogrified on McDougall's say-so into an official with the title of "lieutenant and conservator of the peace in Rupert's Land." As such, he had managed to raise a small company of volunteers to accompany him to the settlement. They ended up taking refuge in a warehouse and were forced to surrender. They were then marched off

to Fort Garry, now in Riel's hands. The next day, on 8 December, Riel hoisted the flag of his provisional government over Fort Garry. Shortly after, Dennis fled to Pembina to join McDougall, whence he, McDougall, and Snow made their way back east. An exasperated John A. Macdonald commented later that "McDougall and Dennis have done their utmost to destroy our chance of a peaceful settlement with these wild people, and now the probability is that ... we must be left to the exhibition of force next spring."[3] And so it was to prove.

On 4 March 1870 Riel brought all hopes of a peaceful settlement to an end by executing Thomas Scott, erstwhile member of Snow's survey party, on a charge of treason against Riel's provisional government. Scott was an Orangeman, and news of his execution was greeted with howls of rage in Ontario with immediate calls for action against the Métis. Two days after Scott was executed, the British government offered their help in putting down what was now being called a rebellion. The offer was accepted, and in mid-May a combined British-Canadian force under the command of Colonel Sir Garnet Wolseley, a veteran of the Crimean War and Indian Mutiny, embarked at Collingwood for Sault Ste. Marie and Thunder Bay. From Thunder Bay, the force would make their way westward using the Red River Route.

By now the Dominion government had taken over survey and construction work on the route. Bridgland's road to Dog Lake was abandoned following further exploratory and road location work in the summer of 1868 by William Browne, acting for the federal government. Browne at that point was something of an anomaly in that he apparently never qualified as a Dominion Land Surveyor and would not qualify as an Ontario provincial land surveyor until 1876. Browne submitted his findings to Dawson in Ottawa, who decided that the route westward from Thunder Bay should be via Shebandowan Lake. Accordingly, work on a road began in the summer of 1869.

From then on, Browne's time was spent supervising the crews working on the road and carrying on location surveys on the Shebandowan–Fort Frances section of the road. In the winter of 1869–70 he travelled some 1500 miles (2400 km) on snow shoes. He was reporting as often as he could to Dawson, preparing his reports in a shed tent and using an upturned toboggan as a drawing table. It was on the basis of Browne's reports that Dawson, from the comfort of his desk in Ottawa, decided on the final line of the route with which his name, somewhat undeservedly one cannot help thinking, became subsequently associated.

Early in 1870 Browne learned by special messenger that Wolseley's expeditionary force was being assembled, and that, on its arrival at Thunder Bay, his work force would be augmented by 1500 men – electrifying news that he must have greeted with mixed feelings. According to his own account,

> I immediately returned to Thunder Bay and engaged all the men I could and started locating road ... I had a party of twenty-five men and it kept us on the jump all the time to get ready for them [the troops] ... When the military arrived we made use of them in construction. The regulars were very anxious to work and kept bothering me to give them work, as we gave them the handsome sum of twenty-five cents a day extra. But the volunteers were not so anxious, but tried to get off.[4]

In spite of the efforts of Browne and his men, it soon became clear that the Dawson Route would take too long to complete, even with the help of the troops. In the end, Wolseley could wait no longer and took to the water, eventually getting his force to Fort Garry by way of Lake Winnipeg and the Red River. They camped outside Fort Garry on 24 August, and it was the sight of their campfires that night that precipitated

Riel's flight to the United States. The first of the two rebellions inspired by Louis Riel was over.

After its exciting beginning, the Dawson Route settled down to a more prosaic existence as westbound immigrants made their way along it, as did numerous lumbermen, prospectors, and miners. When the route was officially opened in June 1871, it consisted of several stretches of roads, one of which covered the 45 miles (72 km) from Thunder Bay to Lake Shebandowan, while another linked Lake of the Woods with Fort Garry 95 miles away.

The transfer of Rupert's Land to Canada finally went through in 1870, to be quickly followed by the creation of the brand-new province of Manitoba. Initially so small that it was derisively described as the "postage stamp province," it centred on and included the disputed land on the Red River. The creation of the new province led the Dominion government to set up the Dominion Lands Branch. Stoughton Dennis – his aberrant behaviour in the west forgiven if not forgotten – was appointed surveyor general of Dominion lands with Lindsay Russell as his first assistant. In 1878 Dennis was appointed deputy minister of the interior under John A. Macdonald. In both this post and that of Dominion surveyor general, Dennis was to serve with distinction until his retirement in 1881 at the age of sixty-one. He died four years later at Kingsmere, Quebec, and was buried at Kingston.

With the creation of the Dominion Land Survey, a new dimension was added to the profession of land surveying in Canada. As of 1875, the Dominion had its own Board of Examiners, successful candidates being allowed to add the prestigious letters "D.L.S." after his name, standing for Dominion Land Surveyor. A year later, the more senior grade of Dominion Topographical Surveyor was introduced, with the letters "D.T.S." earned by those who passed a series of extremely rigorous exams. Very few were to qualify as Dominion Topographical Surveyors, only thirty-two being appointed in the course of the next eighty years.

For the great majority, the letters "D.L.S." added cachet enough. In fact, they marked a land surveyor as having more get-up-and-go than most.

Many Ontario Land Surveyors went on to become Dominion Land Surveyors. Apart from anything else, it got them away from the everlasting trees of Ontario and on to the western plains where, travelling by horse-drawn carts, land surveyors could do their work – and earn their money – with comparative ease. One of the many who went surveying in the west in the early 1880s was John Snow. On returning from the Red River, he had gone back to private practice in Hull. In 1877 he went out west again, this time as a Dominion Land Surveyor where he worked both on the prairies and in British Columbia. Returning east in 1886, he died in Ottawa two years later of pneumonia at the age of sixty-two. His son, also John, who qualified as a provincial land surveyor in 1874 and who also worked out west as a Dominion Land Surveyor, outlived his father by only two years, dying of what was diagnosed as heart disease at the age of only thirty-eight.

All this activity in the northwest on the part of the federal government was being watched with increasing uneasiness by an Ontario that considered the northwest its own. But where exactly did Ontario's boundary lie? Curiously enough the British North America Act of 1867 had little to say about it, being content to leave the definition as it was when the Constitutional Act of 1791 divided the old Province of Quebec into Upper and Lower Canada. The western boundary was left undefined, the province being said to include "all the territory to the westward and northward of the said line to the utmost extent of the country commonly called or known by the name of Canada."

A precise definition of Ontario's western boundary was fast becoming a matter of urgency. The increasing number of immigrants moving westward to the Red River via Thunder Bay called for a clarification of jurisdictions in the northwest. Not only that, from 1865 onward, major discoveries of silver on and about Thunder Bay was drawing attention to the region's mineral wealth. A rich vein of silver found in 1866 and an even richer one on Silver Islet near the tip of the Sibley Peninsula in 1868 triggered the start of a mining boom centred on the future Port Arthur, a boom that was given added impetus in 1871 by the discovery of gold. A little later, there would be major discoveries of gold, silver, iron, nickel, and lead in the Lake of the Woods area.

In July 1871, with the transfer of Rupert's Land imminent, John Sandfield Macdonald, Ontario's first premier, made an appeal to the Dominion government for immediate action. In November a two-man boundary commission was appointed with Eugene Taché and William McDougall representing the Dominion and Ontario respectively. Much depended on the interpretation of the description of the boundaries of the old province of Quebec as defined in the Quebec Act of 1774. In that act the boundary was traced eastward from the Atlantic to the Ohio River and then "along the bank of the said river westward to the banks of the Mississippi, and northward to the southern boundary of the territory granted to the Merchant Adventurers of England trading to Hudson's Bay." Arguing for the Dominion, Taché maintained that "northward" meant due north from the confluence of the Ohio and Mississippi rivers, and that therefore the historic boundary of the old French province, out of which Upper Canada (and later Ontario) was carved, lay along longitude 89°9'30"W, which would place Ontario's western boundary a few miles east of Thunder Bay – unthinkable from Ontario's point of view, particularly in view of the now burgeoning mining operations in the area.

Arguing for Ontario, McDougall contended that "northward" meant north along the eastern bank of the

Mississippi to that river's source in Lake Itaska and *then* due north to what was then Hudson's Bay Company territory, and that this had been tacitly recognized by the Treaty of Versailles of 1783, which, in giving the American colonies their independence had recognized that the western boundary of the United States lay along the Mississippi River. He also argued that subsequently that boundary had been extended north to the Northwest Angle, the position

of which, it will be recalled, had been first determined by David Thompson in the early 1820s. Thus, argued McDougall, Ontario's western boundary should extend northward from the Northwest Angle along longitude 95°13'48"W, which would place that boundary 275 miles (443 km) farther west (see figure 13.1).

There was also disagreement over Ontario's northern boundary. The Dominion maintained that it lay

along the height of land north of Lakes Superior and Huron, which marked the southern limits of the territory once held by the Hudson's Bay Company. Ontario felt it should be farther north. With no agreement reached, negotiations were broken off in May 1872.

A year later, in 1873, on the assumption that the territory under dispute belonged to Ontario, the Department of Crown Lands had reacted to the discovery of silver and gold around Thunder Bay by establishing the Lake Superior Mining Division and by laying out a number of townships in the area with mining locations principally in mind, though some were to have a dual purpose: part mining, part farming. Though of the 640-acre sectional, Pattern 2 type, these townships were anomalously large, with boundaries that tended to conform with natural features.

The first two of these special townships were McIntyre, fronting Thunder Bay just to the north of Neebing laid out by Herrick nine years earlier, and McTavish, at the base of the Sibley Peninsula. Both townships were completed in 1870 by Andrew Scott and Hugh Wilson respectively. In 1871 Hugh Wilson was back on Thunder Bay laying out lots in the town plot of Prince Arthur's Landing. A year later he laid out the townships of Blake and Crooks, which fronted the Thunder Bay shoreline south of Fort William, together with Pardee, an inland township.

To reach Prince Arthur's Landing and start these surveys, Wilson left Toronto in early February, travelled to Duluth, Minnesota, and then, hugging the shoreline, *walked* the 250 miles (400 km) to Port Arthur on the coastal ice. All three townships were laid out in 320-acre parcels with mining locations in mind. The 20-mile wide township of McGregor, which fronted Lake Superior between Prince Arthur's Landing and the Sibley Peninsula, had been designed as a dual-purpose township. However, Cosford Forneri, who surveyed it, reported that he could find no good agricultural land in it – he found only bare

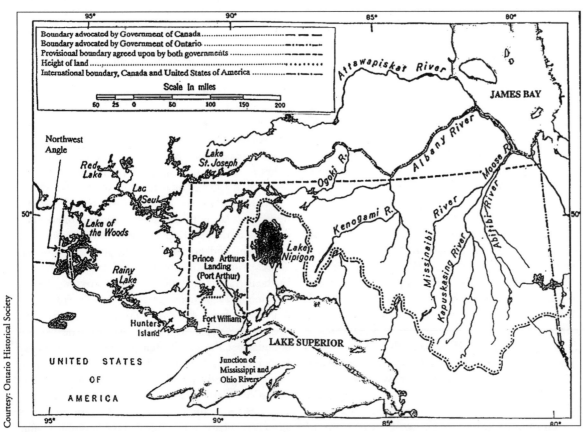

Figure 13.1 The Ontario boundary dispute. Note north-south line just east of Fort William advocated by the Dominion. Ontario argued that its western boundary ran north from the Northwest Angle. (Based on map in Nicholson, *The Boundaries of Canada, its Provinces and Territories*.)

Hugh Wilson, who laid out one of the first dual-purpose townships (part mining, part farming) on Thunder Bay. To reach Thunder Bay in February 1872 he walked up the shoreline from Duluth, Minnesota. Courtesy: AOLS Archives

rock or soil that was so thin as to amount to the same thing.

By 1874 six more townships had been completed at Thunder Bay. Scott had laid out Dorion Township north of existing McTavish, together with Nipigon at the mouth of the Nipigon River, while Wilson had surveyed Sibley Township, that is, the Sibley Peninsula, though it is now a provincial park. From Wilson's survey report for Sibley Township, we learn

that at that point there were five hundred people in the mining community on Silver Islet and that they, like the seven hundred at Prince Arthur's Landing, were totally dependent on food brought in by ship from Collingwood, Sarnia, and Detroit.

Oliver Township, west of Prince Arthur's Landing, had been surveyed by J.J. Francis, while in 1874 an anomalous narrow strip of a township, known as the "Dawson Road Lots," flanking the road to Shebandowan, had been laid out by Forneri. In a direct challenge to the federal government, the Dawson Road lots were placed on the list of free-grant townships – as had other lots in other townships in Algoma. Following all this surveying activity, no more townships would be laid out at Thunder Bay until the early 1890s.

In that same year of 1874 another attempt was made to finalize Ontario's boundaries. There was now a Liberal government in power in both Ottawa and Ontario, the premier of the latter since 1872 being Oliver Mowat, who was to preside over the fortunes of Ontario for nearly a quarter of a century. A provisional provincial boundary was agreed upon. Ontario's northern boundary would extend westward along the fifty-first parallel from the southernmost tip of James Bay to a point on the north shore of Lake St. Joseph and thence due south at about 91°W to reach the American border at the eastern tip of Hunter's Island, in what is now Quetico Park. While the western border of Ontario was some 200 miles to the east of Lake of the Woods, it still kept Thunder Bay in the province.

Meanwhile, it had been with no little disquiet that a suspicious Ontario had watched the Dominion government, starting in the mid-1870s, lay twenty-one townships in the Rainy River District. The townships, which lay along the international border from Fort Frances west to Rainy River, were Canada's response to American settlement activity on their side of the border – and incidentally served to reinforce Dominion claims in the West. They were laid out on the 640-acre sectional, Pattern 1 system and are the

only townships of their kind in the province.

The agreement between the Dominion and Ontario governments on the position of Ontario's western boundary remained in force for four years. Finally, on 1 August 1878, a three-man arbitration board met in Ottawa, with R.A. Harrison, chief justice of Ontario, representing the province, and Sir Francis Hincks, the federal government. The third and neutral member of the board was Sir Edward Thornton, Britain's representative in Washington. After a scant three days the board announced its findings. Just as Ontario wanted, the western boundary would lie on a meridian line extended north from the Northwest Angle until it met the English River. Ontario's northern boundary would be moved north from the height of land to the Albany River. Shifting the boundary westward from where the federal government wanted it back in 1871 meant a gain to Ontario of some 110 000 square miles (285 000 km²). But Ontario's triumph was short-lived. Two months after the board announced its decision, in August 1878, the Conservatives swept back into power in Ottawa. Sir John A. Macdonald refused to ratify the award, and everything was in the melting pot once again.

The running battle between Ontario and the Dominion over the position of the province's boundaries was resumed in 1881, when, in what has been described as a wily move, Macdonald brought in an act to enlarge Manitoba. Manitoba's eastern border was now to lie east of Thunder Bay on the old "due north'" line. Compounding Ontario's woes was the fact that when the federal government created Manitoba in 1870 it retained the rights to all her natural resources, so that, even if Ontario *had* been awarded the disputed territory, as Macdonald was quoted as saying, there would be "not one stick of timber, one acre of land or one lump of lead, iron or gold that does not belong to the Dominion."[5]

Macdonald's action had served only to deepen the chaos already existing in the disputed territory, where both provinces and the Dominion were granting liquor licenses. Already incensed by what was seen to be the wholesale cutting of timber by the Canadian Pacific Railway (CPR), who had timber rights on a 20-mile-wide swathe on each side of the line, then under construction, Ontario's fury deepened when the Dominion began the indiscriminate granting of timber berths and mining licences. When a provincial magistrate in Thunder Bay tried to bring a defiant railway contractor to task, he found his bailiff arrested and thrown into jail by federal agents. This farcical state of affairs intensified when Manitoba was brought onto the scene. In Kenora, then known as Rat Portage, three police forces kept themselves busy arresting each other's constables. A jail operated by Manitoba was stormed by a mob and burned down. When both Ontario and Manitoba held provincial elections in 1883, candidates from both provinces ran in the town.

Finally, to anticipate, all parties agreed in 1884 to refer the dispute over Ontario's boundaries to the Judicial Committee of the Privy Council, the highest court of appeal in the British Empire. All the old arguments were trotted out at the hearing, with Manitoba claiming – as the Dominion had done in 1871 – that the boundary lay along a line running due north from the junction of the Ohio and Mississippi rivers, while Ontario maintained that it should extend north from the Northwest Angle.

To the immense surprise and consternation of both the Dominion and Manitoba, Ontario won her case. It was presented by Oliver Mowat himself, and when he returned home he was hailed as a conquering hero with an estimated 12 000 people marching in a triumphal procession in Toronto. In upholding Ontario's case for her western boundary, the Privy Council also agreed with Ontario that her northern boundary should lie along the line of the English and Albany rivers. There it would lie until 1912.

In 1870 the Department of Crown Lands decided it was time to conduct further exploratory surveys of the north shore of Lake Superior, the first since Herrick's prodigious exploratory survey of a decade earlier. There were to be two parties, one led by John Fleming of Collingwood, the other by Walter Beatty, later notable for his work with the Dominion Land Survey in the West. This was Beatty's first and last foray into northern Ontario. He arrived at Red Rock at the mouth of the Nipigon River in June 1870 along with a party of nineteen, including two "explorers" and two chainmen. There he detached two men who were to cache half the supplies on Long Lake – the 43-mile-long lake that runs southwest from Longlac. He took the main party up the Nipigon "to Herrick's line" and then surveyed the river northward to Lake Nipigon. Arriving on Lake Nipigon, he surveyed its eastern shore as far north as latitude 50°N, that is, well over half that lake's 50-mile shoreline, completing the job at the beginning of August. Of the country bordering Lake Nipigon his only comment was "very rough."

With the survey of the lake completed, Beatty started his main exploration on a southeasterly bearing towards Long Lake about 37 miles (60 km) away. Leaving his party to get on with laying out the line, Beatty took himself off by canoe to get to Long Lake, following a route that involved fifteen portages. He made a track survey as he went, keeping an eye open for arable land, of which he found little. He then explored and traversed the country around Long Lake, covering some 240 miles in all. He dismissed the country southeast of Long Lake as "extremely rough," which just about summed up all the country he passed through.

Fleming had better luck finding arable land east of the Pic River. "North of the Black River the soil is clay loam, level and well wooded. About eight miles above the Black River, a tract of most excellent farming land begins."[6] Fleming covered some 500 miles (800 km) of ground and water that summer, his progress on rivers

and lakes speeded, as he proudly pointed out, by "Massey's Patent Propeller Log," which he used to measure distances run. For determining latitudes he used a Hadley's Sextant "reading to five seconds" and an artificial horizon.

Two years after these exploratory surveys, the contiguous (and completely isolated) townships of Byron (in part) and Homer were laid out near the mouth of the Pukaskwa River, which flows into Lake Superior at the point where the shore of the lake turns abruptly east above Michipoceten Island. Byron Township, along with those of Dorion and Nipigon at Thunder Bay, were the first to be laid out according to the 640-acre sectional, Pattern 3 system. This system would remain the standard in Ontario until 1906.

In 1873 the township of Pic was laid out at the mouth of the River Pic, this by Hugh Wilson. Pic, as were Byron and Homer, was put in with mining activities in mind. These were the only townships to be laid out on a 50-mile (80-km) stretch of the Lake Superior shore that is still virtually uninhabited and which is now part of the Lake Superior Provincial Park. And while, much later, a series of uncompleted townships would come to line the north shore of Lake Superior along the route of Highway 11 and a range of townships would be laid out 50 miles to the north, flanking the Canadian Pacific Railway's right-of-way between Longlac and Lake Nipigon, no townships would be laid out in the rugged country between them.

The early 1870s saw no more new townships going in around Sault Ste. Marie. Along the North Shore (the northern shore of Georgian Bay), however, Shedden and Victoria townships were completed, as well as Plummer, and then Plummer Additional the next year. The township of Victoria was laid out by Albert Salter himself. It seems to have been his last survey. A life-long and enthusiastic advocate of the development of both northern Ontario and the northwest and the first land surveyor in the province to press for the adoption of the American system of laying out townships, he died in Sandwich on 4 September 1874 at the age of fifty-eight.

After a lull of a few years, surveying activities along the North Shore were resumed, with Thessalon Township completed in 1877, together with that of Kirkwood to its north. By 1879, a block of six townships had been completed east of Kirkwood, four between Salter's Line and the lake, and two above that line. Meanwhile, in 1878 further townships had been laid out in the vicinity of Sault Ste. Marie, with a block of seven townships completed to the northeast, while in the late 1870s and mid-1880s a few other townships were completed above Salter's Line north of Thessalon. Thereafter, no more townships would be laid out in that part of northern Ontario until the mid-1890s. Meanwhile, Manitoulin Island had been completely subdivided into townships, sixteen in all, eighteen if Cockburn and Barrie Islands are included.

However, as far as the laying out of new townships went, in the 1870s the Department of Crown Lands placed its most concerted effort into the district of Parry Sound. With the completion of Himsworth at the southeastern end of Lake Nipissing in the early 1880s, all of Parry Sound's forty-six townships had been laid out except one. That was Henvey Township, south of the mouth of the French River, which would not be completed until 1912.

The 1870s also saw a start made on running Ontario's boundary with Quebec. Over that boundary there was no dispute. The general course of the boundary had been accepted for many years, though only the leg between the St. Lawrence and Ottawa rivers had been defined with any precision. When Upper Canada was established in 1791, it had been proclaimed that the boundary between Upper and Lower Canada commenced at a "stone boundary on the north bank of Lake St. Francis at the cove west of the Pointe au Baudet, in the limit of Lancaster and the Seigneurie of New Longueil, running the said limit in the direction of north, thirty four degrees west to the westernmost

angle of the seigneurie of New Longueil; thence along the northwestern boundary of the seigneurie of Vaudreuil, running north twenty five degrees east, until it strikes the Ottawa River."[7] This stretch of the boundary had been run several times with varying results, magnetic compasses being what they are, but lines run in 1862 were accepted as final.

The 1791 version of the boundary from the Ottawa River northward merely stated that it ran up the Ottawa to Lake Temiskaming and thence from the head of that lake due north to Hudson Bay. On Confederation, a map of the Ottawa River made by the Ottawa Ship Canal Company, was accepted as being the most accurate then available, and this was used to establish the Ontario-Quebec boundary along the Ottawa, such being approved in June 1867.

From Mattawa northward, however, the exact location of the boundary remained undetermined. Accordingly, on 1 October 1872 instructions were issued to W. O'Dwyer and John O'Hanly to run the boundary from the junction of the Mattawa and Ottawa rivers up the Ottawa to Lake Temiskaming and thence to the head of that lake. River and lake shores were to be traversed, with the two surveyors working on opposite shores, O'Dwyer acting for Quebec, O'Hanly for Ontario. Leaving Ottawa on 6 November, O'Hanly arrived at Mattawa on the thirteenth and, after forwarding supplies, started work on 2 December. He had a party of sixteen with him, of whom four were classified as "staff." From time to time he and O'Dwyer on the French side connected their surveys, with the two preparing a joint plan at the conclusion of the survey.

In the fall of that same year, the same two surveyors were instructed to continue the boundary due north from a point on the northeastern arm of Lake Temiskaming (as described in the relevant provincial statute) to the shore of Hudson's Bay, some 270 miles (435 km) away. Stone monuments were to be built every mile, with "Ontario" incised on one side,

"Quebec" on the other. A substantial wooden post was to be planted alongside with nearby "witness" trees appropriately marked. In addition, the line was to be cleared of all trees, initially to a depth of 15 feet on both sides. All in all a formidable undertaking. However, in view of the dispute over the position of Ontario's northern boundary, the original instructions were subsequently amended. The surveyors, who were to work together, were to run the line north for 50 miles, or to the height of land if they reached that first.

The surveyors left Ottawa on 4 November 1873 and were on Lake Temiskaming by the twenty-third. After waiting for a few days for the ice on the lake to firm up, they reached the head of the lake and started work on 12 December. With O'Hanly were sixteen men, of which eleven were "labourers" and one a stonemason. In the event, after running some 42 miles (68 km) of line, they crossed the height of land at Labyrinth Lake (east and a bit north of Kirkland Lake) and ran the line another 3 miles north. The survey was not completed, however, until April 1874 at which time a large stone monument was placed near the shoreline on Lake Temiskaming, marking the southern end of the north-south line. Another large stone was placed on an island offshore, marking the boundary at that point, while two monuments of cut stone were placed at the northern end of the line. One was planted at the height of land, the other just to the north of it, inscribed with the surveyors' names and the latitude, that is, latitude 48°10'24"N (see figure 13.2).

What with running the line itself, clearing a swathe down it's full length (though only 8 feet [2.5 m] wide), bad weather, waiting for skies to clear so that astronomic observations could be made, portaging, moving camp, and travel delays generally, the survey took 207 days. Only one-third of the time was actually spent working on the line. As finalized, the boundary on the Ottawa River and up Lake Temiskaming appeared on a plan dated 27 December 1875, which was signed by the

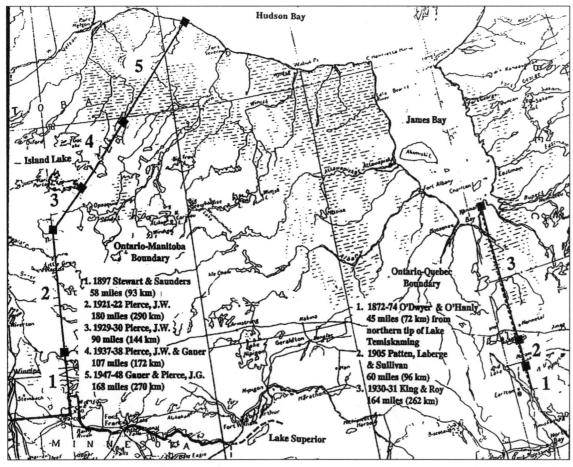

Hudson Bay

5

4

Island Lake

3

Ontario-Manitoba
Boundary

2

1. 1897 Stewart & Saunders
58 miles (93 km)
2. 1921-22 Pierce, J.W.
180 miles (290 km)
3. 1929-30 Pierce, J.W.
90 miles (144 km)
4. 1937-38 Pierce, J.W. & Gauer
107 miles (172 km)
5. 1947-48 Gauer & Pierce, J.G.
168 miles (270 km)

1

James Bay

Ontario-Quebec
Boundary

1. 1872-74 O'Dwyer & O'Hanly
45 miles (72 km) from
northern tip of Lake
Temiskaming
2. 1905 Patten, Laberge
& Sullivan
60 miles (96 km)
3. 1930-31 King & Roy
164 miles (262 km)

3

2

1

Lake Superior

Figure 13.2 A semi-diagramatic representation of the Ontario-Quebec and Ontario-Manitoba boundary surveys. The boundaries were surveyed in stages from south to north, as numbered. The base map is modern.

commissioners of crown lands for the two provinces. A second plan, showing the line north of Lake Temiskaming, was signed by both O'Hanly and O'Dwyer. But between them these otherwise meticulous land surveyors forgot to put a date on it.

Since Confederation, faith in the policy of economic growth through settlement had been sustained by the popularity of the free-grant townships with both immigrants and would-be settlers from other parts of the province. The colonization roads were seen as essential to the free-grant program. And only by providing ready access to newly opened townships and by

improving communications in the older townships could the flow of settlers be maintained. Thus as the number of free-grant townships grew steadily from fifteen in 1868 to ninety-four in 1878, so did the extent of the colonization road program.

In 1872 there were thirty-seven designated colonization roads and the number subsequently grew. Money went not just to building new roads, some of them major, some minor, but also to the repair of old ones and the building of bridges – and to rebuilding them when they fell down, which many did. By 1878, the department was involved in seventy-four road projects of one sort or another. Most were in "old" Ontario, south of the French and Mattawa rivers, but many were in the north. By 1885 the department was spending over $120,000 annually on its road-building program, an enormous sum in those days. Then, in the early 1880s the railways came – the Canadian Pacific Railway (CPR) and what was then known as the Northern and Pacific Junction Railway, which reached north from Gravenhurst to join the CPR just north of Callander.

The railway was immediately seized on as a timely extension of the colonization road system that could transport settlers by the thousands into the country south of Lake Nipissing and, more importantly, into northern Ontario itself. As soon as the proposed route of the CPR became known, there was a rush to lay out townships along or near to it, with over forty completed in five years. A number of these along the North Shore were laid out with reference to Salter's Line, with the surveyors much hampered by the absence of the relevant posts – which had been burned in a massive forest fire some years before.

In general, the longed-for agricultural land was proving to be elusive as ever. Thus, Francis Bolger, for example, working on Ratter Township, reported that "the face of the country is rocky and stony, with light sandy soil."[8] Frank Purvis of Eganville found little more to say of Hagar Township west of Ratter than

"Moose, deer, bears and beavers were frequently met with on the survey."[9] Awrey Township was dismissed by Alexander Niven in a few paragraphs. "I cannot report favorably of this township," he wrote, "there being very little good land or timber in it."[10] Bolger said much the same of Dryden Township (just to the west of present-day Sudbury). He found the country "rough, broken, and rocky and as a whole unfitted for agricultural purposes ... Along the line of the Canadian Pacific Railway a few farms may be cultivated, but no settlement of any size can be formed."[11]

Of Hallam and May townships, surveyed in the spring of 1883, Elihu Stewart reported in the case of the former that much of the land was burnt over, though perhaps 20 percent was fit for agriculture. Of May Township, he wrote, "The surface of the whole township is very broken by irregular hills or mountains of rock, varying in height from fifteen or twenty to one hundred feet."[12] Thomas Speight dismissed Merritt Township (where Espanola now stands) in a brief report, which stated baldly that it contained little or no agricultural land.

Both Elihu Stewart and Thomas Speight were then at the beginning of their distinguished careers, Speight at the very beginning. Licensed in 1882 as both a Dominion and provincial land surveyor, Speight was born in 1859 in Yorkshire, where his father was a shoemaker, and was nine when his family emigrated to Ontario a year after Confederation to settle in Fisherville in York County. He served his articles with Silas James, the superintendent of roads in York County, who was both a Dominion and provincial land surveyor, and who took on Speight as a partner when he qualified. In 1885, two years after his survey of Merritt Township, Speight entered into a new partnership with Anthony van Nostrand, who had qualified the same year as he had, the result being a firm that became known internationally and which today, over a hundred years later, is still in business as Speight, van Nostrand & Gibson, Ltd.

Born in Lambton County in 1844, whither his father had been brought in 1804 from his native Scotland by Lord Selkirk to the ill-fated Baldoon settlement, Elihu Stewart had qualified both as a Dominion and provincial land surveyor in 1872. After working out west he returned to Ontario where, in 1875, he married and went to work in Collingwood, of which he was later to become mayor. That same year, he surveyed the township of Machar in the Parry Sound District. A year later, he made the first of his many surveys in northern Ontario when he laid out three townships opposite St. Joseph Island. Other surveys in Algoma and Parry Sound followed, and then in 1881 he laid out Mack Township, one of the block of seven townships that was laid out that year west of the Serpent River. Later he would be a prime mover in the formation of the Spruce Falls Pulp and Paper Company with its mill in Kapuskasing.

Bolger, reporting on McKim Township, which he surveyed in 1883, gives us a glimpse of Sudbury almost at the moment of that city's birth. He, too, found a township that had been ravaged by fire, "the bush fires having made a clean sweep of every bit of vegetation." There was little arable land, though no doubt settlers would take up land along the railway right-of-way "as many facilities will be offered to the farmer to get his produce to market. A nucleus of a town has already been formed at Sudbury Junction, where the Railway Company have erected about a dozen houses ... The best land met with in the township is in the vicinity of the junction. There is some excellent farming land met with here."[13]

Later in that summer of 1883, a blacksmith working near the line 3 miles (5 km) west of Sudbury Junction came across some reddish rock that he thought might contain copper. His find sparked a rush of prospectors, merchants, contractors, and fortune hunters to the area who, during the following winter, floundered through the snow to lay claims, almost all of which were to be acquired for a total of $100,000 by

The Surveyor Who Collected Butterflies

"Thursday, July 1, 1886: Dominion Day. Surveyed lots for Presbyterian Church at Sudbury 9–1 P.M. Went out with butterfly net in afternoon for a couple of hours." *"Monday, June 6, 1887*: All day exploring over the Little Pic River iron location ... Butterflies very numerous" (John Dunlap Evans's diary, Inco. Co. Archives, Sudbury). Such were typical entries in Evans's diary, a provincial land surveyor who went on to become chief engineer and then general manager of the Canadian Copper Company, the forerunner of International Nickel.

Born in Goderich in 1843, Evans went to Upper Canada College in the late 1850s, and was commissioned a provincial land surveyor in 1864. After practising in Belleville he became chief engineer for the Central Ontario Railway (COR) and moved to Trenton. In 1886 he makes an entry of note for 23 February that reads: "Started for Toronto by the 6 A.M. train. Attended meeting of Prov. L. Surveyors in afternoon to form an Association."

The president of the COR was Samuel Ritchie. After nearly going bankrupt in an iron ore venture, he took himself and Evans north to Sudbury and its copper deposits, with the incorporation of the Canadian Copper Company in 1886 as a result. Ritchie made Evans chief engineer and surveyor of his new company and, in 1890, its general manager. And all the while, Evans was collecting butterflies and other insects. His collection of 60 000 eventually ended up in the Victoria Museum in Ottawa, since absorbed by the Canadian Museum of Nature. One-time president of the Entomological Society of Ontario, Evans had a hitherto unknown insect named after him.

S.J. Ritchie, an industrialist and mining speculator from Ohio then constructing the Central Ontario Railroad into the bog iron country north of Trenton. And so the mineral wealth of Sudbury passed into American hands, to be developed by the Canadian Copper Company formed in 1886 and which, in spite of its name, had its headquarters in Cleveland.

By 1885 the CPR was passing through surveyed townships all the way from Sturgeon Falls to Sault Ste. Marie, and in hopes, presumably, that the two railways now converging on North Bay would bring settlers flocking to the region, six townships were laid out above the Mattawa River in the mid-1880s. With the completion in 1885 of Olrig Township between Phelps and the long-established township of Mattawan, all the land fronting on the Mattawa River was now subdivided into townships.

Thought was also being given to opening up the region between Lakes Nipissing and Temiskaming. Thus Alexander Niven was instructed in 1881 to run base and exploration lines into the area. He had William Johnston with him as an "explorer," his duty to explore the country for 6 miles (10 km) on each side of the survey lines. From his point of commencement at the northeast corner of Field Township, northwest of Sturgeon Falls, Niven outlined further tiers of townships ending up a little to the west of the southern end of Lake Temagami. He then ran his base line to Lake Temiskaming. Reaching the lake, his observations placed the base line on latitude 46°49'2"N. He completed his survey with a line running due south. He summarized his observations on the very broken, lake-strewn country he passed through by suggesting it was more fitted for lumbering than agriculture.

Four years later Niven ran a meridian line to the west of Lake Temiskaming and, at its northern end, surveyed the township of Lorrain – on Lake Temiskaming east and south of present-day Cobalt. Now it had so happened that in the early 1880s, the Quebec government had implemented a mass settle-ment scheme on the eastward extension of what would become known in Ontario as the Little Clay Belt, and it wasn't long before French Canadian settlers had drifted across the provincial boundary into Ontario. Thus in 1885 when Niven came to lay out the township of Lorrain in 40 by 80 chain lots, he found a squatter there, one Camille Latour, who after Niven had surveyed the township, found himself, no doubt somewhat to his surprise, the occupier of Lot 15 in the Second Concession of the Ontario township of Lorrain.

Niven also found a French mission, complete with a church and a bell on what became Lot 16 in the Fourth Concession. While Niven characterized the township as a whole as "rough, rocky and broken," he noted that there were pockets of fertile clay that produced excellent crops, as indeed he had seen on Latour's farm and in a couple of clearings that the mission fathers had made. This fertile clay land was confined to the flats and valleys along the north and northeasterly parts of the township. "However," he wrote in his report, "from the northern boundary of the township I could see a large tract of level land around the head of Lake Temsikamingue, which I was informed was excellent clay soil ... and I have no doubt from what I've heard of it, that [there] are a number of townships there that would be taken up as soon as surveyed, settlement to some extent [having] already taken place."[14]

To summarize, in northern Ontario by the end of 1885, that's to say the year before the inaugural meeting of what is now the Association of Ontario Land Surveyors, there was the isolated township of Lorrain near the head of Lake Temiskaming, six townships along the Mattawa east of North Bay, and a cluster of nine townships east and north of Sturgeon Falls. From this cluster of townships westward, there was a narrow strip of townships, one township wide and some five townships long, hugging the CPR line to present-day Sudbury, with another cluster to the southwest and so to another one-township-wide strip along the Serpent River.

From there westward there was a single, sometimes a double, tier of townships extending along the North Shore to become three tiers and then four tiers deep in the vicinity of Thessalon. West of that there were some forty townships roughly centred on Sault Ste. Marie. East of Sault Ste. Marie, there were the three isolated townships on the northeast shore of Lake Superior, eighteen on Thunder Bay, and twenty-one townships laid out along the international border in the Rainy River District. All in all, as of 1885 there were some 140 townships in northern Ontario, not many considering that northern Ontario is some 800 miles (1200 km) from east to west.

In the Nipissing District, south of the French and Mattawa rivers, there were perhaps only fifteen or so townships yet to be laid out, most of them in what is now Algonquin Park. All would be dutifully laid out in farm-sized, 100-acre lots – lakes, rocky outcrops, barren rock, and all – with the last of them surveyed in the early 1890s.

As it turned out, despite all the efforts of the Ontario government, the Canadian Pacific Railway brought few farmers to northern Ontario. Westbound settlers got on the train in Montreal – and stayed on it until they reached Manitoba.

However, fears that the economic growth of the province would be stunted for want of good land on which to place settlers soon proved nugatory. By the time of Confederation, lumbering had replaced agriculture as the province's leading money spinner. And agriculture itself was changing. While the principal crop was still wheat in the 1880s, what is now known as the "fluid milk industry" started to emerge as towns and cities grew too large to be supplied with milk by local farmers making casual deliveries. Speeding the growth of that industry was the introduction, in 1881, of Holstein Friesian cattle, the breed that now dominates the Canadian dairy industry, and by the introduction of the silo, which solved the age-old problem of feeding cattle during the winter. Farmers were experimenting with new crops and getting better yields from old ones. And, particularly in southwestern Ontario, drainage schemes were bringing extensive areas of once useless waterlogged land into production, a scheme in which a number of provincial land surveyors played a leading role.

While Ontario in the 1880s was still predominantly rural, industrial growth was drawing more and more people to the towns and cities. In 1871, four years after Confederation, Ontario's population stood at 1.6 million, 22 percent of whom were classified as urban. By 1881 that percentage had already risen to 30 percent. As in all industrialized western countries, the flight to the city had begun. Thus by the mid-1880s, the typical provincial land surveyor was an urbanite – a top-hatted gentleman taking his sights along some street in town (see frontispiece). He had his private practice, leavened perhaps by the occasional assignment from the Department of Crown Lands to subdi-

vide or resurvey a lot or two. A land surveyor might hold the post of town or township engineer, in which his time would be spent on drainage work or on the location or relocation of roads, bridges, and the like, combined perhaps with the engineering aspects of their construction – there were as yet very few qualified civil engineers. What was to be an on-going struggle between land surveyors and civil engineers, as to who should be doing what, was just beginning.

Comparatively few of the perhaps two hundred land surveyors active in the province in the 1880s were now carrying out crown surveys in the bush – which by this time was becoming synonymous with working in the north. This would be increasingly left to the young and more adventurous, or to those such as Alexander Niven and Thomas Speight who were expert at it. However, a number of Ontario land surveyors were working for the federal government in the west. When the second Riel rebellion broke out in 1885, most of the fifty-three Dominion Land Surveyors who served in a hastily formed Dominion Land Surveyors' Intelligence

Corps were from Ontario, including Walter Beatty, James Milne, and Thomas Fawcett. Fawcett was wounded at Batoche, and Alexander Kippen of Perth was killed, the corps' only fatal casualty.

That same year of 1885 also saw the death of John Stoughton Dennis. Charles Rankin would die a year later. James Bridgland, who had long presided over the colonization roads scheme, had died in 1880. And by this time other land surveyors who had helped open up the Ottawa-Huron Tract were in retirement. In 1885 Michael Deane, for example, was in his mid-sixties. In short, the last of the pioneer land surveyors who had opened up "old" Ontario were passing from the scene. It was at this juncture, then, with southern Ontario all but completely laid out into townships, with the survey of northern Ontario scarcely begun, and with the land-surveying profession becoming an essentially urban one, that what became the Association of Provincial Land Surveyors of Ontario was formed.

On Draining Agricultural Land

By the early 1880s a number of provincial land surveyors had become township "engineers," some of whom had no formal training in engineering. This tended to rile some surveyors, such as Willis Chipman, who did hold degrees in engineering. Township engineers were often called upon to deal with drainage problems, not in the household sense, but rather those connected with draining agricultural land whose productivity could be increased thereby.

The long and tortuous legislative history of drainage began in 1845 with the passage of An Act to Provide for the Regulation of Line Fences and Watercourses in Upper Canada (8 Vict., c. 20). In 1859 the act was amended and became Chapter 57 of the *Consolidated Statutes of Upper Canada* in 1859 and it was further amended following Confederation.

The Act Respecting Ditching and Watercourses (38 Vict., c. 26) of 1874 repealed and replaced all previous legislation. It brought provincial land surveyors into the judicial drainage arena for the first time. Surveyors could now be empowered to take levels and prepare the plans to be followed when digging a ditch or drain. The act of 1874 was amended four times in four years.

A fresh start was made with an act (46 Vict., c. 27) passed in 1883. The most important feature of this act was that municipal councils were required to appoint an "engineer" who was to inspect the

work, approve it after completion, and award contracts if necessary. Henceforth, municipal drainage work would become a lucrative source of employment for many surveyors.

The act of 1883 was amended three times in as many years and was consolidated again in 1887. There were amendments in 1888, 1889, and 1890, and some further consolidation in 1894. So far so good. But in 1859 a Municipal Act had been passed that also touched on drainage matters. So from then on, the drainage clauses in the Municipal Act with its successive amendments co-existed with the successive versions of the ditches and watercourses act.

An amendment to the Municipal Act in 1866, together with the Provincial Drainage Act of 1872, allowed municipal councils to borrow money for drainage work. Following these amendments, major arterial drainage schemes were carried out. Especially benefiting were Russell County in the East and Middlesex, Lambton, and other counties in the west.

Benefiting most of all, though, was Essex County, where Patrick McNiff was so often up to his knees in "mudd." It was stated in 1880, "The *Ontario Drainage Act* for the reclamation of wet lands has done wonders for Essex. Under this act thousands of acres have been brought into cultivation, and are today yielding a profitable return from land that was, till recently, all but worthless" (quoted in Jones, *History of Agriculture in Ontario, 1613–1880*, 315). It was a remarkable achievement and one that says much for the skills of the many provincial land surveyors involved.

CHAPTER
FOURTEEN

The
Association
Is Born

Following the formation in 1846 by Rankin, Fleming, Passmore, and Browne of the association that became the Royal Canadian Institute, there was no further attempt by land surveyors to form a professional association until 1859, when the Association of Architects, Civil Engineers and Provincial Land Surveyors of Upper Canada was formed. It soon faded.

In 1873 another attempt was made by a now unknown number of provincial land surveyors who met in London to form a provincial association called "The Surveyors' Association of Western Ontario." In spite of its name all provincial land surveyors in Ontario were invited to join. Recommended fees were $8 plus expenses for office and field work; $5 for astronomical observations; and $2 for descriptions. The meeting broke up with a general agreement that the association would meet again, in London, a year later. Whether or not that meeting took place remains unknown, as does the subsequent history, if any, of this association.

In 1874, a meeting of eleven federal deputy land surveyors took place, which would eventually lead to an association in the newly formed province of Manitoba. These eleven surveyors proposed to the surveyor general in Ottawa that the term "Deputy Surveyor" be changed to "Dominion Land Surveyor" – which proposal was accepted. Hence the suffix "D.L.S." that many surveyors were to use so proudly in the years to come. The Manitoban association met again in 1880, leading to the birth of the Association of Dominion Land Surveyors of Manitoba and the North-West Territories, which in 1882 was incorporated in Manitoba as the Association of Provincial Land Surveyors. That same year also saw the formation of the Corporation des Arpenteurs-Géomètres de la Province de Quebec.

The Association of Dominion Land Surveyors was also formed in 1882. It arose from what was apparently a spontaneous meeting to discuss poor rates

Willis Chipman on being commissioned in 1881. Five years later he played a leading role in the formation of the association. Courtesy: AOLS Archives

of pay. Otto Klotz chaired the first, clearly very informal, meeting and was elected president by acclamation. He held this position until 1886 when he was succeeded by Thomas Fawcett. The association was to accomplish much in the years ahead. Very soon after its formation it was urging the federal government to undertake a long overdue national geodetic survey.

Meanwhile in Ontario another attempt had been made to form a provincial association. In 1878 a circular regarding the formation of an association went out to surveyors. Just what the circular proposed and who its authors were remains unknown. The proposal provoked a curious response from Lindsay Russell, who was appointed Dominion surveyor general that same year. From a letter to Francis Lynch-Staunton, who was presumably one of the proponents of the new association, it can be inferred that some stress was laid on the incorporation of the proposed association.

Lindsay Russell cautioned against this:

> While I sympathise in all efforts to raise the standard of ... our profession, I cannot see that is practicable to do anything in [that] direction by legislation ... The only legitimate means of raising the status of the profession consists in the effort of each individual thereof ... If as a class they [surveyors] are held in slight esteem by the public, it is because they do not merit more.[1]

It may be that Russell's discouraging words had the effect of aborting the embryonic association. Nothing more was heard of it, and so yet another attempt at forming a provincial association came to nothing. Quoted later at the inaugural meeting of the Association of Provincial Land Surveyors of Ontario in 1886, Russell's letter put an effective damper on any immediate move towards incorporation.

It wasn't long before at least some surveyors in Ontario were thinking of attempting yet again to form their own provincial association. Among those was Willis Chipman, who in 1886 played a leading role in founding the association that, on its incorporation in 1892, would become the Association of Ontario Land Surveyors.

Willis Chipman was born on 1 October 1855 near Elgin, a village some 19 miles (30 km) north of Gananoque. He went to public school in Farmersville, which, as time went by, was to acquire not only a public and secondary school but a normal school as well,

whereupon in 1888 – presumably dazzled by its own intellectual pretensions – it renamed itself Athens. Chipman graduated from McGill in civil and mechanical engineering with first-class honours in 1876, the same year that his family moved to Brockville. He taught high-school mathematics in Napanee before

The first page of Chipman's report to David Beatty on the survey of Biggar township. (AO, Letterbooks, Willis Chipman, Letterbook 1882-85, MU 3285.)

Courtesy: Archives of Ontario

moving to Toronto where he worked as an assistant engineer at a Toronto waterworks, then in the course of construction. In 1880 he married Angeline Dennison and decided to broaden his horizons by becoming a surveyor, articling himself for a year to George Abrey of Manitoulin Island and going on to

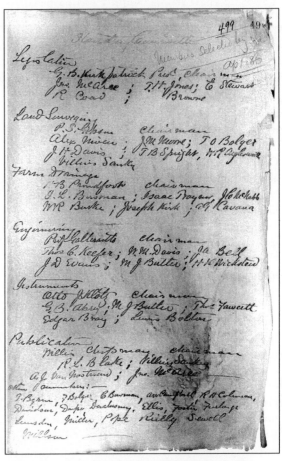

The only reference to the founding of the association in Chipman's letterbook for 1882–85 is a list (on the back inside cover) of possible committee members. "Members selected by me, Ap1 1886" can be faintly discerned top right. (From Chipman, *Letterbook, 1882–85.*)

survey out west, qualifying as a Dominion Land Surveyor in May 1881. He then studied under Peter Gibson to qualify as a provincial land surveyor five months later. By November 1881, when he was twenty-six, he hung up his shingle in Brockville. The following summer, he carried out the survey of Biggar Township (now in Algonquin Park) on behalf of David Beatty, who was surveying in the west.

With a wife and soon a baby son to support, Chipman, who was perennially short of money and perhaps more thrusting than most, lost no opportunity to try and swell his purse by offering to "do" (copy?) Thomas Byrne's field notes for him, stressing that he had "first class drawing instruments, office, etc." Said office, according to his letterhead at this time, was "Opposite Post Office," which would now place it in Court House Square in the centre of Brockville. He also took on a job doing appraisals for a Toronto-based loan and savings company, a position his father had held until his death.

Having learned that Brockville was to build its own waterworks and have a town plan compiled, Chipman bid $1,200 on the latter job and got it. He had eighteen months to complete the plan, so he spent the summer of 1883 surveying in what is now western Saskatchewan. His homecoming in the fall of 1883 could not have been a happy one. His wife, Angeline, had died while he was away, leaving him with two infant children – the couple had been married less than three years. On getting back, he undertook a number of lot or parcel descriptions, while the next summer saw him back in Nipissing, north of the Mattawa this time, surveying Mulock Township to the east of North Bay. Meanwhile he had been awarded the job of preparing a town plan for Prescott.

But, to an increasing extent, Chipman was turning to engineering work, particularly in regard to the design and construction of water and sewage systems, the field in which he was ultimately to make an international name for himself. By the end of 1884 he was supervising engineer of the Brockville waterworks, then under construction, and was widening his engineering horizons by offering his (and the waterworks') expertise to the village of Iroquois in connection with "a water supply to afford a fire protection to your village ... the only cost [to you] will be an annual rental of so much per hydrant ... [it being] needless to point out to you the superior advantages of a water supply of this kind over any steam or horse engine."

In December 1885, he submitted a bid on the installation of a sewage system for Brockville. Chipman's preamble to his proposal, which might well grace a similar proposal made today, ran as follows:

> However beautiful and healthful the situation of the town of Brockville and however pure the breezes of [the] St. Lawrence we cannot close our eyes to the fact that we are accumulating in our midst all the elements necessary for the spread of preventable disease – pure air, pure water and a pure soil are the requisites necessary for the longevity of the human race. Pure air can only be obtained when the soil is pure, as emanations from an impure, polluted soil must contaminate the air with which it is in contact.[2]

None of all this hints at Chipman's emergence in January 1886 as one of the prime movers in the formation of the Association of Provincial Land Surveyors of Ontario, the forerunner of the present association. However, we do know that during December 1885 he corresponded with eleven others, including Otto Klotz, George Kirkpatrick, and Peter Gibson, with a view to forming such an association. And it is on record that as a result of that correspondence a circular over the names of the eleven conveners was sent out not long afterward. It read as follows:

Compiling Town Plans

Having landed the job of compiling a town plan for Brockville, Chipman immediately found himself out of his depth. Thus, there is a note of urgency, even alarm, in the letter he wrote to his mentor, Peter Gibson, asking for advice. He refers to earlier very badly done surveys, and subsequent subdivisions of lots that had caused further discrepancies – one such amounting to 3 feet (1 m) in less than 500. Such errors and discrepancies would become the bane of late-nineteenth-century surveyors attempting to compile town plans. Chipman summarized his many perplexities as follows:

> The Town may be divided into four divisions, viz:
> 1. That part which has never been laid down on any plan whatsoever – (This includes the main business part of town)
> 2. That part that has been surveyed and laid down on plans but not done by a legally qualified surveyor but plans in Registry Office
> 3. That part which has been planned and laid down and deeds drawn to conform thereto but no plans filed –
> 4. That part (about one fourth of town) which has been legally surveyed and plans filed according to Registry Act.

He added "Please explain in full and return your charges ... Will begin work next week" (Willis Chipman, "Letterbook 1882–85," MU 3285, AO). Gibson charged three dollars for his advice. While such a sum may seem picayune to us today, this was about half a day's earnings. One hundred dollars per month was then considered good pay by land surveyors.

We, the undersigned provincial land surveyors, deem it advisable, for the purpose of improving ourselves and maintaining and elevating the standard of our profession, to organise an Association of provincial land surveyors in Ontario.

. . .

A meeting for organization will be held at Toronto, on Tuesday, 23rd February, 1886, at 2 p.m. Arrangements have been made for meeting in the Crown Lands Department.

It is desirable that all P.L.Surveyors should attend this meeting, that a Constitution may be adopted that will meet with the approval of the majority of the profession. Those who may find it impossible to attend will oblige the conveners by communicating their views to Willis Chipman, Brockville, Secretary *pro tem*.[3]

And so the first steps were taken in yet another attempt to draw together the surveyors of Ontario into a professional association. This time the attempt was to succeed.

The first meeting took place on 23 February 1886, not in the Crown Lands Department as advertised, but in the Private Bills Committee Room of the Parliament Buildings. The precursor of the present building in Queen's Park, the Parliament Building was then a two-storey, brick building standing on Front Street between Simcoe and John streets, now the site of the Canadian Broadcasting Corporation's new building.

Thirty-six surveyors came to the inaugural meeting. Was this a good turnout? The answer depends on the answer to another question, namely: how many surveyors were working in the province at that time? The question admits of no firm answer. While the department kept a list of the names and addresses of qualified land surveyors, it did not know how many were still active. George Kirkpatrick, director of surveys in the Department of Crown Lands, estimated that about 250 were active; Willis Chipman estimated about 180. Thus, very roughly, one surveyor in five showed up.

Of the thirty-six, twelve, or one-third, came from Toronto or its environs. The rest came from all parts of southern Ontario, with the exception of the far eastern and far southwestern portions of it. Considering the time of year, it was an excellent turnout and "thoroughly representative," as Chipman himself put it in his preface to the minutes of the meeting. According to him the meeting was a "very enthusiastic one" with "many letters of encouragement and hearty approval ... from members of the profession who were unable to be present."

However, it is clear that the inaugural meeting owed its success not so much to the size of the turnout and satisfactory geographical distribution, as to the presence of such heavyweights of the profession as Peter Gibson, Alexander Niven, Otto Klotz, Thomas Fawcett, and Elihu Stewart, while the presence of George Kirkpatrick from the Department of Crown

---

The Gibsons

David Gibson had four sons who all worked as land surveyors under their father, though only two of them, James A. and Peter Silas, became provincial land surveyors. James qualified in 1855 and worked with his father until the latter died. He then moved to Oshawa and opened a book and stationery store. Born in 1827, Peter Silas went to the University of Michigan where he studied science and civil engineering, taking a year off in 1858 to qualify as a provincial land surveyor. He worked out of Willowdale and became one of the founding members of what is now the Association of Ontario Land Surveyors in 1886.

Marrying in 1868, Peter Silas had ten children. Three of his sons became Ontario Land Surveyors: Harold Holmes, Wilbert Silas, and Morton Milne, who were licensed in 1891, 1898, and 1912 respectively. Morton Milne became a Dominion Land Surveyor, worked in northern Ontario, and subsequently practised out of Whitby and then Agincourt. Harold H. worked in the States, mostly in Kentucky, and returned to Toronto in 1916. His son, Ansel Bee Gibson was licensed in 1924 and practised in Toronto. Wilbert Silas formed a surveying firm known as W.S. Gibson & Sons, which did much subdivision work in northern Toronto, the sons being Silas Eldon and Charles W., licensed in 1930 and 1942 respectively. At the 1930 annual meeting, five of the ninety-five present were Gibsons. From 1972 to 1991 W.S. Gibson and Sons, Ltd., worked with Speight, van Nostrand, Anderson & Currie when the two firms merged to become Speight, van Nostrand & Gibson, Ltd.

Toronto in 1886

With a population of about 90 000 the city of Toronto in 1886 was bounded, very roughly, by Bloor Street to the north, Dufferin Street to the west, the Don Valley to the east, and, of course, Lake Ontario to the south. King Street was the main business street. Beyond the Don, the jail stood in lonely splendour on a hilltop, while to the southeast of it, where Queen Street meets Kingston Road, was what Polk's Toronto Directory calls the "suburban village" of Norway, now a district in the city of Toronto. There were five other such "suburban villages": Carlton West, Deer Park, Parkdale, West Toronto Junction, and Seaton Village on Bathurst north of Bloor. The waterfront had long since been pushed south of The Esplanade, on which a start had been made in 1840. It was scarcely finished when it was appropriated by the railway.

Lands gave an official stamp of approval to the gathering. Kirkpatrick was then in his early fifties, as were both Niven and Gibson. Gibson was by now the most experienced and widely known of the urban land surveyors.

Otto Klotz was thirty-four in 1886. As a Dominion Topographical Surveyor he was already one of the most highly qualified surveyors in the Dominion, as well as being experienced at government in-fighting, as witness the part he played in forming the Dominion association. Thomas Fawcett, D.T.S., wounded the year before at Batoche, was English-born and in his late thirties. Fawcett had succeeded Klotz as president of the Dominion association the year before. Also at the meeting was Villiers Sankey. Born in Ireland, Sankey had taken and passed the entrance exam for the Royal Indian Engineering College at Sandhurst but had then failed the medical, following which he came to Ontario in about 1875, so he had been in the country for only about ten years at the time of the 1886 meeting. Qualifying as a provincial land surveyor in 1878, he joined the firm that before long became that of Unwin, Browne and Sankey. A military man at heart, it seems he had a reputation for efficiency. At any rate, on the formation of the association, he was to land the job of chairing one of the most important of the standing committees, that on land surveying.

The inaugural meeting got under way with Peter Gibson in the chair and with Chipman, predictably, secretary *pro tem.* Gibson asked Chipman to read the circular and extracts from "replies received thereto." How many replies there were and what they said remains unknown. Gibson then gave his own, surely rather low-key reasons for going ahead with the formation of a "P.L.S. Association." The object of such an association, in his view, would be the revision and improvement of the various provincial acts pertaining to land surveying. The association might also suggest to the Board of Examiners that they amend the list of subjects upon which candidates were then being exam-

ined. He concluded by asking for a general expression of opinion.

Otto Klotz was the first to speak. "There is," he said, "material among the provincial land surveyors of Ontario to form an Association creditable to themselves and to the country which [striking a note that reminds us that in those optimistic days men still believed in the ultimate Triumph of Reason] will ever bear 'Progress,' the watchword of the nineteenth century, on its banner." He then read the letter (from which an extract was quoted earlier) that the (now late) Lindsay Russell had written in 1878 deploring the notion of incorporation – a letter which reinforced his own views on the inadvisability of pressing for immediate incorporation. Klotz then relinquished the floor to Thomas Fawcett.

Fawcett pointed out that he had not practised in the province for many years. Nevertheless, "any movement that had for its object the elevation of the standard of the profession met with his entire approval." He observed that other groups, professional and otherwise, "have found it advantageous to form themselves into societies for the means of self-protection, and for the purpose of better securing their rights. There was no reason," he went on, "why the provincial land surveyors of this Province should be an exception to that rule." He stressed the educational value of such an association to its members, as did others later in the meeting who described the benefits resulting from informal contacts with fellow members. Fawcett was thus the first to point out the importance of what we would now call professional development. Lewis Bolton spoke briefly in favour of forming an association, as did Alexander Niven, who stressed that the Surveyors Act could do with amending.

In all this the only sour note was struck by William Spry of Toronto. Spry, whose pinched-up face – at least judging by a contemporary portrait – suggests a certain parsimony if not narrow-mindedness, had qualified as a provincial land surveyor in 1858 but had

spent most of his working life as a construction engineer with various railway companies. He had not practised as a land surveyor for twenty years, he told the meeting.

However, this did not deter him from pronouncing on the state of the profession and the future of the proposed association, about which he was not "sanguine ... unless it was a very inexpensive one." He said that unlike the legal and medical professions "which were constantly increasing and becoming more lucrative" the profession of surveying was "dying out." The reason; that there were no "prizes [pecuniary?] to be looked forward to, as in law or medicine." Further, in his view, there were already too many surveyors. He claimed he "could attend to all the local surveying in one or two counties" himself, adding cryptically, if he "had a horse." One senses that Spry must have sat down to an uncomfortable silence, and that perhaps the less charitable might have eyed him curiously, wondering whether it would be worthwhile giving Spry a horse just to see what he could do with it.

Spry was followed by Elihu Stewart. Perhaps anxious to quench any doubts that Spry might have raised, he suggested that the fact that so many surveyors had come to the meeting was in itself sufficient evidence that an association was thought to be desirable. He, too, drew attention to shortcomings in the Surveyors Act, which should be examined by "those best acquainted with the subject, viz, the surveyors themselves." He proposed that a committee of the association should be set up to examine certain sections of the act with a view to recommending changes. Stewart then moved: "That we proceed at once to organise." The motion was seconded by Lewis Bolton.

Speaking in favour of the motion, George Kirkpatrick threw his considerable professional weight behind the proposed association. "At present," he said, "the surveyors were strangers to each other, but meeting as often as was proposed, yearly or oftener, for the discussion of matters of interest to the profession, and for the reading of papers of practical utility to them in their work, they would improve themselves, and an interest would be stirred among them to advance the profession as was hardly possible in any other way."

Kirkpatrick also suggested that "some of the older members [should] ... give the younger men the benefit of their experience in some of the disputed cases that have come up before our courts from time to time." He then suggested that they should dine together at their annual meeting "as was usual in similar associations." At such dinners, he added elegantly, "the interchange of thought and the feeling of union that would be evoked could not fail to have a most happy effect."

Kirkpatrick was followed by Archibald Campbell of St. Thomas who was in favour of forming an association. He, too, mentioned the Surveyors Act and its shortcomings, and stressed the need to keep an eye on amendments, which, according to him, were "constantly being introduced by inexperienced men." He also referred to the three-year-old Ditches and Watercourses Act, which he said "has opened up to us a new field of labour and a new class of work under its provisions, the great necessity of certain amendments is evident, in justice to the surveyor and in order that the work may be satisfactorily carried out."

Campbell then wished "the movement every success," following which the motion to form an association was put to the vote. The motion was carried. And so, sometime in the late afternoon or early evening of 23 February 1886 the Association of Provincial Land Surveyors of Ontario was brought into being.

History does not tell us whether or not the disgruntled William Spry abstained from voting. He eventually became a member in 1893.

No time was lost in setting the infant association on its feet. A committee of eight was struck to draft a constitution and prepare a set of bylaws. These were produced so quickly that one suspects that someone, Chipman perhaps, had come prepared with a draft constitution and some bylaws in his back pocket. Be that as it may, such were duly submitted to the meeting and, after some amendments, were adopted as a whole.

The constitution gave the association its name, the Association of Provincial Land Surveyors of Ontario, and stated its objectives, which were "the promotion of the general interests, and elevation of the standard of the profession." It also defined three types of members: active (those who were provincial land surveyors); associate (articled students); and honorary ("those distinguished by professional attainments") – these last to be exempt from dues. However, only a year passed before articled students became known as junior members, while associate membership was redefined as being applicable to "those persons not provincial land surveyors who may be elected as hereinafter provided."

There was to be a president, a vice-president, a secretary-treasurer, and three councilors, who together would form an executive committee, "which shall have the management of the affairs of the Association." Three members of the committee would form a quorum, which was also charged with striking standing committees as required. General meetings were to be held annually in Toronto and would start on the fourth Tuesday in February – with some exceptions this day is still adhered to. Fifteen active members would form a quorum. Amendments to the constitution would require a vote of two-thirds of the active membership, such votes "to be taken by letter ballot." There were to be two auditors, selected by ballot, who would report at the annual meeting. Lastly a fee of $3 was payable by active and associate members on joining, with an annual fee of $2 thereafter (very soon upped to $3), such to reach the secretary-treasurer by 1 April each year. Such fees corresponded roughly to what a qualified surveyor was paid in those days for perhaps half a day's work.

A provisional executive committee was appointed consisting of Professor Galbraith,[4] John McAree, and Willis Chipman. There was then a call for nominations for the offices of president, vice-president, secretary-treasurer, and councilors. As it turned out, both Frederick Passmore, then in his seventies and perhaps with his name put forward out of respect, and Peter Gibson lost out to George Kirkpatrick for the office of president. Galbraith beat Niven and Abrey for the position of vice-president. Willis Chipman had been the only nominee for secretary-treasurer, which was hardly surprising.

The first meeting apparently closed with a report of the provisional executive committee. "We congratulate you," Chipman said, "upon the successful formation and organization of our Association upon what we consider a proper basis." Chipman then touched on the reasons why the association had been formed at an opportune time. He then went on to observe that

some few of us may be members of the Institute of Civil Engineers of Great Britain or of the American Society of Civil Engineers [while others may] have the advantage of practicing in the vicinity of the Dominion or Provincial capitals, thereby being able to exchange views and opinions on professional topics [but] the vast majority ... of our provincial land surveyors are without the advantages arising from association with fellow-professional men, which state of things must cease to exist before they can expect to accomplish much towards their advancement.

As for incorporation, Chipman comments that "We must first become a united body, and be able to present our request to the Legislature so intelligently, so justly, and so forcibly, that they cannot do otherwise than comply."

Chipman then announced the standing committees that the provisional executive had decided should be struck: committees on land survey, land drainage, municipal engineering, instruments, legislation, and publication. The committee on land survey would prepare papers for edification of the membership. These might cover "difficulties experienced in interpreting the 'Lands Act' and 'Registry Act'; field-work practice; means of attaining a uniformity in notes and plans;

investigating decisions of Courts, etc., etc." This committee's annual report, Chipman added, would soon become a valuable document, alone "worth our annual subscription."

"Upon examination of Appeal Reports for the last few years," Chipman averred, the committee on land drainage would realize "the muddle into which our legislators and our judiciary have managed to get this matter." The Municipal Act, and Drainage and

Watercourses Act should be examined with a view to rectifying the situation. The work of the committee on municipal engineering "will be, probably, more interesting to a large part of our Association than that of any other." Sewerage, water supply, street paving, roads, and bridges would all come within its purview.

The committee on instruments would keep the members up-to-date on both field instruments and office appliances, as well as on the recording of field

George Kirkpatrick, director of surveys in the Department of Crown Lands, who was the first president of the newly formed association. In 1900 he would initiate the landmark exploratory survey of northern Ontario. Courtesy: AOLS Archives

Peter Gibson. Working out of the Gibson family home in Willowdale he was perhaps the most respected surveyor of his day. Courtesy: AOLS Archives

William Spry. The only man to vote against the formation of the association, he would join it later.
Courtesy: AOLS Archives

notes and methods of perpetuating boundaries. The committee would also encourage manufacturers to exhibit their instruments at annual meetings, while members would be urged to bring in their own instruments for examination by the membership.

The most important committee of all, Chipman observed, was the legislation committee because the usefulness of the association would depend on its work. Its duties would be "to draft and present to our legislators any bills that this Association may wish to become law, and endeavour to secure the passing of the same with as little mutilation as possible. They should also guard the interest of the profession by discouraging legislation thought to be unwise, unjust, or impracticable." The committee would also act on the recommendations of the committees on drainage, municipal engineering, and instruments.

As for the committee on publication, it would report directly to the executive and would concern itself with the publication of the proceedings, besides soliciting advertising from "instrument manufacturers, bridge companies, drain tile manufacturers, stationers, etc."

In what is the only direct reference to the new association in Chipman's letterbook, he lists on its inside cover the members of each committee. At the top right, written faintly in pencil, are the words "Members selected by me, Ap. 1, 86."[5] He didn't get his way with all the committees. For example, though he had selected Peter Gibson as chairman of the committee on land surveying, the post came to be filled by Villiers Sankey. And he had Kirkpatrick down as chairman of the committee on legislation, which position came to be filled by Elihu Stewart.

The provisional executive concluded the inaugural meeting with these words:

To the very clever surveyor we would say that you will undoubtedly become a "crank" unless you occasionally rub up against your professional brethren and get the "corners" polished off. To the "rusty" brother, we think there is no better way of brightening you up than by joining what we are confident is the permanent organization of the "Association of Provincial Land Surveyors of Ontario."

CHAPTER FIFTEEN

The Association: Getting into Stride and on to Incorporation

The second annual meeting of the association was held in Toronto from 1 March to 3 March 1887 after a *pro forma* meeting had been held and adjourned on 22 February to comply with the constitution. There were forty-nine members present. The meeting had been scheduled to take place in the Parliament Building as before, but the House was in session so the venue was changed to the library of the Canadian Institute, then situated at 58 Richmond Street East. It was an appropriate place to hold a meeting of land surveyors, it being land surveyors who had played a leading role in bringing the institute into existence.

In a short preface to the proceedings of the second meeting Chipman wrote, "The Proceedings of our Association at its first meeting were well received by our members ... Our young association is manifesting great energy, and we urge all members to aid the officers and the several committees in carrying on the work of the Association."[1]

Much had been accomplished in the year. Seven hundred copies of the proceedings of the first meeting had been mailed out. Four hundred and twenty copies had been sent to civil engineering and surveying associations in Michigan, Ohio, and Indiana, who sent copies of their annual reports in exchange. Copies of these plus the association's own proceedings had been sent to about three hundred provincial land surveyors. Chipman had referred to these earlier as the "cream of professional literature." The association's officers had processed over forty new members, handled the election of officers by letter-ballot, and set up the various standing committees, the members of which had got together in the intervening months.

Meeting participants were informed that "a meridian has been carefully laid down on the grounds of the Parliament Buildings for testing solars."* There

was to be a dinner at the Walker House on the Wednesday evening. There was also to be an exhibition of instruments to which members had been urged to bring any instruments that they thought would be of interest to their fellow surveyors.

Chipman's secretary-treasurer's report came early in the program. Membership had risen from an initial twenty-five to seventy, as of 1 January 1887. In Chipman's words they were "seventy surveyors, live men, fully awakened to the benefits of organization." Of the thirty-six surveyors at the first meeting, only six had seen fit not to join the infant association. Turning to financial matters, Chipman reported that fees had brought in $210.00 and that $47.00 worth of advertisements in the proceedings had been sold, to give total receipts of $257.00. The major outlay, $98.80, had been spent on the preparation, printing, and mailing of the proceedings. Other expenses included $6.00 for advertising the first meeting in the *Mail* and the *Globe;* about $18.00 on stationery, ballots, circulars, and postage; and $2.00 for the "Minute Book and Lettering." Thus, reported Chipman, contrary to the gloomy forecasts by "prophets who foretold pecuniary embarrassment," he was happy to report a substantial surplus of $106.05.

On Chipman sitting down, no doubt to resounding applause, Otto Klotz moved that Chipman be awarded a $40 honorarium as a small remuneration. The granting of such an honorarium (increasing with the years) became an established custom until the first paid help was recruited in the 1920s.

George Kirkpatrick of the Department of Crown Lands then gave his presidential address. He congratulated the members on the "successful inauguration of a society, the want of which has long been felt ... Union and co-operation," he continued, "are magical watchwords in other branches of work, and the time has come when, if we wish to succeed in elevating the profession of a land surveyor, we must unite, and no longer remain isolated and unknown to one another."

*Presumably a reference to either Burt's solar compass or to a "solar attachment," a device adapted from Burt's instrument, which could be attached to a transit.

He went on to observe that "a general advance in knowledge is taking place all along the line ... If we do not as a body advance with the rest, we shall find ourselves hopelessly overmatched and dragged down from the position which a well-educated and practical set of men should occupy in the community."

Kirkpatrick then gave some statistics on the number of surveyors in the province, in the past and at the time he spoke. Unfortunately there are discrepancies in his figures – at least as quoted. He apparently stated that from 1784 to 1886 a total of 697 land surveyors had been appointed in the province. Of these, he estimated that 260 were dead. This, according to him, left 372 surveyors "unaccounted for." But of course it doesn't. It leaves 437. Be that as it may, he estimated that 250 were practising surveyors in 1887. It seems that the true figure was nearer two rather then three hundred.

Kirkpatrick urged all surveyors in the province to join the association. Then warming to his theme of unite or perish, he described his version of the ideal surveyor, whom he felt all surveyors of the 1880s should strive to emulate:

> The time has gone by when with a compass and Jacob's staff a surveyor was considered to be fully equipped for his professional duties. At the present time every surveyor should be a well-read man: the subjects on which his opinion are often asked are varied. He should be able intelligently and composedly to give evidence in our courts of law, to stand his ground ... [during] cross-examination, to understand the law of evidence and to be able, impartially, to sift the wheat from the chaff ... when getting up a case.

In addition, Kirkpatrick went on, he must know his municipal law and be able to advise municipal councils on roads, bridges, ditches, and watercourses. He

should impress municipalities and individuals with the advantages of "availing themselves of the provisions for securing permanence to the limits of their lots," of draining their "swamp land," and of improving it in other ways. "In a word he has to combine the practical with the scientific." He urged young surveyors to keep good records.

He also urged the association to compile biographical sketches of early surveyors, complete with photographs if such were to be had. "With care ... we may rescue a goodly number from oblivion." And so it is to George Kirkpatrick that we owe the enviable wealth of biographical material that the association possesses today in its annual proceedings.

Then, recalling the modern reader sharply to the realities of surveying a hundred years ago, Kirkpatrick suggested that if there was time there should be a discussion of the durability of wooden posts planted "in earlier days" and how this varied with the kind of wood used and the type of soil in which they stood. Also to be discussed was whether or not the number of growth rings in trees growing in a blaze was an "absolute and unfailing proof of the age of a survey."

He then went on to read "as an interesting contribution to the history of our profession" extracts from some twenty or so eighteenth-century documents, some of them lengthy, relating to the first days of surveying in what became Ontario. In all they totalled, very roughly, between 4000 and 5000 words. One

wonders whether a modern audience would sit through that much unadulterated historical writing with the same degree of attention that Kirkpatrick apparently got.

No papers had been read at the inaugural meeting in 1886. However, a few papers had been hurriedly written, apparently by request, so that they could appear in the proceedings of that meeting, presumably to give the members something to chew on. One of them, on the history of the Surveyors Act, was written by Villiers Sankey, who had emerged, as we have seen, as the chairman of the surveying committee. Preparing his paper as background material to the discussions he assumed would come, he prefaced it by enveighing against the Surveyors Act's lack of clarity and conciseness. He suggested that the rapid strides made by the

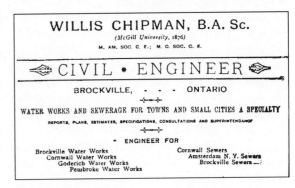

Willis Chipman advertises in the *AOLS Proceedings, 1889.*

"means and methods" of surveying in the previous twenty-five or thirty years of the nineteenth century had outpaced the act itself, which "will be found to be practically the same that it was in 1849, and many of its sections date back as far as 1818 and 1798."

Sankey then went on to the meat of his paper, a brief chronological history of the Act Respecting Land Surveyors and the Survey of Lands, Chapter 146 of the Revised Statutes of Ontario, the act that surveyors were labouring under as of 1886. He concluded with a suggestion that the committee on surveying should put a "series of questions" to the membership that they might consider before the annual meeting. This, he suggested, launching grandly into a surveying simile that surveyors of the time seemed to delight in, "would have the effect of bringing the whole matter to a focus. The back picket, as it were, would stand out clearly, and the cross-hairs being readily adjusted, the front picket would be placed true and plumb."

Following up on his paper of the year before, Sankey reported at the second meeting on the work of his committee on land surveying. With a consolidation of provincial legislation due to be undertaken by the legislature in 1887, the committee had held a two-day meeting the previous December that had been attended by seven members of the association along with several others. Apparently they amended and redrafted the entire act. There seems to be no record of what the amendments were. However, we do know that by May 1887, only three months later, the redrafted act was accepted by the legislature in its entirety – an early demonstration of the power of the association and the respect in which it was already held. And in a postscript to the 1887 proceedings the commissioner of crown lands is thanked for helping to bring the efforts of the association to such a satisfactory conclusion; though, as will be seen, the Act Respecting Land Surveyors and the Survey of Lands (50 Vict., c. 25)

was scarcely in place before the association was considering further amendments.

The drainage committee had met with only partial success with their proposed amendments to the "Drainage Acts." Though the proposals were duly approved and adopted by the executive and membership, the association had no success at all in trying to get the Municipal Act itself amended, though it was commended by the legislature for its suggestion that a special court of appeal should be set up to rule on drainage cases.

Reporting for the committee on instruments, George Abrey admitted to failure in his efforts to solicit papers in this "open, wide, and ... interesting and useful" field. But he did organize the exhibition of instruments, asking Toronto instrument makers to display their wares, as well as Hearn and Harrison of Montreal. The latter did not respond, but Charles Potter and James Foster of Toronto put on a show. Seven members brought their own instruments to display, while Abrey himself displayed over twenty of his own instruments. He had hopes that American instrument manufacturers might take part in the exhibition. However, when they discovered that they would have to pay duty, only partly recoverable, on instruments brought in for display purposes, they declined to participate.

In spite of this, the exhibition of instruments was pronounced a great success. But that success was to be short-lived. With some exceptions, members were disinclined to lug their instruments to Toronto for subsequent meetings, while Toronto manufacturers were to plead that they had little to show members that they hadn't seen before. As for American manufacturers, customs regulations continued to be an effective deterrent to their participation in such exhibitions. And so the idea of having an annual exhibition of instruments died, though it would be revived later.

Eight papers were presented at the second meeting. Galbraith gave an abstruse paper on trussed

beams. Chipman himself gave a closely reasoned paper on "The Assessment of Benefits in Drainage Surveys" in which he referred to drainage work as "ditch making," which could hardly have endeared him to the many township engineers present. There were six other papers, ranging from "The Micrometer Measurement of Distances" to "Mining in the Port Arthur District" to "Electric Lighting of Small Towns."

One of the matters that came before the meeting was a draft bill proposed by William Olgivie, D.T.S., of Ottawa and seconded by Abrey, that was to be set before the legislature. In effect this called for the revival of the board of boundary-line commissioners that had been set up in the late 1830s to settle boundary disputes. This was to be brought up again at several subsequent annual meetings before the idea was finally dropped – only to be revived again in the twentieth century.

The third annual meeting, in February 1888, was again held in the library of the Canadian Institute. Having found a home there, so to speak, the association held its annual meetings at the institute until 1895, following which the venue was changed to a room in the new Parliament Buildings.

In his welcoming address as out-going president, Kirkpatrick noted with satisfaction that under the revised Surveyors Act the qualifying examination for admission to practise now included the subjects of railway surveying and drainage work, and he urged members to obtain more business in the property evaluation field as well as become proficient in forestry and mining.

George Abrey acknowledged the many women who had accompanied their husbands to the annual meeting. "The wife of a surveyor is as a rule isolated from the society of her husband a great deal of the time in consequence of his professional duties calling him away from home," he observed. He went on to suggest that the association might arrange some events of interest for these women. The question was passed on to the entertainment committee, which apparently had been formed sometime between the second and third meeting.

One matter of fundamental importance came up at the third meeting, in 1888, and that was the responsibility of the surveyor under the Registry Act, a matter that had surfaced the previous year when a subcommittee had been struck to look into possible amendments to it. That the act was indeed in urgent need of amendment – and that the conduct of some surveyors needed looking into – was brought home by a letter written by Joseph Cozens of the Soo to the president just before the 1888 meeting:

Will you, at the association meeting next week, bring up the question of surveyors signing plans of subdivision which have no existence?

I made outline survey of a 75-acre block. The owner sends me an elaborate plan of subdivision and requests me to register the same. I refuse to do so unless I make sub-division. His solicitor then writes me "We do not intend placing any sub-division posts, or having any such survey made. The law does not require more than a certificate by a P.L.S." I, *of course*, refuse to certify, and say, that under the circumstances "no Surveyor of any standing would do so." In reply I receive a letter saying "The plans are registered by this time, so ..."

Now, is it according to the ethics of the profession for a surveyor to certify to plans of a survey of a block of land nearly a thousand miles away, *which he has never seen*, and plans of subdivision of which have been got up in an architect's office? Pray have this question ventilated.

The central point at issue, as stated by Villiers Sankey, the chairman of both the committee on land surveying and the subcommittee set up to examine the whole question of registered plans, was "Who was responsible for the correctness of a registered plan, the surveyor or the Registrar?" Sankey pointed out that under the Registry Act the surveyor was, of course, responsible. And in the same vein, Scott, the Master of Titles, had written:

I trust the Association will take such steps as are necessary to see all surveyors are informed that it is alike contrary to professional duty and the law for any surveyor to certify, under the Registry Act or the Land Titles' Act, to the correctness of any plan where he has not actually surveyed the land on the ground. I cannot understand how any surveyor can have formed a different idea of his duty, as any contrary practice would make the certificates of surveyors attached to plans simply worthless.

Scott then touched on the question of how much work a surveyor should do on the ground before certifying a plan. He suggested that a limit be placed on the size of parcels beyond which no "paper divisions" should be made. He noted that where there were a number of lots of the same width, surveyors were in the habit of noting that width "at each end" with the intervening lots left unmarked. He reminded the association, in the person of Sankey, that the law required that the width of each lot be shown.

These discussions resulted in a series of guidelines: yes, an outline survey was necessary in all cases; with regard to subdivision surveys "paper subdivision" was permissible on flat land not exceeding 10 acres, no side of which should exceed 20 chains; where boundaries were irregular, sufficient subdivision surveys were advisable to determine "all broken distances and irreg-

ular courses"; governing lines must be clearly shown as such on plans and whether bearings were astronomic or magnetic should also be made clear; plans must be "properly drafted" and not lithographed; any monuments planted should be shown on the plan; and, finally, it should be made clear whether subdivision had gone forward or whether it was merely proposed. A copy of the guidelines was forwarded to Cozens for his information and there, for the time being at least, the whole matter of registered plans was left.

The committee on legislation had little to report in 1888. In view of the amendments recently made to the Surveying Act and the Ditches and Watercourses Act (partly at the instigation of the association) they deemed it unwise to urge any further changes at that time.

The engineering committee, which under Galbraith had been moribund from the outset, had nothing to report, but the drainage committee had had a busy if frustrating year. On the subject of appeals from the Municipal Drainage Act and the Ditches and Watercourses Act, it was felt that these should be heard by a panel of three competent persons, one of whom should be a provincial land surveyor, instead of by a judge of the county court. This and other ideas had, in fact, already been submitted to the legislature the previous year, but, in the words of Hume Proudfoot of Clinton, "they had not been carried through the House as there were too many lawyers there."

The final session on the afternoon of 1 March saw Alexander Niven elected as president for the coming year, this by acclamation. And, having clearly impressed everyone by his performance as chairman of the committee on land surveying, Villiers Sankey was elected vice-president, again by acclamation, his place on the committee being taken by Elihu Stewart.

Niven moved that Willis Chipman be re-elected as secretary-treasurer: "It does not require any words of mine to inform this Association of Mr. Chipman's worth. I quite agree with all that has been said about him. I don't know any one who could take his place. I would not undertake it for quite a consideration. I think we ought to elect him without opposition." And this they did.

The fourth annual meeting in 1889 was, to quote Chipman's preface to the proceedings of that year, "the most successful yet held, the registered attendance was greater than at any preceding meeting, and great interest was taken in the subjects discussed, while the discussions were more to the point than at any former meeting. Much of the success of this meeting is to be attributed to the exertions of the entertainment committee."

The entertainment committee had got into its stride at the 1888 meeting the year before, but catering arrangements for the annual dinner held that year had failed "to give entire satisfaction." In 1889, however, everything went swimmingly, to use a suitably liquid metaphor. The association had been given an official welcome by the city of Toronto and so members assembled at City Hall to hear a "neat little speech" by Alderman Frankland. They then clambered aboard ten sleighs provided by the city and were taken on a tour that included the new Parliament Buildings, the Rose Hill Reservoir, the Gerrard Street Bridge, and the Toronto waterworks.

Later they dined at the Reform Club – a classy establishment. After "justice had been done to the good things provided" came a series of toasts, beginning of course with "The Queen," followed by the singing of "God Save the Queen." After this they repaired to the anteroom of the club for some entertainment or, to be more precise, to entertain themselves in the manner of the times. Alexander Niven obliged with two songs: "Annie Laurie" and "Bonnie Dundee"; Otto Klotz sang a German song and gave a piano solo; a Captain Manley contributed two songs:

"Never Take the Horse-shoe from the Door" and "Just Before the Battle, Mother," a typical Victorian tearjerker by the sound of it. Another guest, the eminent architect and engineer Kivas Tully, came out with "The Low-Backed Car." Villiers Sankey sang an Irish song. And then, surprisingly, someone gave a talk on "Amateur Photography." Halfway through the evening they all thumped out "Rule Britannia" and at the end they sang "Auld Lang Syne" and, for good measure, "God Save the Queen" for a second time.

The fourth meeting of 1889 was notable for what must have been one of the earliest attempts to establish a metric system of linear measurement in Canada, or at least an approximation of it. This arose out of paper given by Sankey on "Decimal vs. Duodecimal Measurements," a matter that he said was "rather a hobby" of his. Sankey went no further, however, than suggesting that parts of a foot be expressed in decimal terms rather than in fractions. Later in his talk he said hopefully, "I cannot think that any difficulty will arise when foot-rules, divided as I suggest, are placed in the hands of the workmen." Aylsworth was less sanguine in the discussion that followed, a discussion that was to be echoed some eighty years later when Canada was in the throes of "going metric." "Good mechanics," Aylsworth stated, "have used the rule divided into eighths and you cannot make them use tenths."

It turned out that Gibson was already using tenths and hundredths of a foot in his work and that he also expressed parts of an acre in decimal terms. But he, like Aylsworth, had doubts about the reaction of the general public. After considerable discussion a committee was set up to consider the question further and to prepare a "short statement," which would be sent to other surveyors' associations for their comments and presumably eliciting their support. And there, for the moment, the matter was left.

The meeting in 1889 also saw the first attempt by the association to bring its weight of professional opinion to bear on the survey and settlement strategy of the provincial government. It was moved by Elihu Stewart that a special subcommittee be set up to "urge on the Ontario Government the desirability of carrying out, in connection with the Surveys Branch of the Crown Lands Department, a system of exploratory surveys in the new territory," that is, northern Ontario. With his deep interest in forestry, he touched on its timber resources, commenting, "It would be much to the advantage of the Government to know what was on these lands before they sell the limits." Stewart also suggested that "mining engineers" should accompany survey parties.

Stewart's motion to set up a subcommittee to take the association's suggestion to the Department of Crown Lands was duly adopted and, as reported in the proceedings for 1890, he and his subcommittee met the commissioner of crown lands and urged "on him the desirability of instituting a regular system of exploratory surveys in our new and unexplored territory." According to Stewart the "honorable gentleman … expressed himself as interested in the idea." Nothing immediate resulted from the association's recommendation. But just over ten years later, in 1900, the Department of Crown Lands launched what has been called "the most ambitious survey of the century," this to explore northern Ontario much as the Elihu Stewart had suggested. And as he had recommended, each of the ten survey parties was accompanied by a geologist and a timber expert.

The 1889 meeting also saw lengthy discussions of two proposed amendments to the Surveyors Act.* These arose out of a paper on "Practical Surveying" given by Alexander Niven at the previous year's meeting in which he had suggested two ways that the act might be usefully amended. He introduced one of them by way of an anecdote that illustrated the gener-

---

*The general reader is reminded at this point that from this time on there are surveyors acts as distinct from surveys acts.

As late as the 1889, James Foster, a prominent Toronto instrument maker was still referring to his scientific instruments as "philosophical" instruments. Shown is part of his advertisement in the *AOLS Proceedings, 1889.*

Charles Potter, a Toronto instrument maker, advertises a transit in the *AOLS Proceedings, 1891.*

al public's lack of understanding, then as now, of what is involved in carrying out an accurate survey – with consequent displeasure at the size of the fee asked for.

Shortly after I commenced practising as a surveyor in the town of St. Mary's – now more than a quarter of a century ago – while walking up the street one day with my instrument on my shoulder, I was accosted by a farmer in this way: "Hallo there, Mr. Surveyor! What do you charge for running a line?" I replied, "Six dollars a day." "But," said he, "I don't want you a day; I've got a post at the corner of my lot, and I want you to start there and go ahead; you can do all I want in two hours."

In vain I explained to him that the law compelled me to go to the end of the concession from which the lots [were] numbered, and get my bearing and angle up to this post, or take an observation before I could start to run his line. "Well," said he, "after you get your bearings at your own expense you can come and run the line at mine." Bidding him good-day, I continued my journey.

"It would simplify surveying very much," Niven added, "if all lines were run on the astronomical course of the original survey of the township" on record in the Department of Crown Lands. He agreed that this would "not answer in the older townships where most of the lines have been run," but asked, "could not this be applied to the northern townships of this Province?"

Niven went on to remark that the original field notes of township surveys should be collected from the families of deceased surveyors, and deposited in the Crown Lands Office for the information of surveyors, and should "thereafter ... [be] used in court for what they are worth."

Niven's suggestions were the subject of a circular sent out to the members some time in 1888. It outlined two proposed amendments to the Surveyors Act along the lines that he suggested and which were discussed at the 1889 meeting. The first, which suggested that division or side lines should be run on the astronomical bearings given in the original survey, met with a mixed response. Kirkpatrick disagreed on the grounds of expense. "A fatal objection," he said, "is that when taking an astronomical observation you would not be able to command the elements. You would have sometimes to wait two or three days until the weather gets fair."

In rebuttal Chipman said that surveyors should try "to do our work in the most scientific way possible – not the cheapest way." He added that he hadn't taken a night observation for five or six years and then went on: "I take them in the daytime. A modern surveyor can take observations just as well during the day as at night." The chairman (not named), however, commented that "the majority of us stick to the night yet."

With no clear consensus emerging, the meeting went on to discuss the second proposed amendment. This was to the effect that the field notes of surveys made for "private parties on concession lines, side lines or other lines defining the boundaries of lots in townships, cities, towns or villages ... be registered" to prevent the loss of "much valuable information," all much as Niven had suggested the year before. It was further suggested that surveyors draw up concise field notes of such surveys, with a plan if necessary, and deposit same in the county Registry Office.

The discussion on the second proposal was led by Sankey, who supported Niven's idea. After a long and somewhat confusing discussion it was obviously with some desperation that Sankey got to the root of the matter when he said, "The principal point is:- Is it the opinion of the Association that it is advisable to preserve a legal record of surveys?" And there the matter seems to have been left, though both of Niven's ideas would eventually bear fruit.

In 1889 Willis Chipman was again re-elected secretary-treasurer. Said Niven who moved his re-election, "Men may come and go, but Mr. Chipman goes on for ever." However, Chipman, in intimating that this would be his last year as secretary, said that "the work of the Secretary is not quite so easy as you might imagine. It is not difficult, but it takes considerable time ... I am afraid that after this year some other aspiring young member will have to accept the office." And so

ended the meeting that Chipman described as "the most successful yet held."

The lack of growth in membership had at first caused some concern. A membership drive following the inaugural meeting of 1886 had brought the number of members up to seventy as of 1 January 1887. By 1888 the number of active members had risen to 118. And it stayed at about that level until 1891. Attendance at the meetings remained relatively constant during the first few years at slightly less than half of the active membership: 49 in 1887, 48 in 1888, 48 in 1889, 39 in 1890, and 43 in 1891. The reduced attendance in 1890 was due "chiefly to the epidemic that prevailed at the time of the meeting."

In an effort to bring more surveyors into the fold a circular was sent out in 1889 to provincial land surveyors who were in active practice but not yet members of the association. Chipman, then in his last year as secretary-treasurer, reported at the 1890 meeting that fifty-seven surveyors had been circularized. This number, added to the number of paid-up members, suggests that less than 180 surveyors were active in the province at that time. This, it may be noted, was much less than previously speculated.

By the late 1880s, however, any fears that the association might founder through a lack of new members had been firmly laid to rest. The membership if not growing was at least broadly based from the professional standpoint. The proceedings for 1889 list 122 active members. Of these, twelve had university degrees in civil engineering, one (William Davis) had attended the Royal Military College at Kingston, and six had attended Toronto's School of Practical Science. A total, then, of eighteen members had what we would now call post-secondary education.

Nearly twenty members of the association at that time were also members of the Canadian Society of Civil Engineers, the American Society of Civil

Engineers, or the Institute of Civil Engineering. In fact fifty men, or nearly half the membership in 1889, were engineers of one sort or another. At least they so described themselves in the membership roll under "Occupation." In all there were twenty-two township engineers, some of whom were also looking after towns or villages and in one case a city as well. Difficult to categorize and so left out of the reckoning is William Aylsworth of Deseronto, who described himself as "Engineer for Tyendinaga, Engineer for Bay of Quinte Railway, etc." Eleven others were "engineers" who worked for various railways. Finally, there was John Galbraith, professor of civil engineering in Toronto's School of Practical Science.

Among the seventy or so who weren't "engineers" were Thomas Fawcett, D.T.S., and William Ogilvie, D.T.S., employed respectively on "Dominion Government Surveys" and the "Exploration Survey, Alaskan Boundary," while Otto Klotz, D.T.S., held the position of astronomer for the Department of the Interior. Also with the Department of the Interior was Arthur Wheeler. Frank Blake was assistant astronomer at the Toronto observatory. And, lastly, there was F. Percy Burt, at one point Willis Chipman's assistant in Brockville. Burt was living in New York, where he worked as chief draughtsman for *Engineering News* and *American Railway Journal*.

Discussing the questions in the "Question Drawer" soon became a popular feature of the annual meetings, the idea apparently originating in the proceedings of the second meeting in 1887, where it was suggested that if any member had "any matter referring to land surveying, drainage, engineering, instruments, legislation, or publication to bring before the Association" they should bring it to the attention of the secretary or to the chairman of the appropriate committee.

The questions themselves – and the answers to them – tell us something about the "state of the art" in the late 1880s. Later, some of the cadastral conundrums presented to the land-surveying committee were to become very abstruse, but the very first question in the Question Drawer was straightforward enough. It concerned the simple matter of determining the precise location of the boundary between two lots separated by a post and board fence. After a lengthy discussion of the alternatives, the consensus was that the "line between posts and the boards [was] the true division line."

The first question put to the committee on legislation concerned certification of compiled plans. As one member put it, "Looking at the Act as to certificates of surveyors as amended at the last session of the Legislature I cannot see how a surveyor can certify to a plan ... which is nothing more than a compilation of old plans, and the surveyor may never have stretched a chain across the land." Elihu Stewart also had doubts about certifying a compiled plan in the absence of a survey, as had Chipman, who went on to observe that the "whole Act respecting the compiling of plans is very defective," and suggested that the committee on legislation look into the matter with a view to suggesting pertinent amendments. The issue of compiled plans also entered into a second question. Were "old errors ... to be perpetuated or corrected?" Chipman again weighed in, citing a case in which he found one too many lots had been registered and would not fit into the plan. What should he have done? He received no clear answer.

Someone asked the committee on instruments about the best way of illuminating the telescope crosshairs at night and what was "the best lamp for night observation generally?" Peter Burnet advised taking the object glass off the telescope and putting a piece of white paper around the inside of the tube. "This," he said, "will act as a capital reflector." As for lamps, Sankey made do with a brick soaked in coal oil, which when lighted should be held "three or four feet from the instrument."

And what about a theodolite seizing up in very cold weather? George Abrey advised using little or no oil. At -50°F he had difficulty if oil had been used, though when he rubbed the spindle with the "oil of a badger" his instrument never bothered him again and he supposed that "the oil of any other animal would be as good." He also advised trying "black lead," that is, graphite.

In late November 1889, Willis Chipman received a letter from his opposite number in the Association of Dominion Land Surveyors regarding possible affiliation of the four associations of land surveyors in the Dominion. The idea was the brainchild of Stoughton Dennis in his capacity as president of the Dominion association. He suggested that the "general welfare" of all of them would be improved by some form of affiliation, pointing out that "any action taken by all the associations ... would carry very much more weight [with the federal government] than the individual actions or representations of associations now do." Finally, he also suggested that his proposal, if carried out, would result in much attention by the press and public alike.

A three-man subcommittee headed by Niven was set up to consider Dennis's proposal. As they reported at the 1890 meeting, while they approved of the idea in principle, they felt that Dennis's scheme as outlined – which involved a single annual joint meeting – was impractical. Following this up, Chipman invited members of the Dominion Land Surveyors' Association to the next annual meeting when the matter could be discussed further. This was done, and on the second day of the 1891 meeting it was addressed by Dennis himself, who came to Toronto at the head of a small deputation.

Dennis reminded his audience that with the "lately formed" association in British Columbia there were now five associations in Canada. As an example of how the Dominion association had helped the provincial associations he mentioned that the previous winter a federal bill had been brought in to create the Geological Survey Department. There was a clause in the bill that would have allowed surveyors working for the Geological Survey to go into any province and make surveys. "We fought that [clause]," said Dennis, "and had the bill amended."

It was decided in the ensuing discussion that, essentially, each association should go its own way but that there would be an annual convention to be held in Toronto and Ottawa alternately, with the first in the latter city in 1892, that is, in the following year. This in fact occurred, with a report on the convention appearing in the association's proceedings for that same year. It took place on 16 February 1892 in the lecture room of the Literary and Scientific Society on Sparks Street in Ottawa. There were twenty-three land surveyors present. Of these, only three, Lewis, Klotz, and Olgivie, represented the provincial association. This was hardly surprising. At the regular annual meeting of the association, scheduled for the following week, the all-important matter of incorporation was due to come up for discussion.

At the 1889 meeting, Niven, quite casually, had introduced the matter of incorporation in his presidential address. It was a question, he said, "that should engage the attention of our Association as a number of our members feel that incorporation would be for the benefit of the profession." At the 1890 meeting, it came out that there was growing dissatisfaction at the number of unqualified persons "running lines," and it was suggested that the executive committee should do something about it. Only incorporation could solve this problem. The meeting then went on to discuss other matters until at Chipman's suggestion the meeting adjourned for ten minutes so that he could take a group photograph. Whether or not there was a hurried discussion on the subject of incorporation we don't know, but, at any rate, following the intermission it was moved by Chipman that "in the opinion of this Association an Act of Incorporation similar to the acts incorporating the other professions in this Province is desirable."

Though the motion was carried, nothing came of it, perhaps because the executive was preoccupied with the idea of affiliating itself with the Dominion association, as touched on above. However, they did invite Joseph Casgrain to come to Toronto and address the association at the 1891 annual meeting on the pros and cons of incorporation, which invitation he accepted.

Villiers Sankey had been acclaimed president, a position he was to hold during the two years that the association was coming to grips with the matter of incorporation. So it was he in his presidential address who introduced the subject of incorporation at the 1891 meeting and who welcomed Casgrain.

The most important subject ... which is to come before us, is that of incorporation. It is one, the consideration of which is the natural result of association. In other Provinces, it has already been inaugurated; in some of these incorporation came first, association naturally followed and I cannot but think that whichever comes first the other is sure to follow, be it sooner or later. A paper on this subject will be presented by our eloquent *confrère*, Mr. J.P.B. Casgrain, who, being a member of the Incorporated Society of Quebec and of the Association of Ontario, will be able to discuss in a practical and clear manner before us.

Casgrain, then in his mid-thirties, was a graduate engineer who had qualified as a provincial land surveyor in Quebec in 1877 and had become a Dominion Land Surveyor in 1881 when he worked in Saskatchewan. In 1887 he had qualified in Ontario and had joined the association on its formation that same year. The scion of a distinguished seigneurial family, his relatives had been active in politics for generations both in Ontario

and Quebec – later he himself would be made a senator. Tearing himself away from a federal election, he came down to Toronto from his home in Morrisburg to talk to the association on a subject about which, in view of the fact that the Quebec association had been incorporated from its start, he was thought to be particularly knowledgeable.

Casgrain began his talk by reminding the association about what incorporation had done for lawyers and doctors, whose advancement had been speeded by the very fact that their organizations were incorporated. That there had also been advances in surveying, he said, no one will deny. "But we must not suppose that there is now no room for advancement and improvement in our profession."

Casgrain then got down to discussing the added advantages that stemmed from incorporation. He listed the various and impressive powers of the Quebec corporation, pointing out that similar powers could accrue to the association if it were similarly incorporated. He dwelt on "the maintenance of discipline" and described how the board of management of the Quebec association dealt with this. He described the way that this board went about examining candidates, how the examiners were paid, and discussed fees and costs generally.

In the discussion that followed, Peter Gibson voiced concern at the plight of those surveyors who did not wish to join an association, a concern he was to express throughout the discussions on incorporation. Was the standing of such men affected by incorporation? Gibson could hardly have found Casgrain's answer encouraging. "Certainly, for they cannot practice ... the Commissioner of Crown Lands gives no work to a surveyor who has not paid his dues." Furthermore, only those who were members in good standing with the Quebec association (and whose names appear on an roll published annually) were legally entitled to practise in the province. And should a surveyor not in good standing appear in court, the judge would refuse to hear the case.

Looking for a buyer, Chipman advertised his Brockville practice in the *AOLS Proceedings, 1891.* It was taken over by Bryce J. Saunders and after passing through several hands was bought by Raymond F. Mucklestone, who sold it to Martin H. Kaldeway in 1977.

That an incorporated association would be the regulatory body of the profession was a concept that some members of the Ontario association apparently found difficult to grasp. Thus James Dickson of Fenelon Falls commented that it was "very unfair if a man has a license from the Government to practice and that Act says ... unless you pay $4 a year [to join the association] you cannot practice as a land surveyor." Seemingly irritated by all this, Chipman replied, "I can't agree with Mr. Dickson in thinking it is a hardship for a member of the profession to have to pay $4 a year into the Association when by so doing he is putting $10 or $20 into the other pocket."

Kirkpatrick thought that incorporating "would be the very best thing that surveyors could do." He pointed out that government was contributing $400 a year towards the expenses of the Board of Examiners, an amount that he thought government would be happy to save.

Gibson, however, was not reassured. "I look upon it as something of an experiment," he said. "There are no surveyors in the world who have the standing of the provincial land surveyors of Ontario ... what would our standing be after having lost our position as Government surveyors? ... If we do get incorporation let us not lose our status as Government surveyors." In reply, Kirkpatrick explained: "At present we are licensed by a Board of Examiners appointed by the Government. If the Association is incorporated they will have the power to appoint their own Board of Examiners and we would be ... simply changing from one board to another." But Kirkpatrick agreed with Gibson that the association should "make haste slowly."

All this was on the morning of the second day of the meeting. In the afternoon, presumably after some intense discussion over lunch, it was moved by William Aylsworth without further ado "That it is desirable to have the provincial land surveyors of the Province of Ontario incorporated as a body corporate and politic, and this Association take steps to have an Act therefore prepared and passed with as little delay as possible." The motion was carried.

Aylsworth's motion was followed by a second to form a committee to take the matter further. Shortly after the meeting, a deputation from this committee went to see the commissioner of crown lands as proposed and explained what the association was intending to do. He suggested that the association postpone action on the matter until the parliamentary session of 1892. In the interim, the committee had met several times and they retained a W.J. McWilliams, barrister-at-law, to draw up a draft bill of incorporation, which was duly submitted to the commissioner of crown lands for his comments. He "kindly consented to take charge of the Bill and bring it in as a public measure." A copy of the bill was also sent to every land surveyor in the province.

Reporting on all this to the 1892 annual meeting, Niven, chairman of the committee, paid tribute to his hard-working committee, singling out Otto Klotz, who "devoted a whole day to preparing some of the clauses in the Bill [and] a good many of his suggestions were adopted." Niven also praised Villiers Sankey who, with Mr. McWilliams, "got the Bill into its final shape."

Leading the discussion on the draft bill, Niven pointed out that it did "not profess to do away with the existing Land Surveyors Act" but merely to amend it where necessary and that the bill dealt with the "regulation and government of the Association," which would be accomplished by "a governing body elected by all the members in Ontario, by officers and a council elected by them." He pointed out that following incorporation, a surveyor with a complaint against an unlicensed surveyor would no longer be on his own, but that he could pass the matter on to the association to be dealt with by "some committee or person whose business it will be to look after this."

Interestingly enough, much of the discussion of the draft bill centred on how land surveyors in Ontario would henceforth style themselves. Matthew Butler of Deseronto, a senior railway engineer, asked, "Is it possible that the well known title of provincial land surveyor would be wiped out by this Bill; would it become Ontario land surveyor?" Aylsworth thought this would be the case. Sankey agreed but suggested that it would be premature to discuss the matter. "There is no reason in the world why we should not keep the old letters 'P.L.S.'"

Niven said that the intention of the committee was to do away with the word "provincial." To his mind, "Ontario Land Surveyor" was better than "provincial land surveyor." Sankey, backing Niven up, pointed out that "with all due respect to the Dominion Land Surveyors present, that the term 'Dominion Land Surveyor' is very misleading to the public. A great many people," he added, "believe that any one who signs 'D.L.S.' can survey anywhere throughout the length and breadth of the Dominion, whereas this

is not the case." Niven tried to end the discussion. "Let it go, I say."

But Gibson wouldn't let it go. He thought that the letters "P.L.S." should be retained. "There may be reasons for the change that I do not understand ... but I am of a conservative turn of mind and I do not like changes." Typically standing up for the minority, he then went on to speak of the bill's effect on older surveyors who would have none of the association,

Villiers Sankey in 1879. As president of the association in 1891 and 1892, he laid the groundwork for the incorporation of the association in 1892. He was drowned in 1905 when on survey in the Rainy River District.
Courtesy: AOLS Archives

incorporated or otherwise. "It seems a little hard," he said, "this trying to force old gentlemen out that won't join us."

Niven spoke again in favour of the proposed bill. As for the title that Ontario Land Surveyors should adopt, it was felt by the committee that "Ontario Land Surveyor" would be preferable to "provincial land surveyor," while someone tried to reassure Gibson by reminding him that there had been a change before. "The old plans are all signed D.P.S." Shortly afterward, a committee was appointed to place the draft bill before the attorney general and the commissioner of crown lands.

The election of officers at the 1892 meeting saw Villiers Sankey retire after two years as president and Elihu Stewart elected in his place. Before the meeting closed, Gibson proposed a vote of thanks to Sankey.

On 14 April 1892 An Act to Incorporate the Association of Ontario Land Surveyors and to Amend the Act Respecting Land Surveyors and the Survey of Land (55 Vict., c. 34) was passed by the legislature and so the Association of Ontario Land Surveyors came into being. As one traces the events that led up to incorporation, it becomes steadily clearer that Sankey played the pivotal role in those events. If Willis Chipman was the founder of the association, then Villiers Sankey was surely the "father of incorporation."

Toronto's School of Practical Science in Toronto regularly advertised in the association's proceedings. In 1892 the secretary of the school was Louis Stewart, both an Ontario Land Surveyor and Dominion Topographical Surveyor.

CHAPTER SIXTEEN

The Association: 1892–1900

Under the terms of the act that brought the Association of Ontario Land Surveyors (AOLS) into existence, the association was to consist of all land surveyors duly authorized to act as such in Ontario, provided they registered with the registrar of the association within six months of the election of that official and had paid the requisite fees. The association so formed was empowered by the act to pass bylaws regarding the "government, discipline and honour of its members," the "management of its property" (which could include $5,000 worth of real estate),* the "examination and admission of candidates for the study or practice of the profession," and "for all such other purposes as may be necessary for the working of the corporation,"[1] such bylaws to be prepared by a Council of Management and ratified at the annual general meeting or at a special meeting called for the purpose.

The council was to consist of the commissioner of crown lands, the president and vice-president of the association, along with six other elected members of the association. The council would be chaired by one of its members, who would hold office for a year. The elective members of the council would serve for one, two, or three years depending on the number of votes received – these to provide an overlap between successive years. The council was empowered to appoint "such other officers as may be necessary for the working of this Act, who shall hold office during the pleasure of the council." One of the duties of the council under the act was to consider applications to join the association of those qualified land surveyors who had omitted to register through "absence, illness or inadvertence" within the statutory six months – which they could do on payment of any fees owing. Another important duty of council was to take disciplinary action against any land surveyor "whom they find guilty of gross negligence or corruption in the execution of the duties of his office."

In order to set the association on its feet, the act specified that the first election would be by a mail-in ballot to take place on 1 July 1892. This for the positions of president, vice-president, secretary-treasurer, two auditors, and the six elective members of the council, with the commissioner of crown lands acting as returning officer. The ballot was to go, interestingly enough, not just to members of the association but to all qualified land surveyors in the province, using the names and addresses as held by the Department of Crown Lands.

Thereafter, the election of the association's officers would take place at an annual general meeting to be held in Toronto on the fourth Tuesday in February of each year. The act did not specify any form of nominating procedure for the initial mail-in ballot, and apparently there wasn't one. Judging from the specimen ballot appended to the act anyone could vote for whomever they pleased. In the event – and quite understandably considering the preponderance of provincial surveyors who were already members of the existing association – the president, vice-president, and secretary-treasurer elected in the mail-in ballot were the same as those elected at the annual meeting that had taken place only a few months earlier, namely Elihu Stewart, Matthew Butler, and Arthur van Nostrand respectively.

The act specified the composition of the Board of Examiners, which was to be responsible "for the admission to study, and also for such other examinations as council may hereafter prescribe for candidates for admission to practice as land surveyors." The board was to consist of the chairman of the council, four members of the association to be appointed by the council, and two appointed by the lieutenant-governor in council. The act went on to specify the duration of these appointments to ensure continuity, as in the case of the council.

---

*In the mid-1880s, $1,500 would buy you an eight-room brick house in Toronto, complete with bath and with gas laid on.

The chairman of the council was also to act as chairman of the Board of Examiners, with three members of the board to form a quorum. Members of the board were to take an oath of performance before a judge of the county court or a justice of the peace. A schedule of fees was laid down: for registration as a qualified land surveyor under the act, $1; for an application for examination, $1; for apprentices sending in their articles to the secretary, $10; and for successful applicants receiving certificates to practise, $30. All fees were to go to the association, which in turn would pay members of the Board of Examiners, as well as its secretary. Annual membership dues to the association were set at $4.

What might be termed the key subsection of the act read in part as follows:

> From and after the first day of January, 1891, no person, unless registered ... shall be entitled to take or use the name of Ontario Land Surveyor, either alone or in combination with any word or words, or any name, title or description implying that he is registered. Any person who, after the above date, not being registered under this Act, takes or uses such name, title or description as aforesaid, shall be liable on summary conviction to a fine not exceeding $20 for the first offence, and not exceeding $50 for each subsequent offence.

The first to apply for registration under the act, or at any rate, the surveyor who gained the honour of being given the registration number 1, was Henry Strange, who was commissioned a provincial land surveyor in 1838 and who carried out surveys on various railways in southwestern Ontario and also laid out part of his hometown of Guelph. Charles Unwin's number was 17, Peter Gibson's 39, Alexander Niven's 48, George Kirkpatrick's 72, and Otto Klotz's 129.

Interestingly enough, Villiers Sankey himself was tardy in registering, and was given the number 154, while Willis Chipman was even tardier. His registration number was 181.

The Council of Management met for the first time in October 1892. Representing the government, as required in the act, was the commissioner of crown lands, the Honourable H.P. Hardy, who had announced previously that the two members appointed by the lieutenant-governor were Kirkpatrick and Butler. Association appointees were Peter Gibson, Alexander Niven, Richard Coad, Maurice Gaviller, John McAree, and Villiers Sankey, with Professor Coleman to stand by as examiner in geology when required. At the first meeting, Sankey was appointed chairman of the council, which proceeded to make up the new Board of Examiners under the terms of the new act.

Council then went on to frame the association's bylaws. One of them laid down the standing committees. These were to be on land surveying, drainage, engineering, entertainment, and publications. In the main, the bylaws dealt with the place and time of annual meetings as already laid down in the act, the number of times council should meet during the year (three), the duties of the various officers of the association, and the rules by which meetings should be conducted, at which at least fifteen members would form a quorum for the conduct of business. For the council, the quorum was placed at three.

Included in the bylaws were the subjects in which prospective apprentices and land surveyors would be examined and the pass marks required. These were mostly as listed in the act of 1887, the act that had been revised with input from the association. However, the subjects were not laid down in the act of 1892 that brought about incorporation. To have done so would have infringed on the independence of the new association. As Elihu Stewart would remind the members in his presidential address to the newly incor-

Henry Strange in 1838. A veteran land surveyor, he was allotted registration number "1" in the newly incorporated association. Courtesy: AOLS Archives

porated association, it was up to the association to maintain its own standards.

The first meeting after incorporation took place in the lecture room of the Royal Canadian Institute, Toronto, and ran three days from Tuesday, 28 February, to Thursday, 2 March 1893. On the morning of the first day, there were meetings of the various standing committees and the newly formed Council of Management. In the afternoon, van Nostrand, the secretary-treasurer, gave his report on the state of the membership following the passage of the new act. A report, it may be added, that may well have been awaited with some anxiety. However, following the mailing during 1892 of the ballot called for by the act to 360 land surveyors whose addresses were known, followed by a circular to 200 who had not responded, membership had jumped from 107 fully paid-up members as of February 1892 (plus 9 members in arrears) to 173.

Twenty others had paid their dollar to register under the act but had made it known that they were no longer practising. Twenty-nine others had registered but had forgotten (presumably) to say whether they were still in practice or not. These, plus three members partly in arrears, gave a total membership of the Association of Ontario Land Surveyors, as it now was, of 225. According to the records in the Department of Crown Lands, this apparently left 136 surveyors unaccounted for, but it was concluded that of these "a large number have left the Province, or are engaged in other occupations" and it was left at that.

Van Nostrand was followed by Elihu Stewart, who gave the president's address. He dwelt briefly on the history of the association up to that point. Noting that incorporation was a very important step, he stressed that the association should proceed "with the utmost caution." He warned against complacency, pointing out that "we have only obtained a vantage ground which will enable us to do more than was possible heretofore for our advancement ... As you are aware, we have now practical control of the examination of candidates desiring to enter the profession, and it will be our own fault if the standard of admission is not kept sufficiently high to enable us to take rank with the other learned professions of the land."

The meeting of 1893 was memorable not just because it was the inaugural meeting of the newly incorporated association but for a remarkable paper given by Willis Chipman. He had got round to examining the "Map of the Province of Ontario, shewing counties, townships, railways and post offices," which the Department of Crown Lands had issued in 1889, and was appalled to find many errors and omissions in it. What resulted from that examination was a detailed critique of the map, which led up to what was in fact the title of his paper, namely "A Plea for a Topographical Survey."

As we have seen, the need for a systematic geodetic and topographic survey of the province had always been considered secondary to the cadastral surveys needed to meet immediate settlement requirements. That something more than cadastral surveys was required must have occurred to many surveyors as they laboured to lay out townships in the rugged terrain of northern Ontario. And, as they struggled to make sense of the geography of this sometimes precipitous and lake-strewn country with its countless rivers and streams, it must have been increasingly exasperating that the government was making no attempt to map the country's topography systematically.

At the same time, the more forward-looking surveyors in Ontario must have undoubtedly followed developments south of the border. In the mid-1850s the U.S. Coast Survey had begun a precise levelling project in connection with the measuring of tide levels in the Hudson River. The Coast Survey went on to plan a triangulation arc to cross the continent at approximately the thirty-ninth parallel, roughly from Washington in the East to San Francisco in the West. The U.S. Coast Survey thus became the Coast and Geodetic Survey. In a parallel development, the United States Geological Survey (USGS) had been founded in 1875, and was subsequently charged with the topographic mapping of the United States. And in 1884 – just two years before the association held its inaugural meeting – the state of Massachusetts, in co-operation with the USGS, had undertaken its own topographical survey.

Thus while Chipman's paper on the need for a topographic survey arose out of his displeasure at the serious shortcomings in the new government map, he undoubtedly used those shortcomings as an excuse for expressing what must have been on many surveyors' minds. Enlarging on the shortcomings of the Department of Crown Lands' map produced just four years before, he noted the absence on the map of a number of lakes and rivers. The interior of Frontenac County, he observed, was so poorly mapped that it might well be labelled *terra incognita*. He mentioned the county maps produced by private enterprise a quarter of a century earlier, which, among other things, showed streams and the position and size of lakes. "Why," he asked, "did not the Crown Lands Department avail itself of these old and comparatively reliable plans in compiling its new plan of the Province?"

Chipman clinched his argument by showing his audience two sketches. One showed the township of Biggar, which he had himself surveyed, as it appeared on the 1889 map, the second showing the lakes and watercourses as he had shown them in his report to the Department of Crown Lands. What is now known as Lake Biggar, which straggles across the northern boundary of the township, was shown on the new map as draining west into Lake Nipissing and thus into Lake Huron, whereas Chipman had shown it quite correctly as draining north to the Mattawa and thence to the Ottawa. Another lake, reported by Chipman as being in the centre of Biggar Township, had completely disappeared. He noted similar errors in two other northern townships he had himself surveyed. He went on to list the many important rivers missing from the Department of Crown Lands' map.

"I think I have adduced sufficient evidence," he continued, "to convince any member of this Association that the best map we have of our Province, and issued by the Department, is grossly incorrect, and is misleading to the settler, the prospector, and the investor." He felt that "the public should know that the surveyors of this Province are not responsible for the grosser errors the map contains."

But the association was also to blame, Chipman asserted, because it had failed to back up the Dominion association in its efforts to persuade the federal government to undertake a triangulation of Canada. "We must have a topographical survey of our Province – the sooner the better," Chipman concluded, "and I believe that this incorporated Association is the proper body to take the initiatory steps." He ended with the suggestion that the committee on engineering be abolished and one on topographical surveying be appointed in its place.

In moving, in his impulsive way, that the engineering committee be replaced by one on topographical surveying, Chipman was evidently attempting to kill two birds with one stone. At earlier meetings, he had made little attempt to hide his irritation at the chronic sluggishness of the engineering committee. In the end, the committee on engineering was given a reprieve and a new committee was struck to look into topographical surveying. The committee's first chairman, not altogether unexpectedly, was Willis Chipman. In the event, as we shall see, it was to be another ten years before a start would be made on a systematic topographic survey in the province.

With the bylaw concerning standing subcommittees duly amended to include one on topographical surveying, the other bylaws were discussed and duly passed. In the course of that discussion, someone asked, in effect: What power had the association under the act to prosecute unlicensed practitioners? Answer: None. All that the association could do was collect the relevant evidence and submit it to the proper authorities for action. No sooner had this question been asked and answered, than the whole matter of unlicensed surveyors came up again in connection with a letter from Frederick Wilkins of Peterborough complaining about the activities of such a surveyor. Following this, James Tyrrell from Hamilton (who would be the first

First Surveyors in the Canadian Arctic

The exploration and mapping of the high Arctic had been left largely in British and American hands. The Canadian government took no active measures to exert Canadian sovereignty in the Far North until 1884 when the first of three expeditions were sent into Hudson Bay in the ship *Neptune* under the command of Lieutenant Andrew Gordon, R.N., who carried out surveying and hydrographic work on behalf of the Canadian government. W.A. Ashe, D.L.S., went along as observer, surveying Ashe Inlet on Big Island off Baffin Island's south coast.

The next year, Gordon commanded a second expedition. This was in the *Alert*, a ship built specifically for a British polar expedition in 1875–76. This time James Tyrrell, D.L.S., O.L.S., went along as hydrographer. He was also on board the *Alert* when she made her third voyage to the Arctic in 1886.

Ontario Land Surveyor in the Arctic) commented that in his district "there are, at least, four such men, who are continually practising, doing anything they can get hold of in the way of surveying." Peter Gibson recommended that cases should be reported to the secretary and that the offender be notified that he was acting illegally. "Probably the best way to get at it is just to frighten them with the majesty of the law," he added, and went on to suggest a list be made up of offenders.

Another subject that surfaced was that of surveyors' fees, with James Dickson from Fenelon Falls – who would later play a leading role in the founding of Algonquin Park – expressing concern that some surveyors worked for less than others and that this wasn't fair. He himself charged six dollars a day as was usual in his district, but he knew that others charged only five.* Was there any way of disciplining those who *did* charge less? Stewart replied that there had been a clause in the draft bill that would have regulated fees chargeable by licensed land surveyors, but that the association had been advised that the inclusion of such a clause in the act might result in the whole act being thrown out

---

*At the rate of $6 per day, a hard-working surveyor – assuming a six-day week and a fifty-week year – could expect to make $1,800 a year. No income tax in those days. For comparison, a first-class mechanic or artisan at this time could expect to earn only $6 or $7 a week, and this by working ten hours a day and six days a week.

by the legislature and so the clause was deleted. The discussion ended with Chipman moving that the matter be referred to the council for consideration.

Touching on a more technical matter, Dickson went on to suggest that it "would be a good thing" if one-chain-long steel tapes were made with links marked on one side and feet on the other; such could be used by individual surveyors for testing their chains. George Abrey pointed out that these were now being issued by the Dominion Lands Office and were already being used out west. In fact, though Abrey did not mention it, the Dominion Lands Office had started replacing chains by steel tapes in 1883. Abrey did add, however, that they cost $8 each, and he presumed any surveyor could buy one. Chipman suggested it would be "a good move" for the Board of Examiners to furnish standard steel tapes. "We have outgrown altogether these pine window sticks that they have sent around for us, furnished with little brass squares on them. I never heard yet of a surveyor comparing his tape with them."

Among the papers presented at the meeting was one on "Timber Surveys and Explorations" by James Whitson of the Crown Lands Department, who set out to "say something that may be of benefit to the younger members ... who have not yet had any experience of this kind of work." Accordingly, much of his paper dwelt on the outfit required for working in the bush, including food supplies, with special emphasis on winter work. He stressed that the whole party should be able to snowshoe, pull a toboggan, and drive a dog-team. As for the dogs,

> three good dogs will draw from 300 to 450 pounds fifteen to thirty-five miles per day, depending on the condition of the trail. They are fed once a day, after their day's work is done, and will consume on an average per day a little over one pound of cornmeal and a third of a pound of tallow per dog; if fed on fish three pounds per day, but will not work so well on the latter as on the former. The dogs should be all chained up at night, as no matter how well they are fed they like a dessert of snowshoes, or [to] poke their nose into the cook's affairs.[2]

Whitson recommended three tents, two of them 8 by 10 feet (2.4 x 3 m), the other 8 by 12, and with 2-foot walls, these to be warmed by stoves of "light Russian iron." There should be two heavy double blankets per man "and if possible each couple of men should secure a rabbit skin blanket, as there is more comfort in one of them than in two woollen ones of double the weight, and without [which] your men are made comfortable you will have no end of trouble through sickness, or men deserting you."

Whitson's paper led members to express their views on how to work and survive in the bush in winter. James Dickson said he had got by quite happily without a heating stove of any kind. He and his men just used blankets, though he agreed that with a stove one would need fewer blankets. Henry Sewell of Port Arthur just used shed tents, with the tents "in pairs, facing the other, with your log fire in the centre ... and I don't think there is anything so comfortable as that."

Kirkpatrick spoke of a surveyor "who is one of those who do not care much for comfort" and who had spent a whole winter in Manitoba "and never had a fire at all. He had a bag, and he shut himself up in it, and lay down in the snow, and he came out of it perfectly well." However, that was not for everybody. Surveyors, he added, "have to take care of their constitutions, because if they don't they will be miserable rheumatic individuals when they are old ... The more comfortable you can make yourself on a winter survey, the better work you will do." He believed in stoves, adding that he had worked north of Superior in 35-degrees-below weather and "we were always just as comfortable as anything, and we never had those beautiful inventions of now-a-days, rabbit-skin blankets."

And so the first meeting of the now incorporated association ended. It was surprisingly low key. No extravagant hopes were held out for the future, and incorporation seemed more of a beginning than an end. There was a quiet, businesslike air to the meeting, with an obvious determination to build upon what had already been accomplished. Not all was business, however. We learn from the proceedings that the annual dinner was held at the Allington Hotel and that it was attended by thirty-one members and five guests. An unspecified but clearly considerable number of toasts were made, responded to, and drunk to, while "Songs were sung at intervals by Messrs. Niven, Sewell, Bowman and Foster."

～～～

Attendance at annual meetings had remained remarkably constant in the 1890s from a high of fifty-three in 1894 to forty in 1897. However, for reasons not clear, only sixteen turned up for the 1898 meeting, so it had to be rescheduled for March, when the attendance was a satisfactory forty-six. The meetings continued to take

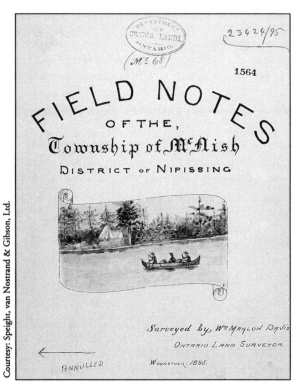

Courtesy: Speight, van Nostrand & Gibson, Ltd.

The drawings and sketches of early surveyors were often of high artistic merit. Above is the cover of one of William M. Davis's field notebooks. The picture on the original is in watercolor. Surveyed by Davis in 1896, McNish Township was one of many townships later legally annulled - see "Annulled" scrawled bottom left.

place at the Royal Canadian Institute until 1895. Then, through the good offices of the commissioner of crown lands, a permanent home was found in the Parliament Buildings, then recently completed. This became known as the "Repository." Furniture was installed, bookshelves put up and appeals were made for something to put on them, this with some success, and before long the association had the nucleus of a respectable reference library.

In 1899 there was a spot of bother about a stepladder. Such a rarity was apparently unobtainable in Toronto, and one had to be purchased in Hamilton at the exorbitant cost of 45 cents, to be brought to Toronto by special express. "When it arrived," van Nostrand told his audience, "it was appropriated by the Surveys Branch, and they had the audacity to put their mark on it. That has been erased, and I have since put the Association mark on it, and it is now in our possession." Whereupon Kirkpatrick quipped: "I would like to ask, has one surveyor the right to remove the marks of another surveyor?"

Other firsts in the decade following incorporation included the production of a surveyors' manual. First discussed in 1899, it reached the members in 1900.

In 1899 the association obtained its first conviction of a surveyor practising illegally. Villiers Sankey, the first chairman of the Council of Management, a post he was to hold until 1900 when he took on the secretaryship instead, first brought up the question of taking action against illegal surveyors in his report of 1895. The following year, he mentioned that several cases had been brought to the board's attention. Most cases of this sort concerned surveyors in the northwest who had put their names to surveys of mining locations that had in fact been made by their apprentices. One case in particular led the association to consider prosecution. However, it was discovered that the association had no power to compel the offender to attend his hearing. This was remedied in 1898, and the next year the association endorsed and helped pay for the

prosecution of an unlicensed surveyor in a case referred to by Sankey as the "action of Foster v. Hall re. unlicensed practice in Rainy River district." He also mentioned that warning letters had been issued to two other offenders, one of which was in connection with the running of timber berth lines by one W.T. Jones, a lumber company employee.

In December 1896 a special meeting was called by Willis Chipman, then president, to discuss proposed amendments to the two principal acts that governed the professional lives of Ontario's land surveyors, the Act Respecting Land Surveyors and the Survey of Land dating from 1887, and the act of 1892 that had brought the association into existence. The thirty members present, having constituted themselves as a committee of the whole, dealt first with the changes they wished brought about in the act of 1892, most of which were duly incorporated in the revised surveyors act of 1897 (60 Vict., c. 27).

The revised act stated that the Board of Examiners should henceforth meet once a year only and that the examination of prospective apprentices should be extended to include history and geography – of Canada in particular – and English grammar. Forestry, elementary botany, and the forest flora of Canada were added to the list of subjects in the final examinations. After articling, a student might take a course of study at Toronto's School of Practical Science or a similar institution, though the apprenticeship must not last longer than four years, three of which must be "in the actual service of a practising Ontario Land Surveyor." Land surveyors who had qualified "in any of Her Majesty's dominions other than this Province" might, at the discretion of the Board of Examiners, be allowed to sit for their final exams without first serving an apprenticeship or at most serving such time as the board thought appropriate.

As far as survey practice went, there were changes spelled out in both the Surveyors Act and the Surveys Act of 1897 (R.S.O. 1897, c. 181) that met with the unqualified approval of the association. One dealt with municipal surveying and the immutability of monuments following surveys or resurveys. After due notice had been given by the commissioner of crown lands of their placement and with time allowed for appeals by those affected, boundaries as established by such monuments were to be deemed unalterable.

The second major change concerned lot boundaries in the districts of Parry Sound, Haliburton, and Nipissing south of the Mattawa River, and in designated townships in several counties bordering the Ottawa-Huron Tract. Much as Niven had suggested at the 1889 meeting, after 1 July 1897 such boundaries were to be run on astronomic courses. The revised act of 1897 also laid down the procedure to be followed where posts or monuments were missing on lands surveyed by the Dominion in the Rainy River District and in other designated townships in northern Ontario townships that had been laid out in the past.

Also discussed at the 1896 meeting was the standard measure of length to be provided by the Board of Examiners to successful candidates. It was decided that "a steel band properly tested and stamped would best serve the purpose, the arrangement of the details being left with the Council." Sankey, in his capacity as chairman of the Board of Examiners, advocated a 33-foot steel tape (that is, half a chain), graduated in feet on one side and links on the other. Though admittedly of little practical use, this could be used by individual surveyors to test the accuracy of their own chains or tapes. In the end, the 33-foot tape as suggested by Sankey was adopted.

Various other acts were passed in 1897 that would have a bearing on the professional life of land surveyors, particularly those principally engaged in municipal work – an increasing number. One was An Act Respecting Disputes Concerning Boundary Lines (R.S.O. 1897, c. 64), which provided for the appointment (by a judge) of an Ontario Land Surveyor to act as a referee in cases where a dispute had arisen over the location of a boundary line between adjoining lands. Having made his survey and taken evidence on oath, the surveyor would then report to the court who would then take the appropriate action, the whole procedure coming under the Arbitration Act.

Another act passed in 1897 was of significance not just to land surveyors but to all residents of the province. Dealing with roads, it was an extract from the Municipal Act (R.S.O. 1897, c. 223) entitled An Act Respecting Municipal Institutions. The act declared that all roads or allowances laid out by crown surveyors and any other roads built and paid for with public monies, including roads passing through native reservations, "shall be deemed common and public highways." And "unless otherwise provided for, the soil and freehold of every highway or road altered, amended or laid out according to law, and every road allowance ... shall be invested in Her Majesty, her heirs and successors." Unless a road or street had already been widened, no municipality was to lay out roads less than 66 feet (20 m) or wider than 100 feet without permission of the county council, the exception being duly incorporated towns and cities. No private roads were to be laid out less than 66 feet wide without municipal permission or the consent of three-quarters of the people living on the land affected.

In townships with double fronts, where road allowances on the side lines running back from their respective "fronts" did not meet – a common enough occurrence – their ends could be joined following a survey made by an Ontario Land Surveyor, who would not only choose the best way of doing this but would also determine the amount of compensation to be paid to those who lost land in the process, such to be paid them by the municipality.

For many land surveyors, however, probably the most important piece of legislation enacted in 1897 was An Act Respecting the Registration of Instruments Relating to Lands (extracted from R.S.O. 1897, c. 136, as amended by 62 Vict. (2), c. 16) or Registry Act for

Land Titles and Registry Offices

In Ontario there are two methods by which privately owned land can be bought and sold. One method is spelled out in the Land Titles Act, the other in the Registry Act. The latter system is a carry-over from Britain where, as the centuries passed, the conveyancing of property became an increasingly tedious and expensive one. In Ontario, the system has been operative virtually since the founding of Upper Canada. Under this system, all the deeds relating to changes of ownership are lodged in a Registry Office. Before a property changes hands, all the relevant deeds have to be "searched" by a lawyer, sometimes a long and costly process.

In 1857 Robert Torrens, registrar of deeds for South Australia, came up with a better way of transferring land. Shares in a company could be transferred by simply passing a certificate of ownership from one person to the next, so why not land? His idea was to establish ownership by a court decree, the validity of the title being guaranteed by the government. Anyone who could read and write could put the transfer through by signing the right form. The system came into use in Australia, New Zealand, and eventually the United States, the U.K., and other European countries.

In 1885 this land titles system was introduced into Ontario where, as defined in the the Land Titles Act, it applied only to Toronto and the county of York. In 1886 it was extended to all crown grants in northern Ontario and the districts of Parry Sound, Musakoka, and Haliburton. With some legislated exceptions, registration under the Land Titles Act is voluntary, provided that the necessary land division has been established by a regulation under the act.

short. This required that all subdivision plans be filed with the registrar within three months of their being surveyed, such plans to be on a scale of not more than four chains to an inch. The front and rear breadth of each lot were to be shown on the plan, as was their length. The plan must also show all posts or monuments and any roads, railways, and other features "together with such other information as is required to show distinctly the position of the said lands." The act also called for the compilation and registration of a plan, under certain conditions, of villages and towns, both incorporated and unincorporated, and spelled out how the preparation of such a plan was to be paid for. But whether the plan was of a new subdivision or of a village or town, its accuracy had to be attested to, in the manner prescribed, by an Ontario Land Surveyor.

Earlier, an alternative method of transferring land had been introduced with the passage of An Act to Simplify Titles and to Facilitate the Transfer of Lands, or Land Titles Act for short. The act called for the deposit, with the treasurer or assessment commissioner of the municipality concerned, of an authenticated duplicate of any plan or survey made in connection with any sale or conveyance of land, the original being deposited with the master or local master of titles.

A schedule of rules accompanied the act. They were quite specific. The plan to be deposited with the master had to be "on a scale not less than one inch to four chains and the scale shall be marked on the plan. The plan shall shew in black India ink the boundaries, numbers and other distinguishing marks of the lots, and shall shew the number of the township, town, or village lots, and range and concession as originally laid out and all the boundary lines thereof within the limits of the land shewn on the said plan." Moreover, where the plan showed land subdivided at an earlier date, such subdivisions had to be shown in "permanent ink of another colour." All roads, streets, adjacent lots, and so on also had to be shown on the plan, along with the

dimensions of the lots. Finally, each such plan had to be certified by an Ontario Land Surveyor.

Having launched the committee on topographical surveying and presumably inspired by the then on-going attempts by the Norwegian Fridtjof Nansen to reach the North Pole, Chipman took another initiative when in 1894 he proposed that the association take an active role in opening up the Canadian Arctic, in which the federal government had been taking an increasing interest since 1884.

"Whereas," Chipman stated in the preamble to a resolution he put to the meeting, "the northerly part of the Dominion of Canada has not yet been thoroughly explored, and its valuable resources are not as yet an available asset; and whereas other nations are turning their attention to this part of our country with views of expropriation; therefore the Association ... deems it desirable that a Special Committee be appointed for the following purposes." These purposes included the examination of the cost and feasibility of running a monumented base line north from a point on the northwestern shore of Baffin's Bay, this in order to further the surveying and exploration of the Arctic.

And so what was called the committee on polar research was set up with Chipman as its chairman. Chipman and his committee had hopes of an Ontario Land Surveyor joining a relief expedition being organized in 1895 by the Geographical Club of Philadelphia to assist Lieutenant Robert Peary, U.S.N., then in Greenland. On those hopes coming to nothing, Chipman then pursued the idea of an all-Canadian polar expedition, meanwhile bringing Peary himself to Toronto to give a lecture – to stir up both the public's and the association's interest in the Far North.

The association, through its polar committee, later joined its voice to those of both the Quebec association and the Royal Society of Canada, calling on

the federal government to take more interest in the Far North. Otherwise Canada would find at least part of the Arctic regions claimed, if not effectively occupied, by other nations, with Norway a leading contender. Meanwhile James Tyrrell, chairman of the polar committee, had learned in 1899 that a Captain Joseph E. Bernier of Quebec was making plans to reach the North Pole via Bering Strait. Tyrrell had hopes that a land surveyor might accompany Bernier's expedition, if and when it left. Thus in February 1901 the committee on polar research, headed by Chipman once more, brought Bernier to Toronto to address the association on his plans to reach the North Pole. But with Bernier's plans hanging fire, the association's polar research committee went into abeyance until 1903.

Following the formation of the committee on topographical surveying in 1893, the association mounted a campaign aimed at both the provincial and federal governments with the object of persuading them to embark on a program of topographic-geodetic surveying. The approach was deliberately low-key. As Chipman, the committee's first chairman, put it at the 1894 meeting, "for a few years, the work of our committee must be of a missionary character."

Accordingly an informal meeting was held in Toronto in December 1894 attended by some half-dozen interested surveyors, including both George Kirkpatrick, director of surveys for the Department of Crown Lands, and Dr. W.F. King, D.T.S., the chief astronomer of the federal Department of the Interior. Here it was decided to continue the missionary work, as Chipman had put it, by acquiring information from other countries on the commercial value of geodetic and topographic surveys. At the 1895 annual meeting Chipman, impatient as always to get things moving, asked that his committee be empowered to take the whole matter up with the Ontario government as soon as the information solicited from other countries was received.

At the 1896 meeting, Chipman reported that some replies from other countries regarding the economic advantages stemming from topographic maps had been received. Armed with these, a deputation had waited upon Kirkpatrick not long before the annual meeting and had "laid before him some facts respecting the work done, and being done, by other civilized countries in mapping their respective countries." He was formally requested to look into the matter.

In the event, all Chipman's efforts and those of his committee came to nothing, at least as far as a strictly provincial topographic survey was concerned, because the Honourable Arthur S. Hardy replaced the Honourable Timothy Pardee as commissioner of crown lands. The gloomy conclusion reached by the association was that nothing more could be accomplished until the next general election, as the government had "not undertaken even to look into the matter."

Otto Klotz, who had taken over the chairmanship of the committee on topographical surveying, had little to tell the membership in either 1897 or 1898, but the following year he drew the members' attention to a proposal made by the head of the U.S. Coast and Geodetic Survey to measure an arc along the ninety-eighth meridian (which passes not far west of Winnipeg) that would extend from the Gulf of Mexico to the Arctic Ocean. The object of the work was to help elucidate the shape and size of the earth. Klotz had been present at a meeting of the Royal Society of Canada where a paper had been read describing the American proposal, which obviously involved the co-operation of the Canadian government. He took the opportunity to draw the attention of the society to earlier submissions to the federal government of the Association of Dominion Land Surveyors regarding the need for a national geodetic survey, adding, for good measure, such information as he and the AOLS had collected.

As a result of all this, the Royal Society addressed a memorial to the governor general urging that not

only should Canada co-operate with the Americans on their proposed measurement of the ninety-eighth meridian but that the Canadian work be widened to include a triangulation of the whole Dominion. It was all to no avail. The Canadian government did not co-operate with the Americans. Nor was it to undertake a national geodetic survey for several years yet, in spite of a growing chorus of pleas, demands, and recommendations from a range of scientific bodies, learned societies, and professional associations, of which the AOLS and the Royal Society were but two.

More to the immediate point as far as northern Ontario was concerned was the formation in 1896 – again at Willis Chipman's instigation – of a committee on exploratory surveys. Its chairman was Elihu Stewart. Reporting for the committee for the first time in 1897, Stewart stated that what was required was a systematic exploration of northern Ontario, with a view to assessing the relative potential of different areas for farming, lumbering, or mining. "Heretofore," he commented, "we have been working in the dark, and in a manner resembling a farmer who, owning a two-hundred acre lot, has never considered it worth his while to examine the character of his possessions beyond the small clearing on the front of the lot."

Stewart went on to suggest that the CPR line could be used as the base line for the exploratory work, noting that "an outline survey" had been made of it "during the last five years ... [which] serves all the purposes of a base line through this district, from which future sub-divisions or other outline surveys can be started." In the subsequent discussion, Stewart reminded those present – which included Kirkpatrick of the Department of Crown Lands – that he had suggested several years before that the surveyor be accompanied by a geologist, as well as by men competent to judge timber quality and agricultural potential. Both this idea and that using the CPR line as a base line would be followed up by the government before long, as will be seen.

Not until 1900 did it become clear that something at last was to come of the association's efforts. Herbert Bowman, in the course of his address as president, commented, "No doubt many of you noted with interest the propositions of the new leader of the Ontario Government, particularly in reference to the appropriation of $40,000 or $50,000 for preliminary exploration work in the northern part of the Province ... for the purpose of obtaining information as to its timber, mines and arable lands." Bowman was referring to a speech made in Whitby by George Ross, who had become premier in October 1899.

Fishing for further information in the course of the discussion that followed his address, Bowman remarked hopefully, "Perhaps some of our members are in the confidence of the government." Kirkpatrick was finally provoked into disgorging what he knew. "Of course," he said, "I do not know what the premier will do; but I was asked some time ago by him to prepare a scheme."

He then revealed that a major stumbling block had been the attitude of the commissioner of crown lands and his immediate advisers. "I always had a good deal of trouble in early days to get the Commissioner to authorize the running of base lines and meridian lines with permanent monuments. They were generally afraid that the expenditure could not be defended in Parliament as readily as money expended in subdividing townships into farm lots."

Kirkpatrick, however, made it clear that he himself was far from making up his mind as to how and when the exploration work should be conducted. This led the chairman of the exploration committee, Maurice Gaviller, who had succeeded Dickson, to say later in the meeting: "Your Committee would earnestly press upon the association, the necessity of, without any delay, discussing, arranging and submitting to the Government a proposed system of exploration" of northern Ontario.

The committee's report was adopted, and that same summer the provincial government carried out a detailed exploration of northern Ontario (described in the next chapter) involving multidisciplinary survey parties and based on the CPR line, much as Elihu Stewart had suggested some years before. And so, with its immediate mission accomplished, the association's committee on exploration went into abeyance, and would not resurface until 1903.

In 1900, after ten years as secretary-treasurer, van Nostrand resigned, to be succeeded by Villiers Sankey. In his final summation, van Nostrand reported that since incorporation, of the 315 land surveyors in Ontario, 60 had withdrawn from the association and 28 had died, to leave an active membership of 227. He left the association with a healthy bank balance of $2,039.15. Concluding his presidential address, Bowman referred to the Boer War, which had seen various Canadian units leaving Canada to serve overseas. He suggested that with so much money in the funds, the association should make a donation to the Patriotic Fund. This it did to the tune of $100 – not an inconsiderable sum at the turn of the century.

CHAPTER SEVENTEEN

Opening Up New Ontario

It will be recalled that in 1886 Alexander Niven reported that to the north and northwest of Lake Timiskaming* lay a belt of flat clay land, admirably suited for agriculture – exactly the sort of land that the government had been hoping to find in northern Ontario all along. In 1886 Niven was sent back to the region to outline seven townships starting at the northwest angle of Lorrain, the only surveyed township in the area thus far. He returned to write enthusiastically "I am happy to report nearly all ... of the seven townships outlined to be good farming land, the soil being clay and the country level and free from stones," adding that, "there is not, in my opinion, the equal of this tract of land left in Ontario." Further, he had explored the land to the north and had found even better land there. He also stressed how easy it now was to reach the northern end of Lake Timiskaming by steamer.[1]

The next year, that of 1887, Niven outlined a further eight townships in the region. And in that same year, Bucke Township – in which Haileybury now stands – was subdivided and released for settlement, as well as five others north of Lake Timiskaming, three of them abutting the Ontario-Quebec border. In 1888 seven more townships were surveyed to the west and north of the head of Lake Timiskaming, and in 1889 a further seven, including that of Dymond, where the town of New Liskeard would grow. In 1889 Niven outlined another eight townships in the region, while other surveyors following in his wake completed the subdivision of those outlined earlier. By 1890 a total of twenty-four townships – or nearly half of the fifty-two townships now comprising the district of Timiskaming – had been laid out in a compact band stretching northwest from Lake Timiskaming in what became known in the early 1900s as the Little Clay Belt to distinguish it from the then recently discovered Great Clay Belt.

By the end of 1890, a further eleven townships had been surveyed, or at least outlined, in the Nipissing District immediately north of the Mattawa. A further fourteen would be added by 1900. And by 1890, all but six townships in the district of Nipissing south of the Mattawa had been surveyed, with the last of them completed by 1896. This was Airy Township, just outside Algonquin Park, where Whitney now stands. With the survey of Airy Township, the subdivision of southern Ontario into townships was virtually complete, this some 110 years after John Collins laid out the first township of Kingston in 1783.

*The modern English name for Lake Timiskaming is used throughout.

Alexander Niven surveyed all or part of many base and meridian lines in northern Ontario. A quiet, unassuming man, he was perhaps the greatest land surveyor in the history of the province. Courtesy: AOLS Archives

Thomas Speight ran a number of base and meridian lines in northern Ontario and was the co-founder of the firm of Speight & van Nostrand, now Speight, van Nostrand & Gibson, Ltd. Courtesy: AOLS Archives

Elihu Stewart. He stressed the need for exploratory surveys of northern Ontario that would include a systematic assessment of mineral and forest resources. His recommendations would be acted on in 1900. Courtesy: AOLS Archives

Henry de Quincy Sewell worked for the Nizam of Hyderabad before coming to Canada. He made many surveys in the Rainy River District and laid down what is now known as the First Base Line. Courtesy: AOLS Archives

In what is now the administrative district of Sudbury,* sixteen more townships had been added by 1890 and fresh deposits of nickel were discovered. Up until about the mid-1880s, little value was attached to the metal. However, with the expansion of the world's navies at about that time, the demand for nickel-steel

---

* Today's administrative districts of Sudbury, Kenora, and Timiskaming were formed in 1907, 1908, and 1912 respectively. That of Cochrane not until 1922. In 1927, Kenora was extended northward to include territory hitherto in the district of Patricia.

armour-plating started to grow. At about the same time, a new method was developed for extracting and refining the nickel in the copper-nickel matte. Thus the discovery of new nickel deposits came at an opportune time, creating so much excitement that the Ontario government was forced to place a temporary ban on the sale of mining lands. With nickel now the big money spinner (the International Nickel Company would be formed in 1902) and with people flocking to the region, a further forty-six townships were surveyed

in the district of Sudbury in the 1890s.

In the district of Algoma, fourteen more townships had been surveyed as gaps in the survey fabric were filled in to the north and east of Sault Ste. Marie. By the turn of the century, almost two hundred townships had been laid out from the shore of Lake Superior west of the Soo to Mattawa in the east. Most of these were in a major agglomeration around Sudbury, stretching eastward from the Spanish River, with townships ten or eleven tiers deep in some places.

Courtesy: L.M. Sebert, C.L.S.

A micrometer-telescope, often referred to simply as a micrometer. Aimed at a graduated staff, the observer could quickly determine the distance between telescope and staff. The instrument made for speedy traverses of rivers and lakeshores and was much used in the north. The paper wrapped around the barrel is the conversion table that came with the instrument.

In contrast to the almost frenetic production of townships in the eastern regions of northern Ontario in the last decades of the nineteenth century, there was comparatively little surveying activity in the west. At the western end of Lake Superior, the late 1880s had seen only seven new townships laid out, these inland from Thunder Bay, while three more went in north of Nipigon. Meanwhile, with mining claims proliferating in the Rainy River area, it was decided in 1887 to run an east-west base line along the extreme southern border of the Rainy River District into which the location of mining claims could be tied. This would be carried out in conjunction with a check survey of the international border itself.

The base line was run by Henry de Quincey Sewell, who, receiving his instructions in December 1887, started laying out the base line the following February in weather that he described as "being the most severe that it has been my lot to experience in this district." Working in continual snow storms that left from four to six feet (2 m) of snow on the ground, he found it difficult to make astronomical observations or to assess the quality of the soil – hardly surprising. From the northwest angle of Strange Township, some 30 miles (50 km) west and south of present-day Thunder Bay, Sewell ran the base line due west to Agnes Lake on Hunter Island nearly 60 miles away and which he eventually reached early in April.

Sewell was also instructed to begin running the boundary between the districts of Thunder Bay and Rainy River (the district then comprising all the extreme western part of northern Ontario). He took a meridian line southward at longitude 91°W to tie in with a traverse – less than 6 miles to the south at that point – that Alexander Lord Russell had been instructed to make of that part of the international boundary.

In 1890, two years after Sewell completed his base line (later called the First Base Line, see figure 12.1), Niven extended the Thunder Bay–Rainy River boundary 120 miles (193 km) northward, placing it, as it was later to become apparent, about three minutes shy of the meridian of 91°, or about 1.2 miles (to the west of it. At his 12-mile post he ran a line east to tie his line

in with the township of Moss, an anomalously large township surveyed in 1878, and at his 33-mile post he ran a 33-mile line to tie in a mining location on Magnetic Lake. Working in rain that fell almost every day for six weeks, he crossed the CPR tracks at about the sixtieth mile at English River, at a point about 7 miles north of Sturgeon Lake.

Niven, by now the Department of Crown Lands' star performer, was to return to the Rainy River District every year for the next seven years. In 1891 he ran what became known as the Second Base Line, which ran 60 miles (97 km) due west from the 30-mile post on the Thunder Bay–Rainy River District boundary he had surveyed in 1890. Every 12 miles, he ran meridians and then ran a parallel base line 6 miles north of the first back to the district boundary, thus outlining, at least in part, the townships in the vicinity of today's Atikokan. The next year, that of 1892, he extended the Second Base Line another 40 miles to the west to reach the shore of Rainy Lake. He went on to tie his line in with the townships (which had been laid out earlier by Dominion Land Surveyors) to the west of the lake.

In 1893 Niven returned to begin what later became known as the Fifth Meridian, running a 54-mile (87-km) line north from the base line he had completed in 1892 to tie in with the CPR 4 miles east of Tache Station – a line he would take farther north in 1897. And in 1894 he ran a 78-mile meridian (part of the Sixth Meridian) north from a point on Red Gut Bay near the western end of his 1892 base (very roughly 25 miles northwest of Fort Frances), which ended a couple of miles north of the Wabigoon River at a point just northwest of present-day Dryden, in the vicinity of which a start was made in laying out a range of townships that same year, beginning with that of Mutrie in 1894.

This would be followed in 1895 by surveys of Van Horne Township (in which Dryden stands) and Wainwright immediately to the north of it, with other townships laid out to the north and west in 1896 and 1897. Meanwhile, in 1895 Niven had run the Seventh Meridian at about 94°W. This ran some 70 miles (110 km) from the northern boundary of the range of townships along the international border laid out by Dominion Land Surveyors in the 1870s and ended on the southern boundary of a township about 20 miles

east of Rat Portage or present-day Kenora. On the way, he tied his line in with the westerly extension of the forty-ninth parallel – also run earlier by Dominion Land Surveyors.

In 1896 Niven was given a job in the east. He was to run an exploration line due north to James Bay that would be a northerly extension of the boundary between the districts of Nipissing and Algoma (out of which the districts of Sudbury, Timiskaming, and Cochrane would later be carved). Starting from the northeast corner of Lumsden Township just northwest of Sudbury, Niven ran the line 120 miles (193 km) due north to reach a latitude roughly that of present-day Timmins, planting wooden posts every mile and 1.25-in. (3-cm) gas pipes every 3 miles, these closed at the top and painted red. He then ran a base line due west for 120 miles.[2]

Two years later, in 1898, Niven was instructed to continue the Algoma-Nipissing boundary line northward to the Moose River, which flows into James Bay. This he did, running his line 4 miles (6 km) north of the river, crossing it at a point about 30 miles upstream from present-day Moosonee. Running through some 300 miles of forest, lake, swamp, and muskeg, the completed boundary line became known as Niven's Meridian. It was the only major meridian line in Ontario to reach salt water and would be the line on which the eastern portion of the massive exploratory survey of 1900 would be based. A provincial historic plaque now marks the spot where Niven's Meridian crosses Highway 11 about 2 miles west of Cochran.

In a paper given at the 1899 annual meeting, Niven gave a typically terse and unemotional account of his survey of the Algoma-Nipissing district boundary, noting that

a little beyond the 100th mile [somewhat to the south of Timmins] we enter upon the good land, the level country that extends to

James Bay, and for the remaining 200 miles of the line the country is almost as smooth as the lawn in front of the Parliament Buildings ... For over 120 miles runs through a splendid tract of farming land, clay soil, often covered with black muck. Parts of it might be called swampy and parts of it muskeg, but taken altogether there are not many places in Ontario where a line can be run for the same distance through such an even uniformly good tract of land.[3]

Such was one of the first comments by a qualified land surveyor on what would become known as the Great Clay Belt, the overrated agricultural potential of which would be a will-o'-the-wisp that would lead successive provincial governments astray for the next thirty years.

Niven's survey ended in tragedy. Leaving Moose Factory in early October, he and his party travelled south via Lake Abitibi, reaching it towards the end of the month to find it frozen but the ice as yet unsafe. Here a native who had worked with Niven for four years was drowned when his canoe struck an ice floe and sank.

Elsewhere, a start had been made on surveying the boundary line between Ontario and Manitoba. The Dominion government had invited the co-operation of Ontario and Manitoba in a tripartite survey of the boundary, with the cost to be split three ways. Still smarting at losing out in the Ontario-Manitoba boundary dispute, a disgruntled Manitoba refused to participate in the survey. But by the late 1890s, with mining claims in the border region proliferating, the need to establish the exact position of the boundary became urgent. So in 1897, the federal government decided – in the face of Manitoba's continuing indifference – to run a joint survey with Ontario only, with the Dominion and Ontario represented by Elihu Stewart and Bryce Saunders[4] respectively (see figure 13.2).

With the monuments planted in 1872 by the international boundary commissioners at the northwest corner of the Lake of the Woods as their point of commencement, Stewart and Saunders started work at the beginning of September 1897 and ran the boundary due north some 58 miles (93 km) to the Winnipeg River, which they reached early in December. The boundary was opened up to sky-line width throughout its length (that is, trees were felled sufficiently far back on each side of the line to afford a clear view of the sky); iron and cedar posts were planted; and as they went they tied in Indian reserves and mining locations adjacent to the boundary. There the Ontario-Manitoba boundary would be left until the early 1920s.

In 1899 Niven ran what is still called "Niven's Base Line." It ran due west from the 120th-mile post on his Algoma-Nipissing boundary at a latitude nearly that of Timmins – to end 120 miles (193 km) away, not far west of Missinaibi Lake northeast of Wawa. The western end of this line would form part of the northernmost boundary of the district of Sudbury. Meanwhile, in 1897 he had returned west to run the southern portion of the Fourth Meridian north from a point just south and east of Ignace on the CPR (the 120-mile length of which would be completed in 1929 by Beatty and Beatty). And in the same year he extended the Fifth Meridian (which he had begun in 1893) north to the fiftieth parallel, which brought him to a point not far southwest of present-day Sioux Lookout, the length of the completed meridian being about 110 miles. By 1900 the apparently indefatigable Niven, now in his mid-sixties, had run well over a thousand miles of base and meridian lines in northern Ontario.

In 1899 the Honourable Arthur Hardy was succeeded as premier by James Whitney, and in the same year the Honourable E.J. Davis took over as commissioner of crown lands. Whitney, somewhat at a loss to revive the waning fortunes of the Liberals, decided – almost for want of a better idea – that it was time the country north of the CPR in northern Ontario was opened to development. And so, in this almost throwaway fashion, the government took steps to implement what the association had long been recommending, the systematic exploration of the north – and this on a scale that must have taken even the most sanguine members of the association by surprise. As described in Kirkpatrick's final report of 1900,[5] no less than ten parties were to be sent out to explore the country from the CPR line north to the provincial boundary, then still lying along the line of the English and Albany rivers, from the Quebec-Ontario border in the east to the Ontario-Manitoba border in the west.

With a single exception, each party would be led by a land surveyor, who would be accompanied – as the association had advocated – by a timber assessor and a geologist. Of the ten districts to be explored, four were in Algoma and Nipissing, that is to say north of the North Channel, Georgian Bay, and Lake Nipissing; four were in Thunder Bay, that is, north of Lake Superior; and two were in Rainy River. Moving from east to west, the districts and the parties that explored them were numbered from 1 to 10 (see figure 17.1).

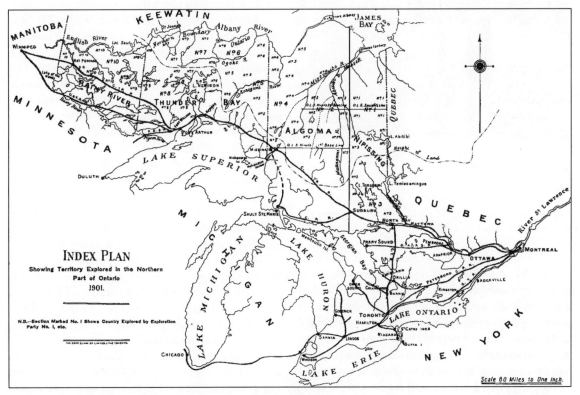

Figure 17.1 Areas allotted to different survey parties in northern Ontario in the great exploratory survey of 1900. (From Government of Ontario, *Report of the Survey and Exploration of Northern Ontario, 1900.*)

The cedar post marking the initial point of the Ontario-Manitoba boundary survey planted by Stewart and Saunders in 1897. Incised on the post are the words "78 chains north of N.W.A.," i.e., the North West Angle. (From the Ontario-Manitoba Boundary Commission Report, 1955.)

The work was done by contract with the conditions fully spelled out. All travelling expenses were paid, while surveyors were expected to provide their own theodolite; pocket sextant with artificial horizon; a steel tape and pins; a compass with a Jacob's staff;[6] a micrometer, that is, a micrometer telescope;[7] and plotting instruments. The government supplied field books; an aneroid barometer; a camera; a tin case for "preserving pressed specimens of the flora of the country"; besides tents, canoes, and packstraps. Surveyors were also furnished with a Kay taffrail log, complete with instructions, for measuring distances travelled by water.

The information to be brought back fell under seven headings: agricultural potential; timber resources; local geology with an estimate of the possible economic importance of any minerals noted; flora, including pressed specimens for subsequent identification; fauna, fur-bearing or otherwise, as well as birds and fish; rivers and lakes from the point of view of possible communication routes; and, finally, information on any "valuable water powers" encountered, including rates and volumes of flow and (presumably with possible dam construction in mind) the nature of the banks on both sides of the river or stream.

Exploration Party No. 1 was led by Thomas Speight, who was instructed to run a base line eastward from the 198th-mile post on Niven's Meridian – the meridian line run by Niven in 1896 and 1898. The point of commencement was, then, the northeast corner of present-day Ireland Township, some 35 miles (56 km) north of Cochrane. The base line was to extend to the Quebec border, reckoned to be 72 miles to the east at that point. Speight in his final report did not mention the latitude of the base line, though Niven, who was in charge of Exploration Party No. 2 and who was to extend the same line westward, placed it at 49°35'30"N – a line, it may be added, that quite fortuitously ran through the heart of the Great Clay Belt.

With Speight were to be two exploring parties, each made up of three men, who were to collect information on timber and soil up to 50 miles north and south of the base line as it went forward. Leaving Toronto on 1 June 1900, it took him five weeks to reach his point of commencement, travelling by train, steamer on Lake Timiskaming, and canoe.

Having run his line, Speight retraced his steps some 20 miles (32 km) and worked his way south along the Burnt Bush River and two other rivers, making track surveys of them as instructed, and eventually, having crossed the height of land, reached lower Lake Abitibi once more – on the way in he had cached supplies there, of which he had *five tons* in all. Discharging some men, Speight then returned to the upper lake and the mouth of the Abitibi River and thence to Iroquois Falls. From there he ran a tie line to the district boundary 18 miles to the west, retraced his journey making a compass and micrometer survey of Abitibi River as he went, returned to lower Abitibi Lake, and traversed its shoreline. Unable to complete a traverse of the upper lake because of the lateness of the season, Speight called it quits.

In Speight's opinion, given adequate drainage, at least one million acres could be "made suitable for farming" in the area he passed through. After speaking with residents in the vicinity, he concluded that "the agricultural resources of Ontario are capable of expansion to an extent hitherto little dreamed of."[8]

Exploration Party No. 2 was headed by Niven, who was instructed to proceed to the same point of commencement as Speight had been, namely the 198th-mile post on the meridian line named after him, and extend Speight's base line west from that point to the Missinaibi River (a tributary of the Moose River flowing into James Bay), with the two exploring parties under him working up to 50 miles (80 km) of the line. He crossed the Missinaibi at the hundredth mile and took the line another 2 miles west of it (labelled "O.L.S. Niven's 2nd Base Line" in figure 17.1). He then travelled upriver, eventually arriving at the end of the base line he had run in 1899 and, as instructed, took it another 24 miles to the west (his "1st Base Line" in figure 17.1). Running a meridian line south to the CPR line, he reached it at a point roughly 30 miles northeast of Wawa. He then tied his line in with an earlier survey made by Elihu Stewart of township boundaries along the CPR. Niven reported as follows:

Summing up the whole line, it may said that ... it runs through as fine a tract of farming land as can be found in Ontario. Where else

Sunday afternoon tea. Height of Land. Party No. 1.

On Lake Abitibi. Party No. 1.

Fawcett's post at head of Albany River, Lake St. Joseph.
Party No. 9.

Party on portage 24, Eaglerock Lake. Party No. 6.

Camp at Lac Seul. Party No. 10.

Dinner Time on Quinze Lake. Party No. 8

The various survey parties in the exploratory survey of northern Ontario brought back many photographs. Above is a selection with the original captions. Party No. 1 was led by Thomas Speight, No. 2 by Alexander Niven, No. 6 by Joseph Tiernan (who died before he was able to write his survey report), No. 8 by David Beatty, No. 9 by James Robertson and No. 10 by John McAree. (All photos from Government of Ontario, *Report of the Survey and Exploration of Northern Ontario, 1900.*)

in Ontario can a tract of land 100 miles square be found, all alike level and good? Muskegs there are in it, of course, but 75% of the whole country (7,800 square miles of it) could be cultivated as soon as cleared and the moss burned off it, and of the 25% remaining, a considerable portion could be drained and cultivated.[9]

Exploration Party No. 3 was led by George Gray. As instructed, he and his party explored "the territory lying east, west and north of Lake Temagami and on either side of the Montreal River and its tributaries east and west of the district line between Nipissing and Algoma."[10] In his final report, Gray stressed that while on the south side of the height of land there was some good agricultural land, the principal assets of the district lay in their timber and mineral resources, noting that the exploitation of the former would be greatly assisted by the abundance of rivers.

The geologist working with the party found "economic minerals ... in nine different places indicating the presence of gold, silver, copper, lead and iron distributed throughout the region," while a "number of valuable water powers were noted, more especially on the Sturgeon and Montreal Rivers." Working independently in the district that summer were two Ontario Land Surveyors, Richard DeMorest and George Silvester, who, leaving Sudbury towards the end of June, worked on until mid-November, exploring and surveying the river and lake systems between Lake Timiskaming and Lake Temagami and those north of the latter as far north as Niven's First Base Line.

Exploration Party No. 4 was led by Alexander Baird of Leamington, a surveyor who specialized in drainage. His appointment as the leader of a party is curious, leading one to suspect that such was the speed with which the great northern survey was planned that Kirkpatrick had difficulty in finding enough veterans

of northern bush work to go around. Licensed in 1877, Baird had played a leading role in laying out the government drains in Essex County, draining the Pelee Marsh, and reclaiming the Holland Marsh, north of Toronto. It was said of him that he had served as an expert witness in every case of litigation – the almost inevitable consequence of any drainage work it seems – in western Ontario since the 1880s.

Baird's assignment was to make a micrometric track survey of the Kabinakagami River, which rises just north of the height of land north of Wawa to flow into and then out of the lake of the same name. He was then to cross over to the Mattawishkwia River and thence down it to the Missinaibi, a tributary of the Moose, the general trend of the whole system being northeasterly. He was then to continue his survey down the Moose River to Moose Factory. Baird's party included a geologist and land and timber estimator, who were to explore the country for 20 miles (32 km) on both sides of the survey line. The jumping-off point of the party was the CPR station at Grasett, almost due north of Wawa, with the point of commencement duly tied in to the railway.

Arriving at Grasett on 20 June, the party was some 6 miles down from the junction of the Mattawishkwia and the Missinaibi by the middle of September. In both these rivers the water was so low that the bottoms of the canoes began to leak after scraping over rocks. "In consequence," Baird wrote in his report, "our provisions and baggage were wringing wet every night, and as the water was getting cold our Indians became discontented with the work of wading and portaging in the rocky bed of the rivers, and refused to proceed further with the work."[11] Thought was given to carrying on the work with fresh men, but as the nearest available source of these was 150 miles away, the survey was brought to a premature halt in mid-September.

Baird had trouble with his Kay's taffrail log, as did other surveyors issued with them. He lost the first one

while testing it. In any case he found it was recording backwards, while its replacement could not be made to work at all. Summarizing the resources of the country passed through, Kirkpatrick, in the final report, dwelt on the volume of valuable timber in the region. As for its agricultural potential, much of the country with its clay and sandy loam soils "can be easily cleared and for farming purposes ... will be equal to the best in the older part of the province."

Two of the four Ontario Land Surveyors placed in charge of the exploration districts north of Lake Superior died of typhoid not long after their return, though there is nothing to suggest that this was anything more than a coincidence beyond the fact that they were working in adjoining districts. Walter Davidson, in charge of Exploration Party No. 5, came from Arkoma in Lambton County, though later he worked out of Sarnia. It seems that like Baird he had little experience in the north. Far from well following his return off survey, he was able to submit only a brief report before dying at his home in Arkona in January 1901 at the age of forty-one. In charge of Exploration Party No. 6 was Joseph Tiernan, who came from Tilbury and was thus, like Baird and Davidson, from western Ontario. Unlike them, however, he had done considerable work for the government in the north and northwest. He died on 20 December 1900 before he was able to report on his survey. He was forty-five.

Davidson was to make a track survey from the CPR station at Jackfish (not far east of Terrace Bay) to Long Lake and then work his way north to the Kenogami River, which he was to follow to its junction with the Albany River. He was then to follow the Albany to its mouth on James Bay some 150 miles (240 km) away. Davidson was thus given a formidable distance to cover, and it was not surprising that he was still on the Kenogami before winter set in. In his perfunctory report – he was already unwell – he noted that before turning back he had covered 100 miles since leaving Long Lake and that there had been nineteen portages.

Tiernan's Exploration Party No. 6 was assigned one major watershed to the west of Davidson's, that of the Ogoki River, which he was to reach via Lake Nipigon. Following instructions, Tiernan travelled down the Ogoki to the Albany and thence some 90 miles (145 km) downstream to its junction with the Kenogami, where he was supposed to tie his survey in with Davidson's. However, as we have seen, Davidson hadn't got that far. Lacking time, Tiernan confined his exploration to 10 miles back from the survey line and, on reaching the Albany, to the south side of the river only. They worked on until late October when, with the rivers icing up, they made their way down the Albany to James Bay and thence via the Moose and Missinaibi rivers to the CPR station at Missanaibi (northeast of Wawa), which they reached on 1 November. Tiernan presumably reached his home in Tilbury a week or so later and a month after that he was dead. Needless to say, neither Davidson nor Tiernan found much arable land, though some mineral deposits of economic worth were found, as were some extensive stands of merchantable timber.

Party No. 7 was led by Hume Blake Proudfoot.[12] The work assigned to Proudfoot's party was the exploration of the country lying on each side of an alleged native canoe route from Lake Nipigon to Lake St. Joseph via the Albany River. It was to be reached by a chain of lakes extending first northwest and then north from Lake Nipigon. However, Proudfoot discovered from natives and Hudson's Bay Company officials that the canoe route to the Albany, as given in his instructions, did not in fact exist. Further, the plan given to him, apparently based on a geological survey made in 1870, was of little help as "the various lakes, etc., shown on the plan, did not in any way resemble the lakes as they are on the ground."[13] Finally, guided by local natives, Proudfoot struck inland, traversing and

mapping as he went, from the head of Wabinosh Bay on the northwestern side of Lake Nipigon to a lake with a name that Proudfoot rendered as Zhooshquabeanahmenis, and which he renamed Smooth Rock Island Lake, since reduced to Smooth Rock Lake. Attempts to find a route to Lake St. Joseph were frustrated by further language problems. "No one in the party knew the name by which the Indians called the lake, and 'St. Joseph' is an 'X' quantity to the Indians."

However, he stumbled on a route that a native guide apparently approved of that took him to the Albany near the eastern outlet of Lake St. Joseph. After a day or so on Lake St. Joseph at a Hudson's Bay Company post, he started southward for Lake Nipigon using a different route, arriving there on 16 October. While Proudfoot's survey did much to elucidate the geography of the region between Lake Nipigon and Lake St. Joseph, little was found by either him or his explorers in the way of arable land, exploitable timber, or minerals.

Working to the south of Proudfoot, David Beatty first took his Exploration Party No. 8 into the watershed of the Gull River, which flows into Lake Nipigon on its west side. With a track survey of the river made, he then moved south to Black Sturgeon Lake surveying as he went. He then moved south to Nonwatin Lake and struck eastward to the northwest corner of the township of Purdom and produced its northern boundary westward to tie it in with his survey of Lake Nonwatin. Then, travelling southwest, he reached and surveyed Dog Lake, which lies roughly 20 miles (30 km) northwest of Thunder Bay. He and his party then took an eastbound train at Kaministiquia to Sprucewood Siding on the Black Sturgeon River, travelled north to the northern boundary of Lyon Township, and then surveyed the river as far as the east-west line he had produced earlier. By September, and with supplies running low and with much time already lost because his patent log did not work (he

had to use a micrometer to make his traverses), he brought the season's work to an end.

"While the country," wrote the ever-optimistic Kirkpatrick, "is not generally adapted for agricultural purposes, its principal characteristics being stone, rock and swamp, it comprises considerable areas of sandy loam which would make good farming land."[14] There was, though, good timber to be had though not in great quantities.

Party No. 9, led by James Robertson, and Party No. 10, led by John McAree, covered the northeastern and northwestern portions respectively of what was then still called the Rainy River District (now lying in the district of Kenora) north of the CPR. Detraining at Ignace, Robertson carried out a track survey of the canoe route to Sturgeon Lake, which lies northeast of Ignace. After making a micrometer survey of the lake, Robertson left it at its southern end to work his way northwest along a chain of lakes to Lac Seul. There he tied his line in with the northern boundary of Indian Reserve No. 28 at the point where it intersected the shore of Lac Seul. He then turned eastward and crossed the height of land to reach Lake St. Joseph. Arriving at the outlet of the Albany River on 31 August, Robertson and his party turned south for the CPR and home. With little good farming land encountered and the timber patchy, the best news came from Robertson's geologist who found gold near Sturgeon Lake.

For the sixty-year-old McAree, heading Exploration Party No. 10, this would be almost his last survey – he would die in 1903.[15] He and his party left Rat Portage by train on 29 June for Margach, not far east down the line, and then headed northeast to Black Sturgeon Lake on the Winnipeg River. He then took his party eastward through a chain of lakes that eventually brought them back to the railway again. Here they boarded a train for Eagle River (about 25 miles east of Dryden) from where they struck north to follow the Wabigoon River to its junction with the English River and then followed the latter river to Lac Seul and the Hudson's Bay Company post at the narrows opposite Indian Reserve No. 28 – where they just missed meeting Robertson and his party who had passed through a few days earlier. McAree then took his party west through a chain of lakes and eventually reached the English River, which they followed down to its confluence with the Winnipeg River. They then went up the Winnipeg, to arrive back at Rat Portage on 12 November, having been on the move for over four months.

Summarizing McAree and his assistants' findings, Kirkpatrick observed that "owing to the rocky character of the greater portion of the area ... the opportunities for agricultural settlement are limited." However, he noted there was much good timber on the English and Wabigoon rivers and their tributaries. Quartz veins were frequent in some localities and "may be found on close examination to contain gold in paying quantities." As for game, this was plentiful, "including moose, caribou and red deer, the latter being a recent arrival, but protection against indiscriminate slaughter," he added, "is urgently required to prevent their extermination."[16]

All in all, the great survey of 1900 was a staggering success and has been described as "a classic of its kind and represents, in resource mapping and in the gathering and presentation of resource information, an achievement seldom equalled anywhere in the world."[17] That the survey was carried out at all owed much to the Association of Ontario Land Surveyors in general, and the committee on exploration in particular, in their on-going effort to have just such a survey made.

Its success was all the more remarkable considering that it was planned so hurriedly and was such a complex operation. Further, with delays in getting parties into the field, it was already high summer before they could begin their work. Much credit is due to George Kirkpatrick, who planned it. And who costed it so accurately that he ran only $518.28 over his $40,000.00 budget – which must have gratified the government in no small measure.

The Department of Crown Lands lost no time in piecing together the reports submitted by the ten survey parties, revealing the presence of what became known as the Little and Great Clay Belts:

It has been established beyond controversy that in the eastern part of the territory north of the height of land there is an immense area of excellent agricultural land, apparently equal in fertility to any in older Ontario, with an equable and temperate climate and an abundance of wood and water, which render the inducements it presents to those in search of homesteads as good as those offered anywhere else on the continent ...

The great clay belt running from the Quebec boundary west through Nipissing and Algoma Districts and into the District of Thunder Bay comprises an area of at least 24,500 square miles ... It is larger than the States of Massachusetts, Connecticut, Rhode Island, New Jersey and Delaware combined, and one-half the size of the State of New York.[18]

The land was reported as being well watered by many rivers, and the climate as presenting "no obstacle to successful agricultural settlement," as the information obtained "completely dispels the erroneous impression that its winters are of Arctic severity and the summers too short to enable crops to mature."

Spurred on by the results of the great survey, new townships were completed in what was now being called New Ontario at an ever increasing rate. Only two townships had been completed in 1901 and eight in 1902. In 1903 the total rose to twenty-one and no less than forty in 1904, their subdivision involving a small army of land surveyors too numerous to mention. Thereafter, the total dropped to thirty-three in 1905 and twenty-one the year after that. These townships were erected on a number of base and meridian lines, laid out for the most part by Niven and Thomas Speight, who by then had emerged as the other heavyweight of northern surveying, indeed of the profession as a whole.

In addition to laying out townships for settlement, there was the need to lay out timber limits in the tracts of exploitable timber that the great survey of 1900 had brought to light. Thus, it was in connection with a "large tract of pine timber" that Niven, acting on instructions received late in 1901, began running a 90-mile (145-km) base line west from the northeast angle of Curtiss Township, about 35 miles northeast of Sault Ste. Marie, to the northwest angle of Craig, some 45 miles northwest of Sudbury, a base line from which he ran a 90-mile meridian due north that brought him out near Woman River Station on the CPR, a survey he would not complete until the summer of 1902.

Meanwhile, Speight had run a 45-mile (72-km) meridian line from the northwest angle of Eby Township, not far from present-day Kirkland Lake, north across the height of land to the Abitibi River. And, acting on instructions received in October 1902, he began laying out the boundary between the districts of Algoma and Thunder Bay, laid down by statute as lying on a meridian line placed at a longitude of 85°20'W. Starting on the shore of Lake Superior west of Michipicoten, Speight took the boundary north about 50 miles. (Niven would take the boundary line another 120 miles north in 1907.) After finishing his work on the boundary line in 1903, Speight went on to outline townships in the vicinity of Timmins, then still in the district of Algoma. To the east of him, William Galbraith and James Robertson were doing the same in northern Nipissing.

In 1904, while the work of subdividing townships in the Clay Belt went on, William Galbraith, Thomas

Thomas Speight's camp when surveying a base line in northern Ontario in 1901 (left). Preparing to take a sight on the same survey (right). Courtesy: AOLS Archives

Speight, and Thaddeus Patten between them laid down nearly 300 miles (500 km) of base and meridian lines that would form the bases of future townships, nearly half that total being the work of Patten.[19] Speight's surveying work in the summer of 1904 was brought to an abrupt end when a large freight canoe carrying 200 pounds (90 kg) of iron bars and 1000 pounds of provisions capsized in rapids on the Abitibi River north of Kirkland Lake. Two men drowned. Discouraged by this incident, most of Speight's men returned to their homes in Mattawa. It now being mid-July, and with no time to hire more men, Speight abandoned the survey.

A year later, Speight laid out three more base and meridian lines in the vicinity of present-day Cochrane, these in continuation of the lines run the previous year by Patten. These lines, in turn, were tied in with Niven's Algoma-Nipissing district boundary. That Patten could not continue his own lines himself was due to his appointment that year as the commissioner for Ontario in the extension northward of the Ontario-Quebec boundary, the location of which had

become a matter of urgency following the discovery of the agricultural potential of the Great Clay Belt, which stretched eastward into Quebec, and the allocation of timber berths in the region, not to mention mining claims and the proposal to build a transcontinental railway through the heart of the belt.

It will be recalled that the boundary had been taken north from Lake Timiskaming to the height of land in 1874. In 1905, messrs. Patten and Laberge, acting for Ontario and Quebec respectively, extended the boundary a further 47 miles (76 km) northward to a point near where the planned railway was expected to cross the boundary. In the following year, Patten, now working with one Sullivan, Q.L.S., extended the boundary northward another 60 miles to intersect a base line that was being run east from Niven's Meridian Line that same year by Thomas Speight. Patten and Sullivan ended the boundary line, now 140 miles north of Lake Timiskaming, in a vast muskeg that, so they were given to understand, stretched north to James Bay and which in some places was considered impassable. No further work would be done on the

Ontario-Quebec boundary until the early 1930s.

Meanwhile, in 1899 the Boer War had broken out, in which some 8000 Canadians saw service. In 1901 an act was passed to reward returning veterans with land on easy terms. With the peopling of New Ontario in mind, a number of townships were set aside for those who had served in the Boer War. Those eligible would be granted 160 acres, with location tickets valid for ten years and no settlement duties or municipal or other taxes to pay. By popular demand, members of the militia who had served during the Riel uprising or in connection with the Fenian raids also became eligible under the scheme, as were not just soldiers, but chaplains, nurses, and the like, as well as their next of kin. The result was a flood of some 18 000 applications, with the Department of Crown Lands having to hire extra staff to deal with them. Nearly 14 000 location tickets were issued, though many were to be surrendered and over a thousand others were to remain unused as late as 1928.

It was largely with the thought of settling these veterans in the Little Clay Belt under the new scheme that the provincial government decided to build its own railway connecting the Little Clay Belt with North Bay, where there was a junction between the Northern Railway and the CPR. Work on the Temiskaming and Northern Railway began at Trout Lake, just north of North Bay, in May 1902 with New Liskeard planned as its first terminus.

In August 1903, when work on the railway was well under way, a couple of timber estimators noticed a glint of ore at a railway cutting at mile 103, a little south of present-day Haileybury. A month later, a blacksmith, apparently working at night, threw a hammer at what he thought were the glowing eyes of a fox, or so the story goes, and was rewarded with chips of what appeared to be copper. Claims were filed, and a provincial geologist arrived on the scene to find great veins of silver. For want of a better name he called the place Cobalt after the reddish tinge of cobalt on the rock. And so the Cobalt mining boom began. By 1904 the Temiskaming and Northern Railway had been pushed north to Englehart, and in 1908 had reached Cochrane, there to join up with the National Transcontinental. Begun in 1906, this coast-to-coast venture (now the CNR) would run though the heart of the Great Clay Belt.

In 1909, six years after the Cobalt find, a prospector named Jack Wilson made a spectacular discovery of gold in Whitney Township not far east of present-day Timmins. In due course this led to the development of the Dome Mines. And not long after that, Benjamin Hollinger and Sandy McIntyre and others working a few miles to the west made the discovery that led to the development of the Hollinger and McIntyre gold mines.

The discovery of gold led to the founding of the small town of South Porcupine. This was destroyed by fire in 1911, whereupon a silver merchant from Mattawa, Noah Timmins, who had done well in the Cobalt silver rush, formed a syndicate that built a new town, incorporated in 1912, to which Noah Timmins gave his own name. About the same time, Harry Oakes (later Sir Harry) and other prospectors started to develop the gold mines in the vicinity of Kirkland Lake

(named after Winifred Kirkland, a secretary in the Department of Mines) that would be the basis of that town's prosperity in the years between the First and Second World Wars.

In 1903, Francis H. Clergue's industrial empire, centred on the Soo, was on the brink of collapse. The story of the growth of Clergue's empire need not be gone into here. Suffice it so say that by the early 1900s its core consisted of a steel plant at the Soo, incorporated in 1902 as Algoma Steel, the Algoma Central Railway, iron mines near Michipicoten Bay, pulpwood concessions, and a sulphite pulp mill. Faced with the prospect of all Clergue's operations falling into American hands – and with them a substantial portion of the province's natural resources – the Liberal provincial government under George Ross attempted to rescue Clergue's holding company with a massive loan. These efforts were to little avail.

The collapse of Clergue's various enterprises was a major blow to the government already facing mounting criticism for its mishandling of the province's natural resources. In 1905 the Liberals under Ross were finally defeated by James Whitney's Conservatives intent on enlarging "the people's share" of those

resources. A minor manifestation of this new policy was the retention by the government of a tract of land south of New Liskeard, known as the Gillies Limit, which was to be developed for the good of the people.

Also as a result of the new policy, the venerable Department of Crown Lands was absorbed by the newly created Department of Lands and Mines. This was soon enlarged to become the Department of Lands, Forests and Mines. In 1906, shortly after his department was reorganized, George Kirkpatrick, who remained director of surveys in the new ministry, recommended the adoption of a new township survey system for New Ontario. He suggested the adoption of what became known as the 1800-acre section system, in effect a modification of the 1000-acre section system that had been introduced, it will be remembered, at the request of the Canada Company.

By now, in the post-Boer period, would-be settlers were pouring in from the United Kingdom and Europe in unprecedented numbers, many of them with little or no experience in farming. Thus, in the 1800-acre section system that Kirkpatrick was proposing, the basic lot would be a nominal 150 acres, each 59.50 chains deep and 25.25 chains wide. Twelve such lots would make up an 1800-acre section, each of which would be closed by the surveyor and with the actual dimensions of each lot recorded as before. Townships under the new system would be 9 miles (15 km) square, twelve concessions deep and twenty-eight lots wide.

There would be surveyed road allowance between each section and as each section was in effect two concessions deep, the end result was much as it was in a double-front township. And, as in a double-front township, the 1800-acre section system resulted, at least in theory, in more compact communities with just over twice the number of homesteads to the square mile compared to the 640-acre section system that had been used in the north up to that time. From the surveying standpoint, one important feature of the

The Gillies Limit

Determined to make the most of various mining properties around Cobalt, the Ontario government disposed of them on favourable terms – with the one exception of the Gillies Limit, which was to be logged, mined, and developed for the "good of the people." The experiment was a failure and the land was eventually auctioned.

In 1906 Homer Sutcliffe and Ernest W. Neelands were asked by two other Ontario surveyors, William J. Blair and D. Sinclair, to complete the survey of the Gillies Limit. This led to the founding of H. Sutcliffe Limited of New Liskeard, a surveying and engineering firm that has been described as the largest of its type north of Toronto and the oldest continuing engineering firm in northern Ontario. The firm holds the survey notes of a number of early northern land surveyors, several of whom went on to become presidents of the association. One of them, Charles Fullerton, would one day become surveyor general.

640-acre section system was retained: the 9-mile-square townships were to be oriented on a north-south, east-west axis (see figure 17.2).

Kirkpatrick's proposal was adopted immediately, with the first three 9-mile-square townships surveyed in 1906. Ten more 9-mile-square townships were completed in 1907, with others to come in the years ahead. However, because of the many base and meridian lines laid down in earlier years with 6-mile square townships in view, these would continue to be completed until the 1930s when the township system was finally abandoned. Thus, between 1906 and 1934, nearly ninety 6-mile-square townships were completed in northern Ontario compared with just over fifty of the "new" 9-mile-square townships.

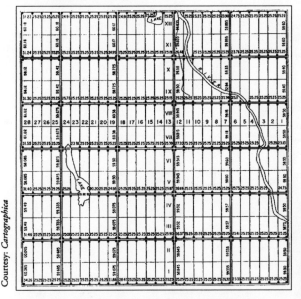

Figure 17.2 The 1800-acre sectional township survey system. This, the last of the township survey systems introduced in the province, was designed with northern Ontario and recent immigrants in mind. Townships were 9-miles square as compared with the 6-mile-square townships laid out in northern Ontario up to that point. Solid black squares indicate survey posts planted.

The year 1906 also saw another 350 miles (560 km) of base and meridian lines laid out in northern Algoma with the new 9-mile-square townships in view, most of them by Niven and the firm of Speight & van Nostrand, in the person of Thomas Speight. The next year, that of 1907, Alexander Niven ran his last major survey line.

Niven was by now seventy-one years old and his health was failing, though he was wont to say that it improved once he was back in the bush. He had been instructed to run the boundary between the districts of Algoma and Thunder Bay from the CPR line north to the Albany River, but had to give up after 120 miles. "The reason for this being," he wrote, "that a number of men in my employ were out of footwear and as the country was very wet from the almost continuous rainfall of the summer, they refused to go further."[20] One has the feeling that Niven himself would have liked to have completed the survey even in bare feet.

Four years later, in 1911, Alexander Niven died in Toronto at the age of seventy-five, some fifty-two years after receiving his commission as a provincial land surveyor in 1859. With him passed perhaps the greatest Ontario Land Surveyor of them all. He was described as "a quiet, dry, slow-talking man" and was "noted among surveyors for his management of men, being famed for getting more line cut in a season than any other surveyor in Ontario."[21]

In that same year of 1911, yet another of Thomas Speight's surveys was interrupted by a fatality. One of his assistants, Alan Anderson, a student at Toronto, suddenly fainted when out on the line, it being an intensely hot June day. He died that same night without regaining consciousness. Speight blamed it on the heat and drinking icy water.

In 1908 the Temiskaming and Northern Ontario Railroad had reached Cochrane, where it linked with the new National Transcontinental (now the CNR). Before long a spur line would connect Cochrane with Moosonee, then envisioned as northern Ontario's own thriving saltwater port. By now there were over 230 "free-grant" townships in which settlers could receive 160 acres, more or less for the asking.

In 1912 the provincial government appropriated $5 million under the newly passed Northern Development Act to speed development in the north. Most of it was spent extending the road system north and south from the National Transcontinental, using a work force of some five thousand men. And in that same year, twelve new 9-mile-square townships were

A Surveying Partnership

In 1868, when he was nine, Thomas Speight emigrated with his parents from Yorkshire, where his father was a shoemaker, and settled in Fisherville. He went straight from school to article with Silas James, D.L.S., P.L.S., and was licensed as a provincial land surveyor in 1881. In 1885 he entered into partnership with Arthur van Nostrand. Van Nostrand's Dutch antecedents had emigrated to America in the 1630s. He became one of Peter Gibson's many students – though he also served for a short time with A.C. Webb out west – and became a provincial land surveyor in the same year as Speight. The partnership between the two men lasted fifty years and only came to an end when they both retired in 1936. In 1905 they had incorporated themselves under the name of Speight & van Nostrand. In 1972 the firm (by then Speight, van Nostrand, Anderson and Currie) joined forces with W.S. Gibson and Son, Ltd. Now Speight, van Nostrand & Gibson, Ltd., the firm remains one of Toronto's leading firms of surveyors.

completed on the Great Clay Belt. Local land agencies were established, and eventually an agency was even established in London, England, to encourage the British emigrant to take up land in northern Ontario (see figure 17.3).

The agricultural potential of the Little Clay Belt was to be amply demonstrated in the years ahead, as would be that of some parts of the Great Clay Belt. But that the Great Clay Belt represented a vast, unbroken stretch of good farmland was doubted by many, almost as soon as that claim was first made by Kirkpatrick in his report of 1900 on the great northern survey. The fertile clay soil was there, all right, in some places, but in others it was covered with many feet of muskeg. Even on the better land, there were likely to be drainage problems, this quite apart from the very short growing season with frosts as late as the first week in June and with the first fall frosts occurring in mid-September.

However, William Hurst, who had become minister of lands, forests and mines in 1911 and who become premier in 1914, was an almost rabid enthusiast when it came to farming the north country. He stated that in northern Ontario "there are millions and millions of acres of the very best agricultural land in the world,"[22] which was pushing it rather. As for its agricultural potential – as opposed to its mining and lumbering potential – it was to be the Ottawa-Huron Tract all over again. As one historian has put it "the north seemed to be a sieve, emptying itself through abandoned farms as new farms were established."[23] It was not until the late 1920s that sober and more scientific thought prevailed and hopes of a clay belt dotted from end to end by thriving farms finally died.

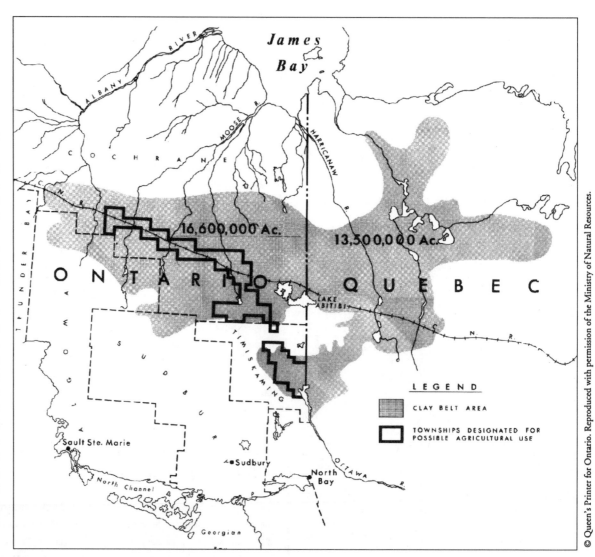

Figure 17.3 The Great Clay Belt and, northwest of Lake Temiskaming, the Little Clay Belt. The presence and extent of the western portion of the Great Clay Belt was brought to light by the exploratory survey of northern Ontario of 1900. In the early 1900s efforts were made to induce immigrants to take up land in the townships designated for agricultural use.

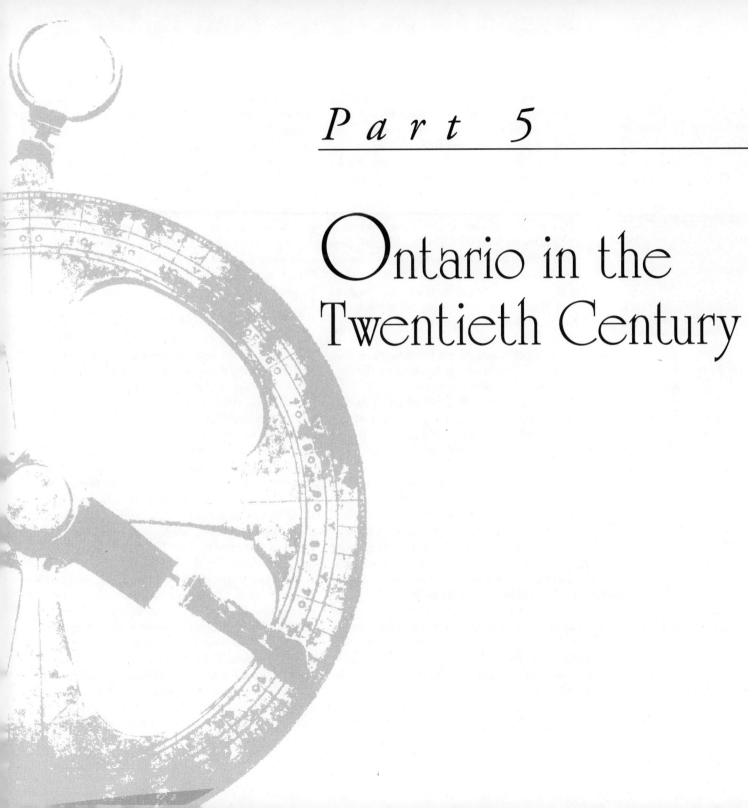

Part 5

Ontario in the Twentieth Century

CHAPTER EIGHTEEN

Boom Years for Land Surveyors

It is arguable that no Ontario Land Surveyor, or anyone for that matter, did more to leave an imprint on the face of modern Ontario than did Archibald Campbell, who was to become known as "Good Roads Campbell." Born of Scots parents in Wardsville in Middlesex County in 1863, Campbell articled with James Bell, who had an extensive land-surveying and civil-engineering practice in St. Thomas and who went on to become its town (later, city) engineer and county engineer for Elgin. In 1891 Bell gave up his city work to become manager of the St. Thomas Pipe and Foundry Company, at which time Campbell succeeded him as city engineer of St. Thomas. Campbell devoted much of his energies to improving St. Thomas's streets. At the same time he was becoming increasingly concerned with the appalling state of neglect into which country roads had been allowed to fall by successive governments besotted by the perceived need for more and more railways.

Thus the year 1894 saw Campbell take a leading role in the formation, under the auspices of the Department of Agriculture, of the Good Roads Association – from which would spring the succession of government departments that eventually became the Ministry of Transportation we have today. In 1896 the Department of Agriculture created the new post of provincial instructor in road-making, and Campbell was appointed to it. He took to his task with enthusiasm, travelling about the province and lecturing as he went, stressing that the cost of well-designed and well-constructed roads would be more than offset by reduced maintenance costs in the future.

Campbell's assistant, William McLean, an Ontario Land Surveyor since 1898, was as dedicated to the cause of good roads as Campbell was. In 1900 Campbell was appointed commissioner of highways in the provincial Department of Public Works, and he took McLean with him. In the same year, the Colonization Roads Branch was transferred from Crown Lands to the Department of Public Works.

The year 1900 also saw Campbell play a leading role in a remarkable publicity stunt financed by an Ottawa Valley newspaperman. This was the "Good Roads Train," which spent the summer touring southern Ontario and carrying the "good roads" message. Railway companies provided the use of their lines and rolling stock. The trains travelled around loaded with road-building machinery and barrels of cement. At each town, the local council was offered one mile of road to be built for nothing then and there, at a location of their own choosing. The indefatigable Campbell accompanied the train and lectured endlessly, often making side trips to smaller villages along the way.

The next year, that of 1901, Campbell persuaded the provincial government to enact the Highway Improvement Act, under which a million dollars was set aside to assist counties in a road-building program, which Campbell and McLean immediately started to plan. It has been said of these two men that they "were vitally instrumental in developing" the provincial highway system we know today.

Meanwhile, in 1896, the first gasoline-powered vehicle had arrived in Ontario. The first vehicle licences were issued in 1903 – 178 of them at $2 apiece. A tag rather than a plate came with the licence. By 1907, with about 2600 motor vehicles on Ontario roads, public interest in building and maintaining better roads was growing fast. Three years later "Good Roads Campbell" was lured to Ottawa, where he became commissioner of highways in the federal Department of Canals and Railways. He made an unsuccessful attempt in 1912 to have the Commons pass Bill 77, the Canada Highway Improvement Act, which would empower the federal government to help finance provincial highways. Eventually passed in 1919 (by which time Campbell had become the federal commissioner of highways), the act set aside $20 million to help provinces pay for highways, provided that a provincial highway system had been established, in which case Ottawa would pay 40 percent of the construction costs.

The first decade or so of the twentieth century were halcyon years for Ontario Land Surveyors and the association. There was New Ontario to be surveyed and opened up, there was plenty of work out west for those who wanted it, the booming mining industry offered new opportunities for surveyors, both above and below ground, while the growing use of hydro-electric power would lead to the need for surveys in connection with the location of long-distance power lines. At the same time, Ontario was becoming urbanized at an ever-growing pace. By 1911, of a total population of over 2.5 million, 53 percent were urban dwellers. The first modern subdivisions were appearing, bringing with them not only more work but a growing volume of legislation, which the land surveyor had to master.

That the years between 1900 and the outbreak in 1914 of the Great War were good times for land surveyors is reflected in the number of surveyors entering the profession. In the first four years of the twentieth century, fifteen Ontario Land Surveyors had received

Dr. Otto Klotz, member of the association and then Canada's most distinguished astronomer, furthered the association's efforts to bring about a national geodetic survey. Courtesy: AOLS Archives

Louis Rorke was secretary of the association from 1912 to 1923 and president in 1925/26. Appointed surveyor general in 1928, he retired in 1935 to serve once more as the association's secretary, a post he held from 1936 until his death in 1942. Courtesy: AOLS Archives

Archibald (Good Roads) Campbell, who laid the groundwork for today's provincial highway system. Courtesy: AOLS Archives

For First-Timers in the Bush

At the 1904 annual meeting, James Robertson gave a paper entitled "Surveys of Crown Lands in New Ontario," primarily for the benefit of the beginner who had never worked in the bush before. Among his recommendations were the following:

Supplies should be calculated at a rate of 100 pounds (45 kg) per man, including instruments, axes, cooking utensils, tents, bedding, and food. The men must be allowed 50 pounds of cereal per month (including beans) and a pound of bacon a day. Condensed milk was fine, but other canned goods weren't worth the trouble of carrying in.

Because of the demand, it was important to book the number of canoes needed well in advance. For transporting supplies, 18- to 19-foot (6-m) Peterborough basswood canoes were best. A lighter 13-foot birchbark canoe should be taken along for work purposes. A large, coarse sponge was useful for bailing out canoes. Arrangements should be made for getting mail into the survey party if this was possible, as this helped keep up morale.

Medical supplies should include cotton bandages, absorbent cotton, surgeons' needles with silk thread, sticking plaster, quinine capsules, a painkiller (an opiate?), essence of Jamaican ginger, chorodyne, and a bottle of lime juice.

"Old clothes should not be taken except the tweed suit to wear in camp or on wet days." Working clothes should include pants of either duck, corduroy, or "full cloth"; a sailor's waterproof jacket; and a soft felt hat. As for firearms: "Revolvers are quite unnecessary and possibly none should be allowed." A rifle and a shotgun would be useful, though should not be depended on for furnishing a part of the supply."

As for black flies and mosquitoes: "A good preparation is made of equal parts of castor oil and sweet oil with as much carbolic acid as the skin will stand. The ingredients may be bottled separately ... and mixed as required ... A more effective preparation is made of equal parts of oil of tar and sweet oil, with a little alcohol and creosote and a sufficient quantity of pennyroyal to perfume the mixture ... If the survey starts early in the season about two quarts of the above will be sufficient."

---

their certificates. The next four years saw twenty-four licensed. Then came a dramatic increase. No less than fifty were licensed from 1908 to 1911, and sixty-four from 1912 to 1915.

Reporting in 1901 as secretary-treasurer, Villiers Sankey announced that the finances of the association were in good shape with few members in arrears. The only unusual outlay, he pointed out, had been $180 for the printing and binding of the association's first surveyors' manual, which had been distributed the previous year. Elected in 1900 to succeed van Nostrand as secretary-treasurer, Sankey created a sensation towards the end of the 1902 meeting when he suddenly announced his resignation after holding office for only

a year. He had no report to present to the association, this, he said, because of pressure of work. His resignation came as such a surprise that Peter Gibson was startled into asking: "You haven't gone mad or anything, have you?" Sankey did stay on, however, as chairman of the Council of Management.

In the summer of 1905, however, the association was stunned by the news that Sankey had been drowned while on survey in the Rainy River District. His body was found a week later and taken to Toronto where, as a reservist, he was buried after a full military funeral. As the principal architect of incorporation, as a staunch and hard-working supporter of the association, and as a wise counsellor, he was sadly missed.

Sankey was succeeded as secretary-treasurer by Killaly Gamble. Irish-born, Gamble had served in the British army for some sixteen years before taking an early retirement and emigrating to Canada in 1882. Here he became a licensed land surveyor in Manitoba and also a Dominion Land Surveyor. Moving to Toronto four years later, he joined the firm of Speight & van Nostrand, of which he was still a member when he was elected secretary-treasurer of the association, a position he was to hold until his sudden death when visiting relatives in England in 1912. Gamble was succeeded as secretary-treasurer by Louis Rorke, who, after graduating from the School of Practical Science, had articled under Elihu Stewart and had become an Ontario Land Surveyor in 1891 and a Dominion Land Surveyor the year after that. Rorke would remain secretary-treasurer until 1923.

The association had, it seemed, a secure home in the repository at the Parliament Buildings. And it was in the repository that the annual meetings continued to be held until 1910, though in 1903 and 1904, evening sessions were held at the rooms of the Engineers' Club at 96 King Street West – a club, it may be mentioned, that Willis Chipman had done much to bring into existence.

Sometime during 1909, however, the association was asked to vacate the repository; the expanding Surveys Branch of what was now the Department of Lands, Forests and Waters needed more space. Thenceforth, the annual meeting was to be held in the Engineers' Club until the late 1920s. Sometime in 1911 the association rented an office in the Temple Building at 701 Bay Street. In 1914 Rorke, then secretary-treasurer, reported that he had moved the office back to the Parliament Buildings, apparently for his own convenience. The library was transferred to the Engineers' Club in 1913, which not long afterwards moved to new quarters.

Around the turn of the century, a matter that was becoming of increasing concern to surveyors was litigation arising from judges' differing interpretations of the phrase "under my personal supervision" that appeared in the certification by surveyors that plans and field notes were correct. Thus, at the annual meeting in 1905, James Whitson gave a paper entitled "Personal Supervision of Surveys," in which he noted that the Department of Crown Lands frowned on surveyors who used their apprentices to carry out the survey work required. Whitson also noted that during the mining boom in northern Ontario in 1897, some surveyors had sent out unqualified assistants to make surveys, and that in one case the Department of Crown Lands had difficulty in compiling plans because it had received three different sets of plans of a set of islands, all filed by the same surveyor. The plans differed markedly. This had led to litigation, and when a resurvey was performed it was found that two of the islands shown on the plans did not, in fact, exist.

As a result, the department directed that in future all plans and field notes should be certified thus: "I hereby certify the foregoing plan and field notes are correct, and are prepared from actual survey made under my personal supervision."[1]

But just what did the key phrase "under my personal supervision" actually mean? Whitson's paper led to a prolonged discussion centring upon the degree of supervision required before a surveyor could conscientiously attest to the accuracy of his work, whether that supervision be that of a qualified assistant or of a student. The Council of Management was requested to look into the matter. The result was the framing and ratification in 1906 of a new bylaw in which the key phrases ran:

The statement in the certificate that the survey has been made by the Surveyor or under his personal supervision means that the survey operations have been carried out under

his personal supervision and direction in such a manner that he is certain of their correct execution. It involves the presence of the Surveyor on the ground. He may assign to his assistants such parts of the work as he may see fit. Any infringement of this By-Law shall render the Surveyor amenable to discipline.[2]

In 1906 Speight, then chairman of the land surveying committee, suggested that the committee on legislation should start thinking about possible revisions to the Surveys Act in view of the impending decennial revision of the Ontario Statutes. This revision (7 Edw. 7, c. 31) resulted in some minor amendments to the Surveys Act, which were assented to in April 1907. As suggested by the association, one of them allowed surveyors, when carrying out a survey at the request of a municipality, to survey "further than the points mentioned in the Council's application," while another dealt with the way surveys relating to the boundaries of roads and highways should be paid for by the municipality requesting them.

These minor revisions were followed in 1911 by more substantial ones affecting both the surveys and surveyors acts. The revised acts incorporated several changes and additions suggested by the association. The Act Respecting Land Surveyors widened the powers of the association to buy and sell real estate. And two new subjects were added to the final examinations: the calculation of the potential horsepower of rivers and streams, and the scaling and measuring of timber. The revisions to the Surveys Act (1 Geo. 5, c. 42) included a new section that provided for a fine of up to $100 for anyone interfering with or obstructing a surveyor in the course of his duties. Other revisions dealt with the minutiae of township surveys.

After 1911 the committee on legislation lay dormant for a couple of years, though at the 1912 meeting Kirkpatrick reported that surveyors were to be provided – at government expense – with copies of the

revised surveys and land surveyors acts, along with extracts from the mining, land titles, registry, and ditches and watercourses acts. The last pieces of legislation affecting land surveyors before the Great War broke out in 1914, concerned an amendment to the Ontario Land Surveyors Act requested by the association, by which the fees for the final examination and certificate to practise were raised to $10 and $20 respectively. There were also minor revisions to the Surveys Act (RSO 1914, c. 166).

It might be supposed, with such a high proportion of land surveyors engaged in drainage work early in this century, that the association's drainage committee would submit long and regular reports. But such was not the case. Perhaps the surveyors were too busy. In some years the committee had nothing to report, while in others brief reference is made to this or that battle then being fought in the courts. Indeed, progress in this particular field of surveying endeavour often seemed to have been measured in terms of legislative battles lost or won rather than in the actual work carried out. This was undoubtedly due to the complexities of the legislation involved. Deploring this in his chairman's report of 1907, George Ross of Welland, whose licence dated back to 1878, observed that drainage legislation had become "merely a fertile source of revenue for the lawyers and an endless trouble and expense for those in whose interest they were framed." He went on: "Every engineer engaged in drainage work has probably experienced the chagrin of having his award set aside owing to some slight technicality of procedure, or the humiliation of having it amended in a manner which he knows to be unjust, by parties wholly incompetent to form a proper conception of the matter at issue."[3]

Ross, who was to remain chairman of the drainage committee for a number of years, called for the appointment of qualified "drainage referees" to resolve drainage disputes. Before long, such referees would indeed be appointed by the province. In 1912 Ross's report consisted of a long technical paper aimed at "our young members, who may not yet have had an opportunity of obtaining much practical experience in drainage engineering." He pointed out that drainage reclamation work fell under three headings: tile or farm underdrainage (the installation of permanent drains under arable land); digging of open ditches to drain swamps or marshes, and widening of streams and rivers or digging of channels to relieve flooded areas; and dyking or levee work. Regarding the underdraining of farm land, he pointed out that this had been done since pioneer days using stones or wooden slabs (actually cedar or pine scoops or cedar rails) and that these had now been superseded by tile, but the "practice of underdrainage spread with comparative slowness."[4]

However, Ross continued, since 1905 the Ontario Agricultural College had been sending teams into the field to encourage farmers to use tile drains. As a result, the total length of tile drains laid down had risen from about 15 million lineal feet in 1905 to about 29 million in 1909, resulting in the underdraining of over 193 000 acres. Ross pointed out that "the surveyor will be called upon much oftener than at present to lay out and take charge of large tile drainage schemes."

In connection with ditch work, he pointed out that a good map of the area was essential, and that the best information was still to be found in the old, commercially produced, county atlases (sad comment on the continuing lack of government topographic maps).

The committee on engineering had resurfaced briefly in 1903 but with little result. It emerged again in 1911 under James Hutcheon, an SPS graduate from Guelph. Hutcheon gave a report on the current state of engineering in Canada. "Probably never before in the history of the country," he said, "has so much work been done in one year, while the prospect for the future appears to be equally promising." He went on to mention the ever-extending hydro lines from Niagara, and the continuing boom in railway construction. He noted the increasing use of concrete for construction

and added that both plain and reinforced concrete were now commonly used for bridges, the spans of which were becoming greater each year. He went on to talk of the many road improvements that had stemmed from increased automobile traffic.

Nothing further is heard of the committee on engineering until it was taken over, presumably sometime in 1914, by Norman Wilson, D.L.S., O.L.S., licensed in 1910, who was head of engineering and surveys for the Toronto Harbour Commission. At the meeting in 1915, Wilson gave a report that provides us with the best picture we have of the kind of work that an Ontario Land Surveyor of the time was engaged in, the sources of his income, and the extent of his involvement in engineering work. Based on fifty-four replies to a questionnaire sent out to the members, Wilson drew up a profile of a typical Ontario Land Surveyor at that time. He found, on average, surveyors earned 54 percent of their income from surveying, 38 percent from general engineering, and 8 percent from general contracting or other business. Of the income earned from surveying, 38.9 percent came from "marking out parcels or lines," carrying out surveys for title, and preparing plans and descriptions; 22.4 percent from subdividing town or city lots and preparing plans for registration; 11.0 percent from township subdivision work; 10.4 percent from hydro and railway right-

of-way surveys; 5.7 percent from running government base lines or other "special" government work; 5.2 percent from surveys of mining claims; and the balance coming from surveys of timber limits, and municipal and court surveys.

The following year, that of 1916, Wilson furnished further statistics relating to the overlap between land surveying and engineering, noting that seventy-five, or 28 percent, of the active members of the association were either active, associated, or student members of the Canadian Society of Civil Engineers.

Thereafter, nothing more would be heard of the engineering committee until 1921, when its chairman briefly noted the efforts then being made by engineers to form their own self-governing association on the lines of the Association of Ontario Land Surveyors. This would come to pass in 1922, when the Professional Engineers' Act was passed. This led to the formation of the Association of Professional Engineers of Ontario – which some 118 members of the Association of Ontario Land Surveyors would promptly join.

Wilson himself was rapidly making a name for himself as a noted land surveyor, having been appointed chief engineer and surveyor to the Toronto Harbour Commission. Established in 1911 by a statute that called for five commissioners, three appointed by the city and two by the federal government, the

---

The Quebec Bridge Disasters

Concluding his report of the committee on engineering for 1911, Hutcheon commented, "The greatest single engineering work now in progress is the Quebec bridge, and it is surely gratifying to the profession to know that one of the great bridges of the world is being built in Canada by a Canadian company."

Somebody should have touched wood. Begun in 1900, the bridge was approaching completion when in August 1907 the southern cantilever span twisted and fell, carrying seventy-five workmen to their deaths. Work on the bridge was resumed after an enquiry – in which John Galbraith, then dean of the School of Practical Science, played a leading role – but in September 1915 a new centre span fell when being hoisted into position and a further thirteen men were killed. The bridge was finally completed the next year.

Norman Wilson. His triangulation of Toronto harbour was the first step in a massive reclamation and construction project undertaken by the Toronto Harbour Commission. He later became an internationally known expert on transportation systems. During the Second World War he was Canada's deputy transit controller.

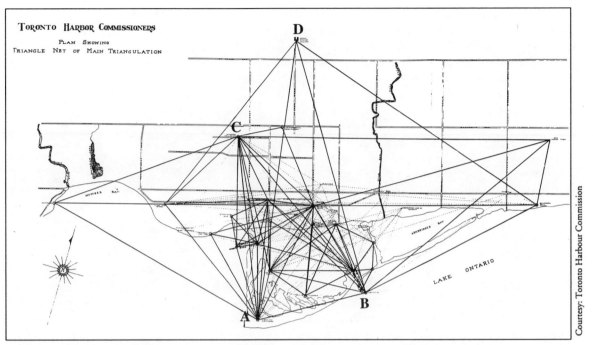

Figure 18.1 Wilson's triangulation of Toronto harbour. His base lines were on piers at the western and eastern gaps (A and B). He tied in his triangulation to the meteorological observatory on Bloor Street (C), the latitude and longitude of which was known. The northernmost survey station was on the tower of Upper Canada College (D). (From the Annual Report of the Toronto Harbour Commissioners, 1913, Toronto Harbour Commission Archives, RG 1/2, Box 1, Folder 2.)

commission was given wide powers: to develop Toronto as a port, to reclaim the marshes on the eastern side of the city for industrial use, and to improve the city's lakefront for recreational purposes. In carrying out its mandate, the commission was to transform the face of Toronto, while the drainage of the marshes would lead not just to an extension of the city's port facilities but to the marinas and extensive parkland around what is now known as Ashbridge's Bay.

Lieutenant-Commander Joseph Bouchette's survey of Toronto harbour in 1793 had been followed by that of Bayfield in 1818. In 1843 the peninsula and the extensive marshes that then lay at the mouth of the Don, called the Ashbridge Marsh, and around the eastern end of the harbour were surveyed by John Howard. In 1867 what is now the Toronto Islands was surveyed by Charles Unwin, who went on to survey the marsh in 1873. Apart from these, no survey of the harbour had ever been made. Thus the first step towards fulfilling the newly formed Toronto Harbour Commission's mandate was to carry out a precise survey of the 12 500 acres of land and water that stretched along the waterfront now falling within the commission's jurisdiction. The job was given to Norman Wilson.

Wilson started work in February 1912 with a detailed survey of all the buildings, wharves, and railway tracks along the 10-mile (16-km) waterfront, together with soundings over the bay and marshes. With four parties at work over several seasons, the survey was carried out in 200 squares using transits and chains and standard traverse methods. This resulted in a series of 100-feet-to-the-inch maps.

A detailed survey of the island had been made in

In a mammoth project undertaken in the early 1900s, the Toronto Harbour Commission reclaimed much of Ashbridge Marsh and constructed modern docks on the eastern side of the harbour. (Left) Surveyor using a dumpy level along the lower Don River. (Bottom) Driving in a survey monument at the foot of Leuty Avenue. (Top) Surveyor on a temporary platform in Ashbridge's Bay uses a dumpy level to check the height of pilings during the construction of the ship canal. Courtesy: Toronto Harbour

1911 by the city surveyor, Tracy Le May, which emphasized property lines and leasehold properties. Following this up, Wilson laid down two range lines on the island and worked from those, the lines being carefully tied into each other by a series of triangles. By 1914 the harbour was surrounded by a network of traverse lines, but, though errors were small, Wilson was not satisfied. So, working from two 2300-foot (700-m) base lines laid down on the piers at the Eastern and Western channels, Wilson then carried out a triangulation of the whole area, one of his stations being the meteorological observatory on Bloor Street, the exact latitude and longitude of which was known, thus allowing Wilson to place all his survey points on a geodetic basis, which were referred to an arbitrarily selected meridian in his final plans (see figure 18.1).

At the same time as this work was going forward, Wilson restored Unwin's 1873 survey of the Ashbridge Marsh, which the commission was anxious to drain

and develop and which contained a number of water lots, the first being granted as early as 1803. In the course of resurveying these lots, Wilson found it necessary to re-establish "The Windmill Line." This was a governing line laid down in the 1830s from a point near the old French Fort Rouillé (the site is now in the CNE grounds) to Gooderham's windmill on Trinity Street on the east side of the city, the windmill having been torn down in the 1850s. The line had been resurveyed by Unwin in 1893. Though he was able to locate only four of the sixty ties Unwin had used, Wilson managed to restore the line, using southerly offsets to get around the various buildings along the waterfront.

Wilson described his work at the 1916 annual meeting. In seconding the vote of thanks to Wilson, Le May commented: "There was a time when the Harbour Commission was first instituted it was suggested that the city surveyor [himself] should perhaps handle the job. After hearing this paper I am more than thankful to Providence that we were not asked to do it."

In their continuing effort to stir up interest in the Canadian Arctic, Chipman's committee on polar research kept a close eye on Captain Bernier's efforts to mount an expedition to the North Pole. Those efforts culminated in 1904, when Bernier was given command of the Canadian Coast Guard ship *Arctic*. Though he never reached the pole, he made voyages between 1906 and 1908 during which formal claim was made in the name of Canada to various regions of the Arctic, with survey monuments placed at a number of locations by members of the Geological Survey.

Chipman never really got over his disappointment that the association did not realize its hope that an Ontario Land Surveyor would play an active role in early polar research and exploration. In his successive annual reports to the association from 1906 onwards, Chipman's accounts of Bernier's voyages dwelt on the exploits of Peary, Nansen, and Amundsen. In 1908

Chipman and his committee even brought Peary (now a commander) to speak at Massey Hall.

With the demise of his committee on polar research in 1913, Chipman turned his abundant energies to the production of biographies. Elected chairman of the standing committee on repository and biography, he made his first report to the association in that capacity in 1914. A few biographies of early surveyors had been compiled earlier, but with Chipman at the helm, the biographies started to pour in.

Chipman urged surveyors in every part of the province to take an interest in the early surveying history of their districts. "Year by year," he said, "a link with the past is forever lost, and what may be obtained today may be unattainable tomorrow." Spurred on by his great love of history, Chipman spared no effort to produce his beloved biographies, co-opting new members to his committee – which tended to get larger and larger. He was also to plead with the older members to deposit their autobiographies with the association, this to ease the task of some future biographer.

Later, in the mid-1920s, by which time the committee on repository and biography had been split into its component parts, he was to declare enthusiastically, "The work of our Committee has all the thrills, pleasures and disappointments of gold mining," a view, one feels, the hard-pressed members of his committee might not always have shared. Ostensibly written anonymously by the committee, Chipman likely wrote many of the biographies himself. The flood of biographies would continue on into the 1920s, with Chipman remaining the enthusiastic chairman of the committee on biography until his death in 1929.

The standing committee on exploration, having seen its principal hope fulfilled by the great northern survey of 1900, lay relatively quiescent until 1909, when Selby passed on a general recommendation by his committee that the government should acquire more precise information on the exact extent of timberlands, the amount of land suitable for agriculture,

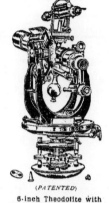

As seen in this advertisement in the association proceedings for 1910, European-made (as opposed to British-made) surveying instruments were starting to enter the American market. They would not reach Canada, however, until after the First World War.

and "the location ... of valuable water-powers" in northern Ontario. Also, in view of the impending transfer to Ontario by the Dominion government of the land north of the Albany River, which, Selby pointed out, would add another 146 000 square miles to the area of the province, his committee advised that "the immediate exploration of this immense territory be commenced, to ascertain what wealth we have in mines and timber, not only for its value but for its protection."

In his report in 1910, Selby recommended that where townships were only outlined an effort should be made to traverse the larger lakes and water courses within the township and that levels be taken along all base and meridian lines. And in 1912, he said that as "large sums have been voted by the government for the development of New Ontario ... the country might be mapped out ... and reported on in detail." And he repeated the call for the taking of levels along base and meridian lines. Selby's report was the last of any substance submitted by the committee on exploration. It finally disappeared in 1918, when it was combined with that on topographical surveying.

The transfer to Ontario by the Dominion government of the land north of the Albany River, to which Selby had referred in 1909, took place in 1912 when the federal government ceded the remaining parts of the Northwest Territories lying south of the sixtieth parallel to Ontario, Quebec, and Manitoba, with all the land lying between the Albany River and Hudson and James Bay handed over to Ontario, which finally assumed the form that we have today, the territory in question becoming known as the district of Patricia.

However, in order to bring the size of Manitoba roughly in line with that of Alberta and Saskatchewan created seven years earlier, the Ontario-Manitoba boundary, as defined in the Boundaries Extension Act, was not to be a continuation northward to the sea of the meridian line begun in 1872 by Stewart and Saunders, but a dog-leg that would augment the size of Manitoba. Following the promulgation of the newly defined boundary, Ontario and Manitoba requested the federal government to run – and finance – a survey of the uncompleted portion of the boundary, but nothing came of this request and no further survey work on the boundary would be carried out until the 1920s.

The association had continued its efforts to bring about a national geodetic survey. By 1905 the committee on topographic surveying was being chaired by Otto Klotz. Klotz was by this time one of Canada's leading scientists and perhaps the association's most distinguished member. He reported, that "after these long years of agitation for the purpose of having a beginning made of a systematic triangulation of Canada, to be followed by topographic and detail surveys, there appears to be now a rift in the clouds and the promised goal in sight."

What had happened was that in 1903 the Royal Society of Canada had submitted a memorandum to the Dominion government asking it to reconsider its decision not to co-operate with the Americans on their proposed work on the ninety-eighth meridian, at the same time calling yet again for a geodetic survey of the country, pointing out that in its absence the same land was being surveyed over and over again by different agencies. In the same year, as part of a reorganization of the Department of Militia and Defence that followed the Boer War, the general officer commanding the department, Major-General the Earl of Dundonald, formed an Intelligence Branch with a Major E.H. Hills, who headed the Topographical Section of the Royal Engineers, arriving from England to examine and report on the state of military mapping in Canada.

Hills supported the Royal Society's recommendation that it was time that a trigonometrical survey of Canada be carried out and that triangulation was the best way of going about it. As a result of his report, a start was made on producing topographical maps for military purposes. By 1904, small, five-man survey parties were working on the Niagara Peninsula, their object the production of maps at a scale of one inch to the mile, with 25-foot contours. From Niagara, the military surveyors moved to the Ottawa area and thence to Montreal, with the work from 1906 to 1914 speeded by the loan of six men of the Royal Engineers sent from Britain.

Meanwhile, the chief geographer in the Department of the Interior had reported on the difficulties he was having in compiling a new map of Canada in view of the many serious errors he had come across in the many maps and plans he was working

Otto Klotz

In 1885 Otto Klotz became closely involved with the systematic determination of longitude using the electric telegraph from the Pacific coast eastward along the so-called Railway Belt. Given telegraphic linkage, the determination of time differences between two places was raised to a new level of accuracy, as was the difference in longitude that could be determined from those time differences. In that same year, Klotz was officially designated "Astronomer," the first in the Department of the Interior.

From 1885 to 1891, Klotz combined surveying with astronomic and longitude work and in 1892 had become heavily involved with the determination of trans-Atlantic longitudes using the newly laid trans-Atlantic cable. By 1904, following the laying of the first trans-Pacific cable, Klotz completed the first "astronomic girdle" of the world, carrying out longitude determinations as he travelled west around the globe.

The Dominion Observatory was completed in 1905, the site being the Central Experimental Farm in Ottawa. Here Klotz was placed in charge of the geophysics unit, which worked on terrestrial magnetism, gravity, and seismology. He died in Ottawa in 1923 at the age of seventy-one.

with. He pointed out that while personally surveying parts of central Ontario he had found errors as much as 2 miles (3 km) in longitude and over 1 mile in latitude.

By 1905 the Dominion government was at last convinced that a national geodetic survey should be undertaken and, having sidled into it by way of geodetic levelling work in connection with a proposed Georgian Bay Ship Canal project, field operations started that same year under Charles Biggar, D.L.S., then on the staff at the Dominion Observatory. In overall charge was the chief astronomer, Dr. King. Though the Geodetic Survey of Canada did not officially exist until an order-in-council brought it into being on 20 April 1909, active work began in the summer of 1905 when the first observation towers for triangulation work were erected in the vicinity of Ottawa. By 1906 other towers were being built along the Ottawa River to the St. Lawrence.

In 1908 Louis Stewart, who was now chairman of the topographic survey committee, reported that the chain of observation towers had got as far as Belleville and that in order to tie in the Canadian triangulation net with the American one, six stations had been built to link Lake Erie and the north shore of Lake Ontario. Precise levelling work was also going ahead along railway lines in eastern Quebec.

In 1910 Thomas Fawcett, D.T.S., who had succeeded Stewart as chairman of the committee, reported that towers had now been built throughout "the greater part of the older district of Ontario." He went on to comment that "the observing of the angles was delayed by the smoke of 1908 [from forest fires], which during that season was unusually bad." Fawcett urged that the provincial government proceed as quickly as possible with the secondary triangulation, pointing out sensibly that it would not be long before the wooden, temporary towers would be unsafe to use. It may be added that in a few years the triangulation net in southern Ontario would consist of some sixty

towers and that angular observations by day were made using a mirror to reflect a beam of sunlight and by night using an acetylene gas lamp.

A year later, Fawcett was reporting that precise levelling work along the railway lines was now going forward throughout the Dominion using copper bolts as permanent benchmarks, either set in concrete or, in cities, drilled into walls of public buildings. In Ontario such marks were now in place from Quebec to Windsor and along the "southerly portion of Ontario." Topographic surveying had also been going ahead along Canada's international boundaries, involving triangulation and other methods. The Department of

Militia and Defence had also embarked on its own topographic surveying program. "We may expect," said Fawcett, "vastly improved maps from this source, as use is being made of the points determined by the Geodetic Survey as a means of control for their maps."

Enlarging on the discussion of railway levelling work in his report to the 1913 meeting, Fawcett said that the levels in Ontario and Quebec were tied in to a benchmark established at Rouse Point, New York, by the U.S. Coast and Geodetic Survey, and that in Ontario the line of levels had been run from Coteau Junction (using both the CPR and Grand Trunk lines) through Prescott, Hamilton, London, Chatham, and

With star globe on the table, Carl Reinhardt of Cobalt, licensed in 1899, works on celestial observations.

thence to Windsor, with a branch to St. Catharines and Bridgeburg.

In 1915 Fawcett mentioned that mapping by the Department of Militia and Defence had come to a halt. This was a reference to a program of survey and mapping by the military begun in 1904 in the vicinity of Niagara. The Geodetic Survey of Canada, however, had begun producing topographic maps with 25-foot contours. A 175-square-mile (453-km²) area around Ottawa was already complete, Fawcett added. That was virtually the committee's last report until the 1914–18 war ended. Said Fawcett in 1917, "The majority of those ... engaged in topographical surveying are either overseas at the front or in training for service at the front."

With the outbreak of the Great War only one year away, Thomas Speight's presidential address at the 1913 annual meeting reflected the optimism then prevailing, not only in the profession, but in the country as a whole, though he struck a sombre note at the beginning of his speech: "War, with its horrors, has smitten parts of Europe with a heavy hand ... the end is not yet." He went on to note, in a more optimistic vein, that the "phenomenal development" in railway construction "had eclipsed all previous records ... This form of progress naturally creates a demand for ... the engineer and surveyor, and the year 1912 may be regarded as the best the country has ever seen."

The services of both surveyors and engineers were also in increased demand in the construction industry, now booming, "particularly in the larger cities ... the present record of sixteen storeys for an office building is now being menaced by one of twenty storeys, reaching 250 feet above ground level." European methods of town planning were now being studied and "great benefits are expected to result in our urban and suburban districts." Then, perhaps not surprisingly since he played a leading role in opening up the region to settlement, Speight dwelt at length on the enormous oppor-

tunities opening up in New Ontario, with its mineral resources and vast tracts of fine farmland.

In a matter of a year, things had started to change for the worse. James Dobie, in his presidential address in 1914, spoke of the war in the Balkans but comforted his audience by dwelling on the progress being made in northern Ontario: the Cobalt silver mines had produced $30 million in the last year, the Porcupine gold mines over $4 million; there was a new pulp and paper plant at Iroquois Falls; the network of railways in the north was nearing completion; and colonization of the Clay Belt was going forward steadily, thanks largely to the Colonization Roads Program.

He went on to observe that "two great avenues are opening up which will afford employment for surveyors for years to come." One was the development of water power north of the height of land in New Ontario. The other was the development of the road system. "There is no question which has assumed such importance in the public mind as that of improving our system of road construction." Older roads were disintegrating under the weight, not only of an increasing number of cars but of trucks. What was needed, he stressed, was not just more roads, but better ones. And what better persons to bring about these desirable ends but Ontario Land Surveyors?

Dobie then proposed that a new standing committee on "Roads and Pavements" be set up. It was a timely suggestion. The Highways Act would be passed by the legislature in 1915, whereby every main road allowance was placed at a minimum of 66 feet (i.e., one chain), with local boards of trustees given the authority to widen such roads up to 20 feet (6 m) on each side or even adopt a more favourable route for the whole road. The following year the Department of Public Works was enlarged to become the Department of Public Works and Highways, being renamed the Department of Public Highways not long after, this under Archibald Campbell's erstwhile associate, William McLean.

In 1916 the new department assumed the first provincial highway, a stretch of about 45 miles (72 km) of the Kingston Road between the county of York and Port Hope – a highway that would be extended eastward to the Quebec boundary following an order-in-council approved by the lieutenant-governor in 1918. In the meantime, work had been going ahead on rebuilding the Lakeshore Road between Toronto and Hamilton. Forty miles long and 18 feet (5 m) wide with 3-foot shoulders, it was the first such road in Canada.

Notwithstanding the general note of optimism that had been struck by Dobie in his presidential address of 1914, the affairs of the association fell into some disarray during the war, particularly on the financial side, and largely caused by a steady increase in the amount of unpaid annual fees. By 1915 one-third of the membership was in arrears with their dues, totalling $1,272, of which $900 was considered impossible to collect. The perilous state of the association's finances notwithstanding, it was decided that same year to donate $400 to the Red Cross Association and the Belgium Relief Fund. By 1917, with many members overseas and exempt from dues, the association actually went into the red to the tune of $430, though only briefly.

Contributing to the association's sorry financial state at that time was a decline in active membership. From a peak of 267 in 1915, it had fallen to only 239 in 1918. Active membership was to remain remarkably constant thereafter, to hover about the 245 mark until the outbreak of the Second World War.

In 1917, such was the financial state of the association that it was decided to raise the annual membership fee to $5 and to increase other fees across the board. For example, the fee for taking the preliminary exam would be increased to $15, that for the final exam would go up to $40. Certificates to practise would be upped to $10, with a further $1 payable for the official notice in the "Ontario Gazette."

These increases required an amendment to the Land Surveyors Act. Accordingly the results of the ways and means committee's deliberations were passed on to the legislation committee for their approval. The committee on legislation had lain virtually dormant since the outbreak of war, but it now came to life again under the chairmanship of Charles Fullerton, D.L.S., O.L.S., who was then superintendent of colonization roads in the Department of Public Works. The committee approved the changes to the Land Surveyors Act proposed by the ways and means committee and came up with some amendments of their own. The association should be given the power to suspend members six years or more in arrears with their fees. And the association should be empowered to discipline members for unprofessional conduct. All except the last would be approved by the legislature within the year – the association would have to fight for that power for another twenty years.

Meanwhile the first reunion for veterans of the association had been held in 1916. Organized by Willis Chipman, with his unfailing sense of history, it was a luncheon to which all members of thirty years'

standing were invited. Thirty-three members were present, eight of whom had been licensed prior to Confederation. Chairing that first veterans' get-together was Charles Unwin, whose licence dated back to 1852. In his latter years, Unwin had confined himself to municipal work in the Toronto area. Following Villiers Sankey's resignation as Toronto's city surveyor in 1905, Unwin succeeded him until he, too, resigned in 1910, though he was still acting as a consultant to the city when he died in 1918 at the age of eighty-eight, two years after he presided at the veterans' luncheon.

Also present on that historic occasion was George Kirkpatrick, whose licence dated back to 1863. Not long retired because of ill-health from the position of director of surveys, which he had held since 1878, Kirkpatrick was eighty-one at the time of the reunion and would die a year later. In the words of his biographer (almost certainly Chipman), "In the death of Mr. Kirkpatrick, the Association of Ontario Land Surveyors loses its best friend, and the Province of Ontario one of its most trusted and capable officials. Through his long service as Director of Surveys he

acquired a knowledge of the early history of surveys and explorations in the Province, possessed by no other professional man."

Kirkpatrick had been succeeded as director of surveys by Lewis Rorke, then fifty-one. Interestingly enough, Rorke continued to act as secretary-treasurer of the association, of which he would be elected president in 1925. And three years after that he would be appointed surveyor general of the province when that long dormant post was revived in 1928.

The veterans' reunion that Chipman had organized was pronounced a great success and "will no doubt become an annual function." As indeed it did.

Forty-five, or about a fifth, of the entire active membership of the association served overseas in the Great War of 1914–18. Making allowances for those members too old to enlist, the proportion of eligible men who saw active service would work out to be much higher. Five Ontario Land Surveyors were killed in action. Others returned disabled. Of the many students who had joined up and their subsequent fate, there were little or no records kept. However, in his presidential address to the annual meeting of 1915, Edward Wilkie read out a letter from one articled student, a Kenneth Campbell, then serving with the artillery in France. It was written, as Wilkie put it, to "one of his late office chums": "Please jog Mr. Wilkie's memory about my O.L.S.," Campbell had asked, "I think under the circumstances the association might let the odd months slide and let me write my finals when I get back. I'm not over here on any giddy pleasure trip." Killed in action, Campbell never did get back to write his finals.

Quite a Complicated Corporate History

Getting on for a century old at the time of writing, one of Toronto's oldest surveying firms, that of Unwin, Murphy & Esten, Ltd., was formed in 1899 and has a corporate history perhaps more tortuous then most. Let's start with Charles Unwin, mentioned elsewhere. Unwin went into partnership with Vernon Wadsworth in the early 1880s. With the departure of Wadsworth and the appearance on the scene of Harry Browne and Villiers Sankey, Wadsworth & Unwin turned into Unwin, Browne & Sankey. Following which, Unwin took on Frederick Foster as his partner.

Enter Charles Murphy, born in Toronto in 1863. He had articled with Villiers Sankey and in the successive offices of Wadsworth & Unwin and Unwin, Browne and Sankey. After obtaining his licence in 1886, Murphy went into partnership with Clement Hanning and Henry Esten to form a firm known as Hanning, Murphy & Esten.

Harry Esten was the son of James Esten, who, as recounted elsewhere, was a surveyor who gave up surveying for the law. Henry, his son, was articled to Charles Unwin and then, having become an Ontario Land Surveyor in 1887, went into partnership with Clement Hanning and Charles Murphy, as noted above. Hanning retired in 1891, whereupon (we are almost there) what was now Murphy and Esten got together with Unwin's firm – which was by then Unwin & Foster – to form a new firm called Unwin, Foster, Murphy & Esten. Foster died in 1899, to leave only Unwin, Murphy & Esten – the firm that is still very much in business today – though no Unwins, Murphys, or Estens are now connected with it.

NAMES OF SURVEYORS IN VETERAN GROUP PHOTO

1.—Charles Unwin.	2.—Thomas Burns.	3.—Henry Smith.	4.—George B. Kirkpatrick.	5.—John D. Evans.
6.—Vernon B. Wandsworth.	7.—Maurice Gaviller.	8.—Hugh D. Lumsden.	9.—Elihu Stewart.	10.—Frank L. Blake.
11.—John Fair.	12.—Richard P. Fairbairn.	13.—George Ross.	14.—Willis Chipman.	15.—Thomas Fawcett.
16.—Charles A. Jones.	17.—Thomas B. Speight.	19.—Alfred P. Walker.	20.—Frederick F. Miller.	21.—James F. Whitson.
22.—Henry King Wicksteed.	23.—Henry L. Esten.	24.—James Hutcheon.		25.—Edward T. Wilkie.

The first veterans' reunion, 1916.

CHAPTER NINETEEN

Between the Wars

Of the 616 560 men and women who served in the Canadian armed services during the First World War, over 242 000 came from Ontario. By the war's end, one in ten was in uniform. As the war drew to a close, the Ontario government gave a great deal of thought to the rehabilitation of ex-service men and women. The closing of munitions plants also threw many out of work.

It seemed a good moment to return to the task of luring settlers to northern Ontario. A Settlers Loan Commission had already been set up in 1916 to lend money to northern settlers at low interest rates, with their farms, goods, and chattels as security. In 1917 the Returned Soldiers and Sailors Settlement Act was passed, whereby veterans were given free grants of land, although unlike the similar and largely ineffective scheme undertaken after the Boer War, there were, very sensibly, settlement duties to perform. Under the act, six 9-mile-square (14-km-square) townships were set aside for veterans in the vicinity of Kapuskasing, where an internment camp had been established near what was then simply a station on the National Intercontinental Railway.

Feeling no doubt that charity should begin closer to home, the sixty Ontario Land Surveyors who attended the annual meeting in 1919 (the first since the cessation of hostilities) drew up a resolution outlining a scheme to settle soldier-farmers on 20-acre lots in the older parts of the province. A copy was sent to the prime minister. Nothing came of this imaginative idea, but much the same type of scheme would be implemented after the Second World War.

Certainly the war was still very much in the minds of members at that first meeting after the war – one of the six papers presented was by Lieutenant J.H. McKnight, O.L.S., D.L.S., who wrote it in hospital where he was recovering from gas-inflicted injuries. The paper had, of course, to be read for him.

In his presidential address, Herbert Beatty paid tribute to members who had served overseas and to those who had been killed, and then observed that "the old days of a surveyor making his living by establishing and defining the boundaries of parcels of land have practically passed away." For the land surveyor there were new priorities. "At present," he said, "the most important programme to which our government has committed itself is that of road building ... [for which] surveyors are peculiarly fitted."[1]

And there was an urgent need both for re-establishing township boundaries and for permanent monumentation. He suggested that the association should take the lead in forming a Dominion Surveyors' Institute, by which the various provincial associations and that of the Dominion could keep in touch with one another. Finally, the association should espouse the cause of town planning.

In 1914 the federal Commission of Conservation had appointed Thomas Adams, a Scottish land surveyor and one of the leading exponents of town planning in the United Kingdom, as its town planning adviser. Adams proved to be as enthusiastic an evangelist for town planning as "Good Roads" Campbell had been for more and better roads, and before long the Town Planning Institute of Canada came into being on an informal basis.

By 1917 most of the provinces had enacted legislation of one sort or another on town planning, some mandatory, as in Saskatchewan, and some permissive, as in Ontario. In the latter, the City and Suburbs Plans Act had been passed in 1912, primarily for the purpose of exercising a measure of control over the hitherto entirely unrestricted right of a landowner to subdivide his property how and when he liked. This was followed by the Planning and Development Act of 1917. However, neither act had anything to say about zoning areas for different uses. Nor did they make it mandatory for municipalities to control development by means of a duly constituted town plan.

In 1919 the Association of Dominion Land Surveyors formed a committee on town planning. For once, the Association of Ontario Land Surveyors was ahead of its Dominion brethren, having set up a similar committee in 1918. Its leading proponent and first enthusiastic chairman was English-born Tracy Le May, city surveyor for Toronto, where from 1912 to 1930 planning was entrusted to the City Surveyor's Office (itself merely a branch of the Municipal Assessment Office). Having drawn the association's attention to some of the inconsistencies between the City and Suburbs Plans Act and the Planning and Development Act, Le May suggested that the association should urge the legislature to amend the latter.

The amendments were accepted, but, as Le May reported in 1919, "It was ... found impossible to secure the inclusion in the Act, of those sections making the delimitations of a Town Planning Zone, and the preparation of a general plan obligatory upon all municipalities, owing principally to the difficulty of enforcement." In the absence of mandatory legislation, what was needed, Le May urged, was "missionary work" to impress upon municipalities the advantages of town planning. And what better missionaries than members of the association, who were all too well acquainted with the result of haphazard development?

It was no doubt due to Le May, elected president of the association in 1920, that town planning was the principal theme of the annual meeting of 1921, with two of the four papers read being devoted to the subject. However, while the association did its best in the next two decades to promote town planning with particular emphasis on zoning, it was to be an uphill struggle. The chairmen of successive town-planning committees in the 1920s and 1930s noted a growing enthusiasm for town planning in other countries and other parts of Canada, but a continuing reluctance on the part of municipalities in Ontario to undertake it.

Tracy Le May himself soon became widely known as a fervent proselyte of town planning. Toronto had an Advisory City Planning Commission by 1929, but with its suggestions rejected by the public it made little headway – though it did manage to impose architectural standards for the buildings along University Avenue, and in so doing contributed to whatever pretensions to stateliness that avenue has today. In the early 1930s, the City Surveyor's Office expanded to become the Department of City Surveying and Planning, but it was to be 1942 before the Toronto City Planning Board was established. As for Le May himself, he would become vice-president of the Town Planning Institute of Canada in 1953.

To return to that first postwar meeting of 1919, it was also Le May who chaired a special committee of the association to consider the question of permanent monumentation. His committee recommended 2-by-2-inch stakes and 1/2-inch-square iron bars for subdivision and general urban work. For township corners and other important points and stations, the committee recommended stone or reinforced concrete monuments, 5 inches square at the top, 8 inches square at the base. For less important stations 1-by-1-inch iron bars should be used and in the case of solid rock, a 1-inch bolt should be cemented or leaded into the rock.

At the same time, James Dobie reported for a separate committee set up to consider permanent monumentation in northern Ontario. They recommended that in all "nine mile" townships where road allowances had been laid out, monuments similar to those used by the Department of the Interior on surveys for the Dominion government be used, with posts planted at the northeast corner of every section or block. Three-foot-square (1-m-square) pits should be dug wherever the posts were planted, placed so that "a straight line will pass through the post and diagonally through each pit, the post being midway between the pits."[2] Wooden posts should be planted beside each iron monument and at lot corners opposite road allowances. No posts should be planted in the centre of road allowances. Both sets of recom-

Tracy Le May led the association's efforts to introduce sound planning laws in Ontario. Courtesy: AOLS Archives

mendations would be incorporated in the Land Surveys Act – Le May's in the act of 1920; Dobie's in a later one.

Bringing the members up to date on topographical surveying at that first meeting after the war, Charles Biggar, the Dominion astronomer and chairman of what was now the committee on topographical and exploratory surveys, summarized the progress made by the Department of Militia and Defence before and during the war. Military mapping had now progressed to the point that 1-inch-to-the-mile maps with 25-foot contours had now been published covering an area of some 25 400 square miles (65 800 km²) along the nation's frontier in Ontario, Quebec, and Nova Scotia, and work was in progress on another 5000 square miles of territory.

The International Boundary Commission, Biggar continued, was making a topographical survey of an approximate half-mile-wide belt along the international boundary along the Pigeon River in Quebec and New Brunswick. He went on to describe the mapping being carried out in Alberta by the Irrigation Branch of the Department of the Interior, while the Geological Survey of Canada had been engaged in the delimitation of the interprovincial boundary between Alberta and B.C.

In the discussion that followed Biggar's report, Le May brought up the subject of city triangulation, in other words, the application of the triangulation and other work carried out in southern Ontario by the Geodetic Survey of Canada to towns and cities. Biggar then mentioned that the Geodetic Survey had hopes of using the spire of what is now Old City Hall in Toronto as a triangulation station, but it was found to move too much in the wind, and when it wasn't windy it moved with changes in temperature. He then let fall that the Geodetic Survey was carrying out a certain amount of secondary transit work on behalf of various cities and had established monuments. Montreal had already applied to have such work done, as had Toronto,[3] Ottawa, and London.

Nothing more was heard of the committee on topographical surveying and exploration until 1921 when the committee was then taken over by John W. Pierce of Peterborough. Born in Eaton Corner, Quebec, in 1885, Pierce was a student in electrical engineering at the University of Toronto when, in the summer of 1906, he worked for James Fitzgerald, Jr., as a chainman. Becoming interested in land surveying, he went on to become both a Dominion and Ontario Land Surveyor in 1909. In 1920 he was commissioned a Manitoba Land Surveyor.

Pierce's report to the association in 1922 mentions among other things that the Geodetic Survey had started on a topographical survey of London, Ontario, in 1921. The Geodetic Survey supplied the equipment and technical personnel, while the city bore most of the costs. In the event, the survey of London would take six years to complete and, as far as the Geodetic Survey was concerned, was an experiment that would not be repeated. The idea of supplying geodetic control to cities would lie fallow until the 1950s.

Pierce's 1922 report to the association was in fact read by a member of his committee as he was at that juncture engaged in his second season of work on the Ontario-Manitoba boundary, a survey that was not only of interest in itself, but because it was the first major survey in Ontario in which aircraft and aerial surveys played a part – albeit a minor one (see figure 13.2).

Wars have always been the forcing-house of scientific invention and the development of new technologies, some of which have revolutionized surveying. As we have seen, the Anglo-French wars did much towards hastening the development of the chronometer and the sextant. The Second World War would bring advances in electronics and methods of ranging that would eventually lead to the virtual disappearance of the transit. The Great War drew surveyors' attention to the possibility of putting aerial photography and topographic mapping to civilian use.

An early attempt to form a Canadian Aviation Corps (with three men) came to nothing when its one and only, second-hand, U.S.-made aircraft was damaged in transit to England and one of the three men was killed in training. Thereafter the only option for air-minded Canadians was to serve with the Royal Flying Corps or Royal Naval Air Service – and some 22 000 Canadians did so. Others had served in the Royal Canadian Air Service, which, equipped with fly-

John W. Pierce worked on Ontario-Manitoba boundary surveys in 1921/22, 1929/30, and 1937/38. He was the first surveyor in the province to use aerial photos.
Courtesy: AOLS Archives

ing boats, had been formed late in 1918 to combat U-boats off the east coast.

Immediately after the war, a distinctive Canadian Air Force was formed, though almost as immediately disbanded. In 1919, however, the British government turned over $5 million worth of aircraft and equipment to Canada, whereupon the Canadian Air Force was re-established in 1920, to be renamed the Royal Canadian Air Force in 1923.

French-born Edouard G. Deville was commissioned a provincial land surveyor in Quebec in 1877 and was appointed surveyor general of Canada in 1885. He directed many of the surveys in the western provinces, pioneered the use of photography in surveying, and was one of the first to realize the important role that aerial photography could play in land surveying. Courtesy: AOLS Archives

Meanwhile, in 1919 an Air Board had been established in Canada to handle matters aeronautical, both civil and military. Thus, the war's end found Canada in an excellent position to venture into the field of aerial surveying, with an administrative infrastructure already in place and with no lack of trained pilots or aircraft, including flying boats that were ideal, at least in summer, for work in the Far North and northwest.

Canada also had, in Edouard Deville, a Dominion surveyor general who had pioneered the use of (horizontal) photography in surveys of the Rocky Mountains in the late 1880s and had written a book on the subject in 1889 called *Photographic Surveying,* subsequently published by the government in 1895.[4] As early as 1918, Deville was at the forefront of air-photography trials carried out in co-operation with the Canadian Naval Air Service. And a year later when the Air Board was formed, an Air Survey Committee chaired by Deville was set up to work with the board. The first experimental aerial survey was made in 1920 in the Ottawa area using Bristol Fighters. Dominion Land Surveyors acted as photographers and navigators.

And that same year, in order to expedite the use of aerial surveying, an interdepartmental conference was held in Ottawa, attended by members of the Air Board, the superintendent of the Geodetic Survey of Canada, and the head of the Topographical Surveys Branch of the Department of the Interior.

Meanwhile one of the pilots attached to the Air Board had drawn the attention of the Ontario Department of Lands and Forests to the possibility of using aircraft for topographical surveying and fire-spotting. This had led to four trial flights, which were made in 1920 from Remi Lake, near Kapuskasing, to James Bay and back, using a flying boat. Edward Ireson, O.L.S., from Toronto, acted as an observer. Encouraged by the amount of information that Ireson brought back, the department mounted a more exten-

Aerial camera mounted in the forward cockpit of a Vickers Viking flying-boat, photo taken in 1924 in northern Ontario.

© Her Majesty the Queen in Right of Canada with permission of the Minister of Supply and Services Canada, 1991.

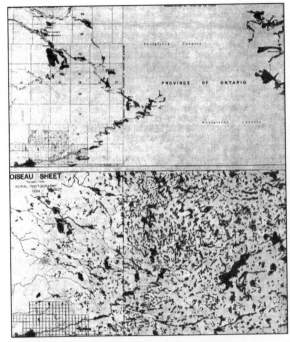

Maps before and after advent of aerial photography
Remarkable example of the advances in mapping made possible by aerial photography. Map of an area in the northwest before the advent of aerial photography (above) and (below) the same area after aerial photography in 1924. (From Pierce, *Adaptation of Aerial Photographs to Surveys and Maps*, 1925.)

sive and systematic experiment the following year using three flying boats loaned by the Air Board. The object was to map different forest types in northwestern Ontario. Two ex-service foresters acted as the mapping team, or, to be more precise, sketching team. The method was as yet crude, with forest types later deduced from oblique photographs taken of the terrain. Even so, the experiment was a resounding success with some 200 000 square miles (500 000 km²) of territory covered between Lake Nipigon and the Manitoba boundary in 1920 and 1921.

In the latter year, one of the foresters reported a forest fire burning in the Sioux Lookout District on the aircraft's return – the first instance of an aircrew detecting a forest fire. In 1922 more aircraft were assigned to fire detection work, and it was primarily with fire detection in mind that the Ontario Provincial Air Service was created in 1924.

As mining activity east of Lake Winnipeg intensified after the war, it became a matter of urgency to take the Ontario-Manitoba boundary farther north. With Manitoba once more refusing to contribute its share, the Dominion and Ontario went it alone. Deville and Rorke, surveyors general for the Dominion and Ontario respectively, were appointed boundary commissioners, agreeing between them that the boundary should be extended to the latitude of the Twelfth Base Line, an east-west line run in Manitoba by Dominion Land Surveyors, that is to say, another 180 miles (290 km) north from where Elihu Stewart and Bryce Saunders had left it in 1897 (see figure 13.2). They decided that a single, carefully selected survey party would suffice, with the cost shared equally between the Dominion and Ontario.

John Pierce led the party. Two other qualified surveyors, Robert Davidson of Alliston and John Carrol of Ottawa, acted as Pierce's senior and junior assistants respectively. Receiving his instructions on 7 March 1921 and working out of Winnipeg, Pierce moved quickly to make the most of what was left of the winter snow to transport to the line the 10 tons of provisions required, along with the camp outfit, instruments, and cement for the monuments. He used horses to haul the loads along such snow-covered roads as there were, and dogsleds along trails when the roads gave out.

A party of twenty-four men were hired in Winnipeg, particular care being taken to select the monument builder "not so much," to use Pierce's own words, "in regard to his ability as his dependability, and to impress on him the importance of his duty and

the necessity that this work be made permanent as well as of pleasing appearance."[5]

Work in the field began on 6 June from the mark left by Stewart and Saunders – which was found to be in poor condition and was eventually replaced by a cement monument – and went on until mid-October, at which time about 70 miles (110 km) of the line had been run. During the winter, supplies were brought in and two main caches established, while a rapid exploratory chain and compass traverse was made of that portion of the boundary still to be run, with the result that the rate of progress during the summer of 1922 was double that of the previous year. Where the boundary line crossed a lake, the line's length and position was determined by traverses and local triangulation.

The number and size of lakes came as an unpleasant surprise to the survey party – it being remembered that the territory they were passing through was virtually unknown. Said Pierce: "So extended did this network of water become that it frequently became a difficulty to know when to stop traversing."[6] Getting around the lakes involved over 1100 miles (1700 km) of traversing, which on average meant over 6 miles of traverse line for every mile of boundary line cut.

It seems that it was because of the number of lakes encountered during the 1921–22 season that it occurred to Pierce that, had he been able to examine aerial photographs of the region before starting the survey and seen how many lakes he would encounter, he would have been much better prepared for what was coming. And so, before starting on the second season's work, he approached the Air Board and invited their co-operation.

Such photos as were produced were limited in both extent and quality. They were, however, in Pierce's words, "sufficient to demonstrate the possibilities of aerial photographs ... in regard to the preparation of topographical maps." And, in the first instance of direct assistance to surveyors in the field, on 3 July 1922, a flying boat flew in to one of the survey camps

On Transits

It was said that Edouard Deville, the Dominion surveyor general, had a marked preference for British-made, as opposed to American-made, transits. Not only that, he rated those made by T. Cooke and Sons Limited over transits manufactured by that firm's major rival, Troughton and Simms, both based in London, England. In consequence, Cooke transits tended to become standard equipment for Dominion Land Surveyors, not a few of whom were also Ontario Land Surveyors. Early in the twentieth century, Deville suddenly switched his allegiance to transits made by yet another English firm, that of E.R. Watts, though he would later take against this firm also.

Meanwhile in Europe, Heinrich Wild and Carl Zeiss each produced new transits. These transits differed markedly from anything seen before, with both horizontal and vertical circles so placed as to allow readings to be taken through a small micrometer telescope placed near the eyepiece of the telescope. These new transits were not only more accurate than other makes of comparable size but were almost half the weight.

In 1921 Wild's Swiss firm of Wild Heerbrugg Ltd. brought out a second model, known as the T2 transit. This was the first Wild transit to reach Canada after the war. Working with a T2 Wild transit, John Rannie, D.T.S., then working with the Geodetic Survey of Canada, realized that the small aperture of the telescope militated against its use in first-order geodetic work. It was largely at his suggestion that the T3 Wild instrument incorporated a larger telescope.

---

and delivered a load of mail, along with the Dominion controller of surveys, who stayed with Pierce and his survey party for four days before being flown out again.

With active work on the line beginning again in the spring of 1922, the latitude corresponding to that of the Twelfth Base Line was finally reached in October of that year. The entire length of the 180-mile (290-km) line was opened up to a sky-line width of 6 feet (2 m), which in practice meant the cutting of a swathe through the forest up to 30 feet wide – no small task. A preliminary line was produced with the venerable 5-inch Cooke transit, while the final alignment of the line was made with a "6 inch reiterating transit of the Block survey type, commonly known as a base line transit."

Final measurements on the ground were made with a steel tape, kept taut in the first season's work by a straining bar, in the second by a 30-pound (14-kg) weight attached to each end. Temperature readings taken at the time of measurement allowed corrections to be made to distances as given by the steel tape. Concrete monoliths marking the boundary were built every 6 miles on average, using hardwood forms brought in for the purpose and using local gravel to mix the concrete. Brass plates, suitably engraved and enamelled with the name and crest of the province, were bolted to the appropriate sides of the monoliths. Standard rock posts or monuments were built between them. Added to the 58 miles, 27.20 chains surveyed by Stewart and Saunders, the total length of the meridian section of the Ontario-Manitoba boundary amounted to 238 miles, 10.37 chains. No further work would be done on the boundary for another seven years.

In 1918, the last year of the war, seven Ontario Land Surveyors were certified to practise. The number then fell in 1919 and 1920, only to rise again to nine in 1921, ten in 1922, and fifteen in 1923, as those students who had served in the armed forces finally got around to sitting for their finals. With this backlog cleared, however, the number of newly licensed Ontario Land Surveyors fell to a trickle. The next six years, up to and including 1929 – the year that the Wall Street stock market crash ushered in the Great Depression – only twenty men entered the profession.

Thereafter, with the Depression deepening and survey work increasingly hard to come by, the number of men qualifying declined still further. From 1930 to 1939 inclusive, only thirty-six men entered the profession, an average of less than four per year in the ten-year period. Small wonder then, that the years of reconstruction that followed the Second World War would find the province in desperate need of land surveyors.

However, the years between the wars saw some significant changes within the profession. These were largely due to the wise and energetic leadership provided by Speight, Rorke, and Le May. Following George Kirkpatrick's death in 1917, Thomas Speight succeeded him both as chairman of the Board of Examiners and as chairman of the Council of Management, which positions Speight held until his retirement in 1929 when he was succeeded by Louis Rorke, who by this time had been appointed surveyor general when that long dormant office was revived in 1928. (See appendix B.) In the meantime, Rorke had stayed on as secretary-treasurer until 1923 when he was succeeded by Le May, who would remain in that post until 1935 – when it would once again revert to Rorke on his retirement as surveyor general.

In the immediate postwar years, the roster of subjects covered in the final examinations was overhauled. Botany and forest flora were dropped and options were introduced, with a candidate offered a choice of three out of six subjects, these being: the Mining Act; the Municipal Drainage Act; the Ditches and Watercourses Act; the principles and methods of highway construction; the method of calculating the horse power of rivers and streams; and the rudiments of geology and mineralogy. Pass marks in the finals were reduced from an unrealistic 70 percent to a more reasonable 60 percent. And in 1923, council also recommended the introduction of an intermediate examination covering mathematics and the ever-widening field of legislation affecting land surveyors. The necessary legislative amendments covering these changes passed into law in 1924. Another proposal, that the preliminary examination be abolished and that school matriculation be accepted in its place, would not be implemented until 1931. Meanwhile, in 1927 the association drew up a Code of Ethics (see sidebar on page 286).

In 1923 the association issued its first modern surveyor's manual. And about this time, the association subscribed to *The Journal of the D.L.S. Association*,[7] which would later be renamed – at John W. Pierce's suggestion – *The Canadian Surveyor*.

Meanwhile, in 1922 a move was made to make women feel more welcome at annual meetings. Wives and guests were invited to listen to a talk on the cities and transportation systems of Brazil and Venezuela given by a civil engineer who had spent some time in South America. It doesn't sound to be the most enthralling of subjects, but at least women got their feet in the door. This led to the formation of the first Ladies' Committee, which organized a program for the 1924 meeting that included a visit to a museum, a "motor ride" around Toronto, a play at the Princes Theatre, and an evening reception at the Engineers' Club, where the women were greeted by the president's wife, Mrs. Herbert Routly. In 1925, following a function at the Grange and a visit to the Toronto Art Gallery, a Ladies Auxiliary was formed at an afternoon tea at the Prince George Hotel, presided over by Mrs. George Abrey. From that year on, the Ladies Auxiliary would play a regular role in the organization of annual meetings.

The association continued to hold its annual meeting at the Engineers' Club until 1927. In 1928 the venue was changed to the Prince George Hotel and then the King Edward Hotel. From 1931 until the outbreak of the Second World War, it was held at the Royal York.

The committee on legislation had been working on

revisions to the Surveys Act of 1914 throughout the Great War. The result was a much more streamlined and succinct act. As befitting the times, the Surveys Act of 1920 (10 & 11, Geo. 5, c. 48) had much to say about road allowances, resurveys, and permanent monumentation of the same. It tightened up provisions relating to road allowances with such posts and boundaries as planted or placed in the original survey being "true and unalterable." And the same was to apply to resurveys of road allowances made under the Registry Act or Land Titles Act, as well as to subdivisions and resurveys of the land itself, in connection with which the type of monumentation required was also specified, with the recommendations of Le May's committee on permanent monumentation adopted virtually *in toto*. Ontario Land Surveyors, in the course of their work, were now empowered not just to pass over private land but to enter any buildings as well, "at a time suitable to the rightful occupant of such building."

The Surveys Act of 1927 contained minor revisions of the substance of the 1920 act. Four years later, in 1931, there were some minor amendments (21 Geo. 5, c. 42) to the act, which provided among other things that within six months of the death of a surveyor, his field notes and records must be lodged with the minister of lands and forests unless they had already been placed in the custody of a surveyor in active practice – something that the association had been advocating for many years. The association's committee on legislation then passed out of existence until the mid-1950s.

Following the formation of the Association of Professional Engineers of Ontario in 1922, the engineering committee, with its long and faltering history, finally got swallowed up by a committee on engineering, roads, and pavements, which kept the members up to date on the progress of road construction in the province. By 1919 there were some 400 miles (700 km) of provincial highways in southern Ontario. What became Highway 2 had been completed from the York

County line to the Ontario-Quebec boundary. Another highway linked Ottawa with Prescott, and a third ran westerly from the Niagara River to London. Also various trunk roads were being built in northern Ontario.

Helped by the Canada Highway Improvement Act, which Campbell had got through the Commons in 1919, Ontario's provincial highway system expanded rapidly. By 1923 there were nearly 2000 miles (3000 km) of surfaced roads in the province. The Department of Public Highways published their first road maps in that year, and a couple of years later the first tax was put on gasoline to help pay for it all. It was 3 cents a gallon. By then, registration fees on vehicles ranged from $31 for a 4-cylinder car to $41 for an 8-cylinder – pretty hefty amounts for those days. Two years after that, in 1927, came the first driver's licence, over 444 000 of which were issued at $1 apiece.

In 1927, what was known as the Ferguson Highway was completed, a fulfilment of an election promise by George Ferguson, an enthusiast of northern expansion. It ran north to Cochrane via Gravenhurst, Bracebridge, Huntsville, Sundridge, North Bay, Cobalt, New Liskeard, and Englehart. In 1937 it became part of Highway 11. By 1930 a number of other trunk roads had been completed in northern Ontario, including the Fort Frances–Rainy River Road and another running west from Fort Frances to the Manitoba border. The International Highway between Port Arthur and Duluth had been completed as early as 1920, as had a trunk road between Sault Ste. Marie and Sudbury, with Sudbury soon linked with North Bay. Yet another trunk road linked North Bay with Pembroke.

What with the difficulty of attracting settlers to northern Ontario – and keeping them there – and the general slowdown of government survey work during the war, few new townships were completed and

released for settlement during the war years: six in 1915, seven in 1916, six in 1917, and only two in 1918. As the vision of a Great Clay Belt peopled from end to end with thriving farmers gradually faded, the number of new townships subdivided or completed for those purposes dwindled to nothing in the decade or so following the Great War. Of the twenty or so new townships surveyed in northern Ontario, most were of the old 640-acre sectional, Pattern 3 type. The last

View down a meridian line. Trees on such a line have to be felled to a sufficient width to allow celestial observations to be made.

three 9-mile-square townships, those of Caron, Horden, and Moose in the vicinity of Moosonee, were surveyed in 1932.

Not long after that the township system was abandoned altogether – at least as a means of land settlement. However, the outlining of unorganized townships would go forward, either in connection with mining activities or, at least at the eastern end of northern Ontario, simply to complete the survey fabric. In connection with these, the laying down of base and meridian lines continued, principally as tie lines or, as mining activities in the northwest intensified, as lines upon which to erect townships in connection with such activities (see figure 12.1).

The war years had seen Edwin Phillips and his business partner, Frederick Benner, both of what was then still Port Arthur, running a base line from the southeast angle of Ledger Township, south of Lake Nipigon, to the Algoma–Thunder Bay boundary that had been surveyed by Speight and Niven in 1902. Some 120 miles (190 km) long, it was completed by Phillips and Benner in 1917. They then went on, between 1918 and 1920, to run the southern portion of what became known as the First Meridian, this due north from the southern end of Eaglehead Lake, some 40 miles north of present-day Thunder Bay. The northern portion of this meridian would not be completed until 1952, when Phillips and Gavin extended it north to the Asheweig River, north of the fifty-third parallel.

Meanwhile, after the war, the Third Meridian, which formed the boundary between the districts of Thunder Bay and Kenora, was continued northward in 1919 by James Dobie to a point some 50 miles (90 km) north of Lake St. Joseph, from which point he started to run a base line westward. A year later, Kenneth Ross of the Soo would extend this base line (the eleventh) eastward to the Thunder Bay–Cochrane district boundary line north of the Albany and westward to the Manitoba border. And in that same year,

Speight & van Nostrand's base line of 1903 was also extended both east and west, Norman MacRostie taking it westward and Herbert Beatty taking it eastward to the Ontario-Quebec boundary. Between 1921 and 1925, Ross would lay down four more base lines of varying length, the Third, Fourth, Fifth, and Sixth, though not in that order, while in 1923 Phillips & Benner ran the Second Meridian, on and to the west of which a range of townships in connection with mining activities would be surveyed south of Lake St. Joseph. And in 1925, Speight & van Nostrand ran a meridian that formed the southern portion of the boundary between the district of Kenora and the district of Cochrane, which had been created three years earlier.

The survey season of 1926 was memorable because, for the first time, aerial photographs, where such were available, were supplied as a matter of course to land surveyors before they took to the field. Speight & van Nostrand ran the Ninth Base Line from the 72-mile post on the Third Meridian that Ross had run in 1920, with meridian lines run north and south in the vicinity of Woman and Red lakes, with the base line intersecting the latter. Both lakes were centres of gold-mining activity, in connection with which 6-mile-square townships would be erected. The base line was continued west to the meridian section of the Ontario-Manitoba boundary, which had been surveyed four years earlier. Working from the 96-mile post on the Third Meridian, 24 miles to the north, Beatty and Beatty (two brothers: Herbert John and Frank Weldon)[8] ran part of the Tenth Base Line east to cross Birch Lake, another centre of mining activity, with meridians again run north and south at 12-mile intervals. Later, Phillips and Benner would take the Tenth Base Line east to intersect the Second Meridian in the vicinity of Pickle Lake, where two isolated 6-mile-square townships would be erected.

While surveyors were being supplied with highly useful aerial photos, the Department of Lands and Forests for its part had ordered that, where base and meridian lines intersected shorelines on certain lakes, the lines be opened well up to make them clearly visible from the air. In other words, the department was waking up to the fact that by co-operating with the RCAF, then engaged in mapping work for the Topographic Surveys of Canada, aerial photos of the unexplored parts of northern Ontario could be obtained at a low cost.[9]

Accordingly, a long-term program was embarked on to lay down principal control lines to which traverses could be tied as the aerial mapping of the north went forward. Niven's Meridian, run in 1896 and 1898, which formed the boundary between the old districts of Nipissing and Algoma, would be retraced and opened up. The Ontario-Quebec boundary would be completed, and the portion of it run earlier would be retraced. A base line would be run clear across northern Ontario from the boundary with Quebec on the east to the Manitoba boundary on the west.

It so happened that in the fall of 1926 gold had been discovered in the vicinity of Savant Lake, northwest of Lake Nipigon. It was decided to outline townships in the area. A base line upon which to erect such townships was required, and it was decided that this base line – the Seventh – should be the one that would be extended across the province in connection with aerial mapping work. Accordingly, instructions were issued in 1927 to run the Seventh Base Line both east and west on 6-mile chords from the 24-mile post on the meridian line run by Dobie in 1919 (the Third Meridian, which marked the boundary between the districts of Thunder Bay and Kenora) in the approximate latitude of 50°24'N.

In 1927 the base line was run west by Phillips & Benner for about 120 miles (193 km), which took it to Lac Seul, while Beatty and Beatty took it east some 115 miles to a point north of Lake Nipigon. The next season, the base line was extended westward to the Ontario-Manitoba boundary line and eastward to the meridian line marking the Thunder Bay–Cochrane

district line. By the end of the 1928 season, the Seventh Base Line had been run roughly halfway across northern Ontario.

In 1929 the Seventh Base Line was extended eastward another 53 miles (85 km) to the old districts of Thunder Bay and Algoma, at which point the line was shifted north a few miles so that it could conform to the southern boundary of the 9-mile-square townships already laid out at the eastern end of Cochrane District. Taken east again in 1930 and 1931, and now on 9-mile instead of 6-mile chords, the Seventh Base Line reached the Ontario-Quebec boundary in the latter year. The only base line to run right across the province, its total length was measured at 690 miles, 6.03 chains (just over 1100 km).[10] In the same year that the Seventh Base Line was completed, Niven's Meridian was rerun and opened up, which the Surveys Branch had envisaged as being the second principal control line in connection with the Dominion's aerial mapping program.

The completion and rerunning of the third major control line, the Ontario-Quebec boundary, commenced in 1930. Shirley King, O.L.S., and Jean-Marie Roy, Q.L.S., acting for Ontario and Quebec respectively, extended the interprovincial boundary another 68 miles from the point where Patten and Sullivan had left it in 1906. They returned in 1931 to complete it, reaching tidewater on James Bay 269 miles, 29.50 chains, from the original point of commencement on Lake Timiskaming. They had retraced portions of the boundary as they went north, and in 1932 they returned to complete the retracement work.

In 1929, meanwhile, with the federal government preparing to hand over the natural resources of the western provinces to their respective owners and with prospectors flocking into the region traversed by the as yet unsurveyed portion of the Ontario-Manitoba boundary, thanks to the increasing availability of aerial photographs of the area, it was decided to start running further sections of that boundary. The section now to

be run was that linking the end of the Twelfth Base Line to the eastern end of Island Lake as specified in the Boundaries Extension Act of 1912.

Manitoba participated for the first time, with G.A. Warrington acting as boundary-line commissioner. The others were Louis Rorke and Frederick Peters, the surveyors general of Ontario and Canada respectively. John W. Pierce was again placed in charge of the survey party. The first step, however, was to determine the exact latitude and longitude of the terminal point of the line on Island Lake. This was carried out in June 1929 by Cecil Ney, D.L.S., of the Geodetic Survey of Canada, who, having flown to the lake in a Vickers Viking, established a temporary mark that he called "Point A." The following year, Ney, again travelling by air, established two intermediate points on the remaining leg of the boundary, and then went on to establish and monument the point on the Hudson Bay shore intersected by the meridian at longitude 89°W, the point that marked the final northern terminus of the boundary.*

Meanwhile Pierce ran a trial line from the Twelfth Base Line, which closed to within 5.1 feet (1.6 m) of Ney's "Point A," which on being made permanent became concrete monument no. 295. Thanks to aerial photos, which cut down on the amount of exploration work required, it took him only seventeen days to cover the 90 miles (145 km). The line between the end of the Twelfth Base Line and Island Lake was finalized by Pierce in the summer of 1930, and in 1932 the 1897 section of the boundary was retraced and monumented. With all this done, work on the boundary was again suspended until 1937, when a start would be made on running the final 280-mile section between Island Lake and Hudson Bay.

---

*Why the eighty-ninth meridian? It was thought this was a gesture in the direction of the historic line running due north from the junction of the Mississippi and Ohio rivers that lay at the core of earlier disputes over the position of Ontario's western boundary.

Ontario had hardly recovered from the depression that followed the First World War before the Wall Street stock market crash of 1929 heralded in the Great Depression. In 1932 the federal government passed the Relief Land Settlement Act by which the federal, provincial, and municipal governments would co-operate in a scheme to resettle families from depressed urban areas in selected townships along the main railways in the vicinity of Thunder Bay, Hearst, and Kapuskasing. Would-be settlers received a $600 grant towards the cost of transportation, land, buildings, and equipment. Some six hundred persons were eventually settled under the act, many of them from the Windsor and Toronto areas, but lacking pioneering skills, less than half were still on their land in 1939, and of these very few were still farming. With the failure of this scheme, hopes of establishing large-scale agricultural settlements in northern Ontario finally faded.

For the members of the association who gathered in Toronto for the annual meeting in 1929, however, of more immediate concern than the stock market crash was the recent death of Willis Chipman. At the Veterans' Luncheon in 1928, Louis Rorke had read a letter from Chipman regretting that, because of illness, he was unable to attend the annual meeting. He died less than a year later, on 3 January 1929. He was seventy-three. Down the years he had gained an international reputation as a waterworks and sewage engineer and in Ontario he had worked on over fifty waterworks and sewage projects, involving just about every city or town of any size in the province. Though at heart an engineer, he remained fiercely loyal to the association he had done so much to bring into being and attended *every* meeting until the one preceding his death. Keen historian as he was, he worked on his beloved biographies almost until the day he died, in all overseeing the production of 274 of them. His home in Toronto, a semi-detached brick house at 103 Spadina Avenue, now lies somewhere under a commercial building that houses ladies' wear shops.

Perhaps it was Chipman's passing, with its reminder that members of the old guard who had helped found the association were dying unhonoured, that led to the decision in 1931 to appoint Vernon B. Wadsworth as honorary president – the association's first. It will be recalled that Wadsworth had studied

Plaque on the monument in MacDonald Park in downtown Kingston commemorating the first survey post planted by John Collins in 1783. Ontario Land Surveyor C. Fraser Aylsworth was instrumental in having the monument erected in 1938.

Commemorating the Land Surveyors

John Collins may be said to have a memorial in a plaque in the city park at Kingston that marks the beginning of crown surveys in the province. Augustus Jones is honoured by a provincial plaque outside the County Court House in Brantford. Mahlon Burwell has one at the Clerk's Office in Port Burwell, which was named after him. Burwell is also remembered on a plaque 3 miles (5 km) west of St. Thomas on Highway 3. It commemorates the Talbot Road, along with Burwell and John Bostwick who surveyed the first road in 1804. Harder to find is the plaque to Charles Rankin, which stands in a small waterfront park in Thornbury. However, Rankin's name is indirectly commemorated by several other provincial plaques in Grey County.

The names of a number of land surveyors live on in other ways. Many townships were named after land surveyors, while some towns and cities have named roads after them. Unwin Avenue, for example, in Toronto's dock land is named after Charles Unwin. Howard Park Avenue, near Toronto's High Park, is named after John Howard, who gave that park to the city. In Scarborough there is a Passmore Avenue, which is named after Frederick Passmore. He is one of four land surveyors who are commemorated in Scarborough in this way. And not so long ago a street in a new development in Collingwood was named Stewart Street after Elihu Stewart.

under J. Stoughton Dennis and was with him when he made his exploratory surveys of Muskoka, Parry Sound, and Nipissing. While Wadsworth had abandoned surveying for the loan and insurance business in 1876, he had remained a faithful member of the association all his life. He would remain an honorary president of the association until his death in 1940 at the age of ninety-eight.

The committee on repository – a separate committee since 1921 – had spent most of the 1920s finding a home for the association's property, which consisted of "the nucleus of a general library ... some ancient surveying instruments and some office furniture." The instruments were offered to the Royal Ontario Museum, but they didn't want them. Finally, in 1927, room for the association's belongings was found in the Parliament Buildings, courtesy of the minister of works, and such books as remained in the Engineers' Club were also placed there. In 1929 the committee reported that some of Willis Chipman's historical material had been added to the association's library. Following this the committee on repository passed out of existence.

The standing committee on land surveying continued to confine its activities to dealing with the practical surveying conundrums submitted to it, while that on drainage had increasingly little to report as the Depression deepened – municipalities just hadn't the money for drainage work, though things started to pick up again by 1936. The mid-thirties saw the committee on town planning still reporting little interest in town planning in Ontario, and still urging the importance of zoning. If anything, town planning had lost ground during the Depression. Reporting for the committee in 1939, James MacKay attributed this to the municipal taxation system. "The only people," he added, "who can plan and really accomplish something are the engineers of the Highway Department and that is solely because they obtain their revenue elsewhere than from real estate." They obtained it, of course,

from the tax on gas and the revenue derived from car and drivers' licences.

The committee on engineering, roads and pavements had increasingly little to report as the Depression deepened and even the relatively rich Department of Highways cut back on construction work. The only bright spot in the provincial economy was the mining industry, a fact reflected by the formation in 1929 of a new committee on mining, with its chairman, Homer Sutcliffe of New Liskeard, giving his first report at the annual meeting of 1930.

The committee on topographical surveys, as it became in the early 1930s when the word "exploration" was dropped from this venerable committee's title – itself an indication of the progress made in land surveying in the province – continued to update the members on surveying and mapping across Canada. By now topographical maps were being produced by a number of agencies. Geological surveying and mapping was going forward at both the federal and provincial level, with the Ontario Department of Mines producing its own series of geological maps. Maps for forestry purposes were being produced by the Ontario Department of Lands and Forests.

At the federal level, there was the National Topographic series that was being continually expanded. In the late 1920s, the Geodetic Survey of Canada had started to use aircraft to speed up its work, using them for, among other things, flying in prefabricated towers to remote locations. Even so, the prodigious distances involved meant the work went ahead slowly, and it would not be until the 1940s that a 600-mile (970-km) gap north of Lake Superior would be closed, thus completing the first-order triangulation network from coast to coast.

Starting in 1932, under the aggressive leadership of Major E.L. Burns, head of the Geographical Section of the Department of National Defence, a start was made on compiling maps for air navigation, using a new type of stereoplotter that Burns himself had

designed in 1935 and which was built by the National Research Council. About the same time, Burns brought to Canada a Zeiss stereoplotter, which in combination with the Zeiss wide-angle-lens aerial camera was considered to be a major breakthrough in aerial map-making. Work went ahead on producing the 8-miles-to-the-inch maps of the Air Navigation Series, with the last of the 221-sheet series coming off the press in 1944.

After twenty-six years as director of surveys and latterly as surveyor general, Louis Rorke retired in 1935, to be succeeded as surveyor general by Charles Fullerton. Following his retirement, Rorke swapped offices in the association with Le May, as already mentioned, with Rorke becoming secretary-treasurer and Le May chairman of council. Rorke thus returned to the office he had held from 1912 to 1924. He remained secretary-treasurer until his death in 1943 at the age of seventy-eight. Le May apparently ran the association from his offices in City Hall, so when Rorke took over as secretary-treasurer, the association rented an office at 331 Bay Street, Toronto.

In July 1935 Elihu Stewart died at the age of ninety-one. It was Stewart, it will be recalled, who spearheaded the association's efforts in the late 1890s to have northern Ontario and its resources systematically explored, efforts which culminated in the great survey of 1900. In 1896 he had been acclaimed mayor of Collingwood, long his home town. With a lifelong interest in forestry, he had headed the Dominion Forestry Service from 1899 to 1907 and was one of the founders of the Canadian Forestry Association of which he was president for several years. He was surveying almost to the last. At the age of eighty-seven, just four years before his death, he re-established some original monuments in Nottawasaga Township.

In 1937 the association celebrated its fiftieth anniversary, with ninety-three members attending the annual meeting at the Royal York Hotel, now recognized as the usual venue. In his presidential address at this historic meeting, Herbert Anderson of North Bay noted that three land surveyors who had been present at the inaugural meeting in 1886 were still alive and on the active list: Thomas B. Speight, then aged seventy-

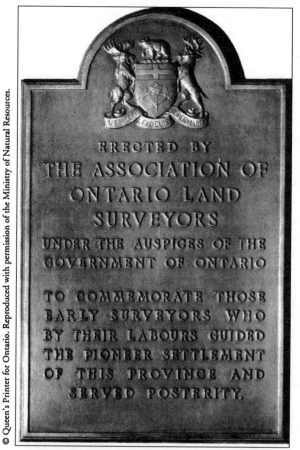

© Queen's Printer for Ontario. Reproduced with permission of the Ministry of Natural Resources.

Plaque in the Parliament Buildings, Queen's Park, unveiled by the lieutenant-governor in 1937 to commemorate the fiftieth anniversary of the the formation of the Association of Land Surveyors of Ontario, later the Association of Ontario Land Surveyors.

eight and who would live on until 1945; Clemens D. Bowman of West Montrose; and Alan G. Cavana of Orillia – with licences dating back to 1881, 1879, and 1887 respectively.

In honour of the association's fiftieth birthday, the CNR arranged an exhibit at the corner of King and Yonge streets, while at 11.30 A.M. on Wednesday, 17 February, this being the second full day of the meeting, "a large gathering of surveyors and friends" watched the lieutenant-governor unveil a plaque that had been put up by the association in the lobby of the Parliament Building on Queen's Park, this "to commemorate," to quote from the plaque (which is still there), "those early surveyors who by their labours guided the pioneer settlement of the Province and served posterity."

As in previous years, the roof garden of the Royal York was the scene of the dinner-dance – the climax of the annual meeting. The entertainment was "a little more elaborate entertainment than usual," being helped by a donation of $100 from the city of Toronto. Thus, "one hundred and twenty-one members, guests and their ladies sat down to dinner at tables tastefully decorated with flowers," the general effect being "colorful and gay." Toasts to "The King" and "Our Guests" were drunk. "A host of good wishes for future success was offered the members and their ladies." Following this (and the dinner, presumably, having been eaten), the "company then moved to the dance floor where the music of the orchestra was calling for dancing feet ... One o'clock came too soon to end another 'Great Surveyors' Ball.'"

The association's fiftieth anniversary year of 1937 also saw the decennial revision of the Surveys Act (RSO 1937, c. 232), which contained no startling changes. More importantly, the legislature passed an amendment to the Land Surveyors Act that at last gave the association the legal right to discipline its members. Thereafter, stated the relevant clause, a surveyor found guilty, after "due enquiry by a committee of the

Association ... of gross negligence or of corruption in the execution of the duties of his office, or of professional misconduct ... or where a surveyor has been convicted in Canada or elsewhere of an indictable offence,"[11] he may be reprimanded or censured by the Council of Management, be suspended for up to one year, or, in extreme cases, might be expelled from the association altogether and his licence cancelled. The amendment also specified an appeal procedure, such to involve a hearing before a judge of the Supreme Court.

The fiftieth anniversary year also saw further work on the Ontario-Manitoba boundary. By this time, the mineral resources of the area through which the boundary ran were being actively developed, and so it was decided to complete the boundary from monument no. 295 on Island Lake to the eastern end of the Eighteenth Base Line in Manitoba, laid down two years earlier by D.N. Sharpe, M.L.S.

By now the use of aircraft to transport men and supplies in this remote region had become commonplace, while the Manitoba government was already using regular commercial flights to further base and meridian line surveys in the northern part of the province. Thus, with the decision taken to carry out work on the interprovincial boundary in the winter of 1937–38, S.E. McColl, then director of surveys for Manitoba, made the momentous suggestion that the survey should rely entirely on air transport, and that dogs and dogsleds, hitherto used for the winter transport of supplies in the region, should be dispensed with altogether.

McColl's suggestion was acted on, and the survey of the 107-mile (172-km) stretch of the line between Island Lake and the end of the Eighteenth Base Line thus became the first land survey in the province to rely entirely on air transport. A Winnipeg-based company was contracted not only to fly men, supplies, and equipment to and from the survey line, but to move survey camps as required. Led as before by John W. Pierce, with Edward Gauer, M.L.S., D.L.S., as his first assistant, the seventeen-man party included a radio operator to operate a portable radio transceiver.

Partly because of the way aircraft speeded progress on the line, partly because aerial photos eased the problem of locating new campsites as the work progressed, and partly because the country became increasingly sparse as the line was taken north, the work was completed by the middle of March 1937, three weeks ahead of schedule. After running the boundary some 7 miles (11 km) north of the Eighteenth Base Line, work was brought to a halt. In contrast to earlier days, when the journey out would have involved weeks of strenuous travel on foot or by canoe, men flew back to Winnipeg and were back at home within a few hours of finishing work on the line. The 1937 survey left 168 miles of the Ontario-Manitoba boundary uncompleted. This would not be done until after the Second World War.

In his very brief presidential address to the annual meeting of 1938, Edward Cavell, O.L.S., a graduate of the School of Practical Science, noted that while "world conditions during the past year had been generally disturbing," things were looking up in Canada where there had been a gradual improvement in the economy. In Ontario this was "due largely to the output of mineral wealth in the northern districts," which, apart from anything else, had improved the lot of Ontario Land Surveyors, who had benefited not only from the many claims that needed surveying but from "the building of plants and the laying out of town sites, etc."

"The surveyors," Cavell added, "also benefit greatly from the large program of the Provincial Highways Surveys Branch, under Mr. W.J. Fullerton. There are now twenty-one Ontario Land Surveyors employed in surveys of highways and lands required for highway purposes." The "large program" referred to had suddenly got even larger when, by an order-in-council dated 27 February 1937, the Department of Northern

A surveyor in the northwest in the 1930s making a celestial observation. Courtesy: AOLS Archives

Development was amalgamated with the Department of Highways, with the latter assuming responsibility for over 2600 miles (4100 km) of roads in northern Ontario.

During that year the Queen Elizabeth Highway (QEW) was nearing completion – up to then the longest continuous divided highway in Canada. As originally designed, it featured a four-lane, 40-foot (12-m) pavement with a median varying from 3 to 10 feet, itself a novel safety measure. The cloverleaf (the first in Canada) at the intersection of this highway and Highway 10 in Port Credit, had been completed in 1937. In June 1939 the QEW would be opened by King George VI and Queen Elizabeth at a ceremony in St. Catharines, though the highway had only got as far as the western end of Niagara Falls.

It was under "New Business" at the 1938 annual meeting that John Ransom, O.L.S., D.L.S., of the Department of Highways in Toronto, created something of a stir when he moved that a multipurpose special committee be set up to investigate and improve working conditions throughout the surveying profession in Ontario. He also hoped the association could find ways to contribute to the success of the Youth Movement, whose object was to alleviate the unemployment problem then being faced by some 150 000 young people across Canada.[12]

As it happened, some seven months after the 1939 meeting, on 10 September 1939, Canada declared war on Germany. For many of the 150 000 unemployed youths – and indeed some Ontario Land Surveyors – the problem of employment was, at least temporarily, solved.

CHAPTER TWENTY

The Second World War and After

Already hard-hit by the Great Depression and its aftermath, the profession in Ontario was brought to a very low ebb indeed by the Second World War. It was fading away, it seemed, for want of new men. In 1941 only six land surveyors were granted licences, only two in 1942, and another two in 1943. In 1944 only one man sat for his finals. He failed, but was granted his licence after taking supplementals. Active membership, already declining from a high of 248 in 1935, had fallen to 222 in 1940. By 1946 it stood at 204.

At the same time, the proportion of members in private practice had been falling. In his presidential address at the annual meeting in 1941, Garnet Berkeley of St. Catharines, commissioned in 1918 and one of the few surviving graduates of the old School of Practical Science, produced some off-the-cuff statistics that showed that, of the 222 members, 90, or nearly half, were employed full time on a salary basis by the Ontario government, the Hydro-Electric Power Commission, a railway company, or another large corporation.

For a couple of years, the association went into a holding pattern. Nathaniel Burwash, president for 1941–42, commissioned in 1905, worked for what was still the Surveys Branch of the Department of Lands and Forests. He said little at the annual meeting of 1942 beyond extending a welcome to the members and commenting that "the outlook for straight land surveying work is very limited," though he noted that some members had found employment in "the war industries."[1] As far as the affairs of the association went, these were thrown into slight disarray by the sudden death, on 3 January 1943, of Louis Rorke, the secretary-treasurer, this a little over a month before the annual meeting. However, Ralph Anderson, an Ontario Land Surveyor since 1911, stepped into the breach and, with the help of Le May, produced the report required of him at the meeting. He stayed on as secretary-treasurer until 1947.

In his presidential address at that same meeting of 1943, Edgar Moore of North Bay could do little more to reassure the members than speak hopefully of opportunities for land surveyors opening up in the fields of urban and rural planning and, surprisingly, in the tourist industry – a reference, perhaps, to the survey of lakeside lots on crown lands, which were then starting to feature in the lands and forests survey program.

Moore went on to observe that many of the original marks and monuments were disappearing, though he noted that, in the eyes of those who considered them imprecise, this was no great loss. In this he begged to differ. "An original post ... is something akin to the Bible ... something to turn to with all faith knowing that it alone cannot be disputed. Let either Bible or post get lost and watch confusion follow." Considering this pronouncement, W. Frederick Weaver's suggestion later in the meeting that "non-essential obliterated townships" be legally annulled must have created something of a sensation.

Weaver, an Ontario Land Surveyor since 1926, was with the Department of Lands and Forests, and was destined one day to become head of the surveys section. He pointed out that no thought had ever been given to actually annulling township surveys where survey lines and posts had been obliterated. He observed that in the 159 years between 1783, when John Collins planted the first survey post in Kingston, and 1942 a total of 1170 townships had been subdivided for settlement purposes. Of these, some 941, or 80.4 percent, had been laid before 1903, when iron posts were introduced. Of the wooden posts used before that, many had disappeared or had been destroyed by fire, lumbermen, or road construction crews. And because of this, "disputes and uncertainty have arisen in the past and will continue to arise regarding the indisputable and true position of original survey points."

Touching on the matter of resolving disputes over boundaries, Weaver mentioned the short-lived

Boundary Line Commissioners Act of 1838. He pointed out that with the rescinding of that act went the only legal machinery for dealing directly with boundary disputes, and that while municipalities – into which about 52 percent of townships were incorporated up to 1942 – had been legally responsible for resurveys since the Surveys Act of 1849, they also had to pay for them. Thus, unless a dispute arose regarding the position of an original corner post, individual municipalities had no interest whatsoever in having resurveys carried out.

Weaver reminded his audience that "when township subdivision surveys have been made ... all subsequent surveys made on Crown or privately owned lands must conform to the original sub-division survey." Now, continued Weaver, for descriptive purposes as required by the Land Titles Office, the surveyor was required to tie his survey of a particular parcel to a lot corner in the township in question. However, in the absence of any survey posts or survey lines, the surveyor, like as not, would project the theoretical position of lot and concession lines from perhaps the one original survey post he has knowledge of – all of which was hardly conducive to accuracy, quite apart from the great expense involved. Weaver also pointed out that much the same, if not worse, difficulties beset the surveyor of a mining claim. In conclusion, said Weaver,

With these facts before us, the practice in retaining and adhering to more or less obliterated townships subdivision surveys ... appears to ... be unwarranted and, I submit, gentlemen, that some of our surveying problems could be eliminated if township subdivision surveys were annulled and new township outlines and control traverses made where it was deemed advisable.[2]

After some discussion, it was moved that the council be authorized to form a special committee to

consider Weaver's idea. The committee's report was presented to the membership a year later. Following much the same line as Weaver's original paper, the report was approved by the association, with the president empowered to appoint a deputation of four to wait upon the deputy minister and the surveyor general (then still Charles Fullerton) to discuss Weaver's proposal. Weaver himself was appointed, along with F. Weldon Beatty, John W. Pierce, and Frederick Benner.

The four duly carried out their instructions and so set in train the process that led to the legal annulment,

Charles H. Fullerton, surveyor general of Ontario from 1935 to 1945, president of the association in 1945 and its secretary from 1947 to 1953. Courtesy: AOLS Archives

in whole or in part, of selected crown township surveys. Beginning in 1947 and up to the time of writing, 101 townships have been wholly annulled and 103 partly annulled. Some of them are in what used to be known as the Ottawa-Huron Tract, most of them in northern Ontario – a sad end to surveys made over the years by innumerable dedicated surveyors, who had sometimes worked in the most rugged of terrains and under the most appalling of conditions to produce those surveys (see figure 20.1).

The 1943 meeting also saw a special committee set up under Edison MacQuarrie of Sault Ste. Marie to consider the future of the profession, and, in particular, how to encourage surveyors to practise in areas where surveyors were lacking. Reporting for the committee in 1944, MacQuarrie came up with the radical idea that perhaps the control and practice of the profession should be taken over holus-bolus by the government. Alternatively, and here the committee struck the first note of a theme that was to become increasingly insistent in the years ahead, the association should raise its educational standards for admittance. A better educated surveyor, he suggested, could supplement his income by practising "some form of engineering or technical science."

That same meeting of 1944 saw Moore's successor as president, Norman Wilson, follow up Weaver's criticisms of the township survey system. Wilson was by now a consulting engineer of some note and at that point was deputy transit controller for wartime Canada. Wilson was an early advocate of co-ordinate systems – he had used one in his prestigious survey for the Toronto Harbour Commission earlier in the century.

Wilson had resigned from the commission in 1923 to go into a partnership with A.E.K. Bunnell, which became the firm of Wilson, Bunnell & Borgstrom Ltd. This firm specialized in city planning and transportation studies, with Garnet Berkeley, O.L.S., heading the survey section. The firm was

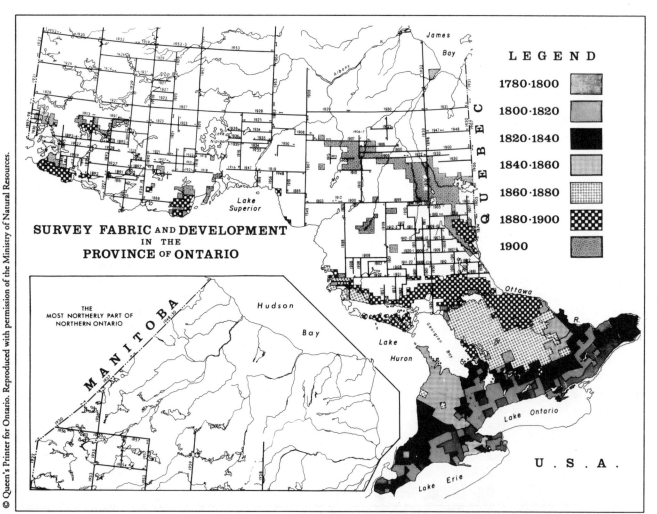

LEGEND

1780·1800

1800·1820

1820·1840

1840·1860

1860·1880

1880·1900

1900

SURVEY FABRIC AND DEVELOPMENT
IN THE
PROVINCE OF ONTARIO

THE
MOST NORTHERLY PART OF
NORTHERN ONTARIO

Figure 20.1 Townships in Ontario laid out over time. These and the principal control lines surveyed in northern Ontario (as of 1967) constitute the "survey fabric" of the province. Some of the base and meridian lines laid down in the 1800s were resurveyed or have passed out of existence.

dissolved in 1930, but Wilson kept up with Bunnell. It was he and Bunnell who submitted a proposal to the Toronto Transit Commission (TTC) in the early 1930s to build a subway under Yonge Street, which they costed at $12.5 million. The city didn't act on the proposal, and it was ridiculed in the press. Wilson would become known internationally for his expertise in the design and construction of subways, designing one in Winnipeg and, when in his seventies, a couple in South America, where he worked on public transit systems in various cities. In connection with the St. Lawrence Seaway,

A Train under a Town?

About Norman Wilson and A.E.K. Bunnell's rejected 1930s proposal for a subway system under Yonge Street in Toronto, the *Toronto Daily Star* had this to say:

> Wilson and Bunnell
> Would build a fine tunnel,
> But isn't it funny
> That Toronto lacks money,
> To pour down a tunnel.

The laugh was on Toronto when Wilson quoted these lines when taking part in the inaugural ride along the Yonge Street subway in 1954, built along much the same route he had suggested, though at many times his original estimate.

Wilson would make the first comprehensive study of the impact of flooding on land use along the upper St. Lawrence.

Said Wilson in his presidential address in 1944: "May I at this time, express what has been my increasing conviction through the years, namely, the very deleterious effect our checker-board township sub-division system has had upon our economy." Expanding on this theme, he posed the question: "How many hundred acre farms have been cleared when actually only a fraction of the average farm was agricultural land? If it had not been that the land was sold in artificial lots, the good land would have been taken up as one proper farm."

It was the same in the northern mining country. What was needed, Wilson pointed out, was a mining claim covering a discrete mineralized area, not an arbitrary 40-acre block. And he deplored the effect that lot lines had had on the Toronto street system, which ran "diagonal to the topography," resulting in "enormous additional cost in city development."

Supporting Weaver's idea, he thought the time had "very definitely come" for the suppression of the township system in unsettled areas. He went further, saying,

More and more through the years have I been led to believe that the purpose behind our system of surveys was threefold: (a) exploratory, (b) to provide a measuring stick by which every settler would obtain approximately the same acreage, (c) to provide a ready means of identifying the parcel granted the settler.

I do not think that there was ever any intent to lay down a mathematically precise mystical system of lots which irrespective of human mistakes and tolerances, would continue to exist in law, or in the inner recesses of the human mind. This idea has been the fetish which has been the surveyor's undoing.[3]

Wilson's remarks presaged the introduction of a province-wide plane co-ordinate system, a subject to which the association would turn its attention after the war.

In his presidential address at the 1945 meeting, William Fulton, O.L.S., then chief surveyor of the Department of Highways, noted that twenty-three members of the association were then serving in the armed forces and that none had been reported as casualties. He went on to consider the future of the association. The problem was not just that there were too few surveyors, but that they were poorly distributed. In 1905, Fulton noted, there was at least one surveyor in eighty-seven different places in the province but in only forty-eight different places in 1944.

During the first year or so of the war, the Queen Elizabeth Way (QEW) had been paved and opened to traffic as far as Thorold, and by 1941 the right of way from Thorold to Fort Erie had been secured and the land graded. About the same time, work was also going ahead on a dual highway from Toronto to Oshawa, and location work was going forward on an easterly extension of the highway against the day when the "St. Lawrence Deep Water Scheme" became a reality. By 1942 the divided highway along the St. Lawrence between Gananoque and Brockville (now the St. Lawrence Parkway) was complete.

In northern Ontario some stretches of roads had been paved, while grading and stoning work on the road between Hearst and Geraldton was going ahead. The work would be completed in 1943, thus closing the last gap in what was already being called the Trans-Canada Highway – what we now call the Trans-Canada would not come into existence until 1949.

By 1944, however, the department – by now far and away the major government employer of surveyors – was doing little work of any kind. Reporting to the association in 1944 on the work of the Department of Highways during the previous year, John Jackson noted that, as far as new construction went, not much had been done except to prepare and file plans and to purchase land with a view to extending the dual highway (later to become part of Highway 401) from Oshawa to Bowmanville, such to be constructed after the war. Observing that the department had been using aerial photos in road-location work since the late 1930s, Jackson noted that by the mid-1940s these were being used in conjunction with ground surveys to make up plans at a scale of 400 feet to the inch "showing roads, buildings, fences, poles, trees, etc., in order to choose the best location for various highways and have these approved, and be ready for construction immediately at the close of the war." A five-year program for upgrading highways was also being prepared, while a start had been made on drawing up a master

plan that would provide a number of divided highways similar to the Queen Elizabeth Way.

In 1945, as the Second World War drew to its close, the Department of Highways found itself with much work to be done and too few surveyors. In response, it set up its own apprenticeship training program, this largely due to the initiative of Harold S. Howden, commissioned in 1935, who had returned to work for the department after serving in the Royal Canadian Air Force and found himself in charge of the department's survey section. Though the program was organized primarily with the needs of the Department of Highways in mind, it was also hoped that graduates of the program would help alleviate the then critical shortage of land surveyors in the private sector. And in the event about two-thirds of the nearly 160 Ontario Land Surveyors that emerged from the program left the department to work in other fields. Similar apprenticeship programs were set up by Ontario Hydro, as well as the Department of Lands and Forests and other government agencies.

As the process of demobilization began, veterans returned to Canada to find both federal and provincial governments generous with rehabilitation schemes and grants of one sort or another. There was a system of loans and allowances for university students, both single and married. For the unqualified would-be university student there were grants and preparatory courses available. In Ontario, helped by generous provincial grants, vocational and technical schools such as the Ryerson Institute in Toronto and the Lakehead Institute suddenly expanded.

Immigration to Canada, which had fallen to a low of a mere 193 000 or so in the ten years between 1937 and 1946, suddenly shot up to over 1.3 million in the next decade. About a third would come to Ontario, which saw its population rise from about 3.8 million in 1941 to nearly 4.6 million ten years later, an increase of 21 percent. With Ontario's economy booming, there were jobs enough for everyone.

For Ontario Land Surveyors, it seemed like a return to the first decade of the twentieth century. But now it was not the urgent need to open up New Ontario that was creating a demand for surveyors but the burgeoning demand for housing, particularly in Toronto and along the Golden Horseshoe where many immigrants were choosing to settle, not to mention the urgent requirements of Ontario Hydro, the Department of Lands and Forests, and, above all, the Department of Highways, now starting to execute the many plans it had drawn up during the war.

The immediate postwar years saw a sharp upswing in the number of students taking out articles. From 1944, when only three students took out articles, the number jumped to twenty-two in 1945 and then to sixty-one in 1946. There was a concomitant rise in the number of active members of the association, though understandably it was slow in coming. From a low of 201 in 1944, the total number of active members would rise to 216 by 1948, and then in a matter of only two years it would shoot up to 268.

But in 1946 the total still stood at 203. At the annual meeting in February of that year, Le May, reporting as chairman of the Council of Management, mentioned that the association "has been under some pressure from various sources ... to admit into the profession by short-cut methods engineers, etc., in areas where there was a dearth of surveyors and where the public suffered on that account." However, he went on, "The council's attitude is that ... it would be wrong and not in the public interest."

In the meantime, Le May reported, the association had been successful in its efforts to have the Department of Veterans' Affairs recognize that apprentices articled to Ontario Land Surveyors were eligible for financial assistance under the "Training on the Job" program. As a result, over eighty ex-servicemen interested in pursuing a career in surveying had so far been interviewed.

It was presumably to expedite the flow of new men into the profession that a special committee on education was set up that same year under the chairmanship of Westcote Cassels of Ottawa. Reporting to the membership a year later, Cassels recommended, among other things, that the Board of Examiners should overhaul the list of subjects covered by the final examination, eliminating some of those covered by senior matriculation and adding others, such as photogrammetry.

The committee suggested that a way should be found to check on the progress of apprentices, while consideration should also be given to lengthening the term of apprenticeship to four years and to two years for pupils with university degrees. And lastly the association should set up its own month-long course of lectures and practical instruction prior to the final exam "with the object of later developing a more extended course of some months at a university, using the institution's facilities, the instruction to be provided by us."

The last suggestion was acted upon quickly. The education committee, which was to become a standing one, initially consisted of Cassels, Weaver, MacKay, Beatty, Baird, Jackson, Anderson, and Fulton, then some of the most prominent members in the association. They set up not one but two courses in January 1947, one at the intermediate level, the other at the final level, attended by forty-nine and thirty-three men respectively. Fourteen members of the association pitched in to prepare and give instruction in a wide range of subjects. "It would be difficult," said Cassels, "to find a more convincing illustration of the esprit de corps of this organization." Four experts in geology and mineralogy from the Mines Department were co-opted to give lectures in their subjects. Finally, the Department of Veterans' Affairs agreed to pay the tuition fees for any ex-servicemen taking one of the courses. Just what these fees were was not stated, but the total cost to the association came to a modest $154.35.

The courses were considered to be so successful that they would be given every year until the associa-

tion finally achieved its long-sought aim of establishing a university course in survey sciences in the early 1970s. The courses would be held in a variety of venues in Toronto, with later ones held at the Glendon Hall campus of York University.

Just how serious the shortage of land surveyors had become was brought home to the association with a jolt when it learned in 1948 that the municipal council of St. Thomas was proposing that a municipal engineer within the bounds of his own bailiwick should have all the powers and privileges granted to Ontario Land Surveyors under the Surveyors Act. The council gave as its reason, its inability to find an Ontario Land Surveyor who could spare the time to speed local transactions in real estate. What was more, representatives from St. Thomas were going to bring the matter up at the annual meeting of the Ontario Municipal Association (OMA), due to take place in Kingston just before Christmas that same year. Here they intended to make a similar proposal in hopes that it would be acted upon by the OMA as a whole.

The crisis was still at its height when Le May told the membership at the 1949 meeting what was going on. Weaver had hurried to Kingston and there had presented "a very excellent brief" to the OMA on behalf of the association, which at least had the effect of delaying the OMA's decision until the meeting of their executive, which was to take place within a few days of the association's own meeting. LeMay told his audience that the association would send a deputation to try and set matters right. If it failed, Le May added, "we have two or three shots in the sling, and will carry it as high as possible, even if we have to go to the Prime Minister."

Fortunately the deputation did not fail. The OMA decided not to proceed with the matter, and all was well. Some surveyors hinted darkly that the St. Thomas municipal officials had been put up to it by the Association of Professional Engineers. That's as may be, but whoever started it, it was, all in all, a near-run thing. At that point in time (1949), active membership stood at 233. But from then on, numbers were to rise rapidly, and fears of a shortage of surveyors receded. Only three years later there were well over 300 active members and in a matter of only four years after that (in 1956) just over 400. By 1960 active membership would stand at 506.

Meanwhile, in 1945 Thomas Speight had died at the age of eighty-six. He had succeeded Vernon Wadsworth as the association's honorary president on the latter's death in 1940. And in 1947, Charles Fullerton, who had resigned as surveyor general the year before (to be succeeded in that office by F. Weldon Beatty), replaced Ralph Anderson as the association's secretary-treasurer.

The various standing committees had comparatively little to report during the war years. Had its development not been hushed up for security reasons, the mining committee would have had much to tell about the Steep Rock iron mine, which was developed during the war. Now largely forgotten, the Steep Rock story, in which Sydney Hancock, O.L.S., played a leading role, remains an exciting one. Steep Rock Lake, so-called because of the high rocky cliffs that lined much of it, was an M-shaped enlargement of the Seine River, which flowed into the right upper corner of the "M." The lake, nearly 330 feet (100 m) deep in places, lay a few kilometres north of Atikokan, some 137 miles (220 km) west of Thunder Bay.

As early as 1897, Dr. W.H.C. Smith of the federal Geological Survey reported that "an iron-bearing horizon, with hematite iron ore of good quality appears to be generally covered by the waters of the lake" – a report that led to a claim-staking rush in the area. But it was not until the winter of 1930–32 that Jules Cross, a veteran prospector and mining engineer from Port Arthur, ventured on the ice and made the first magnetic survey of the lake. Encouraged by his findings, Cross found backers to form a small exploration company in 1938. Working through some 130 feet (40 m) of

water, holes were drilled into the bottom of the lake and one of them struck a very rich ore body indeed.

That same year, Roy S. Kirkup, O.L.S., of the Fort William of the time, was contracted to survey the first mining claims for what in 1939 would become the Steep Rock Iron Mines, Ltd. His assistant was Sydney Hancock. Born in Fort William and educated there and in England, Hancock articled with Kirkup and was commissioned an Ontario Land Surveyor in 1937, the year before the Steep Rock survey. While the iron-ore deposits found at Steep Rock were rich and extensive enough to supply all of Canada's needs for some time to come, investors had little interest in iron-ore covered by many metres of water.

Then the Second World War broke out. With 85 percent of ore carriers from South America being torpedoed, the United States was starting to run short of high-grade iron ore. The development of Steep Rock excited the interest of Canadian-born Cyrus S. Eaton of Cleveland, prominent financier and steel-man, who had an abiding faith in Canada. With Eaton's backing and that of the U.S. government, Steep Rock engineers came up with a scheme that involved nothing less than diverting the Seine River and pumping out Steep Rock Lake in order to expose the ore beneath.

In 1941 Hancock became a field engineer with Steep Rock and ran the preliminary surveys of the Seine River diversion. A year later, as a mine engineer, he was working on the diversion itself, which involved draining a lake by making two 1800-foot (550-m) cuts through rock, the drilling of a tunnel over 10 feet in diameter and 1200 feet long, and an 1800-foot long, 130-foot deep excavation in a gravel hill.

. Following the successful diversion of the Seine River, the pumping out began of an estimated 118 billion gallons of water in Steep Rock Lake, which was done with fourteen 24-inch pumps mounted on steel barges. In mid-1944, with the level of the lake lowered by over 66 feet, dredging of ore-slurry began in the shallowest part of the lake using two mammoth electric

dredgers, which had been transported piecemeal from Boston, Chicago, and California and reassembled on the partly drained lake. In August of that year, Steep Rock crews sighted ore for the first time; what had been Steep Rock Lake started to become an open-cast mine.

In 1946 Hancock became the superintendent of mining and stripping operations. Two years later he was put in general charge of both dredging and the development of housing in the quickly growing Atikokan. From 1956 to 1963 he was assistant to the general manager, from which he went on to become the president's assistant. Meanwhile, from 1942 onward he had not only carried out all the land-survey work for Steep Rock, but carried on a private survey business as well. Among other things, he surveyed the town site of Atikokan, by 1952 a planned community of 3200. Serving on the town council of Atikokan from 1953 onward, he eventually became its reeve.

In 1947 the committee on engineering, roads, and pavements produced a report that included an update on the activities of the Department of Highways, given by Harold Howden. One of the main undertakings in 1946 had been the completion of the location survey of the "Toronto-Barrie Controlled Access Highway" – later Highway 400. By early 1947, grading was almost complete, though bridges, subways, and cloverleafs were yet to be built. A start had been made on paving a new four-lane 18.5-mile (30-km) highway from Highland Creek in Scarborough to Oshawa. It would be opened in December of that year. First called Highway 2A, it would later be incorporated into Highway 401.

Much survey work had been done and some land purchased in connection with the "East and West Toronto By-Pass," linking Highway 2 near the Rouge River on the east with Highway 27 on the west. (It would be opened to traffic in 1956 and would also become part of Highway 401.) In northern Ontario, a location survey had been completed and grading was half complete on an 85-mile (137-km) stretch of Highway 17 (now mostly Highway 105) between

Vermilion Bay, about 60 miles east of Kenora, to Red Lake, this to provide access to the mining area.

Reporting for the committee in 1948, Garnet Berkeley of Smiths Falls noted that one lane of the "scenic highway" (later named the Thousand Islands Parkway) between Gananoque and Brockville had been paved, while that between Highland Creek and Oshawa had now been opened, thus completing the first section of the "proposed dual highway extending easterly to the Quebec boundary." (Location work would be well advanced on what was then known as the Toronto-Windsor Highway by 1951). The Toronto-Barrie Highway had now been graded, while in northern Ontario the Vermilion Bay–Red Lake Highway had been opened with much fanfare, the minister of highways himself leading a parade of cars into Red Lake.

In 1949 comes the first mention of the Trans-Canada Highway as we now know it. Following a meeting of federal and provincial officials, the Trans-Canada Highway Act had been passed in December 1949 by which the federal government agreed to pay 50 percent of the total cost of the highway, provided that the highway met certain minimum standards. In addition, the federal government agreed to pay the provinces 90 percent of construction costs on a mileage *pro rata* basis to help close gaps in the highway. It was agreed that in Ontario the main federally sponsored route should run from near Point Fortune on the Ontario-Quebec boundary to Ottawa, thence to Perth (via Highway 7) to Peterborough and Lindsay, from where it would strike north to Orillia, Parry Sound, and thence to Sudbury. Then, following present-day Highway 17 all the way, it would continue to Sault Ste. Marie, Wawa, Marathon, Nipigon, Thunder Bay, and Dryden and thence to the Manitoba border. In all it would cover over 1400 miles (2200 km) of highway. Using provincial funds, the Ontario Department of Highways would also start building alternative Trans-Canada Highways to the same basic standards.

It would take ten years to complete the federally sponsored Trans-Canada Highway. Meanwhile, all four lanes of Highway 400 had been opened to traffic in 1952 and with the paving of the final section of the Queen Elizabeth Way from Fort Erie to the Peace River Bridge, the entire 90 miles (145 km) or so of the QEW was finally complete. The Macdonald-Cartier Freeway, or Highway 401, would not be opened officially until 1965.

In the course of a talk he gave to the association in 1955 on the history and work of the Department of Highways, Howden noted that the department's Land Surveys Branch then had from sixty-five to seventy-five survey parties in the field. He also noted that of the 8000 miles (13 000 km) of provincial highways built up to that time, no legal surveys had yet been made for three thousand of them – the department was overwhelmed by the amount of work to be done. "Legislation was enacted which permitted hundreds of miles of existing roads to be assumed in one fell swoop. With the reconstruction of these roads, widening of the right-of-way became necessary and surveys for the widening were carried out under the supervision of engineers ... their main interest being the engineering features."

Nobody thought of registering plans "until one W.J. Fulton, O.L.S. [then director of surveys], finally convinced the authorities that the Department was getting into an appalling mess."[4] Even so, the department's Surveys Branch grew slowly until it became imperative to draw up legal records and to erect permanent monuments. All land purchased by the department was now being surveyed, Howden continued, with plans and descriptions lodged in the Registry or Land Titles Office. But such was proving a lengthy business, as any one stretch of highway might involve a large number of landowners. To standardize surveying procedures and improve efficiency, a manual was written and was now being issued to all party chiefs.

Some of the department's woes, Howden explained, dated back to the four years between 1919 and 1923 when the department arbitrarily widened thousands of miles of highway in southern Ontario to 86 feet (26 m). This was done by simply moving fences back from the edges of the original one-chain or 66-foot road allowance. Options were taken on land to be acquired, and the land was paid for, sometimes in a casual settlement that saw a farmer happy to have the department erect a new fence in exchange for his land. In any case, no deeds were prepared or land plans registered, thus leaving the ownership of the land in question. This problem was being dealt with, but some 1500 miles (2400 km) of old highways would have to be surveyed.

Reporting in 1956, the chairman of the committee on engineering, roads, and pavements spoke of the work then going forward on the St. Lawrence Seaway, calling it "the project of 1955 which dwarfs all others." The seaway had been a long time coming. In 1895 the Canadian and U.S. governments set up an International Commission with the idea of simply gouging out a deep-water channel from the Great Lakes to the sea. Two years later the commission came up with a plan. Nothing came of it, but in 1909 the United States and Canada signed a treaty that set up the International Joint Commission. It was largely in hopes that the seaway would soon be a reality that the Toronto Harbour Commission embarked on the port enlargement scheme that transformed Toronto's waterfront. Then came the First World War and everything came to a halt.

By the 1920s the seaway wasn't just a matter of a deep-water channel; particularly as far as Ontario was concerned, it now meant hydro power as well. Thus it was Sir Adam Beck, chairman of Ontario's Hydro-Electric Power Commission (HEPC), who led a deputation to Ottawa in 1924 asking for federal support for what was then known as the "Morrisburg project," a system of locks and power dams, which could not go forward without U.S. approval. What with political changes in Ontario, a violently opposed Quebec, a dithering federal government, and arguments centred mostly on who would sell what amount of electricity to whom, the project went on hold during the mid-1930s. It was revived in 1938 when the United States submitted a draft treaty to Canada, outlining a scheme for the joint development of a seaway and its power potential that would involve damming the upper St. Lawrence. Ontario under the tempestuous Mitch Hepburn wanted no part of it. But come the late 1940s, with a new government and now short of power, Ontario quickly changed its tune. However, opposition from the port of New York and some New England states managed to stall the project once again.

In the meantime, land surveyors first entered into the picture in the person of Norman Wilson, who in 1943 – the same year he was the association's president – produced the "Wilson Report," a comprehensive, if preliminary, study of the effects of damming the St. Lawrence just above Cornwall. He noted that the CNR already had plans to relocate some 35 miles (56 km) of track that would be inundated with water. He suggested new sites for the many villages that would be flooded and recommended locations for deep-water dockage facilities where it might be expected that industries would spring up. He suggested that an immediate start might be made on giving certain sites a river-side character by clearing and widening existing creek beds. He came up with a site for a new cemetery to replace the fifteen that would go under water. And he suggested that a Dominion-Provincial Commission be set up to supervise the rehabilitation of the many that would lose their homes – a suggestion that led eight years later to the formation of the St. Lawrence Seaway Authority.

In 1951 Premier Leslie Frost of an Ontario now determined to develop her own power in the international section of the seaway told his federal ally, Prime Minister St. Laurent, that Ontario would go ahead on the project, with or without the Americans. St. Laurent passed this on to President Truman, telling him, in turn, that Canada would build an all-Canadian seaway.

He created the St. Lawrence Seaway Authority as a crown corporation that same year. New York state, hungry for more and cheaper power, was in favour of the seaway. Opposed to it were American ports as far away as the Gulf of Mexico, railroad and coal companies, and even mining and railway unions. Eisenhower replaced Truman and Congress finally agreed to participate, beginning with; active construction work on the Long Sault Dam in August 1954. The seaway would be officially opened in 1959.

It was an enormous project by any standard. There were seven sets of new locks on the Montreal–St. Lawrence section of the seaway alone, these designed to raise westbound ships about 213 feet (65 m) between Montreal and Iroquois, Ontario. The centrepiece of the project was the Long Sault Dam, behind which the head pond would build up to drive the thirty-two generating units located in the centre of the dam, half of them Canadian, half American. Under the water of a new 32-mile lake created by the dam would go 10 000 acres of land on which stood all of Iroquois, about a third of Morrisburg, seven smaller villages, many farmhouses and farm buildings, not to mention summer cottages, schools, churches, and cemeteries.

There were some sixty-five hundred people to be relocated. To help house them, two new communities were designed and built at Ingleside and Long Sault. Sites had to be found for five hundred houses, which would be moved in their entirety, not to mention cemeteries to receive the many bodily remains that were exhumed and re-interred. About 30 miles of CNR track and about the same length of Highway 2 had to be relocated, these last by surveyors with the CNR and Department of Highways respectively. However, much of the survey work in connection with the creation of the head pond itself was carried out by engineers and surveyors of the HEPC, with the staff of the Geodetic Survey of Canada called on as required.

The project required three classes of survey: hydrographic, topographic, and cadastral. The hydrographic surveys were required to provide the data for the construction of a hydraulic model of the head pond. This in turn would yield the data necessary for the design and planning of the dam itself. The hydraulic model was also needed to ascertain the eventual size of the head pond and to help plan channel improvements and the location of buildings on the eventual edges of the pond. These surveys were carried out by a specialized group of HEPC surveyors and engineers, who first checked the results of earlier hydrographic and hydrometric surveys along the international-rapids stretch of the river.

With precise horizontal and vertical control as their objective, use was made of international boundary monuments as well as previously established monuments established by the International Waterways Commission. Three reference monuments were selected early in 1953, and local co-ordinate grids were constructed to allow survey work to go forward in crucial localities. Meanwhile, discussions with the Americans led to an agreement that the entire project would be controlled by a plane rectangular co-ordinate system referenced to the meridian of longitude passing through a single selected international boundary monument (no. 11).

Using precision echo sounders, the depth along a 45-mile (72-km) stretch of the river was plotted along lines at right-angles to the direction of flow at eighty different locations. The location of each sounding line was established by second- and third-order triangulation using Wild T-1 theodolites. In unmonumented channels remote from the international boundary, the position of the lines of soundings were established by precision traverses. Levels were tied in with U.S. Lake Surveys Datum as adjusted in 1935.

The plane rectangular co-ordinate system proved so successful that it was decided to extend it to the topographic mapping of a strip about 2 miles in depth along the northern bank of the river, and to the cadastral surveys that followed. Precision traverses, tied in to the river survey, were made along the centres of concession and side roads to establish a first-order triangulation network. Secondary control was obtained by additional traverses with points then tied in to aerial photos. Levels were established with Zeiss automatic levels at 350 points.

The end result were maps at a scale of 400 feet to the inch with 5-foot contours. These were used in the cadastral retracement survey of some 20 000 acres of land, of which 17 000 were to be purchased. Rather than invoking the original single-front township system, it was decided to consolidate the individual parcels bought into blocks, survey their outlines, and then redivide them, again using the co-ordinate system, with plans so obtained duly registered according to the Registry Act. Field observations were reduced to a standard form in the HEPC's Cornwall office, and teletyped to their computer in Toronto where the co-ordinates of each survey station were calculated and transmitted back to Cornwall.

Charles Lloyd of Newmarket, a special projects surveyor with the HEPC and chairman of the association's committee on land surveying, in describing the surveys made in connection with the St. Lawrence Seaway given at the association's 1957 meeting, spoke of the many advantages of the plane co-ordinate system, in which, as will be seen, the association was just beginning to become interested. Among those advantages – to use Lloyd's own words – "drafting is facilitated; balancing and distribution of errors is made easy; major errors are spotted immediately and corrected; check chainage can be practically eliminated; missing courses can be readily predicted. Hence trial lines are practically eliminated; large areas can be divided mathematically with confidence. Field time is therefore conserved; time is saved in proving closures as the number of courses in each is usually reduced."[5]

Meanwhile, in 1951, J.M. Riddell, an engineer with the Geodetic Survey of Canada, gave a long paper at the annual meeting on the use of geodetic control for city mapping and on the advantages of the plane co-ordinate system. Geodetic control had got a lot further in the United States than it had in Canada, he told his audience, and had now reached the stage where the U.S. Coast and Geodetic Survey had introduced "State Plane Co-ordinates" by which the geographical position of geodetic stations were being transformed into plane rectangular co-ordinates on a series of grids for each state. Riddell suggested that a similar system applied to each province "would be of inestimable value, not only for city mapping, but for various other undertakings as well."[6]

Riddell made it clear that the federal government would carry out the geodetic surveying required only where the Dominion was directly affected, such as in Fort William and Port Arthur where the federal Department of Public Works and Transport had a direct interest. In the geodetic survey of London, carried out in the 1920s, he pointed out that the city had borne most of the cost, though the Geodetic Survey had supplied equipment, men, and expertise.

Riddell also discussed the factors affecting the choice of map projection upon which to base the co-ordinate system, comparing the Modified Transverse Mercator projection with the Lambert Conformal. It was basically a question of balancing accuracy against the dimensions of the area to be surveyed. Given any system, the greater the area to be covered by a single grid, the greater the error. Thus, with the two systems mentioned, Riddell explained, the north-south and east-west dimensions should not be more than 158 miles (254 km) if the departure from the true scale was to be within 1:10 000.

Concluding his talk, Riddell suggested that as further experience was gained in the geodetic survey of cities, the time required to make such surveys would be progressively reduced and it could be reduced still fur-

ther through the use of electronic devices then coming on the market. As for the legality of surveys made according to a co-ordinate system, he doubted that the law, as it then stood, would allow a Registry Office to accept plans drawn up using a co-ordinate system, even if the co-ordinates were tied in to the marks made in the original cadastral survey. But, he suggested, if a member of the geodetic survey team that had worked on the London survey had also been an Ontario Land Surveyor, and had he been given the authority to endorse the records, such might have been acceptable to the Registry Office. Alternatively, a local Ontario Land Surveyor might have worked along with the team and made ties between the geodetic survey points and original cadastral marks.

Riddell's paper was to have far-reaching consequences and would eventually lead the association to press the Ontario government to adopt a province-wide co-ordinate system for the location of survey points. At the time, however, the association showed little interest, though it did set up a special committee to look into the matter of geodetic control for city surveys, this under Oscar Marshall, professor of civil engineering at the University of Toronto, who had been licensed as an Ontario Land Surveyor the previous year.

The committee saw itself as a fact-finding body. It produced a report in 1952 dealing with the London geodetic survey and the co-ordinate system there, as well as similar work then in progress in Tillsonburg and Kitchener. Kitchener had just doubled its size by annexing portions of Waterloo County. Much of the latter had been settled and subdivided by the German Company at the turn of the eighteenth century and thus had never been surveyed by the Crown. It seemed appropriate, therefore, to carry out a geodetic survey of the whole area and lay down a co-ordinate grid.

In 1953 Marshall reported on the progress being made at Kitchener and Tillsonburg. He quoted W. Harvey Hall, O.L.S., who was directing the

Kitchener project, as saying that the new control survey had shown that many plans compiled from deeds registered under the Registry Act "have only a slight resemblance to existing ground conditions." Marshall observed: "The proper planning of the modern rapidly expanding urban municipality is very directly dependent on accurate plans." In 1954 Marshall commented on the on-going work at Kitchener and congratulated Hall, who deserved much credit for a "pioneering job in Ontario." The association made Marshall's committee permanent, though nothing would be heard from it for a couple of years.

By this time, surveys in connection with the St. Lawrence Seaway, as described above, had been in progress for some time. As members of the association were actively involved in those surveys, it is reasonable to suppose that an increasing number of surveyors were being made aware of the advantages offered by plane co-ordinate systems. Be that as it may, in 1957 the committee on geodetic control of city surveys was renamed the committee on control surveys and acquired a new chairman. This was

Robert G. Code, O.L.S., an engineer and a future surveyor general.[7]

In 1958 Code gave a paper that reawakened the association's interest in control surveys and plane co-ordinate systems. This outlined a theoretical scheme, thought out by Bruce Wright of the Department of Highways, by which a co-ordinate system could be used in the 1000-acre townships, many of which had by now been annulled, in (to use the old name) the Ottawa-Huron Tract. Such a system was to be tied in with geodetic survey points established on three sides of it. Code was succeeded as chairman of the control surveys committee by Patrick Monaghan, then in partnership with Oscar Marshall and Harold Macklin.[8] And with Monaghan's paper given at the 1959 annual meeting, the move towards the establishment of a province-wide co-ordinate system may be said to have begun.

In his paper, Monaghan listed the many advantages of the co-ordinate system and outlined a two-stage scheme whereby, in the first stage, the federal government would be responsible for establishing (or

re-establishing, because possibly 50 percent of the original first- and second-order monuments placed in the early 1900s by the Geodetic Survey had disappeared) the first-order geodetic stations in Ontario, with the second- and third-order stations established by the province and local municipal surveyors respectively – much, it may be added, as Willis Chipman had suggested at the association meeting of 1894.

These stations would provide the framework for the establishment of a province-wide system of plane co-ordinates. The second stage would be the legislative implementation of the first, the establishment of a provincial authority to oversee the second-order work and the drawing up of the requirements to be met by local surveyors tying into the system, with all survey points referred to an agreed-upon co-ordinate system.

Monaghan's report resulted in a recommendation that the association approach the provincial government with a view to implementing the scheme. This led to several high-level meetings, but it would be 1970 before the government finally acted on the matter.

In the postwar years, several base and meridian lines in the northwest were either extended or laid out for the first time, several of the surveys being made by Frank McKergow, a graduate of R.M.C. commissioned in 1948, who, besides working on the Fifteenth Base Line from 1955 to 1957, had extended the Eleventh Base Line westward to the Manitoba border in 1952. In 1953 he had taken the Third Meridian (the boundary between Kenora and Thunder Bay) farther north, and had run the Thirteenth Base Line east from the Manitoba boundary to the Sixth Meridian – whence it would be taken farther east to the Third Meridian by Marshall Macklin Monaghan, of whom more elsewhere, in 1954. Elsewhere in northern Ontario in those years, Phillips and Gavin of Port Arthur had taken the First Meridian (running north, roughly speaking, from Thunder Bay) farther north, which

---

Roughing It

At the 1957 meeting, Frank McKergow showed a film made by a Lands and Forests employee of base and meridian line surveys in the far northwest. From McKergow's running commentary, it appears that most of the film was made in 1955, apparently when McKergow himself was running the Fifteenth Base Line and part of the Sixth Meridian. Their "jumping off place" was Sioux Lookout, from where the party was flown into the survey area by Beaver aircraft. "We had a helicopter on the job," said McKergow. "They certainly have a very definite place in winter surveys, that's for sure." He complained that, before the helicopter arrived, the party had to walk the 5 miles (8 km) to and from work each day. He mentioned a portable radio: "They work very well these days and you shouldn't be without one ever."

He mentioned air mattresses – and eiderdowns. "Those eiderdowns you see are the type that Colonel Hunt used when he climbed Everest:* the bed rolls he used were made by Howards in Ottawa, and we had ours made there." As for clothes, "First you need a parka [and] some thermal boots" which were "dandy on snowshoes ... That white hat you see ... is a thermo hat." Helicopters, walkie-talkies, portable radios, eiderdowns, thermal boots and hats, a 5-mile walk to the line – one wonders what men such as Albert Salter, Alexander Niven, and Thomas Speight, for that matter, would have thought of it all.

---
* Col. John Hunt led the expedition that put Edmund Hilary and Tenzing Norgay on the top of Mount Everest on 29 May 1953.

Boundary monument on the shore of Hudson Bay. The monument on the shore of Hudson Bay marking the terminus of the Ontario-Manitoba boundary survey (foreground). Behind it is the post planted by Ney in 1930 (with a target above it) at which the surveyors had been aiming using a predetermined bearing over a distance of 282 miles. The error was less than 16 feet. The Ontario and Manitoba governments accepted the boundary as surveyed. (From the Ontario-Manitoba Boundary Commission Report, 1955.)

would be taken farther north again in 1959. In 1953, John Pierce, Jr., had taken the boundary between Thunder Bay and Cochrane (Speight & van Nostrand's Meridian) farther north, which would be taken still farther north by Marshall Macklin Monaghan in 1958.

Meanwhile, in 1947–48 the Ontario-Manitoba boundary had been completed in its entirety. It will be recalled that following John W. Pierce and Edward Gaure's survey of 1937, there was still some 168 miles (270 km) to take the boundary to Hudson Bay. John W. Pierce, who had worked on and off on the boundary since 1921, had hopes of completing it himself, but he was now in his sixties and in poor health, and so it

John G. Pierce on the Ontario-Manitoba boundary survey of 1947–48. Pierce was president of the association in 1962 and received the association's Professional Recognition Award in 1976. Courtesy: AOLS Archives

was Edward Gaure, M.L.S., who led the party that began work on the line in December 1947. However, Gauer's first assistant was John G. Pierce, John W.'s son, which must have been some consolation to his father (see figure 13.2).

For lack of suitable landing sites, dog teams had to be used in the early stages of the survey, but aircraft came into their own again later in the survey, covering over 34 000 miles (55 000 km) in some 470 flights. The survey was completed on 6 April 1948 when, as John G. Pierce described it, "it was indeed a thrill" to see through the telescope of his transit the 15-foot-high beacon on the shore of Hudson Bay that Cecil Ney had placed behind the monument he had built in 1930 and which marked the northern terminus of the boundary.

In essence, the survey of the last leg of the boundary involved completing the 282-mile (454-km) line on a predetermined bearing that joined the two points that Ney had previously established: one on Island Lake, the other on Hudson Bay. Following his account of the survey given at the annual meeting of 1949, Pierce was asked how the required bearing was calculated. Pierce passed the question on to his father, John W., who was also present at the meeting and who had run the first part of the line. Pierce, Sr., explained: "The problem was to run the arc over a great circle which would join the initial points ... We [he and Ney] computed the direction of the great circle, and incidently we had four miles of line run when the information came in and our calculations showed we were 4 or 5 seconds off the computed direction, but I decided to keep it straight. So I went ahead ... without any deflection ... and it hits 15.8 feet off [the mark established on Hudson Bay]. I always thought it was luck, and I still think it is, though my son did not altogether agree with that." He went on to say, "One of the disappointments in my life was when it was necessary to complete that line that I was no longer able to carry on."[9] Less than a month after that meeting, on 8 March 1949, John W. Pierce died at his home in Peterborough.

The completed Ontario-Manitoba boundary about 50 miles south of Hudson Bay. (Photo from *AOLS Proceedings, 1949*.)

Asked about the instruments used on that last stretch of line, John G. Pierce replied that they relied on a Dominion "transit of 1913 pattern developed by Troughton and Simms for base line work," adding, "as a matter of interest" that they had "one of those newer Zeiss transits, which we took hoping for great things. It was ... a very compact machine with all the internal focussing, etc. ... but when you start to fool around with those fine sensitive knobs and your teeth are already rattling, it is a difficult job. The mirrors frosted up readily and we finally had to forget about it."[10]

That the completed line had closed the point on Hudson Bay to within less than 16 feet (5 m) was a remarkable achievement. After consultation among the three governments concerned, it was decided to accept the boundary as surveyed as the true boundary, and the last stretch of it was duly monumented as such in the summer of 1950. And so ended the story of the running of the 607.5 mile Ontario-Manitoba boundary, begun by Elihu Stewart and Bryce Saunders over half a century before.[11]

The committee on topographical and exploration surveys had increasingly little to report during the war years. In 1941 John W. Pierce noted that the federal aerial mapping program had come to a complete halt because all RCAF aircraft had been withdrawn for war service. This wasn't quite correct. Public knowledge of a rush to complete the 8-miles-to-the-inch maps of the province was being suppressed for security reasons. These maps were urgently needed for air navigation,

the twenty-six-sheet series being completed in 1943. As of 1941, the work of the Surveys Branch of the Department of Lands and Forests was confined to surveys of mining claims, parcels of crown land in summer cottage country, portions of highways in northern Ontario, and the running of a limited number of ground control lines for aerial photography. It was to be much the same story for the next three years, though from 1944 on, the Division of Surveys and Engineering[12] of the Department of Lands and Forests stepped up their resurveying activities.

In 1947, the same year that Gaure and John G. Pierce started running what remained of the Ontario-Manitoba boundary the committee on topographical and exploration surveys was declared obsolete, and its name was changed to the committee on aerial surveys and mapping. And with that committee's first report in 1948 came the first mention of shoran (standing, more or less, for short range aid to navigation), a system developed by the RCAF during the war for use by allied aircraft.

As early as 1935, Sir Robert Watson-Watt developed an airborne electronic pulse-type system called hiran, which an aircraft could use to determine its position from two ground stations. The war years spawned a number of similar systems, shoran included. All worked on the same basic principle: the time it took a high-frequency signal to travel from an aircraft to a ground station and back was electronically converted (with an allowance made for the aircraft's height) into horizontal distance.

Soon after the war ended in 1945, the National Research Council's (NRC's) Associate Committee on Survey Research started to consider the feasibility of using shoran both for geodetic surveys and as a means of providing horizontal control in air-survey work. With the co-operation of the RCAF, the NRC, and the Army Survey Establishment, the Geodetic Survey of Canada experimented with shoran in 1947 and 1948.

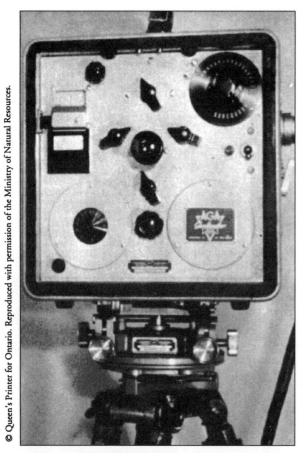

An early model of geodimeter. Using a retrodirective prism as the target, it measured distances between transmitter and target by means of modulated light.

In 1949 and 1950 a major field trial was mounted. Working from a geodetic base line in Alberta, an 1100-mile (1770-km) shoran net was extended by the Geodetic Survey into northern Saskatchewan in 1949 and 1950. This was tied into another base line in Alberta with an encouraging accuracy of 1:59 000. The following year, trials began in the Ottawa area in which shoran was used to pinpoint an aircraft's position at the moment that an aerial photo was taken. It was found that the accuracy obtained was sufficient to control aerial mapping at a 1:250 000 scale, while satisfactory reconnaissance maps at a scale of 1:50 000 could be obtained by an adaptation of the shoran system.

Following these successes, a start was made on covering the whole of mainland Canada with a shoran net. This was completed by 1953, by which time 100 000 square miles (260 000 km²) in the northwest had been surveyed from the air using shoran as the horizontal control. Following this, shoran-controlled aerial photographic coverage was extended into the Canadian Arctic. In effect, what became known as shoran trilateration replaced the old method of geodetic surveying by triangulation. Whereas, in the latter, angles were all-important, in shoran trilateration it was distance as represented by the length of the sides of triangles that counted. And these could be as much as 400 miles long.

While shoran trilateration proved to be of immense use in large-scale survey work, it was not applicable to small areas. It just wasn't accurate enough. In the mid-1950s, however, two other novel instruments appeared in Canada that – in their improved versions – could perform much the same function as the transit but with greater speed and accuracy. One was the geodimeter, the other the tellurometer. Devised in 1952 by Dr. E. Bergstrand of the Geographical Survey of Sweden, the geodimeter used a narrow beam of modulated light sent out by the transmitter (the transit, as it might be), which was reflected back to the transmitter by a mirror or retrodirective prism at the other end of the line or course. The distance between transmitter and reflector was given by the elapsed time translated into distance by means of a photo-electric cell. As first tested by the Geodetic Survey of Canada in the summer of 1956, the transmitter was a cumbersome affair that required a truck to transport it. Furthermore, to minimize interference from other sources of light, observing could only be done at night. Nevertheless, the Geodetic Survey was impressed by its accuracy and capabilities over distances of about 5 miles (8 km), and improved, lighter versions of the geodimeter became widely used. It must be quickly added that geodimeters on the market today are very sophisticated instruments indeed and of negligible weight.

About 1955, there was great excitement among North American land surveyors when they learned of a light and portable distance-measuring instrument called a tellurometer that had been invented in South Africa by T.L. Wadley and developed by the Telecommunications Research Laboratory of the South African Council for Scientific and Industrial Research. An NRC scientist and the director of the federal Surveys and Mapping Branch hurried to South Africa to have a look at it, as did senior surveyors in the United States. Using high frequency radio waves and an appropriate reflector, an early version of the tellurometer could be used for distances from 500 feet (152 m) to 20 miles (32 km). And unlike the geodimeter at that time, the transmitter and the remote station, which resembled it, weighed only 24 pounds (11 kg), with a further 10 pounds for the power unit and 9 pounds for the tripod.

Three tellurometers were quickly ordered, which were assigned to the Surveys and Mapping Branch, the Army Survey Establishment, and the NRC. Tests were made in the summer of 1956. When these appeared to be successful, the Geodetic Survey used tellurometers to strengthen their triangulation network by directly measuring the distance between stations, while new stations were established in the Lake of the Woods area of northern Ontario. Tests were also made on the prairies as to the usefulness of tellurometers on traverse work. Using helicopters, the Army Survey Establishment and the Topographic Survey extended their tellurometer surveys into the Arctic. With newer and lighter versions coming on the market, tellurometers came to be used widely in land-survey work. The Ontario Department of Highways bought its first

Invented in South Africa, the tellurometer used high frequency radio waves to measure distances. This and the geodimeter ushered in a new age of electronic land surveying.

The cover for that year's proceedings were suitably embellished with a picture of Queen Victoria and Queen Elizabeth, along with Britain's Union Jack. The meeting had been held at the Royal York since 1931, but in 1956, with the number of attending members topping two hundred for the first time, it was decided to look for a new venue; in 1957 and 1958 the meeting was held at the King Edward Hotel.

Emboldened perhaps by this break in a twenty-six-year-old tradition, the association membership decided to hold the next meeting outside Toronto. Following the necessary amendment to the Land Surveyors Act and the passage of a new bylaw enabling council to select the place and time of the annual meeting, the members were polled to see where they would like to meet in 1959. They plumped for Niagara Falls. The year after that it was Hamilton. In 1961 it was Windsor; in 1962, London. Then it was back to the King Edward in Toronto in 1963. Thereafter, a pattern was established whereby Toronto alternated with an out-of-town venue, with the first meeting in northern Ontario held in Sudbury in 1966. Attended by 160 surveyors, 85 of them with wives, there wasn't room enough for all in the Nickel Range Hotel, so some had to stay at two other hotels.

In his presidential address at the 1954 meeting, Archibald Gillies of Timmins mentioned the crowning of Queen Elizabeth II the previous year, the ending of the war in Korea, and the death of Stalin. He paid tribute to Charles Fullerton, who, now turning eighty, had had to resign as secretary-treasurer in mid-term. Fullerton's assistant, the recently retired Albert Chase, commissioned in 1909, took over his job but was at it for only a year before his health failed and he also resigned. Vernon Davies, O.L.S., was elected secretary-treasurer in his place.

Davies was the first to suggest that the association should acquire its own building. He was also the first secretary-treasurer to receive a salary, as opposed to the honorarium that was annually voted on and which had

tellurometer in 1960 and an improved model of the geodimeter a year later, using both to carry out horizontal control surveys.

As far as aerial photography itself went, an important advance stemming from the wartime developments in radar was the Airborne Profile Recorder (APR), which in effect was levelling by means of a radar mounted in an aircraft. With data on land elevation in northern Canada and the Arctic urgently needed in connection with air navigation charts, experiments began in 1943 using RCAF equipment, but the results were unreliable. After the war, however, the NRC produced a continuous recording radar altimeter, which used pulsed transmissions on a 1.3-inch (3.2-cm) wavelength that gave errors over land of less than fifty feet (15 m). By reducing the wavelength of the radar to 0.5 inches, the error was reduced still further. In the mid-1950s 90 000 miles (145 000 km) of APR line was flown for the federal government by the RCAF and air survey companies.

Meanwhile, the association had celebrated its Diamond Jubilee in 1952 – the sixtieth year since incorporation.

risen to $1,200 by 1954. However, like his predecessor, Davies lasted only a year. It was following his departure in 1956 that the membership decided that the association could no longer rely on part-time help to keep the office going, and the first full-time assistant-secretary was hired.

Davies was succeeded as secretary-treasurer by Russell Grant, commissioned in 1911, and then on the retired list. Grant's health, however, gave out in October of that same year, whereupon Herbert Anderson took over in mid-term. Then, to cap it all, Anderson died suddenly after he had been in the job for only a year. Wilmot J. Baird was hurriedly elected in his place. Baird remained secretary-treasurer until 1962, thus re-establishing a measure of administrative continuity. This rapid succession of secretary-treasurers in the mid-1950s was accompanied by changes, just as rapid, in the location of the association's business office. For many years this had been at 331 Bay Street. In 1954 the office moved to Room 55, 171 Yonge Street (at Yonge and Queen), only to move back to 255 Bay Street in 1956.

Meanwhile, Le May had died in 1954 at the age of seventy. Few men had done as much for the association. He had served at various times as chairman of the entertainment committee, as a member of council, as chairman of council, as the association's secretary-treasurer, as a member of the Board of Examiners, as chairman of this board, and as chairman of the town-planning committee. Town planning was Le May's greatest love. Appointed Toronto's city surveyor in 1910, he also became its traffic engineer and, in succession, director of the City of Toronto Planning Board, director of the Toronto and York Planning Board, and, finally in 1953, director of the Metropolitan Planning Board. And in his spare time he was a director and one-time president of the Toronto Anglers' and Hunters' Association and a director of the Canadian National Sportsman's Show.

Starting in 1953, the committee on legislation began a major, long-needed overhaul of the Surveys Act. The act of 1937 had been amended in minor ways in 1940, 1941, 1944, 1946, and 1947. These amendments had been incorporated in the act of 1950 (R.S.O. 1950, c. 381), itself amended in 1957. The committee's work led, after several years' work and prolonged consultation with the Department of the Attorney General and solicitors to the Department of Lands and Forests, to the much streamlined Surveys Act of 1958 (R.S.O. 1958, c. 107). Gone under the new act was the venerable term "undisputed angle" denoting a corner of a lot. There was now a "lot corner" established during an original survey, or during a survey of a subdivision plan under the Land Titles Act or the Registry Act if the original post no longer existed – or had never existed – and could not be reliably re-established. And there was the new term "ascertainable point," meaning any point found or re-established in its original position on a line or boundary as originally surveyed or in a subdivision survey made under the two acts just mentioned. The word "concession" now meant a tier of township lots. And many of the sections dealing with survey procedures in townships of various types were tidied up or amended.

Courtesy: Ontario Ministry of Transportation

Locating a new highway in the 1960s. Oil painting by M. Markovich, dated 1961, entitled *Survey Party: Location for Highway 500, North East of Bancroft.*

The most important addition to the new act empowered the lieutenant-governor-in-council to draw up and issue regulations regarding the methods to be used in making surveys, with sketches if need be – which got round the difficulties that had arisen when use was made of a new method that was not covered in the act as it stood. Regulations could now also be issued prescribing the kind and form of monuments, where they were to be used, and how they were to be designated on plans. Finally, in a "catch-all" subsection, regulations could also be issued "respecting any matter necessary or advisable to carry out effectively the intent and purposes of this Act." All of which gave the act of 1958 a new flexibility that was in keeping with the rapidly changing times. Two years after it was passed, the act of 1958 was reprinted as the Surveys Act of 1960 (R.S.O., c. 390), to which an amendment was made the following year that called for the appearance on a plan of the position and type of monument or mark planted during a survey.

By this time, the matter of falling standards within the profession was reaching a crisis point. Said R. Blake Irwin in his presidential address to the 1959 meeting: "It has come to my attention from three separate sources in the legal profession that the standard of work produced by this profession as a whole has reached its lowest ebb." He went on to quote a "prominent lawyer," who had said, "There was a day when a plan of survey signed by an Ontario Land Surveyor was accepted by my firm as a reliable document. I regret to say that our experience today is otherwise." The situation had grown so serious, Irwin noted, that the Director of Titles was employing an inspection staff under the provisions of the Certification of Titles Act. "Whether we like it or not," Irwin said, "the inspection staff set up under the Director of Land Titles is an absolute necessity caused by deterioration in our standards of survey."

At this point inspection of surveys made under the Land Titles Act had in fact been going on for some time. Not long after his discharge from the army in 1946, W. Marsh Magwood, Q.C., was appointed Master of Titles for Toronto and the county of York. In about 1954, though legal authority was still lacking, Magwood appointed a draftsman technician to examine old records, redraft the worst of old subdivision plans, and examine new applications.

In 1956 the Land Titles Act was amended to include a section providing for a Director of Titles who

F. Weldon Beatty on being commissioned in 1920. He was an early advocate of higher educational qualifications for surveyors and helped set up the association's training courses after the Second World War. He was president of the association in 1939 and surveyor general of Ontario from 1946 to 1962. Courtesy: AOLS Archives

W. Frederick Weaver (right) being presented with the Professional Recognition Award in 1971 by President David T. Humphries. Weaver was president of the association in 1949. He became supervisor of surveys in what was then the Department of Lands and Forests.

was to "supervise and determine all matters relating to the titles of land to which this Act applies."[13] Whereupon Magwood was appointed that director. Later that same year, David W. Lambden, O.L.S., C.L.S.,[14] then practising in northwestern Ontario, had occasion to raise an issue connected with registration with Magwood. This led to discussions on the shortcomings of survey records across the province, in which Ralph Anderson, O.L.S., also joined. Early in 1957, Lambden was invited to join Magwood's staff. Then, with the creation of the position of examiner of surveys following a further amendment to the Land Titles Act in 1958, Lambden was appointed to that position.

By April 1958, Lambden was heading a newly created Surveys Division, with an assistant and a staff that included two technicians. The principal aim of the new division was to ensure that an individual landowner had an absolute title based on a cadastral survey that was incontrovertible. Later that same year, as instructed by Magwood, Lambden drew up a code of standards and procedures for surveys and plans, which came into force as a regulation under the Land Titles Act. The regulation also had the effect of extending the activities of the examiner of surveys to cover all the Land Titles offices. With local Masters of Titles referring title survey problems to the examiner, his division was soon inundated with work. To ease the workload, Samuel Mercer, O.L.S., the local Master of Titles in North Bay, was also appointed an assistant examiner of surveys.

In the meantime, in order to expedite the processing of documents, Lambden had initiated a system of description reference plans. A "reference plan" was based on an actual survey and on boundaries as observed on the ground. Reference plans were soon replacing written descriptions by "metes and bounds," whereby a parcel of land was described by a litany of distances and angles. The use of reference plans greatly reduced the time hitherto required to search for individual descriptions, speeded up entries in the land titles register, and simplified the documentation required.

Meanwhile Magwood had been grappling with the problem of poor descriptions under the registry system, the general reader being reminded at this point that there are two systems by which land in the province may be owned and transferred. One solution is to make the land titles system compulsory. However, Magwood came up with a compromise, as represented by the Certification of Titles Act, promulgated in 1958, by which all titles in Registry Office areas had to be certified by the Director of Titles, thus providing a stepping stone to secure title in those parts of the province still exclusively under the Registry Act. The passage of the Certification of Titles Act had the effect of further increasing the amount of work to be handled by Lambden's Surveys Division, with recourse taken to a computing firm to determine and correct mathematical errors in closures.

Following a prolonged study of ways and means of dealing with disputed boundaries, Lambden went on to draft legislation that resulted in the passage in 1959 of the Boundaries Act. Applying to land held under both the Registry Act and Land Titles Act, a boundary dispute could be referred to the Director of Titles, with the examiner of surveys advising the director in hearings, as provided for in the new act, on the true position of the boundary. Following this a confirmed plan was registered in the appropriate Registry or Land Titles office. And so, more than century after the Boundary Line Commissioners Act of 1838 was repealed, the province once more had a legal mechanism for dealing directly with boundary disputes.

That surveys carried out in areas of the province where only the Registry Act applied constituted a major loophole was recognized by Irwin (to return to the annual meeting of 1959). He noted that there was still no way of inspecting subdivision plans *before* they reached the Registry Office, and while the association had passed a bylaw in 1956 that listed standards for subdivision surveys, there was still no way of enforcing them.

Irwin attributed the decline in standards to the great demand for land surveyors coupled with low fees, which had tempted some surveyors to "cut corners." Others in the association saw it differently. In their view, the trouble lay with the inadequate training received by many trainees under the apprenticeship system as it then stood. Some surveyors just hadn't kept up with the times – and had passed their lack of knowledge on to their apprentices. Basically, the fault lay with the low educational standard required of land surveyors, aggravated by the rapid technological advances then being made.

At that time, concern over the educational shortcomings of surveyors was by no means confined to Ontario. It was being felt all over Canada and indeed all over the British Commonwealth. In 1955 the mat-

Frederick J. Pearce was the first to suggest that the association should form regional branches. Known as "Mr. Survey Education," he did much to bring about a course in survey science at the University of Toronto and was an enthusiastic promoter of the Canadian Council of Land Surveyors. He was president of the association in 1968 and received the Professional Recognition Award in 1973.
Courtesy: AOLS Archives

ter had loomed large at the quadrennial Conference of Commonwealth Survey Officers held in Cambridge, England. It had been attended by F. Weldon Beatty in his capacity as Ontario's surveyor general. He was particularly impressed with the emphasis placed in some other Commonwealth countries on raising educational standards for land surveyors. As he reported to the annual meeting in 1956, degrees in land surveying were now available at two universities in Australia and one in South Africa. In Britain, appointments to the Colonial Survey Service, for example, required not only a degree in geography plus training in topographic and geodetic training but a full year at the School of Military Survey with exams at the end of it.

In 1959 a Colloquium on Survey Education, jointly sponsored by the Canadian Institute of Surveying, the National Research Council and the federal Department of Mines and Technical Surveys, brought together eighty-five of Canada's most experienced and influential men in the fields of surveying, mapping, and survey education. The colloquium was to have a major effect on the establishment of university programs across Canada. At that point, only Laval University offered a degree in surveying, this being a prerequisite for writing the examination for licensing as a Quebec Land Surveyor. No other universities in Canada were offering surveying subjects, with the exception of Toronto and McGill, which then offered options in geodetic sciences in their civil engineering courses. However, as was noted at the colloquium, few engineers were interested in taking surveying options. Civil engineering and surveying, once so closely joined, were now going their separate ways, the result being that, from the educational standpoint, land surveyors had been left out in the cold.

Describing the situation as it then stood in Ontario, John G. Pierce, then chairman of the association's committee on education, characterized the typical Ontario Land Surveyor of the day as a man in his late thirties who had some fifteen years of well-paid, boom-time work and was thus comfortably well off. As such, he was tempted to take shortcuts or to shy away from tough or unusual jobs. Pierce warned that, as his typical surveyor lacked a university education, he was unlikely to agree that a university degree be made a prerequisite for acceptance as an Ontario Land Surveyor. A few months after the colloquium on education ended, the University of New Brunswick announced that it would be offering a four-year course in surveying engineering, starting in the fall of 1960. Meanwhile, the association's committee on education had been working towards the establishment in Ontario of a university course leading to a degree in surveying and had got as far as drafting an outline of a four-year course. However it would be more than another decade before the association succeeded in getting such a course put in place. In the meantime, it grappled with the interrelated problems of falling professional standards and a poor public image.

Improving the Profession's Image and Survey Education

It had taken only five years in the early 1950s for active membership in the association to increase from three to four hundred. The next five years saw another hundred land surveyors join the association, to give a total active membership of five hundred by the beginning of 1960. However, from that year on, the net annual increase in membership fell dramatically. The postwar "baby boom" in land surveyors was over.

There were not only fewer apprentices taking out articles, but many were changing their minds about completing them. In 1961 secretary-treasurer Wilmot Baird reported that thirty-seven students had cancelled their articles, while a year later he complained that of the 178 students then registered, many were making no effort to complete their qualifications. Land surveying was no longer, it seemed, a vocation worth pursuing.

That same year, in hopes of improving the image of the profession and to foster a sense of professionalism among its members, the association adopted a revised code of ethics and, a year later, an official seal to be used on plans and documents. A committee on public relations was also formed, with Grenville Rogers of Sudbury, commissioned in 1951, as its chairman. Brochures on the association and its value to the general public were prepared for distribution by individual members. And an abortive attempt was made to establish a museum on surveying, in the form of a surveyor's office at Black Creek Pioneer Village (a reconstruction of an early community).

It was about this time that the association learned that the long-time Toronto home of the Gibson family – at 5172 Yonge Street in North York – was in imminent danger of being demolished to make way for a highrise. Opposed was the North York Historical Society. Thanks largely to William Yates of Scarborough, commissioned in 1949, the association's publicity committee rushed to the society's support: letters were written to the local council and the provincial government, and presentations were made at ratepayers' meetings and the planning board concerned. As a result, the Gibson House – with which the association maintains an on-going connection – was saved. In 1964 it was placed in the hands of the North York Historical Society. All of which was excellent publicity for the association.

With John Bradbury at the head, the committee on public relations moved into high gear. Members arriving at the Chateau Laurier Hotel in Ottawa for the 1964 meeting found a display waiting for them in the lobby that included brochures and a picture of the Gibson House in Willowdale. The display excited the membership so much that when Bradbury started his report by moving that the history of surveying be included as a subject in the final examination, it was promptly seconded by Weaver. However, after some discussion, it was thought some oral questions would suffice.

Bradbury also attended a careers exposition at Galt as a guest of the Canadian Institute of Surveyors, which had a booth there. Deeply impressed by the interest shown in the booth by many of the students, Bradbury urged the association to mount displays at the Canadian National Exhibition and the Ottawa Exhibition. He also had ideas on the upcoming Canadian centennial of 1967. He broadcast over local radio stations, distributed brochures to high schools, and even had film strips made. Such activities were continued by the public relations committee under Vernon McCutcheon of North Bay, who succeeded Bradbury as chairman.

In 1965 the publicity committee suggested that to improve land surveyors' professional self-esteem the association should formally recognize surveyors of outstanding merit. A special committee on awards was set up, and in 1968 the first Professional Recognition Award (for those "judged to have contributed substantially to the status of the profession of land surveying") was presented to John E. Jackson. A graduate of SPS in 1909, Jackson had been an Ontario Land Surveyor since 1911 and later became a Dominion Land Surveyor. After working privately and with the federal Department of the Interior, he spent twenty-one years with the Ontario Department of Highways. Besides being a member of various committees from 1933 to 1963, his particular contribution had been the chairing from 1948 to 1963 of the committee on education, which had been set up to run the courses mentioned in the previous chapter. Up to the time of writing nine members of the association have received the Professional Recognition Award (see appendix E).

The early 1960s also saw a major change in the internal structure of the association, namely the formation of regional groups. During the postwar years, as the number of land surveying and engineering firms proliferated in the Toronto area, a group of land surveyors had got together and formed what they called the Toronto Guild, this according to E.W. Petzold,[1] one of those involved, "without the blessing of the Association of Ontario Land Surveyors, but not without their knowledge."[2] At about the same time, land surveyors in northeastern Ontario decided to form their own regional branch.

That the association should form regional branches was first formally suggested at the 1959 meeting by one Frederick J. Pearce during a discussion about difficulties with registered plans.[3] He said he himself had had no difficulties in connection with registered plans and even if he had, he didn't think it fair "to have the whole Association ... listen to my discussion of that problem. If the Metropolitan area has a difficulty that isn't inherent to my district, then I am wasting my time listening to them discussing their problem." He suggested that regional "districts could be formed."[4]

A year later, in 1960, the association brought in a bylaw, ratified the following year, that regulated the establishment, organization, and operation of what were to be called "regional groups." By 1966 seven regional groups had not only been formed but were reporting to the parent organization: the South Central; the North Eastern; the North Western; the Kawartha-Haliburton; the Eastern; the Hamilton and District; and the South Western. A Georgian Bay branch formed later, to make a total of eight regional groups.

Another important development in the early 1960s was the formation of an association of survey technicians. Fred Marsh, a technician with the Department of Highways, approached Maurice Hewett, O.L.S., then in private practise in Owen Sound, with a view to obtaining the association's blessing and practical help in setting up a technician's association. Hewett, in turn, approached Petzold, who readily agreed to help, with the founding of the Association of Survey Technicians of Ontario (ASTO) as a result.

Marsh died suddenly in 1961 shortly after the ASTO was formed, with his place taken by S.C. Geneja. Addressing the AOLS for the first time in 1963, Geneja stressed the importance of having well-trained, well-educated survey technicians. Doctors and lawyers have "trained and efficient personnel" in their employ, why not land surveyors? He thanked Petzold and R. Lawson of the Provincial Institute of Trades for helping his association set up their first training courses. Reporting to the AOLS in 1964, Geneja stated that there were then about 1500 surveyors' assistants in Ontario.

The ASTO had hoped to set up province-wide night-school courses, under the auspices of the Department of Education. But due to a shortfall in enrolment, only one course had been held – at the Provincial Institute of Trades in Toronto. In 1965 Geneja reported that a course had been held at North Bay as well. These were being financed by the ASTO itself. Geneja appealed to the Association of Ontario Land Surveyors for assistance.

The response of the association was to set up a liaison committee to advise on the financing of the technician's association and to help it obtain a provin-cial charter. Late in 1966, thanks largely to the efforts of Petzold, Pearce, and Ralph Smith, the Association of Certified Survey Technicians and Technologists of Ontario (ACSTTO) received their charter. Petzold and Bradbury were appointed ex-officio members of the ACSTTO's board of directors, while the AOLS set up a special committee on the certification and education of survey technicians to oversee the operations of the ACSTTO and to vet the qualifications of survey technicians and technologists.

By 1968 the AOLS liaison committee had helped organize a survey technology course at the Ryerson Polytechnical Institute and a survey technician's course at the Provincial Institute for Trades in Toronto, with Ontario Land Surveyors giving lectures at both. By 1969, the Department of Education had acted on an association brief and set up similar courses at seven community colleges. The Association of Ontario Land Surveyors continued to liaise with the ACSTTO until the mid-1980s, after which the two associations parted company.

To anticipate, in 1987 the association would found the Institute of Survey Technology as a separate corporation to provide a professional umbrella for those assisting or working under land surveyors. And in 1989, the institute started to classify members of the institute as Ontario survey technicians and technologists and to hold seminars for them.

To return to the 1960s, it was possibly Bradbury's lively performance as chairman of the public relations committee that led to his appointment as full-time secretary-treasurer on Alexander McEwen's resignation in mid-1964. McEwen had been in the job only two years, having taken over from Baird in 1962. By then the association had acquired a new office, namely Suite 903 in the Royal Bank Building, 8 King Street East, the lease on the Bay Street office having expired in 1961.

A panel discussion on the topic "Where Are We Headed?" that took place at the 1966 annual meeting gives us an overview of the concerns of the profession as of the mid-1960s. There were four men on the panel. One was William D. Ratz, O.L.S., who had been one of Harold Howden's many pupils and was then superintendent of surveys for the Department of Highways, which at that point was employing about fifty Ontario Land Surveyors (roughly a tenth of the active membership). Ratz was there to give his views on the shortage of trained technicians.

Representing the private sector were John D. Barnes and Christopher M. Armstrong. John Barnes, commissioned in 1950, had built up a large survey practice in Toronto. At that point he had a staff of forty-five, including six Ontario Land Surveyors. J.D. Barnes, Ltd., it may be added, remains one of Toronto's largest survey firms. The other surveyor from the private sector, C.M. Armstrong had articled with his father, Russell Armstrong, was commissioned in 1950, and joined his father in a surveying and engineering firm in Windsor, which at that point employed over seventy people.

Representing the government on the panel was Stephen B. Panting, O.L.S., who at that point was supervisor of the surveys section in the Department of Lands and Forests and who would go on to become surveyor general in 1985.[5] The fourth man on the panel was John D. Bogart, the association's solicitor. The discussion was moderated by John G. Pierce of Peterborough.[6] The discussion was held, it must be added, at a time when the University of Toronto was offering a surveying option in its civil engineering course and the association, in a state of euphoria, had responded by amending the Surveyors Act to upgrade the entrance requirements of apprentices.

Ratz noted that for several years the objective of the Department of Highways' training program had been to have all of its sixty or so survey parties headed by land surveyors, but the closest they had come to meeting that objective was to have forty-five parties led by either qualified surveyors or apprentices. By 1966,

however, over half the department's survey parties were led by surveyors other than land surveyors; if the trend continued, Ratz speculated, such surveyors would lead all of the department's field parties – as they would in many other organizations concerned with surveying.

With the specialization that would result from the rapid advances in technology and the increased educational qualifications that would be required of the surveyor of the future, Ratz felt that, for a start, the association should do everything it could to back the Association of Survey Technicians of Ontario (at that point just struggling into life) with the object of increasing both the quantity and quality of such technicians.

John Barnes said that while his firm was closely involved with surveys in connection with transportation systems and complex underground services, their primary concern was with the cadastral surveying of small to very large parcels of land in urban or rapidly urbanizing areas. Having noted the "explosive" rise in population and thus the growing demand for cadastral surveys, he posed the question "Are today's survey systems and methods good enough to competently serve the public in the future growth of this country?"

In suggesting that they weren't, Barnes outlined a "worst case" scenario in which surveys of two neighbouring lots conflict. This leads to a costly court case involving not only the lot owners, but perhaps two or more surveyors. To alleviate such problems, Barnes suggested four things. First, the abolition of the system of registering land under the Registry Act and integration of the system under the Land Title Act. Second, the establishment of a central registry office where all land surveyors should be forced to record their notes and plans, such to be computerized to make them easily accessible. In Metro, he observed, a voluntary indexing system was already in place whereby every two months surveyors were handing in a list of the surveys they'd made to a central authority. Third, Barnes suggested the appointment of district survey referees to

John D. Barnes, the founder of J.D. Barnes Ltd. In 1986 the association would name a scholarship at Erindale College of the University of Toronto in Barnes's honour.

Courtesy: AOLS Archives

settle boundary disputes. And fourth, the adoption of a plane co-ordinate control system in urban areas. In fact, the association was already pressing for this.

For his part, Armstrong suggested that the size of survey firms was bound to grow, if for no other reason than the exhorbitant cost of new instrumentation. Either that or there would be a trend towards surveying firms specializing in different sorts of services.

Panting, too, made this point and, like Armstrong, brought up the question of liability, which might become a thorny issue in the case of a specialist firm.

Bogart, the association's solicitor, discounted Barnes's idea of abolishing registry offices. Apart from anything else, the cost of changing the system would be too great. And if change was to come, it would have to be in response to a public outcry at delays in the present system, not to the urging of any one professional association. He warned the members to expect an increase both in the volume and complexity in the regulations regarding ownership and property, and he suggested that the association should consider retraining for land surveyors who had been in practice for some years. Both Armstrong and Panting had suggested and dismissed the possibility that the provincial government would take on a greater measure of responsibility for land surveying than it already had. Bogart agreed. With medicare and the "Welfare State" looming, it was unlikely, in his opinion, that land surveyors will become servants of the Crown in the foreseeable future.

However, Bogart suggested, there were areas of weakness in the association's own administration. The regional group system was an excellent one, but the association should beware of complicating its administrative structure to the point that the association as a whole might lose its sense of direction.

Finally, Bogart urged the association to do more towards publicizing the land-surveying profession. "I feel," Bogart said, "that a large segment of the public do not appreciate the services you are able to provide. Often the cost of a survey is not contemplated by a young couple buying a house on a limited budget. Lawyer's fees are always considered and so should surveyor's fees. The public should be made aware of this."

The index of survey notes and records that Barnes had mentioned as already being tried in the Toronto area had been set up as the result of the work of a special committee of the association. This index led to a pilot project in the South Central Region, using the services of a commercial computing firm. Not all sixty-five surveying firms then in the Toronto area co-operated in the project, but the result was encouraging nonetheless. The special committee was made a standing one, and in 1968 a bylaw was ratified that stated that where 75 percent of the members in private practice in any one region petitioned council for an index of survey notes and records to be set up for that region, such would be established by the association, this to be based on monthly returns of surveys completed by each member.

Barnes's worst case scenario undoubtedly helped arouse the interest of the members in setting up the index, while it came out in subsequent discussions that surveyors in the Ottawa area had gone further and had set up a central registry of the actual survey notes and records, much as Barnes had suggested. Barnes's presentation may also have led to the establishment that same year of a special committee to handle complaints from the public.

In 1969 A.F. Allman, who had succeeded Bradbury as secretary-treasurer the year before and who had now taken over the complaints committee, urged that while some of the complaints might seem trivial – a tree damaged by a surveyor, for example – the association must take such complaints seriously. "What else have we, as Ontario Land Surveyors, got to sell, other than service?"[7] Allman asked. He went on to suggest that the complaints committee be made a standing one, which it was.

Since the war, the standing committees on land surveying and drainage functioned much as they always had. That on land surveying centred on the presentation of practical surveying problems. In the 1950s and early 1960s, surveyors involved in drainage work continued to grapple with the complexities of the Ditches and Watercourses Act, the Municipal Drainage Act, and the Municipal Drainage Aid Act. Then in 1963 these acts were swept away to be replaced with a single Drainage Act, this to the relief to those who had laboured so long in the welter of legislation that had bedeviled their work for over a century. In the meantime, the establishment of conservation authorities following Hurricane Hazel in 1954 widened the work of local town and township engineers, while to an increasing extent the amount of drainage work rose or fell with the changing fortunes of farmers.

Surveyors concerned in mining-claim surveys continued to have their own problems, some of which the mining committee had successfully alleviated by bringing about improvements in regulations and getting amendments made to the Mining Act. The mining industry had had its ups and downs since the war. The postwar boom was followed by a depression at the time of the military action in Korea. Mining claims were cancelled and fewer surveyed. Meanwhile, the airborne magnetometer and aerial maps had started to revolutionize the search for metals.

Business picked up again in the mid-1950s with the search for uranium. In 1956 nearly 48 000 mining claims were staked. A growing difficulty was the destruction of claim survey lines by timber operators. In some cases the surveyor concerned had been unable to close his survey because by the time he had got back to his point of commencement, said point was now buried under a mound of newly felled timber.

In 1963 the committee on legislation started to overhaul the Surveyors Act, which had not been revised since 1931. To an increasing extent, what amounted to a rewriting of the act became involved with the mounting need to upgrade the educational requirements of those entering the profession. In 1960, amendments to the act that resulted in the Land Surveyors Act (R.S.O. 1960, c. 389) increased the term of apprenticeship to four years, this in a belated attempt to upgrade the qualifications of students sitting for their finals. Graduates in civil or mining engineering and forestry from any university in Ontario only needed to serve two years, as did graduates in any educational course deemed to be the equivalent of a university course.

In that same year, largely because of the interest aroused by John G. Pierce's report on the colloquium on survey education, the association called for council to seek ways of establishing a university course in Ontario. Later, Charles Stauffer was to say "that day of February 16, 1960 was a turning point ... in the history of the Association. I, and I'm sure very many others, felt a glow of pride in that we were members of a progressive, forward-looking Association leading the way for Canadian surveyors to upgrade their profession."[8]

In fact, New Brunswick was to beat Ontario to it, as we have seen. Be that as it may, in 1961 the committee on education under the chairmanship of John Pierce asked the University of Toronto to set up a surveying program. The university responded by establishing a two-year specialization option under the Department of Civil Engineering, which was offered for the first time in the calendar for 1962–63. One of those taking the surveying option in 1969, it might added, was P.L. Finos, a future surveyor general. While the Faculty of Applied Science and Engineering agreed to set up a surveying option, there was a *quid pro quo*. The association had to agree to drop its own course at the intermediate level, together with certain subjects at the final level. In 1965 the final course would be dropped in its entirety. Admission requirements were to be lowered for graduates from the new university program.

Early in 1965, with the survey option course now in place at the University of Toronto, the association approved a new surveyors act, which sought to bring about a dramatic change in the educational requirements for would-be apprentices. Henceforward they would have to be graduates of a university course in civil or mining engineering, applied geology, or forestry, or have taken the surveying option in the civil

engineering course at the University of Toronto.

After various delays, the association was ready in 1966 to present the amended version of the new act to the minister of lands and forests. But by this time he had resigned. Faced with having to get the act with its successive amendments approved by a new minister and with interest in the survey option program at the University of Toronto already starting to dwindle, yet another amendment to the new act was brought before the 1967 meeting to expedite its passage. All references to university degrees or their equivalent as a prerequisite for articling were to be eliminated. Now all that was to be required of surveying students was what amounted to a grade 13 certificate.

The proposal to bring in this amendment provoked Stauffer to fury. He accused the members of having "gone chicken" and that they had allowed themselves "to be intimidated by a highly vocal, self-seeking majority who are afraid of progress."[9] After much heated argument, the vote was taken. Against the amendment was Stauffer, John Pierce, and twenty-five others. For it were 156. And so the new Surveyors Act (R.S.O. 1970, c. 453) passed into law on 1 January 1970, some seven years after the committee on legislation first started working on it – but without the stipulation that university degrees or their equivalent were a prerequisite for articling.

However, even as the association was grappling with the final version of the Surveyors Act, it was confronted with what became known for short as the McRuer Report. In 1964 the Ontario government had appointed the Honourable J. Chalmers McRuer, chief justice of the High Court of Ontario, to head a Royal Commission Inquiry into Civil Rights. His terms of reference were to study and inquire into the laws of Ontario, including statutes and regulations as they affected the personal freedom, rights, and liberties of the citizens of Ontario. Made public early in 1968, the McRuer Report contained a section dealing with the statutes governing the "Self-Governing Professions

and Occupations," of which nearly twenty were listed, the association among them. The association set up a special committee, which, in consultation with the surveyor general, was to consider ways of incorporating McRuer's recommendations into the Surveyors Act.

Anticipating that a statutory power procedure act would be enacted as McRuer had recommended, the association immediately set to work effecting various changes in the Surveyors Act. Among them was the adoption of the secret ballot in elections. And, henceforward, a lawyer of ten years' standing would sit on the disciplinary committee, while he and a layman would be members of the Council of Management. Members would have the right to incorporate under certain conditions, and the code of ethics was to be sent to all members, besides being made available free of charge to the public. These and other changes would come into law with an amendment to the Surveyors Act passed in 1973.

Meanwhile, in 1969 the Department of Civil Engineering at the University of Toronto had dropped all options from its curriculum. This placed the association in a dilemma. Both of the association's own courses had been discontinued, and it had already ratified a bylaw by which the subjects covered in Part One of the final examination were those taken by university students in the now defunct survey option.

Both of the association's courses were hastily reinstated pending a new university course on surveying. At the same time, a new committee was formed. Called simply the committee on a university survey course, when it was formed in 1969, it was renamed the committee on geodetic sciences by the time it presented its first report the following year. Its chairman was Frederick Pearce. Indefatigable in his efforts to promote survey education at all levels, he was said to have known the president of every community college personally. To them and to members of the association he became known as "Mr. Survey Education."

With the object of writing a brief urging that a course covering surveying in all its aspects be set up at an Ontario university, Pearce and his committee conferred with university and provincial government officials in both Ontario and eastern Canada, representatives of several institutes connected with either surveying or education, the staff of Ryerson, a firm of educational consultants, a professor from the surveying department of a South African university, and even a lawyer who gave instruction in legal surveying in Australia. Pearce's committee then drew up a tentative curriculum, costed the founding and operation of a course, and defined the association's role in setting up and running such a course. The completed brief was presented to the commission on post-secondary education in 1971.

In the meantime, a proposal to establish an expanded course in surveying under the umbrella of the earth sciences gained the enthusiastic support of Dr. J. Tuzo Wilson, then principal of Erindale College, with Dr. Gordon Gracie appointed by the university to work with Pearce's committee to work out the details of the curriculum of the proposed four-year course. The course was approved by the senate of the university early in 1972, and the first students were admitted in the fall of that year. The association for its part gave its official approval to the new course as one that would lead to academic qualifications that satisfied the entrance requirements of the association.

The first graduates received their B.Sc. degrees from the survey science course at Erindale in 1976, with the first graduates completing their articles and qualifying as Ontario Land Surveyors in 1978. In all, 134 graduated from the program in the first ten years of its existence. Of these, forty-three became Ontario Land Surveyors, four became Canada Lands Surveyors, and three of them Alberta Land Surveyors.

Meanwhile, throughout the decade the pace of technological change had been quickening. In 1959 the committee on aerial surveys and mapping reported extensive aerial survey work carried out on behalf of Ontario Hydro during the previous year in connection with the location of present and future transmission lines. A field trial had shown that the tellurometer had shown it to be fast and accurate when used in control traverses in connection with aerial mapping. By 1960 the chairman of the committee, Charles O'Dale, commissioned in 1947 and then in private practice in Midland, was urging his audience to keep up with the times:

We, as the trail blazers in our country's expanding economy, are still inclined to be in favour of the proven survey instruments and techniques of a century ago. Fortunately, or unfortunately, we are now in the electronic age and every year new surveying instruments and techniques are being developed, tested and improved upon.

Land surveyors, and especially those in private practice, he declared, "are fast becoming obsolete and are considered only a necessary evil to the public when land is transferred." He urged every private land surveyor to acquire a good stereoscope and start familiarizing themselves with aerial photographs and their interpretation, adding that advance information from aerial photographs would save them much time and money.

In 1961 the chairman of the committee on aerial surveying and mapping reported that shoran was giving way to the tellurometer in ground control surveys and that increasing use was being made of helicopters, portable observation towers, and computers. In that same year, a Canadian-designed airborne tellurometer system was designed and tested, while in 1962 the commercial version of the airborne tellurometer, called the "Aerodist," arrived in Canada and would be used until the early 1970s by the federal Surveys and Mapping Branch to extend their coverage in the 1:50 000 map series. The mapping of Ontario at this scale (about 1.25 miles to an inch) would not be completed until 1990. However, coverage of the province in the 1:250 000 series (about four miles to an inch) was completed by 1966.

The early 1960s also saw the arrival of gyrotheodolites on the market. Based on the gyroscopic guidance systems used in ships and tanks, the gyrotheodolite combined the conventional theodolite with an electrically powered gyroscope, which, given time to settle, would indicate the north. They were expensive, but some mining companies bought them for use in underground work.

The mid-1960s also saw the arrival of the first satellite survey system. Developed by the U.S. Coast and Geodetic Survey, the system used two passive satellites, Echo 1 and Echo 2 – in effect nothing more than targets – that orbited the earth with their position in relation to the stars being observed from at least two ground stations out of a number established by the U.S. government around the world. With the position of the satellites established for any one set of observations, that of the observation stations concerned could be computed by triangulation.

In 1965 the association's committee on aerial surveys and mapping sent out a questionnaire designed to elicit information on the extent to which land surveyors were making use of aerial maps and what they were using them for.[10] Of the 135 respondents, a third used them frequently, the rest infrequently or not at all. Listed in order of importance, their uses included retracement surveys to help locate old property boundaries, planning work, discussing a proposed survey with a client, or in costing a survey, checking for gross errors in angles and distances, or using them in legal surveys – a term that was to come into increasing use in the years ahead.

It will be recalled that in 1961 a brief was presented to the provincial government on the desirability of introducing a province-wide plane co-ordinate system.

The association continued to press for this. Meanwhile, the Department of Highways, having bought a tellurometer in 1960 and a geodimeter a year later, had gone ahead on its own and started to lay down local co-ordinate grid systems to provide horizontal control for specific projects, while in 1960, as requested by Metropolitan Toronto, the Geodetic Survey of Canada began establishing twenty-four first-order triangulation stations in and around Metro Toronto as the first step in providing the city with a horizontal control system.

In March 1962, with the co-operation of the Metropolitan Department of Roads, the establishment of second-order monuments began with 230 such monuments put in during the ensuing summer. Distances of up to 4 miles were obtained using a geodimeter at night, tellurometers for distances of more than 4 miles. Angles were measured with a Wild T-2 transit. Using a computer program then being developed by the federal Geodetic Survey, it was hoped that it would be easy to convert geographic positions into rectangular co-ordinates when such were introduced by the province. By 1965 similar control surveys had been completed for Hamilton and Sudbury.

Meanwhile, in 1964, following discussions between Surveyor General Robert Code, who had succeeded F. Weldon Beatty two years earlier, and repre-sentatives from the Attorney General's Office, the Department of Highways, and other government departments involved, the decision was made to adopt the Transverse Mercator projection in three-degree zones for the province of Ontario. The following year, the surveyor general consulted Professor Marshall on the application of the co-ordinate system to the province, while the Department of Highways undertook a departmental study of control surveys. As a result of this, the department started working with the federal Department of Mines and Technical Surveys and began establishing second-order control monuments along major highways.

In 1967 the first step was taken by the province towards the inauguration of a co-ordinate system: the government amended the Surveys Act to provide regulations for setting up and governing just such a system. The surveyor general assured the association that it would be put in place as soon as staff and budget were available. In that same year, the government had formed an informal advisory committee to advise on the implementation of the new legislation.

In describing the activities of the committee at the 1969 annual meeting, Panting, who had been made deputy surveyor general the year before, pointed out that the major difficulty to be overcome was to integrate the legal and control surveys with minimum disruption and minimum cost. There was no question of taking an arbitrary step to tie all cadastral surveys into control points at any one point in time. It had to be a gradual process.

And from the economic standpoint, the obvious place to start, said Panting, was in areas having a sufficient density of control points. These co-ordinate control areas would be enlarged and merged. "The public," Panting added, "cannot be expected to endure forever the cost of resurveys ... Salvation undoubtedly is the indestructible co-ordinate which will not decay and become obliterated or lost."[11]

In 1969, regulations were promulgated under an amendment to the Surveys Act governing what is known as the Ontario Co-ordinate System, based on the Transverse Mercator projection in 3-degree zones, a system that was also being considered by the Surveys and Mapping Branch of the federal Department of Energy, Mines and Resources, as well as by some of the other provinces.

There were to be first-, second-, third-, and fourth-order surveys. The regulations did not cover first-order surveys, which remained the responsibility of the federal government. The regulations recognized that traverses would be required for integrated control in many areas, while other methods such as triangulation, trilateration, photogrammetry, Doppler satellite observation, and inertial survey systems might all be used, so long as the required degree of accuracy (expressed in terms of statistical confidence limits) was adhered to. This list, it might be added, illustrates the increasing technical complexity of modern surveying.

The regulations also covered the choice of station sites, types of monuments, referencing, and the identification of stations by means of a nine-digit number. In this number, the first three digits were to indicate the agency responsible for placing the monument. This agency might be a federal or provincial agency, a municipality, a railway company, or – as the list then

---

The Ontario Land Surveyor

By the mid-1950s, *Telescope Topics*, a newsletter, was being sent to association members to help them keep in touch with the activities of the association and the latest technological developments. Its successor, *The Ontario Land Surveyor*, first came out in July 1958.

The first editor was Charles Stauffer, chief surveyor for Ontario Hydro. In 1962 he reported that the most popular article to date was "Short Distance Measurement with the Tellurometer" by D.H. Richardson. The Tellurometer Company requested 3000 reprints of the article, of which 250 were sent to Australia and 200 to South Africa, with another batch to Hong Kong. Once, when appealing to the membership for contributions, Stauffer observed that the lack of them could not be for want of imagination. After all, he pointed out, land surveyors often used their imagination when writing descriptions ...

---

stood – Bell Telephone or the International Nickel Company. The next two digits were to stand for the year of installation, while the last four digits constituted an identification number for the year in question, issued by the agency concerned.*

In the event, the use of the Ontario Co-ordinate System was never made mandatory, though it came to be used by some government departments and by various agencies (see figure 21.1). Based on a cost-benefit analysis made by the Ontario Treasury, an application to fund the implementation of the system was turned down. And there matters were to stand until the 1980s when the Universal Transverse Mercator projection (UTM) with a 6-degree zone was officially adopted by the government.

At the instigation of Sydney Hancock, president for 1972–73, the internal organization of the association underwent a drastic change with the introduction of "zones" in 1972. Each of the twenty or so committees were slotted into one or another of six zones: legislation, finance, education, administration, surveying, and services. Each zone was to be headed by a chairman; together, the chairmen would act, as it were, as a cabinet for a prime minister. The analogy was Hancock's. The number of individual committees, he explained, had grown to the point that there were just too many for a president to keep an eye on.

What with the successful (albeit symbolic) conclusion of the campaign to have a provincial co-ordinate system set up, the inauguration of the course at Erindale, and the internal re-organization of the association's committee system, the year 1972 was a climactic one for the association. To cap it all, the association purchased its own building at 6070 Yonge Street in Willowdale. Faced with space problems and escalating

The Association's 1972 Council and Its Minister

The association's Council of Management in 1972, the Honourable Leo Bernier, minister of lands and forests, in centre. Flanking him (left) is Sydney G. Hancock and (right) Eathel W. Petzold, presidents of the association in 1972 and 1973 respectively. Bottom left is Robert G. Code, surveyor general of Ontario from 1962 to 1983. Second from right (top) is Stephen B. Panting, surveyor general from 1985 to 1990.

---

*The reader, if he or she lives in a town or city, may well find a small bronze plug at a street corner not far away, with just such a number on it. Look for them on the sidewalk or in the road, close to the curb. This is a survey station, whose position is precisely known, from which a surveyor will begin a local survey.

Figure 21.1 A modern intergrated survey. In 1973 the city municipality of Timmins was created covering thirty-four townships. By 1975 a survey was completed that led to the production of topographic maps, the establishment of permanent horizontal and vertical control networks, and the re-establishment of township corners. Several federal and provincial government agencies and aerial survey firms were involved. (From Rody, *Integrated Surveys*.)

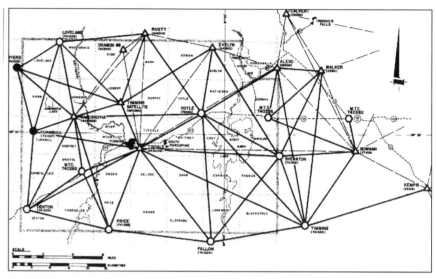

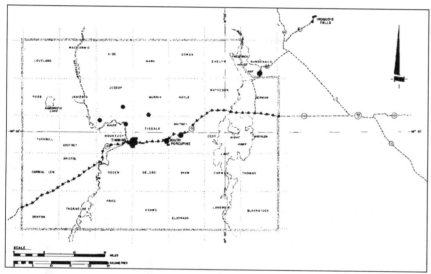

Working from existing first-order stations (triangles), new first-order stations were established by the Ministry of Natural Resources with the co-operation of the Geodetic Survey of Canada (circles). Using tellurometers, second order stations were then established by the Ministry of Natural Resources (solid circles) and the Ministry of Transportation and Communications (pentagons). A high density network of third-order stations was then built up to provide horizontal control for mapping purposes.

Limits of the new city shown hatched. Already in place were benchmarks established by the Ministry of Transportation and Communication along Highway 101 (triangles), the Topographic Survey of Canada (circles), and the Geodetic Survey of Canada (pentagons). Working from these, precision levelling led to the establishment of a network of benchmarks in the central portion of the city.

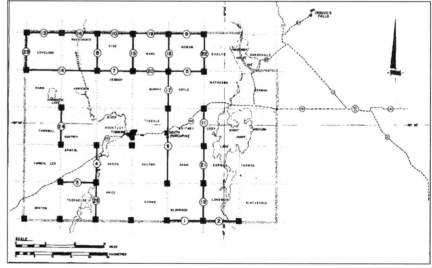

(Right) The position of twenty-nine township corners forming the basic legal framework within the city were re-established using aerial photography and aerial triangulation (solid squares). Positions were expressed in terms of the Ontario Co-ordinate System. Heavy lines denote township boundaries re-established.

rentals, the council felt it had made a good decision. In his presidential address to the 1973 annual meeting at the Royal York, Hancock said "We believe this is a sound investment and marks a big step forward, both as to the image and the stature of our Association ... the time for action was long overdue."[12]

Meanwhile, the late 1960s had seen a woman become an Ontario Land Surveyor: the first female land surveyor in Canada. Women had worked as surveyors in other countries since the mid-1950s. For instance, Wilmot Baird had noted in his presidential address at the 1957 annual meeting of the association that a Mabel Milton had been licensed to practise in the state of New Jersey. He also mentioned that France's first female surveyor, Jeanne Missonnier, who had been licensed in 1955, had received a special commendation from the president of the Order of Surveyors for her willingness to work in a difficult and mountainous area where a surveyor was badly needed.

The same year saw a Miss Pickman of Whangarei, New Zealand, apprenticed to her father. This had provoked the editor of *The New Zealand Surveyor* into commenting:

We understand that certain members of the old brigade, covered with the honorable scars of their long and arduous battles with forests, mountains and inspectors, and proud of their he-man profession, were more than somewhat disturbed when the news broke on their astonished ears. Possibly the news of similar decadence in other countries may help soften the blow.[13]

Evidence that such "decadence" was now affecting Canada came to light at the 1966 annual meeting of the association when Harry D. Currie of Richmond Hill reported for the Board of Examiners, which approves prospective students:

One of the approvals has made history, in that the applicant was from what is alleged to be the gentler sex. The applicant, Mrs. Nancy Lorraine Setterington, is the wife of William J. Setterington, who was commissioned as an Ontario Land Surveyor in 1959. As you may expect, this was discussed thoroughly before approval was granted ... The secretary was instructed to inform all parties concerned that there was to be no reduction in the time spent in the field.

Happily, skepticism such as this was to change as women proved their worth in the field.

Destined to become not only the first woman to qualify as a land surveyor in Canada but the association's executive director, Lorraine Setterington was born in Sudbury, where her father worked for International Nickel. Of English-Irish stock, his surname was Gladstone. The mother of two small children (a third would arrive later), Setterington had worked as her husband's unqualified assistant for six months before deciding to become an Ontario Land Surveyor. She submitted her articles in the spring of 1965; they were finally approved in November. She was commissioned in 1969, having gained top marks in the finals and winning the Samuel Holland Award that year.

Setterington moved to Toronto, where she taught surveying at George Brown Community College and then went on to become a lecturer in the University of Toronto's survey science course at Erindale College. Meanwhile, Setterington had been helping out on a voluntary basis at the association's office on Yonge Street. On the resignation of Allman, the secretary-treasurer, in April 1976, she was asked to run the association's office. She accepted and was appointed executive secretary (later executive director) of the association in July 1976, a post she would occupy for sixteen years. It has been said of her that

her passion, dedication, and determination proved to be just what the profession needed as it moved into the 1980s.

CHAPTER TWENTY-TWO

On to the Future

At the time of the earliest settlements, deputy land surveyors not only carried out the surveys but played an active role in the allocation of the lots they had surveyed. Come the nineteenth century, the latter role was taken over by crown land agents, and increasingly the transfer of land became a matter of private transaction between private owner and buyer. The twentieth century saw the full flowering of our industrialized society, with real estate becoming a cornerstone of the modern economy. But throughout all, the precise spatial definition and location of that all-important commodity – land – has remained with legally authorized land surveyors, be they in their time deputy land surveyors, provincial land surveyors, or, since 1892, Ontario Land Surveyors. That they alone have the legal right to carry out the work upon which so much else rests has understandably always been a source of pride to the land surveyor and it has been a right that has always been jealously guarded.

However, with the growth of the air survey industry since the Second World War and the emergence of new and more accurate methods of geodetic surveying techniques, land surveyors in legal surveying found they were becoming increasingly dependent on the photogrammetrist and the geodetic surveyor. Should these specialists be admitted to the Association of Ontario Land Surveyors? Whether they should or should not proved to be perhaps the most divisive issue in the history of the association.

While the idea had first been scouted by the education committee in 1967, it was not until the annual meeting in 1970 that the matter was brought up before the membership, this by John D. Barber of Toronto, commissioned in 1964, in his capacity as chairman of the committee on aerial survey and mapping:

At the present time, most surveyors have not the proper educational background to fulfil

their obligations in the field of photogrammetric surveying. It seems apparent that unless we show more interest and initiative in our spheres of responsibility, which include not only cadastral surveying, but also photogrammetric, geodetic and engineering surveying, then it is inevitable that our Association will gradually deteriorate.

His committee then recommended that a committee be established "to re-organize the structure and policy of our Association and to approach all professional surveyors outside of our Association with the aim of incorporating these surveyors into our Association."[1]

Barber's suggestion seemingly fell on deaf ears. At any rate it provoked no immediate comment. The Council of Management, however, had taken note of it and later that year set up a study committee to examine both the advisability and feasibility of "restructuring," as it became known for short. This led to a much heralded panel discussion that was the highlight of the annual meeting held in Ottawa in 1971, where it soon became clear that some members were violently opposed to the idea.

The panel was composed of Don McLarty, then president of The Canadian Association of Aerial Surveyors, George Babbage, chief of the Horizontal Control Section of the Geodetic Survey of Canada, while from the association itself were Herbert Todgham, then on the Board of Examiners and two members of the study committee: Kenneth McConnell and William J. MacLean.

Leading the discussion, MacLean, commissioned in 1953 and then with the National Capital Commission in Ottawa, noted that land surveying was changing. The examination curricula as revised by Bylaw 95 and ratified in 1969, had, among other things, made the subjects of photogrammetry, geodesy, geodetic adjustments, and geodetic astronomy mandatory in the final examinations. He observed that even in his own span of experience "the emphasis has changed in legal, geodetic and photogrammetric surveying." Both the geodetic surveyor and the photogrammetrist, he stressed, were now involved in cadastral surveying in one way or another and should

therefore be allowed to join the association. But, he continued, restructuring would not be that easy. "Our studies and our meetings (with the regional groups) have told us that it may be more difficult to revise the present structure of the association than it was to create the original one."[2] Events almost proved him right.

Speaking for the photogrammetrists, McLarty noted that Canada's air survey industry then consisted of seventeen firms employing some fourteen hundred people and that it had an annual turnover of $17 million, of which nearly half was earned overseas.* He went on to say that while about five hundred people were involved directly in the "photogrammetric process," only twenty-five might seek membership in the association in the first instance.

He pointed out that restructuring the association raised a number of problems, among them the relationship of the photogrammetrist to legal surveying. For those who were worried about this, McLarty assured them that photogrammetrists posed no threat. "Not one ... photogrammetrist," he said, "is interested in practicing legal surveying. We have enough problems of our own." He left the members with a final thought. "If the cadastral survey of the future," he said, "is to be performed more efficiently by taking advantage of a higher content of the photogrammetric process, then this will happen irrespective of whether or not the photogrammetrist is a member of the A.O.L.S."[3]

McLarty was followed by Babbage of the Geodetic Survey of Canada. He pointed out that of the survey's staff of one hundred and three, only fifty-six could be considered "legitimate" geodetic or control surveyors. And of these only twenty-one were commissioned land surveyors, consisting of two Dominion Topographical Surveyors, eleven Dominion Land Surveyors, and provincial land surveyors from Nova Scotia, Ontario, Quebec, and New Brunswick. For the most part, he said, the staff of the Geodetic Survey were indifferent to the idea of restructuring, though some were enthusiastic, as he was himself. Like

Edwin P.A. Phillips, commissioned in 1910, was presented posthumously with the Professional Recognition Award in 1972. In 1911 Phillips and his survey party narrowly escaped death in a forest fire. Phillips was appointed city surveyor of Port Arthur in 1913 and worked extensively in northwestern Ontario. He was in partnership with Frederick J. Benner for thirty-eight years and entered his final partnership with Thomas L. Wilson and Peter R. Milton when he was eighty-three. Courtesy: AOLS Archives

Frederick J. Benner, Edwin Phillips' partner for thirty-eight years and president of the association in 1947.
Courtesy: AOLS Archives

---

* Canada had been a world leader in air survey work ever since the ending of the Second World War.

McClarty before him, Babbage ended on a warning note. Unless the association was restructured, it would simply be bypassed.

The subsequent discussion centred on two motions, with the second contingent on the fate of the first. The first was to the effect that the association should recognize that land surveying included, among other things, "activity at the professional level in the fields of geodesy and photogrammetry." As this had been a self-evident fact for the past twenty or more years, the motion could hardly fail to pass. And it did, though not without some stonewalling on the part of some members. One member who could not attend the meeting wrote a letter that concluded: "For approximately eighty years, the Association has been able to administer its own affairs in its own way in accordance with the needs of its particular discipline. We would be complete and utter fools to permit any change in this Association by accepting proposals of doubtful merit which might be prejudicial to us and to our position in society."[4]

The second motion called on the Council of Management to examine and make recommendations on "the legal and administrative procedures required to incorporate the said principle (i.e., restructuring) within the structure of the Association." It was passed. Thereupon one member exclaimed: "You've just committed suicide."

About a year later, council voted to establish a committee on restructuring with James Dearden of Orillia as its head. In choosing members to serve on his committee, Dearden "considered it vitally important that [they] be leaders in the Association and active in its development. I was fortunate to secure the services of three past presidents, namely, Messrs. Dave Humphries, Fred Pearce, John Pierce, and our vice-president, Mr. 'Red' Petzold." The committee met nine times in the summer of 1972, one of the meetings being with the Honourable Leo Bernier, then minister of lands and forests. Dearden's committee recommended to council that a bylaw (73-3) be passed that would extend membership to land surveyors in the fields of photogrammetry, geodesy, and hydrography and regulate the manner in which their applications for membership be processed, such bylaw to come into effect on 1 January 1974.[5]

In his presidential address at the annual meeting of 1974, Petzold noted that Bylaw 73-3 had met with a largely negative response at the previous meeting. However, as instructed by the membership, he had followed up the work of the committee on restructuring by setting up a task force to examine the problem in all its ramifications. This led to a white paper on the subject, written by George Babbage. This was circulated to the members prior to the 1975 meeting, which was held in Sudbury. Following a heated discussion at the meeting, it was decided that the problem should be studied further in the ensuing year. Subsequently a ballot was held on whether or not the association should proceed with reconstruction. It was rejected – though only by a narrow margin. The committee on restructuring was dissolved and the task force disbanded.

Meanwhile the various provincial associations of land surveyors, of which there were then ten, had been drawing closer together in a process that culminated in the formation of the Canadian Council of Land Surveyors. When on his way to a Canadian Institute of Surveying convention in Edmonton in 1968, it struck John Pope, a past president of the Association of Nova Scotia Land Surveyors, that it would be a good idea if the presidents of the provincial associations should meet from time to time to discuss problems of mutual interest. His idea was acted on, with the first such meeting held in Ottawa in 1969, with eight provincial associations represented, those of Quebec, New Brunswick, Nova Scotia, Newfoundland, Manitoba, Saskatchewan, Alberta, and Ontario, the latter represented by F.J. Pearce. The presidents of the British Columbia and Prince Edward Island associations were absent.

The presidents met twice in 1970 and twice in 1971, and it was at the second of these meetings that the formation of a national organization of associations came up for serious discussion following a strong presentation by Professor O.J. Marshall on the self-governing professions in Ontario. A resolution was passed that called for the matter to be taken up by the provincial associations, the preamble to the resolution recognizing the "need for continual discussion on education, licensing, standards and ethics."[6] Marshall was nominated to investigate ways and means of setting up a permanent co-ordinating body.

At a meeting of the presidents in February 1972, a draft letters patent for incorporating an association was drawn up and discussed though no decisions were taken. At the second meeting, held in September of that year, however, a resolution was passed that among other things called for the approval in principle by the provincial associations of the formation of a "Canadian Council of Professional Land Surveyors." At a further meeting of presidents held in 1973, it was reported that six provincial associations had already approved of the proposed council.

A major problem – and the source of much discussion – had been the overlap in jurisdiction and function of the proposed council with the Canadian Institute of Surveying. However, this problem was eventually resolved and at a subsequent meeting of association presidents, held in Ottawa in 1976, it was reported by the chairman, Grenville Rogers of Ontario, that all that remained was to finalize the details of the incorporation of what was now being called the Canadian Council of Land Surveyors (not to be confused with the Association of Canada Lands Surveyors). The council was incorporated under federal letters patent on 10 February 1976 in the names *pro tem* of F.J. Pearce for Ontario, who had been an enthusiastic promoter of the council right from the start, L.R. Feetham for Nova Scotia, and R. Blanchet for Quebec. Following meetings held in Winnipeg in May 1976, the council became operational.

In an on-going process, the council has formulated and distributed to its ten member associations a national code of ethics, adopted a reciprocity policy regarding qualifications, inaugurated a university accreditation program, drawn up a policy on the procurement of surveying services, established a professional liability insurance program, established national standards, maintained an active education committee, and co-operated with the Canadian Institute of Surveying and Mapping on such projects as a textbook on survey law in Canada.

In the meantime, pressure on the Association of Ontario Land Surveyors to restructure itself had been growing. In 1977, the year after the Canadian Council of Land Surveyors came formally into being, the third colloquium on survey education was held at Lac Delage in Quebec. (There had been a second colloquium in 1966.) Much emphasis was placed at the third colloquium on restructuring. It was noted that the Canada Lands Surveys Act had just been passed by Parliament and would be proclaimed in 1978. As spelled out in the Canada Lands Surveys Act, Dominion Land Surveyors were to become Canada Lands Surveyors and the category of Dominion Topographical Surveyor was to be abolished. The new act also provided for a board of five members, including experts on legal surveying, geodesy, hydrography, and photogrammetry, who set the examinations for the Canada Lands Surveyor commission. The exams covered surveying in all its aspects. And, as such, represented the first attempt to restructure the profession at the federal level. The colloquium went on record as supporting the concept of restructuring at the horizontal level (that is, with no one branch of land surveying considered subordinate to any other) and urged that the Canadian Council of Land Surveyors should encourage all its member associations to take immediate steps towards restructuring.

The same year that the Canada Lands Surveys Act was proclaimed, the council of the Association of Ontario Land Surveyors moved that a task force on the role of the surveyor should "be asked to recommend routes by which professional surveyors, whose field of expertise does not include cadastral surveying can become members of the A.O.L.S." Two years later, in 1980, George J. Zubek[7] stated in his presidential address that he considered restructuring the "Number One priority for 1980." Later that year the membership was polled: 66 percent voted for restructuring. Thereupon the association, on becoming involved in the process of amending the Surveyors Act, started to pursue the matter with the Ministry of Natural Resources and representatives from the fields of photogrammetry, geodesy, and hydrography.

The final act in the restructuring drama may said to have been played out with the passage, after several years' delay, of a new Surveyors Act (R.S.O. 1987, c. 6), which was proclaimed in 1988 (later re-enacted as R.S.O. 1990, c. S.29). The new act, under which the Association of Ontario Land Surveyors functions at the time of writing, defined the "practice of professional land surveying" as "the determination of natural and man-made features of the surface of the earth and the storage and representation of such features on a chart, map, or graphic representation, and includes the practice of cadastral surveying," while cadastral surveying itself consisted of "advising on, reporting on, conducting or supervising the conducting of surveys to establish, locate, define or describe lines, boundaries or corners of parcels of land or land covered with water."

The new act swept away the venerable Board of Examiners and replaced it with the Academic and Experience Requirements Committee, one of the functions of which is to pronounce upon the admission to the association of surveyors, whatever their specialty. Surveyors whose field of expertise lay in fields other than the cadastral were to be granted certificates of registration, of which 107 had been granted by February 1992.

～৩৫৬~

Even as the association was struggling to adjust itself to the changes brought about by technological change, new electronic surveying systems were appearing. In 1973 the Geodetic Survey of Canada started testing the feasibility of using the U.S. Navy's Navigational Satellite System for survey work. The system depended on five polar-orbiting satellites. Unlike the passive satellites used in the mid-1960s, these were active, transmitting a coded identification signal on a stable

---

The Association of Canada Lands Surveyors

Formed in 1985, the ACLS is a voluntary association open to all practising and retired Canada Lands Surveyors. It seeks to promote, in the words of its fact sheet, "the application of the Canada Lands Surveyor commission to the professional fields of cadastral, geodetic, hydrographic and photogrammetric surveying of 'Canada Lands' as defined in the Canada Lands Survey Act." It also promotes uniform standards of knowledge, skill, conduct, and ethics among its Canada-wide membership. From time to time the association makes recommendations to the surveyor general of Canada regarding these standards. It also keeps an eye on the qualifying requirements and standards for Canada Lands Surveyors, besides promoting public awareness of the role played by these professionals. It encourages their professional development "in order to best serve the public and surveying profession." Provincial land surveyors are encouraged to qualify as Canada Lands Surveyors. It is anticipated that when there are enough Canada Lands Surveyors in any given area, the surveyor general of Canada will be asked to "declare that all survey work on Canada Lands in that area must be carried out by holders of the C.L.S. commission."

Past Presidents
Back Row: E.W. Petzold, F.J.S. Pearce, M.J.M. Maughan, W.J.G. Wadsworth,
J.D. Barber, D.T. Humphries, J.C. Kirkup, M. Hewett
Front Row: E.C. Brisco, G.T. Rogers S.G. Hancock, H.D.G. Currie, D.W. Endleman
(Present but missed picture M.N. Simpson, J.D. Dearden, J.G. Pierce)

Some past presidents of the association at the 1980 annual meeting. (From *AOLS Proceedings, 1980*)

used ISS for various special projects and for establishing 120 new survey stations in Central Ontario in connection with 1:50 000 mapping, later going on to use the system to interpolate survey points between established Doppler stations.

In the early eighties, the Global Positioning System (GPS) made its appearance in Canada. Originally developed by the U.S. Department of Defence for military navigational purposes, and intended to replace the Doppler system, which would be allowed to fall into disuse as the satellites ran down, GPS depends on a number of satellites that orbit the earth at a height of about eleven thousand miles (18 000 km). There were seven satellites functioning by 1986, with plans to have twenty-one in place by 1993, plus three spares. Moving in six orbital planes relative to the earth, the satellites are co-ordinated so that at least four satellites will be above the horizon at any one time.

The radio signals transmitted by the satellites can be used in two different ways. In one, the so-called pseudo range from satellite to receiver is given by the time taken for the signal to travel from satellite to observer, expressed in terms of distance, with a correction made for clock errors in the receiver. In the other, differences in the phase of the transmitted signal and the receiver are measured. Observations on at least three different satellites must be made to determine the observer's position and altitude, this, mathematically speaking, through a combination of celestial triangulation and trilateration. However, if the altitude of the observer is known, as on a ship at sea, for example, observations of only two satellites may suffice.

Using the pseudo range, an instant readout of the observer's geographical position can be obtained from a single receiver to within about three hundred feet (100 m), generally speaking. Errors in altitude are larger because the distances yielded by the system are to the centre of the earth, and the earth of course is not a perfect sphere. On the face of it, such degrees of accuracy would appear to preclude the use of GPS for

frequency. Distances from satellite to ground station were measured by means of the Doppler shift in the signal transmitted, from which the position of the receiver on the ground could be accurately ascertained.

In 1974 the Geodetic Survey mounted a major operation in which Doppler stations were established – many of them on the sites of existing shoran stations – along the entire east coast of Canada, including Newfoundland, and as far north as the Arctic mainland, with complete coverage of the Arctic Islands. With the co-operation of the Danish government, this geodetic network was tied in to three points in Greenland. In 1975 a start was made on extending the Doppler network across mainland

Canada, a project that would eventually be completed in the mid-1980s.

Another system tested in the mid-1970s by the Geodetic Survey was the Inertial Survey System (ISS). This involved two gyroscopes that oriented themselves north-south and east-west respectively, combined with accelerometers that sensed both horizontal and vertical movement. A built-in computer integrated the readings from the gyros and accelerometers, with elapsed time giving the distance travelled by the instrument, which could be transported in a van or helicopter. However, the system was initially extremely expensive and only some oil companies and the federal government could afford it. In 1975 the Geodetic Survey

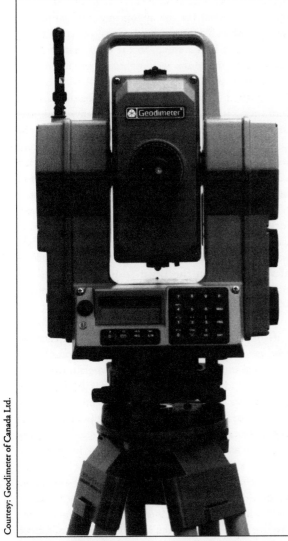

A modern total station. Used in combination with a reflector station, total stations now not only give extremely accurate distances and angles but carry out a variety of calculations in a built-in computer.

surveying work. However, in what is known as relative geodetic positioning, by using carrier phase measurements and observations from several widely spaced receivers (the geographical position of at least some of which are accurately known), errors are so small that they are now being measured in less than one part per million.[8] Extremely expensive in the mid-eighties, the receivers are already getting cheaper, while at the same time getting smaller and thus more portable – receivers may soon be no bigger than a cigarette pack.

By 1986 the Geodetic Survey of Canada was working on specifications that would be attached to the new system, while at the same time plans were being made to establish a number of monitoring stations to track the movements of the satellites, this with the object of furnishing information that would be useful in planning GPS observational work. By the mid-eighties, several companies on contract had already used GPS on a variety of projects, including the feasibility of using the system to establish control points within municipalities.

With its light, portable receivers and extreme accuracy, the Global Positioning System is now in the process of revolutionizing land surveying. However, like shoran and the Doppler system before it, GPS cannot as yet be used by the land surveyor in his everyday work. Apart from anything else, the proximity of tall buildings may interfere with GPS observations. But as computers became increasingly miniaturized and as electronics developed, the venerable transit began to be replaced by increasingly compact and extremely accurate instruments using ranging systems based on various types of transmissions, which, with an appropriate reflector at the remote station, give both distances and angles to a hitherto undreamed of accuracy. Known as "total stations" and with distances and both vertical and horizontal angles appearing on a digital display, some of these instruments are smaller than a shoe box. Today their various manufacturers vie with each other as they bring out successive models replete with new

features designed to ease the task of the land surveyor and to increase the accuracy of results. And there is talk of combining such instruments with a GPS receiver, thus giving surveyors the best of both worlds.

It will be recalled that since the late 1950s, the accuracy of surveys under the Land Titles Act had been checked by the Legal Surveys Division of the office of the director of titles. This division's ever-increasing workload had increased still further with the passage in 1958 of the Certification of Titles Act. This problem had been at least partly alleviated by the introduction of the reference plan system and, in the early 1960s, by the appointment of assistant examiners in the land titles offices in Bracebridge, Sudbury, Sault Ste. Marie, and Kenora.

However, the situation regarding plans lodged with registry offices had changed little. While regulations regarding the standard of surveys made under the Registry Act had been promulgated in 1964, checking for compliance could not be carried out as registrars of deeds and their staffs lacked the necessary training to examine plans. Thus, heavy reliance was still being placed on certificates submitted by the surveyors themselves.

In 1972, in order to bring the administration of the two systems of land registration closer together, both the Land Titles Act and the Registry Act were amended with the result that, as of 1 April 1973, all subdivision plans in a land titles area had to be registered under the Land Titles Act. Land titles offices, including combined registry and land titles offices, were renamed land registry offices. And the reference plan system was extended to registry office records.

Also in 1972, the Legal Surveys Division of the office of the director of titles was made a branch of the Property Rights Division of the newly formed Ministry of Consumer and Commercial Relations. The new branch was given the responsibility of exercising

Courtesy: Geodimeter of Canada Ltd.

control, not only over the quality of plans submitted under the Land Titles Act, the Certification of Titles Act, the Boundaries Act, and the Condominium Act, but those entering the registry system as well. Regional assistant examiners were appointed in London and Ottawa, but even so, to cope with the increased number of plans to be examined, a new approach was required.

Known as "submission analysis," the approach that replaced the detailed in-depth analysis of all plans submitted was based on the assumption that the quality of work carried out by most Ontario Land Surveyors could be relied upon. Those surveyors who were known by past experience to turn in quality work would need only occasional monitoring. Thus, plans submitted by such surveyors could be examined and pronounced upon relatively speedily. Only if a submission was substandard was an in-depth examination to be carried out.

All this had placed the association, a self-regulatory body by statute, in the invidious position (where in fact it had been since the mid-1950s) of having the accuracy of its members' work scrutinized by an outside body – something that struck at the very roots of the association's *raison-d'être*. In 1970 the association took the first active step towards rectifying the situation by establishing a professional standards committee. Its prime function was to evaluate and report on the quality of surveys and plans made by its members "in order that the public interest may be served and protected."

Over a five-year period, this committee, in co-operation with the ministry and the land registry offices, carried out an exhaustive study of many plans deposited or registered under the Registry Act. Continuously poor work was monitored with recommendations for remedial action made to individual members and to the association's complaints committee. In 1975, however, the committee was discontinued despite considerable progress made in upgrading

standards. Overloaded with work as it was, the committee had asked for the appointment of a full-time member of staff to assist in checking plans, but such had not been forthcoming. In the years that followed, disciplinary procedures were tightened up and retraining seminars were held by the association.

In 1983 the association took a major step towards confirming its commitment to high quality work with the endorsement by a substantial majority of its members of a document entitled "Standards for Surveys," which was incorporated within the "Code of Ethics" and the "Standards of Conduct" already published by the association. Two years later, in 1985, Vernon S. McCutcheon (commissioned in 1951 and now retired) was commissioned by the Ministry of Consumer and Commercial Relations to review the whole matter of plan examination and the utilization of survey staff in the Legal and Survey Standards Branch of the ministry. As a preliminary, McCutcheon interviewed some sixty practising land surveyors, as well as officers of the association and the staff of various government agencies. His findings soon made it clear that while the examination of plans had done much towards improving their quality, just as much had been accomplished by appealing to the professional pride of the surveyors themselves. Most importantly, he found that it was the opinion of many in the association that the time had come for the association to assume a greater responsibility for the quality of work carried out by its members.

Accordingly, as of 1 January 1986, the association set up a Survey Review Department (SRD) by agreement with the ministry. In effect, the association took over from the ministry the responsibility of examining and approving reference plans deposited under the Land Titles Act and the Registry Act, such plans constituting the bulk of plans submitted under those acts. At the time of writing, plans registered under the Boundaries Act, the Certification of Titles Act, and the Condominium Act still require ministry approval, as do first registrations under the Land Titles Act and three-dimensional reference plans.

To cover the start-up costs for the new department, the association was given a one-time grant by the ministry, while on-going expenses of the department are covered by the sale of stickers, which must be affixed to all plans registered or deposited in land registry and land titles offices, of which there are now sixty-seven across the province. The number of stickers sold gives a good idea of the volume of land surveying work being carried out in the province – and, it may be observed, of the prevailing state of the development and construction industry and thus of the province's economy. Nearly thirty-three thousand stickers were sold in 1988, a total that rose to almost thirty-seven thousand in 1989 and which fell to twenty-eight thousand in 1990.

The Survey Review Department, managed at the time of writing by Andrea E. Tieman, O.L.S., receives prints of all stickered reference plans deposited in land titles and registry offices, as well as private plans that do not enter the land registration system. These prints are filed alphabetically by firm, of which there were over 360 in Ontario in 1991. The SRD carries out two types of review: a "systematic" and a "comprehensive." In the former, at least one plan from every firm in the province is examined each year. In the latter, eight or more of a firm's plans, which include both reference and private plans and which must be accompanied by supporting information, are examined in detail. The office of the surveyor concerned is visited and the field work in connection with some of the plans is checked out on the ground. The SRD aims to carry out a comprehensive review of a survey firm's work at least once every five years.

Following a comprehensive review, the SRD reports its findings to the firm in question, and suggestions and recommendations for improvement are made. For an individual surveyor who is found wanting, either in surveying principles or knowledge of the relevant statutes, the association has a system for retraining.

Setting up the Survey Review Department forced the association to look for new premises. For many years, the association had been using only part of the building they owned at 6070 Yonge Street in Willowdale. But with the number of staff increasing, it had taken over the whole building in 1980. With no room to house the new department in the old building, the association moved its office on 2 December 1985 to its present location at 1043 McNicoll Avenue in Scarborough.

Meanwhile, beginning in the fall of 1987, in anticipation of the passage of the new Surveyors Act with its implicit recognition that photogrammetry, geodesy, and hydrography were now playing an essential role in land surveying, a start was made on revising the curriculum of the survey science course held at the Erindale campus of the University of Toronto. While maintaining a common core of subjects for all students, a study program could be followed in one of four streams: cadastral surveying; mapping and land management information, including photogrammetry; hydrographic surveying; and geodetic surveying. The Centre for Surveying Science, as it is now called, has a teaching staff of seven resident professors, four adjunct professors, and part-time assistants. The director is Dr. Gordon Gracie. As of March 1992, 359 students have graduated from the course at Erindale, about 85 percent of whom have gone on to qualify as Ontario Land Surveyors.

It will be recalled that in the late 1960s, regulations for the use of the Ontario Co-ordinate System were promulgated but were never made mandatory. In 1973 the Surveys and Mapping Branch of what had become the Ministry of Natural Resources, proposed that a three-year study be made to find better ways of recording, storing, and displaying information on the dimensions, features, and natural resources of the province. This led, in 1974, to a Task Force on

Harold S. Howden, who was chief surveyor for the Ministry of Transportation and Communications and assistant deputy minister, received the association's Professional Recognition Award in 1991.

Geographical Referencing, which conducted a comprehensive study of the mapping needs of the various government ministries and agencies concerned with land use and water use, as well as the requirements of municipalities. After several years of deliberation, to which the geodetic committee of the association contributed significantly, the task force recommended the adoption of the Ontario Geographical Referencing Grid, which is based on the Universal Transverse

Mercator projection (UTM) with a 6-degree, as opposed to a 3-degree, zone as used in the Ontario Co-ordinate System. The specifications for the UTM system were introduced in 1979, together with guidelines – there were no statutory regulations.

The decision to proceed with UTM with its 6-degree zones was not without its detractors. Most map projections require a correction factor if the grid co-ordinates are to yield an accurate geographical position on the earth's curved surface. Some land surveyors argued that, given narrow enough zones, the difference between distance as shown on the grid and the actual distance would be so small that it could be ignored for most practical purposes. In the UTM system, a correction factor must indeed be applied, but this is hardly an onerous procedure. In the event, the decision to proceed with the UTM system was backed by a number of provincial ministries. However, the overriding argument for the introduction of the UTM system in Ontario was almost certainly that the federal government had already adopted it.

At the time of writing, the province's surveyor general is Pier L. Finos,[9] who succeeded to the post in February 1990 following the retirement of S.B. Panting. The Surveyor General's Office, now part of the Land and Resource Information Branch of the Ministry of Natural Resources, is responsible for all surveys of crown lands as it always has been. And, as in the past, it prepares letters patent and other legal documents in connection with changes in the status of crown land. Today, in an on-going process, a computer index to all crown survey records is being developed and refined.

The Surveyor General's Office also remains responsible for the provincial system of horizontal and vertical control survey networks, maintains the data base of geodetic survey data supplied by various agencies, and makes such data available to users. While the position of each control station is defined as its precise latitude and longitude, it is done in such a way that plane co-ordinates can be extracted for use on either the Ontario Co-ordinate System with its 3-degree zones or the official Ontario Geographic Referencing Grid with its 6-degree zones.

The Surveyor General's Office also administers the Surveys Act, the Surveyors Act, and the Geographic Names Board Act and the regulations under those acts. Under the surveys and surveyors acts, the surveyor general continues to play a significant role in the affairs of the Association of Ontario Land Surveyors.

Other branches of the Ministry of Natural Resources are also very much concerned with maps and mapping. The prime responsibility of the Provincial Mapping Office, for example, is the administration of the Ontario Basic Mapping Program. The work of the task force on geographic referencing in the mid-1970s had made it clear that there was growing concern that topographic mapping activity across the province, of which there was a great deal, was uncoordinated in that it lacked a common approach to the description of features making up the land mass of the province. What was required was provincial leadership, and it was this that the Ontario Basic Mapping Program set out to provide.

Inaugurated by the Ministry of Natural Resources in 1977, the object of the program, as its name implies, was to set topographic mapping standards and to produce base maps covering the province at scales that would best meet the diverse needs of the many would-be users of such maps, both government and otherwise. For southern Ontario, a scale of 1:10 000 was chosen, that is, 1 cm on the map equals 0.10 km on the ground. For northern Ontario the scale would be 1:20 000, that is, 1 cm:0.20 km. For municipalities the much larger scale of 1:2 000 was selected (1 cm:20 m).

In this on-going program, the Provincial Mapping Office of the Ministry of Natural Resources oversees the field work, which is tendered out to approved private land and air survey companies. Municipalities contribute to the costs of the large-scale maps on a sliding scale dependent on the size of their population. The ministry remains responsible for the production of the base maps themselves, which are produced as hard-copy topographic maps in black and white. The maps, which utilize the Ontario Geographical Referencing Grid, are now being used by ten provincial ministries, as well as by the federal government, utility companies, municipalities, educational institutions, private companies, and the general public. Since 1988 three-dimensional topographic information throughout the province has been computerized in digital form, which allows for automated applications. And for the large-scale surveys of municipalities, separate computer files are created and made available to them.

The Ontario Centre for Remote Sensing also comes under the aegis of the ministry. It provides a provincial focus for developing new ways of using information derived from satellites and airborne equipment to manage natural resources and the environment. Thus, the centre supported a National Aeronautics and Space Administration (NASA) remote-sensing program that evaluated forest decline using advanced imaging spectrometers, while at present the centre is participating in an international project undertaken to study the production of greenhouse gases from northern wetlands. Other projects in which the centre is involved include the use of remote-sensing technology in compiling soil maps and in the delineation of wildlife habitat.

March 1992 saw the retirement of Lorraine Petzold, the association's long-time executive director. (Lorraine Setterington had become Lorraine Petzold on her second marriage to E.W. Petzold.) She had held the post for sixteen years. One of her first tasks on being appointed had been to determine the status of ninety articled students, most of whom the association had not heard from for several years. Following this she made recommendations as to how student surveyors could be encouraged to complete their articles, and she went on to develop a highly effective monitoring procedure whereby what was then the Board of Examiners could keep track of and encourage articled students. She introduced the first *Student's Handbook* and also instituted a swearing-in ceremony for newly commissioned land surveyors.

Right from the start, Petzold had been relentless in her determination to upgrade the standards of the profession. On taking office she had found that the association was appealing a judicial case arising out of a disciplinary ruling. On looking into it, she found that the association was at fault in twenty-six of the twenty-seven infractions cited. Later she would go on to revise disciplinary procedures so that, at hearings, up to five years of a surveyor's work would be considered rather than just a single survey. By November 1990 she had prepared some thirty-five cases against land surveyors involving incompetence or unethical behaviour. She won all of them.

With her eye always on the future, Petzold became heavily involved with high schools, community colleges, and universities in an on-going effort to attract and retain high-quality recruits to the surveying profession. And, pursuing her goal of improving the professional image of the land surveyor, she lectured to land survey associations in the United States, the Caribbean, England, and Australia, her theme being methods of building up the professional background of the land surveyor.

Perhaps first and foremost, Petzold was tireless in her efforts to improve the status of land surveyors *vis-à-vis* the legal profession, taking part in Canadian Bar Association seminars and giving lectures in the Law Society of Upper Canada's bar admission course. Out of these came papers that are now quoted by lawyers in case law. And in 1983 she toured the province giving lectures to county bar associations. As Petzold's reputation spread, she was invited to speak to lawyers' groups in Nova Scotia, Newfoundland, and British Columbia. And in 1989, her efforts and those of like-minded colleagues culminated in the publication of Canada's first textbook on survey law. In the meantime, at the annual meeting of the Canadian Council of Land Surveyors in 1987, she was presented with the Champlain Award "for outstanding service to the land surveying profession," while at the annual meeting that marked the end of the association's centennial year, she was honoured with the association's Professional Recognition Award. Lorraine Petzold had indeed proved to be the right person in the right place at the right time, and she prepared the association well for what lay ahead in the 1990s.

In 1988–89 the federal government produced the last maps in the 1:50 000 National Topographic Series. These were photomaps of the southwest corner of Hudson Bay, and were the last of the 1124 sheets in the series that covered Ontario. Here the mapping of the province may be said to have come to a symbolic end, this some 380 years after Henry Hudson produced his first crude chart of Hudson Bay and Samuel

Lorraine Setterington (now Lorraine Petzold), Canada's first woman surveyor. Executive director of the Association of Ontario Land Surveyors, she retired in 1992 after holding the position for sixteen years.
Courtesy: Lorraine Petzold, O.L.S.

The Geographic Names Board

Liaising with the Canadian Permanent Committee on Geographical Names, the Geographic Names Board rules on the admissibility or otherwise of geographic names in Ontario and how they should be spelled – dealing with a problem, it may be added, that Lord Dorchester first grappled with in the 1780s. The board maintains a provincial data base of official, unofficial, and alternate names for geographical features and places, as well as collect and collate their historical background. It also provides identifier codes for some 12 000 bodies of water in the province to serve as a key to Ontario's Fisheries Information System. There are now some fifty-seven thousand entries on the board's list of official geographic names.

de Champlain made his first maps of the land that one day would become Ontario.

A wide range of maps are now available from the Natural Resources Information Centre of the Ontario Ministry of Natural Resources. A series of seven maps that cover the province at a scale of 1:600 000 shows such features as major rivers and roads, cities, towns, districts, counties, and townships. Another series at a scale of 1:100 000 that covers only the southern part of northern Ontario shows a wide range of features. And Ontario Basic Maps in black and white are now available for much of the province. Contours at 10-metre intervals are shown on the 1:20 000 maps of northern Ontario; on the 1:10 000 maps of southern Ontario, the contours are at 5-metre intervals. No more *terra incognita!* Willis Chipman and other land surveyors who fought so hard for the topographic mapping of the province would have been well pleased.

In 1992, the Association of Ontario Land Surveyors celebrated the hundredth anniversary of its incorporation. As of April 1992 the association had 798 active members, of which 21 were women. The registration numbers being allotted to newly qualified land surveyors are now in the sixteen hundreds. In other words, over sixteen hundred men and women have became Ontario Land Surveyors since the association was incorporated in 1892. Add the perhaps four hundred deputy and provincial land surveyors of earlier days, and one arrives at a total number of land surveyors working in the province since the coming of the Loyalists that is in the region of two thousand. Of these, nearly three-quarters were licensed since the Second World War, an indication of the explosion in the size of the profession since the war. With all due respect to the modern surveyor, much honour is due to the remaining quarter of that two thousand who opened up the province and contributed so much to its development.

Like its predecessors down the years, the present Surveys Act (R.S.O. 1990, c. S.30) is the lineal descen-dent of the ordinance issued in 1785. The act itself testifies to the long history of land surveying in the province, dealing as it does with the land-surveying procedures to be followed in the various types of townships laid out in the course of more than two centuries. In the mid-1980s, the Ministry of Natural Resources completed a resurvey program to restore the corners and re-establish the boundaries of townships in southern Ontario, something long advocated by the association. A long-range program to do the same for the townships of northern Ontario is now in place and should be complete by the year 2000, funds permitting.

So the old townships are still very much with us, an essential part of both the survey fabric of the province and its administrative structure. With us, too, are the other abiding monuments to the work of the land surveyors of Ontario: our cities and towns, our farms, our roads and highways, our dams and hydro lines, our railways and mines, and, for that matter, the lots on which our homes now stand.

APPENDICES

Appendix A
Lists of Deputy and Provincial Land Surveyors

There are only a few of these lists still extant. Those given here are to be found in the Archives of Ontario, RG1 CB-1 (Survey Diaries and Field Notes, 1790–1928), box 43, miscellaneous records.

1. List of Deputy Surveyors, dated 25 April 1805

(Rearranged alphabetically)

Cockerel, Richard
Fortune, William
Fortune, Joseph
Fraser, Thomas
Grant, Lewis
Greeley, Aaron
Iredell, William
Jones, Augustus
Rider (sic), John
Sherwood, Reuben
Smith, Henry
Stevens, Solomon
Welch, Thomas
Wilmot, Samuel

2. The jacket of this list reads "Schedule of Dep. Surveyors in the Province of Upper Canada, S.G. Office, 6 July 1838." It is reproduced here as it was written.

List of Deputy Surveyors now resident in Upper Canada

Eastern District

Bower, Thomas J.	Osnabruck
Brown, William	Cornwall
Bruce, John S.	Osnabruck
Cattanach, Angus	Dalhousie Mills, Lancaster
McDonell, Duncan	Charlottenburgh
McDonell, Niels	Kenyon
McGillis, John	Williamstown
McDonald, William	Cornwall

Ottawa District

Swalwell, Anthony	Bytown
McNaughton, John	Bytown

Bathurst District

Curry, Robert	Lanark
Rickey, Josias	Perth
	Drummond
Robertson, John	Fitzroy Harbour

Johnstown Distt [sic]

	Address
Blakeley, John	Post Of. Killey Bastard
Booth, John	P.O. Brockville Elizabethtown
Campbell, William	P.O. Merrickville Oxford
Fraser, William	P.O. Prescot [sic] Edwardsburgh
Landon, Asa	Augusta
McDonald, John S.	Leeds
West, James	P.O. Kemptville Oxford

Midland District

Benson, Samuel M.	Belleville
Bruce, George	Kingston
Burke, William	Kingston
Beckwith, Adolphus J.	Marmora
Burroughs, Thomas	Kingston Mills
Clapp, Gilbert S.	Napanee
Campbell, Alexander	Richmond
Emerson, John	Thurlow
Fairfield, William S.	Bath
Fraser, Thomas	Township of Kingston
Kilborn, William H.	Kingston
Nickalls, James	do
Rider, John	Marmora
Smith, John	do

Prince Edward District

Conger, Wilson	Hallowell
Elmore, Publius V.S.	Picton

District of Newcastle

Birdsall, Richard	Asphodel Otonabee
Dennehy (sp?), J. Thomas	do
Huston, John S.	Cavan
Rubidge, Fredk P.	Cobourg
Merriman, Isaiah	Cramahe
Reid, John	Douro
Sanders, George	Cobourg
Wilmot, S.S.	Clarke
Wright, Richard	Cobourg

Home District

Callahan, Patrick	Gore of Toronto
Castle, Henry James	City of Toronto
Chewett, James G.	do
Devine, John	Streetsville
Ewing, Henry	Whitby
Farquharson, John	do
Goesman, John	Markham
Hughes, Christopher	Township of Toronto
Hawkins, Williams [sic]	City of Toronto
Howard, J.S.(?)	do
Kelly, Thomas	do
McLean, Neil	Medonte
Ridout, Samuel	Toronto
Rankin, Charles	do
Scott, John	Innisfil
Lount, George	Holland Landing

Nelson, John — Markham
Hamilton, James — Toronto
White, John Edward — Thorah
Galbraith, John — Brock Pickering
Ridout, Edwd Jacques — Toronto
Richardson, Samuel — Barrie

Gore District

Allchin, Thomas — Wilmot
Black, Hugh — Norval
Blythe, Thomas Allen — Hamilton
Burwell, Lewis — Brantford
Cleaver, James — Nelson
Kerr, Robert — Dundas
Kirkpatrick, James — W. Flamborough
Lind, Joshua — Hamilton
McMahon, Hugh — Guelph
Marlet, Adrian — Dundas
Miller, Andrew — Hamilton
Rees, Richard — Barton
Ryckman, Samuel — do
Tiffany, George S. — Hamilton
Sterrett, James
Burt, John — Erin
Smith, John — Ancaster
Walker, William — Brantford

Niagara District

Ball, George A. — St. Catharines
Ball, Jesse P. — Niagara
Fell, Charles K. — Pelham
DeCou, Edward — Cayuga
Fell, Zenos — St. John's in Pelham
Misner, Jacob — Mainfleet
Kykert, George — St. Catharines
Kennedy, Charles — Gainsborough

London District

Burwell, Mahlon — Port Talbot
Carroll, Peter — Oxford

Hanney, Daniel — St. Thomas
Bostwick, John — Port Stanley
Springer, Benjamin — Delaware
O'Mara, John
Lynn, Robert — Woodstock
McDonald, John — Goderich
Harris, John — London

Talbot District

Walsh, Frances [sic] S. — Vittoria

Western District

McIntosh, Alexander — Chatham
Wilkinson, John Alexr — Sandwich

Keating, John W. — Island of St. Joseph

Finis

3. List of Provincial Land Surveyors to 31 October 1857

(Accompanying circular issued by the Crown Lands Department, December, 1857.)

Note: The original list is in columns with names listed alphabetically, "Date of Appointment," "Residence," and "Remarks." For the sake of brevity, place of residence and remarks have been omitted. I have rearranged the names by the date of licensing. A number of these dates are missing on the list. I have supplied some, which are marked with an asterisk. The remainder are listed separately in alphabetical order at the bottom of the list. "D" indicates surveyors listed as deceased. Many more must have been so.

Name	Year Licensed	
Collins, John	1764	D
Chewett, William	1774	D
Tinling, (William)	1783*	
Kotte, Lewis	1783*	D
Peachy (sic), (James)	1783*	D
Jessup, (Edward)	1784?*	D
McNiff, Patrick	1784	D
Frey, Phillip	1785*	D
Aitken, Alexander	1785	D
Dies, Mathew	1786?*	D
McDonell, Hugh	1788	D
Pennoyer, Jesse	1788	D
Marcoullier, Pierre	1788	
Hazen, Daniel	1788	D
Fortune, William	1788	D
Perrault, Louis	1789	D
Devens, Marie d.d.G.	1789	
Depensier, Theodore	1789	
Rankin, James	1789	D
Vondenvelden, William	1790*	
Stegman, John	1790	D
Coffin, Nathaniel	1790	D
Bedard, J.B.	1790	
Beaupre, Pierre	1791	
Bouchette, Joseph	1791	D
Jones, Augustus	1791	D
Grant, Lewis	1792*	D
Legendre, Francois	1792	D
Turgeon, Charles	1792	D
Demers, Jean B.	1792	D
Dezery, Amable	1792	D
Antill, John C.	1793	D
Welch, Thomas	1793*	D
Hambly, William	1795	D
Watkins, Seth	1795	D
Barris, Josiah	1795	
Fortune, Joseph	1796	D
Whiting, Charles	1796	
Root, Azariah	1796	
McDonald, Allan	1796	D
Lawe, William Parren	1797	D
Greely, Aaron	1797	D
Sherwood, Reuben	1799*?	D
Smith, Thomas	1799	D
Iredell, Abraham	1799*	D
Ryckman, Samuel	1800	D
Rider (Ryder?), John	1800*	D
Wilmot, Samuel S.	1804	D
Ridout, Samuel	1806	D
Rogers, Jonathan	1808	
McDonell, Duncan	1808	
Graves, William	1809	D
Burwell, Mahlon	1809	D
Watson, Simon Z.	1810	D
McLean, Robert	1811	D
Conger, Wilson	1811	D
Everitt, Daniel	1811	D
Park, Shubal	1812	D
Kilborn, Joseph	1813	D
Caldwell, Thomas	1816	
Booth, John	1816	
Nickalls, James	1817	D
Bristol, Richard	1818	D
Burwell, Lewis	1818	
White, John E.	1819	D
Richey, Josias	1819	
Preston, Reuben	1819	
Landon, Asa	1819	
Kennedy, Charles	1819	D
Hudson, John H.	1819	D
Harris, John	1819	D
Galbraith, John	1819	
Chewett, James G.	1819	
Bostwick, John	1819	D
Lount, Gabriel	1819	D
Birdsall, Richard	1819	D
Benson, Samuel M.	1819	
Smith, Samuel	1820	
Rankin, Charles	1820	
Mount, Rosswell	1820	D
McDonald, William	1820	
Lount, George	1820	

Name	Year		Name	Year		Name	Year		Name	Year	
Huston, John	1820	D	Cusack, Rheddy	1827	D	Smiley, William	1836		McDermott, Michael	1843	
Hanchette, Hiram	1820	D	Carroll, Peter	1828		Robertson, John	1836		McClary, William	1843	
Ewing, Henry	1820	D	Springer, Benjamin	1830		Ridout, Edmund J.	1836	D	Kirk, Joseph	1843	
Cattanack, Angus	1820		Fell, Zenas	1830		Rankin, Arthur	1836		Haslett, John J.	1843	
Black, Hugh	1820	D	Farquharson, John	1830	D	McMillan, William	1836		Bell, Robert	1843	
Devine, John	1820	D	Campbell, Alexander	1830		McMahon, Hugh	1836	D	Shier, John	1844	
Rykert, George	1821					Kerr, Robert W.	1836		Salter, Albert P.	1844	
Richardson, Samuel	1821	D	Blakely, John	1830	D	Howard, John G.	1836		Roney, John J.	1844	
Pennock, John	1821	D	Rubidge, Frederick P.	1831		Hood, Andrew	1836		Liddy, George P.	1844	
McNaughton, John	1821		Lind, Joshua	1831	D	Dennehy, John	1836		Kerr, Francis	1844	
Malcolm, Eliakim	1821		Kelly, Thomas	1831		DeCew, Edmund	1836		Gibbard, William	1844	
Kilborn, William H.	1821		Fell, Charles K.	1831		Blyth, Thomas A.	1836		Daniell, John D.	1844	
Goesman, John	1821	D	Burrows, Thomas	1831		Sanders, George	1837	D	Conger, John O.	1844	
Egan, Michael R.	1821		Tidey, John A.	1832		Reid, John	1837		Brough, Allan P.	1844	D
Elmore, Publius V.	1821		Scott, John	1832	D	Allchin, Thomas	1837		Bridgland, James W.	1844	
Quin, Owen	1822	D	Keating, John W.	1832		Strange, Henry	1838		Ambrose, Charles	1844	
Miller, Andrew	1822		Hawkins, William	1832					Tully, John	1845	
Merriman, Isaiah	1822	D	Harley, William	1832		Young, Humphrey	1840	D	Sinclair, Duncan	1845	
McDonald, John S.	1822	D	Hanvey, Daniel	1832		Keefer, Thomas C.	1840		Pollock, James	1845	
Hughes, Christopher	1822	D	Clements, Edgar	1832		Jones, Francis	1840		McDonell, John R.	1845	
Fairfield, W.J.	1822		Castle, Henry J.	1832		Bartley, Onesiphorus	1840		Clendinen, James K.	1845	D
Currie, Robert	1822	D	Ross, Robert	1833		Walsh, Robert	1841	D	Austin, George	1845 ?	
Wright, Richard	1823	D	O'Mara, John	1833		Ryle, Mathew	1841		Salter, Phiboleth D.	1846	D
Swallwell, Anthony	1823		McLeod, John	1833		Roche, John K.	1841		Robinson, William	1846	
Smith, Christopher	1823	D	Emerson, John	1833		Falls, Hugh	1841	D	Passmore, Frederick F.	1846	
McDonald, John	1823		Callaghan, Patrick	1833		Gibbs, Thomas F.	1841*		McNab, Archibald	1846	
Kirkpatrick. James	1823		Bruce, George	1833		White, Henry	1842		McLennan, Roderick	1846	
Dennison, John	1823		Ball, Jesse P.	1833		Wells, Alphonso	1842	D	Devine, Thomas	1846	
Campbell, William	1823		Smyth, John	1834	D	Walsh, Thomas W.	1842		Cromwell, Joseph M.O.	1846	
Burt, John	1823	D	Shurtliff, Lemuel	1834		Vidal, Alexander	1842		Caddy, Edward C.	1846	
Gill, Valentine	1824		Ball, George A.	1834		Peterson, Joseph S.	1842		Booth, Norman	1846	
Cleaver, James	1824		Wilkinson, John A.	1835	D	Perry, Aylesworth B.	1842		Snow, John Allen	1847	
West, James	1825		Walker, William	1835		Newman, John	1842		Morris, John	1847	
Tiffany, George S.	1825	D	Rees, Richard	1835		Ivory, Patrick	1842		Miller, Chisholm	1847	D
Smith, John Jr.	1825		Nelson, John	1835	D	Harper, John S.	1842		Lyons, James	1847	
McIntosh, Alexander	1825	D	Moore, James	1835	D	Galbraith, William	1842		Fraser, Charles	1847	
McGillis, John	1825	D	McLean, Neal	1835	D	Fletcher, Edward T.	1842		Fraser, William	1847	D
McDonald, Neill	1825	D	Lynn, Robert	1835		Dennis, John S.	1842		Deane, William H.	1847	
Hall, James	1825		Hamilton, James	1835		Carroll, William	1842		Wonham, William G.	1847	
Gibson, David	1825		Fell, James W.	1835		Wilkinson, Alexander	1843		Smith, William	1848	
Fraser, Thomas	1825	D	Clapp, Gilbert S.	1835		Sparke, John F.	1843	D	Savigny, H.P.	1848	
Sterrett, James B.	1826		Bruce, John S.	1835		Schofield, Milton C.	1843		Ryan, John	1848	
Bower, Thomas T.	1826		Boyce, George	1835		Richey, James	1843		Rombough, W.R.	1848	
Misner, Jacob	1827		Tracey, William	1836		Parr, Richard	1843	D	Rath, William	1848	

McPhillips, George	1848	Wood, Henry O.	1855
McLaren, Peter	1848	McConnell, William	1855
Hamilton, Robert	1848	Kingsford, William	1855
Grant, John	1848	Johnston, James	1855
Deane, Michael	1848	Hobson, Joseph	1855
Browne, John O.	1848	Haskins, William	1855
Slater, James Dyson	1849	Gibson, James A.	1855
Rubidge, Tom S.	1849	Forrest, Alfred Guy	1855
McCallum, James, Jr.	1849	Donovan, Thomas	1855
Maxwell, John	1849	Boultbee, William	1855
Kertland, Ed. Henry	1849	Bay, Andrew	1855
Fleming, Sandford A.	1849	Wheelock, C.J.	1856
Donnelly, Phillip S.	1849	Weatherald, Thomas	1856
Black, James Jr.	1849	Simpson, Alexander W.	1856
		Shortt, Lawrence H.	1856
Sinclair, Donald	1850	Northcote, Henry	1856
Prosser, Thomas C.	1850	Mercer, William	1856
Jones, E. Robert	1850	McLeod, Henry A.F.	1856
Driscoll, Alfred	1850	McCallum, F.C.	1856
Brown, David R.	1850	Lynch, F.H.	1856
Peters, Samuel	1851	Low, Hamilton	1856
Molesworth, Thomas N.	1851	Low, N.E.	1856
Bristow, Arthur	1851	Jack, John Ross	1856
Unwin, Charles	1852	Herrick, Thomas W.	1856
Stewart, George A.	1852	Gilmour, Robert	1856
Rykert, George Z.	1852	Gardner, Peter	1856
Perceval, William	1852	Dobbie, Thomas W.	1856
Davies, Charles L.	1852	Cheesman, Thomas	1856
Burton, Richard G.	1852	Brady, F.C.C.	1856
Burchill, John	1852	Sproatt, Alexander	1857
Brown, John Smith	1852	Sanders, William	1857
Winter, Henry	1853	Napier, William H.E.	1857
Wallbridge, William	1853	Miles, Edward	1857
McIntosh, James	1853	McDonald, William J.	1857
Lillie, Henry	1853	Lindsay, John	1857
Johnstone, Quinton	1853	Hughes, Thomas	1857
Horsey, Henry H.	1853	Howitt, Alfred	1857
Yarnold, William E.	1854	Herman, Royal W.	1857
Robinson, Orpheus	1854	Hawkins, William	1857
O'Hanly, John L.P.	1854	Hamlin, Latham B.	1857
Nash, Thomas W.	1854	Hallen, Skeeler W.	1857
McDonald, Alexander	1854	Fitzgerald, James W.	1857
Fox, Edward	1854	Esten, James H.	1857
Creswicke, Henry	1854	Ellis, William Henry	1857

Drennan, William	1857
DeCew, John	1857
Clementi, Vincent M.	1857
Burke, Joseph W.	1857
Boulton, William S.	1857
Gossage, Brooks W.	1858

Surveyors listed without a date of licence
(Arranged alphabetically)

Beckwith, Adolphus J.	?	
Browne, William	?	D
Burch, John	?	D
Burke, William	>1838	
Chapman, Amos	?	D
Cockrell, Richard	?	D
Guy, Louis	?	
Hanchette, William	?	D
Jones, Robert	?	
Lawe, George	?	D
Marlett, Adrian	?	D
McCarthy, Jeremiah	?	D
McDonell, James	?	D
McDonell, Robert	?	
O'Hara, Felix	?	D
Pauling, Jesse	?	D
Smith, Henry	?	D
Shaw, Claudius	?	
Treadwell, Charles	?	D
Tuffe, ?	?	

Appendix B
Surveyors General

Upper Canada

April-Sept., 1792 (acting)	William Chewett
Sept., 1792–98	David W. Smith (acting)
1798–1802	David W. Smith
1802–05	William Chewett and Thomas Ridout (acting)
1805–1807	C.B. Wyatt
1807–10	Thomas Ridout (acting)
1810–29	Thomas Ridout
1829–32	William Chewett (acting)
1832–35	Samuel Hurd
1836–38	John Macaulay
1838–41	Robert Sullivan

Canada West

1841–45	Thomas Parke

Office abolished.

Ontario

Office revived.

1928–35	Louis V. Rorke
1935–45	Charles H. Fullerton
1946–62	Frank Weldon Beatty
1962–83	Robert G. Code
1983–85	J.H. O'Donnell
1985–90	Stephen B. Panting
1990–	Pier L. Finos

Appendic C
Past Presidents of the Association

Association of Provincial Land Surveyors

1886–87 George B. Kirkpatrick
1888–89 Alexander Niven
1890–91 Villiers Sankey

Association of Ontario Land Surveyors

1892–93	Elihu Stewart
1894	Matthew J. Butler
1895	Maurice Gaviller
1896	Willis Chipman
1897	T. Harry Jones
1898	Peter S. Gibson
1899	Herbert J. Bowman

1900	George Ross
1901	James Dickson
1902–1903	William R. Aylsworth
1904	Charles A. Jones
1905	James W. Tyrrell
1906	Otto J. Klotz
1907	Thomas Fawcett
1908	Arthur J. van Nostrand
1909	Lewis Bolton
1910	Henry W. Selby
1911	James F. Whitson
1912	Thomas B. Speight
1913	James S. Dobie
1914	James W. Fitzgerald
1915	Edward T. Wilkie
1916	Charles J. Murphy
1917	James J. Mackay
1918	Herbert J. Beatty
1919	C. Fraser Aylsworth
1920	Tracy D. Le May
1921	George A. McCubbin
1922	George Hogarth
1923	Herbert T. Routly
1924	William G. McGeorge
1925	Louis V. Rorke
1926	Norman B. MacRostie
1927	Homer W. Sutcliffe
1928	John J. Newman
1929	Acheson T. Ward
1930	Roger M. Lee
1931	John van Nostrand
1932	John W. Pierce
1933	John M. Empey
1934	Ralph M. Anderson
1935	Ernest G. Mackay
1936	Herbert M. Anderson
1937	Edward Cavell
1938	Roy S. Kirkup
1939	Frank W. Beatty
1940	Garnet L. Berkeley
1941	Nathaniel A. Burwash
1942	Edgar L. Moore
1943	Norman D. Wilson
1944	William J. Fulton

1945	Charles H. Fullerton
1946	Ernest W. Neelands
1947	James K. Benner
1948	Hugh G. Rose
1949	W. Frederick Weaver
1950	Samuel W. Archibald
1951	Christopher G.R. Armstrong
1952	A.L. Stanley Nash
1953	Archibald Gillies
1954	Wilfred G. Ure
1955	John E. Jackson
1956	Wilmot J. Baird
1957	W. Harry Williams
1958	R. Blake Irwin
1959	Raymond F. Mucklestone
1960	Harry D.G. Currie
1961	Maurice Hewett
1962	John G. Pierce
1963	E.C. (Bill) Brisco
1964	Michael J. McAlpine
1965	Rowland W. Brotherhood
1966	W.J. Gordon Wadsworth
1967	Robert R. Smith
1968	Frederick J.S. Pearce
1969	M. Neil Simpson
1970	David T. Humphries
1971	John C. Kirkup
1972	Sydney G. Hancock
1973	Eathel W. Petzold
1974	James D. Dearden
1975	Grenville T. Rogers
1976	John D. Barber
1977	Michael J.M. Maughan
1978	Donald W. Endleman
1979	Thomas E. Lyons
1980	George J. Zubek
1981	Donald F. Yates
1982	Howard M. Graham
1983	Bryan T. Davies
1984	Wayne D. Brubacher

1985	Robert J. Meisner
1986	Harry R. Whale
1987	Lawrence U. Maughan
1988	Jack K. Young
1989	Michael J. O'Sullivan
1990	Talson E. Rody
1991	James W. Nicholson
1992	S. James Statham

Appendix D
Past Secretaries of the Association

Association of Provincial Land Surveyors

1886–89	Willis Chipman
1890–92	A.J. van Nostrand

Association of Ontario Land Surveyors

1893–99	A.J. van Nostrand
1900–1901	Villiers Sankey
1902–11	Killaly Gamble
1912–23	Louis V. Rorke
1924–35	Tracy D. Le May
1936–42	Louis V. Rorke
1943–46	Ralph M. Anderson
1947–53	Charles H. Fullerton
1954	Albert V. Chase
1955	Vernon R. Davies
1956	Russell R. Grant
1957	Herbert M. Anderson
1958–62	Wilmot J. Baird
1963–64	Alexander C. McEwen
1965–68	John N. Bradbury
1969–75	A.F. Allman
1976–92	N. Lorraine (Setterington) Petzold

Appendix E
Recipients of the Professional Recognition Award

1968	John Edwin Jackson
1971	William Frederick Weaver
1972	Edwin Percy Argall Phillips
1973	Frederick John Sidney Pearce
1976	John Gourley Pierce
1980	Herbert Harvey Todgham
1984	John Donald Barber
1991	Harold Stewart Howden
1992	Nancy Lorraine Petzold

NOTES

The following abbreviations are used throughout the Notes and Bibliography:

AO: Archives of Ontario

AC: Archival Committee of the Association of Ontario Land Surveyors

ACSM: American Congress on Surveying and Mapping

APLS: Proceedings of the Association of Provincial Land Surveyors (of Ontario), 1886–1892

AOLS: Proceedings of the Association of Ontario Land Surveyors, 1893 to the present

MNR: Ontario Ministry of Natural Resources

RG1, A-I-1: Letters received by the Surveyor-General, 1766–1913

RG1, A-I-6: Letters received by the Surveyor-General and Commissioner, 1786–1905

INTRODUCTION

1   Quoted (in translation) in Kiely, *Surveying Instruments*, 43–44.
2   This is not to say that triangulation as a method had never been used in Canada. As early as 1685, Jean Deshayes, on the orders of the French government, commenced a triangulation of the lower St. Lawrence with a view to improving existing charts. Having observed a lunar eclipse to establish the longitude of Quebec, Deshayes laid out two base lines on the river ice and then a final 8.25 mile (13.25 km) base line on the north shore. Using this and a survey vessel, he worked 350 miles (563 km) downstream to Sept Isles, laying out some 300 triangles as he went, the locations of which are now lost.
3   Quoted in various places. See, for example, Kiely, *Surveying Instruments*, 182.
4   Quoted in Berton, *The Arctic Grail*, 16.

CHAPTER ONE: SAMUEL DE CHAMPLAIN

1   Biggar, ed., *The Works of Samuel de Champlain*, vol. 1, 152.
2   Ibid., 153–55.
3   Biggar, ed., *The Works of Samuel de Champlain*, vol. 2, 259.
4   Ibid., 266.
5   Ibid., 273–75.
6   Biggar, ed., *The works of Samuel de Champlain*, vol. 3, 37–38.
7   Ibid., 45–46.

CHAPTER TWO:
THE JESUITS AND OTHER EXPLORERS

1   Quoted (in translation) in Lajeunesse, *The Windsor Border Region*, 3.
2   Mealing, ed., *The Jesuit Relations*, 94–95.
3   Quoted in Céline Dupré, Cavalier de La Salle, and René-Robert, *Dictionary of Canadian Biography*, vol. 1, 173.
4   René Brehant de Gallinée, *Découvertes*, vol. 1, 112–66, trans. and ed. James Coyne, Ontario Historical Society, Papers and Records, 4 (Toronto, 1903); quoted in Lajeunesse, *The Windsor Border Region*, 6.
5   Ibid., 6.
6   Ibid., 8.

CHAPTER THREE: THE FIRST LAND SURVEY IN THE PROVINCE AND THE ANGLO-FRENCH WARS

1   The sextant consists essentially of a swinging arm, attached at the apex of a graduated arc. Attached to the arm is a mirror by which the image of a heavenly body is reflected in another split mirror, which allows both it (the object being viewed) and the horizon to be viewed at the same time. By moving the arm, the object can be made to coincide with the horizon, with the altitude of the former being read off the scale on the graduated arc.
2   Quoted in Lajeunesse, *The Windsor Border Region*, 43.
3   Ibid., 45.

CHAPTER FOUR:
HOLLAND, COLLINS, AND HALDIMAND

1   Thomson, *Men and Meridians*, vol. 1, 98.
2   The Lords Commissioners of Trade and Plantations to the King, 4 February 1764, AO, MNR, RG1 A-I-1, vol. 1, items 27 and 28.
3   Ibid.
4   Submission to the King in Council, 10 February 1764, AO, MNR, RG1 A-I-1, vol. 1, items 29 and 30.
5   Samuel Holland to John Pownall, 20 November 1764, quoted in Thomson, *Men and Meridians*, vol. 1, 101.
6   Samuel Holland to John Collins, 8 September 1764, quoted in Kirkpatrick, *AOLS, 1886*, 29.
7   See extracts from Murray's instructions quoted in Fraser, *Third Report of the Bureau of Archives for the Province of Ontario*, liv–lx. Subsequent quotations from Murray's instructions will be found herein.
8   Patterson, *Land Settlement in Upper Canada*, Sixteenth Report of the Department of Archives for the Province of Ontario (1920), 20.
9   Labaree, *Royal Instructions to British Colonial Governors: 1670–1776*, 538.
10 John Collins, account delivered 3 April 1766, AO, MNR, RG1 A-I-1, vol. 2, item 44.
11 Quoted in Murphy, *First Surveys in the Province of Ontario*, 198.
12 Samuel Holland to Hugh Finlay, 31 January 1791, quoted in Kirkpatrick, *APLS, 1886*, 24–25.
13 Ibid.
14 Lajeunesse, *The Windsor Border Region*, 68.
15 Mason Bolton to Frederick Haldimand, 7 October 1778, quoted in Cruickshank, *The Story of Butler's Rangers and the Settlement of Niagara*, 59.
16 Frederick Haldimand to Lord Germain, 25 September 1779, quoted in Cruickshank, *A Collection of Documents Relating to the First Settlement, 1778–83*, 8.
17 Frederick Haldimand to Mason Bolton, 7 July 1780, quoted in Cruickshank, *A Collection of Documents Relating to the First Settlement*, 88–89.
18 Ibid., 51.

CHAPTER FIVE:
HALDIMAND AND THE FIRST TOWNSHIPS

1   Brant's native name was spelled variously as Thayendanegea, Thayendanegen, and Thayeadanegea. I have used his English name throughout for simplicity.
2   Frederick Haldimand to Samuel Holland,

26 May 1783, in Cruickshank, *Settlement of the United Empire Loyalists*, 1–2.

3   This and subsequent extracts from Holland's report quoted in Murphy, "First Surveys in the Province of Ontario," *AOLS, 1898*, 199–201; also in Cruickshank.

4   Holland is referring to Fort Haldimand on Carleton Island. The new British fort at Cataraqui never became known as Fort Haldimand, and when, many years later, a new fort was built across the Cataraqui River from Kingston, it was called Fort Henry, after Henry Hamilton, the name by which it is known to this day. By and large, posterity could have dealt more kindly with Haldimand.

5   Murphy, "First Surveys in the Province of Ontario," *AOLS, 1898*, 202–3.

6   Frederick Haldimand to Sir John Johnson, 1 September 1783. Cruickshank, *Settlement of the United Empire Loyalists*, 6–7.

7   This and subsequent extracts from Haldimand's instructions to Collins originate in AO, MNR, RG1 A-I-1, vol. 2, item 140; also in Cruickshank and Murphy.

8   Variously spelled Cotté, Kotté, and Cotte.

9   Justus Sherwood to Robert Mathews, 11 October 1783, quoted in Cruickshank, *Settlement of the United Empire Loyalists*, 25–26.

10 Fraser, *Third Report*, 1905, lxii–lxiii.

11 Justus Sherwood to Robert Mathews, 2 July 1784, in Cruickshank, *Settlement of the United Empire Loyalists*, 130.

12 John Ross to Frederick Haldimand, 10 October 1784, in Cruickshank, *Settlement of the United Empire Loyalists*, 171.

CHAPTER SIX: SETTLING IN

1   Samuel Holland to Phillip Frey. Quoted in Kirkpatrick, "President's Address," *APLS, 1887*, 31–32.

2   Ibid., 31.

3   John Collins to Frederick Haldimand, 18 June 1785, AO, MNR, RG1 A-I-1, vol. 3.

4   John Collins to Patrick McNiff, 18 June 1785, AO, MNR, RG1 A-I-1, vol 2, item 43.

5   Samuel Holland, "Instructions to

Surveyors," 18 January 1786, AO, MNR, RG1 A-I-1, vol. 2, item 48.

6   Ibid.

7   Ibid.

8   Copied by Alexander Aitken, 10 December 1798, "List of Alignments made by J. Collins Esqr. at the Little Lake, 25th July, 1785," AO, MNR, RG1 A-I-1, vol. 9.

9   William Chewett to Samuel Holland (?), AO, MNR, RG1 A-I-1, vol. 1, item 49.

10 It was not until their centenary in 1883 that the "United Empire Loyalists" formed themselves into an association – an association, that, then as now, some find overly jingoistic.

11 A.P. Walker, "William Fortune," in *AOLS, 1932*.

12 John Collins to Jesse Pennoyer, 15 November 1791, AO, MNR, RG1 A-I-1, vol. 2, item 80.

13 John Smith to John Collins, 27 March 1791, AO, MNR, RG1 A-I-1, vol 1, item 187.

14 Samuel Holland to William Fortune, 2 July 1792, AO, MNR, RG1 A-I-1, vol. 2, item 123.

15 Samuel Collins (?) to Theodore De Pencier, 5 February 1791, AO, MNR, RG1 A-I-1, vol. 2, item 131.

16 Ibid.

17 Samuel Collins to the Land Committee, "Surveys proposed for the Present Year" (filed 14 April 1790), AO, MNR, RG1 A-I-1, vol. 2, items 132–38.

18 Ibid.

19 John Collins to Philip Frey, 31 July 1788, quoted in George B. Kirkpatrick, "President's Address," in *APLS, 1887*.

20 AC, "Augustus Jones," in *AOLS, 1923*.

21 John Collins to James Rankin, 21 February 1791, AO, MNR, RG1 A-I-1, vol. 2, item 110.

22 John Collins to James Rankin, 28 May 1791, AO, MNR, RG1 A-I-1, vol. 2, item 32.

23 John Collins to Jesse Pennoyer, 21 June 1791, AO, MNR, RG1 A-I-1, vol. 2, item 75.

24 Theodore De Pencier to John Collins, 13 August 1791, AO, MNR, RG1 A-I-1, vol. 2, item 161.

25 John Collins to Theodore De Pencier, 5

September 1791, AO, MNR, RG1 A-I-1, vol. 2, item 82.

26 Lord Dorchester, 2 February 1791, AO, MNR, RG1 A-I-1, vol. 2, item 67.

27. Ibid.

28 William Chewitt to Samuel Holland (?), 4 November 1791, AO, MNR, RG1 A-I-1, vol. 2, item 55.

29 Patrick McNiff to John Collins, 30 September 1791, AO, MNR, RG1 A-I-1, vol. 2, item 72.

30 Public Accounts, 3 September 1793, AO, MNR, RG1 A-I-1, vol. 2, items 46 and 47.

31 AC, "Biographical Sketch of the Late Colonel Chewett," in *APLS, 1890*.

CHAPTER SEVEN: JOHN GRAVES SIMCOE

1   Patterson, *Land Settlement*, 41.

2   Quoted in Thomson, *Men and Meridians*, vol. 1, 227.

3   Ibid., 226.

4   AC, "Biographical Sketch of the Late Colonel Chewett," in *APLS, 1890*.

5   Ibid.

6   Circular to Deputy Surveyors, 26 June 1792, AO, MNR, RG1 A-I-1, vol. 1, item 112.

7   George Kirkpatrick, "President's Address," in *APLS, 1887*.

8   John Stegman to D.H. Smith, 27 October 1792, AO, MNR, RG1 A-I-1, vol. 36.

9   These numbers are based on the alphabetical list of geographic townships, as given in successive editions of the manual issued by the Association of Ontario Land Surveyors. I have used the list in the 1974 edition. These figures, in turn, are based on official records. The historian, however, may run into difficulties with the basic list of townships and the dates of survey given. First, some areas were surveyed and later divided into townships. Second, some townships were laid out, named, and subsequently divided into two townships. Thus, total numbers of townships as shown on the modern list may exceed those initially laid out.

The numbers are subject to other qualifications. While in some cases a township might be laid out and subdivided in its entirety, in many others the township was completed in stages, as we have seen. A

further difficulty arises with townships laid out in the latter part of the eighteenth century, when surveyors' returns were being checked for accuracy, or "audited" as it was called. Thus a certain township might not be considered completed until a year or so after the actual survey was made.

10 Patrick McNiff to Land Board, 2 March 1795, *Third Report of the Archives of Ontario, 1905*, 224–25; also see, Lajeunesse, 182.

11 Report from the Deputy Surveyor re Lots on Streams Flowing into Lake St. Clair, 11 April 1793. *Third Report of the Archives of Ontario, 1905*; see also Lajeunesse, 184.

12 Patrick McNiff to D.W. Smith, 31 May 1792, in *Third Report of the Archives of Ontario*, 187–88; also see Lajeunesse, 179–80.

13 Innis, *Mrs. Simcoe's Diary*, 89.

14 Firth, *The Town of York, 1793–1815*, 3.

15 Innis, *Mrs. Simcoe's Diary*, 102.

16 Ibid., 104.

17 Ibid., 174.

18 Champion, *Markham, 1793–1900*, 91.

CHAPTER EIGHT:
BEFORE AND DURING THE WAR OF 1812

1   Quoted in R.M. Anderson, "The Founding of Toronto," in *AOLS, 1933*.

2   John Stegman to D.H. Smith, AO, MNR, RG1 A-I-1, vol. 36.

3   Stegman, receipt, 6 August 1804, AO, MNR, RG1 A-I-1, vol. 36.

4   John Stegman to William Chewett and Thomas Ridout, 28 August 1804, AO, MNR, RG1 A-I-1, vol. 36.

5   Quoted in Archibald Blue, "Colonel Mahlon Burwell," in *AOLS, 1909*, 11.

6   Quoted in Thomson, *Men and Meridians*, vol. 1, 239.

CHAPTER NINE: POSTWAR EXPANSION

1   Thomson, *Men and Meridians*, vol. 1, 187.

2   Quoted in Klotz, "The Northwest Angle," in *AOLS, 1902*, 107.

3   Ibid., 108–9.

4   Quoted in Lambert, *Renewing Nature's Wealth*, 57.

5   Public Records Office, W.O. 55/864, quoted in Murray, *Muskoka and Haliburton*, 48.

6 Murray, *Muskoka and Haliburton*, 52.

7 Charles Sherriff, Public Archives of Canada, C 48, 2–14, quoted in Murray, *Muskoka and Haliburton*, 60–62.

8 From extracts of Alexander Sherriff's report in Murray, *Muskoka and Haliburton*, 63–71.

9 AO, Macaulay Papers, quoted in Murray, *Muskoka and Haliburton*, 84–85.

CHAPTER TEN: THE SHIELD,
THE RAILWAYS, AND A NEW PROFESSIONALISM

1 Wallace, *The Royal Canadian Institute Centennial Volume, 1849–1949*, 131.

2 John Huston to Samuel Ridout, quoted in Murray, *Muskoka and Haliburton*, 133–34

3 D.P. Papineau to Publius Elmore, 8 July 1847, quoted in Aylsworth, *The Hastings Colonization Road*, 181–84.

4 Ibid.

5 Robert Bell, "Diary of a Survey, Madawaska River to the Home District," quoted in Murray, *Muskoka and Haliburton*, 136–46. Further quotations come from these same pages.

6 Robert Bell to commissioner of crown lands, J.H. Price, 6 September 1848, ibid., 148–49.

7 Schull, *Ontario Since 1867*, 28.

8 Quoted in "Alexander Vidal," in *AOLS, 1922*.

9 Alexander Vidal to commissioner, 15 January 1849, AO, MNR, A-I-1, Government Letterbooks, 1842–52, vol. 49, 213.

10 Commissioner to Alexander Vidal, 4 May 1849, AO, MNR, RG1 A-I-2, Government Letterbooks, vol. 49, 1842–52, 235.

11 Commissioner to David Gibson, 20 October 1849, AO, MNR, RG1 A-I-2, Government Letterbooks, vol. 49, 1842–52.

12 Albert P. Salter and John Wilkinson to the commissioner of crown lands, 13 February 1846, AO, MNR, RG1 A-I-1, vol. 25.

13 J. Woods to D.B. Papineau, 8 April 1846, AO, MNR, RG1 A-I-6, vol. 26.

14 James Henderson to D.B. Papineau, 30 April 1846, AO, MNR, RG1 A-I-6, vol. 25.

15 Report by Albert P. Salter, 6 October 1849, AO, MNR, RG1 Series CB-1 (box 29).

16 Reader, *Life in Victorian England*, 2.

17 See Sebert, *Land Surveys of Ontario*.

18 Thomson, *Men and Meridians*, vol. 1, 295.

CHAPTER ELEVEN: THE OTTAWA-HURON TRACT,
MUSKOKA, AND PARRY SOUND

1 Born in Downsview of English parents, Bridgland had studied under Stoughton and qualified in 1844. He would go on to become Superintendent of colonization roads in 1856, a position he would continue to hold after Confederation.

2 J.W. Bridgland, "Report of ... Exploring Lines from the Eldon Portage to the Mouth of the River Muskako," 31 January 1853, quoted in Murray, *Muskoka and Haliburton*, 133–34.

3 Lambert, *Renewing Nature's Wealth*, 88.

4 C. Fraser Aylsworth, "The Hastings Colonization Road," in *AOLS, 1925*.

5 Vernon Wadsworth, "Reminiscences of Surveys," in *AOLS, 1926*.

6 J. Stoughton Dennis, "Report ... of the Survey of the Muskoka Road Line, North of Grand Falls, Parry Sound Road Line, & Exploration to Mouth of Muskoka River," dated 19 April 1861; quoted in Murray *Muskoka and Haliburton*, 167–72.

7 Ibid.

8 Ibid.

CHAPTER TWELVE: UPGRADING THE PROFESSION
AND ON TO THE NORTHWEST

1 *Report of the Commissioner of Crown Lands for the Year 1856*; also see appendix 25, JLA, Fifth Provincial Parliament, Third Session, 1857.

2 Ibid.; also in his report for 1861, 160–62.

3 Ibid.; also in his report for 1861, 160–62.

4 *Report of the Commissioner of Crown Lands for the Year 1856*, appendix X.

5 Ibid., appendix X.

6 AO, MNR, RG1 CB-1, box 43, miscellaneous records.

7 The name changed from the Crown Lands Department to the Department of Crown Lands in 1860, this by an act passed by the legislature. The act also directed the commissioner to issue an annual report covering all the activities of his department.

8 *Report of the Commissioner of Crown Lands for the Year 1860*, appendix 36.

9 William Gibbard, "Report of Inspection of Mining Locations on Lakes Huron and Superior," appendix 29, *Report of the Commissioner of Crown Lands for the Year 1860*.

10 Albert Salter to Joseph Cauchon, quoted in *The Report of the Commissioner of Crown Lands for the Year 1856*, appendix 37.

11 Ibid., appendix R.

12 Salter's Meridian of 1856 is commemorated in a provincial historic plaque at Naughton, on Regional Road 55, about 11 miles (17 km) southwest of Sudbury. Erected close to the meridian line itself, the plaque also records Salter's discovery of nickel and the subsequent establishment of the Creighton Mine.

13 Both Thomas Herrick and Thomas Molesworth were graduates of Trinity College, Dublin, and both became involved in railway work on coming to Upper Canada, with Herrick working on the St. Marys to London section of the Grand Trunk Railway before he qualified as a provincial land surveyor in 1856. Not long after, he would carry out the first exploratory survey of the country north of Lake Superior. Molesworth had been apprenticed to a civil engineer before emigrating to Upper Canada in 1848 where he taught school at Trafalgar, a village just north of Oakville – now nothing more than the intersection of Trafalgar Road and Highway 5. In 1850 he moved to Goderich, qualifying a year later. Between 1852 and 1854 he was involved in the first township surveys on St. Joseph Island and two years after that laid out the town of Wingham.

14 T.N. Molesworth, "Report of the Survey and Exploration of the North Shore of Lake Huron," 3 December 1857, quoted in *The Report of the Commissioner of Crown Lands for the Year 1872*.

15 Arthur Jones, "Report on Township Boundary Lines, North Shore of Lake Huron," 27 May 1859, quoted in *The Report of the Commissioner of Crown Lands for the Year 1872*.

16 Albert Salter, Survey Report, 20 January 1858, quoted in *The Report of the Commissioner of Crown Lands for the Year 1857*, appendix T.

17 *The Report of the Commissioner of Crown Lands for the Year 1856*.

18 Quoted in Thomson, *Men and Meridians*, 215.

19 This and following quotes are from T. Herrick, *Report and Field Notes of the Survey of the Exploration Line from Sault St. Mary to Fort William, North Shore of Lake Superior*, 2 vols., nos. 1896 and 1908, Survey Records, MNR.

20 Taking Lennox and Addington to be one county, excluding Haliburton, and before the introduction of regional municipalities.

CHAPTER THIRTEEN: ONTARIO'S BOUNDARIES,
NORTHERN SURVEYS, AND THE CPR

1 Villiers Sankey, "The Surveyor's Act," in *APLS, 1886*.

2 Quoted in Thomson, *Men and Meridians*, vol. 2, 15.

3 Ibid., 16.

4 John Browne, "The Dawson Route," in *AOLS, 1895*, 100.

5 Quoted in Schull, *Ontario Since 1867*, 99.

6 Fleming, "Exploratory Survey, North Shore of Lake Superior," quoted in "The Report of the Commissioner, 1870," AO.

7 Quoted in Alexander Niven, "Ontario Boundaries," in *AOLS, 1896*, 108.

8 Quoted in *The Report of the Commissioner, 1882*.

9 Ibid.

10 Ibid.

11 Ibid.

12 Quoted in *The Report of the Commissioner, 1883*.

13 Ibid.

14 Quoted in *The Report of the Commissioner, 1885*.

CHAPTER FOURTEEN: THE ASSOCIATION IS BORN

1 Quoted in *APLS, 1886*.

2 Willis Chipman, "Letterbook 1882–85," MU 3285, AO.

3 *APLS, 1886.* All further quotations from the minutes of this inaugural meeting come from this source.

4 When the School of Practical Science in Toronto was founded in 1878, John Galbraith was appointed to the chair in engineering, a position he held at the time of the association's first meeting. He was destined to become the "father" of professional engineering in Canada. The School of Practical Science (SPS) received its first full-time instructor in surveying in 1888. This was Louis B. Stewart, D.T.S., later O.L.S. The school would eventually be attached to the University of Toronto as the Faculty of Applied Science and Engineering.

5 Willis Chipman, "Letterbook 1882–85," MU 3285, AO.

CHAPTER FIFTEEN:
THE ASSOCIATION: GETTING INTO STRIDE AND ON TO INCORPORATION

1 In the pages to follow there are numerous quotations from *Proceedings of the Association of Provincial Land Surveyors (of Ontario).* Where a citation is lacking, the reader is referred to the proceedings for the year in question and the relevant address or committee report, as may be inferred from the text.

CHAPTER SIXTEEN:
THE ASSOCIATION: 1892–1900

1 In the pages to follow there are numerous quotations from *Proceedings of the Association of Provincial Land Surveyors (of Ontario).* Where a citation is lacking, the reader is referred to the proceedings for the year in question and the relevant address or committee report, as may be inferred from the text.

2 *AOLS, 1893,* 71–72.

CHAPTER SEVENTEEN:
OPENING UP NEW ONTARIO

1 Quoted in *The Report of the Commissioner of Crown Lands, 1886.*

2 Because of the curvature of the earth, such long base lines were usually run on 6-mile (10-km) chords in order to approximate the true latitude in 6-mile-square (15-km²) townships. Where 9-mile-square (23-km²) townships were laid out, base lines were run on nine-mile (140-km) chords.

3 Alexander Niven, "Survey of the Boundary Line between Algoma and Nipissing Districts," in *AOLS, 1899.*

4 Born in 1680 in Lyndhurst in Leeds County, Saunders was of Scottish stock. After attending the School of Practical Science in Toronto, he came a Dominion Land Surveyor in 1884, a provincial land surveyor a year later. He graduated in engineering at McGill in 1886, becoming Willis Chipman's partner in Brockville a couple of years later. On Chipman giving up his practice in Brockville in 1892 and moving to Toronto, Saunders took his place as town engineer, later becoming engineer for the county. He moved to Fort William in 1896; this helps account for his participation in running the Ontario-Manitoba boundary. Saunders later moved and worked out west and at the time of his death in 1926 was president of the Alberta Land Surveyors' Association.

5 Ontario Department of Crown Lands, *The Survey of Northern Ontario, 1900,* Toronto: King's Printer, 1901.

6 The history of surveying is devilled by changes in the nomenclature of instruments. As noted earlier, the "Jacob's staff" was invented by Levi ben Gerson in the 1300s and was used for measuring distances, heights, and angles. By the late nineteenth century it was simply a pole that was stuck in the ground to support a compass. A "surveyor's staff" also meant different things down the centuries. According to a surveying text published in 1901, a surveyor's staff was a pole surmounted by a ring with notches cut in it at right-angles to allow the speedy laying out of the same.

7 Commonly used for traversing, the micrometer telescope was used for measuring distances. It consisted of a tripod-mounted telescope, fitted with adjustable hairs, which was aimed at two targets exactly 1/10 chain apart (i.e., 6.6 feet). Distances corresponding to the micrometer angle observed were obtained from a table.

8 Ontario Department of Crown Lands, *The Survey of Northern Ontario, 1900,* 8.

9 Ibid., 53.

10 Ibid., 89.

11 Ibid., 115.

12 Born in Hamilton in 1858, Proudfoot took civil engineering at the University of Toronto and qualified both as an Ontario Land Surveyor and a Domionio Land Surveyor in 1882 He then combined private practise in Huron County with township surveys in Northern Ontario, mostly in the Rainy River District. In the early 1900s he moved to Manitoba and remained there until the outbreak of war in 1914, in which his only son was killed. He then returned to practise in Ontario and Nova Scotia, eventually dying in Toronto in 1935 at the age of seventy-seven. His brother, Hart William, went with him on his survey of 1900 as a private prospector. He qualified as an Ontario Land Surveyor in 1905, only to die a year later at the age of thirty.

13 Crown Lands, *The Survey, 1900,* 174.

14 Ibid., xxii.

15 A provincial land surveyor since 1867 and a Dominion Topographical Surveyor since 1844, McAree worked out of Toronto until 1896 when he moved to Rat Portage, now Kenora. For several years he was engaged in mine location, prospecting, and assay work in the Rainy River District, and then went back to survey work in the West. Returning east from Moosejaw late in 1903, he would die in Toronto from typhoid complicated by pneumonia shortly after his arrival.

16 Crown Lands, *The Survey, 1900,* xxiii.

17 Thomson, *Men and Meridians,* vol. 3, 288.

18 Ontario Department of Crown Lands, *Report on Northern Ontario, 1900,* xvi.

19 Thaddeus Patten, who became both an Ontario Land Surveyor and Dominion Land Surveyor in 1883, was from Little Current and trained under his brother-in-law, George Abrey. Patten's antecedents had some interesting connections with old Toronto and its environs. In the mid-1800s, his grandfather, William Burr, built the "Old Mill" on the Humber River, now a well-known restaurant. His wife, Hester, was a L'Amoreaux of Huguenot descent, whose forebear, Joshue or Joshua L'Amoreaux, fled north as a Loyalist in 1783 and eventually settled on Lot 33 in the Third Concession of Scarborough Township and thus gave his name to what is now a district in the city of Scarborough.

20 AC, "Alexander Niven," in *AOLS, 1911.*

21 Ibid., 21.

22 Quoted in Schull, *Ontario Since 1867,* 175.

23 Schull, *Ontario Since 1867,* 176.

CHAPTER EIGHTEEN:
BOOM YEARS FOR LAND SURVEYORS

1 In the pages to follow there are numerous quotations from *Proceedings of the Association of Provincial Land Surveyors (of Ontario) (AOLS).* Where a citation is lacking, the reader is referred to the proceedings for the year in question and the relevant address or committee report, as may be inferred from the text.

2 "Report of the Council of Management for the year 1905," in *AOLS, 1905,* 42–43.

3 George Ross, "The Report of the Committee on Drainage," in *AOLS, 1907,* 41.

4 Tiles for underdrainage had become available as early as 1860. But few farmers used them because of their cost. In 1878 the Ontario Tile Drainage Act was passed. This allowed farmers to borrow up to $1000 for tile drains from local council, such to be repaid over twenty years (the council recovering the money from the province). Even so, tile drains took a long time to catch on.

CHAPTER NINETEEN: BETWEEN THE WARS

1 In the pages to follow there are numerous quotations from *Proceedings of the Association of Provincial Land Surveyors of Ontario.* Where a citation is lacking, the reader is referred to the proceedings for the year in question and the relevant address or

committee report, as may be inferred from the text.

2 James Dobie, "Report of Committee on Permanent Monuments in Northern Ontario," in *AOLS, 1919,* 59.

3 Under Biggar's direction, a ring of secondary monuments was established around Toronto. Commenting on these monuments many years later, Le May said that they had never been used.

4 The first aerial photos in Canada were taken in 1883. These were vertical photos of the barracks in Halifax and were made by a Captain Henry Elsdale, R.E., using a remote-control camera attached to a balloon tethered above the barracks.

5 John Pierce, "The Survey of the Ontario-Manitoba Boundary," in *AOLS, 1923,* 193.

6 Ibid., 199.

7 The Association of Dominion Land Surveyors became the Canadian Institute of Surveying in 1934. In 1950 the name was changed to the Canadian Institute of Surveying and Photogrammetry, and later still the Canadian Institute of Surveying and Mapping.

8 In 1926 Herbert John and Frank Weldon Beatty were partners in Pembroke. Herbert was a graduate of SPS and became an Ontario Land Surveyor in 1893. Weldon Beatty graduated in civil engineering at U. of T. in 1913, became a Dominion Land Surveyor a year later and then served overseas. After the war he rejoined the Dominion Topographical Surveys Branch but left it after becoming an Ontario Land Surveyor in 1923 when he entered into partnership with his brother. Walter and David Beatty, provincial land surveyors from Eganville and Parry Sound respectively, were cousins of Herbert and Frank Beatty's father.

9 All this more or less coincided with the inauguration of the National Topographic Series (NTS) of maps put out by the Topographical Survey of Canada. Aimed at producing maps at 1, 2, 4, and 8 miles to an inch, depending on the importance of the area, the NTS had its formal beginning in 1927.

10 This was the distance given by F.W. Beatty in his paper, the "Seventh Base Line," in *AOLS, 1933,* 114. A distance of 632 miles, 29.24 chains, given by N.A. Burwash in *AOLS, 1932,* 192 seems to have been a preliminary estimate. Even rough measurements made on a small-scale map show it to be erroneous. The length of the line is now accepted at 1110.5 km.

11 The Land Surveyors Amendment Act, 1937, quoted in *AOLS, 1937,* 198–200.

12 John Ransom, *AOLS, 1938,* 29.

CHAPTER TWENTY:
THE SECOND WORLD WAR AND AFTER

1 In the pages to follow there are numerous quotations from *Proceedings of the Association of Provincial Land Surveyors (of Ontario)* (AOLS). Where a citation is lacking, the reader is referred to the proceedings for the year in question and the relevant address or committee report, as may be inferred from the text.

2 W.F. Weaver, "Annulment of Non-Essential Obliterated Township Surveys," in *AOLS, 1943,* 121–26.

3 N.D. Wilson, "President's Address," in *AOLS, 1944,* 17.

4 Harold S. Howden, "King's Highway Surveys," in *AOLS, 1955,* 144.

5 Charles Lloyd, "Control on the St. Lawrence," in *AOLS, 1957,* 159–60.

6 J.M. Riddell, "Geodetic Control for City Mapping," in *AOLS, 1951,* 137.

7 The Code family holds a land-surveying record, in that all five brothers of an earlier generation were Ontario Land Surveyors. A. Silas Code, commissioned in 1896, worked in private practice in Alveston. His brother, Thomas George Code, commissioned in 1907, went into partnership in Cobalt with another brother, Richard Stanley. Richard Stanley's son, R. Bryce Code, also became an Ontario Land Surveyor in 1947. Robert G. Code, surveyor general from 1962 to 1983, was the son of a fourth brother, Robert Wilmot Code, who was commissioned in 1911 and was in private practice in Windsor. The fifth brother was Charles Edward Code

who practised in Iroquois Falls.

8 Oscar J. Marshall, a professor in civil engineering at U. of T., was commissioned in 1950. The next year he formed a partnership with Harold L. Macklin, who also taught engineering at U. of T. and who was licensed that same year. In 1952 they invited Patrick A. Monaghan, a graduate engineer from U. of Sask., to join the partnership. Monaghan was licensed an Ontario Land Surveyor in 1953. Both Macklin and Monaghan also became Dominion Land Surveyors. Today, Marshall Macklin Monaghan Ontario Ltd. is a leader in surveying, digital surveying, and geographic information systems.

9 John W. Pierce, *AOLS, 1949,* 40.

10 John G. Pierce, *AOLS, 1949,* 42.

11 The survey of the Ontario-Manitoba boundary is the subject of a video recently completed by the Association of Ontario Land Surveyors.

12 A massive reorganization of the Department of Lands and Forests, starting in 1941, had eliminated a number of anomalies. Surveys and aerial mapping, for example, had previously been carried out by different branches.

13 Quoted in Krebs, "Quality Control: Plans and Descriptions" (Seminar on Land Registration), *Ontario Today,* 1978.

14 Graduating in forestry from U.N.B. in 1950, David Lambden became an Ontario Land Surveyor in 1953 and a Canadian Lands Surveyor a year later. He is also licensed to practise in three Australian states and in New Zealand and now teaches survey law at the Centre for Surveying Science on the Erindale campus of the University of Toronto.

CHAPTER TWENTY-ONE: IMPROVING THE PROFESSION'S IMAGE AND SURVEY EDUCATION

1 After service overseas with the RCAF during the Second World War, Eathel W. Petzold took engineering at Queen's University, and became an Ontario Land Surveyor in 1953. After two years working for Ontario Hydro, which saw him at work on the St. Lawrence

Seaway among other things, he went into private practice in Toronto with Douglas Brouse in 1956.

2 E.W. Petzold, personal communication with the author, 17 November 1989.

3 Frederick J. Pearce joined the RCAF in 1940, to be shot down over Germany and taken prisoner of war. Released in 1945, he joined the Department of Highways and qualified in 1949. After this he went into private practice in Stratford. The press sometimes confused him with John Pierce of Ontario–Manitoba-boundary fame. Making a joke of this, Pearce once confessed that sometimes he went along with the idea and on one occasion gave a graphic description of how he had run the boundary up to Hudson Bay.

4 Frederick J. Pearce, "Open Forum," in *AOLS, 1959,* 58.

5 Completing his schooling after his discharge from the armed forces in 1946, Stephen Bernard (Barney) Panting went on to graduate in civil engineering from U. of T. in 1952. Articled to Professor O.J. Marshall, he was commissioned in 1953, following which he worked with Marshall, Macklin, Monaghan and then went into private practice in Sudbury. He joined the Dept. of Lands and Forests in 1958, succeeding F.W. Weaver as supervisor of the surveys section in 1962. Appointed deputy surveyor general in 1968 and supervisor of engineering services in 1972, he returned to surveying in 1979 as general manger of surveying services. He succeeded J.H. O'Donnell as surveyor general in 1985 and retired in 1990.

6 For the discussion, see "Where Are We Headed?" in *AOLS, 1966,* 129–47.

7 In the pages to follow there are numerous quotations from *Proceedings of the Association of Provincial Land Surveyors (of Ontario).* Where a citation is lacking, the reader is referred to the proceedings for the year in question and the relevant address or committee report, as may be inferred from the text.

8 Charles Stauffer, in *AOLS, 1967,* in 123.

9 Ibid.

10 "Report of the Committee on Aerial Surveys and Mapping," in *AOLS, 1965*, 54–58.

11 Stephan Panting, "The Ontario Co-ordinate System: A Preview of Pertinent Legislation and Regulations," in *AOLS, 1969*, 158–59.

12 Sydney Hancock, "President's Address," in *AOLS, 1973*, 2–3.

13 Quoted in Wilmont Baird, "President's Message," in *AOLS, 1957*, 19.

CHAPTER TWENTY-TWO: ON TO THE FUTURE

1 J.D. Barber, "Report of the Committee on Aerial Surveying and Mapping," in *AOLS, 1970*, 46–47.

2 Don McLarty, "Panel Discussion on Restructuring," in *AOLS, 1971*, 44–46.

3 Ibid.

4 In the pages to follow there are numerous quotations from *Proceedings of the Association of Provincial Land Surveyors (of Ontario)*. Where a citation is lacking, the reader is referred to the proceedings for the year in question and the relevant address or committee report, as may be inferred from the text.

5 James Dearden, "Report of the Restructuring Committee," in *AOLS, 1973*, 106–6.

6 Quoted in R.O. Semper, "Background Notes on the Canadian Council of Land Surveyors," personal communication with the author, 21 January 1992.

7 In 1963 Zubek, commissioned in 1961, formed a partnership with Ronald J. Emo, licensed in 1962, which was subsequently joined by Lynn H. Patten, licensed in 1975, to form what is now Zubek, Emo & Patten Ltd., Collingwood's only surveying firm. The firm holds Elihu Stewart's survey records and is now located on Stewart Road.

8 Using relative positioning, GPS-equipped aircraft can estimate their position to within about 4 inches (10 cm), moving land vehicles to less that 0.5 inch (1 cm).

9 Ontario's surveyor general at the time of writing, Pier (Peter) L. Finos, graduated in civil engineering, taking the surveying option, in 1969. After articling with W.D. Ratz he became an Ontario Land Surveyor in 1971. He was licensed a Canadian Lands Surveyor in 1982. After a number of years with what had become the Ministry of Transportation, of which he was chief surveyor from 1985 to 1989, Finos moved to the MNR and succeeded S.B. Panting as surveyor general in 1990.

BIBLIOGRAPHY

SURVEYORS' BIOGRAPHIES

Biographies of Surveyors in *AOLS Proceedings*

The proceedings include many biographies. Most were written by archival or biographical committees. Among these, the following (listed alphabetically by surname) have been consulted:

Aitken, Alexander. In *AOLS, 1932.*
Baird, Alexander. In *AOLS, 1931.*
Bell, Robert, AOLS. In *AOLS, 1925.*
Benson, Samuel M. In *AOLS, 1928.*
Bouchette, Joseph. In *AOLS, 1895.*
Bridgland, James W. In *AOLS, 1927.*
Browne, John O. In *AOLS, 1917.*
Burke, Joseph William. In *AOLS, 1920.*
Burwell, Lewis. In *AOLS, 1924.*
Campbell, A.W. In *AOLS, 1928.*
Carroll, Peter. In *AOLS, 1920.*
Cattanach, Angus. In *AOLS, 1934.*
Chewett, James Grant. In *AOLS, 1921.*
Chewett, William. In *AOLS, 1890.*
Code, A.S. In *AOLS, 1935.*
Code, Robert Wilmot. In *AOLS, 1961.*
Coffin, Nathaniel. In *AOLS, 1929.*
Collins, John, (deputy surveyor general). In *AOLS, 1932.*
Davidson, Walter S. In *AOLS, 1915.*
Deane, Michael, (obituary). In *AOLS, 1897.*
Deane, Michael Hunt. In *AOLS, 1934.*
DeCew, Edmund. In *AOLS, 1922.*
Dickson, James. In *AOLS, 1927.*
Donnelly, Phillip S. In *AOLS, 1927.*
Elmore, Publius Virgilius. In *AOLS, 1925.*
Fairfield, William J. In *AOLS, 1928.*
Fleming, Sandford. In *AOLS, 1916.*
Gamble, Killaly. In *AOLS, 1912.*
Gibbard, William. In *AOLS, 1920.*
Gibson, David. In *AOLS, 1916.*
Gibson, Peter Silas. In *AOLS, 1917.*
Greeley, Aaron. In *AOLS, 1924.*
Herrick, T.W. In *AOLS, 1919.*
Howard, John George. In *AOLS, 1918.*
Jones, Augustus. In *AOLS, 1923.*
Kennedy, Charles. In *AOLS, 1926.*
Kirkpatrick, George Brownly. In *AOLS, 1918.*
Lount, James. In *AOLS, 1925.*
McAree, John. In *AOLS, 1919.*
Macdonell [*sic*], Hugh. In *AOLS, 1922.*
McNaughton, John. In *AOLS, 1921.*

Molesworth, Balfour Nepean. In *AOLS, 1932.*
Molesworth, Thomas Nepean. In *AOLS, 1920.*
Niven, Alexander, (autobiographical (?) sketch of). In *AOLS, 1911.*
de Pencier, Theodore. In *AOLS, 1924.*
Pennoyer, Jesse. In *AOLS, 1932.*
Perry, Aylsworth Bowen. In *AOLS, 1919.*
Pierce, John Wesley. In *AOLS, 1950.*
Prince, Septimus R. In *AOLS, 1922.*
Proudfoot, Hume Blake. In *AOLS, 1936.*
Richey, Josias. In *AOLS, 1922.*
Roche, John Knatchbul. In *AOLS, 1916.*
Ryder, John. In *AOLS, 1930.*
Salter, Albert Pellew. In *AOLS, 1915.*
Saunders, Bryce J. In *AOLS, 1927.*
Sherwood, Reuben Sherwood. In *AOLS, 1886.*
Smith, David William (surveyor-general of Upper Canada, etc., biographical sketch of). In *AOLS, 1894.*
Speight, Thomas Bailey. In *AOLS, 1947.*
Stewart, Elihu. In *AOLS, 1936.*
Tiernan, Joseph Martin. In *AOLS, 1938.*
Vidal, Alexander. In *AOLS, 1922.*
Wadsworth, Vernon Bayley. In *AOLS, 1941.*
Welch, Thomas. In *AOLS, 1919.*
West, James. In *AOLS, 1925.*
Wilkinson, Alexander John Armit. In *AOLS, 1922.*

Some biographies in the association proceedings were written by individuals. Among those consulted (listed by author) were the following:

Anderson, R.M. "Henry Lionel Esten." In *AOLS, 1935.*
Blue, Archibald. "Colonel Mahlon Burwell." In *AOLS, 1909.*
Burwash, N.A. "Louis Valentine Rorke." In *AOLS, 1943.*
Code, R.S. "Thomas George Code." In *AOLS, 1944.*
Esten, H.L. "Balfour Nepean Molesworth." In *AOLS, 1932.*
———. "C.J. Murphy." In *AOLS, 1922.*
———. "Charles Unwin." In *AOLS, 1918.*
———. "James Hutchison Esten." In *AOLS, 1916.*
———. "John Dunlap Evans, O.L.S." In *AOLS, 1931.*
Fitzgerald, J.W., Jr. "J.W. Fitzgerald, Sen." In *AOLS, 1918.*

Fitzgerald, Edward. "J.W. Fitzgerald." In *AOLS, 1926.*
McCubbin, G.A. "The Late Jas. A. Bell." In *AOLS, 1930.*
Miles, C.F. "Edward Madan Miles." In *AOLS, 1918.*
Outram, A.A. "Norman Douglas Wilson." In *AOLS, 1967.*
Passmore, A.C. "Frederick F. Passmore." In *AOLS, 1918.*
Patten, Thaddeus James. Autobiography. In *AOLS, 1939.*
Proudfoot, H.B., and A.J. van Nostrand. "Hart William Proudfoot." In *AOLS, 1933.*
Ridout, John. "Biographical Sketch of Samuel Ridout." In *APLS, 1887.*
Sewell, H.C. "Henry De Quincey Sewell." In *AOLS, 1936.*
Simpson, D.B. "Major Samuel Street Wilmot." In *AOLS, 1921.*
Unwin, Charles. "Autobiographical Sketch of Charles Unwin, O.L.S." In *AOLS, 1910.*
Ure, W.G. Untitled obituary of Tracy Le May. In *AOLS, 1955.*
van Nostrand, Arther J. Autobiography. In *AOLS, 1940.*
———. "James A. Gibson." In *AOLS, 1931.*
———. "Willis Chipman." In *AOLS, 1930.*
Walker, A.P. "William Fortune." In *AOLS, 1932.*
Walker, A.P., and R.W. Code. "Patrick McNiff." In *AOLS, 1931.*
Weaver, W.F. "Frank Weldon Beatty." In *AOLS, 1966.*
Wicksteed, H.K. "Alexander Lord Russell." In *AOLS, 1923.*

OTHER SURVEYORS' BIOGRAPHIES

Armstrong, Frederick H. "Alexander Aitken." In *Dictionary of Canadian Biography.* Vol. 4. Toronto: University of Toronto Press, 1979.

Burns, Robert J. "Thomas Ridout." In *Dictionary of Canadian Biography.* Vol. 6. Toronto: University of Toronto Press, 1987.
Cameron, Wendy. "Roswell Mount." In *Dictionary of Canadian Biography.* Vol. 6. Toronto: University of Toronto Press, 1987.
Clarke, John. "Mahlon Burwell." In *Dictionary of Canadian Biography.* Vol. 7. Toronto: University of Toronto Press, 1988.

Haywood, Robert J. "John Collins." In *Dictionary of Canadian Biography*. Vol. 4. Toronto: University of Toronto Press, 1979.

McKenzie, Ruth. "Henry Wolsey Bayfield." In *Dictionary of Canadian Biography*. Vol. 11. Toronto: University of Toronto Press, 1982.

Nicks, John S. "David Thompson." In *The Canadian Encyclopedia*. Edmonton: Hurtig Publishers, 1985.

Pilon, Henri. "Robert Bell." In *Dictionary of Canadian Biography*. Vol. 10. Toronto: University of Toronto Press, 1972.

Smith, Donald. "Augustus Jones." In *Dictionary of Canadian Biography*. Vol. 7. Toronto: University of Toronto Press, 1988.

Stagg, Ronald J. "David Gibson." In *Dictionary of Canadian Biography*. Vol. 9. Toronto: University of Toronto Press, 1976.

Thorpe, F.J. "Samuel Johannes Holland." In *Dictionary of Canadian Biography*. Vol. 5. Toronto: University of Toronto Press, 1983.

GENERAL BIBLIOGRAPHY

Anderson, R.M. "The Founding of Toronto." In *AOLS, 1933*.

———. "The Development of Township Surveys in Ontario." *Canadian Surveyor* 5, 8 (1936).

Anderson, Bern. *The Life and Voyages of Captain George Vancouver*. Toronto: University of Toronto Press, 1966.

Armstrong, Frederick H., and Neil C. Hultin. "The Anglo-American Magazine Looks at Urban Upper Canada on the Eve of the Railway Era." In *Profiles of a Province*. Ontario Historical Society, 1967.

Armstrong, Joe C.W. *Champlain*. Toronto: Macmillan of Canada, 1987.

Arrian. *Life of Alexander The Great*. Translated by Aubrey de Selincourt. Harmondsworth: Penguin Books, 1962.

Arthur, Eric. *From Front Street to Queen's Park: The Story of Ontario's Parliament Buildings*. Toronto: McClelland and Stewart, 1979.

Ashley, Maurice. *England in the Seventeenth Century*. Harmondsworth: Penguin Books, 1961

Aylsworth, C.F. "A History of the Hastings Colonization Road." In *AOLS, 1925*.

Barry, James P. *Georgian Bay: The Sixth Great Lake*. Toronto: Clarke, Irwin and Company, Ltd., 1978.

Beatty, F.W. "Observations: Conference of Commonwealth Survey Officers." In *AOLS, 1956*.

———. "Seventh Base Line." In *AOLS, 1933*.

Bell, George G., and Andrew D. Pascoe. *The Ontario Government: Structure and Functions*. Toronto: Wall & Thompson, 1988.

Benn, Carl. *Ontario History*. Vol. 81, no. 4, *The Military Context of the Founding of Toronto*. 1989.

———. *The Battle of York*. Belleville: The Mika Publishing Company, 1984.

Berkeley, Edmund, and Dorothy Smith Berkeley. *Dr. John Mitchell: The Man Who Made the Map*. Chapel Hill: University of North Carolina Press, 1974.

Berry, Ralph R. "History of Geodetic Levelling in the United States." *ACSM Journal of Surveying and Mapping*, June 1976.

Berton, Pierre. *The Arctic Grail: The Quest for the North West Passage and the North Pole, 1818 to 1909*. Toronto: McLelland and Stewart, 1988.

Biggar, H.P., ed. *The Voyages of Jacques Cartier*. Publications of the Public Archives of Canada, no. 11. Ottawa: The King's Printer, 1924.

———, ed. *A Collection of Documents Relating to Jacques Cartier and the Sieur de Roberval*. Publications of the Public Archives of Canada, no. 14. Ottawa: Public Archives of Canada, 1930.

———, ed. *The Works of Samuel de Champlain*. 6 vols. Toronto: The Champlain Society, 1922, 1925, 1929, 1932, 1933, and 1936.

Bindoff, S.T. *Tudor England*. Harmondsworth: Penguin Books, 1961.

Blair, E. *Loyalists of Lancaster Township*. Glengarry Historical Society, 1982.

Boardman, John, et al., eds. *The Roman World*. Oxford: Oxford University Press, 1988.

Bonis, Robert R. *A History of Scarborough*. Scarborough, Ontario: Scarborough Public Library, 1968.

Boyer, George W. *Early Days in Muskoka*. Bracebridge: Herald-Gazette Press, 1970.

Boyer, Robert J. *Early Exploration and Surveying of Muskoka District*. Bracebridge: Herald-Gazette Press, 1979.

Brunger, Alan G. "Thomas Talbot." In *Dictionary of Canadian Biography*. vol. 8. Toronto: University of Toronto Press, 1985.

Bumsted, J.M. *Land, Settlement, and Politics on Eighteenth-Century Prince Edward Island*. Kingston and Montreal: McGill–Queen's University Press, 1987.

Canadian War Museum. *The Loyal Americans*. 1983.

Carstensen, Vernon. "Patterns on the American Land." *ACSM Journal of Surveying and Mapping*, 1976.

Cavell, E. "The Holland Marsh." In *AOLS, 1935*.

Champion, Isabel, ed. *Markham, 1793–1900*. Markham Historical Society, 1979.

Chipman, Willis. *Letterbook, 1882–85*. AO. Letterbooks. MU 3285.

———. Will dated 31 November 1928. AO, RG2, York County Estate Files, MS584.

Clement, Donald B. "Public Land Surveys: History and Accomplishments." *ACSM Journal of Mapping and Surveying*, June 1958.

Coleman, Thelma. *The Canada Company*. Stratford: County of Perth and Cumming Publishers, 1978.

Coley, Noel. "Halley & Post-Restoration Science." *History Today* 36 (September 1986).

Cooksley, R.J. "The St.Lawrence Power Project." In *AOLS, 1956*.

Coudy, Julien, ed. *The Huguenot Wars*. Philadelphia: Chilton Book Company, 1969.

Craig, Gerald M. *Upper Canada: The Formative Years, 1784–1841*. Toronto: McClelland and Stewart, 1963.

Creighton, Donald. *Dominion of the North: A History of Canada*. Toronto: Macmillan of Canada, 1972.

Cressy, David. "Elizabethan America." *History Today* 36 (July 1986).

Cruickshank, E.A. ed. *The Correspondence of Lieut. Governor John Graves Simcoe, 1789–1796*. 5 vols. Toronto: Ontario Historical Society, 1923 to 1931.

———. *Lieut. Governor Simcoe in Canada; A Chronological Record*. Vol. 26. Ontario Historical Society, 1930.

Cruickshank, Ernest A. "The Navy Island Memorial." In *Welland County Historical Society, Papers and Records*. Vol. 5. 1938.

———. "The King's Royal Regiment of New York." In *Ontario Historical Society Papers and Records*. Vol. 27. 1931. Reprint. Toronto, 1984.

———. "A Collection of Documents Relating to the First Settlement, 1778–1783." In *Niagara Historical Society, Records of Niagara*. No. 38, 1927.

———. "A Collection of Documents Relating to the First Settlement, 1784–1787." In *Niagara Historical Society, Records of Niagara*. No. 39, 1928.

———. *Settlement of the United Empire Loyalists on the Upper St. Lawrence and Bay of Quinte in 1784: A Documentary Record*. Ontario Historical Society, 1934. Reprint. 1966.

———. "The Story of Butler's Rangers and the Settlement of Niagara." In *Lundy's Lane Historical Society*. 1893. Reprint. Owen Sound: Richardson, Bond & Wright, 1975.

———. "Ten Years of the Colony of Niagara, 1780–1790." In *Niagara Historical Society, Records of Niagara*. No. 17. 1908.

Davis, A.R. "The Addington Road." In *AOLS, 1925*.

———. "Land Surveyors in Reconstruction." In *AOLS, 1919*.

Dobie, James S. "The Past Half-Century in Northern Ontario." In *AOLS, 1937*.

Dupré, Céline. "René-Robert, Cavelier de La Salle." In *Dictionary of Canadian Biography*. Vol. 1. Toronto: University of Toronto Press, 1966.

Eccles, W.J. *The Ordeal of New France*. The Canadian Broadcasting Corporation, 1967.

———. "Louis de Buade de Frontenac et de Palluau." In *Dictionary of Canadian Biography*. Vol. 1. Toronto: University of Toronto Press, 1966.

Elliott, Bruce S. "Baseline Phantom Lot Steeped in History." *Nepean Advance*, 29 February 1988.

———. Private communication with the author, December 1988.

Erwin, Robert E. "Reclamation of the Holland River Marsh." In *AOLS, 1927*.

Feetham, L.R. *History of the Canadian Council of Land Surveyors*. undated.

Firth, Edith G. "Peter Russell." In *Dictionary of Canadian Biography*. Vol. 5. Toronto: University of Toronto Press, 1983.

———, ed. *The Town of York, 1793–1815*. Toronto: University of Toronto Press, 1962.

———, ed. *The Town of York, 1815–1834*. Toronto: University of Toronto Press, 1966.

Fox, W. Sherwood. *The Bruce Beckons*. Revised. Toronto: University of Toronto Press, 1962.

Fraser, Alexander. *Third Report of the Bureau of Archives for the Province of Ontario*. 1905.

Fryer, Mary Beacock, and William Smy. *Rolls of the Provincial (Loyalist) Corps, Canadian Command, American Revolutionary Period.* Toronto: Dundurn Press, 1981.

Fyfe, Douglas. "David Gibson's Involvement in the Rebellion in Upper Canada." Paper presented at The 1837 Rebellion Remembered Conference, Ontario Historical Society, 1987.

Gamble, S.G. "Some Applications of Electronics to Canadian Surveying." In *AOLS, 1957.*

Gates, Lillian F. *Land Policies of Upper Canada.* Toronto: University of Toronto Press, 1968.

Gentilcore, Louis and Kate Donkin. "Land Surveys of Southern Ontario." *Cartographica,* monograph no. 8 (1973).

Goodspeed, D.J., ed. *The Armed Forces of Canada: 1867–1967.* At the Directorate of History, Canadian Forces Headquarters, Ottawa. 1967.

Graham, W.H. *The Tiger of Canada West.* Toronto: Clarke, Irwin and Company Ltd., 1965.

Graymont, Barbara. "Thayendanegea." In *Dictionary of Canadian Biography.* Vol. 5. Toronto: University of Toronto Press, 1983.

Guillet, Edwin C., ed. *Valley of the Trent.* Toronto: Champlain Society, 1957.

Gunn, R.C. "Report on the Erindale Program." In *AOLS, 1983.*

Gynn, Robin. "England's 'First Refugees.' " *History Today* 35 (May 1985).

Haldimand, Frederick. *Official and Private Correspondence and Papers of General Sir Frederick Haldimand, 1758–1784.* AO, MS622, Additional MSS 21827-29.

Hancock, S.G. "The Development of Steep Rock Iron Mines." In *AOLS, 1953.*

Harlow, William, and Ellwood Harrar. *Textbook of Dendrology.* New York: McGraw-Hill, 1941.

Harris, R. Cole, ed. *Historical Atlas of Canada.* Vol. 1, *From the Beginning to 1800.* Toronto: University of Toronto Press, 1987.

Heidenreich, Conrad. *Huronia: A History and Geography of the Huron Indians, 1600–1650.* Toronto: McClelland and Stewart, 1971.

Higbee, L.D. "Historical Notes on the Divided Circle." *ACSM Journal of Surveying and Mapping,* March 1953.

Hodgkiss, A.G. *Discovering Antique Maps.* Tring, England: Shire Publications, 1971.

Hogg, T.H. "St. Lawrence River." In *AOLS, 1935.*

Howden, H.S. "King's Highway Surveys." In *AOLS, 1955.*

Innis, Mary Quale, ed. *Mrs. Simcoe's Diary.* Toronto: Macmillan of Canada, 1965.

Jackson, J. Hampden, ed. *A Short History of France.* Cambridge, England: Cambridge University Press, 1961.

Jernigan, Marcus W. *The American Colonies, 1492–1750.* New York: Frederick Ungar Publishing Co., 1964.

Johnson, Leo A. *History of Guelph: 1827–1927.* Guelph Historical Society, 1977.

Jones, Robert Leslie. *History of Agriculture in Ontario: 1613–1880.* Toronto: University of Toronto Press, 1946.

Jurgens, Olga. "Étienne Brûlé." In *Dictionary of Canadian Biography.* Vol. 1. Toronto: University of Toronto Press, 1966.

Laver, James. *A Concise History of Costume.* London: Thames and Hudson, 1973.

Kenyon, W.A., and J.R. Turnbull. *The Battle for James Bay.* Toronto: Macmillan of Canada, 1971.

Kiely, Edmond R. *Surveying Instruments: Their History.* The National Council of Teachers of Mathematics, Inc., 1947. Reprint. Columbus, Ohio: Carben Surveying Reprints, 1979.

King, Shirley. "The Ontario-Quebec Boundary: Lake Temiskaming to James Bay." In *AOLS, 1934.*

Kish, George. "Centuriato: The Roman Rectangular Land Survey." *ACSM Journal of Surveying and Mapping,* June 1962.

Klotz, Otto J. "The Northwest Angle." In *AOLS, 1902.*

Krebs, H. "Quality Control: Plans and Descriptions." Paper presented at the OLS/ACSTO seminar on Land Registration in Ontario Today, 28 October 1978, Toronto: AOLS.

Labaree, Leonard W. ed. *Royal Instructions to British Colonial Governors: 1670–1776.* 2 vols. New York: Octagon Books, 1967.

Ladell, John and Monica Ladell. *Inheritance: Ontario's Century Farms, Past & Present.* Toronto: Dundurn Press, 1986.

———. *A Farm in the Family: The Many Faces of Ontario Agriculture over the Centuries.* Toronto: Dundurn Press, 1985.

Lafrenière, Normand. *Canal Building on the St. Lawrence River, 1779–1959.* Parks Canada, Coteau-du-Lac Historic Park Series, booklet no. 1. 1983.

Lajeunesse, Ernest J. *The Windsor Border Region.* Toronto: University of Toronto Press, 1960.

Lambert, Richard S. with Paul Pross. *Renewing Nature's Wealth.* Ontario Department of Lands and Forests, 1967.

Lanctot, Gustave. *A History of Canada.* Vol. 1. Cambridge, Massachusetts: Harvard University Press, 1963.

Langley, Michael. "John Harrison: The Hero of Longitude." *History Today* 26 (December 1976).

Leick, Alfred. *GPS Satellite Surveying.* New York: John Wiley & Sons, 1990.

Lewis, G. Malcolm. "Changing National Perspectives and the Mapping of the Great Lakes between 1755 and 1795." *Cartographica* 17, 3 (1980).

Lloyd, C.W. "Control on the St. Lawrence." In *AOLS, 1957.*

MacKirdy, Kenneth A. *Ontario History.* Vol. 51, *National vs. Provincial Loyalty: The Ontario Boundary Dispute, 1883–1884.* 1959.

Manucy, Albert. "Changing Traditions in St. Augustine Architecture." *El Escribano* 19 (1982).

Mathieu, Jacques. "Seigneurial System." In *The Canadian Encyclopedia.* Hurtig Publishers, 1985.

McEvedy, Colin. *The Penguin Atlas of Medieval History.* Harmondsworth: Penguin Books, 1981.

———. *The Penguin Atlas of Modern History.* Harmondsworth: Penguin Books, 1983.

McGergow, F.C. "Winter Surveys in Northern Ontario." In *AOLS, 1957.*

Mealing, S.R. "David William Smith." In *Dictionary of Canadian Biography.* Vol. 7. Toronto: University of Toronto Press, 1988.

———, ed. *The Jesuit Relations and Allied Documents: A Selection.* Toronto: McClelland and Stewart, 1963.

Mendenhall, Herbert D. "The History of Land Surveying in Florida." *ACSM Journal of Surveying and Mapping,* December 1950.

Mettam, Roger. "Louis XIV and the Huguenots." *History Today* 35 (May 1985).

Ministry of Culture and Recreation. *Ontario Historic Sites, Museums, Galleries and Plaques.* undated.

Minnick, Roy, ed. "The College of William and Mary and Surveying in Early Virginia." *ACSM Journal of Surveying and Mapping,* June 1958.

Moore, E.S. "Special Features of the Geology of Ontario." In *AOLS, 1934.*

Morison, Samuel Eliot. *The Oxford History of the American People.* Vols. 1 and 2. New York and Scarborough, Ontario: Mentor Books, 1972.

Morrison, J.C. "Oliver Mowatt and the Development of Provincial Rights in Ontario: A Study in Dominion-Provincial Relations." In *Three History Theses.* Ontario Department of Public Records and Archives, 1961.

Mowatt, Charles L. *East Florida as a British Province: 1763–1784.* 1943. Facsimile reproduction. Gainesville: University of Florida Press, 1964.

Mucklestone, F.H. "The Torrens System." In *AOLS, 1938.*

Multhauf, Robert P. "Early Instruments in the History of Surveying: Their Use and Their Invention." *ACSM Journal of Surveying and Mapping,* December 1958.

Murphy, J.J. "A Documentary History of the First Surveys in the Province of Ontario." In *AOLS, 1898.*

Murray, Florence B. "Agricultural Settlement on the Canadian Shield: Ottawa River to Georgian Bay." In *Profiles of a Province.* Toronto: Ontario Historical Society, 1967.

———, ed. *Muskoka and Haliburton: 1615–1875.* The Champlain Society for the Government of Ontario. Toronto: University of Toronto Press, 1963.

Museum of London. *The Quiet Conquest: The Huguenots, 1685 to 1985.* 1985.

Newman, J.J. "A Short History of the Ditches and Watercourses Act." In *AOLS, 1928.*

———. "A Talk on the Historical Development of the Drainage Laws in Ontario." In *AOLS, 1938.*

Nicholson, Norman L. *The Boundaries of Canada, its Provinces and Territories.* Department of Mines and Technical Surveys, Geographical Branch. Memoir no. 2, Ottawa: 1964.

Nish, Cameron, ed. and trans. *The French Regime.* Scarborough, Ontario: Prentice-Hall, 1965.

Nute, Grace Lee. "Médard Chouart des Groseilliers." In *Dictionary of Canadian Biography.* Vol. 2. Toronto: University of Toronto Press, 1969.

———. "Pierre-Esprit Radisson." In *Dictionary of Canadian Biography.* Vol. 1. Toronto: University of Toronto Press, 1966.

Olgivie, William. "Micrometer Measurement of Distances." In *AOLS, 1887.*

Ontario Ministry of Natural Resources: Surveys, Mapping and Remote Sensing Branch. Report presented to the 1991 meeting of the Canadian Council on Geomatics, 14 October 1991.

Ontario Ministry of Transportation and Communications. *Footpaths to Freeways: The Story of Ontario's Roads.* 1984.

Ontario Department of Agriculture. *Hints to Settlers in Northern Ontario.* Bulletin 244. December 1916.

Ontario Department of Crown Lands. *Report on the Survey and Exploration of Northern Ontario, 1900.* Toronto: The King's Printer, 1901.

Paddon, Wayne. *The Story of the Talbot Settlement, 1803–1840.* Published privately, 1975.

Panting, S.B. *The Effect of Original Surveys Urban Development in Ontario.* Ontario Department of Lands and Forests, 1962.

———. "The Ontario Co-ordinate System: A Preview of Pertinent Legislation and Regulations." In *AOLS, 1969.*

Parks Canada, *Canal Building on the St. Lawrence River, 1779–1959.* Coteau-du-Lac National Historic Park Series. Booklet 1. 1983.

Patten, T.J. "The Solar Compass." In *AOLS, 1906.*

Patterson, Gilbert. *Land Settlement in Upper Canada.* Sixteenth Report of the Department of Archives for the Province of Ontario, 1920.

Pearce, Frederick J. *Matters Pertinent to the Incorporation of the Canadian Council of Land Surveyors, 1973(?).*

Pelton, L.E. "The Control Survey of Metropolitan Toronto." In *AOLS, 1963.*

"Peter Hunter." In *Dictionary of Canadian Biography.* Vol. 5. Toronto: University of Toronto Press, 1983.

Petzold, E.W. Personal communication with the author, 17 November 1989.

Peyton, Harry J., Jr. "Early Development of Horizontal Angle-Measuring Instruments." *ACSM Journal of Surveying and Mapping,* December 1951.

Phelps, Edward. *Foundations of the Canadian Oil Industry, 1850–1866.* Profiles of a Province. Toronto: Ontario Historical Society, 1967.

Pierce, John G. "Ontario/Manitoba Boundary: 'On to the Bay.' " In *AOLS, 1949.*

Pierce, J.W. "The Adaptation of Aerial Photographs to Surveys and Maps." In AOLS, 1925. 168–79.

———. "The Ontario-Manitoba Boundary." In *AOLS, 1938.*

———. "The Survey of the Ontario-Manitoba Boundary." In *AOLS, 1923.*

Potter, Jonathan. *Antique Maps.* London: Country Life Books, 1988.

Pouliot, Leon. "Claude Allouez." In *Dictionary of Canadian Biography.* Vol. 1. Toronto: University of Toronto Press, 1966.

Ravenhill, William. "Mapping a United Kingdom." *History Today* 35 (October 1985).

Reader, W.J. *Life in Victorian England.* London: B.T. Batsford, 1964.

Reid, D. "G.P.S. and the Surveyor: Where Are We Now?" In *AOLS, 1987.*

Richeson, A.W. *English Land Measuring to 1800: Instruments and Practices.* The Society for the History of Technology and The M.I.T. Press, 1966.

Riddell, J.M. "Geodetic Control for City Mapping." In *AOLS, 1951.*

Robertson, James. "Surveys of Crown Lands in New Ontario." In *AOLS, 1904.*

Robertson, J. Ross. *The Diary of Mrs. John Graves Simcoe.* Toronto: William Briggs, 1911.

Rodger, N.A.M. *The Wooden World: An Anatomy of the Georgian Navy.* Fontana Press, 1988.

Rody, Talson E. "Intergrated Surveys: A Practical Example from Northern Omtario." In *AOLS, 1975.* 251–72.

Schull, Joseph. *Ontario Since 1867.* Toronto: McClelland and Stewart, 1978

Sebert, L.M. "The Boards of Boundary Line Commissioners." *The Ontario Land Surveyor,* Spring 1980.

———. "Early Surveying Techniques." *Journal of the Canadian Institute of Surveying and Mapping* 45, 4 (Winter 1991): 614–15.

———. "The Land Surveys of Ontario 1750–1980." *Cartographica* 17, 3 (1980).

———. *The Mapping of Northern Ontario.* Association of Canadian Map Libraries. Bulletin 47. June 1983.

Semper, Robert O. *Background Notes on the Canadian Council of Land Surveyors,* Personal communication with the author, 21 January 1992.

Sewell, Henry D. "Mining in the Port Arthur District." In *AOLS, 1887.*

Shennan, J.H. "History of France." In *The New Encyclopedia Britannica,* 15th ed. 1988.

Siebert, R.Q. "The Temporary Settlement of Loyalists at Machiche, P.Q." In *Proceedings and Transactions of the Royal Society of Canada.* Third series. Vol. 8. 1914.

Smart, Michael B. "The Role of the Land Surveyor in Geographic Feature and Place Naming in Ontario." In *AOLS, 1973.*

Smith, W.H. *Canadian Gazetteer.* Toronto: H. & W. Rowsell, 1846. Reprint. Coles Canadiana Collection, 1970.

Smith, Donald B. "Tekarihogen." In *Dictionary of Canadian Biography.* Vol. 6. Toronto: University of Toronto Press, 1987.

Spreckly, R.Q. "The Origin of the Rectangular System of Survey." *Canadian Surveyor* 4, 4 (1932).

Stagg, Ronald J. "William Bercsy." In *Dictionary of Canadian Biography.* Vol. 5. Toronto: University of Toronto Press, 1983.

Stanley, William F. *Surveying and Levelling Instruments.* 3d ed. London: E. & F. Spon and W.F. Stanley & Co. Ltd., 1901.

Stauffer, C.E. "Report of the Editor of 'The Ontario Land Surveyor.' " In *AOLS, 1962.*

Stretton, W.D. "From Compass to Satellite." *The Canadian Surveyor* 36, 4 (December 1982).

Survey Review Department. *The Ontario Land Surveyor* 28, 4 (Fall 1985).

Sutherland, Stuart, Pierre Tousignant, and Madeleine Dionne-Tousignant. "Sir Frederick Haldimand." In *Dictionary of Canadian Biography.* Vol. 5. Toronto: University of Toronto Press, 1983.

Theberge, Clifford B., and Elaine Theberge. *The Trent-Severn Waterway.* Toronto: Samuel Stevens, 1978.

Thomson, Don W. *Men and Meridians.* 3 vols. Ottawa: The Queen's Printer, 1966, 1967, and 1969.

Thwaites, Reuben Gold, ed. *Jesuit Relations and Allied Documents,* 74 vols. Cleveland: Burrows, 1896–1901.

Tieman, Andrea E. Personal communication with the author, 27 March 1991.

Trudel, Marcel. "Samuel de Champlain." In *Dictionary of Canadian Biography.* Vol. 1. Toronto: University of Toronto Press, 1966.

U.S. Department of the Interior, National Park Service. *Fort Raleigh.* 1987.

Vachon, André. "Louis Jolliet." In *Dictionary of Canadian Biography.* Vol. 1. Toronto: University of Toronto Press, 1966.

Wadsworth, V.B. "History of Exploratory Surveys Conducted by John Stoughton Dennis, Provincial Land Surveyor, in the Muskoka, Parry Sound and Nipissing District, 1860–1865." In *AOLS, 1926.*

Wallace, W. Stewart, ed. *The Macmillan Dictionary of Canadian Biography.* 4th ed. Toronto: Macmillan of Canada, 1978.

———, ed. *The Royal Canadian Institute Centennial Volume, 1849–1949.* Toronto: Royal Canadian Institute, 1949.

Weaver, W.F. "Annulment of Non-Essential Obliterated Township Surveys." In *AOLS, 1943.*

———. *Crown Surveys in Ontario.* Ontario Department of Lands and Forests, 1962.

Wells, Colin. *The Roman Empire.* Stanford, California: Stanford University Press, 1984.

White, Randall. *Ontario, 1610–1985.* Toronto: Dundurn Press, 1985.

Whitson, J.F. "Personal Supervision of Surveys." In *AOLS, 1905.*

Whitten, Charles A. "Surveying: 1776 to 1976." *ACSM Proceedings,* Fall Convention, September 1976.

Wilkie, E.T. "The Seigniory of Longueuil." In *AOLS, 1909,* 153.

Wilson, Norman D. "Report of the Committee on Engineering." In *AOLS, 1915.*

———. "Toronto Harbor Surveys." In *AOLS, 1916.*

Zaslow, Morris. "The Ontario Boundary Question." In *Profiles of a Province: Studies in the History of Ontario.* Ontario Historical Society, 1967.

SPONSORS OF *THEY LEFT THEIR MARK*

Annis, O'Sullivan & Vollebekk Ltd.

Arnett Kennedy Riddell & Jason Surveying Ltd.

Donald W. Baird, O.L.S.
(In Memory of Wilmot J. Baird, O.L.S.)

Bennett & Norgrove Ltd.

George W. Bracken Ltd.

Brown & Coggan Limited

T.A. Bunker Surveying Limited

T.O. Callon Company Limited

Chambers, Miller & Wall Limited

Clancy & Hopkins Surveying Ltd.

A.J. Clarke & Associates Ltd.

R.E. Clipsham Limited

Robert G. Code, O.L.S.

Ivan Dinsmore Ltd.

Donevan & Fleischmann Co. Ltd.

D.S. Dorland Ltd.

D. Eberhardt Surveying Ltd.

B.K. Edwards Surveying Limited

Fairhall, Moffatt & Woodland Limited

D.H. Galbraith, O.L.S.

R.A. Garden Limited

Gord Good Surveying Inc.

Harold S. Howden, O.L.S.

Humphries & Burgham Ltd.

William Jackson Surveying Ltd.

Clare W.A. Jones, O.L.S.

Anton Kikas Ltd.

R.R. Krupowicz Surveying Ltd.

McBain & Carmichael

McConnell Maughan Ltd.

MacKay, MacKay & Peters Limited

R.G. McKibbon Limited

Marshall Macklin Monaghan Ontario Ltd.

Matthews & Cameron Limited

L.U. Maughan Co. Ltd.

Ontario Ministry of Natural Resources

S.B. Nicholson, O.L.S.

Guido Papa Surveying Ltd.

Jean-Guy Payette Ltd.

E.W. (Red) Petzold, O.L.S.

Pierce & Lyons Inc.

R.A. Preiss Surveying Ltd.

P.D. Reitsma Surveying Ltd.

T.E. Rody Limited

Edwin Rowan Surveying Ltd.

William J. Salter, O.L.S.

Schaeffer & Reinthaler Ltd.

David B. Searles Surveying Ltd.

Simpson and Osborne Surveying Inc.

Ronald H. Smith Ltd.

Speight, van Nostrand & Gibson Limited
(In Memory of H.S. Bradstock, O.L.S.)

Stidwill & Smith

Sury, Rowe & Kasprzak Ltd.

B. Tompsett Limited

Verhaegen Stubberfield Hartley Brewer Bezaire Inc.

Webster & Simmonds Surveying Ltd.

John C. Wood Ltd.

Yates & Yates Limited

Young & Young Surveying Inc.

Zubek, Emo & Patten Ltd.

INDEX

(EN) Endnote
(FN) Footnote
(FIG) Figure

GENERAL

EXPLORATORY SURVEYORS, HYDROGRAPHERS AND DEPUTY, PROVINCIAL, ONTARIO, AND OTHER LAND SURVEYORS.

TOWNSHIPS